D0435549

GB

The Great Ideas

SENATVS
POPVLVS QVE ROMANVS
DIVO TITO DIVI VESPASIANI F
VESPASIANO AVGVSTO

Rome: The Arch of Titus, painting by Canaletto signed and dated 1742.

Translated, the inscription reads: "(from) *The Roman Senate and People, To the Divine Titus, (son of the Divine Vespasian), Emperor"*

The
Great Ideas
Today

1981

Encyclopædia Britannica, Inc.

Chicago • Geneva • London • Manila • Paris • Rome • Seoul • Sydney • Tokyo • Toronto

Contents

A NOTE ON REFERENCE STYLE

In the following pages, passages in *Great Books of the Western World* are referred to by the initials '*GBWW*,' followed by volume, page number, and page section. Thus, '*GBWW*, Vol. 39, p. 210b' refers to page 210 in Adam Smith's *The Wealth of Nations*, which is Volume 39 in *Great Books of the Western World*. The small letter 'b' indicates the page section. In books printed in single column, 'a' and 'b' refer to the upper and lower halves of the page. In books printed in double column, 'a' and 'b' refer to the upper and lower halves of the left column, 'c' and 'd' to the upper and lower halves of the right column. For example, 'Vol. 53, p. 210b' refers to the lower half of page 210, since Volume 53, James's *Principles of Psychology,* is printed in single column. On the other hand, 'Vol. 7, p. 210b' refers to the lower left quarter of the page, since Volume 7, Plato's *Dialogues,* is printed in double column.

    Gateway to the Great Books is referred to by the initials '*GGB*,' followed by volume and page number. Thus, '*GGB*, Vol. 10, pp. 39-57' refers to pages 39 through 57 of Volume 10 of *Gateway to the Great Books,* which is James's essay, "The Will to Believe."

    The Great Ideas Today is referred to by the initials '*GIT*,' followed by the year and page number. Thus '*GIT* 1968, p. 210' refers to page 210 of the 1968 edition of *The Great Ideas Today*.

Preface

This year's issue of *The Great Ideas Today* is different from those that have appeared over the past decade or so. The difference is in our substitution for the usual symposium of a group of book reviews written by members of the editorial staff and others. In so doing, we have carried out a plan announced two years ago of offering critiques of recent books that raise issues of interest to our readers. At that time our contributing editor, William Gorman, was available to offer such critiques, as he did, but as he could not do the year following because of illness. Now it has seemed worthwhile to try the experiment on a larger scale, and to make room for it by eliminating, at least temporarily, our usual featured symposium in which recognized authorities discuss a topic of current interest.

These reviews take up Part IV of the present volume. The books discussed there are *Does God Exist?* by Hans Küng, the distinguished Catholic theologian; *Mathematics—The Loss of Certainty*, by Morris Kline, a noted mathematician; and *Sociobiology Examined*, a collection of essays written by fifteen different scientists representing various fields and edited by Ashley Montagu, himself an anthropologist.

The issues raised by two of these books are indicated by their titles. In the case of the first of them, it is the existence of God. A critique of this is offered by two reviewers: Mortimer J. Adler, editor in chief of *The Great Ideas Today*, who writes on the philosophical aspects of the subject, and Wayne F. Moquin, who discusses the theological ones. The question of certainty in mathematics, the issue raised by Morris Kline, is taken up by Charles Van Doren, assistant director of the Institute for Philosophical Research and vice-president/editorial of Encyclopædia Britannica, Inc., who will be recalled by some of our readers as the author of a two-part discussion of the idea of freedom that appeared in our issues for 1972–1973. Professor Montagu's collection of articles, challenging as it does the claims of representatives of the new science of sociobiology, raises the questions about the nature of man, and particularly the question of human freedom, both of which are considered by John Van Doren, executive editor of *The Great Ideas Today*.

In the rest of the volume are, first, two essays on the arts and sciences. One of these is a discussion of the twentieth-century theatre by Norris Houghton, who is equally well known for his achievements as a director of theatre productions, as a teacher, and as a writer. The other is by Stephen

1

Toulmin, who has appeared in these pages before (*see* "The Year's Developments in the Physical Sciences" in our issue of 1967), and who here writes of the profound changes he perceives as having overtaken the scientific enterprise in our time.

Following these is an essay on Gibbon's *Decline and Fall of the Roman Empire* by Hugh Trevor-Roper that is interesting not only as praise by one distinguished historian for another, but that at the same time proves to be a rigorous analysis of Gibbon's aims in writing his great work.

There is also in this volume an essay by Otto Bird, our consulting editor, that discusses recent writings on ethics and treats them as expressions of a permissive society. Mr. Bird, who was executive editor of *The Great Ideas Today* from 1964 to 1970, has appeared before in its pages, notably as the author of "The Idea of Justice" in 1974.

Along with these essays and reviews, this issue presents "Additions to the Great Books Library," as follows:

Lucian's *True History,* a madcap tall tale by a first-century Syrian of whom very little is known, but who was apparently the author of a number of works that have survived, among them this forerunner of *Gulliver's Travels* and the stories of Baron Münchausen;

An Essay on Criticism, by Alexander Pope, which describes the rules of literature that were accepted by the Augustan age, of which Pope was the supreme poet, and who writes here in rhymed couplets of dazzling brilliance and variety;

The Autobiography of Edward Gibbon, in which the author of the *Decline and Fall* applies to his own life the ironic style of thought and expression that on a grander scale is found in his history;

Candide, by Voltaire—the best-known and best-liked tale of one of the great spirits of the eighteenth century, who incidentally pokes a good deal of scornful fun at great books;

"The Great Instauration," by Francis Bacon, which sets forth the plan of the new philosophy that its author hoped to undertake, of which he finished only *The Novum Organum* (see *GBWW,* vol. 30);

"On the Aims and Instruments of Scientific Thought," by William Kingdon Clifford, an essay on the limits of scientific exactitude and certainty that is of particular interest in the light of Stephen Toulmin's essay and the discussion of Morris Kline's book on mathematics by Charles Van Doren.

PART ONE

Current Developments in the Arts and Sciences

Theatre in the Twentieth Century

Norris Houghton

Norris Houghton is well known as a man of the theatre. Beginning shortly after he graduated from Princeton in 1931, he directed or stage-managed Broadway productions for twenty-five years. In 1953 he founded the off-Broadway Phoenix Theatre, where he directed some seventy-five productions over the succeeding decade. He has been president of both the American Theatre Conference (1969–71) and the American Council for the Arts in Education (1973–75).

Mr. Houghton has had a distinguished academic career as well. This began in 1941 when he was a lecturer in drama at Princeton and has brought him to Harvard, Yale, Columbia, and Vassar as professor of drama and literature. He spent thirteen years as dean of the Theatre Arts department at the State University of New York, Purchase, N.Y., and is now visiting professor of English at New York University.

The author of a number of books, among which are *Advance from Broadway, But Not Forgotten,* and *The Exploding Stage,* Mr. Houghton has also published articles in *The New Yorker,* the *Saturday Review,* and the *American Scholar,* among other magazines. A signal contribution to the understanding of modern theatre is his study of post-revolutionary Russian theatre which he explores in two works entitled *Moscow Rehearsals* (1936) and *Return Engagement* (1962), written after numerous trips to the Soviet Union.

Forerunners

As the nineteenth century came to a close, Ibsen and the century's other two great dramatists, August Strindberg and Anton Chekhov, were still alive, but two of them were failing fast. Ibsen was recovering from erysipelas and about to suffer the first of three strokes (the last one fatal); Chekhov was spitting blood in a race for time against tuberculosis. It seems unlikely that they were very merry on the New Year's Eve of 1900.

Had the three of them looked back at their accomplishment, they would have perceived the end of the Romantic movement, which they had replaced with Realism. To have been able to look ahead would have been to foresee a century in which the theatre would become as fragmented as a piece of porcelain dropped on tiles. Realism would be assaulted by Symbolists, Expressionists, Surrealists, Constructivists, Marxists, Existentialists, Absurdists, vigorously pulling the stage first one way and then another—all within less than one hundred years. (In fact, Ibsen and Strindberg had already made some anti-Realistic moves themselves!)

The spectacle of fragmentation would have been unfamiliar. In past centuries the stage had come through each of them much in one piece. There had been the Classical age, then the Renaissance which did look two ways—one toward the Court, the other toward the street corner and inn-yard; then in their own century Neo-classicism had been pushed aside by the Romantics whom they themselves in turn displaced. These were orderly transitions, however, compared to what was to come.

Probably it could not be otherwise. The stage's age-old obligation has been to reflect the world about it. Certainly the century ahead would be fragmented as never before: by two world wars of unparalleled ferocity, by the arrival of the Atomic Age, by great political upheavals—the Bolshevik and Chinese Communist revolutions—by readjustments to be made to the revelations of Darwin and Freud that would cause some people even to begin to re-think the very existence of God.

Fragmentation is an apt word to describe it. But there is a better one which has entered common usage only in our own era—fission. The dictionary points out that this can be used to mean more than just a "cleaving into parts"—it adds the idea of "the release of large amounts of energy." That makes it a better word to describe the twentieth-century theatre, in which great energy is manifest. The question arises: for good or ill? Has it improved on Ibsen, Strindberg, and Chekhov, or not? That has been the challenge for our generation.

The new Realism those three dramatists introduced, like most "isms" in art, had little to do with substance. Such a term describes the *way* the playwrights projected their ideas, the kind of mirror they held up to nature. The more important question to ask is: what do they have to say? Later, though, we must examine how they say it and explore the matter of style.

What Ibsen, Strindberg, and Chekhov had to say to twentieth-century man was very much what he would find he had to say to himself. They foresaw many of his problems and anxieties. If these three masters dramatized these more effectively than most of their successors, it was because they were greater playwrights.

Although Ibsen, the earliest of the three, never wrote a line of dialogue in the 1900s, he anticipated our modern desire to explore the contradictions and frailties of our society as well as in ourselves, to search for causes behind effects, to assail hypocrisy and compromise, to put a finger on pretense and prejudice, to focus a spotlight on corrupting relationships within the family and between the sexes, to embark on the search for one's identity, to point out the dangers that accompany lies and illusions and the equal danger to those fragile spirits whose self-delusions are forcibly stripped from them in the name of facing reality.

This list of preoccupations seems incredibly long, but Ibsen did indeed address himself to all the items it contains in one or another of his mature works, often to more than one at a time.

The author of *A Doll's House* has been traditionally thought of, for instance, as a heralding proponent of "equal opportunity," the emancipation of women. (This conclusion has been reached without regard for Ibsen's own statement delivered in response to a toast at a testimonial dinner given by the Norwegian League for Women's Rights in 1898. He said: "Whatever I have written has been without any conscious thought of making propaganda. I have been more the poet and less the social philosopher than has been generally believed. . . . I must disclaim the honor of having consciously worked for the women's rights movement. I am not even quite clear as to just what this women's rights movement really is!") But such remarks do not alter the fact that, as James Huneker once remarked, when writing about the ending of *A Doll's House,* "that slammed door reverberated across the roof of the world." And the twentieth century can find other reverberations beyond the one Huneker intended. Before the door slammed after Nora as she walked out on her home and family, she had established some truths and struck down some falsehoods about marriage that troubled the nineteenth century, but today we recognize that it was not that she walked out, nor what she walked out on, but what she walked *into* that counted: a quest for self, claming the right of the individual to find her own freedom. "I shall never get to know myself," says Nora to her husband, "I shall never learn to face reality—unless I stand alone. . . . I believe that before all else I am a human being, just as you are—or at least I should try and become one. . . . I must think things out for myself."

Earlier, Ibsen had described a young man's search for self-realization in his picaresque fantasy, *Peer Gynt.* That play described a journey that took its protagonist round about from Scandinavia to Africa through a lifetime of deception and self-deception, of hypocrisy and compromise, but brought him home at the end to find salvation in love—a more conventional conclusion, certainly, than Nora's departure from home to find truth in herself.

Ibsen thus forecast twenty years before the end of his century a theme that has gripped the stage with ever increasing strength in our own era: the search for identity.

Ibsen's *The Wild Duck* is likewise astonishing in its contemporaneity. An insistent confrontation in twentieth-century drama will be that between reality and illusion: the pressure on modern men and women to "face the facts," to "be realistic," colliding with a frequently overwhelming urge to avoid those very things and take refuge in the reassurance of dreams and illusions. Ibsen had already established that Nora and her husband had lived in their "doll's house" of illusion, a house she realized she must leave.

The Wild Duck takes its title from the symbol of the wild fowl which, when wounded, "dives to the bottom and bites itself fast in the undergrowth." To Gregers Werle this image epitomizes the Ekdal family, whose members he feels impelled like a dog to pull out of the water of their deceptions. The parallel, of course, breaks down, for the family, unlike the bird, are not drowned, nor do they need resuscitation. It is only that the husband is ignorant of the fact that his wife has given him a daughter by another man. Granted their relationship is based on falsehood, yet—Ibsen contends—lies can often be more comforting than truth, indeed truth does not in every circumstance set man free. As Dr. Relling, the play's *raisonneur,* observes: "Illusion is the stimulating principle." Eugene O'Neill came to the same conclusion a half-century later; so have other dramatists done in our time.

Even more striking are August Strindberg's excursions into the Freudian realm of the subconscious and of dreams. His extraordinary *A Dream Play* was written in 1902, only two years after the publication of Freud's *The Interpretation of Dreams.* It seems less important to try to make a direct connection than to note that as far back as 1888 Strindberg had written in his Preface to *Miss Julie* concerning his creation of characters: "My souls are conglomerations of past and present civilizations, bits from books and newspapers, scraps of humanity, rags and tatters of fine clothing, patched together as is the human soul." And in the Preface to *A Dream Play* he announced that he

> sought to reproduce the disconnected but apparently logical form of a
> dream; . . . . on a slight groundwork of reality, imagination spins and
> weaves new patterns made up of memories, experiences, unfettered
> fantasies, absurdities and improvisations. The characters are split,
> double and multiply; they evaporate, crystallize, scatter and converge.

(Above) Henrik Ibsen,
lithograph by Edvard
Munch, 1902. (Right)
Anton Chekhov, 1902.

August Strindberg, lithograph
by Edvard Munch, 1896.

But a single consciousness holds sway over them all—that is the
dreamer.

These words reveal sophisticated knowledge of modern research into the
psyche, and properly so, for Strindberg was himself what could be dubbed
a psychopathological case, and one who was aware of his own illness. In 1894
he had entered what has come to be known as his "inferno," a spiritual and
mental crisis of two years duration. Because he was one of the most subjective of writers, his own agonies find voice in his greatest plays. These
masochistic torments grew into paranoia that was fed by sex, by doubt of
his sanity, of God, of his own soul—by, in sum, all the tortures of the
damned. These doubts burst forth in play after play: *The Father, Miss Julie,
The Dance of Death, Comrades,* even *The Ghost Sonata,* each providing a battleground on which the duel between the sexes is bloodily waged, now natura-
listically, now symbolically.

Maurice Valency, in his book about Ibsen and Strindberg, *The Flower and
the Castle,* proposes an arresting likeness between the latter and Vincent Van
Gogh. Strindberg had no more interest in representing nature as it appeared to others than did the Dutch painter. Both saw life "in unusual
shapes and colors, peopled with strange beings, ruled by occult forces,
vibrant with such terrors as most people never feel." Valency notes that

9

both reported not only what they saw but what they felt, dreamed, surmised, and imagined, without bothering to distinguish between external and internal life. Both, it is true, were propelled by tensions we recognize, which when repressed lead toward madness.

Anton Chekhov was far from being a madman; he was, in fact, a physician. His interest was in diagnosing the ills of others, not in using his own ills as his raw material. Like Ibsen and Strindberg he saw life with a poet's vision, but no three poets ever presented more diverse images. Of the three, Chekhov evoked the greatest sympathy for the "human condition," because he made the fewest value judgments; indeed, he had few to make, for he backed no causes and aired no prejudices (unlike Ibsen) but looked at his fellow men with clear and judicious eyes (unlike Strindberg).

Chekhov prefigured our century's battle between illusion and reality in *The Cherry Orchard* as accurately as did Ibsen in *The Wild Duck*. He also penned in his masterpieces a dozen portraits of the disintegrating power of boredom—the want of an object in life—as accurately as did Ibsen in *Hedda Gabler*. If Chekhov did not, like Strindberg, depict the world as a fiery battleground between the sexes, he nonetheless understood the tensions, frustrations, the terrors and the joys, of unrequited and requited love. Whereas Ibsen used the stage often didactically to present man's role in society and to assert his notions of truth, Chekhov worked obliquely to mirror accurately a rather limited group of his fellow men and women. Mirror may be the wrong verb: Chekhov X-rayed his characters, revealing unexpected truths hidden beneath familiar facades. The Russian playwright had extraordinary insights into the psychological motivations of human actions and an uncanny capacity to catch the inner throb of the human heart.

Chekhov was aware, as Ibsen was, but as Strindberg was not, of disruptive external pressures on the family, which he regarded as the basic unit of our society. With Ibsen, he seems to have recognized that the family was but a microcosm of the social structure, but he did not have Ibsen's revolutionary fervor. Indeed, whether or not Chekhov had ever read Marx, certainly he was no socialist. But his plays were full of an awareness that Russia was on the brink of an upheaval. Character after character speaks eloquently of the future, of better days to come. The sale of the cherry orchard, the departure of its owners and all their household save the ancient retainer, Firs— himself as much a metaphor as the axes outside—provide vivid and poignant stage images of social evolution. Ibsen thought change would come if man put his house in order or, better still, tore it down and rebuilt it on firmer foundations of truth. For Chekhov, whether man worked at it or not, change was inevitable and, as such, had both its poignant and its hopeful aspects.

Chekhov's attitude was affectionately captured by his fellow-dramatist, Maksim Gorky, in *Reminiscences of Tolstoy, Chekhov and Andreyev:*

... he looked at all these dreary inhabitants of his country, and, with a sad smile, with a tone of gentle but deep reproach, with anguish in his face and in his heart, in a beautiful and sincere voice, he said to them: "You live badly, my friends. It is shameful to live like that."

Bernard Shaw: one foot in each century

George Bernard Shaw was far from ailing on New Year's Eve of 1900. He was forty-four years old and feeling in top form. He would, in fact, live to be ninety-four, thus nearly straddling two centuries. His first play had not been produced until 1892, but since then he had delivered himself of ten masterpieces.

Shaw may have been prepared to echo Chekhov's "You live badly, my friends," but there was no "gentle but deep reproach," no "anguish" in his voice when he tackled his fellow Britons. "My conscience is the genuine pulpit article," he announced. "If you don't like my preaching you must lump it." He was prepared to out-Ibsen Ibsen if he could. In an encyclopaedia entry, the author of *The Quintessence of Ibsenism* is reputed to have written about himself: "Mr. Bernard Shaw substituted the theatre for the platform as his chief means of propaganda."

To be sure, Ibsen, as you recall, had told his audience of ladies that he had been "more the poet and less the social philosopher than has been generally believed." Shaw, too, is quite ready in his next breath to say, "My plays are no more economic treatises than Shakespear's." Ibsen may appear today as less the social reformer than his contemporaries—outstandingly, Shaw himself—thought him, and more eager to fathom the modern enigma of personality. Shaw's ideas, his "social philosophy proper," may seem to the present generation as having "always been confused and uncertain" (the position that Edmund Wilson took, adding, "The real Shaw has thus never been the single-minded crusader that people at one time used to think him"). Nonetheless, both dramatists acquired fame by at any rate appearing to espouse causes, often unpopular ones.

Eric Bentley has made the point that "no one will ever be able to say how many minds Shaw changed in the generation growing up in the early years of this century, how many young men and women under his spell began to question marriage, the family, science, religion, and above all, capitalism." One cannot gainsay that Shaw employed his comedic genius to debunk the glamour of war (in *Arms and the Man*), to twit the medical profession (in *The Doctor's Dilemma*) and the Irish question (*John Bull's Other Island*), to challenge the cliché that "poverty is no crime" (*Major Barbara*), to discuss sex, love, and marriage in unorthodox terms (in a number of plays culminating in *Man and Superman*), and to write a "fantasia in the Russian manner" (*Heartbreak House*) in order to expose the scintillating but fatuous aimlessness of "cultured leisured Europe before the War."

Out of this broad range of themes, a central one does emerge, binding many of them together. Shaw's principal objective was to show that most of the mores and many of the thoughts of his contemporaries were based on cherished sets of illusions; that those young men and women of whom Bentley spoke must toss away their comforting self-deceptions in order to take their places in the modern world—at least in the World According to Shaw.

But reassessment, whether by the writer himself or by a later critic, does not alter the fact that both Ibsen and Shaw were primarily concerned with the interaction of man to man, of how we can live together fruitfully and truthfully. Shaw's talk about "the Life Force" may echo Ibsen's "claim of the Ideal" in its rhetorical flourish, but their plays continue to vibrate with life, not because of such sententious philosophical catch phrases or even because of what they imply, but because the plays are inhabited by fascinating characters involved in interesting relationships: Eilert Lovborg with Hedda Gabler, Solness with Hilda Wangel, Rebecca West and her Rosmer, Mrs. Alving and Pastor Manders; Dick Dudgeon, John Tanner, Hesione Hushabye, Eliza Doolittle, and such historical figures as Caesar and Cleopatra, Saint Joan, Napoleon.

What it comes down to is that both Ibsen and Shaw were first and foremost dramatists, and only secondly thinkers or philosophers. Ibsen took the "well-made play" he inherited from Eugène Scribe, with its emphasis on plot and situation; he then enriched it with character and applied to it a thesis. Shaw did it backwards; he saw Ibsen's theses as of first importance, used his own idea as his point of departure and worked it out in terms of characters, situations, and plot, creating plays with an intoxicating gift for language. To recall that Ibsen wrote something like tragedies (not, to be sure, of the Greek sort) and Shaw comedies (save for *Saint Joan*) is only to point out the difference in means, not in ends. For great playwrights "the play's the thing," no matter how effectively they may persuade themselves and their publics that it is the idea—the moral, economic or social philosophy—that counts. Shaw himself seemed to agree. (He was always contradicting himself, as everyone knows). "Would any one but a buffle-headed idiot of a university professor infer that all my plays were written as economic essays and not as plays of life, character and human destiny like those of Shakespear or Euripides?"

The twentieth century: preoccupations and fragmentations

Twentieth-century drama is built upon the cornerstones laid by these three master-builders and their iconoclastic junior partner. It inherits their social agenda, the intensifying preoccupation with materialism that went forward apace after the Industrial Revolution with readjustments to newly evolving class lines, until the rich against the poor became a confrontation between the "proletariat" and the "bourgeoisie" while science and technology acquired ever increasing momentum.

Twentieth-century drama inherits also, and perhaps more significantly, the mental and spiritual traumas which haunted the last couple of decades

Minnie Maddern Fiske with George Arliss in Ibsen's *Hedda Gabler,* 1904. *"Mrs. Fiske, who had become a legend in our theatre, . . . was an intelligent and talented performer who won considerable distinction by introducing Ibsen to America."*

of the 1800s. It is those which have been especially noted in the paragraphs devoted to Ibsen, Strindberg, Chekhov, with words about reality and illusion, the search for identity, the acknowledgement of the power of the subconscious and sexuality (all subjects not exactly ignored by Shaw either, be it noted). Read or reread *A Doll's House, The Wild Duck, Ghosts, Hedda Gabler, The Master Builder; The Father, The Dance of Death, A Dream Play, To Damascus; The Seagull, The Three Sisters, Uncle Vanya, The Cherry Orchard.* This staggeringly rich output of the last quarter of the last century draws us straight into the heart of modern drama with its quest for reality and for meaning to life, its search for the realization of self and the means of protecting the self against an increasingly mechanistic, technological world. Modern drama pushes constantly toward the unmasking of each man's true identity and the establishment of his individual responsibility. It does so with mounting anxiety as it portrays a fragmenting culture with its crises of faith—in God, in the relevance or even existence of moral absolutes, in the self itself. Eugene O'Neill testified to this, summing up his own agenda and establishing his own priorities in a letter to his friend, the critic George Jean Nathan:

> The playwright of today must dig at the roots of the sickness of today
> as he feels it—the death of the old God and the failure of science and

materialism to give any satisfactory new one for the surviving primitive religious instinct to find a meaning for life in and to comfort its fears of death with. It seems to me that anyone trying to do big work nowadays must have this big subject behind all the little subjects of his plays or novels, or he is scribbling around the surface of things.

These more or less metaphysical and psychogenic preoccupations, already manifest when our century began, soon become overpowering. And why not? Twentieth-century man arrived on the scene just as Nietzsche's thundering assertion that God is dead was still reverberating, as Freud was unveiling a hitherto unfathomed world of the subconscious, as science and technology were in full gallop carrying us, hats askew and veils flying, breathlessly toward the nuclear age.

How could the stage mirror the confusion? How could its sound track pierce through the cacophony? John Dryden once said that a "play ought to be a just and lively image of human nature." The chronicler of our century's drama can hope only to arrest that "just image," to keep his eye on man, a reeling figure buffeted by world wars, by political and social revolutions, by challenges to his mind and imagination, who sees and hears sights and sounds in the ether such as have never been experienced before.

The ten or a dozen twentieth-century dramatists who kept their eyes fixed most clearly on human nature in these terms, and who thus serve as prime interpreters of our century are Shaw (already on the scene), Pirandello, Gorky, Synge, O'Casey, O'Neill, Brecht, Williams, Miller, Sartre, and Beckett. There have been others, of course, but these will suffice to mention. Of them, four are Irishmen, three Americans, one is an Italian, one a Russian, one a Frenchman, and one a German. All across the West, then, voices of dramatists have been raised to sound again the alarms concerning the human condition that were heard on the stages of Ibsen, Strindberg, and Chekhov.

Pirandello: philosopher of "being and seeming"

Luigi Pirandello provides another example of a dramatist who was hailed as a philosopher in his lifetime, but whose contribution on review has been, like Shaw's, revised so as to upgrade his dramaturgy and downgrade his ideas. At the time the ideas were admittedly echoes of already familiar themes, but with new variations.

It was in the waning days of World War I and the decade which followed that Pirandello, by then already past fifty, began to be taken seriously by the cognoscenti. (It would be incorrect to say that he ever enjoyed the broad popularity of, say, Shaw.) He himself demanded to be treated with gravity. In the Preface to *Six Characters in Search of an Author,* he introduced himself as an author to whom "it was never enough to present a man or a woman and what is special and characteristic about them simply for the pleasure of presenting them." Rather he felt a kinship with writers who "feel a more profound spiritual need.... These are, more precisely, philosophical writers. I have the misfortune to belong to these last."

In *Right You Are (If You Think So)* Pirandello had begun his dramatic studies of the enigma surrounding reality and illusion—not just the use men and women make of these phenomena but the meaning of the words themselves: what *is* reality? what is illusion? May they be the same thing, or perhaps interchangeable? Or variable, not fixed?

The Ibsen-Strindberg-Chekhov triumvirate, and Shaw too, had frequently pondered the roles reality and illusion play in individual personalities, making some people face and others evade their responsibilities to society or in their most intimate personal relationships. Pirandello was not concerned with these matters; he was pondering what is truth. It is an important question, but one that might have seemed intractable to dramatic treatment.

Pirandello proved it otherwise. Creating almost melodramatic situations, he constructed plots and invented characters who dramatized those very questions. Who is Signora Ponza in *Right You Are*? Her husband claims she is his second wife, his first having died. The wife's mother claims Ponza is deluded: her daughter still lives, is still married to him. Who is the deluded one—mother-in-law or husband? We never find out. Is the title character in *Henry IV* mad, as everyone in the play assumes, or rational, as the audience is led by the writer to conclude? Have the Six Characters possibly a more fixed reality than the actors who impersonate them in the play within the play? Or have they no reality at all except in their author's imagination? Is Cia, the focal character in *As You Desire Me*, a wife who disappeared from her home during the war and is rediscovered? Or is she some other woman altogether? All these questions are posed with extraordinary ambiguity and evoke powerful suspense. Truth, Pirandello seems to argue over and over, is what you believe it to be. Like beauty, it is in the eye of the beholder. No wonder these plays have been called "dramas of being and seeming."

This Italian, who won the Nobel Prize for Literature in 1934, two years before his death, was undoubtedly an intellectual, but a rare one. He himself once pointed out that "one of the novelties I have given to the modern drama consists in converting the intellect into passion." The statement is somewhat ambiguous. Exciting as is his action, paradoxical as are his dilemmas, and evasive as are his denouements, his plays seem saturated by a sort of "ironical realism"; the dramatist himself remains uncommitted. Is it, then, his own intellect that is converted into passion, is it the intellect of his characters, or does the process occur in the audience? Toward what, in brief, is the passion directed?

Pirandello spoke for the thoughtful in the generation of the 1920s, not only in his own country but throughout the West, the first generation to be seriously affected by Freud, one beginning to re-evaluate the enigma of personality in the modern context. A half-century later we return to his plays more because they are engrossing and original than because truth is to be found there with a capital T. Today we are less impressed by what he made of his own questions: what is reality? illusion? for the answer seems to be simply, "It all depends."

Dramas of the Common Man: Synge, O'Casey, the Soviets, Brecht

"The sixteenth century is the Century of the Common Man," observes the one-man Chorus in Robert Bolt's *A Man for All Seasons*. After a pause he adds dryly, "Like all the other centuries." For us viewing the twentieth, it is possible to rephrase Bolt's line: *ours* is the Century of the Common Man. We say it without his irony and with a conviction born of witnessing the Bolshevik Revolution of 1917, the establishment of the "dictatorships of the proletariat" in Eastern Europe after 1945, the Chinese Communist revolution that began in 1949.

Prior to 1900, drama was written first to mirror its aristocratic audience, then to cater to the tastes and sensibilities of a rising middle class; still later, as we have noted especially in Ibsen, Chekhov, and Shaw, it served to attack that middle class's cultural and social prejudices and values. (Continuing middle class domination of the theatre is in large measure also responsible for the survival of Realism as the form most congenial to the taste of the twentieth-century public.)

Our century was in its earliest infancy when authentic common men came into view onstage, first from the eastern, then from the western perimeters of Europe — Russia and Ireland. In 1902 Maksim Gorky, urged by Chekhov to apply his considerable talent toward writing for the stage, presented the world with a masterpiece, *The Lower Depths*. The play's characters — a locksmith and his dying wife, a hat-maker, a vendor of meat pies, a couple of longshoremen, a policeman, a shoemaker, a thief, an alcoholic former actor, a seedy "Baron," a pilgrim, a man about whom nothing is known, and the couple who run the flophouse where this group is lodged — depict with intense realism the underside of society, which is portrayed with the authority of one who has known that world and with the sympathy of a man who cares deeply about its inhabitants.

Gorky was a revolutionist. In fact, he wrote one of his plays in prison while serving a political sentence. By 1906 he had to flee abroad, becoming a political exile for the next eight years. But *The Lower Depths* is not properly a political play. It is, in fact, one of the major dramas to deal with the familiar theme of reality and illusion. Although one of its most affecting and eloquent characters (Luka, the pilgrim) encourages illusions among these derelicts, his voice is not the author's. That belongs to Satine, the man with the shadowy past, who believes that "lying is the religion of slaves and masters," who says, "Truth is the god of the free man." It is a proper position for a champion of the proletariat. Dreamers do not act; Gorky's is a veiled call to action: "Arise, ye prisoners of starvation!"

And as Chekhov urged Gorky to write for the theatre, so William Butler

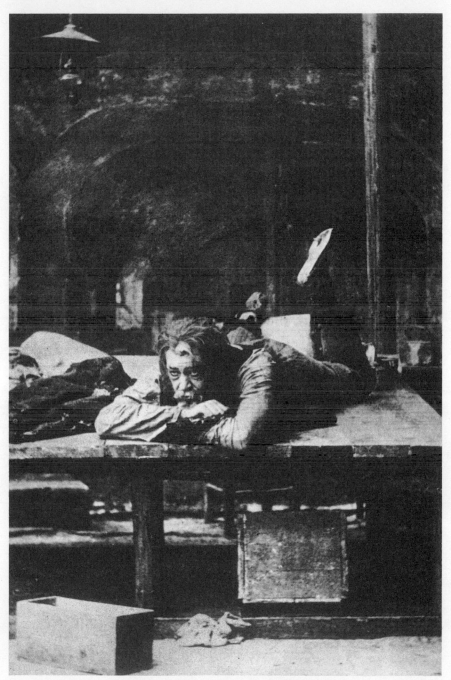

Konstantin Stanislavsky in Maksim Gorky's *The Lower Depths*, 1902.

Yeats at about the same time was counseling John Millington Synge. "Go West, young man!" cried Yeats. Synge obeyed, journeyed to the bleak Aran Islands and the green cloudswept West Country of his native land, and produced a handful of plays which contain some of the most beautiful lines written in our language. His subject? The fisherfolk and peasants of Ireland.

Synge himself was no more interested in proletarian political and social upheavals than were the characters who inhabited his cottages and pubs— Pegeen Mike and Christy Mahon, the Widow Quinn, Maurya who lost five sons to the sea, her daughters Nora and Cathleen. Life is hard for these folk, but it is lived joyously and freely in *The Playboy of the Western World*, stoically and with fortitude in *Riders to the Sea*, Synge's two masterpieces. His people may sleep in ditches or haylofts, run races on the sands, drink "poteen" by the fire—some industrious, some lazing away their days in fine talk—but they possess, as their creator wrote, "a popular imagination that is fiery and magnificent, and tender." The common man never had a more lyrical portraitist than the Irish prose-poet.

Synge's characters peopled the countryside; those of his compatriot, young Sean O'Casey, dwelt in the Dublin slums. The latter more resemble what we think of as the twentieth-century proletariat, doubtless because our world is also less dominantly agrarian, and because O'Casey's folk are engaged in revolution and urban barricades: the snipers and their grenades provide more recognizably modern street sights and sounds. However, one must remember that "a play ought to be a just and lively image of human nature." So the Easter Rebellion, which was a poignant reality to O'Casey himself and claimed the blood of so many of his characters, provides only the background for an elbowing crowd of raffish, roguish, laughing, weeping common people—Joxer and Captain Boyle in *Juno and the Paycock*, Fluther and The Covey and Bessie Burgess in *The Plough and the Stars*, Minnie and Daveron in *The Shadow of a Gunman*.

To these dramas celebrating the common man, we must add the not inconsiderable body of work that has all but engulfed the stage in those parts of the world where a Communist government has taken power in the name of the people, where there exists what is usually called proletarian drama. It may seem surprising that the Soviet portion of this has gone all but unnoticed in the outside world between 1917 and the present. Certainly it has not been for lack of output. Dozens of Russian playwrights have turned out hundreds of plays in the past sixty-odd years, but only the most determined American playgoer has seen more than a half-dozen of them on our stages during as many decades.

Quality has not kept up with quantity. No first-rate dramatist has appeared since Gorky died in 1936. Vladimir Mayakovsky, a talented futurist poet with a gift for satire, had a meteoric success during the first dozen years after the Revolution, but he committed suicide in 1930. Mikhail Bulgakov and Yevgenny Shvarts, both also now dead, had considerable talent. The former's *The Days of the Turbins* and *Molière* added to the literary fame he acquired through his novel, *The Master and Margarita*. Shvarts's reputation rests on a series of dramatized fairy stories, mostly adapted from Andersen and the Grimms (notably *The Naked King, The Shadow, The Dragon*), ostensibly written for children but which were in fact fashioned into sharply critical satires of Soviet life and values. The reason these two dramatists caused tremors outside Russia was because they found metaphors through which to express with eloquent conviction their faith in the freedom of the human spirit.

The main body of proletarian drama has been disregarded outside the U.S.S.R. because it has been picturing a life-style and values irrelevant or unsympathetic to Western eyes. For at least two generations it toed the Party line too closely for Western taste. Neither early Soviet plays about collective farming and hydroelectric plants nor later ones depicting the new heroes' and heroines' struggles (which they inevitably won) against so-called anti-revolutionary forces aroused much enthusiasm in parts of the world where these preoccupations seemed less than cosmic. But the real trouble lay in the depiction of a sterile world where man was not free to question, to think, to fulfill himself. Not until the 1970s did a Soviet generation begin to feel less constraint in subject matter and at long last try to create "a just and lively image of human nature."

"The theatre entered the province of the philosopher—at any rate, the sort of philosopher who wanted not only to explain the world but also to change it. Hence the theatre philosophized; hence it instructed." So wrote Bertold Brecht shortly before his death in 1956. Brecht was himself a philosophical dramatist who wanted to change the world. He was also a poet, a Marxist, a cynic, a nihilist, a moralist with more than a touch of the polemicist. He was a man of paradoxes: committed yet alienated, active yet passive, pessimistic yet hopeful. In his contradictions Brecht comes closer than most playwrights to epitomizing the plight of the artist in this fractured, fragmented world of the twentieth century. The concluding verse of his *St. Joan of the Stockyards* addresses his confused generation of whatever political hue and simultaneously reveals his own ambivalence:

> Humanity! two souls abide
> Within thy breast!
> Do not set either one aside:
> To live with both is best!
> Be torn apart with constant care!
> Be two in one! Be here, be there!
> Hold the low one, hold the high one—
> Hold the straight one, hold the sly one—
> Hold the pair!

Whatever the extent of his Marxist commitment (and the Russian Communists have been slow to hail him as a true comrade), Brecht became a champion of the common man and an ardent opponent of capitalism. His

Setting for a scene in *Mother Courage and Her Children* (*Mutter Courage und ihre Kinder*), staged by Bertolt Brecht for the 1949 production by the Berliner Ensemble.

early plays, epitomized by *In the Jungle of the Cities,* assert that in the modern materialistic world dominated by each man's greed, society resembles nothing so much as a pack of wolves preying on itself. We are all beasts, he seems to say, and there is no health in us. Such pessimism is, of course, alien to the Marxist, who purports to have faith in the perfectibility of both the individual and society. Brecht demanded that the world be changed, but even as he uttered the challenge, he questioned the possibility of its fulfillment.

This paradox set him apart from his Communist brethren. For them it was obvious that if capitalism is "The Great Satan," saving grace can be found only in its demolition and replacement by socialism. The basic sociopolitical conflict of our century has revolved around the confrontation and partial accommodation of these two systems. But, like many others, Brecht could not quite choose his side. The indignity of the human condition he felt was attributable in part to frailties and pressures within and without the social and economic structure, but man's own waywardness played a part. Furthermore, there was no saving grace to be expected from heaven. Even in *The Good Woman of Setzuan,* his Chinese gods, saying farewell to Shen Te, the "good woman," depart on their pink cloud mouthing ironic and ambiguous platitudes: "Should the world be changed? How? By whom? No! Everything is in order. . . . Just be good and everything will turn out well!"

In play after play Brecht pursued his paradoxes. *The Threepenny Opera,* probably his most warmly received work, written with composer Kurt Weill, draws upon the black world of whores, pimps, and robbers who mouth obscenities and practice cynical betrayals of each other and the world, "with the double-cross as the leit-motif." All this is contrapuntally set to the accompaniment of one of Weill's most hauntingly sweet scores—"a lark singing above battlefield corpses."

Mother Courage and Her Children, Galileo, The Good Woman of Setzuan, The Caucasian Chalk Circle, Brecht's four major dramas, provide little light to guide us through the dark streets of the poet's imagination. Whether he writes of the Thirty Years' War, as in *Mother Courage,* or the Inquisition setting out to muzzle Galileo, the man of science, or offers us ironic Chinese parables, his characters are repeatedly drawn into intolerable situations, either through their own cupidity and cynicism (as in *Mother Courage*) or as the victim of others' ignorance and reactionary pigheadedness (as in *Galileo*), hypocrisy and rapacity (as in *The Good Woman*). For Brecht, the twentieth century is not a happy or a hopeful time to live.

American drama comes of age: O'Neill—Williams—Miller

The twentieth century was not a happy or a hopeful time for Eugene O'Neill, either, although his despair bore no relationship to the class struggle. "Who wants to see life as it is if they can help it?" cries Edmund Tyrone in *Long Day's Journey into Night.* For "Edmund" we read "Eugene," for the

Eugene O'Neill.

play is about the author's family, and the younger son is himself. To look at a photograph of America's only Nobel Prize-winning dramatist, taken during the last decade of his life — the decade during which that line was penned — is to see the face of a sensitive, pain-ridden, brooding human being. The pain could be attributable to the Parkinson's Disease which was slowly eroding his body and mind; the sensitivity and brooding had been his throughout most of his life, and they were bred of the spirit. In the same play the same character continues his agonizing self-analysis:

> It was a great mistake, my being born a man, I would have been much
> more successful as a seagull or a fish. As it is, I will always be a
> stranger who never feels at home, who does not really want and is not
> really wanted, who can never belong, who must always be a little in
> love with death.

O'Neill was one of the few American dramatists whose work increased in power and stature as he grew older. His last great quartet, *Long Day's Journey into Night, The Iceman Cometh, A Moon for the Misbegotten, A Touch of the Poet,* provided the world with arresting insights into the spiritual malaise of our century. They are not couched in glowing poetry or trenchant wit (or even very fine prose). They are at odds with America's widely held optimism, even its humor. They are oblivious to political, social, or economic theories. They rise from the dark night of the soul when a man ponders his role in the cosmic scheme.

In his initial full-length play, *Beyond the Horizon,* which won for him his first Pulitzer Prize in 1921, O'Neill revealed how seriously he took the theatre as a vehicle for his brooding, and how somber was to be his palette. Two or three themes are present. (He returned to them time and again.) First, there is the haunting question that keeps being asked by modern dramatists: what shall a man live by, the dream or the fact? The playwright indicates at once his position: "In *Beyond the Horizon* there are three acts of two scenes each. One scene is out of doors, showing the horizon, suggesting the man's desire and dream. The other is indoors, the horizon gone — suggesting what has come between him and his dreams." Life is too painful to be dealt with head-on. One must try to find some protection. In *The Iceman Cometh* and *A Moon for the Misbegotten* alcohol seems to sustain the "pipe dream"; in *Long Day's Journey* it is morphine for at least one character, drink for the others. And fog. In play after play, O'Neill, a great lover of the sea, uses fog as his symbol for illusion. "I really love fog. It hides you from the world and the world from you," says Mary Tyrone, and her younger son echoes her: "Fog is where I wanted to be.... Everything looked and sounded unreal."

A second theme asserts itself in *Beyond the Horizon:* the conflicting aims and values of the materialist and the artist. More than one American dramatist of this century has been attracted to the problem of reconciling the two. George S. Kaufman and Marc Connelly wrote a satiric fantasy on the subject, *Beggar on Horseback;* Philip Barry, Maxwell Anderson, and S. N. Behrman had refreshingly amusing ideas concerning the clash in such plays as *Holiday, High Tor, The Second Man.* Abroad, Jean Anouilh made it a major theme of his work. But no one more insistently probed it than O'Neill, in *Marco Millions, The Great God Brown, Dynamo, Days without End.* One could say that this is merely a restatement of the reality/illusion motif, with the materialist-businessman cast in the role of realist, the poet-artist as the dreamer. However you look at it, the conflict is between basic values, whether consciously pursued or unconsciously induced. A balanced culture requires both, but America has not become aware of this, O'Neill seems to say, and continues to weigh the scale in favor of the materialist.

A sense of "belonging," or, more correctly, of not belonging (another way of saying "alienation"), also absorbed O'Neill in his first play. Two brothers, whose conflict of interest sparks the action, are drawn by circumstance to exchange roles, with near-tragic consequences for both as the dreamer tries to adapt to the reality of running a farm and the doer is destined to wander aimlessly. The search for one's place in life also underlies *The Hairy Ape,* where Yank, a maladjusted stoker on an ocean liner, finds his only fulfillment in the fatal embrace of a gorilla at the zoo.

To these three themes can be added a fourth: psychosexual relationships within the family. In O'Neill's two closest approximations to tragedy, *Desire Under the Elms* and *Mourning Becomes Electra,* he turns to father-son, mother-son, father-daughter relationships to dramatize the destructive drives that have disrupted nature and invited calamity from the Greeks to our own day. *Desire Under the Elms* also embraces these twin basic urges of man—to possess his own piece of land and to pass it on to his offspring. The denial of these desires, combined with the sexual complications between son and stepmother, could well have led to tragedy, but the play falls short of that because the characters lack grandeur of soul and their creator lacks the language to compensate.

As O'Neill recognized, his version of the *Oresteia, Mourning Becomes Electra,* also lacks a critical component. Aeschylus explored the relationship of man to God—the divine conundrum—and of justice clashing with mercy. The twentieth-century playwright, having lost touch with God, falls back on Freud as a surrogate Athene, and the result is less than satisfactory.

It has been said of Ibsen, Shaw, and Pirandello that the judgments of their contemporaries have been overturned by time, that their excellences may be judged as deriving more from their technical prowess as playwrights than from the power of their ideas. I suspect that O'Neill will experience the reverse: his skill as a dramatist will be recognized as inferior to the profundity of his subject matter. Even now one rereads most of his early works with growing consternation at the melodramatic strains he places upon his situations and the ineptitude of his language, but one finds in his later plays a substantial grasp of the truly meaningful problems and dilemmas faced by twentieth-century man.

Laurette Taylor, right, playing the part of the mother, Amanda, in Williams's *The Glass Menagerie,* 1945, makes a dress long enough to hide the limp of daughter Laura (Julie Haydon). *"The women of* The Glass Menagerie *are stranded, their lives unresolved, in Williams's 'play of memory', much like the unresolved lives of the young Prozorov women in Chekhov's* The Three Sisters.*"*

O'Neill was not the only one to confront such themes. The guns of World War II were scarcely stilled when America's two most thoughtful dramatic interpreters of our postwar world took center stage. Tennessee Williams was thirty-four, Arthur Miller twenty-nine. During the following decade they hopscotched through the theatrical seasons. Williams turned out first *The Glass Menagerie* in 1944, then *A Streetcar Named Desire* in 1947, *The Rose Tattoo* in 1950, *Cat on a Hot Tin Roof* in 1955; Miller produced *All My Sons* in 1947, then *Death of a Salesman* in 1949, *The Crucible* in 1953, *A View from the Bridge* in 1955. With those eight plays the two dramatists vied to inherit the mantle of O'Neill. In the end, they tore it down the middle.

Their first major works defined their lineages and their differences. Williams sprang from Chekhov, Miller from Ibsen. Williams staked his claim to the psychological understanding, poetic insight, and felicity of expression of the Russian, Miller to the sense of social responsibility and cry of conscience that animated the Norwegian. Williams used indirection and an amalgam of laughter and tears to win sympathy for his harrowed humans. Miller roused passion blended with indignation to hold his audiences transfixed. He hoped, as he put it, that "by the route of passion may be opened up new relationships between a man and men, and between men and Man." This he accomplished.

Both playwrights inherited from their spiritual progenitors one common concern—the ongoing conflict between reality and self-delusion which had attracted Ibsen in *The Wild Duck* and Chekhov in *The Cherry Orchard*. In both *The Glass Menagerie* and *A Streetcar Named Desire*, Williams, like Chekhov, painted portraits of women who, reminscent of Madame Ranevsky, cannot bear to face the harsh facts of changing life. Amanda Wingfield takes refuge in a "magnolia-scented past," her daughter, Laura, in her collection of old phonograph records and glass animals. Blanche Du Bois in *Streetcar* is haunted in her dreams by strains of the Varsoviana and pursuing admirers who never materialize. The women of *The Glass Menagerie* are stranded, their lives unresolved, in Williams's "play of memory," much like the unresolved lives of the young Prozorov women in Chekhov's *The Three Sisters*. Blanche's life ends in the confinement of a lunatic asylum. In Williams's view, escape from reality may sometimes be essential to retain one's sanity.

In *Death of a Salesman,* Willy Loman's self-delusion is deeply ingrained and his unconscious effort to instill it in his sons is in large measure responsible for the wreckage of all three lives. In Miller's earlier play, *All My Sons,* another father deludes himself that he can avoid responsibility for past crimes by formally refusing to admit guilt, but the author sternly allows his protagonist no way out but suicide. Conscience, along with the acceptance of social responsibility for one's actions, would seem to be for Miller twin imperatives of moral behavior. Their assumption leads John Proctor, the protagonist of *The Crucible,* to choose death rather than deny his conscience and his responsibility; Eddie Carbone, the leading character in *A View from the Bridge,* finally recognizes that to have denied those forces requires expiation with his life.

It may be a truism to observe that characters plagued by conscience are also anguished with guilt. Certainly in Miller's work the two necessarily and constantly interact. Public conscience stems from private guilts, regularly sexual in origin. The discovery by Willy Loman's son, Biff, that his father has had extra-marital affairs is responsible for the growing alienation between the two. So, too, John Proctor's guilt over his adulterous liaison with his servant girl, Abigail Williams, and his subsequent rejection of her leads directly to the central catastrophe of *The Crucible.* Again, the unwilling recognition by Eddie Carbone of his incestuous desire for his niece motivates his suicide. The expiation of guilt is as necessary to these dramas' resolution as is fidelity to conscience.

Death of a Salesman is concerned, however, with more than the themes of reality and illusion, conscience and guilt. It focuses with equal force on the disastrous consequences of lives dedicated to false values. Willy Loman is persuaded that material success transcends all else. He is prepared to cheat and lie and to encourage his sons to do likewise, on the theory that the end justifies the means. He never realizes that the end is unworthy. He believes that with a smile and a shoeshine he can conquer the world, not only liked but well-liked, unaware that integrity, maintained at higher cost, pays better dividends. Be on guard, warns Miller, lest the American dream, wrongly interpreted, lead only to bankruptcy of the spirit. *Salesman* is redeemed finally by love, by the author's posthumous reprieve for his hero: at his graveside Willy's best friend reminds his sons that "a salesman is got to dream, boy. It comes with the territory." What counts is the kind of dream it is.

Tennessee Williams also understands that a man or woman "is got to dream." He understands, too, something of the desperation that is felt by those who suffer from loneliness, from the inability to communicate with their fellows. He understands sexual hunger and deprivation. These matters are not always explicitly expounded; they are dealt with much as Chekhov did, by indirection. Williams does not judge and condemn his characters as Miller does. No more did Chekhov. Like the latter, Williams sympathizes with them, laughs at their foibles, but never sentimentalizes. John Mason Brown, an eminent critic of the time, recognized Williams's resemblance to Chekhov. Writing of Blanche in his review of *Streetcar,* Brown said: "Mr. Williams understands and would have us understand what has brought about her decline. He passes no moral judgment. He does not condemn her. He allows her to destroy herself and invites us to watch her in the process."

Finally, like Chekhov, Williams writes prose that is warmly lyrical. This gift bathes even the most sordid of his scenes (and one cannot deny that there is much that is sordid and perverse) in an incandescent glow. He has a sharp ear for the common speech, especially of his native South, and he has the knack of being able to reproduce it; but more, he can heighten it until it takes on the condition of poetry, much as Synge and O'Casey could do.

To what extent are these two American dramatists of the 1940s and 1950s true interpreters of their time? What have they contributed to better understanding of the preoccupations of their fellow men through their work in the theatre of the twentieth century? It is difficult to pass judgment on one's contemporaries when both are still alive and writing. Nonetheless, their best work to date was done almost a quarter-century ago, so some perspective should be possible.

Unexpectedly, both writers seem oblivious to the aftermath of the world's greatest convulsion, World War II. True, in Miller's *All My Sons*, the protagonist is involved in a wartime scandal concerning the manufacture of faulty airplane parts sold to the government; but this is really only a timely device to illustrate the author's principal point that "no man is an island." Loman's career in selling is in no way affected by the war or postwar reaction. It comes to an end because Willy can no longer deliver the goods. His sons Biff and Happy grow up in a world unclouded by impending war or by the preceding Depression years.

The world of Tennessee Williams is equally insulated. Only a few lines spoken by the son in the prologue and epilogue to *The Glass Menagerie* establish any connection with the world outside. Says Tom:

> I turn back time ... to that quaint period, the thirties, when the huge
> middle class of America was matriculating in a school for the blind....
> In Spain there was revolution. Here there was only shouting and
> confusion. In Spain there was Guernica. Here there were disturbances
> of labor, sometimes pretty violent, in otherwise peaceful cities such as
> Chicago, Cleveland, St. Louis.

And at the end; "Nowadays the world is lit by lightning! Blow out your candles, Laura...." Nothing about *A Streetcar Named Desire* or *The Rose Tattoo* or *Cat on a Hot Tin Roof* or any other Williams or Miller play written between 1947 and 1952 bears any relation to America's contemporary social, political, or economic concerns or to its mental or spiritual traumas deriving therefrom. Just as one would not know that Chekhov's world was on the brink of the Russian Revolution of 1905, so Williams's works could have as well been written ten years earlier or ten years later than they were. It seems merely a matter of the author's personal maturation.

The thundering exception is Miller's *The Crucible*. If there had been no House Un-American Activities Committee, no Senator Joseph McCarthy, there would have been no *Crucible*. Those black and hypocritical days fired Miller to fury and from that white heat emerged this one superb drama. The parallel of the seventeenth-century Salem witch-trials to the blacklists of the early 1950s and the personal betrayals that occurred under political pressure seems so apt once Miller has hit upon it that one can only assent to the leap of imagination by which he arrived there.

For Williams and Miller, man is and must always be the subject of drama. Not scientific progress, not political revolution or social evolution, not wars and rumors of wars, but man—how he conducts himself, how he grows or shrivels, how he faces life and death. They are seeking Dryden's "just and lively image of human nature."

Sartre and Beckett: philosopher-playwrights of existentialism

The American theatre has not been hospitable to philosophers, at any rate not as some European theatres have. Americans have fairly successfully kept their eyes on man, but they have not assigned him a role in the divine comedy; they have spent little time or energy seeking to define him or relate him to God. To see that, we must turn to France, especially during these same early postwar Williams-Miller years.

France and America experienced very different wars. We never felt ours arose from any paralysis of national will. We were never invaded and occupied. We had few collaborators, needed no *Résistance*. How otherwise it was for the French, among them Jean-Paul Sartre, who began writing for the theatre in 1943 after serving in a German prison camp, and in whom the war evoked profound reactions which he shared with his disillusioned French compatriots. In their humiliation he and they found existentialism a congenial philosophy.

It is surely unnecessary here to attempt its definition. Suffice it to say that in denying the existence of God, of any fixed standards of conduct or verifiable moral codes, "the just image of human nature" takes on new meaning. Without values external to him, and with no given human nature, man must create his own values, the existentialists said. He must make his own choices and accept responsibility for them. As a totally "free" being, man has the necessity, Sartre wrote in *Forgers of Myths* (1946), an essay on existential drama, "of having to work and die, of being hurled into a life already complete which yet is his own enterprise and in which he can never have a second chance; where he must play his cards and take risks no matter what the cost."

For Sartre, the stage was the ideal medium through which to disseminate this philosophy: the very nature of the dramatic form lent itself to the spectacle of man's existential situation, of the necessity to *act*. In *No Exit* and in his next play, *The Flies*, a reworking of the Electra-Orestes-Clytemnestra legend, this philosopher-playwright accomplished the extraordinary feat of dramatizing his philosophical position far more explicitly than had Pirandello. In *No Exit*, Sartre presents us with three persons locked in a room from which there is no escape. They are dead and in hell, condemned to re-live together through eternity the choices made during their lifetimes. By the final curtain, hope has been eliminated.

The Flies also possesses its own symbolistic system. The plague of flies with which Argos is afflicted (a Sartrean invention) is the plague of guilts which, Sartre felt, were sucking the life blood of France at that time, even as they had done in the ancient kingdom. The land can be saved only if these guilts—avenging furies—can be exorcised. It is this action that Orestes takes upon himself, one vastly more significant than avenging his father's death by killing his mother. He both succeeds and fails in his self-appointed mission: he finds freedom for himself, but ironically at the cost of banishment by his fellow countrymen and disavowal by his sister. Both plays are grim, pessimistic readings of the human condition.

To many American dramatists, Sartre's use of the theatre, like Pirandello's, seems alien: to start with a philosophical concept and then invent a drama to explicate and illustrate it. The American writer is much happier working in reverse fashion, drawing a picture and then looking to see whether it illustrates anything beyond itself—whether, keeping the intellect out of it, his subconscious may have endowed the work with more than he was aware.

Sartre and Pirandello are now both dead. The twentieth-century theatre feels their loss, for there are no other dramatists of the next generation who have chosen to try to dramatize metaphysics. Perhaps the filmmaker Ingmar Bergman comes closer to doing that than any writer for the stage.

Samuel Beckett, 1965.

Samuel Beckett, however, is still alive and while not of the next generation he belongs, certainly, in the company of philosophical dramatists. But
there is a distinction. Sartre's plays have a polemical ring; they seem to have
been written to persuade the spectator to accept Sartre's philosophical
position. They take the focus off man and transfer it to the *idea* of man.
Beckett simply dramatizes the human condition, finding metaphors for
what he feels its state to be. This may be why Beckett's work has acquired
more universal favor than Sartre's, even though his conclusion is equally
bleak.

Born in Dublin, living in Paris and writing in French, Beckett first astonished the world with *Waiting for Godot,* which appeared in 1953. It had an
original run of four hundred performances (in an admittedly tiny theatre),
and has been translated into more than twenty languages. During the five
years after its première, more than a million people, it has been claimed,
succumbed to its peculiar appeal, and goodness knows how many more
have done so since then.

Many interpretations have been offered of this ambiguous drama. For
Peter Brook, the English stage director, the play is a symbol "in an exact
sense of the word." Pursuing his point he continues: "When we say 'symbolic' we often mean something drearily obscure: a true symbol is specific; it
is the only form a certain truth can take." Brook is right. The whole work
is, indeed, a symbol: the *waiting* of Estragon and Vladimir is as much a
symbol as the *Godot* for whom they wait, or the tree beneath which their vigil
takes place, or the couple, Lucky and Pozzo, who interrupt their dialogue.

So it is in all Beckett's work. The parents in the dustbins of *Endgame,* the
blindness of Hamm, its protagonist; the emptiness of its landscape, are all
symbolic and together create a total symbol—for the emptiness of existence.
So does the lady buried to her waist in the sand in *Happy Days,* as do the
tape *and* the man in *Krapp's Last Tape.*

Harold Hobson, the distinguished critic of *The Times* of London, some
years ago wrote, "The feeling which Mr. Beckett expresses on the stage is
a note heard nowhere else in contemporary drama. . . . He is without hope
and without faith." I disagree. Hobson overlooked, in the first place, the
much more nihilistic dramas of Sartre and Albert Camus. In *Waiting for
Godot,* the fact is that man does *not* give up his vigil, he does put off suicide
until tomorrow, he continues to wait, offering meanwhile loyalty, kindness,
and concern for his fellow man. "We have kept our appointment," says
Vladimir. "We are not saints, but we have kept our appointment." Beckett
is not without faith, not without hope.

Reflections on the state of tragedy and comedy

When Dickens wrote his oft-quoted paradoxical opening paragraph to *A
Tale of Two Cities,* remarking that not only was it "the best of times; it was
the worst of times. . . . It was the spring of hope; it was the winter of despair,"
he might well have been summarizing the pages that have preceded, except

that there has been significantly more emphasis on the "worst" than the "best," on incredulity, darkness, and despair rather than on belief, light, and hope. That being the case, it is worthwhile looking again to see, if possible, a more balanced picture.

Comedy is the inverse of tragedy, laughter the antidote for tears. So it has always been said. But in twentieth-century dramatic writing we find a breakdown of these formerly accepted categories. That is why Dickens's paradoxes are relevant: it has been *both* the best and worst of times, simultaneously a season of light and of darkness. Chekhov was saying that when he called his serious *The Seagull* and *The Cherry Orchard* "comedies"; so was Beckett when he filled his bleak *Waiting for Godot* with ancient slapstick comic devices and turned his no-man's land into a haven for Charlie Chaplins. Even as O'Casey was recording tribulation and death in Dublin's back streets, he was evoking wild Irish mirth in the doings and sayings of his collection of drunks and scalliwags. And then, of course, there was Shaw, treating with his coruscating wit many of the most serious subjects bedeviling the age.

There are those who say that tragedy had already disappeared before the nineteenth century. Certainly, by the end of that hundred years men and women had abandoned their faith in moral absolutes. But with the denial of good and evil, there was no longer a frame of reference by which to judge men's actions. Black and white were mixed in a wave of gray. Gray may avoid despair; it cannot induce exaltation. From the days of Aeschylus and Sophocles to our own, without exaltation there has rarely been tragedy.

I would argue that Ibsen never wrote a tragedy (although some claim *Ghosts* comes close); *Miss Julie* and *The Father* are not tragedies; and in our own century neither is *Saint Joan*, nor *Mourning Becomes Electra*, nor *A Streetcar Named Desire. Death of a Salesman* may be an exception because of the sense of the universality it evokes. The admirers of Robert Bolt's *A Man for All Seasons* can make an excellent case for that play. Surely the spectacle of Sir Thomas More preferring death to the sacrifice of his own integrity reminds us once again of that greatness of spirit through which pain can be transmuted into glory. But the dramas of Brecht, Sartre, and Beckett by no means fulfill the properly rigorous requirements: serious, troubled, despairing even, but tragic—no. As Edith Hamilton puts it in her deceptively simple little book, *The Greek Way*, "When humanity is seen as devoid of dignity and significance, trivial, mean and sunk in dreary hopelessness, then the spirit of tragedy departs."

So, whether one likes it or not, one is bound to conclude that in the past hundred years tragedy has all but slipped away, to be replaced by serious dramas, problem plays, and a few philosophical works that have often portrayed man as helpless, but seldom as heroic.

Poetry has also all but disappeared from the stage in this century. During the periods of its greatness—Greece, Elizabethan England, France in the days of *le roi soleil*—dramatists turned instinctively to poetry as their mode of expression. For more than a hundred and fifty years now our stages have reverbrated to no "mighty line," no lyrical outpourings. Pushkin and Goethe were the last major poets to assay the drama with any success and both of them, like T. S. Eliot and Yeats a century later, were better poets than playwrights.

"It is inescapable," Maxwell Anderson pointed out in his *The Essence of Tragedy,* "that prose is the language of information, poetry the language of emotion." From the moment that our dramatists became absorbed in facts as a substitute for truth, Realism as the most accurate expression of reality, science as the new god, wonder and mystery disappeared. "To be or not to be? That is the question," muses Hamlet. "My way of life has fallen into the sere, the yellow leaf," sighs Macbeth. "Ah'm tired of livin' and feared of dyin'," sings Joe in *Showboat.* The twentieth-century songwriter speaks explicitly, stating a fact; Shakespeare turns the same world-weariness into poetry.

Something else has happened to push poetry off the stage. Today's audience has lost its hearing. The twentieth is the century of the communications revolution, by this is meant principally the invention of the mass media, films, and television; by this is meant, in turn, the replacement of the word by the visual image. Motion *pictures* and tele*vision* bear considerable blame for robbing our stage of its poetry, and that may be one reason it lacks the emotional power required for great tragedy.

What of comedy? Tragedy may have disappeared or suffered a sea-change, but surely comedy is still at home on our twentieth-century stages? The difficulty with this is that comedy presupposes a fixed society with certain accepted norms of behavior. It is deviations from the norm of custom and conduct, whether they be those of Alceste or Harpagon, Sir Politick Would-Be or Sir Andrew Aguecheek, Khlestakov, the fake Inspector General or Fancourt Babberly, Charley's fake aunt from Brazil, that evoke our laughter. But society in our century has been nothing if not fluid. Its frames of reference with regard to accepted behavior have changed with incredible speed. What seemed funny in the 1880s draws yawns in the 1980s; comedies and musicals of the 1920s are revived only for their quaintness. *H.M.S. Pinafore* charms today because of its Sullivan score and the intricacy of Gilbert's verse-patterns, not because of the fun it pokes at the Royal Navy: there isn't enough Navy left to laugh at.

As comedy is supposed to reflect the state of society, and as the mores of Moscow and Monte Carlo have little in common, those Russians who laughed at Katayev's *Squaring the Circle* in the 1930s would almost certainly have found little to roll in the aisles over at Coward's *Private Lives,* produced in the same decade. So, place works against comedy as well as time does. So does the social order. Admittedly, one can learn more from Restoration comedy about the high life of late seventeenth-century London than can be culled from the history books, but the Wits offer us in their mirrors no reflections but their own; we get no images of Midland farmers, say, or Cornish fishermen in 1690.

To be sure, certain comedies defy time, place, and custom. They exist independently in an artificial climate that parodies real life but does not reflect it. Oscar Wilde's *The Importance of Being Earnest* is the classic example. Then there are some farces of Feydeau and Pinero, and Labiche's *The Italian Straw Hat* (*Le Chapeau de Paille d'Italie*). Again, there are comedies founded on basically ludicrous situations, such as mistaken identity or some fatuous presumption. Plautus's *Menaechmi* becomes Shakespeare's *The Comedy of Errors*, then turns into Rodgers's and Hart's *The Boys from Syracuse*. The Roman *Miles Gloriosus* becomes first Sir John Falstaff, then twentieth-century Aubrey Piper in George Kelly's *The Show-Off*. The point is that these comedies are based on sure-fire laugh-provoking complications or human caricatures; they are nearer to farce than comedy in that they mock our society but do not illuminate it.

So, then, satire and "social" comedy would not alter serious drama's conclusions concerning the stage's interpretation of the century. Most of our comedians under cover of laughter would lead us to equally bleak conclusions. In recent times we have become familiar with an appellation that seems to fit: "black comedy." Was not Louis Kronenberger correct when he announced that comedy is not to be confused with optimism? That it is "much more reasonably associated with pessimism?" After all, who in the present generation would say with Robert Browning's Pippa (he did not say it himself) that "God's in His Heaven/ All's right with the world."

The interpreters

Said Hamlet, "The play's the thing/ Wherein I'll catch the conscience of the king." But the idea did not occur to him until the Players appeared. Thus far, Ibsen and some of his successor playwrights down to Beckett have held our attention. Now it is time for the players, and with them all the other contributors to the event.

There is only so much a dramatist—even Ibsen—can do on his own. Of course, what he does is basic; but without playhouses and players, without nowadays a director's guiding hand and designers of setting, lighting, and costumes, his creation remains literary, it is not theatre—and theatre is our subject.

Having begun this retrospective with the great dramatists of the last twenty years of the 1800s, the spotlight now swings back to refocus on those same two decades, but this time on the theatrical styles that prevailed.

There is always an organic relationship between form and content in any art, or there should be. In the performing arts we find that save for composers and dramatists, artists are interpreters, rarely creators. Thus, in the

John Barrymore, 1922 (left, above), Alexander Moissi, 1925 (left), and John Gielgud, during the 1930s (above), use their ''truth to life'' interpretations of Shakespeare's *Hamlet*.

David Garrick, costumed for the role of Richard III; engraving by William Hogarth, 1746. *"More than a hundred years earlier David Garrick had astounded English audiences by his true-to-life style of acting."*

theatre, the only necessity for actors, directors, and designers is to find ways to express the intent of the dramatists, to adapt their skills to the task of exploring the most effective means for giving life to the play and enhancing the style of the playwright.

Realism rules the stage

Unquestionably the new style of the 1880s was Realism. After the fustian and grandiloquence of the Romantic afflatus, it was refreshing to plunge into the chilling waters of "truth to life," wherever that current might draw one. In 1873 Zola had asserted, in the Preface to his dramatization of *Thérèse Raquin,* that "there should no longer be any school, no more formulas, no standards of any sort; there is only life itself.... We must delve into the living drama of the two-fold life of the character and its environment, bereft of every nursery tale, historical trapping and the usual conventional stupidities." In the same place he said that "the experimental and scientific spirit of the century will enter the domain of the drama and . . . in it lies its only possible salvation."

"Truth to life" is a perilously simplistic phrase. It assumes there is common agreement as to what "truth" is, as to what is meant by "life." For the nineteenth-century Realists—and their nephews, the Naturalists—truth was regularly thought to be based on acceptance of the outwardly observable facts that the new "scientific spirit" revealed; "life" for them was still mankind, but now living in and conditioned by an environment that encompassed "new" concepts of moral, social, and political order whose influences must be understood and taken into account.

I have long been attracted to the notion that in those ages when things of the spirit are held most precious (as in the Middle Ages and the early Renaissance), art turns away from the depiction of life's externals. It seeks to find symbols and abstractions to express the unseen and a language — poetry, to be precise — that can lift us out of the give-and-take of daily life. On the other hand, at those times when materialism dominates — the days, say, of the later Roman Empire, the Jacobean and Restoration ages in England, and much of the West after the Industrial Revolution — the most congenial artistic attitude is Realism, of which prose seems the appropriate expression.

If this notion is valid, it goes a long way toward explaining why Realism was the style the theatre embraced with such enthusiasm in the last decades of the nineteenth century and which it has had such difficulty letting go in our own time. It helps to explain, too, why both Ibsen's "social" plays and Chekhov's "scenes of country life" found their natural expression in prose; equally, why Strindberg cast off Realism and Naturalism in favor of Symbolism and Expressionism when the subconscious or mystical experience took over in *A Dream Play, The Ghost Sonata, To Damascus.*

Arthur Miller has his own favorite notion to account for the hold Realism has had since Ibsen. "I have come to wonder whether the force or pressure that makes for Realism, that even requires it, is the magnetic force of the family relationship within the play," he says. I confess I have some difficulty with this. The family has been with us since the House of Atreus, but Aeschylus had his mind less on family relationships than on the Almighty, and Shakespeare was more concerned with the nature of evil and man's capacity to become "habituated to sin" than in the domestic ties of Macbeth to his lady-wife.

Nevertheless, it is true that Ibsen, Strindberg, Chekhov (and Shaw much of the time) did develop their theses in terms of the family: Ibsen's Alvings and Ekdals, Chekhov's Prozorovs and Ranevskys, Shaw's Morells and Undershafts. So today do O'Neill, Williams, and Miller himself. But when Ibsen wants to present "a man seen alone," Miller continues, "confronting non-familial openly social relationships and forces," he sends Peer Gynt out of the living room and into a world of poetic fantasy. Not only does the form of the language change from prose to poetry; so does the style of the whole play. And when O'Neill, Brecht, Sartre, and Beckett take as their subject man not in familial but in broadly social or philosophical terms, Realism does not seem to satisfy them either, and new forms must be explored. And as the intent of dramatists alters, acting styles must also change. Realistic drama requires realistic performances. When the concern ceases to be with idealized kings and queens, and warriors and courtesans are

Eleonora Duse, 1896. *". . . what inner radiance and spirituality this Italian artist possessed!"*

replaced by middle-class parents and their offspring, by salesmen and schoolteachers, by day laborers and farmers, the very timbre of the voice changes, the body moves differently. The same is true of the environment. The palace becomes a parlor, a bedroom, and a bath, the battlefield a bench in a public park.

It was not easy for nineteenth-century actors, accustomed to roles of heroic proportions and a great vocal demand, to scale their performances down to life size. The abolition of the soliloquy and the aside required the actor to find a way of expressing his inner unspoken feelings and thoughts without recourse to the convention of direct address to the audience. For designers schooled by the Bibienas, those masters of Baroque scene design, it was equally difficult to become reconciled to representations of kitchens or garrets; but the requirements of the new Realism offered no alternative.

"Truth to life": Stanislavsky, Saxe-Meiningen, Antoine, the Americans

A few actors had prepared the way for the transition. More than a hundred years earlier David Garrick had astounded English audiences by his true-to-life style of acting. Commented a contemporary critic: "Garrick's imagination was so strong and powerful that he transformed himself into the man he represented." Another observed that he performed his roles "so naturally as that in Truth they are not perform'd at all. . . ." In succeeding generations Salvini in Italy, Schröder in Germany, Shchepkin in Russia, and Sarah Bernhardt in France mesmerized the public by the truth of their acting. (It is possible to wonder, rather churlishly, as one reads eyewitness accounts of their performances, how true to actual behavior their technique would seem to a late twentieth-century audience.) But the transition from romantic excess to realistic spareness was long and difficult. It took quite altered technique to bring acting into step with modern realistic stage behavior.

Out of time stood Eleanora Duse. In 1900 she was already in her forties, a figure of infinite mystery whose technique appeared (like Garrick's?) to consist in doing nothing. But, according to those who saw her, what inner radiance and spirituality this Italian artist possessed! And how deceptive was her simplicity. It derived from total immersion in her role and the capacity to winnow out everything that was extraneous to the realization of truth. The only performer I have ever seen in this country who shared that precious gift was Laurette Taylor, and even she had not Duse's courage to abandon the artifice of the rouge-pot and perform without the aid of any makeup whatever!

Aside from the clowns—Chaplin and W. C. Fields in America, Jouvet in France, Petrolini in Italy, Beatrice Lillie in England—who in any case must be judged as performers rather than as actors, only a handful can be recalled who lifted their art to the highest level of realism where "truth to life" was fully achieved. Among these would certainly be Kachalov and Moskvin in Russia, Moissi in Germany, Barrault in France, Edith Evans,

Konstantin Stanislavsky (left), one of the founders of the Moscow Art Theatre, an influential theorist and "towering stage personality," posed with his wife, Lilina (right), an actress in the theatre, and playwright Maksim Gorky in 1900. (*See* page 17 for a photograph of Stanislavsky in Gorky's *Lower Depths*.)

Olivier, and Gielgud in England, John Barrymore and a few others subsequently in America.

Stanislavsky is one of the towering stage personalities of the past hundred years, as influential a figure in this account as his fellow countryman, Chekhov. He was both theorist and practitioner (as director and actor). In the present context he appears as a theorist with "Truth to life" his battle cry. Stanislavsky formulated and formalized a system through the mastery of which actors could attain a close approximation of that objective. He based his system on acceptance of the idea that truth to life could only be attained by discovering the "true" psychological motivations of action. Consequently, he demanded that the actor reach into his inner depths of psychic experience, fortifying it with his creative imagination and producing a stage image in which he—and his audience—could totally believe. An elaborate set of exercises was devised to assist the actor in the discovery of this inner truth.

Stanislavsky was the right man at the right time. The Realistic plays of Ibsen were already the talk of Europe. Soon, by way of the Moscow Art Theatre that Stanislavsky was himself to create, would come works by Tolstoy, Gorky, and Chekhov. As the late nineteenth-century Realistic playwrights were succeeded by those of the twentieth, so the system of Stanislavsky, altered in various ways by various interpreters and disciples, became the cornerstone of twentieth-century acting.

The Russian believed, however, that his system would work not only to enhance performance of the contemporary drama but would be equally appropriate to the interpretation of all drama. Insisting on so broad an application of his theories, he lost some disciples. Their contention was that, while psychological truth might be valuable as a key to unlock the door to the new Realism, it was a well-nigh useless tool to apply to non-Realistic plays. It worked perfectly for Chekhov and well for Ibsen; it would be equally useful when applied later to Tennessee Williams and Arthur Miller and other Realistic dramatists; but it could annihilate the theatre-theatrical, the theatre of the Symbolists and Expressionists, the exaggerations of farce, and for that matter the fantasy of *A Midsummer Night's Dream* or *The Tempest*. As the century moved forward, the number of those who became aware of these limitations would increase. One might conclude, nonetheless, that Realistic plays came to dominate our century's stage as much because of Stanislavsky's discovery of a way to perform them as because of playwrights' conversion to the slice-of-life style.

Stanislavsky was a triple-threat man of the theatre—not only a theorist, but a director and an actor as well. It is in his role as director that he must be considered next. (Incidentally, only in the past hundred years has the need to appraise the director's contribution arisen, for the profession, as such, did not exist before then. But this has become the century of the stage director, and close to the top of the list of great figures of that kind, by almost common consent, would stand the name of Stanislavsky.) He had only one forerunner in that capacity. (The Prince of Denmark once gave

Scene from Shakespeare's *Julius Caesar,* as performed by the Meininger
Company, 1881; founded by a German prince named George II, grand duke of
Saxe-Meiningen, *''The Meininger Company became a sensation throughout Europe
with no great actors. Instead, it provided the first inkling of what ''total theatre''
might become—a new look at scenery, a fresh approach to costumes, illumination,
stage properties, an unexpected emphasis on mob scenes, all directed toward
intensifying verisimilitude.''*

a famous lesson in acting, but he was, it turned out, a fictitious character. Besides, he was really only interested in the way actors read their lines.) The forerunner was a German prince named George II, grand duke of Saxe-Meiningen. He was Stanislavsky's direct predecessor and (in absentia) his mentor.

In his autobiography, *My Life in Art,* the Russian pays deserved tribute to the German grand duke, whose touring troupe, under the direction of one Ludwig Chronegk, visited Moscow in the late 1880s. (Stanislavsky was still in his twenties). By a happy coincidence, during the decade when Ibsen was writing *Ghosts, An Enemy of the People, The Wild Duck, Rosmersholm,* and *Hedda Gabler,* the ducal producer and his director in Germany were preparing the stage to receive the Norwegian dramatist's plays. Realistic acting and staging were as basic to their artistic credo as Realistic writing was to his.

The Meininger Players were an ensemble with no stars. If there had been no other deviation from nineteenth century stage traditions, that fact alone would have established the Players as avant-garde. For the nineteenth century continued the practice of the eighteenth (and fortunately had the talents available) in building the performance around a star. For almost two hundred years, luminous and talented personalities followed one another across the stages of Europe. No need for a director or ensemble playing when all eyes were fixed on Garrick or Mrs. Siddons, the Kembles, Macready and Kean, Mlles Dumésnil, Clairon, Rachel, Mme Vestris.

The Meininger Company became a sensation throughout Europe with no great actors. Instead, it provided the first inkling of what "total theatre" might become—a new look at scenery, a fresh approach to costumes, illumination, stage properties, an unexpected emphasis on mob scenes, all directed toward intensifying verisimilitude. Beyond that, there was the very conscious intention of welding everything into an artistic whole.

Today, it is hard to realize that this conception of staging was revolutionary. But when young Stanislavsky first beheld it, he was electrified. He recognized at once that a single guiding hand was essential. He perceived that the illusion of reality possessed a power, when single-mindedly undertaken, which not only satisfied spectators heretofore accustomed to the self-conscious bravura performance of a star but provided a new experience deriving from recognition and identification. He began to think too about "orchestration" and from there to the contribution of the conductor.

Late in life Stanislavsky was to say that the director exists only to serve the actors. Examination of his own prompt books and stenographic transcripts of his rehearsals belie his claim. Unquestionably he appreciated the importance of the individual's training, the sensitivity and imagination each actor brought to the realization of his character. But Stanislavsky never forgot that the production was his own conception, his unique interpretation, that the excellence of the orchestra depended greatly on the talent of the conductor.

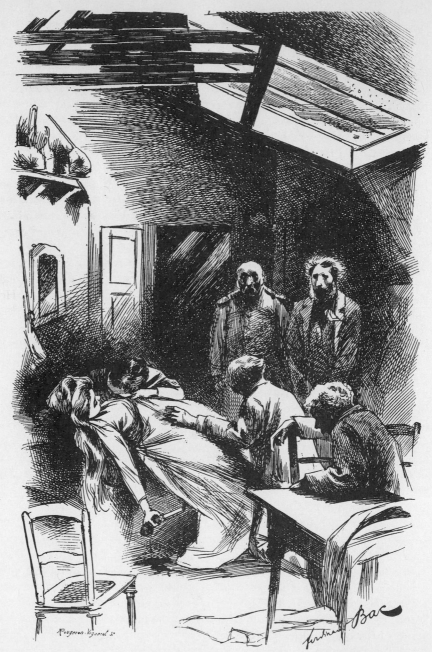

"André Antoine . . . established his Théâtre Libre *in 1887; his influence spread throughout western Europe."* Shown above is a scene from Ibsen's *The Wild Duck* as produced at the *Théâtre Libre*.

To the company that went forth from that little grand duchy in Eastern Germany the twentieth century owes a profound debt. Stanislavsky was not the only young artist whom it inspired. In France there was André Antoine, an obscure clerk in the Paris Gas Company, who had been satisfying his craving for the stage by appearing in amateur theatricals and by "renting his manual strength to the Comédie Française," as John Mason Brown wittily put it; that is, he was member of that company's *claque*. Thus, by constant watchful attendance, he gained familiarity with the workings of the foremost theatrical establishment of his day and acquired an awareness of what artistic overhaul was needed. The example of the Meininger Players showed him how that overhaul might be brought to pass.

Antoine's is one of the great success stories of the modern theatre. From the tiny hall situated on a back passage somewhere in the labyrinth of Montmartre, where the erstwhile gas company clerk established his *Théâtre Libre* in 1887, his influence spread throughout western Europe. Fiercely dedicated to the new *tranche-de-vie* Naturalism, to the abolition of the star system, to the verisimilitude of the scenic environment, to the new playwrights whose works required actors to behave exactly as people do in real life, Antoine made his theatre synonymous with the "New Movement." He himself summed up the artistic principles behind that movement in his *Memories of the Théâtre Libre:*

> The characters are people like ourselves, not living in vast rooms the size of cathedrals, but in interiors such as our own, by their firesides, beneath their lamps, around their tables; . . . their voices are like our own and their language of our everyday life, with its elisions and familiarities and nothing of the rhetoric and noble style of our Classics. . . . In these modern plays, written in a truthful and natural movement and in which the theory of the environment and the influence of external things plays so important a part, is not the setting the indispensable complement of the work? . . . It is certainly never completely naturalistic, since there must always be in the theatre—no one will deny it—a minimum of convention, but why not make an effort to reduce this minimum? . . .

In the eight subsequent seasons before Antoine dissolved the *Théâtre Libre,* he presented for the first time in Paris *Ghosts* and *The Wild Duck, Miss Julie,* and Tolstoy's *The Power of Darkness,* not to mention first performances of plays by Porto-Riche, Edmond de Goncourt, Brieux, Becque. Without Antoine the Realistic movement might never have got off the ground. What avails it to write plays that do not get produced? What point is there in being produced unless there is an understanding interpreter?

From Paris the new "Free Theatre" movement spread first to Berlin, then to London, and shortly thereafter to Dublin. In Berlin, Otto Brahm and associates created the *Freie Bühne,* whose opening presentation in 1889 was *Ghosts.* The Independent Theatre opened in London in 1891; its initial

"David Belasco was a flamboyant practitioner of Realism, especially in scenic effects." Shown above is his setting from the New York production of *Tiger Rose*, 1917.

production was *Ghosts*. The next season it would present the premiere of Shaw's first play, *Widowers' Houses*. The movement spread then to Dublin where William Butler Yeats, Lady Gregory, and their colleagues formed the Irish Literary Theatre to provide a hearing for the new generation of dramatists, among them John Millington Synge and later Sean O'Casey. So it was that the new drama of Realism found stages and producers sympathetic to its aesthetic aims. It must be remembered that all of these theatres were tiny (the Independent in London, for instance, never had more than seventy-five subscribers), and they were considered very avant-garde in the last years of the nineteenth century.

If one were to single out two Americans who embodied the new Realism at the turn of the century, one would be the actress, Minnie Maddern Fiske, the other the producer-director-playwright, David Belasco. Mrs. Fiske, who had become a legend in our theatre by the time of her death in 1932, was an intelligent and talented performer who won considerable distinction by introducing Ibsen to America. Scarcely a man is now alive who remembers her original presentations of *A Doll's House, Hedda Gabler, Rosmersholm, Pillars of Society, Ghosts*. But some of us still cherish memories of her revivals of them. My own recollection is of her Mrs. Alving the year before she died. She was a tiny lady with bright eyes, a husky voice and great stage presence. She underplayed, but with great intensity and unerring believability.

Stage design by Jo Mielziner for a scene in Arthur Miller's *Death of a Salesman*, 1949, a unit setting in which different parts of a house are visible at the same time.

Belasco was a flamboyant practitioner of Realism, especially in scenic effects. Some readers will doubtless recall growing up on stories of Belasco productions: *The Easiest Way*, for which we are told the producer purchased the contents of a boarding house, including the wallpaper, and transferred it to his stage; *The Governor's Lady*, wherein a Child's Restaurant was reproduced on stage, with the smell of Child's famous griddle cakes wafted across the footlights. The succession of sunsets, dawns, and moonlit nights which Belasco and his electrician concocted was eye-boggling. Here was a man who loved to reproduce "life" on stage, but whose understanding of the word was limited largely to its externals.

From Belasco's day to our own, Realism has continued to be the dominant style of the American theatre in playwriting, acting, directing, scenery, lighting, and costuming. Sometimes the plays have been travesties of any serious search for the meaning of life; the acting has often been stereotyped and only skin-deep, the directing mechanical, the physical production overly literal.

But there have been magnificent exceptions. Three outstanding dramatists and one or two actors have been mentioned. In an effort to provide an overview of a whole century of theatre, we dare not lose altitude by dropping down too close in order to identify all the practitioners deserving of mention. But one or two artists must be singled out: Robert Edmond Jones and Arthur Hopkins, who in the 1920s designed and directed John Barrymore's great *Hamlet* and his brother Lionel's *Macbeth*; Elia Kazan and Jo Mielziner, who respectively directed and designed *Death of a Salesman* and

47

Two designs by Robert Edmond Jones for Arthur Hopkins's production of *Hamlet* with John Barrymore.
Act III, Scene 3.
Hamlet: *Now might I do it pat, now he is praying;*
And now I'll do't. And so he goes to heaven;
And so am I revenged.

A Streetcar Named Desire in the 1940s. All of them, with apparent effortlessness, lifted Broadway for a moment above its usual Realism and infused it with poetry.

Russian foes of realism: Meyerhold — Vakhtangov

Realism was the twentieth century's great stylistic inheritance from the nineteenth. We have made it our own because the materialism that engendered it and the scientific age that justified it as an art form are still asserting their primacy. So long as in both East and West power is generated by wealth, and progress is measured by scientific and technological breakthroughs, Realism will continue to dominate our stages.

The theatre, however, is an art. It has much more on its mind than material and scientific matters: life and death, for example. And while it may talk about life and death in "realistic" terms in realistically minded ages, it has also talked about them in non-Realistic ones and perhaps then with greater power—witness *Everyman*. Today the theatre possesses great artists who are not interested in photographing life or in fashioning reproductions of it. To be sure, in the past hundred years they have been in the minority, but there comes a time when even the Realists themselves become

Act V, Scene 2.
Fortinbras: *Let your captains*
Bear Hamlet, like a soldier, to the stage.

disenchanted with their images of "real life," when they sense that there is so much more to it than meets the eye; then they become Symbolists.

As certainly as Stanislavsky became the champion of Realism, so did another Russian, a contemporary and sometime colleague, Vsevolod Meyerhold, become the standard-bearer of the opposition. An original member of the Moscow Art Theatre in 1898, he quickly concluded that its creative path would lead in precisely the opposite direction from the way he wanted to go. He left Stanislavsky, went to St. Petersburg in 1902, and in the years immediately preceding and following the Bolshevik Revolution of 1917 carved out a place for himself as the most brilliant exponent of the theatre-theatrical in Europe.

Meyerhold started by saying, in effect, that one goes to the theatre to engage in a special experience, not to be asked to forget one is there (a state of mind which Stanislavsky encouraged). What one sees on the stage must *not* be imitation of life but a transmutation of life through the use of an artistic vocabulary and visual images so composed and juxtaposed that they do not explicitly reproduce the comfortably recognizable. "Truth to life" is, in fact, impossible to attain in the theatre. Nor is it desirable.

Trompe l'oeil is acceptable accomplishment in painting, but it attracts us principally because of the technical virtuosity exhibited. It provides no new insights. Impressionism, Expressionism, Surrealism, indeed all the "isms" of modern and post-modern art rest on the principle that the function of

49

painting and sculpture, as perceived today, is to translate nature, not reproduce it, to react to it, not explain it, to discover the true meaning of reality through art.

This seems easier to accomplish in the visual and plastic arts than in the theatre, and the reason is obvious. The theatre's principal material is living human beings, not immobile paint and canvas, not marble, metal, or wood. Arbitrary selection of forms brought together to create an artistic composition, whether in dance or theatre, must always be conditioned by that living human factor, the performer, who is never fixed, who can never be anything but human.

It is much easier to make a man look like a man, sound like a man, act like a man, than to turn him into a symbol or an abstraction. That is why the anti-Realistic, nonrepresentational theatre is quite as difficult as "Truth to life" theatre (perhaps both are finally impossible). But it is the challenge Meyerhold accepted. It meant creating a new kind of actor who moved and responded in new ways to new stimuli, a new approach to scenery, costume, and lighting, a new relationship with the spectator, a new organization of theatrical space. For thirty years Meyerhold worked toward the realization of these objectives. When he started, it seemed as though he, like Stanislavsky, was the right man at the right time. But history betrayed him. The Soviet Communist party could not tolerate Meyerhold's revolution. He was "liquidated" artistically in 1938 and subsequently died in confinement on some unknown day at some unknown place.

The twentieth-century theatre was never the same after him. Even the staunchest Realists had to rewrite their credos. Theatre could try to be "True to life," but it could not evade the fact that it was *not* life, it was theatre. If Meyerhold accomplished nothing else, he established that incontrovertibly.

Meyerhold insisted that his aesthetic was built on the past. From the Greeks, for example, he derived a conviction that the proscenium arch was inhibiting, that a semicircle of spectators gathered around a performance space was preferable to their being seated in parallel rows. The Greeks used masks and high-platformed shoes to make their heroes seem larger than life; they employed a chorus which interrupted the story with song and dance. Of course, none of this was true to life, but the early Greeks did not write Realistic plays, so the matter was irrelevant.

From the *commedia dell'arte* of the Italian Renaissance, Meyerhold seized the notion that actors must be able to tumble, jump, sing, strut, and improvise. They must be prepared to respond to interruptions and sallies from their street-corner audience. They must be comfortable in masks and traditionally unrealistic garb (think of Harlequin's patchwork pajamas). These accoutrements were intended to convey the idea by a sort of visual shorthand that characters were types, not individuals. Pantalone was always Pantalone, the archetypal old man, no matter what actor might be wearing his costume and mask in any dramatic situation. The play was *not* the thing;

indeed it scarcely existed; so there was nothing to interpret. The performance was the whole creation.

In the oriental theatre Meyerhold also found masks and stylized make-ups, a use of music and sound as an almost constant accompaniment to action.

All these borrowings the Russian *régisseur* employed in one or another of his productions. Each stressed the fact that the theatre was art, not life—at least not life as we are accustomed to see it and live it.

Meyerhold's pre-revolutionary heyday coincided with the short-lived Expressionist-Constructivist-Surrealist attempts to capture the stage. Meyerhold made frequent use of Constructivism, and his work came close to Expressionism, if by the term is meant a style that eschewed, as it were, the Kodak in favor of the X-ray camera in order to take a look at what lay behind externals. This latter "ism" came up with but a handful of good dramatists, notably Hasenclever and Kaiser prior to World War I, Toller and Mayakovsky after it. But Meyerhold was not dependent on new plays. Reinterpretation of the classics was an even greater challenge to him and provided better opportunity to illustrate his special brand of theatricality. So his productions of Pushkin's *The Queen of Spades* and *Boris Godunov,* Lermontov's *Masquerade,* Gogol's *Inspector General,* Dumas's *Camille,* and Chekhov's short "vaudevilles" have become textbook examples of the theatre-theatrical. Whether they were Romantic poetic dramas like those of Pushkin, Lermontov, and Dumas, or Realistic satires like Gogol's and Chekhov's mattered little to Meyerhold. He repossessed them, made them his own. It seemed almost by chance that the Romantic pieces became epitomes of the Romantic, the satires funnier than they had ever seemed before.

There was a third great Russian stage creator in our century who led subsequent generations down their most satisfyingly productive avenue. Named Yevgenny Vakhtangov, he died in 1922 before he was forty. His master was Stanislavsky but, like Meyerhold, he could not totally subscribe to the tenets of Realism. He was drawn to Meyerhold's aesthetic position but could not bring himself to full acceptance of anti-Realism either. His compromise was to build on the core of Stanislavsky's psychological truth in characterization a complex of light, airy *jeux de théâtre.* He had it both ways, varying the proportion of ingredients from play to play.

Most contemporary stage directors, designers, and actors are unaware of the debt they owe to Vakhtangov, whose definitive production of *The Dybbuk* for the Habima Theatre in Israel (still in its repertoire) is the only work of his they may have seen. But there are few of our contemporary artists, although certainly all the best, whose performances, settings, or *mises-en-scènes* have not benefited by embracing some part of the Vakhtangov compromise. On the stages of London, Paris, New York, and throughout America—and, yes, in Moscow, too—nineteenth-century Realism has been tempered and modified by a coating of theatrical sparkle. "Selective Real-

Anti-Realistic stage of Vsevolod Meyerhold designed for his production of *Revizor* (*The Inspector General*) by Gogol, Moscow, 1926.

ism" we term the result in America. It is our common coinage, and we owe it to the young Vakhtangov.

Western foes of realism: from Maeterlinck to Brook

Again we must return to the 1890s, once more retracing our steps to Paris. There we encounter a precocious seventeen-year-old named Paul Fort. It is exactly 1890, and he has just founded his *Théâtre d'Art*. He is what might be called a neo-romanticist, alienated by the *Théâtre Libre* and its grubby naturalistic kitchen sinks. He longs for poetry in the theatre. Unfortunately, no major talents are available. Instead, he finds he can channel his poetic longings into providing his stage with new visual effects. He has persuaded several of the major Impressionists to contribute their talents to design settings, costumes, programs, posters, for never-mind-what plays: Toulouse-Lautrec, Vuillard, Bonnard, Denis, Redon, and others. In so doing he ties the theatre (at least his *Théâtre d'Art*) to the new movement in modern painting—a not inconsiderable feat for a teenager.

Theodore Komisarjevsky has recalled that "the scenery at the *Théâtre d'Art* was a pure ornamental fiction, independent of anything concrete. It had to fulfill one function only—to complete . . . the aesthetic illusion created by the poetry of the play. Sometimes the scenery of the Symbolists was 'independent' to such an extent that the stagehands were in the habit of setting it up upside down."

Fort's theatre existed for only two years, a casualty of its own preciosity. But the campaign against Antoine and his Realists and Naturalists was picked up and carried on by another Parisian, Lugné-Poe, whose *Théâtre l'Oeuvre,* dedicated to Symbolism, took over where Fort's left off. There Ibsen's *The Lady from the Sea,* Maurice Maeterlinck's *Pelléas and Mélisande,* and later Alfred Jarry's *Ubu Roi,* major milestones in the break with realism, were presented.

Maeterlinck and Jarry were minor dramatists, but they brilliantly articulated and illustrated the line of the anti-Realists. The former attacked the theatre of the establishment in a famous passage in his *Le Tragique Quotidien:*

> When I go to a theatre I feel as though I were spending a few hours
> with my ancestors, who conceived life as something that was primitive,
> arid and brutal . . . I am shown a deceived husband killing his wife, a
> woman poisoning her lover, a son avenging his father . . . murdered
> kings, ravished virgins, imprisoned citizens—in a word, all the
> sublimity of tradition, but alas, how superficial and material. . . . I was
> yearning for one of the strange moments of a higher life that flit
> unperceived through my dreariest hours; whereas, almost invariably,
> all that I beheld was but a man who would tell me at wearisome
> length, why he was jealous, why he poisoned or why he killed.

To oppose the theatre of action, Maeterlinck proposed a "static" theatre:

I have grown to believe that an old man seated in his armchair,
waiting patiently, with his lamp beside him; giving unconscious ear to
all the eternal laws that reign about his house, interpreting, without
comprehending, the silence of doors and windows and the quivering
voice of light, submitting with bent head to the presence of his soul
and his destiny—an old man, who conceives not that all the powers of
this world, like so many heedful servants, are mingling and keeping
vigil in his room, who suspects not that the very sun itself is supporting
in space that table against which he leans, or that every star in heaven
and every fibre of his soul are directly concerned in the movement of
an eyelid that closes, or a thought that springs to birth—I have grown
to believe that he, motionless as he is, does yet live in reality a deeper,
more human, and more universal life than the lover who strangles his
mistress, the captain who conquers in battle, or the husband who
avenges his honor.

Maeterlinck proceeded to put his theory to the test in a series of short
plays, *The Intruder, The Interior, The Blind,* and several full-length ones in
addition to *Pelléas and Mélisande: The Death of Tintagiles, The Seven Princesses,
The Blue Bird.* These are odd somnambulistic dramas; silence is as important
in them as speech. Was Maeterlinck prefiguring the so-called "non-verbal"
plays of a later day? Such language as he used was evocative of invisible
action—the so-called "Maeterlinckean Beyond," as it was dubbed by his
contemporaries. Debussy's score for the operatic version of *Pelléas and Mélisande* captures exactly the quality of Maeterlinck's work.

Jarry's *Ubu Roi,* by contrast, is noisy, shocking, funny, irreverent, a rebellion of adolescence—not surprising, since Jarry was but fifteen years old
when he conceived the idea. The play tells of a stupid amoral man, Ubu,
who installs himself as King of Poland and holds onto his throne by the
simple expedient of killing and torturing all opposition until he is finally
driven from the land—a preposterous but terrifying nightmare of a play,
and with prophetic overtones of later dictators. (Interestingly enough, it
had a successful revival in postwar Poland.) Dramatic historians point out
that although Jarry's impact was slight at the time the play was produced
(1896), by the 1920s he was belatedly hailed as a prophet of the "Theatre
of the Absurd." His may be a name to forget, but not the impulses he
engendered.

These two dramatists should possibly have been dealt with along with
other writers. They were passed over then because their significance lies
not in their writing but in their influence in effecting a changing form of
theatre.

Throughout the Western world, all contemporary stage designers acknowledge their debt to Adolphe Appia and Gordon Craig. To most laymen these names are probably no better known than Jarry, Vakhtangov,
or even, I fear, Meyerhold. Both men taught by precept rather than example. Appia was born in Switzerland in 1862; Craig was born ten years later, the

Design for the forum scene in Shakespeare's *Julius Caesar* by Edward Gordon Craig, 1922.

"Most of his life was devoted to a 'theatre of the future', and the inspiration behind much of today's theatre practice and theory clearly stems from Craig's pioneering work" (from *Encyclopaedia Britannica,* 1981).

son of the great English actress, Ellen Terry. He and Appia were never collaborators, but the similarity of their views about the theatre was striking.

Realism had placed its principal burden on the actor. Symbolism, indeed anti-Realism in general, depended on the director and designer to evoke the appropriate mood. Appia came to the stage by way of Richard Wagner. His first book, in fact, was *The Staging of the Wagnerian Drama* in 1895, and in his famous drawings for *Tristan and Isolde* and the *Ring* cycle it became evident that he could evoke mood solely by form and light, composed in harmony with the quality of the music.

Appia, however, was disturbed by something more fundamental: how to reconcile the three-dimensional actor to his two-dimensional environment, the painted scenery of the day. Appia's answer was, like all major discoveries, disarmingly simple: make the environment three-dimensional. In the theatre he envisioned, the painter would be thrown out, to be replaced by the sculptor, or rather, the fashioner of three-dimensional architectonic forms that would occupy stage space vertically, horizontally, and in depth — steps, ramps, cubes, platforms. Let color be provided by light rather than pigment.

Craig came to many of the same conclusions which he stated in his first book, *On the Art of the Theatre*, and also in issues of *The Mask*, a periodical for which he began to write in 1908. In them he echoed Appia's conclusion that "artistic unity requires that one person control all the elements of production." Thus, the two of them strengthened the role of the director, that twentieth-century newcomer to the stage. Craig, however, went further than Appia: eventually, he argued, the dramatist could be dispensed with! "When he [the director] will have mastered the uses of actions, words, line, colour, and rhythm then . . . we shall no longer need the assistance of the playwright — for our art will then be self-reliant." He went still further: "The actor must go," he declared, "and in his place must come the inanimate figure — the *übermarionette* we may well call him, until he has won for himself a better name."

Craig's proposals were never put to the test, of course, but by his and Appia's arguments at least a unified conception of a production under the guidance of a single creator was given new credence. (To be sure, Saxe-Meiningen had paved the way.) Moreover, their drawings, especially Craig's — many of them unrealized in the theatre, alas — have served as inspiration to stage designers throughout the century. When Craig died at the age of ninety-four in 1966, he could take satisfaction in the way the look of the stage had altered in his lifetime, thanks to himself and to Appia.

Two Germans working together from the early 1920s until the rise of Hitler, Bertold Brecht and Erwin Piscator, were even more closely bound than Craig and Appia; their relationship more resembled that of Chekhov to Stanislavsky. Piscator was an underrated genius of a stage director; Brecht, as we know, was essentially a playwright and theatrical theorist. The two of them, who became the outstanding theatrical spokesmen of the hour,

Sketches by Adolphe Appia for Wagner's *Die Walküre*, 1892 (top), and *Tristan and Isolde*, 1896 (bottom). *"In the theatre he envisioned, the painter would be thrown out, to be replaced by the sculptor, or rather, the fashioner of three-dimensional architectonic forms that would occupy stage space vertically, horizontally, and in depth—steps, ramps, cubes, platforms. Let color be provided by light rather than pigment."*

devoted their stage first to attacking capitalism, then to offering their alternative.

The difference lay in the way they approached their propaganda objective. Ibsen, you recall, had sought to persuade men and women to rebuild society by depicting it principally in terms of family crises. His dramas evoked a deep emotional and empathic response. Shaw's sermons had been couched in the comic vein; whether talking in family terms or working on a broader social canvas, laughter had been his weapon.

Brecht and Piscator wanted to eliminate emotion from their theatre, and since they had no great comedic gifts, they did not seek laughter either. They demanded that their audience be made to think, to learn, to have their old complacence challenged intellectually—*but not to feel.* To change the world requires clear heads. So the public must listen and be stimulated by what it sees and hears without experiencing any Aristotelian purgation of the emotions.

This objective would be accomplished, announced Brecht the Theorist, by imposing a sense of "alienation" on both spectator and performer. The former must never forget he is in the theatre, never cross the fine line into empathic or sympathetic response to characters or situation. The actor too must never imagine that he *is* the character he impersonates; he must at all times stand outside it, reacting objectively. To keep the spectator aware of his whereabouts and prevent his "engagement," Piscator employed means that Meyerhold had used to the same end with tremendous effect: photographic slides, film clips, interpolated songs accompanied by an orchestra visible on the stage, direct address to the audience, no effort to conceal the stage mechanics—a bare back wall, lighting equipment in full view (such scenery as there was changed before the spectator's eyes). Clear white light was used, for color, it was claimed, evokes moods and stimulates emotions; it plays on the senses and distracts the mind. And it was the mind, I repeat, that these two theorists were out to capture.

At Piscator's theatre in Berlin, the *Volksbühne,* and after the war in the playhouse of the company assembled by Brecht in East Berlin, the *Berliner Ensemble,* their theories came to life. The debt owed to Meyerhold is apparent, and the stylistic debt our contemporary stage owes to these Germans is equally apparent. The only postscript that need be written is to record that Brecht's theory of alienation does not always work: it is impossible to see *Mother Courage* or *Galileo* in East Berlin (or elsewhere) without being profoundly moved. That may be because forty years have passed. Or, more probably, it is because Brecht was a poet, and poets cannot help speaking to the heart, whether they will or not.

One more theorist of the twentieth-century theatre remains to be considered—Antonin Artaud, exponent of the "Theatre of Cruelty." Martin Esslin has said of him: "One of the most extraordinary men of his age, actor, director, prophet, blasphemer, saint, madman—and a great poet—Artaud's imagination may have outrun his practical achievement in the

George Grosz, the German artist who brought new intensities to caricature and painting to provide some of the most vitriolic social criticism of his time, was commissioned by director Erwin Piscator to ''use the stage as a drawing board'' for the production of Haŝek's *The Good Soldier Schweik,* 1928.

theatre. But his vision of a stage of magic beauty and mythical power remains, to this day, one of the most active leavens in the theatre."

A Frenchman, born just before the turn of the century, Artaud's importance to this review rests on his authorship of a single book, *Le Théâtre et Son Double* (an ambiguous title), which was published in 1938 and which Robert Brustein has properly called "one of the most influential, as well as one of the most inflammatory documents of our time."

There are too few rebels in our era—rebels, that is, who truly turn the tide of artistic history. A half dozen dramatists who have done it have been under our scrutiny, along with another half dozen prophets and practitioners. For the true rebel is a "nay-sayer," as Brecht, himself one, once phrased it. But, to turn the tide, he must also be a "yea-sayer." Artaud was certain he knew what must be destroyed; he also had a clear vision of what must replace it. Alongside his platform those of Brecht, Craig, Meyerhold, Strindberg—the cream of the rebel crop—seem almost innocuous.

What Artaud really wanted was to throw out the theatre of the day and start over again. Not Ibsen, Stanislavsky, or O'Neill wanted to go that far. Artaud repudiated the past, even Molière and Shakespeare, because he asserted they were "culturally ineffective" in today's world. He turned equally against highbrows and middle-brows because, in directing its attention to them, the theatre, he claimed, had alienated itself from the "general public," by which he meant "the masses." Without them, no renewal of culture would be possible. Instead, "the great public looks to the movies, the music hall or the circus for violent satisfactions." The theatre must find a way to bring the masses back to itself, Artaud insisted:

> Our long habit of seeking diversion has made us forget the idea of a
> serious theatre, which . . . inspires us with the fiery magnetism of its
> images and acts upon us like a spiritual therapeutic whose touch can
> never be forgotten. Everything that acts is a cruelty. It is upon this idea
> of extreme action, pushed beyond all limits, that theatre must be
> rebuilt.

Becoming somewhat more specific he added:

> The theatre will never find itself again . . . except by furnishing the
> spectator with the truthful precipitate of dreams, in which his taste for
> crime, his erotic obsessions, his savagery, his chimeras, his utopian
> sense of life and matter, even his cannibalism pour out on a level not
> counterfeit and illusory but interior.

None of these fevered dreams did Artaud realize in his lifetime (he died in 1948), and not a great deal of attention was paid to his little book when it first appeared. But twenty years later in France, heralds of the new "Theatre of the Absurd" (notably Jean Genet) hailed it as their inspiration; so did leaders of the avant-garde in the American theatre of the 1960s, Julian Beck and Judith Malina, whose Living Theatre productions of *Para-*

Antonin Artaud, 1948. He was a dramatist, poet, actor, theoretician, and author of a book entitled *Le Théâtre et Son Double,* *"which was published in 1938 and which Robert Brustein has properly called 'one of the most influential, as well as one of the most inflammatory documents of our time'."*

dise Now, Antigone, and *Frankenstein* received their inspiration from some of Artaud's fiery injunctions. Richard Schechner's Performance Group's *Dionysus in '69* and Joseph Chaikin's Open Theatre were other responses. In Poland, Jerzy Grotowski owed an enormous debt to Artaud; so did Peter Weiss in Germany when he wrote *The Persecution and Assassination of Jean-Paul Marat as Performed by the Inmates of the Asylum of Charenton under the Direction of the Marquis de Sade* (nicknamed *Marat/Sade*).

Peter Brook, who staged the Weiss drama in London and New York and for motion pictures, understood Artaud's dream better than most. In his book, *The Empty Space,* Brook articulated the Frenchman's intent:

> He wanted a theatre . . . served by a band of dedicated actors and directors who would create out of their own natures an unending succession of violent stage images, bringing about such powerful immediate explosions of human matter that no one would ever again revert to a theatre of anecdote and talk. He wanted the theatre to contain all that normally is reserved for crime and war. He wanted an audience that would drop all its defenses, that would allow itself to be perforated, shocked, startled, and raped, so that at the same time it could be filled with a powerful new charge.

Brook himself must be among the creative theatrical personalities about whom something is said here. In the second half of our century the career of this English director has summed up the journey of a whole generation. He has served as artistic director of the Royal Shakespeare Company of Great Britain, has brought to the stage distinguished revivals of ten or more of Shakespeare's plays—finding, for example, with the help of Jan Kott, a fresh interpretation of *King Lear* in a production that starred Paul Scofield in 1962, and a controversial and unforgettable anti-Realistic *Midsummer Night's Dream* in 1970. When the next year Brook left England to form a multilingual, multinational troupe in Paris, *Le Centre International de Créations Théâtrales,* with which he could explore new paths into the future, it seemed the beckoning ghost of Artaud who led him on. Brook, in turn, beckons the upcoming generation to make new experiments, dream new dreams.

Ensembles follow the stars

In contradistinction to the star system, which dominated the eighteenth and nineteenth centuries, the "New Movement" in the European theatre, as we have seen, began with companies dedicated to reducing the individual actor's importance in favor of the ensemble. In the past few generations this tendency toward collective creation has significantly increased.

The Saxe-Meiningen troupe was the first step in that direction since the Renaissance. In sixteenth-century London The Lord Admiral's Men, The Lord Chamberlain's Men, The Queen's Men occupied the Swan, the Globe, and other Elizabethan playhouses. *The Comédie Française* came into being in

Paris in the following century. These were, of course, the companies for which Shakespeare and Marlowe, Molière and Racine wrote. They had their leading performers, to be sure, but beyond that, they developed collective personalities through the interaction of players and playwrights. The French company, as the world knows, still survives; the London ones collapsed even before Cromwell's Commonwealth darkened all British stages.

The Russians are in the vanguard today—Moscow alone has more than twenty repertory companies—but significant ones also exist in the West: the Royal Shakespeare Company and the National Theatre in Great Britain, a spate of resident regional groups across America and in Canada, collectives headed by Jerzy Grotowski in Poland and Peter Brook in Paris, Peter Stein at the Schaubühne in West Berlin, as well as the *Berliner Ensemble* in East Berlin.

It is not a coincidence that this revival occurred simultaneously with the arrival of the stage director on the scene. Not much is known about the acting company that performed at the *Théâtre Libre* in Paris, but we know a great deal about the Moscow Art Theatre ensemble that worked with Stanislavsky and his co-founder, Nemirovich-Danchenko. We also know that out of the Irish Literary Theatre emerged the Abbey Theatre's acting company—Sara Allgood, Barry Fitzgerald, and others. Meyerhold trained his company in a new acting method he called "bio-mechanics," which set it apart from all others; Vakhtangov left a group of disciples who carried on his work after his untimely death; Brecht's *Berliner Ensemble,* headed by his widow, Helene Weigel, has preserved the principles of "epic" theatre.

In the United States the Group Theatre, formed in 1931 by Harold Clurman, Lee Strasberg, and Cheryl Crawford, imported the artistic principles of the Moscow Art Theatre and fused them with the strong social consciousness which ran high in that American decade to produce the most significant theatrical collective our theatre has known. The Group Theatre came to an end in 1941, but its artistic principles have been perpetuated in the training offered by Strasberg's Actors' Studio, a remarkably successful training ground for young talent.

The interaction between director and ensemble has, then, supplanted that between stars and supporting casts. Indeed, a majority of the creative leadership of our century owes its eminence to the companies those artists established. It has not been enough for a group of actors, no matter how talented, to wish simply to band themselves into a collective. There has been, and always must be, a powerfully creative leader with his own clearly defined aesthetic objectives, a person of vision and dedication who can hold the troops in line for sufficient time to weld them into a unit. When this is done, the stage can come close to realizing its highest potential. History has proved it.

Theatre in the age of media

Architects are not artists of the theatre, but the art they serve is intimately bound to it. Since 1900 an evolution has taken place in the physical, architectural environment of the Western theatre.

One hundred years ago the theatre was rigidly corseted into playhouses inherited from the eighteenth century. We know what they looked like, those proscenium theatres, for they are still all around us. The spatial relationships between stage and auditorium have remained much the same throughout these two centuries, and they have served very well for the peep-show "slice-of-life" Realistic plays of Ibsen, Chekhov, Shaw, and their followers, housed in so-called box sets.

As Realism gradually loosened its grip, however, new spatial relationships required different ground plans. By mid-century the "arena" stage, which placed the performers in the center of a space with audience surrounding them, began to be encountered more frequently. "Thrust" stages appeared, contemporary adaptations of the ground plan of playhouses from the Greeks to the Elizabethans. Experiments were undertaken in "open space" arrangements—large areas resembling lofts or warehouses—that had no fixed performance space at all but could be altered from play to play, the audience being forced to adjust to a different perspective with each new presentation. The Russians and Germans led the way in these experiments, aimed principally at breaking down the rigidity of the spectator-performer relationship.

The revolt against illusion in the theatre has not, however, been the only reason for altering the shapes of our playhouses, possibly not even the principal one. It is my conjecture that today's more creative and far-seeing theatre artists, some consciously, some unconsciously, have been facing the necessity of redefining their medium in a world increasingly dominated by films and television. They have been asking themselves what the living stage possesses that these media do not. Unless they could identify that and capitalize on it, cease borrowing "cinematic techniques," it would be hard for them to hold their own—just as Artaud foresaw.

As the great American stage designer, Robert Edmond Jones, once remarked, "Nothing is so photographic as a photograph." The Realists in their anxiety to be "true to life" have, in effect, been trying to beat the photographers at their own game, paying little attention to the warning of drama critic Walter Kerr that "it is never wise to battle a competing medium in terms of what it can do best; it is much shrewder to offer, by way of competition, what you can do best."

What the theatre can do best, what its uniqueness vis-a-vis film and television is, is childishly obvious: only in it do—and can—the performer and the spectator come together at the same time in the same place. True *rapport* can never be established with an electronic or filmic image. Only in

65

the living theatre can the kind of "communion" between actors and public be accomplished that Meyerhold and his talented disciple, Nikolai Okhlopkov, used to talk about fifty years ago in Moscow. That is why those Russians began then to lead the way toward demolishing the proscenium arch, the orchestra pit, footlights — all physical deterrents that separated the stage from the spectators.

There are still dramatists, as everyone knows, who write scenes that can be transposed unharmed from stage to screen; not infrequently the close-up can, for example, even add impact. Few who saw *A Streetcar Named Desire,* both in the theatre and as a film, would claim that the latter did not stand up satisfactorily to the original. But, on the other hand, no one who saw *Our Town* in both media could assert that Thornton Wilder's play, depending so profoundly on establishing direct communication between characters and spectators, really worked as a movie.

It is necessary, then, for writers, directors, designers, architects of playhouses, and theatre audiences consciously to join hands to insure that as the century comes toward its close, there is still a theatre that is uniquely itself, worth passing on to future generations, a theatre the movies and TV can never replace, one vastly more complex than that which we inherited from the nineteenth century, as well as drama equally insightful in recording the human condition.

Conclusion

This overview of the theatre in the twentieth century has resembled a landscape observed from high altitude: some bright peaks, some dark valleys, a patchwork of fields and forests — in other words, no clear spectacle of homogeneous terrain. Early in this essay it was remarked that the most apt words to characterize our century's theatre might well be "fragmentation" and "fission." These still seem appropriate.

To remark on the acceleration of speed with which our civilization alters course is doubtless trite. But it is not the less true. Never have the arts as a whole so rapidly grasped and then cast aside one mode of expression after another as in the past eighty to a hundred years. And the stage has kept pace with the rest.

If any discernible line has emerged, it has been in the direction moving away from the Realism that was the principal heritage of the nineteenth century. Verisimilitude as the instrument chosen to pierce the illusion of reality has been gradually blunted, partly by over-use, partly by a growing realization that indeed it might well be the wrong instrument to employ. By the end of the first third of the century, this was growing into a widely held conviction. It may have been one result of the Great Depression, which forced much of the West to reorganize its priorities, reassess its faith in materialism and science, release itself from the preoccupation with "things."

What to replace Realism with became the problem. At this point the fragmentation set in. There were numerous directions in which to turn; paths had already been cleared during the preceding decades. The theatre explored several of these. Fifty years later, however, although the main thrust of Realism has been dissipated, no single clearly discernible successor to it—no one "ism"—has emerged triumphant. An eclectic theatre may reflect the eclectic spirit of the times: no one standard of taste governs, no definitive norm of behavior exists, no credo dominates.

What the theatre seems to be undergoing, then, is a period of transition. No sure battle plan exists to win a war against the electronics that threaten to swallow it up. No conviction has taken hold that language is the best weapon, or that, contrariwise, "non-verbal" stress on physical action is the way to go. It is not settled that abstractions, properly selected, can reveal reality. What legacy the twentieth-century theatre will leave to the twenty-first remains today uncertain.

It is not quite the same with the drama. Our century's playwrights inherited a number of preoccupations and problems with which the nineteenth-century dramatists had wrestled. Ibsen and his generation found no sure answers. In many cases there *were* no answers. So they passed the questions on to their descendants, down to Beckett's generation: questions about God, reality and illusion, the realization of self, family relations, social and moral responsibility, conscience, the good life.

Drama's terrain may seem at first glance no more homogeneous than the theatre's, as ideas clash with ideas, but it does possess a greater sense of continuity with the past and within the present. John Dryden's advice to seventeenth-century playwrights holds for today: "A play ought to be a just and lively image of human nature." Our best dramatists, I am persuaded, still aspire to obey that advice. They will continue to do so.

The Emergence of Post-Modern Science

Stephen Toulmin

Stephen Toulmin is a previous contributor to *The Great Ideas Today.* His first article, titled "The Physical Sciences," appeared in the issue for 1967.

Mr. Toulmin was born in London in 1922. He received his doctorate in philosophy, after studying under Ludwig Wittgenstein, from Cambridge University where he was a Fellow of King's College. In 1949 he became a University Lecturer in the Philosophy of Science at Oxford University and continued there until 1955. He then became Professor of Philosophy and head of the philosophy department at the University of Leeds where he remained until 1959. From 1960 to 1965 he was the Director of the Unit of the History of Ideas for the Nuffield Foundation, and for the following eight years he taught at Brandeis, Michigan State University, and the University of California at Santa Cruz. In 1973 the University of Chicago appointed him professor of social thought and philosophy. He has taught in the capacity of visiting professor at Columbia, New York University, Dartmouth, and Hebrew University. From 1966 to 1975 he was counsellor for the Smithsonian.

Mr. Toulmin has written many books, some of which are collaborative efforts with his wife, Dr. June Goodfield. Since he last appeared in these pages, he has published *Human Understanding* (1972), *Knowing and Acting* (1976), and co-authored with Allen Janik *Wittgenstein's Vienna* (1973). His latest book, *Introduction to Reasoning,* which he wrote with Allen Janik and Richard Rieke, was published in 1979.

1. Introduction

How does the science of the middle and late twentieth century differ most profoundly and significantly from that of earlier periods: e.g., the late seventeenth or mid-nineteenth centuries?

If asked that question, we can answer in one or another of two superficial ways. On the one hand, we may be tempted to emphasize the sheer *quantity* of scientific work that has been done over the years since 1945. After all, the scale of the contemporary scientific enterprise is justly impressive; and the late Robert Oppenheimer underlined it by quoting Derek J. deSolla Price's striking observation that "90% of all the scientists who have ever lived are alive today." Yet this reply is a superficial one, because it overlooks the crucial point of the analysis by which Price established his conclusion. The point is that, from the year 1700 on, the novel enterprise of "modern science" was a freely growing activity and began to display the statistical peculiarities shared by *all* activities of that kind. As a result, the "90%" conclusion has been true ever since the early eighteenth century: It was true in A.D. 1750 as it was in A.D. 1950 that 90% of all the scientists who had ever lived were alive *then*! What is peculiar about the scale of the contemporary scientific enterprise, indeed, is that this "90%" doctrine is *ceasing* to be correct. Modern industrial societies are at last beginning to exhaust their supplies, both of people who are capable of doing serious scientific work and also of revenues to support it. At least in those societies, the level of scientific activities has begun to reach saturation.

On the other hand, we may be tempted to emphasize the *quality* of recent scientific work: picking on one or more of the spectacular local advances made within particular branches of science, during the last seventy-five years, as being the crucial change, or changes, that characterize twentieth-century science. Has this not been the century of relativity and quantum mechanics; of nuclear energy and computers; of DNA and antibiotics, brain physiology and neurosurgery; of psychoanalysis, behavior therapy, and the first steps toward a true science of human nature? Yet this second kind of reply also runs the risk of superficiality, because it concentrates on individual scientific discoveries and innovations, while overlooking the deeper, more general and far-reaching changes within the larger enterprise of science. Many of those discoveries and innovations have played noteworthy parts in the development of our contemporary stock of scientific ideas, and there is no virtue in downplaying their importance for science. But, if we reflect for a moment on the sources of their significance, the further question must surely present itself: "What is it that makes these novelties so important? Do not other, profounder changes within the scientific enterprise underlie, and lend significance to, all these individual changes, in fundamental physics and biochemistry, in neurophysiology, medicine, and psychology?"

The purpose of this essay is to look behind the everyday activities of twentieth-century science, and to dig below the specific novelties characteristic of particular branches of science, in the hope of bringing to light some fundamental changes that have modified the guiding aims of the whole scientific enterprise. Since the year 1900, I shall argue, the natural and human sciences have been redirected toward some fundamentally new goals, and their methods of thought and investigation have been modified to accommodate that change of direction. In one way or another, the resulting reorientation has affected all the different branches and disciplines of science, and it has involved a real break with the whole tradition that we have come to know by the name of "modern science"—i.e., the intellectual enterprise that was conceived and launched in the course of the seventeenth century, by such philosophically and theologically minded scientists as Galileo, Descartes, and Newton.

If that argument is sound, we are rapidly moving into a quite novel phase in the historical development of science, whose characteristic features warrant a correspondingly new name. So, following Frederick Ferré, I shall speak of the scientific goals and methods characteristic of this new phase as belonging to *post-modern science*. The "modern" science that developed during the 250 years from A.D. 1650 on has begun, in the course of the twentieth century, to be superseded by "post-modern" science; and in certain crucial respects, as a result, scientists have broken through bounds and restrictions that were placed on the scientific enterprise by its original founders. Initially, as we shall see, those restrictions facilitated the rapid advance of physics, chemistry, and physiology, at least during the eighteenth and nineteenth centuries. But in our own time, as our interests have expanded to include also such sciences as psychology and ecology, those restrictions have become more of a hindrance than a help; and they now have to be outgrown in order that scientists can freely expand their inquiries and speculations into new areas of thought.

What was the character of those initial restrictions? At first, the modern scientists of the seventeenth and eighteenth centuries—the "new mathematical and experimental philosophers," as they called themselves—simplified their intellectual tasks by adopting one very particular theoretical stance. This stance quickly came to dominate the inquiries both of eighteenth-century "classical" Newtonian physicists and of the chemists and physiologists who subsequently modeled their investigations on those of classical physics. The stance in question involved a particular conception of the scientist's situation *vis-à-vis* his objects of study as being—at least in principle—a detached and external one. For the purposes of scientific investigation and theorizing, it was the scientist's duty to place himself and his rational speculations outside the world of nature that was his subject matter. This requirement shaped the basic character of a truly "scientific" attitude to nature and determined the ideals of scientific objectivity to which modern scientists aspired. Correspondingly, the scientific world picture that was gradually built up, by adopting this attitude and procedure, depicted nature as a self-contained, deterministic mechanism, from the influence of whose processes and forces humanity was somehow excluded or exempted.

During the twentieth century, the momentum of scientific change has at last obliged scientists to change their intellectual stance, together with their associated attitudes, methods, and criteria of objectivity. Even in point of theory (it turns out), human beings can place themselves "outside" the world of nature and view its processes and forces from the standpoint of detached onlookers, only to a strictly limited extent; and, to the extent that they do so, they unavoidably narrow down the range of topics and activities that can be brought within the scope of science. If those limitations are to be overcome, and the scope of scientific understanding is to reach beyond them, scientists must learn to view their situation *vis-à-vis* the world of nature in a new way. They must see themselves not just as spectators looking on at the world of nature from outside but also as participants with roles to play from within that world. The scientific world picture that is in the course of being developed, as a result, will be correspondingly less mechanistic and deterministic. This picture will reintegrate humanity with nature— the human observer, as agent, with the natural processes that he both studies and influences. Correspondingly, the rational imagination and activities, both of scientists and other human beings, will themselves have to be recognized as active elements within the operations of nature.

This dual change, in the basic theoretical stance of scientists and in the associated scientific world picture, is the fundamental underlying feature that differentiates the "post-modern" science of the late twentieth century from the "modern" science of earlier years. It is this difference that lends a basic philosophical significance to the theoretical innovations of twentieth-century physics, opens up the possibility of bringing human psychology into harmony with the theories of the other natural sciences, and has helped to diminish the gap between science and technology that was so characteristic of the classical, or "modern" period. And it is this transition, from the modern to the post-modern phases in the historical development of science —the emergence of "post-modern science" from the "modern science" that preceded it—that I shall be attempting to map and analyze in the sections that follow.

2. Theory and practice in the classical scientific tradition

If we are to understand just what point science has reached in our own time, it is first necessary to recognize with some precision where that science has been coming from. The leading features of post-modern science can best be explained by setting them against the background of the classical, or "modern," scientific tradition out of which they were grown. We can usefully begin by considering four characteristic features, all of which played major parts in shaping the program and results of classical science, but all of which have also had to be reappraised during the last seventy-five years. They are:

(a) the traditional separation of scientific thought from technological practice,

(b) the philosophical foundations of the modern scientific tradition, as established by René Descartes and his successors,

(c) the assumed link between scientific objectivity and "value neutrality," and

(d) the professional organization of scientific work, especially as it developed in the course of the nineteenth century.

Each of those features needs to be discussed and defined with some care so as to show how it contributed to the dissociation of the scientific observer from the natural processes and mechanisms he observed. This observation was at the heart of the classical program for the advancement of scientific understanding.

a. Technological practice and scientific theory

To most American ears, the suggestion that technology and natural science either can be or should be treated as quite distinct and separate enterprises —not to say that they *must* be so treated—has never sounded at all attractive or convincing. The goals and methods of scientific investigation have always been thought of in more practical or pragmatic terms on the American side of the Atlantic than on the European side: so much so that, in the United States, the public mind has rarely distinguished science from technology. In the eighteenth-century American colonies, for example, the prototypical scientist of everyday imagination was not the severely aloof and intellectual Isaac Newton, but the jolly and practical minded Benjamin Franklin; and the American Philosophical Society was established in colonial Philadelphia with the declared purpose of promoting "useful knowledge" quite as much as "natural philosophy." From the beginning (that is to say), American science was fueled and inspired by the technological promises of Francis Bacon, quite as much as it was by the philosophical maxims of René Descartes or the theological dreams of Isaac Newton. (To this day, indeed, Americans tend to speak of the engineering problems of interplanetary travel and communications as being the concern of "space science.") So it will be necessary to remind ourselves how early and deeply the program and methods of modern science, as pursued in Europe, became allied with the intellectual preoccupations of theology and philosophy, rather than with the practical concerns of technology.

At the outset, around the year 1650, it was not at all certain which way the development of science would take it. Francis Bacon had provided scientists with a highly attractive manifesto, according to which the advancement of scientific learning could be expected to yield both "light" and "fruit"—both improved intellectual understanding *of* nature and improved technical command *over* nature; and the "new philosophers" were not above appealing to these Baconian promises in their dealings with potential patrons. Some early support for the Royal Society of London was obtained from King Charles II, in return for an understanding that the Fellows of the new Society would, among other things, attack the unsolved practical problems of transoceanic navigation, particularly the problem of determining longitude in a reliable manner. But these technological prophecies were quickly found to be overoptimistic. Once Newton had published his great *Principia**, it soon became evident that, among the central problems of science, the most tractable ones were by no means those that had direct technological implications for human life and society. So, from 1690 on, the Royal Society became progressively less concerned with practical issues, and more and more with abstract questions of "natural philosophy." By the 1740s, it was found necessary to establish in London a parallel institution, called the Royal Society of Arts, with the duty and the financial resources to promote and reward industrial innovations. (In the event, the full "technological spin-off" from better natural science that Francis Bacon had promised around A.D. 1600 began to be fully realized only after some 300 years, during our own twentieth century.)

In England and Europe, accordingly, eighteenth-century natural science put down its deepest roots in theology and metaphysics, rather than in engineering and the other practical arts. In Newton's own eyes, the theories of planetary astronomy, which were the core of his *Principia* and provided the chief corroboration for his more general ideas about the laws of motion, force, and gravitation, were significant above all because they demonstrated the rationality of the Divine Design for Nature. First and foremost, the "laws" of motion and gravitation were evidence of God's Plan for the Creation: any practical advantages that might be gained by putting our understanding of those laws to use, in the service of engineering or the like, were incidental and uncovenanted. Scientists could not afford to base decisions about the relative priorities of their inquiries on considerations of technological relevance or value. The agenda of the natural sciences must be decided by allowing the theoretical problems of (e.g.) physics to develop out of one another in their own way. Any attempt to force the pace of science

---

* *GBWW*, Vol. 34.

by emphasizing problems of direct human concern would be in vain—as much as when King Canute put his flattering courtiers to shame by sitting at the sea's edge, and ordering the tide to recede before the natural time had come for it to do so.

In the end, what was generally true of European science became largely true of natural science in the United States as well. For all its initial declarations of purpose, the American Philosophical Society soon became, almost as much as its European counterparts, a center for the discussion of theoretical problems, rather than for the pursuit of technological innovations. Franklin's own experimental investigations into electricity, for instance, were motivated almost entirely by intellectual curiosity rather than by any prophetic vision of electric light or motors, to say nothing of electronics and other such "useful arts." Despite the continued wish of Americans to find practical applications for scientific knowledge, the sciences achieved actual intellectual progress in the United States only by following along the same abstract, theoretical paths that had already been marked out in Europe. In his role as Secretary of the Smithsonian Institution, Joseph Henry might work for (say) the establishment of lighthouses and other navigational aids; but, as in his parallel role as a scientific student of electricity, he could follow no other road than that taken in Europe by Priestley and Faraday, Ampère and Poisson. Similarly, when Louis Agassiz and Asa Gray debated the problems of geological change and the theory of organic evolution, they had its cosmological rather than its practical implications in mind. How far did the evidence about the Earth's crust testify to the Divine Plan and confirm "the veracity of Moses as an historian?" Was Evolution compatible with Creation or with Design? For those protagonists, as for their Bostonian listeners up on Beacon Hill, the immediate consequences of that debate were not technical or practical but philosophical and theological.

So, for some 200 years after Newton's major work, the natural sciences made progress independently and on their own, by abstracting themselves from the demands of practical techniques and following out their own sequences of intellectual problems. Questions about the planetary orbits, for instance, led on to questions about gravitation, and these in turn gave rise to questions about other "central forces," such as those involved in magnetic attraction and molecular bonding. Questions about chemical combination, likewise, led on to questions about atomic weight and structure, and these in turn gave rise to questions about the nature of heat and the kinetic theory of matter. In all the natural sciences, it seemed as if scientists simply had to follow up the available clues and problems and see where they led. Only after the year 1870 or thereabouts did the new picture of nature, built up as an outcome of two centuries of scientific investigation, become sufficiently precise and detailed to yield any substantial harvest of technological fruit.

It is only from the mid-nineteenth century—first, with the electric telegraph, subsequently with the development of artificial dyestuffs and other industrial chemicals—that we can recognize the beginnings of the alliance between science and technology which by now many people have come to take for granted, and which is frequently (though mistakenly) viewed as a permanent feature of both enterprises. Throughout the crucial two centuries from 1670 on, during which "modern science" was finding its proper mission and taking on its basic character, the central topics for scientific investigation and speculation remained the academic ones known traditionally—and significantly—by the name of "natural philosophy."

b. Scientific theory and the rational spectator

What were the fundamental themes and presuppositions of this new "natural philosophy"? How did these theories and presuppositions shape the working methodology of modern science, or the world picture in terms of which the physicists and biologists of the eighteenth and nineteenth centuries framed their inquiries? Those are the questions to which we must now pay closer attention.

To begin with, the separation between technology and scientific theory that appeared during the late seventeenth century represented not just the general victory of a philosophical program for science over a more pragmatic one. Rather, it was the outcome of one quite specific constellation of philosophical views. In particular, the philosophical foundation of the modern scientific movement was a set of doctrines and distinctions that justified the new mathematical and experimental philosophers in abstracting, for separate investigation and discussion, the concepts, questions, and relationships appropriate to the science of mechanics. As formulated by Galileo, Kepler, and Descartes in the early years of the seventeenth century and brought to fulfillment by Newton in his *Principia*, the central tasks and problems of physics involved the ideas of "force," "mass," and "motion"; and a scientific conception of nature could claim to be philosophically sound, in their eyes, only if it was constructed around a mechanical account of all the chief processes of Nature.

So conceived, Descartes's novel program for developing a mechanistic picture of nature was not just an epistemologist's fantasy thought up in the spirit of pure inquiry. It was intended quite as much to justify a particular ideal of scientific explanation, one that was to dominate theoretical debate in seventeenth-century physics. Descartes himself (it appears) saw as his *magnum opus*—the crowning point in his own philosophical output—not the shorter *Meditations* and *Discourse on Method** to which students of philosophy turn first today, but the four-volume *Principles of Philosophy* in which he worked out in a comprehensive manner his own mechanistic analysis of the workings of the physical world. In this vast work, published in both French and Latin, Descartes set out to expand the scientific insights of his early

---

* *GBWW*, Vol. 31.

hero, Galileo, so as to generate a complete system of physics and cosmology. With this in mind, it can be quite misleading to discuss the arguments of René Descartes, the epistemologist and metaphysician, as though they could be isolated from the explanatory procedures of René Descartes, the physicist. The general program of seventeenth-century philosophy, which Descartes analyzed and expounded most fully and explicitly, was a program designed to make sense, at one and the same time, both of the "outer" processes and mechanisms of Nature and also of the "inner" activities of Mind, through which alone human beings could come to a knowledge of Nature. In the long run, an account of epistemology could thus be satisfactory, only if it warranted a scientific methodology that proved fruitful in physics and biology.

Bearing in mind this close alliance between seventeenth-century mechanics and epistemology, we can usefully look next at two specific features of the new program for "natural philosophy." The first of these had to do with the essentially theoretical character which the new philosophy inherited from Aristotle and the other philosophers of Antiquity. The second had to do, more particularly, with the implications for scientific methodology of *dualism:* i.e., of Descartes's famous (or notorious) dichotomy between the "two substances," Mind and Matter.

To begin with Aristotle, we already find the philosophers of classical Athens taking it as self-evident that human beings are capable of adopting an entirely detached attitude toward the world in which they find themselves, and engaging in abstract speculation about that world without intervening in its processes or otherwise influencing it. The key word that Aristotle chose for this particular mode of philosophical thought was *theoria,* or "contemplation," and he even presented a life devoted to contemplation as his ideal mode of human life. In this connection, the etymological origins of the Greek word *theoria,* and of its Latin counterpart *contemplatio,* are of some interest. Historically speaking, a *theoros* was, in the first place, a delegate sent from a city to the Oracle to consult the Sibyl: as such, the delegate was a *the-oros,* or "divicure," i.e., one who "had a care for the god." Subsequently, the same word was used for the city's delegates to the intercity games (e.g., the Olympic Games), who observed the proceedings officially without themselves participating in the athletic action. Finally, the word *theoros* came to be used as a quite general word for a spectator or onlooker; and *theoria* became the corresponding abstract noun, meaning "spectating" or "looking on." By a somewhat similar transformation in Latin, a *contemplator* was originally the surveyor who marked out the area of a shrine (or *templum*) in preparation for a religious ceremony, as contrasted with the *augur,* who conducted the actual ceremony; and, subsequently, the terms *contemplator* and *contemplatio* became generalized to cover the activities of those who merely observed the mysteries and reflected on them, without directly affecting their course. In both languages, accordingly, a true "theorist" or "contemplative" was one who chose to withdraw from the world and devote his life to *theoria* or *contemplatio*, i.e., a life given over to prayer and reflection, without attempting to exert any direct influence on the things taking place in the world.

Aristotle had taken it for granted that the option of *theoria* is, in fact, open to us. For Descartes, by contrast, the availability of this option became a genuinely problematic issue. How can the mental operations of any human observer give him reliable knowledge about the physical world, without being caught up in the deterministic network of nature, or reacting back on the processes of that world, and so altering them? Aristotle's program for natural philosophy assumed a *one-way interaction* between the human observer and the observed phenomenon: the scientist's thoughts and perceptions were thought to be occasioned by the phenomena of nature, on which it was not supposed that they exerted any counter-influence. The question for Descartes was, how the existence of any such one-way interaction could be squared with the rest of his scientific and philosophical conceptions.

It is at this point that Descartes's dualism of mind and matter displays its scientific significance. On the one hand, all the processes going on in the "outer" (or physical) world were presumably causal, mechanical processes, conforming to rigorous, deterministic mathematical principles and relations: on the other hand, the intellectual procedures characteristic of a human observer's "inner" (or mental) world were presumably rational, and so exempt from mechanical causality. Whereas the phenomena of physical nature were linked together in one single, vast, material, and mechanical world system, the free mental activities of rational beings apparently went on "outside" that system. The sphere of causality was matter; the sphere of rationality was mind; and the possibility of *theoria* depended on the possibility of separating these two distinct realms, or "substances." So, for Descartes, the mind-matter dualism appeared necessary, not simply as the outcome of epistemological analysis, but also as a precondition for the development of any effective natural philosophy, in which the causal processes of a mechanistic Nature can become known to rational human beings. In the course of separating mind from matter and setting one against the other, rational thought became separated from causal process, and by extension, so was the world of humanity—the realm of rationality and mind—from the world of nature, which was the realm of causality and matter. The only point of union between these two realms lay in the depths of the brain, where the "material" processes bringing signals from the outer world, along the nerves of the human frame, finally (though in an intrinsically mysterious way) reached the "mental" territory of the inner *sensorium*.

This epistemological image of the human mind as making contact with the physical world of matter and mechanism only internally, within the inner cerebral theatre of the sensorium, rapidly won general acceptance among most of the "new philosophers." In this respect (it seems) Descartes was simply articulating openly notions that were already implicit in the scientific procedures and epistemological assumptions of his distinguished predecessors, such as Galileo and Kepler. The image in question is clearly to be found in the writings of Isaac Newton. In the closing paragraph of the General Scholium that Newton added to the second edition of the *Principia*, we find him speaking of "the organs of sense" being carried up the afferent, sensory nerves in the form of "electric and elastic" influences, to meet the mind ("that which in us perceives and thinks") in the depths of the brain, and of the "command of the will" being carried back by similar mechanisms down the efferent, motor nerves, to stimulate the motions of the muscles. The same general model also played a central part in the philosophical arguments of John Locke and the other British empiricist philosophers, right up to the time of Kant; and its philosophical influence is not exhausted even today. From John Stuart Mill and Thomas Henry Huxley, up through Bertrand Russell to Sir John Eccles and other contemporary neurophysiologists, we can trace its continuing influence in the nineteenth- and twentieth-century epistemological debate.

How did this model, or image, make itself influential in the actual work and methods of physical science? In the first place, it gave scientists the assurance they needed that they could achieve a genuine objectivity in their studies of nature. The earlier alchemists (for instance) had always been exposed to the fear that their own spiritual state, of purity or defilement, might affect the success of their procedures; but the new scientists of the seventeenth century now seemed to have a guarantee that, by using appropriate mathematical and experimental methods, they could arrive at knowledge of the laws and principles of the natural world of a kind that would be quite unaffected by their own subjective mental states and operations. In this way, they could fully achieve the status of rational spectators: looking on at the phenomena of nature, and drawing inferences about the workings of the underlying world system, without affecting those phenomena or workings in the process.

So, within the program of the new natural philosophy, the notion of rational scientific objectivity came to take a very particular form. Instead of the term "objective" implying merely an absence of bias, prejudice, or other distortions of judgment, it came to denote one special kind of knowledge: namely, that which is available only to an onlooker, who observes his objects of knowledge from a position of detachment—"clinically," to use another metaphor—and formulates judgments about them on the basis of such detached observation, not otherwise interacting with them. And this notion of "objectivity" eventually became an ideal to which scientists in other new fields of work might aspire. (Much of the attraction of behaviorism to academic psychologists, for instance, has lain in its declared intention of introducing just this kind of spectator's "objectivity" into the analysis of human actions and responses.)

Eventually, the Cartesian model of rational natural philosophy culminated in the work of Pierre Simon, Marquis de Laplace, whose exhaustive mathematical analysis of astronomical theory completed and corrected the mechanical account of the planetary system first developed by Newton in the *Principia.* In a famous declaration about the deterministic implications of Descartes's world picture, Laplace spelled out clearly the connection between the methodology of Newtonian physics and the philosophical demand that the scientist should aim at placing himself outside the world which is his object of study. Let us imagine (he proposed) an observer possessed of a calculating mind of unlimited power, who looks on at the entire universe from outside it—what we may call an Omniscient Calculator. If this Calculator were simply presented with data telling him the position and velocities of every atom in the universe at the moment of the Creation, then by a straightforward application of Newton's laws of motion and gravitation (Laplace argued) he would understand the mechanical operations of the world system completely and could in principle foretell the entire subsequent history of the universe.

Laplace did not, of course, suggest that actual human scientists would ever be able to achieve the position of Omniscient Calculator. But he did imply both that this is the ideal to which all scientists should be aspiring, and also that whatever objective scientific knowledge they do in fact achieve will be of the same general kind as the Calculator's knowledge: i.e., a more or less complete knowledge, on the one hand, of the unchanging "laws" of the Creation and, on the other hand, of the specific variables and boundary conditions relevant to any particular physical system. Newton had been the first to succeed in this task, even approximately. His analysis of the structure of the planetary system—together with his formulation of the "inverse square" law of gravitation—had enabled him to forecast the movements of the planets, with justified confidence, for thousands of years ahead. Now, Newton's successors should apply the same procedure to other more complex systems and so extend their own powers of prediction in the direction of the imaginary Calculator's omniscience.

Laplace's expression of the Cartesian ideal underlying the methods of Newtonian physics has been immensely influential. At the same time, it was subject from the start to certain restrictions and qualifications which were not at first properly appreciated. It was directly influential within the physical sciences, because it reinforced the physicists' conviction that their work was proceeding along the right lines and that they could press ahead with every expectation of continued successes. It was indirectly influential, also, because the interests of Laplace himself extended far beyond astronomy, into the newly emerging human and social sciences. For more than a century, as a result, sociologists and social theorists vied with one another to discover the "laws" of social and historical change, to bring social phenomena within the scope of calculation and prediction and thus to become the Newton of the human sciences. Along with Condorcet and Saint-Simon, Laplace himself was one of the major figures in French social and political theory at the close of the eighteenth century, and his *Philosophical Essay on*

*Probabilities** was one of the great founding documents of statistical theory. ("Statistics" was first conceived of as the science of the "state," i.e., the science of social phenomena involving the overall behavior of human beings in very large numbers.)

Finally, Laplace's image was profoundly influential within philosophy. It exerted that influence, first, on the metaphysical level. The entire intellectual system of determinism and mechanical materialism that mid-nineteenth-century thinkers found so enticing (or threatening) depended on taking Laplace's image, not as the expression of an explanatory ideal, but rather as a statement about the actual character of the natural world. So understood, it appeared as though Newton had "proved" that Descartes in fact was right, and that the whole physical world of matter and forces is indeed a single comprehensive "machine" grinding out future events in an ineluctably predetermined manner. (Physical determinism thus took over the role previously played among, e.g., Calvinist theologians, by God's foreknowledge as an excuse for fatalism.) Even when philosophers had become more skeptical about the credentials of this metaphysical scheme, Laplace's view retained its influence over the epistemological debate, especially in the philosophy of science; and right up to the 1950s, the "axiomatic" and the "hypothetico-deductive" analyses of scientific explanation given by the logical empiricists and others perpetuated Laplace's conviction that Newton had discovered not just one but the only proper method for explaining natural phenomena.

From the beginning, however, a more careful and effective reading of Laplace's position would have brought its limitations to light. For those restrictions lay at the heart of the argument and were self-imposed. The Omniscient Calculator studied the historical development of the universe from outside it, and without himself being a part of it. Like a classical Greek *theoros*, he obtained the data he needed for predicting the course of its development wihout participating in its activities or influencing its processes. Thus, inevitably, his success as a Cosmic Forecaster depended entirely on the possibility of interacting with his objects of study in this one-way manner. When Newton "broke the code" of the Solar System, he was of course in that position: neither the astronomical observations to which he appealed in explaining the facts of planetary motion, nor the theoretical calculations which he himself performed, could have had any effect on this motion. To that extent, Newton's method of explaining phenomena mathematically, and from outside, was well adapted to his particular problem. What few people before the twentieth century paused to inquire explicitly was whether the same stance was appropriate to scientific problems of all kinds and in all fields. That is a question which the subsequent development of the natural sciences, especially from the 1920s on, has at last compelled us to face.

---

* *GGB,* Vol. 9.

c. Scientific objectivity and value neutrality

The radical separation of the human observer from observed nature that was central to the methodology of classical, or "modern," science had one further important consequence. Once the world of nature had been set apart from the world of human affairs and interests as an object for detached study by "rational spectators," it could be treated as a world made up of morally indifferent or neutral "facts." Human thoughts and feelings, wishes and regrets, ceased to be elements within nature: instead, they became obstacles to a proper understanding of nature's laws. ("Things are as they are, and their consequences will be what they will be," said Bishop Butler, "Why, then, should we seek to be deceived?") As a result, the ideal of scientific objectivity current during the reign of "modern" science was not merely that of a spectator's knowledge; it was a kind of knowledge that confined itself to "the facts" and ignored all questions about human values and preferences. To employ a phrase that in due course became a byword —especially among those social scientists who sought to emulate the rigor of the physical sciences in their own work—it was the modern scientist's duty to aim at "value neutrality." The true scientist should not allow his concern with the relationships involved, either in natural or in human affairs, to be deflected by any value commitments or other prejudices from reporting those "objective" facts with unvarnished precision.

This demand for value neutrality played two separate roles in the sciences. On the one hand, it required the modern scientist to approach all the intellectual problems that properly fell within the scope of his methods with a clear head and a cool heart. On the other hand, it served to demarcate those issues that were properly the subjects for "scientific" investigation and discussion from those that were, rather, matters of human taste, choice, or decision. To begin with, these two aspects were not always distinguished in people's minds. As a result, for a long time the limited scope of this demand was no more fully appreciated than were the intrinsic limitations of Laplacean determinism.

The first aspect was, of course, scarcely open to challenge. Given a problem whose status as a topic for scientific inquiry according to the methods of modern science is not in serious doubt, the scientist is under a clear obligation to attack that problem in a disinterested (or impartial) way, as well as from a detached standpoint. In studying or speculating about the movements of the planets around the sun or of blood corpuscles through the capillaries, the course of chemical reactions or physiological processes, and the historical transformation of the earth's crust or the populations of organisms inhabiting it—all of which are in themselves unresponsive to, and uninfluenced by, the scientist's attentions—it will do no good to let one's scientific ideas be influenced by a wish for one result rather than another. In those cases, evidently enough, human feelings and interests can indeed act as "prejudices" and so come between the scientist and his proper goal.

81

To this day, one of the standard ways of criticizing any piece of scientific work, throughout all of physics and most of biology, is to argue that the investigator concerned brought prior preconceptions to his investigations and approached his subject matter in a prejudiced manner, so that his mind was not truly open or impartial and his view of the facts was correspondingly subject to distortion.

However, this extreme kind of disinterest (or "value neutrality") remains unquestionably appropriate only for so long as we confine our attention to natural objects, systems, and processes that lend themselves to such purely "objective" (i.e., detached) study. At first, it was not recognized how far this placed significant limits on the range of subject matter that scientists could hope to bring under the wing of "modern science." The flow of the blood, the chemical processes of oxidation, and the history of the earth may be proper objects of scientific study just because they involve those passive unresponsive "objects" of kinds that are almost entirely unmoved and uninfluenced by our observation of them. To that extent, we do well to study them from a purely detached, factual standpoint, in the passionless clinical manner associated with the classical ideal of "value neutrality." But it is not so clear that the same methods and maxims hold good in all cases, particularly in the case of human beings. Whether we study the behavior of our fellow humans individually or in groups, it is far from obvious that we can do so fruitfully and effectively—if at all—by viewing them from a purely detached viewpoint, confining our attention to what we can discover about them on a one-way basis, without their even knowing that we are studying them. In short, it is not at all certain that our fellow humans do usefully lend themselves to scientific study as simple "objects," without our also considering their capacity to interact with us on a two-way basis, to respond to our investigations as "subjects" in their own right.

Consequently, it is not at all certain that the demand for value neutrality, which may be appropriate enough in astronomy or organic chemistry, can be carried over to psychology and the social sciences. There, the methods of investigation that were developed around the year 1700, in the heyday of Newtonian physics, and were subsequently applied to other kinds of research, may run up against their natural limits and cease to provide the uniquely "scientific" way of approaching our investigations. We should once again note that the demand for "value neutrality" brought with it certain inescapable restrictions on the proper scope of science. If rational, scientific objectivity, unclouded by human wishes and prejudices, was to be achieved only by refusing to attend to anything but "cold, hard facts," that alone had the effect of setting bounds to the scope of "scientific" investigation—at least, so long as "science" was understood to mean science undertaken in the classical, Cartesian, or Newtonian spirit.

For much of the nineteenth and early twentieth century, of course, the equation of impartiality with detached disinterest embodied in the classical conception of "scientific objectivity" remained unchallenged. The general sense of this conception has by now entered the vocabulary of colloquial speech. If, for instance, a novelist speaks of one character looking at another with a "scientific" eye, we immediately understand what he means: a "scientific" attitude toward other people, like its fellow-stereotype, a "clinical" interest in their welfare or their affairs, is popularly taken to involve the deliberate suppression of all affective concern for, or any genuinely personal interest in, the people who are its object. For the sake of knowledge (it is implied), the true scientist should be prepared to experiment on his own mother as coolly as he would experiment on a guinea pig.

By taking Mind out of the world of Nature (it seemed) Descartes had denied the scientific "reality" or significance of the passions, except, of course, as objects to be studied in turn by the physiological psychologists. So, an ideal of "rationality" was put into circulation which denied any possibility that the passions themselves could be a source of knowledge or rational understanding; and when David Hume put forth his famous epigram in reaction against this exaggeration—"The Reason both is, and ought to be, a Slave of the Passions"—that declaration was brushed aside lightly, as a piece of mischievous fun intended only to shock respectable opinion. It was another hundred years, at least, before Hume's successors began to take with any real seriousness his realization that all thought and action, even the most ideally "rational" and "objective," have some basis in the affective part of our human nature.

d. *Professionalism and scientific detachment*

Before long, the philosophical arguments for suppressing our human interests and affective responses, in the interest of achieving rational, scientific objectivity, were reinforced by other developments of a more sociological kind. By the end of the eighteenth century, the level of scientific activity had grown to a point at which science could no longer remain what it had predominantly been since the mid-seventeenth century; namely, an occupation for individual gentlemen of leisure and curiosity, or for physicians and clergymen with plenty of spare time. From the year 1800 on, the enterprise of modern science began to develop its own particular institutions, and these institutions—whether colleges of pharmacy, physiological laboratories, centers of chemical research, or whatever—soon followed the path of all institutions. They specialized and differentiated. Adam Smith had been right (it turned out) in science quite as much as in manufacture. Intellectual productivity, quite as much as industrial productivity, was promoted by the division of labor.

This specialization and differentiation of science was not a sociological phenomenon alone. Even as a matter of method, the new experimental and mathematical philosophers quickly found that the first step toward discovering intelligible general mechanisms in nature was to recognize and abstract natural processes of particular varieties, and to concentrate on each variety separately. Some natural processes obeyed purely mechanical principles; others involved gravitational forces; others again were electrical or magnetic, chemical or physiological; and no purpose was served by trying to generalize about all these different kinds of processes before they had first been studied and understood one at a time. So, there came into existence that profusion of scientific disciplines and subdisciplines with which we are familiar in the twentieth century. Initially, at least, it was most effective to study electrical phenomena, optical phenomena, physiological phenomena, and the rest separately and independently, as the subject matters of distinct disciplines; and, as time went on, this increasingly came to mean also that they could be most effectively studied by becoming the concerns of different groups of people. In this way, the specialization of scientific disciplines and ideas brought in its train a corresponding differentiation of scientific professions, journals, and institutions. Each discipline was perceived as defining, and as defined by, its own distinct research agenda, and the tasks on that agenda became the professional concern of an equally specialized group of scientists.

Notice that word, "scientists." The invention and rapid acceptance of this term serves as a good historical index of the moment at which the specialization and professionalization of the natural sciences became unmistakable. Throughout the seventeenth and eighteenth centuries, the word "scientist" was unknown. Half a dozen other terms were used in referring to those people whose curiosity led them to investigate the structure and workings of the natural world. Some of these terms were naturalized into English from other languages, e.g., French (*savant*) and Italian (*virtuoso*). Others carried over into the new era of modern science the scholastic terminology of earlier times, e.g., the widely used phrase "natural philosopher." But, once their concern with science began to be recognized not merely as a taste, or an attitude of mind, but also as an occupation, even as a "job," such usages became inadequate. As William Whewell argued in his Presidential Address to the British Association for the Advancement of Science for the year 1840, a new word was needed which would register this change in the status of scientific investigation: a term that would mark off original scientific discoveries as the products of a specific kind of professional work and individual, in the same way that the much more ancient and accepted term "artist" marks off original artistic creations as the products of a specific kind of professional work and individual. And it was in fact Whewell who, in that 1840 lecture, deliberately coined and launched the neologism "scientist," using the term "artist" as his model.

Thus, it was only in the second half of the nineteenth century that the different natural sciences began to be recognized at all generally as defining particular professional roles. Once the drive toward disciplinary and professional fragmentation was well under way, however, it quickly gathered speed: with "physicists" doing specialized work in physics, "biologists" in biology, and eventually even, in our own day, magnetohydrodynamicists specializing in magnetohydrodynamics. Furthermore, this separation of scientific inquiries into distinct groups only strengthened the tendency to define the tasks of science in "objective" terms, by encouraging scientists to divide up and classify the kinds of objects and processes available for detached observation, study, and reflective theorizing in a taxonomy of "natural kinds." Nature provided the scientific onlooker with a spectacle comprising a dozen quite different kinds of processes and objects; and what distinguished physicists from biologists, or physicists of different sorts from one another, was the particular aspects of nature on which they respectively chose to concentrate their detached rational scrutiny. Just as there were several different sorts of engineers and other practitioners, whose professional task was to develop improved techniques for controlling and changing their respective aspects of nature, so now there were different sorts of scientists, whose professional task was to develop improved ways of understanding them; and in addition—at any rate, in Europe—a certain lingering assumption that science was a more genteel occupation than engineering helped to sharpen the contrast between those whose mastery was merely practical (i.e., who had useful techniques) and those whose mastery was fully intellectual (i.e., who had correct ideas). Manipulating the world of nature for practical purposes was a mechanic's province; a gentleman's concern was to contemplate the works and wonders of nature from a more theoretical and supposedly "higher" standpoint. So, Aristotle's conception of *theoria* (or philosophical contemplation) as the highest mode of human life and activity had social implications in the world of modern science.

Considerations of these four features of "modern" science—its distinction between theory and application, the dualism formulated by Descartes, the assumption of a link between objectivity and "value neutrality," and the professional (and academic) organization of scientific endeavor—worked together to establish and confirm the central methodological feature of "classical" or "modern" natural science that was launched by Descartes and Newton and remained dominant in Western thought about nature until the early years of the twentieth century. Above all, this "modern" science aspired, so far as was practicable, to achieve the theoretical ideals that the new philosophers of the seventeenth century had inherited from their Athenian forerunners. Their account of nature was to be a *spectator's* account, which reported and analyzed the operations of nature "from outside," i.e., without influencing or altering them. No doubt, the extent to which this could be done *in fact* was limited by the coarseness of our instruments and procedures, but that did nothing to undermine the theoretical ideal. It was not until well into the twentieth century that the scientists of Western Europe and North America seriously faced the possibility that this central intellectual ambition might be unrealizable, not, or not merely, because it was out of human reach for practical reasons, but also because it was *misconceived in principle.*

3. The crisis of objectivity in the development of modern science

If it had not been for the disciplinary fragmentation of the natural sciences, the challenges to the "classical" ideal of scientific objectivity might have been recognized and faced earlier on. From the very beginning, as Karl Popper has recently pointed out, there were fundamental reasons for questioning whether the basic program of modern science could be fully carried through. But, so long as the intellectual agenda of science as a whole was simply thought of as the sum of the agendas of all the different subdisciplines (or "special sciences"), there was no way in which these limitations could force themselves on the attention of scientists, unless and until their consequences made themselves apparent to people working on the particular problems of one or another special science. Given the accepted division of labor involved in "doing science," criticisms of the program that were stated only in general philosophical terms could be ignored, or at least shelved, in the absence of more specific problems and difficulties—preferably, ones with empirical implications.

In retrospect (Popper has argued) we can see that the program of Descartes and Newton, particularly as generalized by Laplace, had fundamental restrictions built into it. These show up soon enough if we consider either (1) the general kinds of subject matter scientists would eventually have to deal with, or (2) the particular problems that arise when we attempt to bring the activities of human beings—including scientists themselves—within the scope of science.

As to (1): it was no accident that the basic subject matter of seventeenth-century physical theory—notably, Newton's mechanics—was "inert Matter." In itself, Descartes had argued, matter was incapable of self-movement. The outcome of all merely physical processes could do no more than transfer between different material bodies some part of the total quantity of motion that God had conferred on the entire Universe at the time of its Creation: they could, in themselves, create no new motion. This passive view of matter was preserved in the theories of Newton and most of his successors. (That made the problem of Life as intractable an issue for philosophical biologists in the eighteenth and nineteenth centuries as the problem of Mind had been to Descartes himself.) Beginning with the movements of the planets and freely falling objects, and going on to embrace mechanical systems of progressively more complex varieties, classical science was able for many years to go on expanding in scope and power without coming up against its own natural boundaries.

In brief: all the varieties of subject matter that initially presented themselves to classical Newtonian scientists as promising topics for study comprised *insensate* objects, systems, and processes. The planets, for example, presumably continued on their elliptical paths around the sun in just the same ways regardless of whether human astronomers were observing them or not. Because they were insensate, they were quite unaware of being observed; because they were so enormous, they were quite uninfluenced by the scientists' procedures and observations; and for both reasons it was legitimate to assume that the behavior they presented to the eye of a rational, detached spectator was typical of their behavior generally. In this paradigmatic case, accordingly, *theoria* was a reliable posture from which to acquire a well-founded knowledge of nature. The same was seemingly true through a great range of cases. Even in the case of the human frame, many bodily processes (e.g., those involved in the flow of the blood through the arteries and veins) could apparently be studied in the same detached and "objective" manner: there was no reason at all, for instance, to suppose that the valves in the circulatory system began opening and closing in significantly different ways the moment their operation came under the scientist's scrutiny.

With respect to (2), some scientists might feel residual doubts about the operations of the human nervous system, which the great Swedish nineteenth-century chemist J. J. Berzelius expected to remain forever opaque to scientific investigation. But, by the beginning of the twentieth century, it had begun to appear to Charles Sherrington and others that, given sufficient care and delicacy, neurological processes, too, could be brought within the purview of the classical scientific concepts and theories. In themselves, after all, the electrical impulses in human nerves are no more sensate, and so no more aware of being subjects of scientific observation and theorizing, than the planets are. All that remained was to devise practical methods of studying neural processes without modifying them in untended and unaccountable respects.

As Descartes had foreseen, the limitations to the theoretical analysis of natural phenomena in terms of "inert Matter" began to make themselves seriously felt only when scientists began to study human perception, experience, and thought. At that point, the problems were grave and remained so; and only their general dissatisfaction with the peculiar consequences of Descartes's dualistic theory of matter and mind excused classical scientists in the Newtonian tradition for ignoring Newton's reservations and assuming that the classical world picture could indeed embrace all natural phenomena whatever within its scope. For, let us simply suppose that Laplace's Omniscient Calculator influences the universe that he is observing in however slight a way, so that the human beings within that universe acquire evidence that their behavior has come under his scrutiny: what is then liable to happen? Alternatively, let us suppose, even more simply, that human beings become aware that their behavior has come under the scrutiny of other human scientists: what is liable to happen in that event? Either way, being sensate and thoughtful, the humans who are under observation have the option of acting in a perverse, counter-suggestible manner and may seek to frustrate the expectations of that observer (whether that observer is human or cosmic makes no difference in this respect). At least in the case of human behavior—as Karl Popper has rightly argued

—it is no longer clear that the goal of complete predictability and determinism was ever really open to us, even during the heyday of classical Newtonian science; and, strictly speaking, the most that could ever have been hoped for from any comprehensive natural philosophy based on the methods and principles of classical physics was an account of the mechanical, and so insensate, part of the universe—leaving aside all those processes that implicated the consciousness and thought of sensate, rational agents.

Karl Popper's point is worth sharpening up further. On the one hand, Laplace's image of the Omniscient Calculator is a true expression of the intellectual goals laid down for classical science by Descartes and Newton. On the other hand, the relevance of this image of the actual tasks of classical science depended on the Calculator's interacting with the world whose history he sought to account for in a strictly unidirectional way. In a phrase, there had to be a purely one-way "coupling" between the cosmic observer and the observed world. It was an axiom of Cartesian theory that, for the purposes of physics, this condition could be satisfied: the movements of the planets influenced the observations and thoughts of the astronomer, without his thoughts and observations influencing the planets in return. But two questions could legitimately be raised. First, one might inquire whether that Cartesian maxim could be relied on to continue holding with complete accuracy within all future scientific theories, *even* for the purposes of physics. Or might it well be that, on a sufficiently refined level, physical processes would themselves turn out to be observable only in ways that involved a two-way coupling? And, second, one might question whether it had ever been possible to enlarge the scope of Cartesian and Newtonian physical science into a comprehensive natural philosophy, including intelligent human behavior alongside the phenomena of planetary movement, the circulation of the blood and the rest. Is not our knowledge of intelligent human behavior inevitably the product of an inquiry based on somewhat different methods and maxims?

From time to time, both these questions were debated in general terms by the philosophers of the eighteenth and nineteenth centuries. Pursuing arguments begun by Ruggero Giuseppe Boscovich, a noted Jesuit philosopher from Ragusa (now Dubrovnik) in Dalmatia, Joseph Priestley claimed in the 1770s that the initial assumption on which the world picture of classical science had been based—the assumption that matter is intrinsically inert—was unfounded. On the contrary, Priestley argued, every individual material particle presents an active point-source of power and influence. In this way, he hinted at an alternative approach to theoretical physics, based on a theory of fields of interaction, which was to be developed in detail and at full length only with the appearance of quantum mechanics in the 1920s; and he tried to use the same argument to undercut Descartes's philosophical dichotomy of mind and matter, also. To be consistent, Priestley argued, Descartes should have been prepared to bring the mental and material aspects of nature within a single system. But Priestley's theoretical proposals were ignored for at least forty years, until they were taken up by Michael Faraday with his theory of electrical fields. As for Priestley's philosophical criticisms: these were generally attacked as involving an impious Epicureanism and materialism, much to the theological embarrassment of the Reverend R. G. Boscovich himself.

A few years later, Immanuel Kant was openly criticizing all attempts to expand the mechanistic theories of classical science with the aim of explaining the higher mental activities of human beings in the same terms as the motions and properties of material objects: It was impossible in principle (he claimed) to turn psychology into a natural science. We would at once qualify this statement of Kant's position, if only to forestall cries of anguish from those late twentieth-century psychologists who would claim "scientific" respectability for their professional enterprises. As Kant used the phrase, the words "natural science" referred to a discipline that was capable of being organized in the form of a coherent mathematical system—his own favorite examples were Euclidean geometry and Newtonian dynamics—and he found it imperative to deny *only* the possibility that one might "calculate" the intelligent behavior of sensate, rational human thinkers and agents using the same kind of exact formal theories as Newton had developed to account for the movements of planets and other insensate material things. In taking this stand, Kant was certainly not denying that human thought and conduct were explicable *in any terms whatever*. He was concerned only that psychological explanations should be given in terms *appropriate to* their specific subject matter and problems; and for this purpose (he saw) the standard model of Newtonian mechanics had nothing to offer. In seeking to understand the trains of thought and action of our fellow human beings, we do not approach them in the purely detached posture of astronomers seeking to account for the movements of the planets. Rather, we have to place ourselves on their level, put ourselves in their places, and decipher the "reasons" motivating their lives in the same terms we use in the case of our own.

So long as the natural scientists of the seventeenth and eighteenth centuries confined their investigations narrowly enough, they could insist on remaining in the posture of rational spectators and stand by the particular criteria of objectivity appropriate to that posture. As soon as their successors tried to expand the application of the spectator's posture beyond the study of insensate or unresponsive systems, however, they entered a new field, in which the appropriateness of employing the classical criteria of scientific objectivity became questionable; and, the moment they presented this limited conception of scientific method as *universal* in scope, they laid themselves and their arguments open to damaging criticism. The methods and criteria of "modern science" had been developed in the course of studying sticks and stones, planets and plants, and for the purpose of such investigations their power and value were unquestioned. When extrapolated without limit and applied to the behavior of human beings—to say nothing of the Universe as a whole—their merits were dubious and remained unproved.

Even so, until well after 1900, the significance of these qualifications was largely speculative and philosophical: they did not affect the practical operations that scientists performed on their experimental subject matter, but only the theoretical manner in which they conceived of their relations with that subject matter. Considered in practical terms, the limitations on the classical view made little difference to the actual conduct of scientific work. By the most natural and legitimate sequence in the world, scientists in the classical, Newtonian tradition began by focusing their attentions on the simplest cases of force and motion, and then, bit by bit, expanded their inquiries outward from that base to include also energy and electricity, molecular structures, chemical reactions, and elementary physiological functions. In this way, while consolidating their understanding of the basic processes of physics and chemistry, they succeeded in keeping the truly problematic issues at arm's length; and, if necessary, they were ready to distract attention from those more difficult areas by dismissing cosmological speculations as theological, and psychological phenomena as subjective.

To this day, there are large areas of the physical sciences in which the classical method remains, for all practical purposes, as effective and fruitful as ever. In the greater part of this work, physicists, chemists, and physiologists can still freely assume that the processes they study are not significantly affected by, or responsive to, our observation of them. Yet, by now, it is also clear that the assumption of a one-way coupling rests on a simplification of the true situation, which may be useful for certain purposes, but is valid only within limits. The moment one seeks to move across those limits, the theoretical basis of that assumption has to be reconsidered. And those scientific enthusiasts in the late nineteenth century who went full steam ahead, without a second thought, were evidently creating the conditions for a crisis in the historical development of science.

By claiming unlimited power and unrestricted application for methods of investigation that had been tested and proved in only a limited range of cases, nineteenth-century scientists placed themselves at risk. For in doing so they begged the answers to two questions which, at the time, had never been thoroughly or critically appraised:

(1) Was there reason to believe that the methods of investigation that had proved fruitful in the case of insensate, unresponsive objects and processes would continue to be effective in the case of sensate and responsive beings? Or were Kant's strictures on all attempts to produce a "mechanics of the mind" a proper warning against such an extrapolation?

(2) Was there even reason to believe that, in their dealings with insensate, unresponsive beings, scientists would always be able to preserve a purely Laplacean "one-way interaction" with their subject matter, by continuing to reduce their causal influence on the systems they studied, without ever reaching any natural limit? Or would a point be reached, in due course,

beyond which even physicists and astronomers could no longer claim to be serving as pure onlookers whose investigations produced (at least in principle) no significant changes in the behavior of the system they were observing?

If all other things had been equal—in particular, if the scientists of the 1830s and 1840s had been as reflective and self-critical about their philosophical presuppositions as their precursors had been, some one hundred or one hundred and fifty years earlier—those issues might already have been confronted before the middle of the nineteenth century. Certainly, there was nothing substantive in the intellectual content of nineteenth-century science that compelled scientists to claim unrestricted application for its theoretical posture and methods.

As things turned out, the division of labor associated with the professionalization of scientific work led to these questions being sidetracked. The extraordinary successes that all of the various physical and biological sciences achieved in turn, each in its own field, gave the spokesmen of science the idea that they had hit on an intellectual method of unlimited fruitfulness. Whatever the subject of investigation might be—from the minutest of atoms to the entire cosmos, from the simplest physical collision to the subtlest of mental experiences—the maxims of scientific method, the criteria of scientific objectivity, and the demands of a truly scientific attitude should (they assumed) be the same.

The enthusiastic advocates of "modern science," accordingly, fell into the habits of exaggeration and self-deception that gave rise to "scientism," not out of any kind of self-interest or other such ulterior motive, but from sheer uncritical extrapolation. As a result, the intellectual crisis whose sources were built into the "classical" conception of scientific detachment and objectivity was postponed until after 1900. Instead of being precipitated and overcome in the lifetime of the Newtonian world picture (as we shall see), it was faced only during the years from 1905 on, when the adequacy of Newton's own theories was at last called in question, even within the heartlands of physics itself.

4. The transformation of the sciences during the twentieth century

How has this crisis affected our twentieth-century ways of thinking about the world? Its unforeseen onset, explicit recognition, and eventual resolution—what I am here calling the transition from modern to post-modern science—have occupied some sixty or seventy tumultuous and productive years of intellectual history. As had happened with the critique of earlier scientific theories of Copernicus and his successors, some three or four hundred years earlier, the first steps in this transition acted like the movement of a single pebble that precipitates an avalanche. Beginning from certain apparently localized difficulties within the formulation of theoretical physics, the resulting changes have spread out and ramified, until they have transformed the intellectual status and character of contemporary science at many points and on many levels. For the purposes of this essay, we may divide up these changes and consider them under three subheadings:

a. Changes in the character and conception of "theory" in science, by which the earlier conception of the scientist, as a rational onlooker detached from his objects of study, has been progressively displaced by a newer conception of the scientist, as a participant involved in the very processes about which he theorizes;

b. Associated changes in the character and conception of technology, arising from the fact that the earlier habit of manipulating and utilizing the seemingly unlimited resources of nature has run up against the limits of those resources, together with the fact that it has become necessary to allow quite consciously and explicitly for the role of human actions *within* the natural processes that are being put to individual or industrial use;

c. The consequent abandonment of "value neutrality" in the actual conduct of the scientific enterprise, together with a novel recognition that the pursuit of science imposes not merely intellectual but also ethical demands on its practitioners.

a. The theorist as participant

We may take as our starting point Albert Einstein's dissatisfaction with late nineteenth-century attempts to link Isaac Newton's system of mechanics with James Clerk Maxwell's theory of electromagnetism, so as to achieve a complete synthesis of physics. It was this critique of Einstein's that acted as the loose pebble which, first, prompted the creation of relativity physics and, not long after, led to the more comprehensive critique by Werner Heisenberg and Niels Bohr of the physical relationship between the "observer" and the "observed." By itself, it is true, Einstein's initial theory of relativity—the so-called "special" theory of relativity, dating from the year 1905—did not require one to reject the earlier picture of the scientist as an onlooker viewing nature from a detached position. Even so, it did introduce one important change to that picture, the long-term intellectual consequences of which were to be momentous. Hitherto, scientists had not merely taken it for granted that they could, at least in principle, observe and describe the world of nature with progressively increasing precision, without influencing its operations in any theoretically significant way; they had also assumed that all of their observations could be compared and correlated in a perfectly straightforward manner, regardless of the actual location in the universe from which those observations were made. According to Newton's theory of mechanics, there existed one or more privileged "frames of reference" (the so-called "inertial" frames) in relation to which mechanical processes of all kinds could be described using especially simple mathematical forms. It was natural enough, therefore, to think of Laplace's

Omniscient Calculator as contemplating the world from just such an "inertial" viewpoint.

The immediate consequence of the new relativity theory was to put that second assumption in doubt. By putting the mathematical system of Maxwell's electromagnetic theory at the heart of physics, in place of Newton's mechanics, Einstein was able to show that—theoretically speaking—all frames of reference were on a par with one another. As he saw things, there was nothing in nature to mark off descriptions given from the standpoint of "inertial" frames of reference as either simpler or otherwise "better" than those given from any other viewpoint. For the purposes of physics, any one viewpoint was as good as any other, and no physical tests could ever serve to pick out any one frame of reference (whether associated with Laplace's ideal observer, or with "absolute space," or with the hypothetical "ether") as defining the ideal standpoint for a detached scientific contemplation of the Universe. The scientist might still dream of observing and describing nature without affecting its operations; but he could do so only by employing physical agencies (e.g., light rays)—there was no longer any way in which these observations could be made entirely "from outside" the world of nature itself. To put the matter bluntly, the relativistic principle implied that any frame of reference was physically as good as any other, i.e., that any physical description of nature must be understood as being given "relative to" some arbitrarily chosen frame of reference *within* the physical world; and this step paved the way for a radical reappraisal of the traditional picture of the scientist as observer.

That deeper critique was forced on physicists only when they turned their attention away from astronomy—the physics of the largest scale processes open to human study—and looked instead at the physics of phenomena on the smallest scale available for scientific investigation. The crucial arguments were those associated with the introduction, by Erwin Schrödinger and Werner Heisenberg, of wave mechanics and quantum mechanics. These new theories were required in order to account for the puzzling properties of the electrons within the newly discovered substructure of individual atoms, and for the processes by which material atoms were found to absorb and emit light and other forms of electromagnetic radiation. (Here, the names of Ernest Rutherford, Niels Bohr, and Louis de Broglie come particularly to mind.) By the late 1930s, as the outcome of a vigorous debate in which Heisenberg and Bohr took the most prominent parts, one fundamental conclusion had been established and had won general acceptance. On the level of subatomic particles, at least, no physical procedures were available by which one could measure all of the specific variables needed for the purposes of perfect Laplacean prediction, without in the process changing the actual values of those variables to an unknowable extent. Roughly speaking, on the subatomic level Nature permitted the physicist to probe her workings only with blunt fingers: the more precisely he attempted to discover and describe those workings, the more seriously he was doomed to intervene in them, and so to change them.

As time went on, it became clear that the resulting principle—viz., that the exact and simultaneous values of all physical variables were inescapably "indeterminable"—was of much more general application. Although it had been recognized first on the subatomic scale, where its consequences were inescapable, there was every reason to suppose that it held good on all other levels of physical magnitude, as well, even where it had no practical consequences of any sort. So, as soon as quantum mechanics had taken its place as one of the foundation stones of the new physics, the old dream of drawing a sharp, precise line between the "observer" and the "observed"—of a one-way interaction between the onlooking scientist and the natural processes of which he was a spectator—had apparently to be abandoned. As a matter of quite basic principle, no such sharp line could be drawn. Even for the purposes of the most fundamental parts of theoretical physics, scientists were now obliged to think of themselves not as spectators looking on *at* nature but as participants involved *within* nature. Whether on the largest, astronomical scale or on the smallest, subatomic scale, their own procedures for observing, measuring, and describing nature would from now on form an essential, uneliminable part of their objects of study. Physicists could no longer retreat to an intellectual "hide" and observe nature like bird-watchers. No such "hide" was any longer available. To observe *was* to influence; and even the most delicate of observations involved a two-way interaction with nature.

Once the earlier assumption of a one-way interaction between the onlooker and his natural objects of study had to be abandoned even in fundamental physical theory, the other limitations on the ideas and methods of "classical" science became easier to recognize. Ever since Descartes, the mathematical exactitude of physical theory had given it a prestige, and also a philosophical centrality, that other sciences apparently lacked. So, in the eyes of most philosophers from Descartes on, the fact that psychology (say) had so much less hope of achieving the kind of theoretical detachment to which physicists could realistically aspire only underlined the impossibility of turning psychology into a truly "exact" science. As a result of Heisenberg's critique, however, this philosophical dichotomy between physics and psychology—between the natural sciences and the human sciences—also came up for reconsideration. There might still be some force in Wilhelm Dilthey's arguments for distinguishing between the explanatory sciences of "causality" (e.g., physics) and the interpretative sciences of "meaning" or "intentionality" (e.g., anthropology and psychology); but the older arguments for considering the ideas of physics as the essential key to all "natural philosophy" no longer held good. The inescapable limitations on absolute exactness of scientific observation created by the two-way interaction between the psycholgist and his subjects now turned out to affect all of the natural sciences, even the most basic. So, there was no longer the same reason to view psychology, philosophically, as a secondary or "inferior" branch of science, destined eventually to be taken over by—or "reduced to"—the more exact and fundamental science of physics.

Even on a theoretical level, twentieth-century changes in science have had a fruitful and liberating effect on the development of psychology. True, among all the schools of psychology, there are still some that stand by the earlier theoretical ideal and continue to dream of achieving the older, Newtonian kind of "objectivity" in their studies of human behavior. The strictest advocates of "radical behaviorism" as the proper method for psychology, for instance, still prefer to think of their research subjects as research *objects* and seek to explain their behavior in terms of exact, onlooker's theories, without resorting to any dubious, interpretive categories such as "meaning." Behaviorism apart, however, most scientific psychologists today are prepared to recognize and accept the fact that, in psychological research, a two-way interaction between the observer and his subjects of study is quite unavoidable, and even fruitful. Indeed, if psychologists were to limit themselves to the kinds of observations of human behavior that can be made by pure spectators, disdaining all two-way interactions and attributions of "meaning" to that behavior, they would be robbing themselves of their most important sources of insight into the character, significance, and purposes of human conduct.

Far from its being a deplorable concession to intellectual prejudice and frailty for the psychologist to intervene in, and interpret the meaning of, the human conduct that he investigates, these are necessary and legitimate procedures for improving his understanding of that behavior. They are necessary procedures, because—for the technical purposes of psychiatry and psychotherapy, above all—discovering how human agents respond in the context of two-way relationships is a necessary step in coming to understand their states of mind; and they are legitimate procedures, because the earlier objections to such standards rested solely on a conception of "scientific objectivity" which is no longer accepted even within physics. If we think seriously for a moment about the methods employed in such enterprises as psychiatry, for instance, we may well ask ourselves how there could ever be any significant "understanding" of human conduct *without* two-way interchanges between the observing psychiatrist and the observed patient. Whether in everyday life or in more clinical contexts, the kind of knowledge and understanding that we have about our fellow human beings is precisely the personal knowledge and understanding that two individuals build up in the course of developing a two-way relationship: the knowledge that rests, not on objective record-keeping and detached prediction, but on personal familiarity and reciprocal expectations; not on unilateral expectations, but on mutual understandings.

Does this mean that the conditions for truly "scientific" observation break down in the study of human behavior and that psychologists must abandon the quest for "objectivity?" That conclusion is forced upon us only if we cling to an outdated conception of scientific "objectivity" which is by its very nature ill-adapted to the goals and methods of psychology. Certainly, psychiatrists, psychoanalysts, and psychologists of many other stripes can all of them strive to avoid or counteract the effects on their investigations of bias, prejudice, and similar distorting influences; and they will, if they are wise, delay drawing any confident theoretical inferences, or presenting any firm practical conclusions, until they have taken care to reflect on the possibility of such distortions. (It is for this very reason, indeed, that psychoanalysts in training are encouraged to recognize, and make allowances for, the effects of "countertransference," i.e., the influences that their own emotional reactions within the analytic situation may have on their interpretation of an analysand's state of mind.)

If the goals and methods of "modern" science, as developed from 1650 till the early twentieth century, made the detached objectivity of the rational onlooker the proper ideal for any science, accordingly, the goals and methods of "post-modern" science now rest on a recognition that, to a greater or lesser degree, all scientific understanding whatever involves uneliminable intervention by the scientist in the processes that he is seeking to understand. Instead of seeking to stand "outside" those processes, scientists have now learned to accept their new status as participants within the very situations they are studying.

The effects of this change on science have already been broad and deep. By choosing to concentrate here on the quantum revolution within physics, at one extreme, and on the rise of psychiatry and other psychological sciences, at the other, we have marked only the two end points of a spectrum. It is at these extremes, of course, that the limitations of the classical approach make themselves most obviously apparent. Yet, to a greater or lesser degree, the same transition from "modern" to "post-modern" can be illustrated all the way across the sciences: in physiology (say) as much as in psychology, and in cybernetics as much as in chemistry. It is not just the sciences that lie close to the central philosophical debate whose ideas and methods have been transformed during the last thirty or forty years. Released from the arbitrary constraints imposed on science by the presuppositions of Cartesian and Newtonian "natural philosophy," all of the sciences—human and natural alike—have been free to rethink their assumptions and procedures, so as to allow for the scientist's own presence in, and involvement with, the world of natural phenomena and processes. In that sense, the whole range of theoretical sciences has, by now, begun to develop in the new, "post-modern" direction.

b. Technology and nature

If during the last fifty years our most basic scientific theories have been redirected in ways that take new account of our human role within nature, something very similar is also true of our industrial and technological practices, and of the scientific ideas that underlie them. Once again, we can conveniently illustrate the effects of the transition in two contrasted enter-prises and areas of experience: ecology, on the one hand, and heavy indus-try, on the other.

Ecology serves as an especially good example of "post-modern" science, for a number of different reasons. To begin with, it is a field of study in which theory and practice are unusually close; then again, it has a method that focuses attention on natural processes that take place on the human scale and are of kinds in which human agents may quite typically be in-volved; finally, it is a science that has been able to achieve intellectual maturity and independence only during the last few decades. To the extent that it requires us, quite specifically, to study and report on the reciprocal interactions between the conduct of human agents and other elements of the natural environment, the subdiscipline of *human* ecology might even be held up as the prototypically "post-modern" science, and it is probably no accident that human ecology has only recently become a serious field of scientific study.

By the standards of earlier times, ecology was scarcely a "science" at all. Instead of emulating the analytical methods of the physical sciences, by bringing to light the minute constituents and processes within individual bodies or systems, considered in abstraction from their natural contexts, the ecologist views naturally occurring systems as complex wholes and is interested in the patterns of interaction that link the parts of such systems together in actual situations. Food chains, predator-prey relationships, population balances between coexisting species, the reciprocal influences of climate, vegetation, and soil, and so on: these are the patterns and elements in terms of which an ecological account of the natural world is to be formulated. Given the character of such preoccupations, the ecologist will find it hard to set himself, and his viewpoint, wholly apart from his objects of study. Not only do human actions and artifacts play a significant, in some situations even a controlling, part in the processes under investigation in ecology: in addition, any ecological experiment is necessarily an interven-tion in those processes. How critical an influence does the level of a particu-lar insect population have on the interspecific relationships in the given environment? In order to investigate this question experimentally, we might (e.g.) introduce a large number of sterile male insects, so cutting down the rate of reproduction of the particular species, and study the consequential changes in the populations of other species. But, clearly enough, such an "experiment" would be successful only to the extent that it *did* involve a modification of the processes that we seek to understand.

Is this to say that ecology is more of a clinical science, like medicine, than it is a theoretical science, like physiology? Not at all. Regarded as a science, ecology is concerned not with the practical management of the environ-ment but with its underlying laws and mechanisms. However, just as physi-ology and medicine borrow each other's methods and learn from each other's experience, so scientific ecology learns from the practical experience of those whose task it is to monitor and manage fish and wildlife, or the forests, or the water quality of rivers and lakes, while at the same time contributing methods and ideas to those practical enterprises. No doubt, it is quite *possible* to study ecological theory without having any particular concern for environmental policy: equally, it is quite possible to play a part in wildlife management, or to engage actively in the politics of the ecology movement, while remaining somewhat indifferent to the theoretical analyses arrived at in scientific ecology. But such one-sided preoccupations as these are much less easy and natural to maintain in the ecological field than they are in the case of (say) physical science and practice, where an intellectual fascination with atomic structure and fundamental-particles theory can very easily be dissociated from any concern with the politics of nuclear engineering, and vice-versa.

The theoretical preoccupations that direct the attention of scientific ecologists have had parallels in other areas of science, too. In recent years there has been a vigorous debate about the respective virtues of "holism" and "reductionism" in the biological sciences, notably in physiology. At times, this controversy has been discussed at a somewhat elevated and metaphysical level, with analytically minded biochemists attacking the advocates of holism for surrendering to "vitalism" and the more holistically minded physiologists criticizing the biochemists for thinking in too "mechanistic" a way. But the discussion has also had genuinely practical implications for physiological method. For example, physiologists have increasingly come to organize their theories of organic functioning around the analysis of entire "systems"—the vasomotor system, the respiratory system, the central nervous system, etc.—rather than focusing exclusively on the biochemical reactions occurring locally at some given point in the physiological frame. By so doing, they have followed the example set originally in the 1860s by Claude Bernard, treating the body's organisms as providing internal environments that have their own inner microecology and microecological systems—that are, as the term is, in homeostasis.

So much for the one extreme. Meanwhile, at the other, the actual practice of modern industry has also had to pay fresh attention to the ways in which human actions and natural processes are reciprocally connected. From early medieval times until well into the twentieth century, the resources of nature had seemed practically inexhaustible. During the High Middle Ages, it was a regular part of Christian doctrine that God had given to man a "dominion" over all of the "lesser Creation," i.e., over the world of nature; and the belief that all minerals, plants, and animals alike were there for human beings to take and use freely was carried over into the modern era by Francis Bacon and the other prophets of modern science and technology. It is true that, in parallel with the biblical exhortation to "be fruitful and multiply," there also went a more moderate doctrine, according to which man's dominion was to be exercised as a "stewardship." Thus, the idea that the exploitation of nature was to be undertaken circumspectly and advised-

ly was not wholly foreign to the traditions of the Church. Still, it would have
been hard for the people of medieval Europe—who were still scratching a
living from the soil in settlements carved out from the forests or mountains
of the Mediterranean region, or harvesting arable land newly won from the
swamps of the northern countries—to conceive of a future time when their
countries would be afflicted with the problems of overpopulation and excess consumption.

In the course of the second millennium A.D., there took place those three
great expansions which, taken together, were to bring about a great transformation in human affairs. These were the two sharp increases in agricultural productivity, the one following the Black Death, the other in the
eighteenth century, which displaced so many rural laborers, prompting
urbanization and later industrialization; and, finally, from the late eighteenth century on, the harnessing of iron, coal, and steel that was associated
with the creation of the factory system of industrial production. In retrospect, it is clear that the attitudes of robust self-confidence that were characteristic of the men whose enterprise initiated the expansions were scarcely
compatible with any great measure of self-restraint. Everywhere, it seemed,
there was territory to be "discovered" and "opened up" to agriculture and
commerce: first, the deep soils of England, Holland, and the North European Plain, later the rediscovered wonders of India and China, together
with the gold and silver mines of Central and South America, and eventually also the fertile plains of the Mississippi Basin, the Rió de la Plata in
Argentina, and the Australian outback, as the other continents were "colo-
nized" in turn. For the time being, all the riches of the earth were netted,
harvested, tilled, mined, and processed without fear or limitation.

How unnecessary it is to belabor the contrast with the position that
humanity faces today! In little more than twenty years, the need to consider
the "environmental impact" of all major new urban and industrial developments, instead of being seen as a bee in the bonnets of a few cranks—a John
Muir, an Aldo Leopold, a Rachel Carson—has become a central issue of
national policy and international politics. The nineteenth-century industri-
alist could watch smoke belching from his factory chimneys and drifting off
into the sky without a moment's anxiety about where it was going thereafter, and he might reflect to himself that a little grime was a small price to
pay for prosperity. (Recall the old Yorkshire saying, "Where there's muck,
there's brass.") But, in the 1980s, a manufacturer (at least in the United
States or Western Europe) whose plant does not have "scrubbers" to clean
the emissions from the chimneys will be continually looking over his shoul-
der at the local government agency responsible for environmental protection, and worrying about the bad publicity that will ensue if it proves that
his particular fumes and wastes are helping to increase the cancer rate in
the immediate neighborhood, or even returning to earth to poison the fish
in lakes a thousand miles away.

On every level, the style and character of twentieth-century industrial technology have forced new questions into the political arena. Some last few manufacturers and trade unionists may still brush environmental issues aside, as a preoccupation of upper middle-class eggheads who do not have to learn a living with their hands. ("The professor's petunias are wilting.") But, by now, this is at best a rearguard action, covering an inevitable retreat. Meanwhile, the complaints continue to flow in. At one end of an economic scale, the Swedish government points an accusing finger at the factories of northern England and the Ruhr, as damaging the natural resources of Scandinavia; Canadians put the increasing acidity of their remotest lakes down to rain adulterated by fumes from the midwestern United States; while the growing populations of northern and southern California, the intermountain states and British Columbia compete for limited water supplies. At the other end, the savannahs and fringes of arable soil around the Sahara are dying back, under the impact of overgrazing and exhaustion, leaving the infertile sands to take over; the last great forest areas of the world are being encroached on and eroded away by the search for minerals, new settlements, and even newsprint; while the very fish, whales, and crustaceae of the oceans can no longer hold their own unaided against the trawls, nets, and harpoon guns of the world's fishing fleets. Where in earlier centuries "the bounty of nature" was a watchword for the supposedly unbounded and self-renewing riches of the earth, during the last half-century human beings have at last begun to learn—both as individuals and as nations—to live like misers, measuring their actions in terms of their impact on a finite store of resources. An ever-increasing gross national product is no longer seen as an unmixed political good; now, it has always to be weighed against the limits to growth.

What this means is that in technology as in science, it is no longer possible for human beings to think of themselves as operating from outside the world of nature. We can no longer *view* nature, as scientists, from the detached standpoint of Laplacean onlookers; and we can no longer *use* nature, as manufacturers, with the carefree assurance of divinely authorized Dominion. In both theoretical and practical terms, we must now accept our rediscovered position as a part of the very nature that we have been viewing and using. To some extent, however slight, all our scientific observations of nature modify the processes we observe; and to some extent, often great, all our technological exploitations of nature involve using up "natural goods" which can no longer be guaranteed to replace themselves. So, we must stop behaving as though we were ourselves the *invisible* part of nature; the detached mind and sovereign hands that can have no significant impact on the overall state of nature and can do no significant harm to it. The survival of that very nature which we both observe critically and rely on practically will from now on depend on our capacity to learn measure and restraint in our interactions with it. The old Greek motto *Mēden Agān*—"Nothing in excess"—has thus acquired a new meaning and relevance for us all.

c. *The ethics of the research enterprise*

The consequences of these transformations have had an impact, not merely on the intellectual and practical effects of the scientific enterprise, but also on its internal conduct. They are compelling scientists at the present time to engage in a critical reappraisal of their whole enterprise from the standpoint of ethics. A hundred years ago (as we saw) it was still possible to claim that the sciences were "value free." The scientist's methods of inquiry were commendable just because they were dispassionate and free of all self-interest. If science had its own special ethical concerns, these had to do only with matters of integrity and truthtelling: the worst sin a scientist could commit was to falsify his observations and so mislead his colleagues. The phrase "value free" may always have involved some element of exaggeration; but, at most, the values of nineteenth-century science were seen as intellectual values. On a deeper level, the scientist's posture of detachment and abstraction seemingly set him outside the scope of any genuinely moral critique. Since the pure onlooker could minimize the effects of his observations on nature, his activities presumably did, in themselves, neither good nor harm in the world. His single-valued pursuit of truth insured that he was, ethically speaking, out of the line of fire. Adopted as a mode of life, *theoria* divorced from *praxis* could still be acclaimed as Aristotle had taught that it should, both as the highest occupation and as a wholly self-validating one.

Here again, the contrast between science then and science now scarcely needs underlining. Since the mid-1960s, the whole enterprise of science has been subjected to a series of ethical challenges, and the claims of complete *Wertfreiheit* ("value-freedom") have been left in tatters. Some of those challenges, it is true, have themselves been open to objections, as uninformed or ill-motivated. The high romantic rhetoric of the "anti-science" movement, based on the counterculture of the late 1960s and early 1970s, echoed themes from the spokesmen of an earlier romantic era, such as Schiller and Blake; and many of the resulting criticisms of science owed more to an enthusiastic political radicalism than they did to the power of a serious historical analysis. Scientists were damned for lending themselves as "co-conspirators" with capitalists and imperialists, and their method of intellectual detachment was caricatured as entailing a posture of callous indifference. For some four or five years, even the most scrupulous and high-minded scientists were thrown onto the defensive, and the calm meetings of scientific academies were liable to be disrupted by invasions from slogan-chanting protestors. (Watching the resulting confrontations from outside was like seeing the unworldly Albert Einstein mobbed by a crowd of infuriated antivivisectionists.) The scientists themselves did not in every case react with proper composure to these attacks: some of them fell back on shrill denunciations of their critics and took refuge in the outdated slogans of an earlier age. Did not the First Amendment give scientists *carte blanche* to do whatever research their intellects could conceive? Should not their own disinterested motives be sufficient protection from the indignities of such politically motivated criticism?

Behind these wild and irrelevant disorders, however, a more serious ethical critique was beginning to take shape. Its first significant outcome had to do with the morality of human experimentation: the conduct of scientific investigation that used human beings—whether medical patients or normal volunteers—as their objects of study, and that in some cases exposed those human beings to more or less risky procedures, which were capable of doing them harm without any countervailing expectation of medical therapy or other comparable benefit. The issue was not, of course, a new one. The testing of new medical agents and procedures had always involved an element of risk, as when Walter Reed used Cuban subjects in his work on the development of a yellow-fever vaccine. But hitherto the task of deciding how far such risks could acceptably be carried had generally been left to the conscience and discretion of the physicians and research scientists themselves. If worst came to worst, the relatives of a deceased research subject could always bring a civil action for tort against the experimenters; no larger public interest was apparently involved.

During the years following the Second World War, however, there was an essential change in the situation. The shameful experience of wartime experiments conducted in German concentration camps brought physicians, research scientists, and governments together in the effort to formulate an internationally recognized code for the conduct of human experiments. From being the private concern of scientific investigators in hospitals, universities, and pharmaceutical companies, medical research involving human subjects rapidly became a matter of public polity, for the reason that the costs of that research were increasingly met out of public tax funds, and because government agencies, such as the United States Food and Drug Administration (FDA) were required to check and validate the substances and devices which were the outcome of that research. How could the electorate be content to stand by and see its taxes spent to pay for research whose methods were morally questionable?

The late 1960s, accordingly, saw the rapid emergence of biomedical ethics as an active field for both theoretical discussion and practical policy. On the one hand, a vigorous public debate sprang up about moral issues in medical practice and research, both in the press and in more sober academic journals and forums; and this debate led to the establishment of several highly influential new periodicals and institutions, such as the Institute of Society, Ethics and the Life Sciences at Hastings-on-Hudson, outside New York City, with its widely circulated monthly, the *Hastings Report*. From being in the late 1940s and '50s the subject of a handful of books and articles at most—and those concerned chiefly with the excesses of the Nazi era—by the 1970s "bioethics" had become an academic and literary industry. On the other hand, within the United States government, the

Public Health Service, whose National Institutes of Health conducted or provided financial support for much of the country's biomedical research, began to demand that all university hospitals and other institutions of medical research establish procedures capable of assuring that all their research projects and methods were planned so as to be free of morally objectionable procedures. There came into being a vast network of "institutional review boards" which were responsible to the P.H.S. for conducting prior reviews of—and, if need be, for recommending prior restraint over—all research involving human experimental subjects in the institution concerned.

For a while, it looked as though the ethical debate about medical experimentation might have even more drastic consequences. The passionate controversy that followed the Supreme Court ruling on abortion spilled over into science and, spurred on by horrifying press reports about experiments supposedly conducted in Finland or Sweden, the United States Congress seriously considered making the use of any human fetus in scientific research a criminal offense. However, faced with the prospect of catastrophic restraint on gynecology and pediatrics, cooler heads prevailed; a National Commission was set up to consider and analyze the conditions on which the use in medical and behavioral research of vulnerable human subjects—whether unborn children, or prisoners, or juveniles, or the insane—should be regarded as either acceptable or inadmissible. In this way, a revived kind of "casuistry" grew up, by which all the possible varieties of human experimentation were submitted to a kind of taxonomic analysis, and a common pattern of case law was established against which research proposals were to be measured in advance.

Before long, this debate about the ethics of scientific research expanded to embrace wider issues, also. The most striking episode in this story was the debate in the mid-1970s about the ethics of research on recombinant DNA. The most noteworthy aspect of this particular controversy was the fact that it originated in an ethical initiative by the research scientists themselves. Previously, the general pattern had been for outside critics to raise cries of alarm, indignation, or anxiety about the supposed ethical implications of scientific research projects which, in the eyes of the scientists themselves, either posed no ethical difficulties at all or were even totally "value free." Now, with the development of new procedures by which the actual structures of the key macromolecules in living cells could be manipulated and modified, molecular biochemists in California and elsewhere found themselves wondering whether the widespread use of such procedures for genetic engineering and other kinds of biotechnology might not expose the public at large to risks of an unpredictable scale and gravity. A first meeting of scientists, lawyers, and journalists at Asilomar, outside Monterey in California, led to a public declaration of self-restraint on behalf of the research community, and was followed by a broader, more public debate, whose outcome was the adoption by the National Institutes of Health of a set of guidelines for research in this area. (Britain and other countries engaged in recombinant DNA research soon followed suit.)

In this case, again, the temper of the public discussion threatened at times to become overheated. Political radicals denounced recombinant DNA research as a wild dream of pharmaceutical multimillionaires egged on by fascist-imperialist politicians. The more conservative scientists, in reply, tore their hair and bewailed unjustifiable political interference in the innocent tasks of natural science. But, when the dust had settled, it was clear that a middle way had emerged, by which legitimate claims for the protection of the larger public against possible new forms of harm were respected, without the scientists themselves being subjected to unreasonable or excessive restraints. By the early 1980s, the use of recombinant DNA techniques for technological ends was beginning to move ahead without being seriously handicapped by conforming to the NIH guidelines; and, for all except a few irreconcilables, the prospect of being able to produce biochemical agents like insulin and interferon industrially, and even to create custom-designed forms of those agents with highly discriminating medical uses, began to weigh heavily in favor of the recombinant techniques.

Finally, going beyond all ethical debates about the actual conduct and immediate hazards of scientific research itself, some wider ethical questions have recently been raised about the political rights and social responsibilities of scientists, within the larger societies of which they are members. So long as science could be thought of as an isolated (if professional) pursuit having no significant impact on the welfare of the larger community, such issues were inconsequential. It was presumably up to each individual scientist to decide for himself in what direction his curiosity drew his intellect and imagination; and, since his activities were free of cost or harm to his fellows, there was no basis for a moral challenge, and so no ethical case for him to answer. Some, indeed, have even argued that this freedom from ethical accountability was, in earlier times, one of the main charms of traditional scientific work. Certainly, most classical scientists took some care to avoid putting themselves in a position from which they might be obliged to justify their activities publicly. Right up until the Second World War, most academic scientists ruled out all thought of seeking financial support for their research from either government or industry. For the most part, they chose to work on rather small-scale projects, the expense for which could be met out of a university's normal budget. (In some cases, the scientists themselves were expected to pay for the cost of any research they did—e.g., the wages of a glassblower—out of their own pockets.) Accepting outside subsidies was widely regarded as compromising the integrity of research: science belonged, not to any single nation or industry, but to an essentially supranational community of rational thinkers, and it should avoid giving even the slightest appearance of being for sale to industrialists and politicians. So when, in January 1939, J. D. Bernal published a striking new book, *The Social Function of Science*, in which he argued strongly for developing a system of governmental finance for science, his proposals were denounced by Michael Polanyi and others as threatening the essential freedoms of science.

In the subsequent forty years, Bernal's speculative proposals have become the actualities of contemporary politics. From holding government and industry at arm's length before the Second World War, academic scientists have moved into a position in which they are largely dependent on such outside support for the costs of their research. The thing that made a crucial difference to their attitudes, in this respect, was their experience from 1939 on. In their wartime work on radar, sonar, nuclear physics, and the rest, they discovered that they could operate within the other institutions of their societies and states, without compromising their intellectual standards or their freedom of judgment; and they were (to tell the truth) happy enough to learn that lesson, given the vastly higher scale of financial resources available in a government research establishment, as contrasted with the private university. With the return to peacetime work from 1945 on, as a result, scientists were ready enough to contrive ways of interesting government, not just in the development of new weapons, but in helping them to pursue their academic research topics also. So, alongside glassblowing and statistics, "grantsmanship" rapidly took its place as an essential addition to the compleat scientist's quiver of skills. And, from around 1950 on, the different agencies of the United States government began to provide some very substantial sums of money to support academic science in American universities. This support has continued to the present day, notably through the National Science Foundation and the National Institutes of Health; though, over the years, the NIH's funds for biomedical research have grown more steadily and reliably than those for other basic sciences.

With rewards, however, there came also responsibilities. The expenditure of public tax money has always to be accounted for, not just in the narrower accountant's sense of that phrase, but also in terms of specific performances and achievements. In line with this, the scientist had to show the government funding agency that he had in fact carried out the scientific work for which a grant had originally been made; and, in due course, larger questions began to be raised about the procedures by which it was decided what projects should be supported at all. Was it sufficient to allow the scientists in any given field to decide by consensus—by what came to be known as "peer review"—which proposals in their field showed most intellectual promise, and so most deserved support? Or should the public's own representatives have an opportunity, either through the Congress or in other ways, of bringing some wider system of social priorities to bear on such funding decisions? Are scientists equipped to decide by themselves and on their own how their research efforts can best benefit the larger community? Or should their fellow citizens have an independent chance to indicate their own preferences, as between (say) environmental medicine and biochemistry, space travel and metallurgy?

This debate has only recently begun to play a large part in the politics of science. It raises all kinds of hard questions: about ways in which the general public might educate itself so as to be capable of expressing informed preferences rather than naive daydreams or prejudices, about the role of Congress and its committees, about the desirability of local initiatives (like the committee of concerned citizens organized at Cambridge, Massachusetts, in the course of the recombinant DNA dispute), and so on. As a result, it is not yet clear whether all the institutions are yet in place for dealing effectively with the social responsibilities of science, or whether new channels of discussion, education, and accountability will be required. But, at least in the United States, a significant dialogue has begun between the scientists and their fellow citizens about the novel social responsibilities that the scientists have had to assume within the new world of publicly financed, post-modern science.

5. The new agenda and responsibilities of science

Once we recognize and accept our novel position, as people for whom the older simplicities of Cartesian and Newtonian science are no longer a genuine option, what future trains of thought and lines of development will open up for us? Evidently enough, the kind of science that we can do, from our new standpoint as participants within nature, will warrant us in retaining neither the same ideals of cool, detached objectivity, nor the same fragmentation of scientific issues into completely separate disciplines, nor the same *Wertfreiheit*—i.e., freedom from moral issues and social accountability—that characterized the natural sciences from the late seventeenth century to the early or mid twentieth century. Instead, we shall have to work (a) toward newer ideas of objectivity, (b) toward a reintegration of scientific issues within a broader world view, and (c) toward a novel conception of the scientist's role within the larger society. All of these interlinked changes are forced upon us as necessary consequences of recovering for humanity its proper place within the world of nature.

a. Objectivity and justice

To begin with the most basic characteristic of a "scientific" attitude, viz., its claim to objectivity: the objectivity of any participant within a larger transaction, who deals with his fellow participants in an equitable, unbiased manner, is inevitably different from the objectivity of the detached observer, who sets himself quite apart from the transactions that he studies and reports on them (as it were) from behind a screen. Throughout the two hundred and fifty to three hundred years' history of modern science, the pursuit of objectivity became equated with the claims of *Wertfreiheit*. The same intellectual stance that allowed earlier scientists to eschew all questions about values and preferences also helped to preserve them against the biases of their own subjectivities. Indeed, for them the best way of assuring objectivity was, simply, to avoid all ethically tinged involvements with their subject matter. By remaining detached, they avoided the chief threat to the free exercise of an objective judgment.

The moment that this posture of detachment is no longer open to us, the problem of objectivity arises in a quite new way. Some people have reacted to the change by suggesting that our position as participants within nature makes true scientific objectivity impossible for us any longer. But this reaction is certainly extreme. Rather, we have to find alternative ways of identifying and counteracting the influence of our own biases on our scientific judgment, which are compatible with acknowledging that we are inescapably involved with the objects and systems that we study. To put the point in a sentence, we have to set aside the "value-free" conception of scientific objectivity as *detachment,* in favor of a "value-laden" conception of scientific objectivity as *justice.* Our task as post-modern scientists is no longer to abstract ourselves in thought from our subject matter and speak about it from outside. Instead, it is to find ways to treating, and thinking about, the other persons, objects, and processes of nature in a fair and equitable manner, without giving undue attention or favor, either to our own personal situation and interests, or even to specifically human situations and human interests at all.

We saw, earlier, what this change of posture and standpoint entails for psychology. To those who sought to carry over the traditional conception of scientific objectivity into the study of human behavior and mental processes, the goals and methods of behaviorism have a special, undeniable appeal. For behaviorists set out, quite explicitly, to devise experiments that would avoid all direct influence by the experimenter on his experimental object. By putting their subjects into carefully designed and rigorously controlled situations, which unfold according to preset schedules, behaviorist experimenters attempt to observe and record their subjects' responses in as detached a manner as any ornithologist who observes and records the nesting and mating behavior of finches from a perfectly protected hide. Other psychologists, however, have not felt able to confine themselves within the limitations of these goals and methods and, as a result, they have had to learn ways of recognizing and making allowances for their own influence on the course of the transactions in which they and their research subjects are jointly involved: recall, e.g., the concept of "countertransference" in the practice of psychoanalysis.

The corresponding problems in such sciences as ecology have been remarked on less frequently. Suppose, for instance, that we set out to understand all the food chains, predator-prey relationships, climatic cycles, and other ecological phenomena in which we are involved, by virtue of our situation within the world of nature: we shall end by building up pictures of all those processes in which human beings, and human agents, coexist alongside bees and mosquitoes, cultivated grain plants and wilderness forests, pesticides and dams, domesticated animals and river fish. Just because our own situations, and our own interests as human beings, are bound up with all those other elements within nature, it is out of the question to imagine that we can take a totally detached view about fellow participants in those processes, or of the processes themselves. So, in that case, the only relevant kind of objectivity consists in seeing and describing our role in the processes of nature fairly, without giving our own concerns an undue emphasis or an unjust protection, at the expense of all the other elements.

This is easier said than done. In ecology and related areas of science, the full demands of scientific objectivity have not yet been faced in all their complexity. To spell out these problems concisely: it is not even easy to describe the ecological *processes* in which we find ourselves, as human beings, in terms that give equal time and equal protection to all the other species and influences involved, far less to devise ecological *policies* for the management of those processes that pay just and equitable respect to all those other fellow participants whose habitat we share. On the contrary, we are subject to a standing temptation to build ecological analyses around human technological projects, instead of vice versa. Seen from that point of view, the problem becomes one of seeing how all other elements in the current ecological situation are liable to affect or be affected by the human projects in question, and so to facilitate or hinder their fulfillment; and, whatever else we may say about that formulation of the problem, it cannot be regarded, by any standard, as "objective."

At the present time, there are some unresolved basic ambiguities in the attitudes that different people bring to the practical problems of ecology and the environment: not just as between industrialists for whom environmental concerns threaten extra expense, and conservationists for whom industrial development is itself the threat, but even among conservationists themselves. On the other hand, there are those people who see incautious development now, in the service of certain current human desires, as being liable to restrict or prevent the subsequent achievement of other, later human desires, and who challenge such hasty development solely on that account. For these people, the basic problem of environmental protection is simply an anthropocentric, utilitarian problem of intelligent resource management in the long-term human interest—aimed at maximizing the number and variety of different human satisfactions achievable with given resources in given situations, and taking special care to make due provision for nonmaterial satisfactions, like the beauty of a view or the taste of fresh springwater. On the other hand, there are those people who seek to widen the discussion and put such anthropocentric concerns into a larger framework. For those other people, it is important to recognize trees, and birds, and other species of organisms as having requirements that need serving and protecting, alongside the requirements of human beings: in their eyes, thinking about the environment in a merely anthropocentric way is plainly inequitable and offends against the basic demands of objectivity, in the wider sense of *justice*.

These ambiguities affect our thinking about ecology on both the theoretical and the practical planes, i.e., from the standpoint both of ecological scientists and of environmental policymakers. Within ecological science, they leave us without any clear procedure for developing a fully impartial and justly proportioned analysis of the habitat—in which due weight is given to the roles of all the species and agents involved—as contrasted with an analysis directed by, and toward, the protection of our own human concerns. Meanwhile, within the realm of ecological policy, it is left correspondingly unclear whether the environmental impact statements that are administratively required in the case of all large-scale development projects must be framed in terms that respect the inherent requirements of, say, a redwood forest, or whether it is sufficient to recognize the investment that human beings themselves have in the survival of such a forest—as a potential source of future lumber and newsprint, of spiritual refreshment, or even of mere peace and quiet.

b. Cosmology and the larger world view

If we have difficulty in resolving these ambiguities today, that fact is no accident. For the task of placing relative priorities on the rights of different agents and participants in a conflict-of-interest situation is, precisely, the sort of problem that could not arise within the program of so-called modern (or Cartesian) science. To be more exact: the division of labor that led to the fragmentation of classical science into distinct disciplines had two complementary outcomes. In the first place, it allowed natural scientists to abstract particular aspects of nature and investigate them separately, apart from the overall complexities of the situations concerned. But at the same time, it bought this advantage at the price of cutting all these different aspects of nature off from one another, so that the complex overall interactions between these distinct aspects, within any situation, belonged to the scientific agenda of no single science and so became, scientifically speaking, nobody's business.

The future agenda of post-modern science will unavoidably differ from that of classical science in this second respect, also. If we are to view nature from within—from a position as participants in the processes of nature—we can no longer afford to chop up our understanding of nature into separate fragments, or confine our attention to one scientific discipline at a time. Instead, we shall need to find ways of fitting these disciplinary aspects back together again, within a broader conception of nature, and of the place of human beings within it. From now on, we shall no longer be able to regard nature merely as an object for detached study and description, from which we are to that extent separated, and even *alienated*. Instead, we shall also be having to consider the world of nature as our *home*. (Interestingly enough, when John Wheeler, the physical cosmologist from Princeton University, gave an address in Washington to celebrate the five-hundredth anniversary of Copernicus's birth, he chose as his title "The Universe as a Home for Man.") And, faced with the question of how we humans can be truly "at home" within nature, we can scarcely continue to study only one disciplinary aspect of our place in nature at a time. There is, for example, no way in which we could be "at home" in nature gravitationally speaking, but not electromagnetically speaking; physiologically speaking, but not neurologically speaking; endocrinologically speaking, but not psychotherapeutically speaking. Either we are "at home" in our actual habitat, or we are not—that is a comprehensive judgment, to be made with an eye to our overall situation. As a result, we need to transcend the fragmentation of classical science into self-contained disciplines, each with its own distinct standpoint, in favor of some more comprehensive point of view, and so build up for ourselves a larger picture of the world, whose merits go beyond the requirements and discoveries of any one science.

This change in the agenda of science, as it moves into its post-modern phase, has some unexpected consequences. In the eyes of its founders, it was one of the greatest merits of modern or Cartesian-Newtonian science that its agenda permitted scientists to set aside—as lying entirely outside science—all general disputes about matters of philosophy and religion and concentrate on narrower topics about which some method of rational investigation and agreement could more easily be achieved. If the broader concerns of philosophy and religion became sidetracked in the process, that was a comparatively small price to pay for progress; and, despite the personal interest that Newton himself, for one, displayed in the philosophical and theological implications of the scientific enterprise, the task of building up a cosmological vision of the world, adapted to our religious as well as our intellectual concerns, took a back place in the plans of modern science.

It had not always been so. During some earlier stages in the historical evolution of ideas about nature, the place of humanity within the overall scheme of things had been a central topic for debate. In late antiquity, for instance, the Epicurean philosophers taught that it was desirable for us to detach ourselves from the aggravations of a life in nature and cultivate the imperturbable attitude of mere onlookers; but the Stoic philosophers emphasized, rather, the importance of integrating our human thoughts and activities into the natural world, and harmonizing our lives with the processes of nature. Considered against this background, the contrast between modern and post-modern science is significantly like the contrast between the Epicurean and Stoic points of view; indeed, in some places, Descartes himself discussed the ethical implications of "the passions" in positively Epicurean terms, claiming for "the rational mind" the power to separate itself from all the turmoil of the senses and the emotions, and to achieve the same kind of imperturbability that Epicurus had valued.

So understood, the program of "post-modern" science involves the revival of certain older, Stoic attitudes. The rationality of human thought and action cannot be shown, or judged, in isolation, solely in terms of their local efficacy in dealing with single, self-contained problems. They must fit in with, and respect the overall harmony of, the larger scheme of nature. To sharpen up the point: The agenda of post-modern science requires us to take seriously, once again, the conception that nature in fact *has*—or even *is*—a larger scheme, rather than an assemblage of separate aspects. One thing about that conception is not yet clear: viz., how, and on what conditions, such notions as harmony and integration are to be given a truly scientific interpretation. After three centuries of scientific investigation that has been devoted predominantly to the analytical study of separate groups of phenomena or aspects of nature, scientists are only now beginning to recognize and redevelop the intellectual procedures needed for thinking about and dealing with large integrated systems. It will certainly take some time before it is possible to reestablish an effective dialogue between scientists, philosophers, and theologians, about the overall scheme of nature, and about the place of humanity within that scheme.

c. The accountability of scientists

Finally, given the place that the new enterprise of post-modern science occupies within the larger framework of human society and culture, scientists can no longer claim that their investigations are value free. Instead, they now have to confront all those social, political, and moral issues that were sidetracked during the heyday of "modern" science and accept a new kind of accountability for their work, their ideas, and, above all, their intellectual priorities. To the extent that the basic theoretical attitudes of classical science were those of detached, rational spectators, rather than those of participants, they set humanity apart from nature; but to the extent that they were also the polite attitudes of gentlemen, rather than practical attitudes of craftsmen or engineers, they set the same scientists apart from their fellow humans as well. Conversely, the transformaton of modern science into post-modern science has had the effect, not only of reinserting humanity into its proper position in the natural world, but in addition of relocating scientists into their proper position within the larger social and political world—which, to be sure, does not always seem eager to make room for them.

So long as the new knowledge built up by natural scientists could still be thought of as entirely pure—i.e., as devoid of immediate technological value or application—scientists could pursue new knowledge in an entirely single-minded, single-valued spirit. Indeed, the English physicist John Ziman has pointed out striking resemblances between the frame of mind that young scientific apprentices have brought to their work in the twentieth century and that of young novices in the medieval monastic orders. Just as talented new Brothers obtained their deepest satisfaction from committing themselves wholly to a life of devotion and service to a priestly Order, and hoped only to win a reputation among their colleagues for their sanctity, so too bright new research scientists in the twentieth century have obtained their satisfaction from committing themselves to a life in devoted service to their Science, and have hoped only to win a professional reputation for their intellectual insight. After Hiroshima, however, monastic attitudes toward the work of science have become increasingly difficult to sustain. Since the 1940s, the professional activities of science have become caught up in the larger activities of society in so many ways that the walls of the scientific monastery have finally crumbled.

Hence arise all those problems about the ethics of the scientific enterprise that we looked at briefly earlier in this essay. From now on, the professional agenda of the sciences will include paying proper attention to the larger social and cultural, economic, and political significance of the new theories and techniques that are being developed in each field. This is not to imply that dramatic political episodes, comparable to the recent controversy about recombinant DNA research, are liable to turn up very often in other sciences also; but it is to imply that scientists in all fields would do well to cultivate the same sense of public responsibility in thinking about their own fields of work that the molecular biochemists displayed when they organized the initial moratorium on recombinant DNA research. They will do well to do so, not just out of a disinterested concern for the public welfare, but also from motives of self-defense. Although the wave of hostility toward science associated with the "counterculture" may have passed its peak, the public at large retains a lingering suspicion of science and scientists which is waiting to be reactivated by future horror stories about reckless development and proliferation of risky new discoveries.

The task of building up new institutions and channels of communication, by which scientists can make their proper contributions to the political debate, must be expected to continue. Furthermore, the increasingly complex character of the technical decisions on which the prosperity of modern industries and nations depends in an age of microprocessors and computer-operated machine tools, of novel weapons systems and energy sources, will only make this task the more urgent. Whether in legislatures or through scientific academies, whether at public inquiries or before oversight committees, scientists are learning to explain their work to representatives of the larger electorate, and to discuss with those representatives the social priorities, economic consequences, and moral constraints that determine the political strengths and weaknesses of the scientific enterprise, and hedge around the fields for fruitful, publicly financed research.

This is a prospect that Michael Polanyi and his colleagues in the Society for Freedom in Science dreaded, as a threat to the very health and vigor of science; but it is a prospect that needs to be faced with maturity and intelligence, rather than flatly denied or refused. By playing an active part in devising the special channels through which they can responsibly collaborate with other political institutions, both nationally and internationally, scientists will be doing themselves, as well as the rest of us, a good turn. An excellent illustration of the contribution that the scientific community has already begun to make in that direction can be found in the history of the Pugwash conferences. These meetings were organized largely on the initiative of physical scientists who were concerned about the nuclear arms race, and they played a significant part in laying the political groundwork for the nuclear nonproliferation treaties of the early 1960s. Held under the sponsorship of Cyrus Eaton at his summer home in Pugwash, Nova Scotia, they brought together scientists and political figures from the United States, the U.S.S.R., and other countries, to discuss nuclear weapons, disarmament, and the like, and they succeeded in establishing a dialogue between the American and Russian governments about the technical problems of contemporary policymaking and weapons development that has helped to strengthen the fragile foundations of world peace at a dangerous time in history.

It is time to bring this essay to a conclusion. Since the time of Aristotle, and even that of Newton, science has come a long way; the transformation that it has been undergoing in the course of the twentieth century is only the culmination of that long journey. The heart of that twentieth-century transformation (we have seen) lies not in the sheer quantity of scientific work being done today, nor in the intellectual quality of particular discoveries, so much as in the increasingly rich and varied ways in which science enters into and influences our lives outside the purely intellectual world of concepts and theories. Even on the intellectual level, the deepest significance of our new twentieth-century theories lies in the contribution they can make to the new "post-modern" image of science as an enterprise that goes on essentially *within* nature, not *outside* it. The Aristotelian image of the natural philosopher as a purely detached theorist, which continued to dominate the underlying aims and ideals of modern science until well into the twentieth century, has finally been superseded. Like the heroes in a Tom Stoppard drama, scientists have found themselves drawn, willy-nilly, out of their seats in the stands and into the dust and action of the actual arena.

This transformation has come, in some respects, as a shock and a surprise; and not all scientists are yet fully reconciled to the resulting changes in their status, their methods, and their mode of life. But these changes have been both deep and broad, and they will not easily be undone. They cover the whole spectrum of science, from relativity and quantum mechanics at one extreme to ecology and psychoanalysis at the other, and they have had the effect of discrediting the very philosophical foundation of "modern" science—the foundation which Descartes laid down for the rational investigation of the physical world in the early seventeenth century, and which Newton and his successors built upon so successfully from the 1680s on. As a result, we may expect scientists—and the sciences themselves—to become, both theoretically and practically, even more deeply involved in the world that they study in the years and centuries to come. The age of one-way interactions with nature is over, probably for good. From now on, both the theories of the sciences and the practical lives of scientists will have to take into account the two-way character of their interactions both with nature and with society. The absolute detachment and self-sufficiency of Aristotle's *theoros*, Descartes's rational Mind, and Laplace's Omniscient Calculator may have been a charming dream; but it proves to have been a dream nonetheless.

PART TWO

The Reconsideration of a Great Book

Edward Gibbon's
Decline and Fall of the Roman Empire

Hugh Trevor-Roper

Hugh Trevor-Roper was born in 1914, in Glanton, Northumberland, a
village under the Cheviot hills, and educated at Charterhouse School
and Christ Church, Oxford, where he studied classics and history. He
wrote his first book, a biography of Charles I's minister Archbishop
Laud, as a Research Fellow of Merton College, Oxford. It was published
in 1940. In the Second World War he served in the Intelligence Corps
(Secret Intelligence). In 1945 he carried out an official investigation into
the disappearance of Adolf Hitler. His report to the Four-Power
Intelligence Committee in Berlin was the basis of his book *The Last
Days of Hitler* (1947), which has been translated into twenty languages.
After the war he returned to Oxford and taught modern history at Christ
Church. He was appointed Regius Professor of Modern History at
Oxford in 1957. In 1980 he was elected Master of Peterhouse,
Cambridge. His published works include *The Rise of Christian Europe*
(1965), *The Philby Affair* (1968), *Religion, The Reformation and Social
Change* (1968), *Princes and Artists* (1976), and *Hermit of Peking*
(1976). He has also edited *Hitler's Table Talk* (1953), *Hitler's War
Directives* (1964), and *The Goebbels Diaries, Last Entries* (1978). He
has contributed regularly to the *Sunday Times,* the *New York Times,*
and other periodicals, writing mainly on history and foreign affairs. He is
a Fellow of the British Academy, a corresponding member of the
American Academy, and Director of Times Newspapers Ltd. He was
made Chevalier de la Legion d'Honneur in 1975 and created Lord
Dacre of Glanton in 1979. He is married to Lady Alexandra Haig,
daughter of Field Marshal Earl Haig.

I. Genesis of the work

Edward Gibbon is, in an important respect, the first modern European historian. That is, he is the first historian of the past whose work is read not merely for pleasure but for instruction. The first volume of his *Decline and Fall of the Roman Empire* appeared in 1776, the last in 1788. It was challenged at the time and has always aroused opposition in some quarters; but no criticism has ever been able to sink it. Its intellectual content remains valid today, and any discussion of the course and causes of the decline of Rome is still dominated by it. Of no other historian writing before 1830 can this be said. Both as a historical scholar in his mastery and judgment and use of the evidence, and as a historical interpreter in his examination of causes and effects, Gibbon is unique in his time.

Of course there are still earlier historians whom we still read and enjoy — Froissart, Commines, Clarendon, St. Simon. But these were chroniclers of their own time, and their value lies largely in the fact that they were contemporary with the events they chronicled. They were irreplaceable eye- or ear-witnesses. But Gibbon did not write contemporary history. The durability of his work owes nothing to the easy advantage, or accident, of direct observation. In looking back on the Roman Empire he enjoyed no technical or adventitious advantage over us. Indeed, we may say, he enjoyed less than we do, for the intervening two centuries have vastly increased the evidence for such study. Nevertheless, this increase of evidence has not driven Gibbon, as it has driven every other eighteenth-century historian, out of the field. He remains modern, surprisingly modern. Later commentators may supplement or modify the detail of his work, but they very seldom detect an error. They cannot improve on the style, and they generally endorse the judgment.

Gibbon's whole life was, effectively, devoted to this great work, and this work supplies the unity of his life. His first and last ambition, as he himself tells us, was to be an historian. His early writings, in themselves unimportant, interest us solely as evidence of the formation of his historical philosophy. When he had chosen the subject of his life's work, he set out consciously to solve the greatest historical problem of his time. Having solved it, he never contemplated another major work. His memoirs, left unfinished at his death, are closely related to his great work. They are a strictly intellectual autobiography: the biography not, except incidentally, of Edward Gibbon, but of the author of *The Decline and Fall of the Roman Empire*. Since he saw his own previous life as a preparation for this task, we must begin with a brief summary of his early years.

Edward Gibbon was born in Putney near London in 1737. His father was a country gentleman of independent though somewhat straitened means, "warm and social" temper, and Tory politics. He had a family estate in Hampshire and represented his neighbors in Parliament. Gibbon was the only surviving child and grew up in solitude. "A puny child, neglected by my mother, starved by my nurse, and of whose being very little care or expectation was entertained," he was brought up by a devoted aunt, to whom he would afterward pay a moving tribute. His mother died when he was ten years old, and although his father remarried (and Gibbon became very attached to his stepmother), this did not occur till Gibbon was already grown up. Of formal education, owing to his constant illness, he had very little, and that little was broken by continual change. Finally, out of "perplexity rather than prudence," his father, "without preparation or delay, carried me to Oxford, and I was matriculated in the university, as a gentleman commoner of Magdalen college, before I had accomplished the fifteenth year of my age."

Gibbon's career at Oxford was disastrous. He has himself given a brilliant, and famous, account of it in his memoirs. Oxford university was not, at that time, distinguished for teaching or learning, and Gibbon, feeling neither encouragement nor discipline, sought to find his own way through "the dangerous mazes" of religious controversy. The result was that "at the age of sixteen, I bewildered myself in the errors of the Church of Rome." This, of course, in 1753, was a fate worse than death. If he should persevere in such a course, Gibbon would be socially ostracized and excluded from the parliamentary life in which it was intended that he should succeed. His horrified father quickly removed him from Oxford, carried him abroad, and deposited him with a Protestant tutor in Lausanne. The tutor was M. Pavilliard, a Swiss pastor, whose function was to keep the young Gibbon under firm discipline, to reclaim him for sound religion, and to give him the formal education of a gentleman. Pavilliard did all this; but he also did much more. He introduced Gibbon to the intellectual life of Lausanne. And Lausanne, as it happened, was the center of a recent revolution in historical philosophy.

Long afterward Gibbon looked back to his removal from Oxford and his years at Lausanne as the formative experience of his life. "Whatsoever have been the fruits of my education," he wrote in his memoirs, "they must be ascribed to the fortunate banishment which placed me in Lausanne . . . If my childish revolt against the religion of my country had not stripped me in time of my academic gown, the five important years, so liberally improved in the studies and conversation of Lausanne, would have been steeped in port and prejudice among the monks of Oxford. Had the fatigue of idleness compelled me to read, the path of learning would not have been enlightened by a ray of philosophic knowledge. I should have grown to manhood ignorant of the life and language of Europe, and my knowledge of the world would have been confined to an English cloister." For Gibbon was convinced that, intellectually, he owed nothing to England, or at least to the England of his early years. Intellectually, it was Lausanne, not England, that had formed him. "Such as I am, in genius or learning or manners, I owe my creation to Lausanne: it was in that school that the statue was found in the block of marble." Without the experience of Lausanne there would have been no *Decline and Fall of the Roman Empire.*

Why was Lausanne so important in the 1750s, and so particularly important to an Englishman? To answer this question we must look at the study of history before Gibbon, both in England and in Europe: to its stagnation in England and to its renaissance in Europe.

Since the Renaissance, European writers had sought to discover general causes in history to replace the theological determinism of the Middle Ages, and the theologians had invariably resisted these attempts. The pioneers were the great Florentines, Machiavelli and Guicciardini, in the early sixteenth century. Machiavelli, in particular, had assumed that there were secular causes in history which, if understood aright, could be seized, controlled, and made to work for a particular political purpose: they could even triumph over the accidents of "fortune" and restore a state and society which had been corrupted or defeated. This presupposed that the citizens of such a society (or, if the corruption had gone too far, a Prince) should possess *virtù,* or public spirit combined with a resolute determination to apply the new science according to its own rules, or "reason of state." It followed that the function of the historian was to discover these rules and define this reason of state.

After the Reformation, both Catholics and Protestants condemned Machiavelli, and the old theological determinism was restored to authority, reinforced, on the Catholic side, by an insistence on continuous Church history and, on the Protestant side, by belief in Providence and millenarian speculations. A few bold spirits challenged this renewed orthodoxy, particularly at the beginning of the seventeenth century. Such were Jacques-Auguste de Thou, the French historian of sixteenth-century Europe, and Paolo Sarpi, known in England as Fra Paolo or Father Paul, the Venetian historian of the Council of Trent. Both de Thou and Sarpi were Catholics, but both were condemned by the Catholic Church. In England, the same secular attitude was shown by the Elizabethan historian William Camden, who enjoyed a European reputation and founded a chair of "civil history" — i.e., secular history, detached from theological interpretation—at Oxford. However, this critical spirit was soon quenched; Camden's chair at Oxford quickly became a sinecure; and "providential history" was strengthened by the struggle of the Thirty Years War, as it had previously been by the Wars of Religion after the Reformation. In France, in the later seventeenth century, Bishop Bossuet would write a "universal history" on a theological base, and in England the most popular historians, from Sir Walter Raleigh to Bishop Burnet, based their historical interpretation on Providence. This interpretation lasted well into the eighteenth century.

Unable to challenge the theological interpretation at its base, the "civil historians," from the beginning, adopted the device of distinguishing between "first" and "second causes." They allowed that the Providence of God was the first and main cause of historical events; but they argued that, in order to achieve its ends, Divine Providence allowed the operation of "second" or "secondary" causes which were purely secular and could properly be studied and judged by unaided human reason. The clergy did not like this distinction, which they regarded as a mere face-saving device by "infidels" and skeptics. They particularly disliked it when it was applied to the history of the Christian Church: a history which was regarded as the direct expression of divine purpose, and beyond the reach of secular explanation. They therefore eyed it vigilantly, ready to pounce on the first sign of open heresy.

The secular explanation of history being unpopular in the seventeenth century, conventional historians took refuge in the accumulation of indisputable, and therefore ideologically safe, facts. This was a great century of erudition: the erudition of individual scholars, who published massive compilations of documents, inscriptions, and other evidence, and the erudition of organized societies, like the Benedictines of the Abbey of St. Germain des Prés in Paris (the Maurists) and the Jesuit society of Bollandists in Flanders. This scholarly accumulation was not necessarily disinterested. Often it was intended to supply ammunition for ideological controversy. However, in the end, its effect was different. Repelled by the sheer mass of often irreconcilable evidence, and wearied by the continuous controversy, scholars were driven back into skepticism. They concluded that historical truth was unattainable and a consistent interpretation therefore impossible. This doctrine was made fashionable by the *émigré* French Huguenot Pierre Bayle, whose *Dictionnaire Historique et critique,* published in 1695–97, is a vast miscellany of "disorderly erudition" (as Gibbon called it), undirected by any positive philosophy. It was known as "Pyrrhonism," from Pyrrho of Elis, the founder of the skeptical school of Greek philosophers.

For the greater part of the eighteenth century, while "Providential" history remained orthodox, Pyrrhonism was the reigning historical philosophy among the intellectuals of Europe. Voltaire ended by accepting it—at least when he could not use history as propaganda. In *Pyrrhonisme de l'histoire* and other works, he argued that nothing was certain and that the only safe guide in history was *le bon sens. Le bon sens,* for instance, proved that ritual prostitution could never have occurred (similarly in the sixteenth century, *le bon sens* had proved, to Bodin, the reality of witchcraft). In England the essence of Pyrrhonism was stated by Dr. Johnson. In 1751, in an article in *The Rambler,* he dwelt on the ease of the historian's task who had "no other labour than to arrange and display the material already put into his hands." It never occurred to him that intellectual power was required to interpret such material. The only question which he asked was why, even in so unexacting a profession, so few have excelled, and, in particular, why there had been no great English historians; for it was, as Gibbon would write, an "old reproach that no British altars had been raised to the Muse of History," and David Hume, a few years later, would describe Camden as the last great English historian. Johnson's answer was that the English neglected the study of history because so effortless a task was beneath them: and he too had to look back to the reign of Elizabeth before he could find a reputable English historian. There he found Richard Knolles, whose *History of the Turks,* he said, was unread only because the subject was so dull. Twenty-four years later, at the Club in London, Johnson would hold forth on the same subject. "We must consider," he said, "how very little history there is; I mean real authentic history. That certain kings reigned, and certain battles were fought, we can depend upon as true; but all the colouring, all the philosophy of history is conjecture." On this occasion Boswell maliciously notes that Gibbon was present but remained silent. Later, in the *Decline and Fall,* Gibbon would take his revenge. Quoting Johnson's praise of Knolles, Gibbon would comment drily that a modern reader of history looked not for "1400 folio pages of speeches and battles" but "some tincture of criticism and philosophy."

Johnson's England was the England in which Gibbon was brought up until his removal from Oxford. It was an England of peculiar intellectual sterility. The greatest of English scholars, Richard Bentley, had died in 1742, the great antiquary Bishop Gibson in 1748. After them a "frivolous and superficial age" of scholarship was dominated by two clergymen: the swashbuckling bully William Warburton and his toady Richard Hurd. Gibbon, as he tells us, from his early youth, *knew* that he "aspired to the character of a historian," but in England he had no models, no preceptors. He read, but in that era of fashionable Pyrrhonism, his reading was "vague and multifarious." He devoured "crude lumps" of history "like so many novels." Before he was sixteen he "had exhausted all that could be learned in English of the Arabs and the Persians, the Tartars and the Turks." At Oxford he wished, but was not allowed, to learn Arabic. Then, on his fall from grace, he carried this "indigested chaos" of historical matter to Lausanne and there discovered, what he had hitherto lacked, an articulating cord.

For while England had been "an intellectual backwater," historical studies on the Continent had undergone a revolution. The revolution had begun in Naples, and its most important product (since Vico remained virtually unnoticed till the nineteenth century) was Pietro Giannone, a lawyer, whose *Civil History of Naples* had been published in 1723. Giannone's work had shown how the power of the Church, having been rooted and institutionalized in the medieval Kingdom of Naples, had become a constant social force, determining the later political history of the Kingdom. The work caused an immediate sensation. While it pleased the lay rulers who were seeking to break the stranglehold of the Church, it enraged the Catholic hierarchy. In the end, the hierarchy proved more powerful. Excommunicated, driven from city to city, Giannone finally took refuge in Calvinist Geneva, where he planned to publish, in Lausanne, a new and more devastating work. His ally was a Calvinist pastor, Jacob Vernet. Giannone did not succeed in his object. Lured into Savoyard territory, he was kidnapped by agents of the Duke of Savoy, who sought to please the Pope by this *coup de main*. He spent the rest of his life in a Savoyard prison; he was forced to recant his heresy; and his unpublished works were suppressed.

In the following generation, Giannone's ideas were adopted and extended by an even more important writer, the President de Montesquieu. Montesquieu was a philosopher of history who explicitly rejected the Pyrrhonism of Bayle and, like Giannone, looked for a social explanation of historical change. About 1730 he wrote in his notebook that he would like to write a "civil history of France" comparable with Giannone's *Civil History of Naples*. He never did this, but he made an intensive study of the civil history of mankind. He distilled his observations, in somewhat miscellaneous aphoristic form, into his greatest work, *de l'Esprit des Lois*, which he published in Geneva in 1748. He too used the services of Giannone's friend, Jacob Vernet, and he too found his work condemned by the Catholic Church.

Montesquieu's *de l'Esprit des Lois* is the beginning of modern sociology. It revolutionized historical study by giving a new "social" dimension to the secular historical philosophy of Machiavelli. Thereby, it ended the defeatist Pyrrhonism of the previous half-century and invited scholars to look for historical explanation not merely in political decisions or ideological slogans but in the complex of forces which together could be described as the "spirit of the laws": that is, the structure and organization of society which conditioned both decisions and events. Men, Montesquieu wrote, are governed not merely by political power nor, *a fortiori*, by divine providence but "by many things: climate, customs, manners; from all which is derived a general spirit"; and his great work was a congeries of general and particular illustrations of this spirit and its differing manifestations.

The effect of Montesquieu's work was immediate and profound. One of those who felt it was Voltaire, who was at this time working on a "universal history" designed to rescue that subject from the theological interpretation of Bossuet and, at the same time, to make it palatable to the taste of his mistress, Madame du Châtelet. Voltaire's work was his *Essai sur les Moeurs*, which he revised to incorporate some of Montesquieu's ideas, and which he published at Geneva in 1756. At this time Voltaire was living in Switzerland, first in Geneva, then in Lausanne. Voltaire too made use of the services of Jacob Vernet.

Thus Geneva and Lausanne, the French cities on Lac Leman, were, in these years, the very center of the new historical revolution, and Calvinist pastors like Vernet were active agents of the scholars and philosophers who resorted thither to publish their books without interference from French or Italian censors. Little did Edward Gibbon senior realize how much he was doing for his erring son when he carried him off from Oxford and deposited him with a Calvinist pastor in Lausanne. There, better than anywhere else in Europe, the young Gibbon could discover a philosophy to organize his vast, undigested historical reading. Gibbon himself soon discovered it. It was in Lausanne that he read Giannone's *Civil History of Naples*, which he would afterward single out as one of the distant tributaries of his own work. It was there that he visited Voltaire, "the most extraordinary man of the age," and attended the private theatre in which Voltaire himself acted in his own plays and declaimed his own poems. But above all it was there that he found "delight in the frequent perusal of Montesquieu, whose energy of style and boldness of hypothesis were powerful to awaken and stimulate the genius of the age."

At the close of his five-year period in Lausanne, Gibbon began his first book. It was a short book, written while he was still, as he admitted, completely under the influence of Montesquieu. Originally, he had designed it as an offering to Suzanne Curchod, to whom he had been engaged in Geneva, but his father obliged him to break off the engagement, and the essay was not published until 1761. By this time he had been in England for three years and had recently been called up for service in the Hampshire militia. He now dedicated it to his father, who had urged him to publish it in the hope that it would recommend the writer for a career in politics. It was written in French and entitled *Essai sur l'Étude de la Littérature*.

Gibbon's juvenile *Essai* is of interest to us solely because it is by him and is the first expression of his historical philosophy. Condensed and aphoristic ("alas" he afterward exclaimed, "how fatal has been the imitation of Montesquieu!"), it is ostensibly a protest against the decline of classical studies into decorative triviality and pedantry, and the consequent contempt in which they had fallen among the fashionable "modern" philosophers in France. As a devotee of ancient literature, Gibbon wished to restore classical studies to the respect which they had enjoyed in the sixteenth century, when the great scholars had sought not merely to conjure with the ancient texts but to understand the whole society which they reflected. Throughout his essay, Gibbon expressed his veneration for the old standards of scholarship and demanded respect for all facts, however small: for who knows? "a Montesquieu, from the meanest of them, will deduce consequences undreamed by ordinary men."

However, while refusing to despise facts, like the French *avant-garde* writers, Gibbon insists that they must be controlled by "philosophy"; and he then expresses his own philosophy of history. He rejects the "useful but also dangerous Pyrrhonism of our age." He sees "philosophy" as a means of understanding and so perhaps controlling the apparently arbitrary course of history. "History, to a philosopher, is what gambling was to the Marquis de Dangeau: he saw a system, relations, consequences, where others saw only the caprice of fortune." Gibbon's ideal of a philosophic historian is Tacitus; for only Tacitus, he says, shows the close connection between institutions and events, between the laws and the destiny of the Roman Republic. This is the connection which has now been philosophically illustrated by Montesquieu. "In the hands of a Montesquieu, the theory of general causes would be a philosophic history of mankind. He would make us see those general causes regulating the rise and fall of empires; assuming successively the guise of fortune, prudence, courage, weakness; acting without the assistance of particular causes, and sometimes even triumphing over them."

"The rise and fall of empires . . ." Already we are moving toward the great work. Or are we? We cannot be certain that this was yet in Gibbon's mind. What we can say is that it had been in Montesquieu's mind, for he had himself written on that subject. In 1734, fourteen years before *de l'Esprit des Lois,* he had published a book of *Considerations on the Romans, their Greatness and Decline.* Indeed, we can go further: we can say that this problem—the problem of the decline of Rome—was on the mind of all the historians of the eighteenth century, and that it was because they were all haunted by it that Montesquieu had himself devised the science which, ultimately, not he but Gibbon would apply to its solution.

Why were the men of the eighteenth century so exercised by the decline of the Roman Empire? Their interest arose naturally out of the new, optimistic philosophy of the Enlightenment and, in particular, its doctrine of progress. Hitherto men had seen history as a record of decline: decline from primitive innocency, said the theologians; decline from the unforgettable age of the apostles, said the Church historians; decline from the political and literary greatness of classical Antiquity, said the humanists. Ambitious men might hope to recover the innocence of man, or the apostolic purity of the Church, or the science and arts of Antiquity, but no more. However, in the later seventeenth century, this conviction of the superiority of the Ancients had been challenged. The "Moderns" had by then gained confidence in themselves: they believed that they had not only caught up with the "Ancients" but had surpassed them. By the eighteenth century, past history wore a new look. After the fall of the Roman Empire there had indeed been a Dark Age of gothic barbarism and superstition. But with "the Revival of Letters" Europe had recovered its vitality, and since then there had been a general "Progress." Thanks to this progress, it was now possible to look critically upon the past—even upon Classical Antiquity and the Early Church—and hopefully to the future. Progress, once secured, was irreversible.

So at least said the ideologues and idealists of the Enlightenment. And yet, it could be asked, was it so certain? Might not a philosopher in imperial Rome have said the same? But he would have been wrong. Who could then have foreseen that the civilization of Antiquity would disappear, destroyed by despised barbarians? Who could then have imagined a Dark Age of a thousand years? And if that could happen once, who could guarantee that it would not happen again? The civilization of the moderns might seem both solid and brilliant; it might be self-confident. But was it proof against the secret disease which had somehow undermined the equally solid, brilliant and self-confident civilization of Antiquity? Might it all happen again?

This was the problem that haunted the more thoughtful philosophers of the Enlightenment. It was a problem which only historians could answer, and they could answer it only by analyzing the causes of the decline of Rome. All of them, to a greater or lesser extent, addressed themselves to the problem; if we think of it as Gibbon's subject, that is only because he eclipsed his predecessors. Giannone in particular had been exercised by it. His study of Roman law, he wrote, had inspired him to consider the great problem of the "origin and changes of the Roman Empire, and how, from its ruins, there arose so many new rulers, laws, customs, kingdoms and republics in Europe." Montesquieu himself wrote on it—but Montesquieu was not an historian and his work, though rich in ideas, lacks historical substance. All the disciples of Montesquieu, even though they did not write formally on the subject, had it on their minds. As one of them wrote, "it was indeed a subject worthy of their genius; for in the whole history of human affairs, no spectacle occurs so wonderful in itself, or so momentous in its effects, as the growth of that system which took its rise from the conquests of the barbarians"; for those conquests, though they spread over the Western world "a thick night of superstition and ignorance which lasted nearly a thousand years," in the end laid the foundation of a state of society uniquely favorable "to the general and permanent happiness of the human race."

The disciples of Montesquieu were to be found, above all, in Scotland. Englishmen—unless, like Gibbon, they went to Switzerland—were too complacent to heed his lessons: their history remained either Pyrrhonist or providential. But in Scotland, a poor and backward country now eager for "improvement," these lessons on the social machinery of progress were eagerly followed. Montesquieu's *de l'Esprit des Lois* was bought, immediately after its publication, by David Hume, then on a diplomatic mission to Turin. Hume brought it back to Scotland, where it was quickly and often reprinted, in both French and English. Hume's friend, William Robertson, became a disciple; and the ideas of Montesquieu yielded their first historical fruit in Hume's *History of England* (1754–62), and in Robertson's *History of Scotland* (1759) and *History of Charles V* (1769), whose first chapter, or rather book, is a long essay on the changes in European society from the Roman Empire to the Renaissance.

When he returned to England from Lausanne, full of the ideas of Montesquieu, Gibbon read the works of both Hume and Robertson and was enchanted by them. "The perfect composition, the nervous language, the

well-turned periods of Dr. Robertson," he wrote, "inflamed me to the ambitious hope that I might one day tread in his footsteps; the calm philosophy,
the careless inimitable beauties of his friend and rival, often forced me to
close the volume with a mixed sensation of delight and despair." Gibbon's
veneration for Hume and Robertson never wavered, and he was always
closer, intellectually, to the *literati* of Scotland, fellow disciples of Montesquieu, than to the literary establishment of London, dominated by Dr.
Johnson and that egregious pair—the poor man's Johnson and Boswell—
Warburton and Hurd.

Having stated his philosophy in his *Essai,* Gibbon now looked around for
an historical subject. A committed classical scholar, deeply in love with
Latin, and then Greek, literature, he continued to study the ancient world,
but, like Hume and Robertson, he at first thought of writing on modern
history. Various modern subjects occurred to him—the history of Sir Walter Raleigh, the French invasion of Italy, Medicean Florence, the history of
the liberty of the Swiss—but none had been seriously taken up when the
end of the war with France, and the disbandment of the militia, enabled
him to exact from his father the fulfillment of an old promise and make—as
every English gentleman of means and culture must make—a Grand Tour
to Italy. He left England, on a boat crowded with English aristocrats panting
for foreign travel, in January 1763.

Gibbon's Grand Tour lasted two and one-half years. It fell into three
stages. First he spent over three months in Paris. His *Essai* had been well
received in France, and he had introductions to the salons and met the
philosophers and men of letters of the time. He also visited the "Benedictine
workshop" of the Maurist abbey of St. Germain des Prés, for whose learned
industry he always expressed admiration. From Paris he moved on to
Switzerland. As he afterward put it, "between the expensive style of Paris
and of Italy, it was prudent to interpose some months of tranquil simplicity."
So he returned to Lausanne. There his old tutor, M. Pavilliard, greeted him
warmly but, having moved to a smaller house, could not give him lodgings.
This was convenient, as he remembered Mme Pavilliard's "uncleanly avarice." Instead Gibbon stayed for a whole year in a country chateau whose
impoverished owner had turned it into a fashionable boarding house for
English visitors. There he made two friends of his own age who were to be
important in his life. One was a regular officer, Captain John Baker Holroyd, afterward first earl of Sheffield, who was to become Gibbon's lifelong
and most intimate friend. The other was William Guise, whom he would
choose to be his companion on the third stage of his tour: the journey to
Rome.

Gibbon kept a diary of his Grand Tour which is full and informative for
the whole period until his arrival in Rome. He and Guise were carried over
the Alps to Turin and then took the route through Milan, Pavia, Genoa,
Parma, Modena, Bologna, Florence. Everywhere they were received by the
great, visited the antiquities, the picture-galleries, the theatres; and always

Gibbon was reading and writing. For his own contribution to historical writing, he was still thinking of the liberty of the Swiss, but his present reading was largely about Italy and the Roman Empire. He carried with him, for relaxation, the Latin poets and, for systematic study, the works of the Roman topographers and the great Renaissance and modern compilers and commentators: Bergier's monumental work on Roman roads, D'Anville's modern geography of the Roman empire, Ezekiel Spanheim's collection of Roman coins and medals. He also wrote several technical essays to clear his own mind: essays on Roman weights and measures, Roman coinage, Roman population, the route taken by Hannibal over the Alps, etc., etc. Clearly the liberty of the Swiss was not in the forefront of his mind at this time. Italy was now competing with Switzerland. As he wrote to his stepmother from Florence, "I have never lost sight of the undertaking I laid the foundations of at Lausanne, and I do not despair of being able one day to produce something by way of a description of ancient Italy which may be of some use to the public and of some credit to myself."

The climax of the tour was of course the visit to Rome, which Gibbon and Guise reached on October 6, 1764. In his *Memoirs,* long afterward, Gibbon recalled the excitement of his arrival there:

> my temper is not very susceptible of enthusiasm, and the enthusiam
> which I do not feel I have ever scorned to affect. But at the distance of
> time I can neither forget nor express the strong emotions which
> agitated my mind as I first approached and entered the *eternal city.*
> After a sleepless night, I trod, with lofty step, the ruins of the Forum;
> each memorable spot where Romulus stood, or Tully spoke, or Caesar
> fell, was at once present to my eye; and several days of intoxication
> were lost or enjoyed before I could descend to a cool and minute
> investigation . . .

Then, nine days after the first arrival, came the moment which is recorded in one of the most famous passages of the *Memoirs:*

> it was at Rome, on the 15th of October 1764, as I sat musing amidst
> the ruins of the Capitol, while the barefooted friars were singing
> vespers in the Temple of Jupiter, that the idea of writing the decline
> and fall of the city first started to my mind.

Recently, doubt has been cast on the reality of Gibbon's revelation in the Capitol. His own diary, to which he explicitly refers for confirmation, is not available for the period after his arrival in Rome, and the brief entries in the diary of his companion Guise, though they mention visits to the Capitol on six of the eight days between October 6 and 13, state only, on the fifteenth, that it "being wet weather this morning," they visited an English painter. However, Gibbon was a veracious and accurate writer, and if he cited a diary, the diary presumably existed even if it has since been lost. He may of course have misread the date—or Guise may have confused dates (diaries are not always immediately written). In any case, Guise only states that the morning was wet, whereas Gibbon clearly states that the visit to the Capitol was at "vespers," in "the gloom of the evening." There is therefore no evidence incompatible with Gibbon's statement, which is entitled to belief. In any case, Gibbon's "enthusiasm" at the first sight of the monuments of ancient Rome is amply borne out by the letters which he wrote to his father three days after arrival. "If it was difficult before to give you or Mrs. Gibbon any account of what I saw, it is impossible here. . . . I am really almost in a dream. Whatever ideas books may have given us of the greatness of that people, their accounts of the most flourishing state of Rome fall infinitely short of the picture of its ruins. I am convinced that there never, never existed such a nation, and I hope for the happiness of mankind that there never will again."

Gibbon's original idea, inspired by the ruins of ancient Roman grandeur, was to write a history of the decline and fall of the city: its gradual destruction or deformation by time, the barbarians and the Christians, from the days of the pagan empire to the sixteenth and seventeenth centuries. This was a subject to which his close study of Roman topographers during his journey had prepared him. It was a subject which he would ultimately treat in the last chapter of the *Decline and Fall*. But at present it was only an idea—and one idea among many which competed for his interest. He may have suspended, but he had not yet given up, the idea of Medicean Florence or the liberty of the Swiss.

Meanwhile, he and Guise pursued their journey to Naples and then returned to Rome. On arrival in Rome he was disagreeably surprised. His banker there showed him a letter from his father suddenly stopping all credit, and he was obliged to cut short his travels. Humiliated by this affront, he began the return journey with Guise, via Venice and Lyon. At Lyon he received a peremptory letter requiring his return for a meeting of the Hampshire militia. Leaving Guise in Lyon, he returned alone to England.

Thus on his return to England in 1765 Gibbon had not yet decided to write the *Decline and Fall of the Roman Empire*. So vast a program could hardly be envisaged on the basis of his present studies, wide though they were. So far, he had acquired a philosophy of interpretation, and a solid understanding of the Roman world, and he had taken particular soundings at various positions in a vast general reading. What he owed to his Italian journey was the addition of a new idea—but an idea of great potential growth: for although at present limited, it could ultimately expand and absorb all the varied interests with which, at present, it competed.

The process of absorption took three years. Gibbon's favored project, in the years immediately after his return, was still the *History of the Liberty of the Swiss*. In this project he was encouraged by his Swiss friend Georges Deyverdun, who was prepared to collaborate by translating the German documents; for Gibbon was not prepared to learn the "barbarous dialect" of German Switzerland. Deyverdun, whose friendship dated from Gibbon's first stay in Lausanne, had now come to England in search of employment, and 1767 he and Gibbon collaborated in publishing a literary review, *Mémoires Littéraires de la Grande Bretagne*. The review ran for two years and contained notices of new books: one of them being the *Essay on the History of Civil Society* by Adam Ferguson, one of the Scottish disciples of Montesquieu. The language of the review, though published in London, was French. Meanwhile, Gibbon wrote, also in French, the first section of his book on the liberty of the Swiss and submitted it, by the hands of Deyverdun, to the judge whom he most admired, David Hume. Hume wrote an appreciative judgment of it but urged Gibbon to write not in French but in English. French, he admitted, was the universal language of the polite world, but would its supremacy last? Hume had himself recently been employed in negotiating the treaty of Paris, which ended the Seven Years' War and incorporated Canada in the British Empire, and he foresaw the ultimate prevalence of the English language. "Our solid and increasing establishments in America," he wrote, "promise a superior stability and endurance to the English language." It is curious to think that, but for this intervention by Hume, Gibbon might have written the *Decline and Fall* in French and thus deprived English literature of a great monument.

For in spite of Hume's approbation, Gibbon did not persevere with the liberty of the Swiss. Other critics were less flattering, and in 1768 he decided to abandon that subject for good and return to classical themes. In 1770, following Hume's advice, he used English, not French, for a new work. This was an attack on the absurd pretensions of the now aged dictator of scholarship, Warburton. In the same year, the death of Gibbon's father made him financially independent. He gradually got rid of the family estate in Hampshire and in 1773 established himself at 7 Bentinck Street in London. There he began to work on the subject which had now replaced the *Liberty of the Swiss* and all other modern topics. He had settled at last for the decline and fall, not now of the city, but of the whole empire of Rome. With this subject he would not only introduce to England the new constructive historical method suggested by Montesquieu. He would also seek to answer the great historical question which haunted the "enlightened" philosophers of the eighteenth century: why did the civilization of Antiquity fail? and, could it all happen again?

II. The Decline and Fall *(1) The Western Empire*

The first volume of the *History of the Decline and Fall of the Roman Empire* was published on February 16, 1776. The publishers were Strahan and Cadell, Gibbon's previous publisher having declined the book. At first Strahan agreed to print 750 copies; then he retreated to 500. But when he saw the finished text, he was so impressed by it that he doubled that figure. Even so, he soon found that he had underestimated the success of the book. It sold, he afterward reported, like a threepenny pamphlet on current affairs. The entire edition had gone in a fortnight, and a second edition of 1500 copies was immediately printed. This too was sold out by the end of the year. Early next year a third edition of 1000 copies was published. Meanwhile a pirated edition had been printed in Dublin.

The instant success of the book surprised and delighted Gibbon, who heard, at first, nothing but praise of it. The praise was the more enthusiastic because no one had expected so remarkable a work. Gibbon himself was by this time well known in London, in literature, politics, and society. He had social tastes. He was a member of fashionable clubs. He was also a member of "the Club," the famous literary society, founded by Sir Joshua Reynolds, dominated by Johnson, and immortalized by Boswell. And he was a member, though a silent member, of Parliament, sitting, since 1774, as member for Liskeard in Cornwall, a "nomination borough" controlled by his cousin, Edward Eliot of Port Eliot. His friends knew that he had been working on a Roman history; but the brilliance of the book, when published, took them all by surprise. "Lo, there is just appeared a truly classic work," Horace Walpole wrote to a friend, adding, of Gibbon, that he "is a member of Parliament and called a whimsical because he votes variously, as his opinion leads him. I know him a little, never suspected the extent of his talents: he is perfectly modest." Lord Camden, the great Lord Chief Justice, wrote to Garrick "in a transport" about the book: "such depth—such perspicuity—such language, force, variety and what not!" The immediate reviews were also uniformly favorable, and the world of fashion was united in its admiration with the world of literature and politics.

More important to Gibbon was the approbation of the world of scholarship. He was delighted by letters from the Scottish *literati* who alone, perhaps, being themselves disciples of Montesquieu, could measure his purpose and achievement. Hume and Robertson—the Tacitus and the Livy of Scotland, as Gibbon called them—both wrote glowing letters. So did Adam Ferguson. To Ferguson, Gibbon wrote back that "your approbation and that of your literary friends in Edinburgh" had given him the greatest pleasure, for "I have always looked up with the most sincere respect towards the northern part of our island, whither taste and philosophy seem to have retired from the smoke and hurry of this immense capital." Of Hume's letter—one of the last letters that Hume wrote—Gibbon would afterwards remark that it "overpaid the labour of ten years."

In this letter to Gibbon, Hume contrasted the brillance of his work with the general sterility of English intellectual life in the middle eighteenth century. "You may smile at this sentiment," he wrote, "but as it seems to me that your countrymen, for almost a whole generation, have given themselves up to barbarous and absurd faction"—he was referring to the internecine politics of the Whig oligarchy—"I no longer expected any valuable production to come from them," he added. But with his praise, he

mingled a note of foreboding. "When I first heard of your undertaking
. . . I own I was a little curious to know how you would extricate yourself
from your last two chapters. I think you have observed a very prudent
temperament; but it was impossible to treat the subject so as not to give
grounds of suspicion against you, and you may expect that a clamour will
arise." Hume's foreboding was perfectly correct. Gibbon's last two chapters
were the famous fifteenth and sixteenth chapters of his work, on the rise
and establishment of Christianity in the Roman Empire during the period
covered by the first volume, from Trajan to Constantine; and they did
indeed cause a dreadful clamor.

From the preceding account, it will be apparent what Gibbon's attitude
to ecclesiastical history must be. He was a "philosophical historian," a "civil
historian," in the semi-heretical tradition which went back through Montesquieu and Giannone to Machiavelli. He himself, in a footnote, would afterward explicitly state his intellectual pedigree: "Guicciardini and Machiavelli," he wrote, "with their worthy successors Fra Paolo and Davila, were justly
esteemed the first historians of modern languages till, in the present age,
Scotland arose to dispute the prize with Italy herself." Neither those Italian
nor these Scottish historians had regarded religious truth as a determining
force in history. The Italians had seen religion as an engine of state; the
Scots, following Montesquieu, had seen it as a social force, the "spirit" of a
particular form of society. In consequence of these views, some of these
historians (or at least those who lived in Catholic societies) had been regarded, and even condemned, as heretical. However, this was not by their wish.
None of them had sought to pick a quarrel or challenge the established
Church: rather, they had conformed with it and hoped to preserve its good
will by distinguishing, in history, between "first" and "second" causes. Of
course, if they wrote explicitly on the relations of Church and State, they
exposed themselves to trouble, especially in strongly Catholic countries.
This had been experienced, even in the eighteenth century, by Giannone
in Italy. But so long as they avoided such a frontal attack, they could hope
to escape unscathed, at least in Protestant countries. However, even there,
caution was needed. The clergy, by now, might no longer be able to perse-
cute, but they could make life uncomfortable.

All this was well known to Hume and his Scottish friends, who had had
some trouble with the bigots of the Scottish church. Consequently they had
trodden very warily. Hume's own skill had been remarkable and had produced remarkable results. Though his *History of England* had been savagely
attacked by political partisans, it was positively commended by the archbish-
ops of Canterbury and Dublin, who relished his support for the established
Church more than they disliked his "infidelity." Robertson even contrived
to combine "philosophical" views, and an expressed admiration for Voltaire, with the position of a Presbyterian minister and Moderator of the
Church of Scotland. He could perform this elegant balancing act because
he steered clear of ecclesiastical history. His historical philosophy was clear

—John Wesley bitterly attacked him for saying nothing of the Providence of God as the true motor of history—but it was implicit, not stated. Gibbon's intellectual position was precisely the same as that of Hume and Robertson, but he was more vulnerable because, like Giannone, he had chosen a far more sensitive topic. The "philosophical historian" of the later Roman Empire could not, like the historian of England or Charles V, evade the issue of the rise of Christianity. It was central to his subject. It had to be faced, and faced frontally.

Gibbon trod at first delicately into this heavily mined area. Although his own skepticism could not be concealed, he was careful never to express any dissent from the opinions of the established Church. Indeed, in an early footnote, he emphasized that the philosophers of Antiquity, Socrates, Epicurus, Cicero, and Plutarch, "had always inculcated decent reverence for the religion of their own country, and of mankind"—and clearly he intended to identify himself with them. Similarly, in all matters of theological interpretation, he avoided any personal commitment: "the duty of an historian," he wrote, when he approached the vexed question of the early Christian miracles, "does not call upon him to interpose his private judgment in this nice and important controversy"; and he would gravely reproach Conyers Middleton, whose famous *Free Enquiry* of 1749 had completely destroyed the credibility of those miracles, for his bold criticism which "approaches the precipice of infidelity." And of course, like his seventeenth-century predecessors, he took care to distinguish between "first" and "second" causes.

At the very beginning of the two famous chapters, Gibbon ceremoniously rolled out the conventional formula. By what means, he asked, did the "pure and humble" Christian faith gradually insinuate itself into the minds of men and insinuate itself so successfully that it not only prevailed over contempt and persecution but "finally erected the triumphant banner of the Cross on the ruins of the Capitol?" The obvious answer, he readily admitted, was "that it was owing to the convincing evidence of the doctrine itself, and to the ruling Providence of its great Author." That, of course, was the First Cause. But, he went on, "as truth and reason seldom find so favourable a reception in the world, and as the wisdom of Providence frequently condescends to use the passions of the human heart, and the general circumstances of mankind, as instruments to execute its purpose, we may still be permitted, though with becoming submission, to ask, not indeed what were the first, but what were the secondary causes of the rapid growth of the Christian Church." With these careful phrases he supposed that he had disarmed the critics. "I had flattered myself," he afterward wrote, "that an age of light and liberty would receive without scandal an inquiry into the human causes of the progress and establishment of Christianity."

Thus reassured, Gibbon strode forward into the most controversial era of Church history. With massive scholarship, magnificently organized and brilliantly set out, but also with polished irony and sometimes devastating wit, he traced the transformation of Christianity from a heretical Jewish sect into a Gentile mystery religion with universal claims; its division into opposing sects armed with increasingly fanciful doctrinal slogans; the gradual incorporation into it of extraneous but politically useful doctrines; its reinforcement by miraculous claims and formidable discipline; its novel cult of virginity; the emergence of a distinct class of clergy, "a celebrated order of men which has furnished the most important, though not always the most edifying subjects for modern history"; the growth of monasticism; and the changing policy of the imperial establishment toward this most persistent of the competing new Oriental superstitions. As Gibbon broached topic after topic in this account of a revolutionary ideology on the way to the capture of power, his ceremonious lip-service to the Providence of God became ever more transparent, and his own views emerged with sparkling and, to some, painful clarity.

The first of these two famous chapters ends with a splendid exercise of sustained irony: Gibbon's grave reproach to the "supine inattention of the pagan and philosophic world" which altogether failed to notice the stupendous miracles of the early Church.

> The lame walked, the blind saw, the sick were healed, the dead were raised, demons were expelled, and the laws of Nature were frequently suspended for the benefit of the Church. But the sages of Greece and Rome turned aside from the awful spectacle, and, pursuing the ordinary occupations of life and study, appeared unconscious of any alterations in the moral or physical government of the world. Under the reign of Tiberius, the whole earth, or at least a celebrated province of the Roman empire, was involved in a preternatural darkness of three hours. Even this miraculous event, which ought to have excited the wonder, the curiosity and the devotion of mankind, passed without notice in an age of science and history. It happened during the lifetime of Seneca and the elder Pliny. . . . Each of these philosophers, in a laborious work, has recorded all the great phenomena of Nature, earthquakes, meteors, comets, and eclipses, which his indefatigable curiosity could collect. Both the one and the other have omitted to mention the greatest phenomenon to which the mortal eye has been witness since the creation of the globe. . . .

The second chapter, after an account of the Roman persecution of the Christians, whose self-imposed penances and deliberately courted martyrdoms were described with more psychological acumen than sympathy, ends with "a melancholy truth which obtrudes itself on the reluctant mind," viz.: that

> even admitting, without hesitation or inquiry, all that history has recorded, or devotion has feigned, on the subject of martyrdoms, it

must still be acknowledged that the Christians, in the course of their
intestine dissensions, have inflicted far greater severities on each other
than they had experienced from the zeal of infidels.

To the philosophical world of the eighteenth century, these statements
were unexceptionable, and the style in which they were expressed was
irresistible. But even in the eighteenth century there were readers who
would be—or would pretend to be—outraged by them; and of course they
were even more outraged by the impossibility either of refuting Gibbon's
statements, which were all impeccably documented, or of convicting him of
the unorthodoxy which he was so careful to disown. By the time the eager
readers of the first volume had reached chapter fifteen, their initial harmony had dissolved and the previous chorus of unanimous approval was
disturbed by a swelling murmur of dissent.

Gibbon's letters at the time reveal the gradual change. "I have the satisfaction of telling you," he wrote to his stepmother on March 26, "that my
book has been very well received, by men of letters, men of the world, and
even by fine feathered ladies; in short, by every set of people, except perhaps by the clergy, who seem (I know not why) to show their teeth on the
occasion." Five weeks later he wrote to Deyverdun reporting the success of
the book but adding that there was "another side to the coin";

> would you suppose, my dear Sir, that anyone would have carried
> injustice so far as to attack the purity of my faith? A cry has been
> raised against me by bishops, and by a number of ladies respectable
> both for years and enlightenment. They have presumed to maintain
> that the last two chapters of my so-called history are nothing less than
> a satire against the Christian religion: a satire all the more dangerous
> because it is disguised by a veil of moderation and impartiality; and
> that the emissary of Satan, having long beguiled the reader by a very
> agreeable narrative, insensibly leads his footsteps into an infernal
> snare. You will appreciate, Monsieur, the full horror of all this, and
> you will understand that I shall maintain only a respectful silence in
> the face of my enemies.

The tone of the ensuing debate had been set by "the Great Cham" of
English letters, Dr. Johnson. We have seen that Johnson was wedded to the
old Pyrrhonist view of history. Born in the reign of Queen Anne, his ideas
had been fixed by the middle of the eighteenth century, and he was unwilling to receive or comprehend the new ideas of Montesquieu. He detested
Hume as an infidel, despised Robertson as a Presbyterian, and was prejudiced against both as Scots. Both he and Boswell disliked Gibbon personally.
They could not see what he was seeking to do and could only see his
"infidelity." On March 20, 1776, a month after the publication of Gibbon's
volume, Johnson and Boswell were at Oxford where, as they admitted, their
orthodoxy was always rekindled by the sight of those venerable spires. "We
talked," says Boswell,

of a work much in vogue at that time, written in a very mellifluous
style, but which, under pretext of another subject, contained much
artful infidelity. I said it was not fair to attack us unexpectedly: he
should have warned us of our danger before we entered his garden of
flowery eloquence, by advertising 'spring-guns and man-traps set here'.
The author had been Oxonian, and was remembered there for having
'turned papist'. I observed that as he had changed several times—from
the Church of England to the Church of Rome, from the Church of
Rome to infidelity—I did not despair yet of seeing him a methodist
preacher. *Johnson* (laughing) 'It is said that his range has been more
extensive, and that he has once been Mahometan. However, now that
he has published his infidelity, he will probably persist in it'.

Unwary footsteps insensibly beguiled into an infernal snare . . . a garden
of flowery eloquence secretly filled with spring-guns and man-traps . . . these
were the regular charges made against Gibbon. Soon they would appear in
print. Already, in June, Gibbon reported that the archbishop of Canterbury's chaplain was "sharpening his goose-quill," and in the autumn the
pamphlets started appearing. For some time Gibbon maintained his "re-
spectful silence," but finally, in 1778, he was stung into action by a particularly impertinent attack both on his scholarship and on his honesty. The
author was H. E. Davies, a young man of Balliol College, and he too accused
Gibbon of seducing "those readers who may heedlessly stray in the flowery
paths of his diction without perceiving the poisonous snake that lurks in the
grass."

At this point Gibbon decided to strike back. Suspending work on his
second volume, he wrote his *Vindication of Some Passages in the Fifteenth and
Sixteenth Chapters of the History of the Decline and Fall of the Roman Empire.* It was
directed against all the critics who had so far attacked him and was published in January 1779.

Gibbon's *Vindication* is a devastating work. He wrote it unwillingly: he
resented the interruption to his work which it entailed, and he was conscious that his enemies were not worth his powder and shot. Victory
over such opponents, he said, was humiliation enough. But once he had decided to counterattack, he decided also to annihilate. And he did annihilate. Abandoning, for once, his customary "grave and temperate irony,"
he let himself go, and, as Dean Milman afterward put it, "with a single
discharge from his ponderous artillery of learning and sarcasm, laid
prostrate the whole disorderly squadron." When the smoke had
cleared, he had no wish to commemorate the battle or set up a trophy. He
asked that "as soon as my readers are convinced of my innocence, they
would forget my *Vindication.*" In order to help them to do so, he had caused
it to be printed in octavo, so that it could not be bound up with his *History,*
which was in quarto. In fact, though his adversaries were forgotten, the
battle was not: it had been too spectacular, too decisive. Nor was the *Vindication:* it contained too many magnificent Gibbonian phrases. It has often

been reprinted, though Gibbon's scholarship no longer needs its defense.

In spite of the *Vindication,* attacks on Gibbon continued. No year passed without some book or pamphlet against him, and nearly sixty books and as many articles against him were published in his lifetime. But from now on, he absolutely refused to notice any of them, and all are now forgotten. One of them, however, raised, and finally settled, a controversy which had long been suppressed by the established Churches. This was the controversy over "the Three Heavenly Witnesses" who are cited in the first epistle of St. John (V. 7). This text is important, for it is the only biblical text which can be cited in support (rather indirect support at best) of the doctrine of the Trinity.

The authenticity of this vital verse was first questioned by Erasmus, who observed that it did not occur in any known Greek or early Latin manuscript of the Bible. He therefore dismissed it as a later interpolation and excluded it from his edition of the New Testament. Afterward, however, he yielded to orthodox pressure and restored the verse, not because he was convinced, but "to remove any pretext for calumny." After this victory for orthodoxy, to reject the verse was to incur the charge of unitarianism or worse, and scholars, in general, concealed their doubts or expressed them in learned privacy. Gibbon cast aside such caution. He rejected the verse openly and emphatically as condemned "by the universal silence of the orthodox Fathers, ancient versions and authentic manuscripts." It was, he said, an interpolation, perhaps from a marginal note, of the fifth century, perpetuated in the manuscript tradition. "After the invention of printing, the editors of the Greek Testament yielded to their own prejudices, or those of the times; and the pious fraud, which was embraced with equal zeal at Rome and at Geneva, has been infinitely multiplied in every country and every language of Europe."

Such a statement inevitably roused the orthodox, and George Travis, archdeacon of Chester, devoted a whole book to the defense of the injured verse. His "brutal insolence" was answered, and refuted, in seven devastating letters by the Greek scholar Richard Porson. Gibbon sat quietly in the wings while "the wretched Travis still smarts under the lash of the merciless Porson." After that, the verse never recovered its authority. It was abandoned by Protestants at the beginning of the nineteenth century, and even by Catholics, at the end.

When the dust had settled, Gibbon, in his *Memoirs,* expressed regret for having provoked the battle which he had so easily won. "Had I believed," he wrote, "that the majority of English readers were so fondly attached even to the name and shadow of Christianity; had I foreseen that the pious, the timid and the prudent would feel, or affect to feel, with such exquisite sensibility, I might perhaps have softened the two invidious chapters, which would create many enemies and conciliate few friends." This statement of regret can be believed. It is very likely that Gibbon, with his foreign education, had misjudged the attitude of his countrymen: that living among "philosophers," men of letters, and men of the world, he had not appreciated the bigotry which slumbered beneath the smooth, rational surface of English intellectual life. Hume had been aware of this and had warned Gibbon against it; but it was too late for Gibbon to heed the warning. As he put it, "the shaft was shot, the alarm was sounded, and I could only rejoice that if the voice of our priests was clamorous and bitter, their hands were disarmed from the powers of persecution."

Gibbon also had another reason to regret the controversy. The provocation of the famous fifteenth and sixteenth chapters had not only involved him in a time-consuming controversy: it had also, to a large extent, distorted his achievement. Gibbon was not, after all, simply a skeptical or an anticlerical writer. If he had been, he would have been forgotten long ago. He positively repudiated the historical skepticism of Bayle and, like Hume, he supported (though from outside) the established Church. What he had set out to write was something which far transcended the content of those two chapters. His book was to be both a great work of modern scholarship and a "philosophical" interpretation of the most important turning point in European history. To such an enterprise, an examination of the social and political function of Christianity was essential, and Gibbon was bound to consider it in those terms. He saw it not as true or false, but as the ideology of a new world order. But ideology was not the only force which had to be considered. There was also the objective condition of the society within which it worked, and which it transformed: secular institutions, economic movements, questions of population, defense, culture and the arts.

Gibbon considered all these, systematically, using modern, comparative methods of interpretation. He was particularly interested in laws as the expression of a social system—in Montesquieu's "spirit of the laws"—and made great use of the Theodosian Code, the series of enactments by which the Emperors from Constantine onward had effected the gradual transformation of a pagan into a Christian state. He used the great edition of Jacques Godefroy, a Huguenot scholar of the seventeenth century. Giannone had also used this "stupendous work" as a key to the understanding of social change. "I used it," says Gibbon, "(and much I used it) as a work of history rather than of jurisprudence; but in every light it may be considered as a full and capacious repository of the political state of the empire in the 4th and 5th centuries." Gibbon's study of the Roman economy, population, and defense shows an astonishing mastery of recondite and scattered sources; and his range extended far beyond the political frontiers of the empire. But all this was ignored by his clerical critics. Exasperated by his treatment of Christianity, they swarmed angrily around him, buzzing feebly about minor details. Gibbon no doubt supposed that, in turning aside to swat them, he was disposing of a marginal nuisance and clearing the way for an objective assessment of his work. But if so, he was mistaken. Although he vindicated his scholarship, he never secured recognition of his real achievement. Even his admirers failed to appreciate it. They praised him for his literary style, his narrative power, his psychological penetration, his wit. They failed to see that he had undertaken a radical reinterpretation of the whole process of European history.

One man who did see it was the greatest of Montesquieu's Scottish disciples, Adam Smith. Smith came to London in 1775 to see to the publication of *The Wealth of Nations,* and his close friendship with Gibbon dated from that visit. They went regularly together to Dr. Hunter's anatomy lectures, and Smith was made a member of the Club, probably on Gibbon's proposal. This did not please Johnson, and it positively enraged Boswell, who now worked himself into hysteria at the mere thought of Gibbon and his "infidelity." Indeed Boswell responded to Smith's election by contemplating secession and the formation of a new Club: it was bad enough to have Gibbon, he observed, but "Smith too is now of our Club. It has lost its select merit." Johnson contented himself with saying that Smith was as dull a dog as any he had met, and that his wine bubbled in his mouth. Smith and Gibbon were close friends till Smith's death. Gibbon regularly gave the highest praise to *The Wealth of Nations,* while Smith regarded the *Decline and Fall* as putting Gibbon "at the very head of the whole literary tribe at present existing in Europe." Smith and Gibbon can hardly have influenced each other's work, as they both published in the same year and only met in that year. But they tackled the same general problem from separate positions, one as a historian and the other as a "political economist"; and they both descended, intellectually, from the same progenitor. As another Scottish "political economist," John Millar, later wrote: "the great Montesquieu showed the way: he was the Lord Bacon in this branch of science. Dr. Smith is the Newton."

It will be convenient to discuss Gibbon's "philosophical" interpretation of the decline of Rome later. At present we may complete the discussion of Gibbon's battle with the clergy by asking, what was Gibbon's personal attitude to religion. Was he, as his enemies maintained, an "infidel"?

The answer is that, strictly speaking, he was not. Like so many men of the Enlightenment—like Voltaire and Benjamin Franklin—he was a deist. To the orthodox this hardly constituted a difference. They regarded deism and infidelity as indistinguishable. But the difference was considerable, and the confusion was greatly resented by the deists themselves. Infidelity was atheism, materialism. Deism was belief in a divine force or "deity" whose existence and qualities were demonstrated by the regularity and complexity of Nature, and neither needed nor would accept any support or definition from Revelation. Voltaire waged a long war against the infidels d'Holbach and La Mettrie, and Gibbon deeply resented the charge of infidelity brought against him, and rudely thrust at him, by the unitarian scientist Joseph Priestley. In general, Gibbon did not express his religious beliefs: "on religion she was rational, that is, silent," he reported, after a visit from his devout aunt, "the holy hermit of Northamptonshire." The most that he would say about them, in his *Memoirs,* is that, after his reconversion from

Catholicism, "I suspended my religious inquiries, acquiescing, with implicit belief, in the tenets and mysteries which are adopted by the general consent of Catholics and Protestants." The position thus described is almost identical with that professed by Benjamin Franklin in his autobiography. It amounts to outward conformity with any Christian Church: the envelope for deism.

Gibbon's deism, though never formally expressed, is implicit in many of his observations. Thus, in his early *Essai,* he describes Lucretius, the Roman poet of uncompromising materialism, as having, "in spite of himself, proved the existence of the deity by tracing up the phenomena of Nature to general laws"; in other words, Lucretius's own arguments prove not atheism, as he himself supposed, but deism. In the *Decline and Fall* Gibbon expresses the same general view. "The God of Nature," he writes, "has written his existence on all his works, and his law in the heart of man"; and again, "the unity of God is an idea most congenial to Nature and Reason"; and of Genghis Khan he remarks that "the Catholic inquisitors of Europe, who defended nonsense by cruelty, might have been confounded by the example of a barbarian, who anticipated the lessons of philosophy, and established by his laws a system of pure theism and perfect toleration. His first and only article of faith was the existence of one God, the author of all good, who fills by his presence the heavens and earth, which he has created by his power."

Within this general deism, Gibbon, like all good deists, rejected sectarian differences. As a conformist, he conformed to the established Church, which he anyway preferred, for the same reason as Hume, viz.: that establishment ensured a higher degree of lay control. This made him a Protestant in England. He anyway preferred Protestantism as being, in his time, more rational and more tolerant than established Catholicism. But he recognized that it was not necessarily or always so. Churches, to him, were to be judged exclusively by their social function. If he allowed that Zwingli, Luther, and Calvin were named "with gratitude, as the deliverers of nations," he would also point out that they enforced, as "the absolute and essential terms of salvation," doctrines which had been prepared by the Catholic Schoolmen, "and many a sober Christian would rather admit that a wafer is God than that God is a cruel and capricious tyrant." And he admitted that "the Catholic superstition, which is always the enemy of reason, is often the parent of the arts."

It was partly on these grounds—his insistence on conformity and tolerance—that Gibbon so disliked his fellow-deist Voltaire. Recalling his early visits at Lausanne, he refers to Voltaire "whom I then rated above his real magnitude." Gibbon had since become disillusioned with Voltaire, partly because of Voltaire's Pyrrhonist philosophy of history, partly because of his superficial scholarship, and his disrespect for erudition, but largely because of his intolerance. He noticed that Voltaire always, regardless of the issue, took the side of the anti-Christians; that he needlessly "insulted the religion of nations"; and that he subordinated his scholarly judgment to his anti-

Christian prejudices. The footnotes to the *Decline and Fall* frequently cite Voltaire and almost always to expose his lack either of scholarship or of objectivity. They point to his "generous" bestowal of the Canary Islands on the Roman Empire; his "excessive" and "ridiculous" partisanship for the Muslims whenever they are opposed to the Christians; and his insistence that the Nestorian inscription in China, which Gibbon rightly declared genuine, was "a Jesuit fraud." On one occasion Gibbon exploded that in some matters "Voltaire was a bigot, an intolerant bigot."

The subtlety, and the tolerance, of Gibbon's religious views were not appreciated by the enraged clergymen who assailed the first volume of the *Decline and Fall;* but after dispatching them with his *Vindication,* Gibbon could afford to ignore them and resume his work. There were other interruptions—an extended visit to Paris, constant attendance in Parliament, political office as Lord Commissioner of Trade, the composition of a memorandum in French to justify the government's foreign policy—but Gibbon did not lose much by these digressions. He worked steadily and methodically. He always rose early and wrote only in the morning. Social and parliamentary distractions positively stimulated him: "I never found my mind more vigorous, nor my composition more happy, than in the winter hurry of society and parliament." By 1780 he had completed two more volumes, and they were published in 1781, followed, a few months later, by a fourth edition of volume I. As frontispiece, they carried an engraving of a portrait of Gibbon painted by his fellow member of the Club, Sir Joshua Reynolds.

With the completion of his third volume Gibbon had now fulfilled his original plan. He had carried the history of the Roman Empire from its greatest extent, in the time of Trajan, to its dissolution in the West in A.D. 476. In the course of those three volumes, he had described, in a narrative of masterly power and lucidity, the whole political history of the Empire— the foundering of the Principate in the disasters of the third century, the incursions of the Goths and later barbarians, the emergence of a military despotism, the establishment of a new devolved empire by Diocletian, the civil wars in which that new system almost foundered, its restoration by the victory of Constantine, Constantine's foundation of Constantinople as the new capital in the east, his patronage of Christianity, the invasions of the barbarians and the revived Persian monarchy, the attempted pagan restoration under Julian, the renewed civil wars and usurpations of the fourth century, the new dynasty of Theodosius the Great, the establishment of Christianity as the only religion of state, the new assaults of the barbarians, and the final abolition of the hopelessly shrunken and enfeebled imperial power. But he had not confined himself to political history, or even to the history of "Rome." He had studied the changing institutions of government, the structure of society, the currents of thought. He had traced the religious changes not merely on the level of doctrine but in their legal and social aspects, seeing the Christianization of the empire not as the victory of an idea but as a profound revolution in society, transforming (and weakening) the very basis of the empire: a change which could not be separated from the parallel bureaucratization of that empire and the weakening of its defenses. He had observed the alterations in Roman culture under the impact of events; and he had studied the origins, the social organization and the character of the various groups of barbarians to whom the Empire had at last succumbed. Finally, in an epilogue entitled "General Observations on the Fall of the Roman Empire in the West," he had given his answer to the two general questions which haunted the men of the Enlightenment: why had that great reversal of civilization happened? and, could such a thing happen again?

To this last question Gibbon gave a cheerful answer. But as this answer depends on his total philosophy, we shall postpone consideration of the process by which he reached it. It is enough, here, to quote its "pleasing conclusion," so acceptable to the hopes, so comforting to the doubts, of the eighteenth century, that a second decline and fall need no longer be apprehended, "that every age of the world has increased and still increases the real wealth, the happiness, the knowledge, and perhaps the virtue, of the human race."

III. The Decline and Fall (2) *The Byzantine Empire*

With the conclusion of his third volume Gibbon could say that he had fulfilled his "first engagement with the public." The work that he had designed was finished, and the "General Observations" were its epilogue, its summing-up. Many reasons now tempted him to rest on the fame which he had already acquired and indulge his private tastes. He had a modest private fortune; but he needed an additional income if he were to live in London maintaining his house in Bentinck Street, his coach and servants. He enjoyed society and had, as he wrote, an "invincible love of reading, which I would not exchange for the treasures of India." This being so, his natural inclination was to stay in politics. He enjoyed parliamentary life, and his unexacting political office as a "Lord of Trade" provided him with the necessary income while leaving him leisure for society and study. At first, he yielded to this temptation. For a whole year after the publication of his third volume, he ceased writing and read, for pleasure, the Greek classics. However, as he put it, "in the luxury of freedom I began to wish for the daily task, the active pursuit, which gave a value to every book, and an object to every inquiry." So, at the end of this delicious year with Homer, Herodotus, Thucydides, and Aristophanes, the tragedians and the philosophers, he resolved to resume his work. In the preface to the fifth edition of his first volume, he announced his decision. This meant, in effect, moving forward from Roman to Byzantine history.

In his last volume Gibbon had left himself this option. At the end of his narrative, he had not taken a formal farewell of his readers. Instead, he had remarked that though the Roman Empire was now extinct, "the history of the Greek emperors may still afford a long series of instructive lessons and interesting revolutions." So he now undertook to set out those lessons, to describe those revolutions: to narrate the whole history of the Byzantine Empire from the fifth century, when it was left as the sole inheritor of Roman tradition, to the fall of Constantinople to the Turks in 1453. The preface in which he made this announcement was dated March 1, 1782. On the very same day he noted in his commonplace-book that the fourth volume of his *History* had been begun.

Before that volume was completed there had been a revolution in Gibbon's way of life. It was caused by the rapid political changes precipitated in England by the American Revolution. In 1781 Parliament had been dissolved, and at the general election which followed, he was not returned for his cousin's pocket borough of Liskeard. As he himself put it, Mr. Eliot had changed his politics, "and the electors of Liskeard are commonly of the same opinion as Mr. Eliot." Thanks to government support, he obtained another seat; but soon afterward the government of Lord North fell, and the new administration, as a measure of economy, abolished the Board of Trade. Gibbon's office as a "Lord of Trade" was thus automatically extinguished. He remained in Parliament, but without salary or any hope of office under the new administration of Lord Shelburne. However, in February 1783 the Shelburne administration was overthrown on a vote, and Lord North returned to power in a coalition with his former enemy Charles James Fox. This reversal gave Gibbon some hope, but he was disappointed. "My vote was counted in the day of battle," he observes, "but I was overlooked in the division of the spoil." He obtained neither the Commissionership of the Excise nor the Secretaryship to the Embassy in Paris.

Without political office, Gibbon could not afford to live in London in the manner to which he had become accustomed, and he had already decided on the only alternative: he must withdraw himself "into a kind of philosophical exile in Switzerland." Providentially, at this moment, his Swiss friend Deyverdun offered a solution. Deyverdun had inherited a large and elegant house, la Grotte, at Lausanne and needed a tenant to share its expenses. He therefore proposed to divide the house with Gibbon. Gibbon accepted the proposal and, to the dismay of his friends, announced his "irrevocable" decision to emigrate to Lausanne.

Gibbon's friends predicted that he would be miserable in Lausanne. Having enjoyed the best society of London and Paris, how could he be content with life in a provincial city? But Gibbon knew his own mind and "never for one moment" regretted his decision. La Grotte, he discovered, was "a Paradise." Once established there, he lived in great comfort and had no further interest in political office. "I have health, friends, an amusing society, and perfect freedom," he wrote to Lord Sheffield: "a commissioner of the Excise! The idea makes me sick." In 1789, when Deyverdun died, he bought a life interest in La Grotte and became "the free master of one of the most delicious spots on the globe." La Grotte remained his home for the rest of his life.

The migration to Lausanne cost Gibbon a year's interruption of his writing, but once his library had arrived, he resumed work and soon finished volume IV. This volume related the history of the Gothic Kingdom of Italy, and, in the East, the long reign of Justinian, with his empress, the famous ex-courtesan Theodora; the misfortunes of Justinian's successors; and the restoration of the Byzantine state by Heraclius. It ended with the death of Heraclius in A.D. 641.

At this point Gibbon decided to change his plan and his pace. The change was imposed by the vast range and complexity of the events which he had now undertaken to narrate. So far, he had covered five centuries of history in four volumes. During the greater part of these centuries, the Roman world had extended from the borders of Persia to the Atlantic and from the Cheviots, the Rhine, and the Danube to the desert of Africa. This huge area, whether it was governed from Rome, Milan, Trier, Nicomedia, or Byzantium, had remained essentially a unit, and its unity had been supplied by its internal lake, the Mediterranean Sea. The fifth century had seen the disintegration of the Western Empire as the barbarians overran Gaul, Spain, and North Africa, and Britain was abandoned, soon to be invaded by the Anglo-Saxons. A little later, the Goths had set up their kingdom in Italy. But, even now, the idea of unity was not lost; the new rulers of the West acknowledged it in theory and sought to preserve Roman institutions in their barbarian kingdoms; and in the sixth century Justinian attempted to restore its reality. For a time he succeeded. Imperial authority was reestablished and secured by Roman fortresses, in Italy, North Africa, and Spain; Roman law was formulated in the greatest of all its codifications; and although the spoken language of Byzantium was Greek, Latin remained the language of imperial government.

However, although Justinian's laws and buildings endured, his conquests did not. The Western Mediterranean had been regained only to be re-lost, and after the Emperor's death in 565 the Eastern Empire itself was threatened. The Lombards invaded Italy; the Avars poured into the Balkan provinces and, in Gibbon's phrase, "alternately bathed their horses in the Euxine and the Adriatic"; and the Persians returned to the attack in Asia Minor, penetrated to the Bosphorus, and laid siege to the capital. The besiegers were finally driven off by the new emperor Heraclius, but the whole structure of the empire had been shaken by these attacks, and it would never be the same. In retrospect, the age of Justinian appears as the Indian summer of the historic Roman Empire, and modern historians see the reign of Heraclius as the beginning of a new "Byzantine" age.

This great historical revolution was emphasized, and made permanent, by events in the East. It was in the reign of Heraclius that Mohammed created a new power in Arabia and that the immediate successors of Mohammed began those lightning conquests which would totally change the age-old political balance of Rome and Persia. Within a few years, Muslim armies destroyed altogether the Persian Empire, severed Syria, Palestine, Egypt, and the Maghreb from Christendom, and left Western Europe to evolve a new "feudal" organization under its barbarian kings. From now on both Rome and Byzantium changed their character. Rome became the spiritual capital of the Western barbarians, Byzantium the last outpost of Greek Christian civilization in the face of successive invaders from North and East.

Having reached this great turning point and observed the vast new panorama before him, Gibbon conceived and announced a new plan. With Byzantine civilization after Heraclius he had little sympathy and would, he said, "have abandoned without regret the Greek slaves and their servile historians." But he reflected "that the fate of the Byzantine monarchy is *passively* connected with the most splendid and important revolutions which have changed the state of the world." He therefore decided, while preserving Byzantine history as the central thread of his work, to examine the history of the various barbarian kingdoms which rose on the ruins of Rome and ultimately built up the modern civilization of Europe; for it is "in their origin and conquests, in their religion and government, that we must explore the causes and effects of the decline and fall of the Eastern Empire." In other words, whereas, in his previous volumes, Gibbon had analyzed the causes of the decline of the Roman Empire, he now shifted his interest, or at least his sympathy, and set out to discover the causes of the rise of modern Europe. Rome and Byzantium, the twin capitals of ancient culture, would still provide his work with its unity; but his enquiring spirit would reach out to embrace the successive barbarians—pagan, Muslim, or Christian—who had threatened or conquered them, and to explain the springs of their dynamism, the "spirit" of their laws. So, while giving a continuous narrative of Byzantine history, he would introduce, in turn, the Franks, the Arabs, the Bulgarians, the Hungarians, the Russians, the Normans, the Latin crusaders, the Mongols, the Seljuk, and then the Ottoman Turks. The final capture of Byzantium would lead to "the restoration of learning in the Western world," and so Gibbon would "return from the captivity of the new to the ruins of ancient Rome; and the venerable name, the interesting theme, will shed a ray of glory on the conclusion of my labours."

It was an ambitious plan and demanded a vast range of knowledge. It also required a quickening of pace. Gibbon's first four volumes had covered five centuries; now eight centuries had to be compressed into the two volumes which were all that he allowed himself for the completion of his work. Nevertheless, that work was punctually completed, according to plan. Never did Gibbon show the sheer power of his mind better than in this extraordinary feat of organization, compression, narrative, and analysis. The sources were now less accessible, more widely scattered; the path, often, less trodden. Whereas the Roman Empire in the West had attracted learned scholars in Europe, the history of the East and of the barbarians was often undocumented, and Gibbon had to rely on arcane and imperfect sources, and on his own judgment. Fortunately, that judgment was seldom at fault. In medieval history, since the archives were as yet hardly opened, it was inevitable that he would make errors; but his errors of fact are still remarkably few, his critical spirit was never dulled, and his narrative is still wonderfully readable. Some of the most brilliant passages of his *History* are in these last two volumes: his account of Mohammed and the rise of Islam; his description of the degradation of the Papacy in the ninth century; his narrative of the Crusades; his excursions into the history of the Mongols and the Turks; his marvelous final chapters on the siege and capture of Constantinople and the history of medieval Rome.

Throughout this history of the Dark and Middle Ages, Gibbon continued the same method which he had used in his first volumes: that is, the method inspired by Montesquieu. Just as he had formerly used the Theodosian Code not as a mere compilation of laws but as a means of understanding the social structure of the Constantinian empire, and thus appreciating the social revolution caused by the adoption of Christianity, so he now used the Code and the Pandects of Justinian, and the Basilics of the "Macedonian" emperors, as means of understanding sixth- and tenth-century Byzantium. He deduced the character of the Visigothic and Lombard societies from their laws, wrote to England to secure the *Institutes* of the Tartar conqueror Timur, or Tamerlane, and plunged into the thicket of the *jus publicum* of feudal Europe. So also, in studying the barbarian societies, he constantly asked the questions which a modern social historian would ask: questions of diet, economy, family structure.

Perhaps the most striking example of this is Gibbon's examination of the structure and motivation of the nomadic society of the steppes: the Huns in the fifth century and the Tartars or Mongols in the thirteenth century. Here he drew on a wide variety of sources—Greek and Roman writers from Herodotus onward, medieval travelers like the Franciscan friars who visited the courts of the great Mongol Khans, the writings of the Jesuits in Peking, and the French translations of Manchu and Chinese documents available in his time. These works he read critically, looking for evidence not merely of political events but of social causation, and he often (as he once wrote in another context) "deduced my own consequences, beyond the holy circle of the author." The result is an extraordinarily modern interpretation. Indeed, the greatest modern authority on the Mongols begins an essay on the social history of Mongol Nomadism with a detailed examination of Gibbon's enquiry into the subject, explaining that "Gibbon is worth quoting at this length because he sets out so many of the facts, and raises so many of the questions, that must still be considered by the social historian who deals with such a people as the Mongols."[1]

---

[1] Owen Lattimore, "The Social History of Mongol Nomadism," in *Historians of China and Japan*, ed. W. G. Beasley and E. G. Pulleyblank (Oxford: Oxford University Press, 1961), pp. 328–31.

Gibbon's treatment of Eastern history is indeed one of the most interesting aspects of his work. We know from his *Memoirs* that he had always been interested in it: that as a boy he had read all that he could find of the Oriental peoples, and that at Oxford he had tried to learn Arabic. Dr. Johnson's *boutade* that he had once been a Mohammedan is no doubt a recollection of that fact. He was also a friend of the greatest of English orientalists, Sir William Jones, who was a fellow member of the Club and a declared disciple of Montesquieu. Gibbon showed both his knowledge and his sure judgment in Oriental history when he insisted, against the prevailing view of the French *philosophes,* that the Nestorian inscription of Si-ngan Fu, or Sian, was genuine, and he was well aware of the interrelation of Eastern and Western history. As a modern Chinese historian has written, "From the Pisgah-height of his universal historical learning, Gibbon could clearly see how the East and West affect each other, and co-relate in a causal nexus events apparently unrelated."[2]

This being so, Gibbon was particularly interested in the most dramatic and important collision of East and West before the final conquest of Constantinople; the Crusades. This was a topic which exercised all the "philosophic historians" of the Enlightenment. In general, these writers had reacted against their theologically minded predecessors, who had seen the Crusades as wars for the true faith, by declaring them to be wild enterprises, the expression of fanaticism, barbarism, and delusion; but they also saw them as economically progressive in one sense, since they enriched the Italian cities by the commerce of the East. This view had been expressed summarily by Voltaire and Robertson, and, more recently, by Adam Smith, who saw "the most destructive frenzy that ever befell the European nations" as "a source of opulence" to the Italian republics.

Gibbon did not agree. To him the Crusades were almost entirely harmful. Even when seen from a parochial Western viewpoint, they "checked rather than forwarded the maturity of Europe." The lives and labors which were buried in the East could have been "more profitably employed in the improvement of their native country"; industry, thus created, "would have overflowed in navigation and trade; and the Latins would have been enriched and enlightened by a friendly correspondence with the climates of the East."

Only in one accidental respect did Gibbon see the Crusades as beneficial "not so much in producing a benefit as in removing an evil": they undermined the "Gothic edifice" of feudalism. The strong language that Gibbon uses shows how much he detested the "oppressive system of feudalism," which was supported by "the arts of the clergy and swords of the barons," while "the larger portion of the inhabitants of Europe was chained to the

---

[2] C. S. Ch'ien, "China in the English Literature of the 18th century," in *Historians of China and Japan,* p. 316.

soil, without freedom, or property or knowledge." He allowed that the authority of the clergy operated "as a salutary antidote: they prevented the total extinction of letters, mitigated the fierceness of the times, sheltered the poor and the defenceless, and preserved or revived the peace and order of civil society." But to the feudal lords he would allow no value whatever. Their "iron weight" oppressed the people and crushed "every hope of industry and improvement." However, he argued, the Crusades, if they achieved nothing else, at least weakened the power of this "martial aristocracy":

> The estates of the barons were dissipated, and their race was often
> extinguished, in these costly and perilous expeditions. Their poverty
> extorted from their pride those charters of freedom which unlocked
> the fetters of the slave, secured the farm of the peasant and the shop
> of the artificer, and gradually restored a substance and a soul to the
> most numerous and useful part of the community. The conflagration
> which destroyed the tall and barren trees of the forest gave air and
> scope to the vegetation of the smaller and nutritive plants of the soil.

Gibbon's chapters on the Crusades express a deeply felt hatred of foreign conquest and of social immobility. It was "contrary to nature and reason," he wrote, "for any power to dominate distant societies against their will"; mercantile progress was to be obtained not by the forcible seizure of monopolies but by "the overflowing" of industrial wealth in navigation and trade; and it is in a tone almost of satisfaction that he records the ultimate failure of that whole imperialist adventure: after two centuries of heroism and barbarity, the Muslims recovered control of Syria and Palestine and "a mournful and solitary silence prevailed along the coast which had so long resounded with the World's Debate."

The Crusades may have been an imperialist or a commercial adventure, but they could not have been launched without the force of religious fanaticism. Throughout his work, Gibbon never spares religious fanaticism. His enemies, of course, attacked him for his irreligion and accused him of consistent hostility to Christianity. But this is unfair. The passage which I have just quoted shows that Gibbon recognized that the medieval Church performed a positive social function; and whenever he could detect that function, he would praise the institution.

Many instances of this could be given. Gibbon's criterion is always social or humanitarian or intellectual: it is never doctrinal. Thus, when the Church champions the poor, defends human dignity, encourages learning, dispenses charity, or opposes cruelty (e.g., in protesting against gladiatorial contests), Gibbon always supports it. When it persecutes heretics or unbelievers, or stifles free thought, or inspires fanaticism, or divides society, he castigates it. Where it preaches nonsense, he is ironical. Where it is lukewarm, rational, or worldly, he is indulgent to it. It is sometimes said that the hero of Gibbon's work is Julian the Apostate. This is not true. Gibbon disliked Julian for seeking to stamp out Christianity by force and exulting in the destruction of its writings, whereas, as he remarks, "it is unworthy of a philosopher to wish that any opinions and arguments the most repugnant to his own should be concealed from the knowledge of mankind." To Julian, Gibbon perhaps preferred that agreeable Christian cleric Synesius, the fifth-century bishop of Ptolemais, who accepted his bishopric on the clear understanding that "he loved profane studies and profane sports; he was incapable of supporting a life of celibacy; he disbelieved the resurrection; and he refused to preach *fables* to the people, unless he might be permitted to *philosophise* at home."

For, in general and essentially, Gibbon is critical of theocratic power, which is never so damaging as when it is exercised by convinced and single-minded priests. He refers to "the austere and dangerous virtues" of the greatest of medieval popes; and after a splendid account of the vices of the less austere popes of the ninth century, culminating in John XII, whose "rapes of virgins and widows had deterred the female pilgrims from visiting the tomb of St. Peter lest, in the devout act, they should be violated by his successor," he adds the general comment that "to a philosophic eye, the vices of the clergy are far less dangerous than their virtues." "Fanatics who torment themselves," he says, when describing the self-imposed penances of St. Simeon Stylites, cannot be presumed "susceptible of any lively affection for the rest of mankind. A cruel, unfeeling temper has distinguished the monks of every age and country"; and it was the "merciless zeal" of the monastic orders which, in the Middle Ages, "strenuously administered" the Roman Inquisition.

In his last chapter, Gibbon summarizes the story of his whole work as "the triumph of barbarism and religion." Overtly, the barbarians of the West destroyed Rome, and the barbarians of the East, a thousand years later, destroyed Byzantium. But in fact, Gibbon insists, in each case, the fatal blows did not come from without. "If all the barbarian conquerors had been annihilated in the same hour," he writes, when dealing with fourth-century Rome, "their total destruction would not have restored the Empire of the West"; and he would have said as much of medieval Byzantium. Both Roman and Byzantine civilization, he believed, had perished inwardly before they were overpowered by their external enemies. Even the cities themselves were destroyed from within. It was not the barbarians who had reduced Rome to ruins. When they captured the city, they had neither the time, nor the strength, nor the will to destroy its monuments. "Their moments were indeed precious. The Goths evacuated Rome on the sixth, the Vandals on the fifteenth day ... Their hasty assault would have made a slight impression on the solid piles of Antiquity ... From these innocent barbarians the reproach may be transferred to the Catholics of Rome"—to *"those* barbarians who alone had time and inclination to execute such laborious destruction." The final destruction was by the upstart popes of the Renaissance: it was they who, to build their new palaces, used the Colosseum as their quarry and enabled Gibbon to muse on the long decline of the city and in "the ruins of the Capitol."

"The triumph of barbarism and religion" . . . This indeed was Gibbon's considered judgment. "I believed, and I still believe," he would write in his memoirs, "that the propagation of the Gospel and the triumph of the Church, are inseparably connected with the decline of the Roman monarchy." How they were connected becomes clear in the course of the great work, as we shall shortly see. Meanwhile, we may return to the external history of that work, which Gibbon completed in Lausanne in the summer of 1787. He had worked regularly, day after day, for three years, quickening his pace at the end by overtime in the evenings. His description of its completion is famous, but the temptation to quote it is irresistible:

> I have presumed to mark the moment of conception: I shall now commemorate the hour of my final deliverance. It was on the day, or rather night, of the 27th of June, 1787, between the hours of eleven and twelve, that I wrote the last lines of the last page, in a summer-house in my garden. After laying down my pen, I took several turns in a *berceau,* or covered walk of acacias, which commands a prospect of the country, the lake, and the mountains. The air was temperate, the sky was serene, the silver orb of the moon was reflected from the waters, and all nature was silent. I will not dissemble the first emotions of joy on recovery of my freedom, and, perhaps, the establishment of my fame. But my pride was soon humbled, and a sober melancholy was spread over my mind, by the idea that I had taken an everlasting leave of an old and agreeable companion, and that whatsoever might be the future date of my *History,* the life of the historian must be short and precarious.

Having completed his work, Gibbon took it to England to be printed. He spent the autumn with Lord Sheffield at his country house, Sheffield Place in Sussex, polishing it for the press. It was published in three volumes, on May 8, 1788, Gibbon's 51st birthday, and the publisher celebrated the occasion by a dinner at which a commendatory ode was read by the poet William Hayley.

Gibbon's fame was by now well-established. The clergy continued their attacks, and indeed extended them: for they now found a new front against which to direct them. This was what even Gibbon's defender, Richard Porson, described as his "rage for indecency": an indecency which Gibbon generally relegated to the footnotes and protected by "the obscurity of a learned language." The most famous of such notes concerned the striptease act of the Empress Theodora in her unreformed days as a prostitute on the stage. Gibbon leaves the quotation in the original Greek of the Byzantine historian Procopius. The clergy were perhaps particularly irritated by his comment, "I have heard that a learned prelate, now deceased, was fond of quoting this passage in conversation." The prelate is said to have been Warburton. The bishop of Norwich was so shocked that he went carefully through the whole of Gibbon's work extracting such passages, in order to hold them up to execration; but he was forestalled by *The Gentleman's Magazine* which published such a list, without comment, and was duly reproached by a correspondent for printing "filthy extracts from a silly book."

Gibbon, as usual, ignored all attacks, and steadfastly resisted all attempts to tempt or bully him into controversy. He returned to Lausanne, where he enjoyed his celebrity and was accepted, according to Maria Holroyd, Lord Sheffield's daughter, who visited him there with her parents, as "King of the place." There he toyed with various literary projects. The most ambitious was a scheme to publish a collection of the English medieval chronicles, which were to be edited by the Scottish antiquary John Pinkerton, with prefaces by Gibbon. The most valuable was his *Memoirs* which he had nearly completed when an event occurred which called him back, for a second visit, to England.

The event was the sudden death of Lady Sheffield in 1793. In order to be with Lord Sheffield at this time, Gibbon hurried across France, between the opposing armies of the French Revolution and the European coalition against it, and spent the summer of 1793 at Sheffield Place. He then visited friends and moved to London during the winter. There he was taken ill and died after two operations on January 16, 1794. His proposed edition of the English chronicles, of which he had just written the prospectus, died with him—though it was resumed, on a larger scale, in the Roll Series in the next century. Lord Sheffield, as his executor, caused his body to be buried in his own family mausoleum in the parish church of Fletching, next to Sheffield Place, and himself edited and published his *Memoirs* and other miscellaneous writings. Gibbon's manuscripts remained in the hands of Lord Sheffield's descendants until 1896, when, on the death of the last Lord Sheffield, they were bought by Lord Rosebery and by him presented to the British Museum.

IV. The philosophy of The Decline and Fall

A great work of "philosophic history" does not set out its philosophy in crude schematic form. A historical work which is written within a doctrinal orthodoxy may do so: history is then determined and corrected by the ideology which it is written to illustrate and support. But a historical philosophy which is genuinely empirical must be seen to emerge from the historical facts, and its emergence must be gradual. What then, we ask, is the philosophy which ultimately emerges from the *Decline and Fall,* and why did Gibbon deduce from it that his own civilization was in no danger of another Dark Age?

An important point is made early in the first book. There, after describing the organization of the Roman Empire at its zenith, in the "age of the Antonines"—or rather, in the whole period extending from A.D. 98 to 180—Gibbon states that "if a man were called to fix the period in the history of the world during which the condition of the human race was most happy and prosperous, he would, without hesitation, name that which elapsed from the death of Domitian to the accession of Commodus." But Gibbon does not, it should be noticed, necessarily endorse this view, which had been expressed by earlier writers—e.g., by Francis Bacon in the *Advancement of Learning*—and which he represents as a truism of the time. Indeed, from the beginning, his praise of the Antonine age is qualified: for he sees, even in that age, in the very structure of the imperial system, the seeds of its decay. For the centralized Roman empire, by its very definition, excluded a certain vitalizing principle necessary to the health of society. That principle was public spirit, what Machiavelli had called *virtù*.

"That public virtue," writes Gibbon, "which among the ancients was denominated patriotism, is derived from a strong sense of our own interest in the preservation and prosperity of the free government of which we are members. Such a sentiment, which had rendered the legions of the Republic almost invincible, could make but a very feeble impression on the mercenary servants of a despotic prince." This animating principle of "public virtue," expressed in active participation in public life, is to Gibbon the great contribution of classical Antiquity, and its extinction, in imperial times, its transfer (as Machiavelli would say) to the "barbarian" successor-states in Western Europe, is a major theme in his work. "In the last moments of her decay," he writes later, "Constantinople was doubtless more opulent and populous than Athens at her most flourishing era" when a far lesser wealth was divided among far fewer citizens. But each Athenian citizen was a freeman who dared to assert the liberty of his thoughts, words, and actions—whose person and property were guarded by equal law; and who exercised his independent vote in the government of the Republic. Against this, "the subjects of the Byzantine empire, who dishonour the names both of Greeks and Romans, present a dead uniformity of abject vices which are neither softened by the weakness of humanity nor animated by the vigour of memorable crimes." It was on this account that Gibbon quickened his pace when dealing with Byzantine history. In Byzantium he could find no evidence of public virtue, or even of Machiavelli's *virtù*, and so he transferred his interest to the barbarians who had in their societies those seeds of growth.

How is this virtue born, how nourished, how stifled and killed? Essentially, it depends upon the discovery, cultivation, and systematic teaching of the natural dignity and equal rights of man. But as man is conditioned by his environment, and the "spirit" of his institutions, there is always a danger that such ideas, which are not native everywhere, and are often inconvenient to rulers, will be suppressed and extinguished by orthodoxy and interested power. For even if power is exercised by liberal rulers, there is always the danger of illiberal successors. A Marcus Aurelius may be followed by a Commodus. For this reason, Gibbon, though he may praise the virtuous emperors, cannot praise the system; and he adds that, under the "Antonine" emperors, excellent rulers though they were, the inherent vices of the system were positively aggravated by "two peculiar circumstances" which exposed the subjects of the Roman empire to a condition "more completely wretched than the victims of tyranny in any other age or country." These two circumstances were the memory of past freedom and the universality of imperial power. "The division of Europe into a number of independent states . . . is productive of the most beneficial consequences to the liberty of mankind." The heretic, the nonconformist, could always find a base, and so ideas and experiments unpopular to present power could not be completely stifled. But the monopoly of the Roman emperors was absolute. They ruled effectively over the entire civilized world. "Wherever you are," said Cicero to the exiled Marcellus, "remember that you are equally within the power of the conqueror."

Virtue therefore depends for assured survival, not only on a continuing tradition of freedom, but also on a plural society, on the division of power between separate authorities. Ideally, it requires independent, competing states, preferably with different political systems; independent authorities within particular states; economic and intellectual competition. In the Roman empire these conditions did not obtain. There the emperor exercised a complete monopoly of power, and this monopoly, by stifling freedom, inevitably stifled all forms of progress. At one moment, Gibbon tells us, in the decline of the Western Empire, the emperor Honorius sought to devolve power in Gaul to provincial assemblies. "If such an institution, which gave the people an interest in their own government, had been universally established by Trajan or the Antonines, the seeds of public wisdom and virtue might have been cherished and propagated in the empire of Rome," which "under the mild and generous influence of liberty" . . . might then "have remained invincible and immortal." But the Antonines had granted no such devolution of powers, and now it was too late. The over-centralization of the Empire had already stifled the spirit of freedom which alone could have revived it, and "the stupendous fabric yielded to the pressure of its own weight."

To Gibbon, virtue, thus defined, is not, as to the Stoics, merely a private possession, enabling a man to bear with equanimity all the blows of fortune. It is essentially an active principle. It depends on freedom, demands freedom, and creates freedom. It expresses itself in public life. It also, since it nourishes science, forwards material progress. Conversely, monopoly of any kind is its enemy: monopoly of power, monopoly of wealth, monopoly of knowledge or of alleged access to truth. The centralized power of the imperial bureaucracy was one such impediment to virtue: by its mere structure "the empire of the Caesars undoubtedly checked the activity and progress of the human mind." The vast hereditary estates of the Roman landlords were another. So was the immobility of labor—the hereditary obligation of the Roman middle class as much as the hereditary serfdom of the early medieval peasant. Gibbon hated all forms of immobilization: mortmain of land, thesaurization of wealth, tied labor. So he would rejoice when the Crusades incidentally broke up baronial wealth and power and would record without pain the sacrilegious dispersal of clerical wealth, "most wickedly converted to the service of mankind." An amusing instance of this strong conviction occurred in his own life. His friend Lord Sheffield suggested that Gibbon should bequeath his library to him, so that it could be preserved as *Bibliotheca Gibboniana* at Sheffield Place. Gibbon refused. "I am a friend to the circulation of property of every kind," he wrote, and as he had built up his library for his own use out of the relics of others, so he wished his own to be broken up and to serve scholars in the same way.

Public spirit, public service—this, to Gibbon, was the human motive force of progress; and it was nourished, in his view, by the kind of society which, in turn, it created and preserved: a plural, mobile society. It had created the city-states of Greece, the republic of Rome; and from those city-states and that Republic—not from the Roman Empire—the ideas had been born which were the intellectual means of its preservation. The centralization, the immobility, the monopoly of the Roman Empire had gradually destroyed that pluralism, stifled those ideas, and so progress had been retarded, public virtue had declined, and in the end an inert, top-heavy political structure had fallen to external blows which a healthier organism could have survived.

Fortunately, modern Europe was not comparable with the Roman Empire. It could indeed be seen as a single cultural unit—all the Western countries had reached "almost the same level of politeness and cultivation"—but, thanks to its national divisions, it was internally not a single monarchy: it was a "great republic" in which healthy competition would lead to continuous improvement; for no barbarians, except a few Calmucks and Uzbeks, were now left to threaten it, and scientific discovery, once made, could not be reversed. So, for the future, Gibbon could only see a prospect of continuing progress. A second decline and fall was not in sight.

It is within this general context that Gibbon's attitude to Christianity and the Church must be seen. Gibbon was not interested in religious doctrine, though he amused himself with its speculative refinements. He had his own belief—deism—and regarded all metaphysical ideas as a waste of time. But religion and Churches, he would admit, are a social and psychological necessity, and the particular forms which they take are important, for they can influence the progress or decline of civilization. Therefore the historical question he asked was, did the ideas of Christianity and the organization of the Church, as adapted to the Roman Empire, generate or stifle public spirit, freedom, and a plural society?

His answer was that they stifled it. If Christianity had first been established in independent city-states like those of Greece, perhaps it would have assumed a different and more useful form—as it eventually did in the communes of Italy and, more successfully, in the Protestant cities of Switzerland. But the very fact of its establishment by imperial power, as an ideological support to that power, made it subservient to a centralized, monopolist system whose organization and absolutism, in its own formative period, it imitated and sustained.

Of course there were exceptions. Occasionally, the organized Church of Rome would find itself the champion of freedom, and its clergy would show, or elicit, signal examples of public spirit. Thus Gibbon would pay a notable tribute to Pope Gregory the Great, whose antique Roman patriotism recreated the virtue of ancient Rome and gave to his city, deserted by its distant Byzantine overlords, a new lease of life. "Like Thebes or Babylon or Carthage," he writes, "the name of Rome might have been erased from the earth, if the city had not been animated by a vital principle, which again restored her to honour and dominion"; and later he praises the popes of the eighth century, thanks to whom he can say that, although the temporal power of the popes "is now confirmed by the reverence of a thousand years," "their noblest title is the free choice of a people whom they had redeemed from slavery." However, in general, Gibbon believed that the Church was opposed to progress. By its very structure—by its adaptation to the centralized, hierarchical system of the Constantinian Empire—it undermined the social basis of public virtue.

In particular, as a cause and symptom of corruption, Gibbon singled out monasticism. Some of his most brilliant chapters, and his most sustained irony, are reserved for the spread of this Egyptian plague, as he called it, over the Roman empire: for "the swarms of monks who arose from the Nile" and "overspread and darkened the face of the Christian world." Monasticism, he wrote roundly, had, in a later age, "counterbalanced all the temporal advantages of Christianity." For monasticism, he believed, was parasitic not only on society but also on the Church, whose "temporal advantages"—i.e., whose constructive social function—he would admit. It withdrew the resources of society, both human and economic, from that free and useful circulation on which progress depended. It condemned men to idleness, immobilized wealth, kept land in mortmain. And it positively undermined the very idea of civic virtue.

Of course there were exceptions here too. Gibbon would always allow the exceptions: he would never forget the learned monks of St. Germain des

Prés. But in general he was always a Protestant in respect of monasticism, from the time when, in Switzerland, he had seen the newly rebuilt abbey of Einsiedeln flaunting its rococo splendor "in the poorest corner of Europe" and described it in his diary as "le comble de la superstition, le chef d'oeuvre de la politiqui ecclesiastique et la honte de l'humanité." Another Swiss abbey, which he had also visited, elicted from him a more summary exposition of his general philosophy. "Within the walls of Vindonissa," he wrote in a footnote to *The Decline and Fall,* "the castle of Hapsburg, the abbey of Königsfeld, and the town of Bruck have successively arisen. The philosophic traveller may compare the monuments of Roman conquest, of feudal or Austrian tyranny, of monkish superstition, and of industrious freedom. If he be truly a philospher, he will applaud the merit and happiness of his own time!"

If Gibbon deplored the permanent social character of monasticism, he was even more opposed to the morality which it preached in its first centuries. For that morality was a complete denial of "public" virtue. Instead of active participation, the early Church preached, and the early monks practiced, positive withdrawal from public life. Such withdrawal was not then justified by any alternative activity, for the monks were not learned, they did not teach, they fulfilled no social function, they founded no industry, they tilled no land, they cleared no waste. Their retreat from activity was absolute, and to Gibbon it was contemptible and disgusting: a degradation of the human spirit, a denial of social duty, a refusal to face the challenge of the time. Nowhere is Gibbon's irony more withering than in his thirty-seventh chapter on the "origin, progress, and effects of the monastic life" which prepares the reader for the final collapse of the Western Empire.

In particular, he pours his scorn on the "Anchorites," those "unhappy exiles from social life," "the monastic saints who excite only the contempt and pity of a philospher," not only by their credulity, their superstition, their "horrid and disgusting" aspect and absurd penances, but because they preached a doctrine destructive of human dignity and, in its consequences, fatal to the progress of society. At a time when the fate of civilization hung in the balance, the Christian clergy "successfully preached the doctrines of patience and pusillanimity; the active virtues of society were discouraged; and the last remains of the military spirit were buried in the cloister." The successors of the barbarians who destroyed the empire might use even the cloister as a means to preserve, through a dark age, the relics of ancient literature; but the monks of the fourth century had no such redeeming virtue. After his splendid account of St. Simeon Stylites, who spent thirty years reiterating his mechanical devotions on a pillar sixty feet high in the Syrian desert, Gibbon concludes: "if it be possible to measure the interval between the philosophic writings of Cicero and the sacred legend of Theodoret, between the character of Cato and that of Simeon, we may appreciate the memorable revolution which was accomplished in the Roman Empire within a period of five hundred years."

Such is the central philosophy of Gibbon's *Decline and Fall:* the positive philosophy which gives it its coherence and unity. But there is also another underlying belief that sophisticates its presentation: a kind of undertow that pulls in the opposite direction. For if Gibbon is confident that scientific advance is irreversible, and that modern Europe has acquired a political structure favorable to continuous progress, he is always aware that the course of history is not conditioned by science but by men, and that human wisdom, like human "virtue," is often at the mercy of unpredictable events. Theoretically, progress is continuous, but in fact human folly, or crime, can create interruptions, and these interruptions can sometimes be disastrous. After the Mongol devastation of Persia "five centuries have not been enough to repair the ravages of four years"; once "active virtue" is lost in a society, as in Byzantium, it is hard to recover, perhaps impossible without radical social change; and the survival of nations may sometimes depend on the life of one man.

When we look back into history, we recall the great ages of humanity, the ages in which "virtue" was generated and generalized. But how brief are those ages? The great age of Athens barely exceeded the span of a single human life. The means of progress may always be at hand, but can we assume that they will always be exploited? Is history, generally speaking, more than the register of the crimes, folly, and misfortunes of mankind?

This melancholy undercurrent is always present in Gibbon's work, giving it depth and maturity, and preventing his confidence in the possibility of progress from degenerating into complacency. Gibbon's heroes, the real martyrs of his church, are those upholders of ancient, classical "virtue" who are overwhelmed by the blind forces of bigotry, barbarism, or corrupted power: men like the senator Boethius, "the last of the Romans whom Cato or Tully could have acknowledged for their countryman." It was because paganism, even in its decline, still professed that ancient virtue, and Christianity, being still raw and radical, attacked it, that his sympathies, in general, were with the former. As he would put it, later, in a letter to Lord Sheffield in which he expressed his horror at the excesses of the French Revolution, "the primitive Church, which I have myself treated with some freedom, was itself at that time an innovation, and I was attached to the old Pagan establishment." For that pagan establishment was the last protection of the old classical virtue.

I have suggested that Gibbon's historical philosophy was not fully appreciated in his time. The clerical critics seized on his "infidelity" (or his indecency) and discredited themselves by attacking his scholarship. Contemporary criticism never moved from this narrow base, and so Gibbon's total philosophy was not effectively discussed. Thus Horace Walpole, though he admired Gibbon's style, declared his work unoriginal in sub-stance: there was nothing in it, he wrote, which could not be found in the work of the bigoted Jansenist scholar of the seventeenth century, Tillemont. Coleridge carried philosophical obtuseness even further. He condemned the work *in toto:* "I do not remember a single philosophical attempt made throughout the work to fathom the ultimate causes of the decline and fall of that empire . . . Gibbon was a man of immense reading, but he had no philosophy . . ."; and Carlyle, whose early historical philosophy—the "Provi-dential" philosophy of a Scotch Presbyterian household—was shattered by it, declared the whole work lacking in "virtue," the style affected and the notes "beastly." What enabled Gibbon to survive that period of eclipse which normally follows the death of an author who has been a classic in his own time was not his philosophy, which was completely misunderstood, but his remarkable accuracy as a scholar, his compelling narrative power and his irresistible style, and particularly his brilliant characterization, which brings the figures of the past to life.

On his scholarship, it is perhaps enough to quote the remark of the ablest modern historian of classical scholarship, who, as a Roman Catholic, would hardly be predisposed in his favor. *The Decline and Fall,* says Rudolf Pfeiffer, is "one of the most impressive books ever written on the ancient world."[3] Gibbon's narrative power received a reluctant tribute even from Carlyle, who saw *The Decline and Fall* as a solitary bridge linking Antiquity with the modern world, "and how gorgeously does it swing across the tumultuary chasm of those dark centuries!" Carlyle incidentally paid a just tribute to the sheer power of Gibbon's writing when he called him "the most strong-minded of historians," the perusal of whose work "forms an epoch in the history of one's mind." Of his characterization, the best witness is another Roman Catholic writer whose philosophy was very different from his, Car-dinal Newman. "The character of St. Athanasium," wrote Newman, "stands out more grandly in the pages of Gibbon than in those of the orthodox Church historians," and he admitted, with reluctance, that "the chief, per-haps the only English writer who has any claim to be considered an ec-clesiastical historian is the unbeliever Gibbon." A similar tribute was paid more recently from a very different point of view by a modern philosopher. "Not long ago," writes Bertrand Russell, "I was reading about Zenobia in the *Cambridge Ancient History,* but I regret to say that she appeared complete-ly uninteresting. I remembered somewhat dimly a much more lively ac-count in Gibbon. I looked it up, and at once the masterful lady came alive . . . Gibbon conveys an extraordinarily vivid sense of the march of events throughout the centuries with which he deals."[4]

---

[3] R. Pfeiffer, *History of Classical Scholarship 1300–1850* (Oxford: Oxford University Press, 1976), p. 162.

[4] Bertrand Russell, *Portraits from Memory and Other Essays* (New York: Touchstone Books, 1969), p. 185.

Whether Gibbon's philosophy, which is his most original contribution to historical thought, is true or not can, of course, be questioned. No historical philosophy has been, or ever can be, proved "true": the most that can be claimed for any such philosophy is that it has not been proved false: that it is still, after a sufficient test of time, debatable. Gibbon's interpretation remains permanently debatable. In spite of another two centuries of historical study, scholars still do not agree about the basic cause of the decline of classical civilization in general and of the Roman Empire in particular. To that great problem there is no answer which was not suggested by Gibbon, and all discussion of it is still, implicitly if not explicitly, a commentary on his work.

PART THREE

The Contemporary Status
of a Great Idea

Ethics in a Permissive Society:

The Controversy Regarding the Objectivity of Moral Values

Otto Bird

Born and raised in Ann Arbor, Michigan, Otto Bird attended the university there, graduating in 1935 with honors in English, to which he added a master's degree in comparative literature the following year. He took his doctorate in philosophy and literature at the University of Toronto in 1939.

From 1947 to 1950 he served as associate editor of the *Syntopicon,* for *Great Books of the Western World,* working with Mortimer Adler. In the latter year he joined the faculty at the University of Notre Dame, where he was director of the General Program of Liberal Studies until 1963. He was executive editor of *The Great Ideas Today* from 1964 to 1970, when he was appointed university professor of arts and letters at Notre Dame, from which he retired in 1980.

He has written four books, *The Canzone d'Amore of Guido Cavalcanti with the Commentary of Dino del Garbo* (1942), *Syllogistic Logic and Its Extensions* (1964), *The Idea of Justice* (1967), and *Cultures in Conflict* (1976), besides articles on the history and theory of the liberal arts. In addition he was a major contributor to the *Propædia,* or Outline of Knowledge, of the current (fifteenth) edition of the *Encyclopædia Britannica.*

Mr. Bird now spends much of the year in Shoals, Indiana, where he has built a house and grows grapes for making wine. He continues to be active in editorial projects of Encyclopædia Britannica, Inc., and remains consulting editor of *The Great Ideas Today,* to which he is a present contributor.

The relation between ideas and society is a complicated one. At times, ideas have clearly formed society, as when they led to the establishment of the great religions, or when they shaped our modern, secular societies, whose very names incorporate the ideas—of freedom, equality, democracy—that brought them into being. Yet, at other times, ideas and the elaboration that they receive seem rather the reflection than the source of the society in which they occur. Such is the case today in the field of moral philosophy and the theory of values. The permissive society has begotten a permissive theory of ethics.

To be permissive is to permit, to allow, to let go, and not to forbid or prohibit. Shakespeare uses the word in this sense and, significantly, lists as characteristic of such a society some of the very traits that are perceived today:

> And liberty plucks justice by the nose;
> The baby beats the nurse, and quite athwart
> Goes all decorum.
>
> —*Measure for Measure*, I. iii. 29–31

Liberty plucking justice by the nose may be said to be what happens when terrorists, acting as they please, do injury to the innocent. Children who turn upon and violate the government of parents or schools that have allowed them to act as they like are beating their nurse. The widespread abandonment of any standard of the decent, proper, and right in speech, dress, and behavior clearly attests that decorum has "gone athwart." Such a state of affairs, Shakespeare goes on to say, is one in which

> . . . evil deeds have their permissive pass. (ibid. 38)

The claim implicit in this statement that such deeds are evil in themselves, objectively, and not just in the opinion of the speaker, is contrary to a permissive ethics. Permissiveness as an ethics should be distinguished from permissiveness as a method. In the latter sense it may well be compatible with a general objective morality in that it advocates allowing an individual to follow a way of discovery as opposed to explicit instruction from another as a method of moral training. As an ethics, however, permissiveness is characterized by the claim that there is no objective right or wrong. Such notions as right and wrong, good and bad, are held to be of man's making, having no root in the nature of things. Ethics, as proclaimed in the subtitle of a recent book, consists in "Inventing Right and Wrong."

This book*, by J. L. Mackie, an Australian and at present a professor at the University of Oxford, merits analyzing in some detail. Besides providing ammunition for a permissive ethics (although as we will see later on, the author is by no means entirely "permissive"), the book raises a larger issue regarding the fundamental basis of moral values and argues for their subjectivity. It is thus opposed to other recent writings that argue for the objectivity of those values. Representative of such writings is *Six Great Ideas,* by Mortimer Adler (New York, 1981), which argues for the objectivity not only of the idea of the good but also for that of truth and of beauty. (The remaining three great ideas that Adler discusses are liberty, equality, and justice.)

From these works of Mackie and Adler it is possible to obtain a clear and summary statement of the issue that divides them. By comparing the two books and identifying the points at which they disagree, one can isolate further issues in the controversy as a whole. Having done that, we can then consider each of these issues in greater detail, reviewing for that purpose some other recent contributions to the controversy; in particular, *The Nature of Morality* (New York, 1977) by Gilbert Harman of Princeton and *Justice and the Human Good* (Chicago, 1980) by William A. Galston, professor at the University of Texas.

The issue

What precisely is at issue when it is claimed that there are no objective values, as Mackie does in the first sentence of his book? Or, to make the same claim in the opposite term, that our values are only subjective?

The question, it should be emphasized, is about the status of values, not about their content: about good and bad, right and wrong, as they exist in the world—not about what things or actions are good or bad, are right or wrong. All of us make judgments and statements about good and bad, right and wrong, about what one should do or should not do. To ask whether such judgments are objective or subjective is to ask about their basis and validation: whether they are based on and validated by something in the objective nature of things apart from the way we think about them, or whether their basis and validity lies merely in the feelings, attitudes, and policies that we choose and adopt. The question, in short, is whether good and bad, right and wrong, value and disvalue, are to be discovered and identified, or whether they can be—and have been—invented and made?

To understand the issue it is necessary to distinguish between descriptive

---

* *Ethics: Inventing Right and Wrong* (New York: Penguin Books, 1977).

and prescriptive judgments. In its simplest form a descriptive statement is one that describes how something is as in ascribing color to an object: "My cat, Yum-Yum, is grey." But it is also possible to make descriptive statements by using evaluative instead of descriptive terms. To make descriptive judgments with evaluative terms is, in fact, a common practice. Thus, as Mackie points out, we have no difficulty in distinguishing between a kind and a cruel action or in describing the difference between the action of a brave man and that of a coward. Judgments about such matters are descriptive and, given what is meant by kindness and cruelty, bravery and cowardice, can be true or false. The prescriptive judgment enters in when we go beyond this to evaluate the actions and claim that kindness and bravery are good and ought to be pursued, whereas cruelty and cowardice are bad and ought to be avoided. It is only with respect to the latter, the prescriptive judgment, that the issue arises regarding the objectivity or subjectivity of values.

Another way of formulating the issue is in terms of truth and falsity: the question is whether prescriptive judgments can be true or false. To claim that they can is to maintain the objectivity of values. To deny that they can is to claim that those values are merely subjective. But again, it is important to note, as Mackie does, that it is the objectivity of the norm or standard that is at stake, and not the judgment made in accordance with the standard. Given the positive law as a standard, a court's decision on a criminal case is a true judgment provided the decision is in accord with the relevant law and the facts of the case. Here the issue concerns the action in question, i.e., the facts of the case, the relevant law, and whether or not the law has been broken and a crime committed. And although both the action and the law and its application are subject to argument and interpretation, the question is objectively answerable and the corresponding judgment true or false. The issue regarding the objectivity of values arises only when we go on to address the law itself: is the law just, and is there any other basis for justice than the choice and policy of men expressed in the positive law? Also, the same question can be asked of justice as of kindness and bravery: why should or ought one to act justly and do the just thing? Is there any objective basis for that "should" and "ought," or is it only a matter for human decision and policy?

The case for the subjectivity of moral values

Moral subjectivism can take both a positive and negative form. Its positive form is found in the account known as the emotive theory of value, the classic expression of which is Charles L. Stevenson's *Ethics and Language* (New Haven, 1944). According to this theory, the normative and prescriptive character of distinctively moral terms and judgments is no more than an expression of the speaker's feelings of approval and a desire to evoke the approval of others. The theory amounts to a positive form of moral subjectivism inasmuch as it claims to provide an explanation of the meaning of moral terms and judgments. Since it reduces that meaning to the feelings of the subject, it also implies the negative form that denies any objective basis to them. In this positive form the theory is compatible with the most extreme permissiveness—which is not to say all proponents of the theory actually subscribe to that doctrine.

Although the positive form implies the negative, the reverse does not hold. In denying objectivity to values, Mackie acknowledges that in our ordinary and common use we make claims to their objectivity, which he regards as false and erroneous. He maintains, however, that moral subjectivism by no means implies the abandonment of morality, and, in arguing the case for being moral as well as in specifying its content, he considerably restricts the ground for mere permissiveness. But before turning to these topics, we will look at his arguments for moral subjectivism.

Mackie offers three main arguments for the claim that moral values have no objective basis, based on (1) the relativity of moral codes such as appears from their variability over time and place, (2) the "queerness" of objective values, if such things existed, both in their status in the world and in our knowledge of them, and (3) the possibility of explaining why values are commonly thought to have some objective basis.

The argument from relativity rests on the fact that moral codes are found to vary widely from one time or place to another—a fact that Mackie takes to be so widely known that he makes no effort to document it. Indeed, he is so struck by the effects of technological change upon human desires and purposes that he declares: "The human race is no longer something determinate whose members have fairly fixed interests in terms of whose satisfaction welfare might be measured and decisions thus morally assessed." With this in mind he tends to dismiss the significance for ethics of such notions as the good for man or basic goods and primary purposes.

The argument from queerness is both more complex and more difficult. It is complex in that Mackie finds both a metaphysical and an epistemological queerness in his subject. He claims that if objective values did exist, they "would be entities or qualities or relations of a very strange sort, utterly different from anything else in the universe." But he says nothing more about the contents of the universe, and one might almost forget that there are many strange things in it, especially in the universe of modern science with its quarks, black holes, and so forth. But another queerness is said to lie in our knowledge of objective moral values—the difficulty of understanding the connection between an act and its wrongness, e.g., between the act of causing pain just for fun and its wrongness, and the additional difficulty (as Mackie claims) of understanding how we can "see" the two together—the act and its moral "consequentiality." Before such "queernesses," Mackie finds it much simpler to identify the "moral quality" with a "subjective response" that has been found socially undesirable.

The third argument rests on the claim that it is easy to understand (hence less "queer"?) why and how people come to believe in the objectivity of values through a process of "objectification." But again the argument is a complex one since, according to Mackie, this phenomenon has more than one source. The phenomenon in question is described as a reversal of direction between desire and its object. We desire an object and then, seeing it is good at satisfying the desire, we mistakenly think that we desire it because it is good. We thus get "the notion of something's being objectively good, or having intrinsic value," and hence as something that ought to be desired, when conditions are suitable, "by reversing the direction of dependence here." We are encouraged in this confusion, Mackie declares, not only by the tendency of the mind to project its feelings upon objects, as in attributing foulness to a fungus because we feel disgust for it, but even more so by the need to "internalize" the pressures and demands that society exerts upon us. If society is to exist, certain patterns of behavior are incumbent upon all its members, and, since the sources of these demands are "indeterminate and diffuse," we tend to attribute an intrinsic prescriptive quality to the demands themselves. Hence, Mackie says, ethics might be considered "a system of law from which the legislator has been removed," and even, given the religious sources of society, "the persistence of a belief in something like divine law when the belief in the divine legislator has faded out."

The relation between morality and society is a topic that calls for further consideration. But here we can conclude our review of the case for moral subjectivism as set forth in this book. In brief, Mackie's argument reduces to the claim that it is easier and simpler to explain moral values with their normative and prescriptive force if we consider them to consist in human feelings, attitudes, and policies rather than in anything objective to which such feelings, attitudes, and policies are a response.

The conventionality of morals

Although Mackie holds that values are subjective and that morality is something that men themselves make, yet he also maintains that the "whole content of morality" cannot and must not be left to the determination of each individual agent. Much of it apparently can, and to this extent he sides with permissiveness. But where morality cannot be left to the individual conscience is in the social arena and the way an individual behaves toward his fellow human beings. Thus Mackie asks us to distinguish between morality in a broad sense, as consisting in the whole code of behavior that an individual follows, and morality in a narrow sense as "a system of a particular sort of constraints on conduct—one whose central task is to protect the interests of persons other than the agent." Mackie dismisses as of no significance the question of which sense is "more correct," yet his main concern is with morality in the narrow sense. In other words, for him, morality is primarily a social matter and a social need that cannot be left up to individual choice.

The reason it cannot lies in both the human situation and the constitution of society. The human situation is everywhere a finite one: our goods, resources, information, and intelligence are all in limited supply; but, more importantly, according to Mackie, our sympathies toward our fellow man are so limited that one person not only endeavors to obtain more than another but will even act with malevolence to do so. Mackie thus agrees with Hobbes that if individuals were left to their own devices the competition among them would amount to a war of all against all, and society would be impossible. The need in such a situation is for some "device to counteract the limitation of men's sympathies," and it is precisely the function of morality, according to Mackie, to provide such a device.

Where does this morality come from? Just as Mackie finds in Hobbes what he takes to be an accurate description of the human situation, so he also finds in Hobbes's account of a social compact the main lines of an answer and a solution. Since the situation is that of violent competition, the main need is to put some limit on that competition. This is accomplished by an agreement to limit the claims against one another and provide a way of enforcing them, namely by the establishment of a sovereign state. Individuals then have a double reason for keeping their bargain: to avoid punishment for breaking it, to obtain benefit by keeping it. Mackie thus interprets Hobbes's "laws of nature" as the fundamental principles of morality. Some of the many "laws" that Hobbes enumerates may call for change with changes in the world and society, but the law that men perform the covenants they have made is declared to be "an eternal and immutable fragment of morality." Agreement, contract, compact, covenant is thus made the foundation stone of society and morality. The contract need not be thought of as explicit historical occurrence; rather it is "implicit in human societies."

It is important to note that morality is thus claimed to have an external and nonarbitrary source: it is an objective condition and requirement for the existence of human society. Yet this fact of itself, Mackie would argue, does not provide any objective prescriptive moral value. Why should or ought one keep one's word? Only in order to avoid punishment or to obtain the benefits of life in society. The only "ought" here is hypothetical and no way categorical as imposing a moral obligation in and by itself.

The case for the objectivity of moral values

Mackie maintains that the argument he advances holds for all values, although in his book on ethics he deals in fact only with moral values. Mortimer Adler, however, in *Six Great Ideas* deals with truth and beauty as well as goodness and presents reasons for believing that all three have an objective basis. In his treatment of goodness and of justice Adler thus provides the material for stating the case for the objectivity of moral values.

This case, as made by Adler, lies in the answers that seem to him to be required by the following questions:

1. Can a true judgment be made about what is good for all men, and not just individuals? Or are there any objects that are really objectively good for all men?

2. Is an object regarded as good simply because it is in fact desired, or is it something that ought to be desired because it is in fact good?

3. How can a prescriptive judgment be true or false when no number of factual truths can ever lead to a prescriptive conclusion?

4. How can there be more than one kind of truth, i.e., a truth different from that found in descriptive statements?

As is evident from the way the questions have been formulated, the argument makes use of the distinction between descriptive and prescriptive judgments, but it goes beyond anything we have discussed in two significant respects: First, it asserts that there are descriptive statements that are true for all men—i.e., facts about mankind. Second, it claims that there exists a prescriptive truth, and that truth therefore is not something that belongs exclusively to descriptive statements.

If it can be shown that there truly are objects that are good for all men, we will have taken the first step toward overcoming the claim that all moral values are subjective. For to assert that they are entirely subjective is to equate them with desires, and desires are the properties of individuals and vary from one individual to another. As dependent upon desires, values are thus made relative to the individual: the good is an object of an individual's desire. Hence, if there is an object that can be shown to be good for all men, it cannot be truly asserted that all good is relative to the individual.

Adler accepts the identification of the good with the desirable: we desire what *appears* to us to be good, so the good is an object that we see as desirable. But Adler denies that this equivalence thereby makes the good relative to the desire of an individual. He bases this denial upon the distinction that can be drawn between natural and acquired desires—the former of which are "needs," the latter "wants." The needs are "inherent in human nature, as all truly specific properties are," and are accordingly "present in all human beings, just as human facial characteristics, human skeletal structure, or human blood types are." Furthermore, these needs "are always operative tendentially or appetitively (that is, they always tend toward or seek fulfillment), whether or not at a given moment we are conscious of such tendencies or drives."

In all three respects wants differ from needs. They are acquired, not natural; they differ from individual to individual, since, as acquired, they depend upon the individual temperaments, experiences, and circumstances; and, third, wants are conscious desires at the time they exert their motivating power.

Adler's argument requires that these common words be understood in their precise meaning. That they must be taken so becomes plain as he notes still a fourth way in which needs differ from wants. Needs, he claims, can never be misguided or excessive, whereas wants obviously can be. This feature enables him to distinguish between "right and wrong desires." A right desire is one that is truly in accord with a human need. A wrong desire is one that mistakes what is required by a human need; it consists in a want for an object, looked upon as good, which in fact will not satisfy the need it seems to serve — as when we think to meet our bodily requirements with what is called "junk food."

It might appear in using such morally charged terms as "right" and "wrong," Adler has departed from the realm of descriptive fact. Yet from the example he adduces, it is clear that he is claiming to be still at the descriptive factual level of the way things are. Thus it is a fact about human nature that knowledge is a need for man: he has an innate capacity for knowing that naturally tends toward fulfillment, and it is a need common to all men. Evidence of this is the fact that all men, with the exception of the handicapped, learn to speak a language. The efforts of a child learning to speak also show how he actively wants to acquire that ability. When this occurs, it is a case of a natural need being met through right desire — "right" in the sense that what it seeks will, in fact, meet the need it seems to serve.

The distinction between needs and wants thus makes it possible to distinguish real from apparent goods: real goods are those that really satisfy natural needs, whereas apparent goods consist of those that are objects of desire, and good in that sense, but that, while perhaps harmless and certainly pleasant, do not correspond to natural needs. We may and often do want the wrong food and drink, or too much or too little of it, for the good of our health.

So far, in identifying natural desires and needs, and even in distinguishing right and wrong desires, and real and apparent goods, we remain at the factual level, have made no prescriptive statement that we claim is true or false. Any statement we might make in a given instance about a need and a right desire is a descriptive statement and is true or false according to the kind of truth appropriate to such statements. The desire is right if it is for an object that is in fact capable of fulfilling the need for a real good, and, if that is the case, the corresponding statement of it is a true one; but, if we are mistaken about either what we take to be a need or the capacity of the given object to satisfy it, the statement is false. However, we still have no basis for making a prescriptive statement that is true.

We have that, according to Adler, only when we see that "we ought to want and seek that which is really good for us (i.e., that which by nature we need)." And we see this, Adler maintains, and also see that it is true, as soon as we understand the meanings of its terms. It is a "self-evident truth" in that it is impossible to think the opposite: "Without knowing in advance which things are in fact really good or bad for us, we do know at once that 'ought to desire' is inseparable in its meaning from the meaning of 'really good,' just as we know at once that the parts of a physical whole are always less than the whole." It is categorical in that it does not depend upon anything other than itself. and "upon this one categorical prescription," Adler asserts, "rest all the prescriptive truths we can validate concerning the real goods that we ought to seek."

The truth of prescriptive judgments thus has a double basis: the prescriptive injunction that is self-evidently true combined with knowledge of the goods that are truly real as satisfying needs of human nature, which is a matter that ultimately has to be determined by factual investigation of that nature. The objectivity of moral values accordingly also rests on a double basis: the existence of real goods which is a matter of objective fact combined with the general prescriptive injunction which is also objectively true in being self-evident and not merely a subjective desire.

Little more can or need be said about the prescriptive injunction. But to complete the case for moral objectivity, more remains to be said about real goods. For unless these goods can be identified as goods needed by all men and not something to be left to be determined by individual wants, the case against the subjectivity of moral values has not been made. But this task, Adler maintains, is readily accomplished. He identifies six real goods, as follows: wealth, health, pleasure, friends or loved ones, liberty or freedom of action, and knowledge and skill in all their forms. About these goods, Adler holds, we know enough to be sure beyond reasonable doubt that they correspond to natural human needs and are common to all human beings.

With this understanding of need and real good, Adler adopts as his own Aristotle's definition of the truth of practical judgments as consisting in conformity with right desire. The statement that one ought to want and seek knowledge is a true practical judgment. It is practical as being regulative of human action in declaring what ought to be done, and it is objectively true in that it calls for an action motivated by a desire for a real good that satisfies a natural need of every human being. Thus, in the human order of desire and action of what ought to be done, objective truth is to be found quite as much as it is in the descriptive order of the way things are. But it is a different kind of truth in that it consists in conformity with right desire rather than in conformity with the way things are.

The points at issue

From even so summary an account of just these two participants in the controversy concerning the objectivity of moral values it is possible to locate and identify the major points at issue. Among these are four that arouse the deepest and most basic disagreement:

(1) the nature of objectivity and whether there is a real and genuine issue posed by the question: is the basis of morality objective or merely subjective?

(2) the test of objectivity: what would count as an adequate way of determining whether values are objective or not?

(3) the moral import of human nature: do the common features of human existence provide a suitable basis for making objective moral judgments?

(4) the basic problem and primary purpose of moral philosophy: is it concerned with what constitutes the human good and how the individual can achieve it, or, instead, is it concerned with how men can live together and enjoy the benefits of political society?

On each of these four questions Mackie and Adler take opposite positions and present arguments in support of them. In this, however, they are not unique, but representative of others who have taken part in the controversy by arguing either for or against the objectivity of moral values. This will become clear as we turn now to consider in greater detail each of these issues and the arguments about them. In doing so, we will have occasion to review the work of some other recent writers on the subject.

Objectivity: a genuine issue?

Objectivity itself constitutes an issue inasmuch as there are differing and opposed positions regarding what it is, what is to count as an objective moral value, and how objectivity is to be distinguished from subjectivity. On this, the most radical position is that which claims that there is no real genuine issue at stake when it is asked whether moral values are objective or not. Such is the position taken by the British philosopher R. M. Hare, who, in the article "Nothing matters," published in his *Applications of Moral Philosophy* (London, 1972), and quoted by Mackie, claims that no real difference can be detected between an objectivist and a subjectivist when they happen to agree on a particular moral judgment. It must be admitted that the two might well agree that a certain course of action is wrong. If so, and if the question of objectivity is a real one, it should be possible to detect some difference between them, Hare argues; but, he declares, none is to be found: "Think of one world into whose fabric values are objectively built; and think of another in which those values have been annihilated. And remember that in both worlds the people in them go on being concerned about the same things—there is no difference in the 'subjective' concern which people have for things, only their 'objective' value. Now I ask, 'What is the difference between the states of affairs in these two worlds'?"; and he then adds, "Can any answer be given except 'None whatever'?" With this he concludes that there is no genuine issue between the objectivist and subjectivist position; the only difference between the two is verbal—they are different names for the same thing.

Heidegger, the German existentialist, would also dismiss this issue, although for very different reasons from those of Hare. He maintains that the issue is wrongly posed in that the distinction between subject and object as it is applied in moral matters is a mistaken one. True and valid thinking about such matters is prior to such a distinction: "Such thinking is neither theoretical nor practical. It occurs before such a differentiation."

Adler and Mackie in common with other objectivists and subjectivists maintain not only that a valid distinction can be drawn between subject and object but also that as applied to morals such a distinction gives rise to a genuine issue on which there can be real and serious disagreement.

The distinction between subject and object and their corresponding judgments seem clear, indeed obvious, when it is made in Adler's terms of want and desire. The statement that I want x is subjective inasmuch as it is a statement about the subject's condition, namely that I as a person feel a certain desire which I am seeking, or will seek, to satisfy. But the statement that I need x is objective in that it states an exigency or requisite of human nature that is quite separate from subjective desire; in fact, I might well have a need for x without actually wanting or desiring it. So far, however, neither statement is distinctly moral and does not become so until there is the added note of prescriptivity, namely that I ought or ought not to seek to obtain x. And whether there is a genuine issue regarding moral objectivity depends upon whether there is a real difference between claiming that this latter judgment has an objective basis apart from the subject or does not.

There is no doubt that in the practical order of human action an objectivist might well agree with a subjectivist in recommending or condemning a certain course of action. Human beings do not have to share identical moral philosophies in order to pursue a common course of action. But that is not the question here. As Mackie points out, in arguing against Hare, the difference that is crucial for showing that there is a real issue is not at the first order level but rather at the second order. The question at issue is whether there is anything in the nature of things apart from individual wantings that provides a basis and justification for the recommendation or for condemnation.

Mackie argues that Hare oversimplifies the situation and so mutes the difference by imagining only the case in which both the subjectivist and the objectivist are agreed upon a particular action. The difference between them becomes more evident when a change in a given policy is being argued. For, as Mackie writes, "if there were something in the fabric of the world that validated certain kinds of concern, then it would be possible to acquire these merely by finding something out, by letting one's thinking be controlled by how things were. But in the world in which objective values have been annihilated the acquiring of some new subjective concern means the development of something new on the emotive side by the person who acquires it."

That there *is* a difference and that it is significant appears also from the fact that it makes a difference for general philosophy as well as morals if values have an objective basis. As we have already seen from Adler's analysis of the truth of prescriptive judgments, to maintain the objectivity of values one must also admit that there is more than one kind of truth, that truth is not limited to descriptive judgments. But with this we are leaving the area of our first issue and entering upon the discussion of the second.

The test of objectivity

Among those who hold that the question of objectivity does indeed pose a genuine issue, there arises at the very start an issue over which there is deep disagreement. That is the question of what is to count as an adequate test of objectivity so that, once successfully concluded, it will serve to confirm that a moral judgment has an objective basis. In other words, what is to count as evidence of moral objectivity? On this matter the sharpest disagreement concerns whether or not the ultimate test has to consist in something like an empirically established observable fact, one that will provide the ground for making a true descriptive judgment, or at least something similar to that. The subjectivist argues that nothing less than such a test is sufficient to validate moral objectivity. The objectivist argues, to the contrary, that no such test as this is needed, since there are other ways, indeed ways more suitable to moral philosophy, that provide all the evidence that is needed.

For the subjectivist case, Mackie again provides a good starting point. He points out that the objectivity of values is sometimes confused with other notions which are not only not the same but which also do not provide a test. Among these the most important are those of intersubjectivity and universalizability.

Many individuals may in fact share the same beliefs about what is good or bad, right or wrong, but that does not mean these values have an objective basis, nor does it provide any evidence that they do. As shared, the values are intersubjective, but they are not for that reason objective. So, too, those sharing such beliefs might well universalize them and claim that all persons in the relevant circumstances should hold them and act accordingly. But this is no more than to advance a claim on the part of those making it and does not entail that those values *are* objective. Mackie admits, however, that the converse does hold: "If there were objective values they would presumably belong to kinds of things or actions or states of affairs, so that the judgments that reported them would be universalizable."

What then for Mackie would count as a test of the objectivity of values?

On this subject, he is not as clear as one might wish. He declares that they would have to be "part of the fabric of the world," and also "perhaps something like Plato's Forms"—those eternally subsistent immaterial Ideas. Also, as we have noted earlier, Mackie emphasizes that they would be very "queer" entities. Presumably by this he means that they would be different from the observable entities of the natural world. And, as we have seen, because of this alleged "queerness" he argues that values cannot be objective.

Whereas the test of observability is only implicit in Mackie's work, it is made explicit and indeed the very keystone of objectivity in another recent book by Princeton professor Gilbert Harman, entitled *The Nature of Morality: An Introduction to Ethics* (New York, 1977). In the first sentence of his first chapter on "Ethics and Observation," Harman asks: "Can moral principles be tested and confirmed in the way scientific principles can?" Since scientific principles are tested by observation, the question is whether moral principles are likewise tested by observation. Harman allows that we do make moral as well as nonmoral observations, where by *observation* he understands an immediate perceptual judgment made without any conscious reasoning. As an example he cites the case of children drenching a cat with gasoline and igniting it; a person observing it could both "see" the action and "see" that it is wrong. Here the first seeing is a nonmoral observation, the second a moral one. The question at issue is whether such moral observations provide a test of the objectivity of moral principles or values.

Harman answers in the negative and offers as support a comparison between this situation and that which holds between observation and theory in scientific practice. A physicist, testing a micro-particle theory, observes a vapor trail and judges immediately that it is a proton. Again there are two "seeings," that of the vapor trail and that of the proton, and these supposedly correspond to the two in the moral example. It should also be noted that in both cases the second "observation" is not as immediately perceived as the first. Harman himself does not make this point, since he maintains that all observations are "theory laden" as presupposing concepts, hypotheses, theories, all of human construction. Yet clearly the wrongness of the act and the proton are not perceptible and hence not perceived in the same way as the children's action and the vapor trail. However, this is not the difference that is Harman's concern. He is concerned to point out that there is a real relation (though this is not his term) between the proton and the vapor trail, whereas there is no such relation between the children's act and its wrongness. There "really was a proton" in the cloud chamber, it is a "physical fact" that causes the vapor trail and has a real effect upon the physicist's "perceptual apparatus," given the particle theory and the other assumptions under which he is operating.

In the moral example, however, there is no such connection between the wrongness and the children's act. The wrongness is not a "moral fact" corresponding to the proton as a "physical fact." Even if the children were perversely acting as they did because they thought it was wrong, this motive only reveals something about their beliefs and is not evidence of the "actual wrongness of the act" as something objective apart from their belief. Scientific observation provides "evidence not only about the observer but also about the physical facts," whereas "a particular moral observation . . . does not seem to be evidence about moral facts, only evidence about you and your moral sensibility." Hence, Harman concludes, "there does not seem to be observational evidence, even indirectly, for basic moral principles."

To the extent, then, that moral values must meet the test of observability, the subjectivist case is buttressed by the failure to find any observational evidence for the existence of moral values. To this argument the objectivist can reply at once that, so phrased, the conclusion is scarcely surprising, since the wrong test is being applied: in short, that objectivity is not exclusively dependent upon observability. For this claim we need look no further than to the argument that Adler makes for objectivity as summarized above.

His argument, as we have seen, rests on a double basis: first, a factual one about human needs rooted in the nature of man and, second, a categorical injunction that the real good ought to be sought. The evidence for objectivity is accordingly double: the facts about human nature and the truth of the categorical injunction. It is this second one that is our concern here; the first will be considered later when we come to discuss the issue regarding the import of human nature for moral judgments.

What evidence is there that the categorical injunction is true? Adler claims, as we have already noted, that its truth is self-evident in that it is impossible to think the opposite. Once the meaning of its terms is understood, that is, of real good and that it ought to be desired, its truth is seen immediately. It thus contains in itself all the evidence that is needed to show its truth. Even without knowing what things are really good, we know that they ought to be desired and that we should not desire what is really bad.

There is more that can be said about self-evident truths, and Adler does so in the chapters of his book that deal with truth and knowledge. Self-evident truths, he claims, constitute the strongest, the most certain, and the most incorrigible knowledge that we have. They thus provide evidence in the strongest sense of that term. Examples of such truths, in addition to the categorical injunction, are the following: nothing can both exist and not exist at the same time, or at that time both have and not have a certain characteristic; the whole of any physical body is greater than any of its parts; no triangle has any diagonals. Although all of these are self-evident, they differ in important ways, and to see how they do enables us to understand better how they are evident and also why they need no other evidence for their truth.

Take first the mathematical example. The truth that no triangle has a diagonal appears at once as soon as it is understood that a triangle is a three-sided plane figure, whereas a diagonal is a straight line drawn between two nonadjacent angles, for a triangle in being three-sided has no nonadjacent angles. Although this truth depends upon the definition of the terms in that one must know what is meant by a triangle and a diagonal, the proposition is not a mere tautology and a matter merely of words. In this it differs from such a proposition as all triangles have three sides, which is true but tells us no more than the definition of a triangle. The proposition about the diagonal is instructive in that it notes a further characteristic about triangles.

More significant for our purposes here, however, are those self-evident truths that involve terms that are themselves indefinable. Such, for example, is the proposition that no part is greater than the whole. We cannot understand what a part is without reference to whole, and vice versa; yet, as soon as we do understand, we see at once that in the case of any finite whole, without any further reasoning or any other evidence, the whole is greater than any of its parts.

The self-evident truths about existence and the moral good resemble this latter proposition rather than the mathematical example. Both are concerned with terms that are indefinable and yet also stand in no need to be defined. For as soon as we come to understand what is meant by existence and the real good, we also see that the same thing cannot both exist and not exist at the same time and that the real good ought to be desired. We see that they are true and that their opposite cannot be and cannot be thought.

With these principles, then, we have reached an ultimate and can go no further. But there is no need to. For they are first principles and underlie all our thinking about existence and morality. And as Aristotle pointed out, it is impossible to define and prove everything; one must ultimately reach an indefinable and unprovable—an ultimate evidence.

But at this point we reach an impasse. For what Aristotle and the objectivists take to be an evidence, the subjectivists deny, claiming that at most it is only a postulate and gains what force it has only from the agreement granted to it by those who accept its use as a principle. Thus Mackie, for example, explicitly denies that any categorical imperative is objectively valid and claims that to think so is just an error; the only basis is human agreement or convention.

With this we come to another issue in the controversy over objectivity. It bears closely upon the question of evidence that we have just been considering. Indeed, as we have just seen from Adler's argument, the evidence for moral objectivity does not rest solely upon the categorical injunction that the real good ought to be sought. It depends also upon the factual nature of human needs. Here the question at issue concerns the import of such needs for moral judgment. Consideration of this issue will also help to prepare the way for facing the question whether morality is ultimately only a matter of human agreement and convention, as the subjectivist holds.

Human nature as a basis for moral judgment

On this issue there is no doubt that the two positions are clearly at odds. The subjectivist doubts and denies that any facts about human nature and its needs provide a sound basis for moral judgment about what men ought to do. The facts, of course, by and of themselves provide no basis for the prescription that human needs ought to be satisfied; the "ought" here, according to Mackie, is a subjective preference smuggled in to pose as an objectively based injunction. The objectivist position, as we have seen from Adler's argument, would agree that the facts of themselves provide no prescriptive "ought." That derives from the self-evident truth of the first principle of the moral order that we have just been considering. But the two positions are also at odds over the relevance for moral judgment of any facts about human nature. The objectivist thinks they are of the greatest importance and relevance, whereas the subjectivist tends to dismiss them as of little or no importance.

Mackie, for example, asserts as a warning against the objectivist that "there may well be more diversity even of fundamental purposes, more variation in what different human beings will find ultimately satisfying, than the terminology of '*the* good for man' would suggest." Indeed, he attaches so much importance to the diversity of the ways in which men satisfy their needs that he tends to deny that they are of any help in establishing the objectivity of moral judgment; in short, he reiterates that the argument from the relativity of morals and mores still holds.

Adler, in arguing the objectivist case, admits the diversity in human behavior but denies that it is so great as to destroy entirely all invariant human needs which provide the basis for objective values. To think that it does, he argues, comes from the failure to differentiate between "a basic human need and what is needed to implement the satisfaction of that need." Thus, such things as mechanical means of transportation, protection against environmental pollution, and extended school systems are all facts that are new to our contemporary technological society; and they are real goods. This is so, Adler says, not because they satisfy needs that are new, but only because in present circumstances they are required as implements for satisfying invariant needs rooted in human nature:

> Wealth, health, and knowledge are always and everywhere real goods, no matter what the circumstances of human life may be. But means of transportation, environmental protection against pollution, and the institution of school systems are not, under all circumstances, required to implement the satisfaction of the basic human needs for the real goods just mentioned.

Strong support for the objectivist case on this issue is also supplied by William A. Galston in his book *Justice and the Human Good* (Chicago, 1980). In this work Galston claims that there is an intimate relation between the good of human nature and the moral virtue of justice. The position he argues for is in inspiration Aristotelian (or "quasi-Aristotelian," as the author prefers) in claiming that "although our ruling *ideas* are anything but Aristotelian, many of our *experiences* and *intuitions* are." Of further importance for our purposes, Galston is especially concerned to argue at some length against the conventionalist and contractarian theory of justice so prevalent today, largely because of the acclaim accorded to *A Theory of Justice* by John Rawls (Cambridge, 1971). As we have seen from reviewing Mackie's position, he has adopted a version of this theory as a basis for the subjectivist position. Galston, in arguing for a natural as opposed to a contractarian basis, provides support for the objectivist position. But more of that later when we come to consider the relation between morality and society.

Against the charge that the concept of human nature is so indeterminate as to be philosophically useless, Galston argues persuasively that not only does it have a determinate content, it provides an actually existing unity that underlies the diversity among human beings. As the most obvious and important traits that men share in common, Galston lists the following:

—a distinctive kind of consciousness, self-awareness, that produces both introspection and the knowledge of mortality;
—a distinctive kind of comprehension, rationality;
—a distinctive kind of communicative competence;
—complex and differentiated passions;
—the interpenetration of reason, passion, and desire that constitutes the moral realm;
—unique kinds of activities, such as artistic expression;
—a distinctive form of association that we call "political" containing enormously complex conventions;
—and, finally, what we may with Rousseau think of as instinctual underdetermination.

Certainly, Galston does not seem to be excessively bold in declaring that "it seems reasonable to assert that something like this ensemble of fundamental characteristics is what we mean by human nature."

Galston argues that these characteristics also provide a basis for determining what constitutes the human good. And this good is not one of subjective desire that varies from one individual to another. There is no "simple and direct equating of individual benefit and individual preference." Here, Galston means by "benefit" a real good that satisfies in Adler's terms a "need," whereas a "preference" corresponds to an individual "want." Thus Galston, like Adler, finds in human nature, which all human beings share in common, the ground on which to base the claim for moral objectivity: in short, the intersubjectivity of human good suffices to overthrow the argument for moral subjectivism. To this end, Galston quotes with approval the followings words of Isaiah Berlin:

> We seem to distinguish subjective from objective appraisal by the
> degree to which the central values conveyed are those which are
> common to human beings as such, that is, for practical purposes, to
> the great majority of men in most places and times. . . . Objectivity of
> moral judgment seems to depend on (almost to consist in) the degree
> of constancy in human responses.

Galston claims that there are four elements that are constitutive of the
human good. They are "ends, states, qualities, and activities that human
beings value for their own sake." In the terminology he uses, there are
principles of worth. There are four such: the worth of existence, the worth
of developed existence, the worth of happiness, and the worth of reason.
For each of these, Galston provides an analysis and a justification to the
extent that a justification is possible, usually by meeting objections raised
against them as constituting real goods or as achievable.

There is no need in such a brief review as this to say any more about the
first, the value of human life. That a human being is endowed with certain
capacities and that it is good that these capacities be developed is equally
obvious. Galston points out that there are many different capacities, some
higher than others, and not all equally shared or at least to the same degree
by all individuals. But it is possible to arrive at a principle of choice that is
objective yet also sensitive to the needs of different individuals, namely:
"Develop one or more of the highest capacities within your power, subject
to the constraints of unity, coherence, and balance between these capacities
and those in other classes." By happiness Galston understands the fulfillment of desire so as to equate it with "the presence of the totality of what
appears to be good." (In this he differs from Adler, for whom happiness
consists in the totality of real—not apparent—goods that satisfy natural
needs.)

The fourth principle, the worth of reason, is of a different sort and
deserves closer consideration because of the important claims that Galston
makes for it, nothing less than that "morality rests" on it.

The principle of rational action on which morality is said to rest is
formulated thus: "Take or do only what you are entitled to. To be entitled
to *x* is to have a warranted claim on *x;* to have a warranted claim is to be
able to advance a satisfactory reason to have or to do *x*." Since Galston is
concerned in this book to propound a theory of justice, it is understandable
that he should emphasize the importance of this principle. However, it is
by no means obvious that all morality rests upon it. Galston points out the
advantages of adopting such a principle: its help in securing agreement,
resolving difficulties, and explaining our actions to one another so that we
have greater insight to ourselves. Ultimately he allows that it implies "the
choice of a particular way of life—a life of self-understanding and -control,
of mutually giving and receiving explanations, of striving for moral knowl-

edge and for human community based on that knowledge." But except for claiming widespread acceptance for it, Galston does not provide any basis for such a choice's having a categorical prescriptive force: for its being a categorical and not merely a hypothetical "ought." Here it looks as though Mackie could say that objectivity is being confused with intersubjectivity.

Yet for this principle, as for the other three, Galston makes strong claims to objectivity. He asserts that all four principles are not "an arbitrary axiomatization, justified only by clarity and simplicity." They are said to be widely acknowledged and to be presupposed by our deeds and judgments. More important, they are said to be ultimate, not only in that they need no further defence, but are themselves "constitutive of the moral sphere," as having their own evidence. Unfortunately, it would not seem that this can be so unless it is also understood that the real good ought to be sought. And about this self-evident principle of the moral order I do not find that Galston has anything to say.

Morality and society

Mackie remarks that his approach to ethics may well seem entirely wide of the mark to those in the Aristotelian tradition. But the reason that he alleges is not the only one—namely, whether human nature provides an adequate basis for ethical choice. An even more basic issue concerns the primary purpose of morality and hence too of moral philosophy. Is it the determination of the human good, and how the individual can achieve that; or is it rather a question of how men can live together and enjoy the benefits of society?

On this issue, as we have already seen, Mackie opts for the second position. Following Hobbes and Hume, he adopts a contractual view of human society and holds that morality is the conventional cement that holds it together. This view is of especial importance for him in that he claims that it provides a nonarbitrary basis for morality. Although Galston makes no mention of Mackie's work, he does argue explicitly against the social and moral theories of Hobbes and Hume. In doing so, he makes telling arguments against the subjectivist case as it is presented by Mackie.

Since Galston's argument here is somewhat complex, it may be helpful at the start to indicate its salient points. First, there is the question whether the political community is entirely produced by choice and agreement among human beings in the way that a contract is made. This raises the question whether agreement is the basic and only justification for that association. Third, is scarcity of goods and resources the primary motivation for morality? And finally, does social need provide a nonarbitrary basis for morality?

The answers given to these questions depend upon the understanding that one has of the relation that holds between the individual and the political community. On all of them Galston presents arguments that seriously undercut the force of the subjectivist case.

Political association has always contained a conventional element arising from human institution and agreement. This is no less true of the ancient city-state than it is of the modern technological nation with its enormous complexities of man-made components. The question is whether convention constitutes the only basis of ethics and whether the convention should be conceived as the kind of agreement found in a business contract.

To do that is seriously to misconstrue, Galston argues, the relation between the individual and the state, and this remains so whether the contract is viewed as a theoretical construction, historical happening, or a practical requirement. "Contract theories," Galston writes,

> see free, independent, fully formed individuals deliberating about the kinds of mutual connections and limitations to which they should severally agree. Each individual, considering personal interest in the context of a general understanding of the empirical requirements of physical and material security, comes to regard as advantageous the sort of society we call *political*. But if these empirical requirements happen to be different, there is no reason to agree to enter into the political community.

Such theories are defective in that they misunderstand the nature of both man and the state and the relation between them. Galston agrees with Aristotle that there is a natural component to the state. The political association is needed for the actuation of human development. Also, human beings as separate existences are related in important ways to one another even before they engage using their minds to construct a common life through consciously entering the political community. In short, contract does not provide a good model of political society.

Nor is it true that agreement willed by men is the only way of justifying basic principles. As Galston notes, "we do not seek answers to mathematical puzzles by asking what various individuals would assent to. Rather, the independently determined answer serves as the criterion of rational assent." So too, principles of justice are agreed to because they are seen to establish what is just and are not as such established by that agreement. Indeed, "many kinds of moral principles rest on noncontractarian grounds" inasmuch as they are seen to be constitutive of, or ancillary to the achievement of, the human good.

The contractarian theory of Hume, to which Mackie also subscribes, rests on the assumption that principles of justice are required only in a situation of scarcity where the selfishness of men has to be obviated in order to prevent the disruption of society. Mackie extends this argument beyond justice to include all of morality.

According to Hume, with respect to questions of justice there are three different cases that must be distinguished: first, that of such abundance that every member of the society is able to obtain the goods that he desires; second, the situation at the other extreme where the scarcity of goods is so great that some must die and all be miserable; third, the case in between these two in which goods are sufficient to enable some, but not all, to obtain what they want. Given the difference between these three situations Hume then goes on to claim that any question about justice disappears whenever the first or second condition prevails. The rules of justice are not needed if abundance provides all that everyone wants, or if the scarcity is so extreme that every individual seeks his own self-preservation before anything else.

Against this argument Galston maintains that the dependence of justice upon scarcity falls, since it can be shown that rules of justice still hold even in the two extreme situations. Take the case of abundance. Hume assumes that justice is concerned only with external goods that, at least potentially, are transferable from one person to another. But, Galston points out, such an assumption is contrary to the facts. Cases arise in which injustice is done even though no individual is deprived of the good in question and when that good cannot be transferred to another. Such is the case of a teacher who conscientiously grades all but one of his students impartially and, with that one exception, gives each the grade he earned except for his favorite to whom he awards a higher one.

Further, there are some goods which are intrinsically scarce, so that even in a time of abundance of material goods, questions of justice may arise with regard to the possession of political power, positions of authority, and the priority among ends to be pursued: "whether we *ought* to do something that we have the power to do." So too in the case of extreme necessity, one course of action may be better, more just, than another even though one member may have to sacrifice himself. Galston cites the case of two men on a raft that can support only one, when one is healthy and the other terminally ill, or one is eighty and the other twenty—situations in which "the appropriate outcome is at least inclined in a particular direction." If there is no relevant difference, then it is just to determine the outcome by lot or chance. It would "be right to use force only to enforce the correct outcome if the other party resists."

From such counter-examples as these, Galston thinks it is clear that even in situations of extreme abundance or of need, principles of justice hold and are needed, even though their application may differ from that made in times of relative sufficiency.

We come now to the fourth question on the issue regarding the relation between morality and society: whether the need of society for morality is sufficient to provide a nonarbitrary basis for morality. An affirmative answer is essential for Mackie's position, since otherwise his morality becomes completely permissive and he loses even that "eternal and immutable fragment of morality" that promises should be kept. To make morality entirely a function of society is to divorce it from any concern for the individual human good and thus leaves the latter without any other basis than individual preference. But even with respect to the political community itself, the principle seems a highly dubious one for reasons that are both factual and moral.

On the factual side there is plenty of evidence that societies continue to survive even when there is widespread disregard for truthfulness and the keeping of promises. The moral argument is even more telling. If morality consists entirely of rules imposed by society for its preservation, there is no ground for judging the society itself to be good or bad. But, as Galston remarks, "one can hardly maintain that the continued existence of every institution, or political regime, or form of life is preferable to its collapse." The argument fails in that it mistakes the direction of the relation between society and the moral good: it is not the needs of society that determines the moral good, but rather the moral good that determines the needs of society and how they should be satisfied. If personal integrity is a good, that is so not because it is indispensable for the existence of society but "because it is essential for a desirable way of life in which individuals can by and large count on each other to act sincerely and to take their commitments seriously."

Conclusion

Disagreements are disagreeable, and one of the ways out of the disagreeability frequently is to try to show that there is no real ground for disagreement, that what seems to be a cause for it is just a mistake. Such would appear to be the ploy of those who attempt to dismiss the controversy over the objectivity of moral values as a mistake. In recent years it has been something of the fad of the therapeutic school of philosophers to attempt to solve philosophical problems by dissolving them. Something of a royal predecessor for such a procedure is supplied by Kant's dismissal of metaphysics. Kant got rid of a disagreeable problem, namely that of metaphysical questions over which there had long been serious disagreement, not by claiming that the issues were false and not genuine, but by asserting that they were not solvable by human reason which, he claimed, was incapable of transcending the limits of experience. And just as Kant's attempt at dismissing metaphysics has proved to be a mistake, so too has the attempt to get rid of the question of the objectivity of values. Metaphysical controversy has continued long after Kant thought he had got rid of it; the question about objectivity likewise continues to excite real and solid philosophical dispute. In fact, all the evidence that is needed to show that the dispute is founded on a genuine issue is supplied by the differences we have found over the other three questions at issue we have identified in the controversy. These differences are real enough and, indeed, at least in the case of one of them so serious that it is difficult to see how they are resolvable. On the other two, all the weight of the argument would seem to be clearly on the side of the objectivist case. The difficult, perhaps even the unresolvable question, concerns the nature of first principles and how they are grasped.

Take the question regarding the evidence for objectivity of moral values and the kind of test that would show that it is so or not. The case for subjectivism as encountered in the review of it here seems to rest on the claim that nothing is objective unless it is observable, or at least capable of being observable if one had the sight to perceive it (e.g., of the microparticle, the proton). It sounds as though values could be accounted as objective, or as having an objective basis, only if they were shown to be something like dogs or men or, even, protons. Yet such a demand is to make a huge assumption of great epistemological and indeed metaphysical consequences. It is to assume that the only valid knowledge that we have is of the kind that experimental science has with its ultimate dependence upon sensible observation, and also that the only kind of truth that there is consists in descriptive statements characterizing the contents of the physical world.

As Aristotle pointed out long ago, we would be mistaken to expect to find that all kinds of truth are the same, or that all kinds have the same degree of exactness. Moral matters cannot be as precise or as exact in the knowledge of which we can have of them as can mathematics, nor is the truth of either of these disciplines dependent ultimately upon experimental and observational evidence. Mathematical truths have practical applications, but then so do moral truths, and both of them can have practical consequences that can be observable. But neither of them in their principles rest upon observables such as chairs, dogs, or men, or even upon protons, if indeed these are observables.

Mathematics depends upon such a principle as the notion of number, which is not an observable; metaphysics depends upon the notion of being, and that x cannot both be and not be at the same time and in the same respect; morality depends upon the notion of the good. None of these is observable as a singular physical entity that we encounter in our walk down the street. Yet, this is no reason for claiming that they are not objective, but only desires, or wishes, or postulates of our own making that have no kind of independence from an individual's human contrivance. Granted that, on the foundations of mathematics and metaphysics as well as of morals, there are fundamental differences and profound disagreements. None of these can operate at all without allowing something more than the mere observables of the physical world.

In short, to claim that the only test of objectivity of moral values is observability is to mistake the nature of the thing being investigated, to cast a net either too small or too big for the kind of fish we seek.

Suppose we agree, however, that observability in the sense just discussed is mistaken, there still remains a serious question. This concerns the status of first principles and how they are grasped. Suppose we claim that the first principles of the moral as well as of the metaphysical order are self-evident, i.e., as soon as one comes to the understanding of the terms in which they are expressed, one will "see" that they are true. As soon as we say this, a subjectivist like Mackie will jump upon that "see" and claim that we are having recourse to an "intuition," which he claims at once drops us into the subjectivist camp. For the truth of the proposition depends upon our "seeing" its truth. And that he can claim is because we will, wish, or want it to be so.

With regard to such first principles then, one side asserts that they are evidences that can be seen; the other, denying this, claims that they are postulates that we freely accept for one reason or another. What kind of resolution is there when one reaches such an impasse? Aristotle met it with Heracleitus: everything changes, nothing remains, everything both is and is not; so what can one do? Speech becomes impossible, Aristotle reported, though one might hold up his finger. But speech nevertheless continues, though fingers may not be up—which brings us to our next point at issue.

The case for the objectivity of moral values rests also upon the claim that it is possible to identify the components of what constitutes the real good for all men at all times. Or, to qualify this formulation of it, that there are goods that are really good for all men as satisfying their natural needs in order to become all that they are capable of becoming. It is also claimed that this is a factual matter. And such it does appear to be. Indeed, it is hard to see why, in general (and in moral philosophy as here we remain at a very general level), such things as life, health, pleasure, friends and loved ones, freedom of action, knowledge, skill, and aesthetic satisfaction are not real goods that do contribute to making a good human life. It also seems on the face of it that such things were goods for the ancient Greeks and Barbarians as they are still for all human beings on the earth today. What then do the subjectivists mean when they claim that human nature is so changeable that the nature itself provides no basis for making moral judgments? Since these are goods as satisfying needs as matters of fact, they must mean that they can be satisfied in different ways. But so what? For health, one needs a nutritious diet, and there are many different foods that provide an equally nutritious diet. No objectivist need claim that everybody must eat Post Toasties or pasta or steak and potatoes in order to be healthy; he claims only that health is necessary for a good human life and that nutritious food is needed for this purpose, not that one is a complete failure if he does not become and remain a healthy person.

That there are real goods answering to natural needs is a factual matter. About them, mistakes may therefore occur, and even among objectivists, disagreements may arise regarding whether a given item is in fact a real good. For example, John Finnis, in his book *Natural Law and Natural Rights,* offers a list of basic goods for all human beings that includes religion along with life, play, aesthetic experience, sociability, practical reasonableness, and knowledge. Yet neither Adler nor Galston, as far as I can find, make any mention of religion, at least as a practice, although they would readily accept the others as real goods. But disagreement over real goods in particular cases does not thereby destroy the case for the objectivity of moral values. For the fact remains that there are many goods that clearly and unmistakenly satisfy natural needs.

Part of the disagreement in the overall controversy concerning the objectivity of values undoubtedly concerns the malleability of human beings, not only in extent, but also in desirability. The subjectivist sometimes talks as though there were no limits at all to the extent to which human beings can be molded and remade, and as if the lack of such limits is all to the good. The objectivist not only sees grave dangers in attempting such remolding but is also much more dubious of the extent to which it is even possible.

The final issue that we have considered in the controversy over the objectivity of moral values concerns the relation between morality and society. On this point it looks as though the disagreement turns about morals and mores: the subjectivist tends to reduce all morals to the condition of mores that are relative in that they vary from one culture and from one time to another, whereas the objectivist claims that at bottom there are certain moral standards not subject to such variation. The mores in the sense of the customs, habits, traditions, conventional ways of behavior undoubtedly depend upon agreement and the ways and customs that have come to be accepted within a given community; and these do indeed differ from one community to another. But the objectivist maintains that underlying all of such societies one will still find that there are common ideas of what is good and what ought to be done: that killing one another at random is not good; that murder is therefore wrong, though there may well be differences about what constitutes a murder; that sexual practices, especially as they result in offspring, need some regulation; that, at least within one's own community, one ought to render to each his own. With changes in conditions and circumstances, it is not such principles that change; it is their application. Patriotism, for example, does not cease to be a virtue, an admirable excellence of character; what changes is the conception of one's country—for Socrates, Athens; for the man of the twenty-first century, perhaps the world.

In summary, we can conclude as follows. Within the context of the four leading questions we have identified as being at the center of the controversy:

The issue concerning the objectivity of moral values is a real and genuine issue. It is not a false issue founded on a question that would make no difference in the answer that is given to it; to claim that there is an objective basis to moral judgments finally *is* different from claiming that the basis is merely subjective.

On two of the remaining three points at issue, the arguments of the objectivist clearly outweigh those of the subjectivist. First, with regard to the relevance of human nature, it is possible to identify goods that are in fact good for satisfying natural human needs and that to this extent are indeed good for all human beings. Second, the human good is determinative of morality and not the needs of society, since, at the simplest level, a society can be judged as good or bad according to the extent to which it achieves the good of its members as well as of the whole society.

This leaves as the fourth question at issue, that of prescriptivity, the source of the *ought*. Is it only a postulate, willed by men, taken for their purposes, whatever they are, whether to preserve society or for some men's conception of the human good. Or is it self-evident, such that its truth is open to anyone to see? With this we do reach an impasse: indeed, the most impassable of all the four issues. But this is scarcely surprising, since with this issue we come to the question of first principles.

PART FOUR

Reviews
of Recent Books

Hans Kung: Does God Exist?

Mortimer J. Adler   Wayne F. Moquin

Mortimer Adler has devoted a lifetime to the teaching and practice of philosophy, which he regards not as an academic specialty but as everybody's business, and to the cause of education through the study of great books. Among numerous books he has written is *How to Think about God: A Guide for the 20th-Century Pagan* (1980), in which he endeavors to set forth what can be said about God by the mind without the aid of revelation. For many years an associate at the University of Chicago of Robert Maynard Hutchins, with whom he edited *Great Books of the Western World,* he has since 1952 been director of the Institute for Philosophical Research in Chicago, and, since 1974, chairman of the Board of Editors of Encyclopædia Britannica, Inc. His latest book is *Six Great Ideas,* in which he distinguishes the ideas we judge by from those we act upon. He is editor in chief of *The Great Ideas Today.*

Wayne F. Moquin was born in Chicago. He attended Luther Theological Seminary (1957) and Chicago Lutheran Theological Seminary. He spent four years in the parish ministry, then left to become education writer for Sacred Design Associates in Minneapolis. In 1964 he returned to Chicago to work for Mortimer Adler at the Institute for Philosophical Research. He has been involved in numerous publishing ventures, including: *Annals of America* (associate editor); editor of *Makers of America, Documentary History of Mexican Americans, Great Documents in American Indian History, Documentary History of Italian Americans,* and *The American Way of Crime;* and associate editor of *Great Treasury of Western Thought.* He is currently on the staff of Encyclopædia Britannica, Inc., as associate editor of *Compton's Encyclopedia.*

I. Exposition of the book

Hans Küng's *Does God Exist?* is a formidable exercise in apologetics, that branch of theology which seeks to defend and assert the message of the churches in the face of contemporary ideologies. Apologetics differs from theological squabbles among the churches, in that, while all the Christian churches share the message of the New Testament, with ideologies of the twentieth century, they do not necessarily have common ground.

Küng's premise in writing this book is that there is in our time a multiplicity of world views, of which some are ideological and some not, but which taken together deny, doubt, or derogate the God of Abraham, Isaac, and Jacob, of Moses and the prophets, the God whom the churches see fully and finally revealed in the Jesus of the New Testament.

The aim of the book is simple: to affirm "by a clear, convinced Yes, justifiable at the bar of critical reason" that God exists. But the journey of more than 700 pages to get to this affirmation is far from simple and involves some serious problems for philosophy and theology. Although *Does God Exist?* is divided into seven sections, A through G, the book is basically in two parts.

The first part, sections A through D, traces the course of modern philosophical/scientific thought from the rationalism of the Enlightenment to the nihilism of Nietzsche, with several detours into the twentieth century. It is here that all the cases against belief in God are made.

The second part, sections E through G, is developed thematically rather than historically, although quite a few historical summaries of philosophical, theological, and scientific positions are outlined. The presentation in the second part begins with an argument for an affirmation of reality (in response to Nietzsche) and proceeds to an affirmation of belief in God in sections F and G.

In section A, Küng "looks back over the dramatic history of reason and faith in modern times, which led to the elimination of God from politics and science." The two thinkers primarily at issue are Descartes and Pascal. It was Descartes who found in reason the basis on which to measure and quantify the whole of empirical reality. Beyond this, he was able to derive the idea of God from the certainty of this same reason.

Pascal, also devoted to reason and faith, rendered an opposite conclusion.

His focus was, however, on man in the universe, "out of which no Creator's voice can be heard." He impugns the certainty of reason yet denies that fundamental uncertainty is inevitable. He challenges man "to take the risk of believing in God." For Pascal, faith becomes the foundation on which reason can operate, for purely rational self-certainty (Descartes's *Cogito, ergo sum*) cannot serve as a basis on which all other certainty can be built.

Section A of Küng's book then goes on to describe the divergence of theology from natural science since the Enlightenment. The blame for this divergence is laid mostly at the doors of the churches, which, in one rear-guard action after another, attempted to preserve the ancient/medieval world view.

As Paul Tillich has noted: the churches "tried to discover gaps in our scientific and historical knowledge in order to find a place for God and his actions within an otherwise completely calculable and 'immanent' world. Whenever our knowledge advanced, another defense position had to be given up." But, in the face of ecclesiastical dogmatizing, natural science fought back, asserting its own claims by virtue of experiment and observation, to the end that God as explanation of anything became less and less necessary.

This, at first only implicit, denial of God receives its corrective by Küng in Section B. With a new scientific view of the world, it was no longer possible, he notes, to stick "to a philosophically obsolete image of God." In the Newtonian world, God became the machine-maker, the God who made the world and put it in operation according to its own natural laws.

With Spinoza comes a departure from this deism to pantheism: God "the one and only divine substance," of which the individual self and all finite things are only modifications. In Spinoza and those influenced by him, there took place a "restoration of the divinity of nature" which had been neglected by the Enlightenment.

This led, perhaps inevitably, to a subjectivizing of God. For Fichte, God became "an immediate, original certainty that is rooted in feeling." When the objectifying of God out of the world by way of deism is set alongside the subjectifying of God into the "inwardness of emotion, of feeling," one may ask (as many did), why bother with a concept of God at all? He is so removed as to be irrelevant or so interiorized that "faith surrenders objective reality." It was Hegel, Küng says, who saw this possibility clearly. And it is Hegel whose thought, and the reactions to it, forms the bulk of Sections B, C, and D of Küng's book. Hegel is, indeed, the pivotal philosopher for Küng. It was Hegel, after all, who took completely seriously the modern world view vis-à-vis the problem of God. He saw the potential for atheism and "perceived exactly the historical context in which must be seen this basic feeling of the religion of modern times that God is dead." And it was Hegel who in his great synthesis sought "a reconciliation of faith and knowledge, of a philosophical and a biblical God."

The synthesis is so impressive to Küng that he seems to wish that it could serve as a modern counterpart to the work of Thomas Aquinas in the thirteenth century. "Hegel—this genius of dialectical synthesis—created a system containing an amazing abundance of material . . . on a scale never before offered to Christianity: a *summa universalis,* and—for that very reason —supremely a *summa theologica.* . . . a miracle in the age of an unbelieving philosophy."

The Hegelian synthesis, unlike the Thomistic one, did not break down because of a new world view. The world simply passed it by in the way of reaction and challenge. In any case, as Küng points out, the possibility of maintaining it was demolished in the course of the nineteenth century. Yet even in the twentieth century, he argues, "important thinkers particularly in the fields of mathematics and natural science [Whitehead and Teilhard de Chardin] are working out alternatives to science without religion and progress without God."

It is in Sections C and D that the decisive challenge to Hegel comes, and the curtain is finally rung up on full-blown and unembarrassed atheism. Section C deals with the thought of Feuerbach, Marx, and Freud. In the matter of atheism, Feuerbach is clearly the leading thinker, for it was he who first published a serious intellectual formulation of the denial of God. And Küng suggests, in his remarks on Marx and Freud, that these two writers never really improved on the groundwork laid by Feuerbach in his *Essence of Christianity:* "Anthropology is the mystery of religion." God is a reflection, a projection, the infinitely lengthened shadow, of mankind. Parenthetically it must be said that Küng mentions but does not explore the tremendous impetus given to atheism and other worldly faiths by the French Revolution.

From rationalism to atheism, all modern intellectual meanderings are seen by Küng as leading inexorably to Nietzsche, "the most dangerous diagnostician of modern man." "Does atheism, thought out to the very end and consistently realized, not finally lead to the reassessment of all values, to the destruction of existing morality and thus to nihilism?" Küng asks. This is the subject of Section D.

It is fitting to end the first part of the book with Nietzsche, for it is impossible to go beyond him in the transformation of thought he ushered in and in the radical denial he made of even basic empirical reality. Preparatory to a full-scale discussion of Nietzsche, Küng describes the work of Darwin, David Friedrich Strauss, and the stern pessimism of Schopenhauer.

Interpreting Nietzsche is not an easy matter, since it is often difficult to delineate between what he is reporting and what he is innovating. But his singular importance for the twentieth century is undeniable. Reminiscent of the opening sentence of the *Communist Manifesto* (1848), Nietzsche announced in *The Gay Science* (1882): "The greatest recent event—that 'God is dead,' that the belief in the Christian God has become unbelievable—is already beginning to cast its first shadows over Europe."

For Küng, that is Nietzsche's most significant contribution: he was willing to announce the consequences of atheism for modern society: "This long plenitude and sequence of breakdown, destruction, ruin, and cataclysm that is now impending." No one would have had more right to say, "I told you so," than Nietzsche, had he lived to observe the events of the twentieth century (he died in 1900).

The consequences of this announcement of the death of God had to be a "meaninglessness which threatens everything," Küng concludes. It has led the world to a point where "all the consequences of belief in God must be overcome." Further, "all previous foundations of human knowledge are to be undermined by depicting them as prejudices of faith." This is the end of any fundamental certainty, the beginning of nihilism, "the conviction of an absolute untenability of existence when it comes to the highest values one recognizes," in sum, "the conviction of the nullity, of the internal contradiction, futility and worthlessness of reality." (Nietzsche himself apparently wanted to put nihilism behind him and move on to something positive: "I want to create something new," he said. But the breakdown of his health prevented him.)

In the first four sections of *Does God Exist?*, Küng is not content to present a "systematic clarification of the problem of God as it has developed in the course of history." Each section also contains a critique: of rationalism, of the Hegelian synthesis, of atheism, and of nihilism.

These subsections, entitled "Interim Results," perform at least two functions. They subject the issues raised to a critical analysis and a "correcting course," and they serve as building blocks for the affirmations the author makes in part II, sections E through G.

In these subsections, Küng's approach is one of overwhelming fairness: he is not a fanatical polemicist on behalf of church or dogma. He notes carefully the failures of the churches over the past few centuries in dealing with the advances of scientific knowledge as well as with social, economic, and political issues.

For instance, in the "theses on modern rationality," he states: "Obviously, not only philosophy and theology but also the natural sciences have great difficulties with changes in the world picture. Neither natural science alone nor philosophy and theology alone can solve these difficulties."

There must be a "radical course correction of Church and theology." Even in the theses on atheism and nihilism, he insists on this "course correction" for the sake of truth.

Küng assesses the results of the first four sections thus: "We did not want to leave anything unquestioned, to conceal anything apologetically, to appeal to any authority beyond further appeal. We tried to think critically and self-critically, in order to perceive and to be certain of the foundation of our knowledge and faith."

Having traced the development of modern atheism and nihilism and found them both "possible, irrefutable but unproved," Küng is ready to make a case for saying Yes to reality and to God.

In Section E, two attitudes to reality are explained: fundamental mistrust and fundamental trust. "Fundamental mistrust means that a person in principle says No to the uncertain reality of himself and the world," Küng writes. But he himself prefers the other attitude. Man is by nature inclined to say Yes, he argues: fundamental trust makes us open to reality, and the Yes can be consistently maintained in practice. The implications of fundamental trust are then explored for the individual, for science, and for ethics and religion.

Having provided a basis for saying Yes to reality, Küng nevertheless acknowledges that fundamental trust is inadequate because: "nihilism is not overcome in principle. The reality on which fundamental trust is based seems itself to be without foundation." The uncertainty of reality remains. Hence "the basic riddle of human life can scarcely be solved if the central question, the question of God, is not faced." It is pointless to reject nihilism unless atheism is also rejected.

This is the task of Section F of the Küng book, a long and complicated treatise in which all the major discussions on the problem of God in modern times are analyzed, not necessarily in chronological order. The main issues and thinkers covered are: transcendence (Ernst Bloch, Max Horkheimer, Heidegger, Sartre, and Wittgenstein); the natural theology controversy (Roman Catholic theology versus Karl Barth); and Kant's critiques of the proofs of God's existence.

Küng concludes his preliminary arguments by admitting that God cannot be proved but goes on to declare that "God as the supposedly all-determining reality will be verified by the experienced reality of man and the world." This is an "indirect verification" by which "it should be possible to give an account of belief in God that will stand up to any kind of criticism and to make clear the relevance of belief in God to the reality of man and the world."

Consequent to this argument, Küng states: "If someone denies God, he does not know why he ultimately trusts in reality." Belief in God therefore is "rationally justified." But this is not "an outward rationality . . . not first a rational knowledge and then confident acknowledgement of God . . . . It is an inward rationality which can offer fundamental certainty." In "boldly trusting God's reality, despite all temptations to doubt, man experiences the reasonableness of his trust."

Lest Küng be accused of rationalism here, he goes on to say that "belief in God, too, is a matter not only of human reason but of the whole concrete, living man, with mind and body, reason and instinct, in his quite particular historical situation." It is a "superrational," but not irrational, trust, a decision "grounded in and related to reality and rationally justified in concrete life. . . . realized in a concrete relationship with our fellow men: without the experience of being accepted by men, it seems difficult to experience acceptance by God."

Hence such trust is "constantly to be freshly realized." Most of all, it is a gift from God "who reveals himself as primal source, primal meaning, and primal value."

Having come this far in his Yes to God, Küng pauses to assess the meaning of his Yes for ethics. His conclusion is that absolute moral norms cannot be justified except by fundamental trust in God. "The unconditionality of the ethical claim . . . can be justified only in the light of an unconditioned . . . God himself."

Finally we arrive, in Section G, at the God of the Bible, after a discussion of the several non-Christian religions. The God of the philosophers is left behind, and the God of Abraham, Isaac, and Jacob appears. It seems fair to state that Küng's thesis here is that the Bible reveals to us a God about whom our information thus far was inadequate, but on the right track.

Section F had given us the God in whom we could trust on the basis of an "indirect verification," the God whom it is reasonable to trust if we want an underpinning for contingent and uncertain reality. It is the God who is revealed (the means of revelation are not discussed) as primal source, meaning, and value.

Now the mask is pulled away, and we learn that the God in whom we trusted was the God of the Bible all the time. While we might have been satisfied with the God of the philosophers, the God-in-general, we realize that such a God, even in the other religions, has no name, no concreteness.

Belief in the God of the Bible, Yahweh, "is also rationally justifiable and has proved itself historically over many thousands of years," Küng writes. This is the God of the cosmos, the Creator, who can yet be addressed as a person by humans. This is the God "who does not operate above the world process, but in the world process. . . . He is himself the all-embracing and all-controlling meaning and ground of the world process, who can of course be accepted only in faith."

What, then, is the relation between the God of the philosophers and the God of the Bible? In Küng's mind they are quite the same, in that we move from one to the other in a direct line of reasoning and clarification. The process involves a deepening of understanding, and hence of trust, that is involved.

First it is affirmed that God is also for the Bible "the primal ground of all reality," and "the primal goal of all reality." Then there is a final assessment that must be quoted in full:

> We have been reflecting once more, then, on the God of the Bible without adopting a biblicist attitude and ignoring the conclusions of philosophy. And we have reflected again on the God of the philosophers without stopping at metaphysics:
> *It proved to be an overhasty reaction simply to dissociate the God of the philosophers from the God of the Bible, as "dialectical theology" attempted to do.
> *It proved to be superficial simply to harmonize the God of the

philosophers and the God of the Bible, as natural theology did.
*The important thing was and is to see the relationship in a truly
dialectical way. In the God of the Bible, the God of the philosophers is
in the best, three-fold sense of the Hegelian term "sublated"—at one
and the same time affirmed, negated, and transcended.

This is the more divine God, before whom modern man, now grown
so critical—without ever having to give up his reason—"can pray and
offer sacrifice, again fall on his knees in awe and sing and dance before
him."

Finally, at the end of Section G, the God of the Bible is revealed as the
God of Jesus: "God himself encounters us in a unique and definitive way
in the activity and the person of Jesus." But not just Jesus; it is the crucified
Christ who, as the living one, "is the ground of faith, the criterion of
freedom. He is the center and norm of what is Christian." Again, "this
Christ Jesus is in person the living, authoritative embodiment of his cause:
embodiment of a new attitude to life and a new life-style." For Küng, this
is God in the world for us, who makes it possible to cope with suffering and
to face the final enemy, death.

The agency in us for trust and obedience to this God is the Holy Spirit,
"never my own possibility, but always the force, power and gift of God." One
receives this Spirit by "opening myself inwardly to the message and thus to
God and his crucified Christ," Küng maintains.

II. Philosophical critique of the argument

So much for Küng's argument. Now let us see what it all adds up to and
what it is worth. Let us first examine it from the point of view of philosophy;
and, after that, from the point of view of religious faith as well as from that
of dogmatic or sacred theology.

In the judgment of the authors of this review, one a philosopher and the
other a theologian, Küng's whole approach to the question of God's existence is unsound and misguided, both philosophically and theologically. It
fails because, with respect to God's existence, it fails to understand the
proper scope and limits of philosophy, on the one hand, and of theology,
on the other. It has all the faults of that queer discipline known as "natural
theology," which is neither a purely philosophical theology nor a dogmatic
theology that draws its inspiration from articles of religious faith and uses
reason, not to prove anything, but only to help faith seek an understanding
of itself.

Philosophical theology begins and ends with what is wholly within the
grasp of reason, with no enlightenment or influence from religious faith. To
whatever extent and with whatever degree of assurance philosophical
theology is able to construct arguments affirming the existence of a su-

preme being, it necessarily falls short of providing reasons for affirming the existence of the God believed in by men of faith and worshiped by religious Jews, Christians, and Muslims.

I will return presently to the gap that separates the God of the philosophers from the God of Abraham, Isaac, and Jacob, of Moses, Jesus, and Mohammed. On the unbridgeability of this chasm, except by an act of faith, Pascal is completely right and Küng, relying on Hegel, is completely wrong.

Dogmatic theology (also denominated "sacred theology" because it has its ultimate source in Sacred Scriptures) begins and ends with what God has revealed to mankind about Himself and about His creatures in relation to Himself. In the development of dogmatic or sacred theology, reason plays a subordinate and ancillary role, not the principal and exclusive role it plays in philosophical theology.

In philosophical theology, reason operates inquisitively and probatively as it operates in metaphysics and in the philosophy of nature. In dogmatic theology, reason does no more than serve faith in its effort to understand what is believed—believed without rational grounds for such belief.

The absence of rational grounds does not make religious belief insecure or uncertain. On the contrary, faith has a certainty greater than any certitude that reason can achieve, because when faith is understood as a gift bestowed upon man by God's grace, the truths it holds, though beyond rational proof, have their security and warranty in the source from which they come.

In the modern world beginning with Descartes and Leibniz what came to be called "natural theology" is an effort on the part of philosophers who are also men of faith to reach by reason the God that is the object of their religious belief.

Modern philosophers who criticized and rejected the efforts of natural theology were justified in doing so; but Küng, who pays undue attention to all the pros and cons of the modern controversy about the merits of arguments for and against God's existence, fails signally to recognize that none of the views expressed, whether favorable or adverse, have any bearing whatsoever either on orthodox religious faith and its dogmatic theology or on a truly philosophical theology which acknowledges that the God it is able to think about and even affirm is not the God believed in and worshiped by religious Jews, Christians, and Muslims.

The discoveries and methods of modern science, especially in the twentieth century, make much of traditional natural theology untenable; but, on the contrary, a truly philosophical theology profits from attention to modern science.

This can be made crystal clear by considering Küng's question: Does God exist?

"Yes" say religious Jews, Christians, and Muslims, not on the basis of any natural knowledge that they have or can acquire and not on the basis of any rational arguments, but solely as an act of faith on their part, which is to be understood not as an exercise of their human will to believe but rather as a supernatural gift bestowed upon them by God's grace. To this affirmation on their part, modern science and philosophy make no contribution and present no obstacles or impediments.

Küng vacillates from one page to another in viewing religious faith, on the one hand, as an exercise of the human will to believe, for whatever motive, emotional or pragmatic, and viewing religious faith, on the other hand, as a supernatural gift, an act of the will not naturally motivated but moved solely by God's grace.

On the former view of faith, the apologetic efforts in which Küng engages for hundreds of pages may be justified by a desire to bolster up the merely human will to believe in God against countervailing motivations to will a disbelief in God. But on the latter view of faith as a supernatural act of the will moved by God's grace, all of Küng's elaborate apologetics are at best nugatory. Why this is so will be made clear in the third and concluding section of this review.

Let us return to Küng's question: Does God exist? When that question is answered affirmatively, without hesitation and with complete assurance, by religious persons, the God about whom the question is asked is the God who has revealed Himself in Holy Writ. The first article of faith is belief in the Divine revelation itself—belief in the supernatural source of the Old Testament and the New, or the Old Testament and the Koran. That these books contain the revealed word of God is both unprovable and irrefutable. That is why the acceptance of them as the revealed word of God must be an act of belief, whether that belief results from our merely human will to believe or consists in the supernatural faith that God's grace bestows.

However, when the question, Does God exist? is answered affirmatively by nonreligious persons who think that they have found philosophical reasons for such affirmation, the God about whom the question is asked is not the God who, according to religious faith, has revealed himself in Holy Writ. The question only appears to be the same question because the same three words are used.

Of those three words, the crucial word is "God." When the question is asked and answered by religious persons, the word "God" signifies not only a supreme being, having aseity and acting as the uncaused cause of the cosmos, without which action the cosmos would not now exist. The word "God" also signifies for them a morally perfect being, benevolent, just, and merciful, providential and caring, concerned with man's salvation, a divinity to be worshiped and trusted, an object of prayer and supplication.

There is only one thin thread of common meaning in the two connotations of the word "God." Both include the note of aseity, a property of the supreme being which has in itself the sufficient reason for its own existence and is, therefore, independent, unconditioned, and infinite in its existence. It is that one thin thread that relates the God of the philosophers to the God of Abraham, Isaac, and Jacob, of Moses, Jesus, and Mohammed. An unbridgeable chasm of difference remains between a God conceived exclusively in metaphysical terms, which are the terms appropriate to philosophical thinking about God, and a God conceived in moral terms, which are the terms appropriate to religious thinking about God.

It is, of course, possible to leap across the chasm, but that one thin thread of connection will not by itself support the leap. The leap requires an act of belief unsupported by reason, either an exercise of the will to believe or an act of supernatural faith.

In either case, the leap must not be misunderstood, as it usually is, as a process of going from no grounds whatsoever for affirming the existence of God to the affirmation of God's existence. Properly understood, it consists in going from a philosophical affirmation of the supreme being's existence to the religious belief that the God whose existence has been affirmed on rational grounds is benevolent, just, merciful, providential, a God to be relied on and prayed to, a God through whose grace man gains salvation.

In a recently published book that is strictly a work in philosophical theology for twentieth-century readers (*How to Think About God*), I have reviewed the major arguments for the existence of God as supreme being and uncaused cause of whatever else exists, and I have also considered the main criticisms of such arguments raised by modern philosophers.

Twentieth-century cosmology and nuclear physics confirm the rationale of philosophical theology in dealing with the question of God's existence. But, with one exception, modern philosophy raises no insuperable difficulties and makes no indispensable contributions.

That one exception is Bertrand Russell's theory of descriptions, which is useful in explaining how Anselm's understanding of God as the being than which no greater can be thought leads to a definite description of God that gives connotative meaning to the word "God" when it is used as the proper name of an object with which we can have no direct acquaintance.

I am not saying that there are no difficulties with even the very best philosophical argument for the existence of the supreme being. There are. The best argument hangs on a premise that is not self-evident, cannot be proved, and yet is more credible than its opposite. Hence the conclusion of the best argument cannot be affirmed beyond the shadow of a doubt, but only beyond a reasonable doubt, or even just by a preponderance of reasons in its favor rather than against it.

What I am saying is that I have found nothing in the thought of Kant, Hegel, Nietzsche, twentieth-century existentialists, and twentieth-century linguistic and analytical philosophers, which presents genuine difficulties to be surmounted. On the contrary, the critical points raised can all be dismissed because they stem from ignorance or misunderstanding of the metaphysical principles on which a sound philosophical argument for God's existence rests; or they can be disregarded because they apply only to the unsound reasoning that is to be found in the efforts of modern natural theology to prove what cannot be proved—the existence of the God who has revealed Himself in Sacred Scriptures.

Only Küng's complete failure to understand the difference between such unsound natural theology and a sound philosophical theology can explain why he devoted so many hundreds of pages to modern philosophical thought, from the onslaughts of which neither a truly philosophical theology nor a truly dogmatic theology needs to be defended.

It is even more important to point out that orthodox religious beliefs— Jewish, Christian, or Muslim—do not need to be rescued from the nihilistic and atheistic attacks of modern thought. Yet Küng spends an inordinate amount of time and effort in trying to save orthodox religion from Nietzsche's nihilistic proclamation that God is dead or that the Christian God has become unbelievable.

This is all the more surprising in view of the fact that Küng explicitly acknowledges that Nietzsche's nihilism is both unprovable and irrefutable. The articles of Jewish, Christian, and Muslim faith are also unprovable and irrefutable. If they were either provable or refutable they would belong to the domain of reason and of knowledge, not to the domain of faith and of belief. In short, they belong in exactly the same domain as Nietzsche's nihilistic proclamations.

Where does that leave us? Whatever is unprovable and irrefutable must be either (1) a self-evident truth, or (2) a belief voluntarily adopted for whatever human motive, emotional or pragmatic, or (3) a belief that is an act of religious faith, supernaturally caused by God's grace.

It is not because what is believed or disbelieved is self-evidently true or false that orthodox religious belief, on the one hand, and Nietzsche's nihilistic disbelief, on the other hand, belong in the sphere of the unprovable and irrefutable. Nietzsche can hardly claim that his nihilism is an act of religious faith on his part. On the contrary, his disbelief in God, his immoderate skepticism about being able to attain any truth, and his total distrust of reality represent nothing but a purely voluntary exercise of his will to disbelieve. It is no better than a personal prejudice without foundation.

When we exercise the will to believe or disbelieve, in the realm of matters that are beyond the reach of reason and evidence, our motivation, as William James pointed out, must be either emotional or pragmatic. James himself advanced good pragmatic reasons for exercising a will to believe that was opposite in tenor to Nietzsche's nihilism. That some pragmatic motivation might be found for such nihilism is difficult if not impossible to imagine. It must, therefore, represent nothing but emotional distemper on Nietzsche's part, and that is certainly not worth paying attention to, especially in view of the fact that Nietzsche himself, like Hume before him, found good pragmatic reasons for abandoning his extreme or immoderate skepticism when it came to the affairs of daily life.

In any case, orthodox religious belief, when it is not mistaken as the exercise of a humanly motivated will to believe, does not operate on the same plane as Nietzsche's nihilistic disbelief. Though it, too, is unprovable and irrefutable, it does not spring from emotional or pragmatic motivations. If it did, all that could be said for religious belief is that, for many persons, it is emotionally more satisfying than Nietzsche's disbelief and that, for most persons, it is pragmatically more justifiable. However, when religious belief is taken as a supernatural act of the will, moved by God's grace, its certainty for those who have such faith is incommensurable with whatever probability is assigned to their beliefs or disbeliefs by persons who allow emotional or pragmatic motives to elicit a will to believe or disbelieve on their part.

Here and there, Küng adopts the orthodox view of faith as a supernatural gift. If this view had completely controlled his thought, he would have written a totally different book or, better still, no book at all on this subject.

Since he lacks the philosophical, and especially the metaphysical, acumen needed to cope with the fundamental errors of modern thought and since he has no contribution at all to make to philosophical thinking about God, Küng's reputation as a theologian, based on the positions he has taken in controversies about certain dogmas of the Roman Catholic Church, might have been preserved by his not having attempted to deal with the question of God's existence.

III. Theological critique of the argument

The theological assessment is in response to two questions. First, is the book viable as an apologetic? Second, on the basis of the most fundamental assumption of the churches about their own message, has Küng succeeded in making a valid case for God?

I say fundamental assumption, because it is not my purpose to pick apart his treatment of single doctrines, such as virgin birth, miracles, resurrection, etc. We must go beyond these to the one belief all the churches share about the God of the Bible: that He reveals Himself. This is the issue that underlies the problem of any apologetic effort.

Apologetics, according to Paul Tillich, is " 'answering theology'. It answers the questions implied in the 'situation' [the scientific, artistic, economic, political, ethical, and social complexities of any era] in the power of the eternal message and with the means provided by the situation whose questions it answers."

This means that apologetics is a theology for the world. But can there be a theology for the world? The churches have never been in agreement on this problem, although apologetic endeavors have been around nearly as long as the churches themselves.

Note that theology and message (preaching the gospel) are not identical. The churches would all agree that they have a message to address to the world in all of its situations. But, to quote Tillich again: "Can the Christian message be adapted to the modern mind without losing its essential and unique character?"

Tillich thinks it can. Others in our time, most notably Karl Barth, have disagreed. According to Barth: "We must treat unbelief [the world] seriously. . . . But faith itself . . . must be taken so seriously that there is no place at all for even an apparent transposition to the standpoint of unbelief, for the pedagogic and playful self-lowering into the sphere of its possibilities." This is to say that it is impossible for the churches to walk hand in hand with the unbelieving world, granting the validity of its premises, concepts, and definitions, yet hoping by clear and rational exposition to lead it into the arena of faith.

In this conflict over apologetics, Küng has chosen to align himself with Tillich. He seems to assume that an unbelieving world can understand the message, if it is explained clearly and cogently enough.

But the Tillich-Barth debate is not either the whole or the final word on the issue of apologetics. First, we must have a clearer understanding of the apologetic task as the churches have understood it, before giving a final assessment of Küng's success or failure. Alan Richardson, in his book, *Christian Apologetics* (1947), has explained the work of apologetics as two-fold. First, it is a task that takes place within and for the churches themselves: "Christian apologetics . . . compels us to examine the methods and conclusions of theological enquiry in the light of our general knowledge of the world around us and of ourselves in relation to that world." In that sense apologetics is a self-clarifying theological effort. Theologians and preachers, in order to formulate their message (ever within the framework of the biblical message), have always had to take stock of the assumptions, beliefs, and opinions commonly at work in the world. This is no more than to say that the churches in every age have lived in specific historical contexts. The churches must be in touch with the time.

Secondly, the churches often have to assume a defensive position against attacks from without, as they do today in lands utterly uncongenial to their message. Here we are back at the heart of the Tillich-Barth debate, and here the whole apologetic endeavor becomes a bit murky. No matter how the churches are in contact with the spirit of the time, the fact is that the churches and the world at large do not operate on congruent sets of assumptions. Thus, the apologetic effort can only succeed up to a point. If the world, through error or misunderstanding, accuses the churches wrongfully, the answer from the churches may help clarify and convince on specific issues. But can apologetics do more? Küng, by his writing of *Does God Exist?*, testifies that he thinks it can. And let it be acknowledged that there is an age-old tradition which agrees with Küng. The tradition stretches from the Acts of the Apostles to Justin Martyr to St. Augustine to St. Anselm to St. Thomas to Tillich and Küng. It is hard to think of any success that it has had. In the Acts of the Apostles, St. Stephen and his hearers certainly shared very common ground in their understanding of the acts of God in the Old Testament, but all Stephen got for his effort was death by stoning. St. Paul did not regard his address to the men of Athens as an unqualified success, in fact, he never again tried to make such common cause with unbelief. And so forth.

Note—unbelief, not reason. For faith is not set by apologetics in opposition to reason or any other intellectual faculty. Faith is always set over against unfaith. The assumption is that the world of unbelief has a light of truth of its own and can therefore more easily be led directly to the greater light of God's truth by critical reason. But that is very hard to accept. As Mr. Adler has correctly noted in the previous section, faith is not the will to believe what reason is able to posit. Faith is always and only the gift of God for those to whom He will give it. What apologetic can move in an unbroken line from unbelief to the God of the Bible, saying Yes at every stage of the argument, and arriving finally at the New Testament faith? Those who think such a reasonable progression is possible should examine carefully the first nine chapters of John's gospel. It is there made very clear that coming to faith is a crisis encounter between humanity and its Lord. The eyes of the blind are not opened by the blind, nor are the "spiritual" leaders of the time convinced by reasonable discourse.

If Küng's apologetic fails, it is for the reason that, according to the churches, God reveals Himself, He is not willed or reasoned to exist. Küng's book, and any other such apologetic, runs aground on the rock of revelation. All the while that he has been saying Yes and Yes and Yes to God, Küng has never noted God's No to humankind. This No is most succinctly stated by St. Paul in Romans 11:32—"For in making all mankind prisoners to disobedience, God's purpose was to show mercy to all mankind." This verse is the concluding statement of an argument St. Paul makes in the first eleven chapters of Romans. First, the case is made against the Gentiles: in their ignorance of God they have turned to worship that which is not God. In other words, their seeking after God is a useless enterprise that leads them to fashion gods after their own understanding (precisely the point that Feuerbach made). Secondly, Paul states that those who, having the Law of God, propose to make themselves just by observance of the Law also fail. They are also under the judgment of God, or as Romans 3:9 puts it: "All men, both Jews and Greeks, are under the power of sin." Hence all approaches to God from humanity's side are closed off. This is made clearer in chapter 4: everything depends on faith "in order that the promise may rest on grace," so that no one may boast either in the pursuit of wisdom or in obedience to Law. In sum, the God of the Bible has caught all mankind in its utter ignorance of Him and in its unavailing striving after a god in its own image. And He has said No to the whole enterprise.

The churches have affirmed from the beginning that without faith there is no reaching God from the direction of humanity. On the contrary, it is

God who comes to the world by his actions in the history of Israel and finally in Jesus.

In this revelation, in this progressive salvation-history, He reveals us to ourselves (that we do not know Him and cannot find Him) and He shows Himself as God-for-us in one man at one time in history. He does not reveal Himself as "ground of being," Supreme Being, unmoved mover. Faith and philosophy may meet and agree in these terms, but faith apprehends first the conviction that it is God who acts, who comes among people as a presence in a person. Having first affirmed this, then faith may try to perceive the activity of God behind His masks in nature and history.

There is always a hiddenness of God in His revelation. Granted, reason may have wished God to stand at the top of a heavenly staircase and announce His presence for all to see. But the deeds and word of God find a response only in faith: the God-given ability to see, hear, and perceive; a faith which is not the will to belief, but which will bend the will to obedience in faith. Unfaith, on the other hand, can perfectly well insist that the whole history of Israel and ministry of Jesus bear within themselves the possibility of being interpreted solely as one more religious contrivance of a misguided few. Both Feuerbach and Freud came to just such a conclusion.

The New Testament is emphatic on the matter of revelation and faith. After St. Peter's great confession ("You are the Christ.") in Matthew 16, Jesus says: "You did not learn that from mortal man; it was revealed to you by my heavenly Father." St. Paul is just as unequivocal in his First Letter to the Corinthians: "Has not God made foolish the wisdom of the world? For since, in the wisdom of God, the world did not know God through wisdom, it pleased God through the folly of what we preach to save those who believe." (1:21–22) And again: " 'What no eye has seen, nor ear heard, nor the heart of man conceived, what God has prepared for those who love him', God has revealed to us through the Spirit." (2:9–10)

The churches therefore insist, on the basis of this conviction about revelation and faith, that between this God of the Bible and the humanity that hears no voice in the silence of the universe, there is a chasm only God can overcome. The churches have also insisted that it is to this humanity that a *message*, not an apologetic, has come. And this God makes possible the believing of His own message, to urge that wager (Pascal), or that leap of faith (Kierkegaard), to risk believing in the face of all evidence to the contrary. Such being so, Küng's assertion that critical reason, having examined all the evidence and pursued a logical course, must conclude, "Yes, the God of the Bible exists," is senseless. If critical reason could reach the end Küng says it can, why would it not long since have done so? Why would there be any bother about revelation and faith? It is not easy to say why Küng has written as if he thought he could sidestep such questions.

Morris Kline: Mathematics—
The Loss of Certainty

Charles Van Doren

Charles Van Doren was born and raised in New York City. In 1947, after service in the Air Force, he graduated from St. John's College, Annapolis, Maryland, and two years later took a master's degree in mathematics from Columbia University, where he also received his doctorate in English literature in 1959, and where he taught literature from 1955 to 1959.

In 1965 he joined the Institute for Philosophical Research in Chicago as associate director under Mortimer Adler. Since 1973 he has also been vice-president, editorial, of Encyclopædia Britannica, Inc.

He is the author of *Lincoln's Command* (1957), *The Idea of Progress* (1967), and several children's books. In addition, he was editor, with Clifton Fadiman, of *The American Treasury* (1955); was executive editor of the twenty-volume *Annals of America* (1967), of which he wrote most of the two-volume *Conspectus;* was one of the General Editors of *Makers of America* (ten vols., 1971); edited, with Mortimer Adler, the *Great Treasury of Western Thought* (1977); and was supervisory editor of four volumes of documents on various aspects of American history edited by Wayne Moquin between 1971 and 1976.

With his wife, Geraldine, he maintains a home now in Chicago and another in Cornwall, Connecticut. They have also recently purchased a small house in Cortona, Italy, which they are able to visit occasionally and where they hope eventually to live a portion of each year.

Science, said Erwin Schrödinger in his wonderful little book, *Nature and the Greeks,* is neither more nor less than "looking at the world in the Greek way." By the "world" he meant, of course, the physical world; and he might have added that the scientific instrument the Greeks developed for looking at that world was mathematics.

The Greeks did not invent mathematics, which was handed down to them by pragmatic Babylonians and Egyptians who used it to measure things and make money. (It is still good for that.) But the Greeks saw within this practical device a hidden glory, their revelation of which is probably their greatest achievement.

It took the Greeks less than two centuries to do everything they could with mathematics. They began by sharpening the clumsy tool they inherited from their Ionian forebears. The Babylonians had been content with approximations that would shock a third-grader today, but the Greeks soon put that right, and made more money than anyone ever had, in the process. But they realized, too, that the very mathematics that measured flooded fields and accounted for jars of wine and oil could also define rich harmonies with tautened strings and track the wanderings of the heavenly bodies. There was something here that the Babylonians had never suspected and perhaps would never have been interested in. The physical world, in short, must be mathematical. Which is to say, it exhibits qualities that the Greeks were the first to see in it.

No one is quite sure why, after their spectacular start, the Greeks ceased to mine the mathematical lodes they were the first to open up. According to Schrödinger's theory, a battle was joined between the "moral philosophers," like Plato and Aristotle, and the "philosophical scientists," like Democritus and Leucippus. The former won, this story goes, and burned the books of their conquered foes.[1] It is true enough that almost nothing

---

[1] Curiously, while Schrödinger may in general be right in setting up an opposition between the "moralists" and the "physicists" in Ancient Greece, it does not seem to apply to the greatest of the so-called moralists, namely, Plato and Aristotle. Plato was doubtless influenced by Pythagoras, who certainly believed that the material world is mathematical and that is why we can comprehend it, but he was not, strictly speaking, a Pythagorean. In the algorithm, as it may be called, of the Divided Line (*Republic* [*GBWW,* Vol. 7]), Plato makes clear that mathematical objects have a different order of being from the being of the "real" world (whichever way "real" is interpreted, as meaning on the one hand material, on the other ideal); and this view pervades *The Timaeus* [*GBWW,* Vol. 7] as well, although a careless reader may not see that. Aristotle's conception of the being of mathematical objects, and their relation to the knowable world, was equally subtle and sophisticated, even modern. But Schrödinger would seem to be correct about most of the Greek philosophers who both preceded and followed Plato and Aristotle. And he is surely right in regretting the loss of the many books of Democritus.

survives of the many remarkable writings of the Greek Atomists, but I doubt that this was a mere quarrel among philosphers. A better theory is that the mathematicians themselves had discovered some disturbing news about the world they were looking at—so disturbing they were afraid to go farther.

This news involved irrationals, or quantities that could not be measured in terms of a given unit. The idea that a line drawn innocently in the sun-drenched sand could be so mysteriously unknowable was a shock to the Greek mind and may have conjured up notions of a dark side of the universe corresponding to the dark side of the soul revealed by Euripides in his *Bacchantes**. What disharmony was here, what incomprehensible danger? At any rate, nearly two millennia had to pass before mathematicians again found the courage and skill to probe the dark the Greeks had left behind. The man who did it was Descartes, and he invented a new tool, the crossed lines of so-called Cartesian coordinates.

The thinking behind the invention was more important than the tool itself. Every place (or point) in the real world is *some* place; every point has a definite location. Is there, Descartes wondered, a mathematical analog of that statement? His coordinates provided the answer, as well as—an unexpected bonus—a family of equations that could describe all the lines, both straight and curved, in the world. The equations were so useful, the fact that solving them often resulted in the same irrationals that had troubled the Greeks was ignored. To say nothing of negative roots. What kind of number was −2? Was it a number at all? Some mathematicians said no, and declared all negative roots of equations illegitimate.

Descartes's mathematical universe was static, but it was evident even to him and certainly to those who followed hard upon his achievement that the real quarry was a moving point, not a stationary one. It took only fifty years to trap it, from the publication in 1637 of *The Discourse on Method*† to the appearance in 1687 of Newton's *Principia*‡. But the mysteries were growing at an equally rapid rate. First there was gravitation itself—the strange power that, in Dante's great phrase, "moves the Sun and the other Stars." It is hardly more revealing to say, as Newton did:

$$F = G \frac{mM}{r^2}$$

which, when translated, states that the force of attraction between any two masses m and M, which are separated by a distance r, decreases by a predictable amount as the distance increases. The key to the equation is the symbol G, which stands for gravity. G is a constant; it is the same number no matter what m and M and r may be.

---

* *GBWW*, Vol. 5.
† *GBWW*, Vol. 31.
‡ *GBWW*, Vol. 34.

Gravity may be, and probably is, physically unknowable. But an ordinary number can be assigned to it, can do its work, as it were, in an equation. Is this not very mysterious?

If so, the puzzlement was swallowed up in an even greater mystery, that of the instrument itself that Newton (and Leibniz) had invented to trap the moving particle. This was the integral and differential calculus, a wonderful example of the strange power of mathematics to accomplish more than has been expected of it. Newton had to calculate the changing force on a moving body at various orbital points, and he did this by employing smaller and smaller units of curved lines and planes. It is worthwhile seeing the method he used, which is apparent in this example. Suppose the problem (one of integration) is to find the area under a curve, AB.

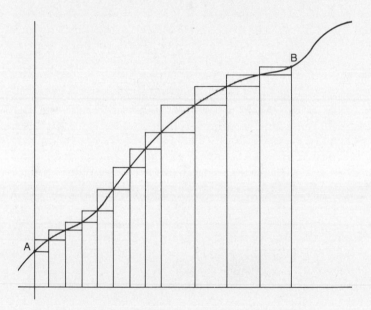

The sum of all the narrow rectangles *beneath* the curve is obviously less than the desired area; the sum of all the narrow rectangles extending *above* the curve is obviously greater. The desired result lies in between the two sums. If the rectangles are made narrower, the difference between the two sums decreases; eventually, when the rectangles have been made "infinitely" narrow, the difference between the two sums disappears, and either sum is the area under the curve.

But what does "infinitely" narrow mean? (The analog in differential calculus is "infinitely" short curved lines, lines so short that they are "practically straight.") Newton himself was not terribly concerned about the question; curiously, he almost alone was more worried about the existential, not to say theological, problem of gravitation. But for a century and more, mathematicians struggled with the puzzle of these infinitesimals.[2]

Newton may have been right to ignore the technical difficulties in the theory of limits that he had created for his pygmy followers. At any rate, it would have been difficult for any man to avoid being swayed by the adulation accorded to Newton, the most admired intellectual that ever was.

> Nature and Nature's *Laws* lay hid in Night;
> God said, Let Newton be, and there was Light.

That was the sort of thing they said about him, even while he lived, even to his face. In short, he seemed to have confirmed that the Greeks were right all along: physical nature really is mathematical, and mathematical reasoning is, or leads to, the highest and most dependable truth.

The Age of Reason never doubted that. But the mathematicians had sowed some Dragon's Teeth. The bone of contention was Euclid's famous parallel postulate. Euclid had been curiously indecisive about this postulate, which seems to say simply that parallel lines never meet. Mathematicians around the time of the French Revolution—perhaps there was something in the air—began to wonder whether they ever did, or rather, what you would have in the way of a geometry if you assumed that parallel lines did meet. In fact, you got something very interesting, or rather two things, two different non-Euclidean geometries: hyperbolic (or Lobachevskian) and elliptic (or Riemannian)—to give the discoverers their due. The old, standard Euclidean geometry we all learned (more or less) in school is then reduced to being parabolic metric geometry, a very special case of a much more general situation.

What were these new geometries? Did they make any sense at all? Actually, they make excellent sense. Hyperbolic geometry, in which parallel lines always diverge, and therefore do not meet even "at infinity," and in which the sum of the angles of every triangle is less than 180°, is the geometry of certain surfaces with double curvature, like a saddle. Elliptic geometry, in which parallel lines always converge and meet twice, and in which the sum of the angles of every triangle is greater than 180°, is the geometry of a sphere, such as the Earth on which we live.

Saddles may not convince anyone that non-Euclidean geometry is a really serious proposition, but the Earth ought to. Riemann pointed out, in fact, that mathematically speaking the generalized surface of a sphere is indistin-

---

[2] Infinitesimals were banned from mathematics at the beginning of the nineteenth century by Cauchy and others who developed a rigorous theory of limits to justify the calculus. More recently, a slightly playful theory, called nonstandard analysis, has employed infinitesimals once more. A positive infinitesimal is defined as a number smaller than any positive real number but larger than zero; a negative infinitesimal is larger than any negative real number but smaller than zero. Using this absolutely inconceivable class of numbers, the basic theorems of the calculus can be proved, and the results are the same as in standard analysis. This also proves that if you give a mathematician an inch, he is very likely to take a mile or even more.

guishable from a Euclidean plane; it is impossible to tell, from the mathematics alone, which surface you are on, a plane or a sphere. This is so, at least, if you allow one assumption about the Euclidean plane: namely, that all parallel lines do meet, in either direction, if they are extended indefinitely (as far as you please). And why should this not be assumed? It is "obviously" true of any two parallel lines in nature, that they meet in the farthest distance; we can "see" it. Again, it seems that the Greeks were right, and the world out there is truly, deeply, credibly mathematical.

The crisis in mathematical thought

Many of the best nineteenth-century mathematicians were not comfortable about what these new developments had revealed about their science. It almost seemed that you could choose whichever geometry was most convenient (this was Poincaré's view) for a particular situation and not have to worry about whether it was "true." But if that was a useful way to proceed, it called in question the old certainty that had surrounded mathematical reasoning. Certainty had been the hallmark of mathematics, the quality that distinguished it from all other sciences, the virtue and power that made it their queen. What would life as a commoner be like?

There were many reasons to question the certainty. First, there was the emergence of non-Euclidean geometry itself. The first shocks were overcome by the efforts of mathematicians who stepped back and viewed the situation from a wider perspective, seeing the various geometries as special cases of one great science, which might be called projective geometry. At the same time, others were busy trying to convert all of geometry into numerical analysis, because numbers, unlike points, lines, planes, were as dependable and certain as they had always been.

But were they? First, there were the irrational numbers—numbers like the square root of 2. Now this number is not definite. It is impossible to write it down in decimal form—although one can of course write it: $\sqrt{2}$—as though that solved the problem! As such, the expression works perfectly well in many situations; for example, one can say that

$$\sqrt{2} \cdot \sqrt{2} = 2.$$

That is precise enough, but it masks the fact that we are claiming the product of two numbers we cannot write is a number we can.

Next, there were negative numbers. These are all very well when they mean, as they often do, "take away" (a certain positive magnitude) from a (larger) positive magnitude, as in the expression $4 - 2 = 2$. In a sense the expression "-2" in that equation is not a negative number; it merely denotes an operation that we can perform on apples or oranges or whatever. The trouble is we cannot leave it at that. Negative numbers are so useful in so many situations that they take on a life of their own, as in $2 - 4 =$

— 2. They become (a mathematical statement) *real*. We cannot do without them.

Then there was that curious entity *i*, the square root of minus one. There is "obviously" no such thing, since the rules of arithmetic require that any negative number multiplied by itself is a positive number, so that no negative number can have an even-numbered root. Again, however, we cannot live without roots of negative numbers. They are essential in a myriad of mathematical situations, and in physical situations as well. (The theory of vectors, without which we have no physics, is expressed in terms of so-called complex numbers, numbers of the form $a+bi$, where a and b are ordinary real numbers—integers, or fractions, or irrationals, or whatever—but i is the square of minus one.) Without them the majority of equations are unsolvable, or solvable only in part. Worst of all, perhaps, there are entire domains of possible mathematics that would have to be discarded if complex numbers were banned. The tyranny of the possible in mathematics is almost absolute. Once a door has been opened, no matter what the perils that may lie behind it, it can never again be closed. Or if it is closed, it is never locked, with the key thrown away; someone knows where the key is hidden.

The worst was still to come. It emerged from the work of Georg Cantor, who early became obsessed with the problems—and opportunities—of mathematical infinity. Infinity for centuries had been a kind of Philosopher's Stone of mathematicians, to be used only in the last extremity (when more normal devices did not suffice), and avoided like the plague when possible. Thus infinitesimals had been used by Newton to construct his System of the World, but they were expunged from analysis as soon as this could be done, a century later, by men like Gauss and Cauchy. Division by zero—which produces an infinite result—was prohibited even in grammar school, and phrases like "as small as you please" or "as large as you please" or "as close as you please to a limit *l*" were invariably taught to young mathematicians. But infinity is not so easily got rid of, as Cantor knew.

Instead of avoiding the beast, he sought it out and tracked it to its lair. His first discovery was that all infinities are not alike. There is a class of mathematical things that is infinite, true, but not as infinite as another class of mathematical things. The first class—which he named aleph-null (the first letter of the Hebrew alphabet with a little zero attached)—comprises many sets of familiar entities. Among them are the integers, both the positive integers—from 1 to ∞—and the negative *plus* the positive integers. Both these sets belong to the same aleph-null class, so they have the same number. There are just as many positive and negative integers as there are positive integers.

In fact, there are just as many positive integers that are the squares of positive integers as there are positive integers. That is, the following sequences have the same number of terms:

$$1, 2, 3, \ 4, \ 5, \ldots$$
$$1, 4, 9, 16, 25, \ldots$$

The reason is obvious: there is one and only one square for every integer, no more, no less. That is the first kind of puzzle that Cantor set us to live with.

The integers are one thing: what about fractions? "Obviously," there are many more fractions than there are integers, since there is an infinite number of fractions in the interval between the integers 1 and 2; and in the sequence of integers there is an infinite number of such intervals, each fillable by an infinity of fractions. So it would seem; but in fact it is not so, because the fractions, the vast infinity of fractions, can be counted; that is, they can be put into a one-to-one relation with the integers, and if so, there are no more fractions than there are integers, nor any fewer.[3]

The fractions, or rational numbers, are, as mathematicians say, denumerably infinite—which only means they can be counted or put in a one-to-one relation with the positive integers; or, as they also say, the set of rational numbers is well-ordered. Question: is every (infinite) set well-ordered? Is there some ingenious way to count every infinite set, as Cantor found the way to count the fractions?

Unfortunately, no—as Cantor also proved. In fact, there is a non-denumerably infinite set of numbers lurking in that very interval between 1 and 2 in which we were able to count an infinite number of fractions. These are

---

[3] Here is the way to count the fractions, as Cantor taught us. Create an array; then start at the corner and count down, in a zigzag. The array includes all the fractions, but you can keep on counting them forever, and you can count them all if you do go on forever.

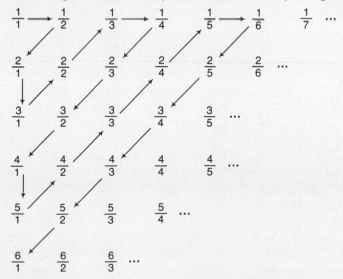

the *real* numbers, which include not only the rationals but also the irrational numbers—the roots to which we have referred several times before, and which had early troubled the Greeks.

Consider carefully this interval between 1 and 2. In the interval there are an infinite number of fractions. These are countable. For every one of those fractions between 1 and 2 there is a square root of it that also belongs in the interval. The square roots of the fractions between 1 and 2 are therefore also countable, being one-for-one. But there are an infinite number of roots of every fraction between 1 and 2—an 11th root of 7/4, for example, or the 4,276th root of 99/50—and the entire array cannot be counted. It is not just that we have not yet found the way; Cantor proved that it can't be done. Thus the class of real numbers deserves another number besides aleph-null, and Cantor named it C.

"C" stands for "continuum." The real numbers constitute a continuous sequence, between 1 and 2, or between 0 and infinity, or between negative infinity through zero and on to positive infinity (the same number, C, applies to each of these infinite sets). These numbers are compact. No other numbers can be inserted between them, as in fact irrationals—an infinity of them—can be inserted in between *any* two rational numbers. The real numbers are as compact, or continuous, as the points on a line (C is also the number of points on a line, short or long or infinite in length, straight or curved in any fantastic, twisted manner possible or desired).

Here it seemed that Cantor was not just playing pleasant games with numbers. Some of his mathematical contemporaries did not like what he was saying and attempted to belittle it; some laymen were shocked at what they felt was almost blasphemy. But most mathematicians, then and now, are aware that it is no longer possible to ban infinity from mathematics, or even to use it only *in extremis*. Infinity is at the heart of mathematical thinking. It cannot go on without it.

It cannot go on very well with it, either—and that has brought about a crisis of mathematical thought in our time. This is the burden of Morris Kline's excellent volume, *Mathematics—The Loss of Certainty*.[4] Kline's history of mathematics is much more detailed than the one I have presented here, and it brings the story down to our own time, to the paradoxes and problems presented to modern thinkers by such men as Russell, Hilbert, and, especially, Kurt Gödel, the Austrian logician who threw the ultimate monkey wrench into the machine of axiomatic reasoning in 1931 when he proved that no axiomatic system is independent, that is, can depend for its consistency only on itself. The reasons for this go beyond the scope of this essay, but they are educed with full clarity by Morris Kline.

One response to the crisis has been an attempt, also described with thoroughness by Kline, to shore upthe fundamentals of mathematics by a

---

[4] *Mathematics—The Loss of Certainty*, by Morris Kline (New York: Oxford University Press, 1980.)

number of methods. Several twentieth-century schools of mathematical fundamentalists have emerged; I will do no more than name them here, as to explain the detailed differences among them would require as many pages as Kline devotes to the matter. Suffice it to say that there have developed over the past century logicism, intuitionism, formalism, and set-theorism, as separate and conflicting schools of fundamentalist thought, and a goodly number of minor modifications and offshoots of each school, as well.

Despite all this activity, none of the programs designed by these schools to establish a solid foundation under the edifice of mathematical thought has turned out to be entirely satisfactory, even to the adherents of the various schools themselves. Bertrand Russell lived long enough to see his and Whitehead's logicism fall into a kind of limbo of belief, in which even Russell would not support it with enthusiam. David Hilbert, probably the greatest pure mathematician of our time, carried to his grave severe doubts about the formalist program he had proposed as early as 1900 and on which he worked, off and on, until his death. The limitations of the set-theoretic program are apparent to all, at the same time that all admit its rich contributions to the total view of mathematics. The Intuitionists, who began by proclaiming a pox on all the opposing schools, are probably today still the most doggedly determined. But their minimal program requires the reworking in extremely difficult and painful ways of almost all classical mathematics, and most mathematicians have simply ignored them.

Indeed, the deliberate avoidance of the crisis by the great majority of mathematicians in our time is the main complaint of Morris Kline. Certainty has been lost; none deny this; but who, he asks, seems to care? However, if mathematical reasoning is not certain, in the old sense; if its underpinnings are rickety and undependable; if the choice of geometry is a mere matter of convenience, and if the number system is beset with logical paradoxes and problems so severe that there is even doubt whether one really *knows* that $2 + 2 = 4$, what then has mathematics become? What kind of mental activity is it? Does it deserve the respect and admiration it still demands from nonmathematicians? Finally, what has happened to the old Greek idea that the world, *because* it is mathematical, is knowable by science?

Mathematics and modern science

Some years ago I made the acquaintance of a rather touching chimpanzee named Mary. Mary was an experimental subject in a laboratory at John Hopkins University, and the chief experimenter, whose name was Jack, enjoyed Mary's company and half-adopted her. Mary thus spent a good deal of time in Jack's living room. I met her there one afternoon.

Jack was sitting on his sofa and Mary was sitting on the floor at his feet, adoring. Suddenly Mary reached out and pulled the ends of Jack's shoelaces, untying them. Jack smiled at me. "Now watch what happens," he said. Mary turned away, frowning, but then turned back, took the laces clumsily between her thick fingers, twisted and turned them on Jack's shoes, and finally laid them down in imitation of the way they had looked when they were tied.

"She can't tie them," said Jack. "But she never stops hoping that when I move my foot, they'll stay the way she put them." He shook his feet, and the laces hung from his shoes. Mary frowned again.

This story suggests a basic truth about mathematics. Let me try to explain by describing three moments in its relatively recent history.

The first example takes us back to the 1860s. Owing to the experimental work of Faraday, the scientific world was fascinated by the prospects, as well as the mysteries, of electricity. At the same time, effective work was being done on magnetism. The result of these efforts, undertaken in isolation, was the discovery of a few mathematical laws about the behavior of each of the two phenomena, considered separately. But no one had yet put them together when the brilliant young Scottish physicist James Clerk Maxwell set his mind to the problem.

It is important to understand just what problem it was that Maxwell set his mind to. Maxwell was a very different man from Faraday. Faraday was a pragmatist with rather dim ideas, but a great ability to follow out his hunches in the laboratory. Maxwell was an extremely acute mathematician. It was the mathematics of electricity and of magnetism that troubled him. Mathematically, there seemed to be a connection, but the fit was not quite right. If he were to *assume* a connection, and array the equations all together, and add a certain term, the thing would come out, the mathematical problem was solved. But this was not only mathematics he was doing. These equations supposedly described, or dealt with, the real world. To what then did the curious added term refer? Without the term the mathematics did not work; the term was needed; but if needed, then it must have an analog in reality. What was it?

The genius of Clerk Maxwell was not only his mathematical ability. It was also the imaginative leap he took in supposing that the added term referred to and helped describe the characteristics of a *field* of magnetic force. From a source of electricity, he concluded, an electromagnetic field or electromagnetic wave must spread out into the surrounding space. This had to be so, because the mathematics required it.

How curious! There was no physical evidence of the field of force, and to this day, strictly speaking, none has been found. Yet no one to this day has questioned Maxwell's mathematics, either. The electromagnetic field equations are considered to be in the class, as a contribution to physics, of Newton's equations of planetary motion and Dirac's equations of quantum mechanics.

And not only are the equations a major contribution to theoretical physics. If, on the basis of Maxwell's mathematics, we assume the existence of an electromagnetic field, we find we can make real, practical things like telephones, phonographs, televisions, and computers.

Question: If, in the course of the feverish efforts of the fundamentalists to erect solid underpinnings of mathematics that make it "true," it is found that the Maxwell equations are false, will our televisions self-destruct?

Second question: What is the difference between the chimpanzee who arranges the shoelaces as they ought to be, and then frowns when they do not stay put—and the mathematician who inserts the missing term, and then smiles when his equations come out?

The second exemplary moment occurred a generation later. The physicist Max Planck was trying to understand some curious results of radiating a "black box," a body that absorbs all the radiation that falls on it. As the amount of radiation on the box continuously increased, the amount of radiant energy emitted by the box increased not continuously but in jumps. This made Planck's equations unsatisfactory; they did not come out. But if he inserted a constant term in the equations, which he called h, the equations did come out.

What then did h signify or refer to in the real world? Not a field of force, but what Planck called a "quantum of action," an irreducible unit of energy such that when less than a certain amount of energy was input the box would continue to emit a constant output, but when the input was increased beyond that certain amount the output would jump.

Some of the most imaginative concepts in twentieth-century physics have been developed to explain h, the tiny constant that Planck had to put in his equations to make them work. There is no physical evidence of the quantum of energy, but when you assume it, you can make atomic bombs. Perhaps they are physical enough.

Again the monkey-mathematician has placed the laces on the shoe and seen them stick.

The third moment occurred a few years later, after Einstein had published his astonishing paper on the special theory of relativity in 1905. He had immediately set to work on a more general theory, but he lacked the mathematical skills to make the equations come out. He turned to his friend Hermann Minkowski, who possessed the mathematics Einstein lacked. Minkowski realized that if Einstein's field equations were converted to homogeneous equations, an interesting physical interpretation would become possible. Homogeneous equations (to make a long story very short) are obtained by dividing all terms in the original equations by a new term, t; and t could stand, said Minkowski, for time. The x's, y's, and z's of the original equations then became the three spatial coordinates, and t the time coordinate of a four-dimensional space-time continuum.

The extraordinary thing about this is that the conversion of standard equations to homogeneous ones is something that practically any German schoolboy could have done in 1905. It is merely a technical conversion of equations from one *form* to another; no change has occurred in the values or, one would think, in the meaning or significance of the equations. But mathematics is often more than it seems. This formal conversion allowed Einstein to proceed in his work, and to develop first the general theory of relativity, and then his unified field theory.

That was perhaps the most triumphant monkey trick of all.

The real crisis of mathematics in our time is that no one, least of all any mathematician, is able to explain why these tricks work.

Work they do. We have telephones and televisions. We have atomic bombs. Einstein's predictions of physical phenomena were confirmed. Why?

There are many answers, none of them satisfactory. Morris Kline presents a number of them at the end of his book. He discusses the views of thinkers such as Kant and Poincaré, Eddington and Jeans, Birkhoff and Einstein, Duhem and Herman Weyl. All are struggling with the great question suggested by the old Greek idea. If the world is essentially mathematical, then there is no wonder that mathematics is able to deal with it, to describe its occurrences, to predict its events. But is that so? Why should the world be mathematical? Is God, after all, a mathematician? Is there a God?

The failure of modern mathematics

These questions are so important that it ought to be the first obligation of every mathematician to struggle to answer them. They are so difficult that most mathematicians are unwilling to try.

There are probably more mathematicians alive today than have lived throughout history. The profession is thriving. Enormous numbers of papers are published, degrees are obtained, courses are offered. Mathematics, like almost every other scientific discipline, has become subdivided so that it is unlikely that any two mathematicians, meeting by chance, can understand each other once they stray off the unimportant matters they have in common. What they consider their important work they share with only a few others. And for the most part they do not care, Morris Kline tells us, whether what they are doing is of any practical use.

Mathematics, faced with a crisis in its fundamental thinking and taking advantage, as other disciplines have also, of the proliferation of academic institutions today, has therefore fundamentally changed its character. It is no longer the queen of the sciences. Queens only have real power as long as they are considered to be really useful. Physicists and chemists and engineers today no longer consider most mathematicians to be partners in the great task of understanding and controlling nature. Mathematicians have become brilliant dilettantes.

Curiously, the same sort of thing seems to have happened to mathematics that happened to painting when photography was invented, in the nineteenth century. For many centuries prior to that painting had possessed a pragmatic as well as aesthetic function. Painters were the recorders of people, places, and events; every soldier, for example, went into battle with a miniature portrait of his loved one, done in oils and carefully framed. This function of painting was soon taken over—although not completely—by photography, which could record real things more accurately and more cheaply. Painting was therefore freed from its roots and allowed to soar. The ultimate result was abstract impressionism, where the painting itself is said to be the "object"; the painting is not *of* anything outside itself.

Similar things have happened to music and even to literature in our time, perhaps under the influence of painting, perhaps for other reasons. Both these ancient arts, which served practical as well as aesthetic ends until about 1900, have severed their ties and been allowed to soar without restraint and, one is tempted to say, without responsibility. Is it because journalism has displaced the pragmatic function that literature used to possess, and electronic music displaced the pragmatic, down-to-earth entertainment aspect of the older music? Perhaps.

The world may be no worse off for lacking objective fine art. At various times in the past, painting and sculpture and music and even literature have become more abstract and then less so, without real harm being done. Recently, the pendulum seems, in the case of painting at least, to have begun to swing the other way, and paintings that look like things have begun, still only tentatively, to be again admired. The novel is not as dead as it was claimed to be a generation ago, nor drama either. The fine arts will probably, perhaps even certainly, survive their being cut off from their mundane roots.

The problems facing mathematics are apparently more serious. There are questions that need to be answered, there is important work that needs to be done. But before it can be well done, before the best mathematical minds can set themselves to it, we have to know whether the world is really mathematical. Or at least we have to know what *kind* of answer to that question would be satisfactory. As yet we do not even know that. Instead, the mathematicians who might be able to answer it or at least give us insight about the answer devote their time to their new publications, and the more of these the better.

It seems that the answer, however complex it may turn out to be, will not involve a banning of the imagination from mathematics. Poetry, the best poets have always known, was never purely imagination or purely reality. The true poet is not, Shakespeare said only as a joke, one who

> gives to airy nothing
> A local habitation and a name.

Poetry that has no basis in reality is never of the best; but poetry that has no touch of the imagination is not so, either. How the two work, both in cooperation and in opposition, is the wonder that poets know. As much could be said about the other fine arts.

Mathematics is not, or is not only, a fine art. But it has some of the characteristics of such an art, and it should not forget this. Perhaps the poets can teach the mathematicians a useful lesson in reminding them that mathematics, like poetry, is a rationalized fiction, a constant interplay between appearance and reality, a never-ending conflict between fact and dream. If this is accepted and believed by the best mathematicians, the artful science—or is it a scientific art?—has the potential of becoming once again a queen.[5]

---

[5] Anyone who is interested in the history of mathematics and in the relation between that history and the history of Western thought in general should read Morris Kline's fine book. But the interested reader should not stop there. No discussion of the crisis of mathematical thought in our time would be complete without reference to one of the most remarkable books of the twentieth century, Scott Buchanan's *Poetry and Mathematics* [*Great Ideas Today* 1974]. In this small volume Buchanan brought to our attention the inextricable interconnections between the two disciplines of his title and showed how mathematics is more like poetry than most people would have thought, and vice versa. Mathematics probably has no chance to emerge from its current doldrums without general recognition of these connections.

Ashley Montagu (ed.):
Sociobiology Examined

John Van Doren

Like his brother, Charles, born and raised in New York City, John Van
Doren graduated from St. John's College, Annapolis, Maryland, in 1947.
Thereafter he studied history at Columbia University, where he got his
doctorate in 1952.

Beginning in 1956, he taught history and English literature at Brandeis
University, was subsequently lecturer in English at Smith College and
assistant professor of English at Boston University.

In 1969 he was managing editor of a 20,000 volume collection of
writings on American history published on microfiche by Library
Resources, Inc., in Chicago, and the following year was made executive
editor of *The Great Ideas Today.* He is also a fellow of the Institute for
Philosophical Research.

His wife is Mira Jedwabnik, an artist and entrepreneur known
especially for her large-scale enamels commissioned for elevator doors
and murals in numerous hotels and office buildings in the United States
and elsewhere. They live in Evanston, Illinois, have a home also in
Connecticut, and another in New York City.

The subject of this book is a familiar one to readers of *The Great Ideas Today*. It was discussed first by William Gorman in the issue for 1979, reviewing *On Human Nature*, by Edward O. Wilson, himself the chief theorist and principal expounder of sociobiology, who in an earlier work by that name claimed to be offering what he called "a new synthesis" of disciplines in the social and biological sciences; and both Wilson and his new science were taken up a second time by Daniel Bell in "The Social Sciences Since the Second World War, Part Two," which appeared in *The Great Ideas Today* last year. Now comes an opportunity for further comment with the appearance of a collection of essays by representatives of various disciplines, chiefly the social and biological sciences—some fifteen of them in all—who declare their opposition, in varying degrees, to the claims of sociobiology, and whose writings on the subject are presented by Ashley Montagu, a distinguished anthropologist who contributes an introduction to the volume.

Such a collection of writings allows us to confront sociobiology rather more directly than either Mr. Gorman or Professor Bell was able to do. The former spoke as a humanist well read in philosophy and religion who could discuss the "impact" that Professor Wilson said sociobiology, as "a truly evolutionary explanation of human behavior," must have on those subjects —and concluded that the impact was slight, at least as far as Professor Wilson, an avowed "scientific materialist," had in his own writings managed to achieve. Professor Bell, for his part, was concerned with the reaction to Professor Wilson's claims in learned circles, particularly the social sciences, over the past decade—a reaction, he said, that had made sociobiology "the storm center of a controversy so vehement as to earn a place in the annals of intellectual history"—and concluded that much of the controversy had been unnecessary, derived as he thought it largely was from propositions misconceived or ideologically motivated. But in neither case did the issue that sociobiology might be thought to raise seem to have been fairly joined, and nothing more than provisional judgments could be offered with respect to it.

Whatever judgments may be arrived at here, the issue itself *is* joined, at least up to a point, in this collection of writings by scientists who challenge sociobiology on its own ground, as an explanation of human behavior—this being understood, it is true, in terms that do not extend very far toward encompassing the speculative and religious activity that was Mr. Gorman's

concern. And where the issue is not joined, it is not from ideological prejudice, nor is it from a failure to engage the topics within Mr. Gorman's range,
but because the philosophical—or, if you please, the scientific—assumptions of both the sociobiologists and the social and biological scientists are
too narrow to allow it. To which should be added that, so far as a settlement
of the disagreements involved depends upon matters of fact that biology is
still investigating, the salient questions must in any case remain open, it
being impossible to say with respect to such matters which among alternative explanations of them is more likely to be right.

The challenge of sociobiology

To recapitulate briefly what the claims of sociobiology are, at least as set
forth by Professor Wilson, they may be said to include these propositions:
(1) that the fundamental patterns of human behavior have been genetically
determined not only in the tendencies that used to be called instincts but
in many social manifestations as well, (2) that the varieties of human social
behavior are the result of adaptive strategies that, while more elaborate
than those of other species, are not essentially different from them, (3) that
where such strategies have established cultural patterns which are at odds
with the demands of evolutionary biology, the patterns must sooner or later
give way to such demands, and (4) that an understanding of how this can
be so is provided by a unified theory embracing observations drawn from
ethology, genetics, ecology, and other biologically grounded sciences.

In Professor Wilson's own words, "the question of interest is no longer
whether human social behavior is genetically determined, it is to what
extent. The accumulated evidence for a large hereditary component is
more detailed and compelling than most persons, including even geneticists, realize. I will go further: it already is decisive." Again, while "the
specific details of culture are nongenetic," and can be "decoupled from the
biological system and arranged beside it," yet culture will be defeated if it
actually tries to escape biology: "there is a limit ... beyond which biological
evolution will begin to pull cultural evolution back to itself." In the same
vein: "The genes hold culture on a leash. The leash is very long, but
inevitably values will be constrained in accordance with their effects upon
the human gene pool." And, finally, with these matters established, "the
humanities and social sciences shrink to specialized branches of biology,"
while "one of the functions of sociobiology" is "to reformulate the foundations of the social sciences" so that they become "truly biologized," making
possible a new science that will amount to "the sociobiology of a single
species."

Professor Wilson is not the only protagonist of sociobiology, of course.
Another writer who has done much to promulgate the science is David
Barash, whose *Sociobiology and Behavior* (1977) is among the better-known

books on the subject. Barash speaks there of "an ultimate biological reason" for cultural behavior, of the ways in which, as he views them, "our deep evolutionary 'sweet-receptors' predominate over our rationality," and of his belief that what he calls "the whole range of characteristic disaffections with modern life" are, in man, the legacy of his attempt to turn himself away from the demands—aggressive, self-serving, violent—of his biological nature.

Along with Barash should be listed R. L. Trivers, who in a number of influential articles has propounded the notion (as Wilson has himself) of "inclusive fitness"—the phenomenon whereby organisms endanger or sacrifice themselves for others of their species which are not close kin when there is some chance of reciprocity—which is thought to be instructive as a biological explanation of human social behavior. There is also W. D. Hamilton, who in some influential articles has worked out the mathematics of natural selection in a way that seems to favor sociobiological assumptions, and there is Richard Dawkins, whose book *The Selfish Gene* (1976) is a popularization of sociobiological thinking.

As Barash, Trivers, Hamilton, and Dawkins are often mentioned by the contributors to this collection, so are the names of certain ethologists whose work is perhaps the principal tributary to the synthesis that sociobiology has attempted to bring about. Among them are Nikolaas Tinbergen, Konrad Lorenz, and Iranaeus Eibl-Eibesfeldt. All have reported on studies of animal behavior and its implications for human beings. In Tinbergen's opinion, human behavior "is not qualitatively different from animals," being characterized by certain innate drives, of which the strongest are aggression, sex, foraging, and parental care. Like Barash, he believes that "there are good grounds for the conclusion that man's limited behavioral adjustability has been outpaced by the culturally determined changes in his social environment, and that this is why man is now a misfit in his own society." This idea is shared by Konrad Lorenz, who has suggested in a widely read book, *On Aggression* (1966), that human social instincts and psychological inhibitions "could not keep pace with the rapid developments of traditional culture, particularly material culture," and that men suffer profound psychological disorders as a result.

Less skeptical of cultural controls is Eibl-Eibesfeldt, who believes that "drives, learning dispositions, and innate releasing mechanisms, can influence man's inclinations in a quite decisive way," but who argues that merely because a disposition is inherited does not mean "it is not amenable to conditioning, nor must it be regarded as natural in the sense that it is still adaptive." Eibl-Eibesfeldt suggests that cooperative behavior among men is quite as much an innate characteristic as any other kind.

To lump the names of these writers is not to insist that they are without their differences. But most of them may be said to subscribe to the fundamental assumptions of sociobiology, which, as an article by Karl Peter and Nicholas Petryszak in the present collection puts it, may be summed up by saying that the "behavior patterns of all living systems are adaptive in an evolutionary sense," and that evolution is the "master paradigm for the analysis of all the life processes." By virtue of their belief in these propositions, all sociobiologists may be said to subscribe to the notion that they are at least in sight of something that Jerome H. Barkow, another contributor here, calls "a new theory of human nature."

The response of the behavioral scientists

Some of the contributors to Professor Montagu's volume oppose not only the assertions of the sociobiologists but take issue as well with the claims of ethologists and geneticists that are accepted by sociobiology as tributary to its synthesis. Among such claims are those arising from studies of animal behavior done over the past generation by ethologists such as Lorenz and described in popular books by Desmond Morris and Robert Ardrey. Their depiction of animal behavior, particularly aggressive behavior, has been taken over by sociobiology as an indication of similar propensities in human beings—where the ethologists have not suggested a connection themselves.

Citing Lorenz to the effect that human social behavior "is still subject to all the laws prevailing in all phylogenetically adapted instinctive behavior," and such remarks of Ardrey's as that "man is a predator with a natural instinct to kill with a weapon," Michael Simon observes that "there is in these accounts a definite undercurrent that suggests that people do what they do . . . because of internal forces that we have all inherited from our remote animal ancestors and which cannot easily be resisted." This is very different, Simon contends, from merely observing that "we are more like animals than we thought we were"; it implies the existence of a determining evolutionary pattern in human beings, a conclusion that is not "warranted by the evidence ethologists have [actually] presented or are ever likely to turn up."

Simon is joined here by S. L. Washburn, who questions whether much can be learned from human beings in the way that human ethologists attempt to do, as if it were impossible to talk to them, and as if their behavior were not affected by the workings of the human cortex. "Human ethology," Washburn writes, "might be defined as the science that pretends humans cannot speak."

In Professor Montagu's collection, objections are made also by Mary Midgley, James C. King, Steven Rose, and others to the genetics of such a writer as Dawkins, whose *The Selfish Gene*, though a work of popularization, has incensed the social scientists and embarrassed the biologists with its depiction of genes as self-serving entities directing human behavior to their advantage. This is a conception as difficult to reconcile with contemporary understanding of what genes actually are and how they function as it is with human behavior as such, for the unselfish aspects of which it is unable to account. It is with Dawkins especially in mind that King characterizes socio-biology as "a shocking attempt to ensnare us all in a set of rules of behavior . . . endowed with a pseudo-scientific apotheosis," constituting "a jerry-built doctrine . . . compounded of old hat genetics that current research has already rendered obsolete," and "sophomorically cynical interpretations of social relations . . ."

The conclusions of Hamilton, Barash, and others whose accounts of kin selection, which are fundamental to sociobiology, and which are based upon a mathematics of heredity, are also questioned—by Washburn—in this volume. Kin selection is the term used to reconcile what biologists call altruistic behavior with the workings of natural selection, which presumably dictate against self-sacrifice in the struggle for existence. Such behavior—whereby certain birds, for example, will call attention to themselves in the presence of a predator so as to protect their young—was difficult for Darwin to explain and for a long time presented problems to evolutionary biology. But evolutionary biology did not suppose it had to account for truly social behavior of the kind that human beings manifest, since it accepted this as consistent with the development of a creature—that is, man—who was so different from other organisms as to be behaviorally unique.

Sociobiology *is* able to account for such behavior, or thinks it is—by extrapolation, it is true, from the behavior of organisms much less complex than man—because what actually happens when the bird sacrifices itself for its young is that it ensures survival not of itself but of its genes, and that is perceived as the driving force behind such acts. Or, to put it another way, the willingness, the capacity, to survive genetically is held to be precisely what natural selection selects. What seems a contradiction to the survival of the fittest is thus perfectly consistent with it, according to the sociobiologists, and—to jump at once to an oversimplified conclusion—human social behavior need therefore no longer be taken as evidence of the difference of man but can be seen as a manifestation of the evolutionary pattern common to all species.

Washburn's objection is that the underlying calculations are false. "The fundamental calculus in sociobiology is based on the genetic resemblance between relatives," he notes, the idea being that "parents share one half of their genes with an offspring, and there is less sharing with more distant relatives." In fact, such a rate of diminution only undermines the claims of the sociobiologists, he suggests, for the number of shared genes diminishes far more narrowly than the range of human social behavior extends. But, Washburn contends, all that is beside the point. "This whole calculus upon which sociobiology is based is grossly misleading," he argues:

> A parent does not share one half of the genes with its offspring; the offspring shares one half of the genes in which the parents differ. If the parents are homozygous for a gene, obviously all offspring will inherit that gene. The issue then becomes, How many shared genes are there within a species such as Homo sapiens?

Washburn cites evidence to indicate that, as the proportion of shared genes between men and chimpanzees is as high as 99 percent, men themselves must share even more, perhaps fifty times as many more. In fact, as each human being shares nearly all his genes with every other human being, those he shares only with his close relatives are at most a minuscule proportion of his biological makeup—which makes nonsense of kin selection as the governing principle of human social behavior.

However, it is with Wilson and others such as Trivers and Dawkins whose names have become synonymous with sociobiology that the contributors here are chiefly at odds. Nearly every article in the collection finds ground of opposition to the first of these, and many do so to the others. What is almost a litany begins with Professor Montagu's assertion that, while Wilson writes well and "has produced a great deal of original work based on his researches which are of fundamental importance," yet "his overweening fault is biologism, his conviction that since humans are animals who have evolved in much the same ways as other animals they must be explicable in much the same way." Mary Midgley calls Wilson "actually right in thinking that attention to evolution can in a special way improve our understanding of culture," but she contends that "because he overstates his claim, this vital but relatively modest point is lost." Karl Peter and Nicholas Petryszak suggest that the "biological boundaries" that Wilson perceives as limiting human culture are "vague and unspecific." James C. King, quoting Wilson to the effect that "sociobiology, if coupled with neurophysiology, might . . . explain the reasons why we make certain moral choices instead of others at particular times," notes the implication that punishment for deviant behavior could be sanctioned by some supposed imperative in the genetic material. King protests "the idea that moral values can be deduced from genetics" on the ground that it "has within it the terrifying threat of the enforcement of scientifically determined righteousness." Other writers here go so far as to call sociobiology "a travesty" of the science of human nature it seeks to become, a theory of "magniloquent" claims, and a conception of man vitiated by its debt to the "lurid fantasies" of ethologists who, having studied other species, conclude that human behavior is fundamentally aggressive.

The opposition to sociobiology

Is it possible to summarize the opposition of the social and biological scientists here to sociobiology? Among sixteen articles, each concerned with some aspect of the subject and offered as a fresh view of it, that is difficult to do. Yet it is not impossible. As certain propositions may be said to lie in most of the arguments *for* sociobiology, so other propositions seem common to the arguments against it. These are (1) that, while there is a genetic basis or component to human behavior, this is for the most part culturally rather than biologically determined; (2) that man is thus unique among organisms that are products, as in other respects he is himself, of biological evolution; (3) that his nature must therefore be understood in historical, rather than merely evolutionary—i.e., biological—terms; and (4) that it is the behavioral sciences, not—or not in the main—the biological ones to which we must turn for an understanding of his behavior.

Some of the contributors are more convinced than others, it is true, of the first of these propositions and are willing to give greater weight to biology than are their colleagues. "The disagreement about the human biogram is entirely a matter of substance rather than principle," writes Marvin Harris. He means to distinguish the social scientists from sociobiology, but the statement holds for differences among the social scientists themselves. At one extreme among them is Washburn, who, after a discussion of man as an animal who learns his behavior, says flatly, "the laws of genetics are not the laws of learning." At the other extreme is Jerome Barkow, who asserts that sociobiology "can readily account for the evolution of such human phenomena as altruism, parent-offspring conflict, the double standard, lying, sex differences in behavior, ethnocentrism and race prejudice, incest taboos, altruism [*sic*], sexual jealousy, and the tendency, in many societies, for a man to pay more attention to his sister's children than to his own"—which would seem to leave very little room between himself and the sociobiologists he undertakes to oppose.

There are also differences with respect to the other propositions, notably the last of them, as to which it must be said that while all the contributors are opposed to sociobiology on *some* ground, some see more reason to oppose it than the threat it poses to social science. Although disarming statements about this last can be found in Wilson's writing, such as the remark, quoted in these pages last year by Professor Bell, that "the social sciences are potentially far richer in content" than biology and will eventually "absorb" its "relevant ideas ... and go on to beggar them by comparison," the essays and chapters that have made him famous are to the opposite effect. In *Human Nature,* Wilson calls biology "the antidiscipline" of the social sciences, by which he means that its function is to reduce to its own level the explanations of those sciences, particularly anthropology, which as they deal with man are thought to be above it. "The essence of the argument," he asserts, is that "the brain exists because it promotes the survival and multiplication of the genes that direct its assembly." This is quite opposite to what Derek Freeman here calls the "anthropological perspective," in which "Man is seen as a primate whose brain ... has undergone an evolution decisively different from that of any other animal species" in that it has been adapted to enact "not only the biological programs of our primate physiology, but also ... cultural and other humanly devised alternatives."

Arguments from other contributors are to the effect that sociobiology requires a response not only from the social sciences but from philosophy as well. Sociobiology embodies logical fallacies, Steven Rose contends, in its ascription to human genes of tendencies such as "altruism" which are a product of social interactions, "as if Newton had defined gravity as a 'property' of the apple, rather than as law describing an aspect of the relation between the apple and the earth." A somewhat similar point is made by Stephen Jay Gould when he argues that Wilson has made "a fundamental error" in looking to human acts, rather than to human tendencies and capacities, for an understanding of the biological basis of human behavior. S. A. Barnett raises the question whether the objection to sociobiological speculations does not lie ultimately in the limitations of science when it comes to understanding "the moral principles of a Confucius, the theories of a Newton, the works of a Shakespeare or a Mozart," none of which could have been predicted by any scientific method.

From such a perspective, it is biology that should be considered tributary to the social sciences, not the other way around, in the effort to account for human behavior. "Contrary to Wilson, I should place all the sciences relating to humans within an anthropological framework," Professor Montagu observes. A further limitation of biology is that it can say little about the characteristically human faculty of speech. "Social science might be defined as the science that studies the nature, complexity, and effectiveness of linguistically mediated behaviors," Washburn suggests. And, in general, the opinion of the contributors is that if human behavior is socially determined, as they believe, then it must be interpreted by social rather than by biological science.

The issue raised by sociobiology

Among the propositions that the sociobiologists have advanced, and among those that are put forward by these social and biological scientists, is it possible to discern the issue that has created the controversy between them? Again, because of the variety of the statements and the number of protagonists involved, it is difficult to do this without reductions that ignore important differences, or, in some cases, elaborations that obscure fundamental agreement. The first of these errors would be committed, certainly, if it were concluded that the division is simply between the proponents of heredity and the proponents of culture as the source of human behavior. Neither argument entirely excludes the other, and on certain terms both can allow great latitude to the principle they nevertheless regard as ultimately subordinate.

What is involved is a somewhat different question, as Professor Bell observed in these pages last year, namely "in what way does genetic inheritance limit the ranges of human behavior; or again, in what way does genetic predisposition facilitate what kinds of change?" If the question is put in still other terms, we can see that, granting some genetic basis to human behavior, the underlying issue is whether human beings can control their biological predisposition, either because they are subject to the different imperatives of culture or from some innate capacity—in a word, whether they are free.

All discussions of sociobiology line up on this issue, which is more or less sharply drawn depending how the terms in it are defined and understood. And it may be noted here that the proponents of sociobiology seem to occupy either an extreme position or an unexceptionable one according to the language they use. Their position is unexceptionable—is, in fact, indistinguishable from standard evolutionary biology—when it asserts that there is a genetic *basis* for human behavior like that which is discernible in other species. As ducks swim, birds fly, and monkeys climb trees, so human beings walk upright on two legs; these are species-specific traits, which everyone accepts. More distinctly social behavior is that of speech, which every normal human being easily learns—which he cannot in most cases be prevented from learning—and which no other species can learn at all. So with other human acts. None of the contributors to Professor Montagu's collection disputes that the human capacities involved are the product of our biological development.

When, however, the sociobiologists say—as they do say when they wish to be clear about what is, after all, their fundamental contention—that human social behavior is actually determined by the human biogram, they go beyond anything that evolutionary biology has ever claimed. For then they are saying that the human social behavior is what it is by virtue of demands and constraints that are embedded in our genetic structure as being most conducive to our survival. By this the sociobiologists mean that quite specific behavioral manifestations—as lying, altruism, race prejudice, incest, and war—are ultimately commanded or prohibited, as the case may be, by our heredity.

None of these restrictions is observable, of course, or could be observed without having witnessed the evolution out of which they are supposed to come. The basis of such assertions is the observed behavior of nonhuman species described by ethologists, and the genetic "calculus" (as Washburn calls it) which has been developed by Hamilton and others. It is by inferences drawn from these and related studies that sociobiology has arrived at its speculative insights.

What the evolutionary perspective leaves out is human culture—the accumulation of experience that makes human beings the one species that has not only an evolution but a history. This encompasses a variety of behavior vastly greater than any process of natural selection would require, comprehending populations far greater than any process of biological kinship would include and extending over different habitats. "In the case of the human species," Derek Freeman writes, "we are dealing with processes that lie beyond the reach of any purely genetic theory of evolution." Human behavior over the last 40,000 years, he points out, has been increasingly, and now is almost entirely, a product of "exogenetic" factors embodied in and transmitted by human culture.

Wilson himself has acknowledged the importance of culture in the formation of human behavior. But whatever weight he gives to it, he regards culture as having developed separately from and parallel to evolution, the effects of which it may suppress (at more or less of psychic cost) but cannot modify. And the opinion of the sociobiologists generally is that man is a creature suffering from futile attempts to deny his mostly violent nature by cultural prohibitions that are either doomed to failure or can succeed only insofar as it is understood that they have scotched the snake, not killed it. In this the sociobiologists follow ethologists such as Lorenz, who has said that "humanity must give up its self-conceit and accept the humility which is the prerequisite for recognizing the natural laws which govern the social behavior of men," and writers such as Ardrey, who contends that "man is a predator with a natural instinct to kill with a weapon," and similar aggressive tendencies. They rely also on those studies in population genetics that suggest the mechanisms by which social—i.e., altruistic—behavior can serve selfish—i.e., gene-preserving—ends, which are regarded as determining of human behavior.

It is not easy to see, therefore, how the bottom line for sociobiology can be anything short of genetic determinism. Whatever acknowledgment the proponents of the science make of cultural factors in human development, they really believe, and indeed they must really believe if they are to be understood as saying anything different from what evolutionary biology has always said—that biology is the dominant force in such behavior, that it is ultimately the human biogram that tells us what to do and what not to do. To argue merely that genetic factors extend farther into the evolution of human kind than has previously been supposed is to claim no more than the behavioral sciences are willing to admit and may be said themselves to have asserted in *Civilization and Its Discontents* and other now classic writings. To maintain (as the literature of sociobiology sometimes seems to do) merely that there exists a sociobiology of *other* species—i.e., a close relationship between species-specific behavior and (presumable) hereditary dispositions—is to claim what the behavioral sciences feel no obligation to deny. The question is whether *human* behavior is influenced to what Wilson has called a "decisive" extent by human biology. To that the sociobiologists must be understood as saying "yes" if they are saying anything very much at all.

Nor should we be surprised, this being so, to find the social and biological scientists in Professor Montagu's volume, who recognize the implications of sociobiological thinking, contesting them at every point. The best of the pieces in the collection, among which should be mentioned those by Washburn, King, Barnett, Gould (a paleontologist, it is true), and N. J. Mackintosh, as well as one by Mary Midgley, do this with energy and eloquence. Granting a hereditary factor in human behavior, they maintain that the human species is unique in having evolved into something that evolution, as a biological process, is insufficient to explain. We are reminded, as to sociobiology, how little it can tell us about the phenomenon of language and how little we can know about human kind in any other terms. The connection between human social behavior and human intelligence is explored, making it clear that the one is inconceivable without the other. The malign moral implications of sociobiology are discussed, among them that obedience to the biological imperative ought to be socially prescriptive (though why it should have to be so is not explained), since any alternative must be futile and confusing. The social consequences of the theory, which are class and race distinctions, are examined, as are the echoes in sociobiological theory of the earlier psychological determinism of Pavlov and B. F. Skinner, which may tell us something about dogs but provide little insight, if any, into human behavior.

Yet the effect of these criticisms, taken together, is not as great as it might be. It is not as great as it might be because the thinking of the social scientists, in particular, is split in much the same way as that of the sociobiologists is. That is to say, as the arguments of the sociobiologists are of either an unexceptionable or an extreme kind, in the sense of being such as the social scientists think it unnecessary to oppose or impossible to accept, so it is also with the social scientists. For the basis of their opposition to sociobiology is that the human species has not only a biology but a culture, and culture appears in their accounts either as a program of behavior operating through mechanisms that have much the same force as the mechanisms of biology, or as a self-defining experience that allows nothing to human kind *except* a history, as if the species had made itself up as it went along. But the first of these conceptions suggest a distinction rather than a difference between culture and biology as the source of human behavior, merely substituting one determinism for another, and that is a result the sociobiologists can accept, at least in spirit—which may account for the fact that Wilson is now and then very cordial to the social scientists. And the second conception, in principle quite opposite, means in effect that there is no such thing as a human *nature* at all, which is a proposition that sociobiologists are not alone in refusing to concede.

Take first the determinist argument. "What the theory—if that is what it may be called—implies," writes Michael Simon of sociobiology, "is that social practices that persist do so not because they are adaptive or because of the weight of cultural tradition but because of propensities that reside in the genes." Against this, the "environmental factors" (to use Professor Montagu's own term) that social theorists prefer to regard as the source of human behavior, like the "weight of cultural tradition," may be outer-directed rather than inner-directed (to adopt some language used a generation ago), but they are directed nonetheless, and the understanding of human behavior is hardly less constrained on the supposition of their power than it is on the assumption that we are controlled by our biology.

"I would emphasize," Derek Freeman writes "that . . . I accept the same 'scientific materialism' as that in which E. O. Wilson places his trust, as also the theory of evolution by means of natural selection in its modern form. . . . But equally, I do not suppose that acceptance of the theory of evolution by means of natural selection is in any way incompatible with the full recognition of the learned behavior and symbolic systems by which human populations have long been characterized, and which depend on the transmission of information by other than genetic means."

It is hard to believe that the difference between what this concedes and what Professor Wilson claims for sociobiology is unbridgeable. Indeed, when Wilson writes that "rather than specify a single trait, human genes prescribe the *capacity* to develop a certain array of traits," the difference would seem largely bridged, though the statement is here cited, by N. J. Mackintosh, as an ultimately misleading admission. The distinction between open and closed systems thus envisaged reminds one of claims that a computer into which a capacity for variable responses had been programmed would have the capacity to think. It is not quite the same, but there is prescription in both cases.

In contrast is the argument against sociobiology based on the conviction that the human species is self-defining. This is a fundamental notion of the behavioral sciences. As one of the articles in Professor Montagu's collection acknowledges, "contemporary social theorists act on the belief, even if they do not always profess it, that man's inner nature is a *tabula rasa* which is fully dependent for its development on the processes of social interaction and socialization. These processes together insure the internalization of society's prescribed values and goals." Such a statement means more than that human beings are without the constraints whereby we say of other species that they are creatures of their evolutionary biology. It means, or at least as developed it becomes the idea, as another article in the collection puts it, that with respect to the human species, "what seems fixed or constant is so only in the historical moment which itself is always in flux, that the human nature of feudal, preindustrial society was not the human nature of the industrial revolution, is not the human nature of today's advanced capitalism—and will not be the human nature of the transformed societies of tomorrow. . . ."

The opening this made for the sociobiologists is apparent. Leaving aside the question how a human species "fully dependent for its development" on the social environment in which it finds itself could ever have created that environment in the first place, as contemporary social theory also assures us, somewhat contradictorily, that it did—leaving aside the further question of how a species conceived as existing only in "flux" could be a species at all, since the only thing specific about it on such terms would be that it was unspecifiable—such a doctrine ignores the constants in human behavior that are everywhere perceived. "Sociobiology has achieved instant popularity," Marvin Harris writes, "in part because the better-known social science research strategies cannot provide scientific causal solutions for the perennial puzzles surrounding phenomena such as warfare, sexism, stratification, and cultural life-styles." The test of any theory of nature, Emerson wrote nearly a century and a half ago, is "that it will explain all phenomena. Now many are thought not only unexplained but inexplicable: as language, sleep, madness, dreams, beasts, sex." Sociobiology may be vulnerable to every sort of criticism, as the contributors to Professor Montagu's collection say with otherwise convincing eloquence, but the sociobiologists have been tempted, as it were—like the psychologists and biologists before them in our century—by a vacuum that the social sciences have not only left unfilled but have tried, in effect, to deny.

Conclusions

While the question raised by the discussion of sociobiology is that of human freedom, and while the contributors to Professor Montagu's volume manage to say a great many interesting and worthwhile things about this—as on their side do the sociobiologists—the issue is not resolved or even perfectly joined. In part, that is because certain questions of a factual nature, as whether the human genetic code really carries the kind of instruction that the sociobiologists think it does, cannot as yet be altogether settled in the present state of research. It is also in part because, as Professor Bell observed in his essay last year, the sociobiologists and their opponents are looking at a common subject from opposite sides, with the one noting the universals in human culture, for which they attempt to derive a biological explantion, and the other concerned with its variety, which they maintain can only be accounted for by the succession of choices that have created human history. But the underlying problem is that the ideas involved are not fully grasped and indeed cannot be fully comprehended within the terms in which the debate is for the most part carried on. The ideas involved are those of freedom and necessity, and the terms are for the most part those of the natural and social sciences, and such ideas are too big for such terms.

A sense of this comes over the layman when he reads a discussion of human necessity that is conceived as a purely biological phenomenon, no less than when he finds human freedom conceived in the plastic and arbitrary fashion of certain of the social scientists. The layman already thinks he knows, or has certainly heard said, that human beings have a nature by which they are bound, and that this involves both moral and social imperatives of duty and of right. There is a distinguished literature to that effect going back to Aquinas, and even further. As this understanding of man is that he is in part an animal, the news that he is constrained by his biology cannot be very startling even if the constraints are now thought to be more extensive than they were formerly. It is only the social scientists who are shocked by such a thought, and they are shocked because their conception of human kind excludes all obligation, having rejected any thought of ends, much as men of the Renaissance were shocked when Machiavelli told them that man in a certain state can be endlessly self-serving, because their conception of man was godlike and they had forgotten about original sin.*

At the same time, if the sociobiologists can be seen as having reintroduced into contemporary thought about human nature the idea of natural constraints (however reductive their conception of these may be), and if that is salutary as a corrective to be called the culturalist position, the culturalists, whatever may be said against their conception of freedom, seem altogether correct in their insistence that the human behavior which is actually perceived by sociobiology as predetermined does little if anything to diminish our sense of human capacities. The longest list of behavioral constraints that any sociobiologist has claimed to see in man is trifling compared to the abundance and variety of human powers, which incidentally include far greater constraints—of a moral, social, or intellectual kind —than any the sociobiologists have proposed. Among these, the most important, such as those of propositional speech and conceptual thought, are not yet even within the possibility of biological explanation, and may never be.

That the controversy has become as heated as it has, seeing that for the most part neither side has hold of more than a piece of the idea it undertakes to serve, suggests that it is inspired by the cultural moment quite as much as it is by the merits of the case. In fact, connections have been perceived to lie between sociobiology and cultural phenomena that it seems to underwrite. "Inherent in the idea of sociobiology as presented by Wilson, and by some of his more extreme followers, such as Richard Dawkins," Professor Montagu writes "is the notion of genetic determinism of . . . individual differences, social differences, the stratification of classes, sexual status, and racism." Thomas Sheehan, one of the contributors to his collection, describes the uses that anti-egalitarian theorists of our day, such as Alain de Benoist in France, have made of sociobiological claims. And perhaps there are other things also in the cultural climate of the moment that help to explain our interest in such theories.

The most important connection, however, would seem to be with cybernetics. Throughout the literature, on both sides of the controversy, the language of the computer is regularly employed, with "program," "system," "information," and related terms turning up frequently. There is not room here to expand very far on this. But it is hard to resist the suspicion that sociobiology provides an instance of relatively modest insights based upon careful observation being swept away by an overpowering metaphor that

---

* For a discussion of the classic literature on the subject of freedom, *see* "The Idea of Freedom" Parts I and II by Charles Van Doren published in *The Great Ideas Today* (1972, 1973).

nowadays commands attention, a metaphor that itself bears some relation to metaphors of former times, as that man is a machine, a system of electrons, the house of a homunculus, and the manifestation of diabolical possession. That some of these metaphors now seem merely quaint does not mean that the current idea of a genetic computer will in time seem so too; for all we know, that fancy may in time prove to be a fact. It does mean that, for the moment, the speculations of sociobiology have got ahead of any evidence it can put forward to substantiate its claims, and that they have touched images and ideas that already exist in the mind of the audience to which they are directed. It is possibly not an accident that Professor Wilson, whatever one may think of his theory, is a writer of more than usual sharpness and force to whom men listen, not so much from a conviction as to the truth of what he says, but from admiration at the way he says it.

PART FIVE

Additions
to the
Great Books Library

The True History

Lucian

Editor's Introduction

Although Lucian had achieved renown in his time and his works have influenced various modern writers, little is known concerning the details of his life. The information available has been reconstructed from his writings, which means that it is not only obscure but uncertain, for he is a satirist who is not always to be taken seriously. However, the portrait of his life which emerges from his works is of a man deeply impressed by classical Greek literature and extremely critical of the literary, philosophical, and intellectual pretensions of his own time.

Lucian was born in Samosata, part of the Roman province of Syria, around A.D. 120, during an era which has been referred to as the Golden Age of the Roman Empire. He was descended from a long line of sculptors and artisans, which probably made his family well-off but not wealthy. As a young boy, he demonstrated talent as an artist and was apprenticed to his uncle, a sculptor. They had an argument, at which point Lucian left home and traveled to western Asia Minor, where his true education and a lifetime of wandering awaited him.

In Asia Minor, Lucian acquired a Greek literary education and was very successful at assimilating himself to the culture and language of the Greeks. He became so adept at Greek oratory that he traveled from city to city displaying his eloquence and rhetorical skills in public lectures and pleading law cases. This took him from Greece to Italy and Gaul where he gained prestige and influence among the Roman officials and became famous in literary circles. The subject matter and style of his oratory during this period are readily detected in surviving texts of speeches, a few of which are found in works by him entitled *In Praise of the Fly*, *The Tyrannicide*, *Phalaris*, *Herodotus*, and *The Scythian*.

After years of wandering about the Roman provinces, Lucian settled in Athens ca. A.D. 155. Here the lover of literature expanded his knowledge of the literary and philosophical works of the ancient Greeks. At this time, Lucian's interest in public speaking waned, and he began to write critical and satirical essays, some of which were written in imitation of Menippus of Gadara, a Cynic philosopher of the third century B.C. whom Lucian admired. Menippus's works are in the form of satirical pamphlets and lampoons, and it is easy to see why Lucian felt a certain affinity to him.

His stay in Athens proved to be a rather prolific period in his life, for during this time, Lucian wrote numerous essays and dialogues. Among these are two of his most famous works: *Dialogues of the Gods* and *Dialogues of the Dead*. The former satirizes various aspects of Greek mythology; the latter provides an ironic portrayal of man's vanity. Throughout this time in Athens, Lucian was able to maintain the reputation he had gained during his oratory days through the writing of *Prometheus, The Tragic Zeus, Dialogues of Courtesans, Zeus Confuted,* and *Nigrinus*. This reputation led him to make the acquaintance of the emperor Verus, whose mistress Lucian flattered in *Imagines*. Although this cannot be certain, Lucian apparently followed Verus to Antioch in A.D. 162 during the emperor's campaign against the Parthians, and he stayed there for some years before returning to Samosata. He later wrote *How to Write History* in response to the histories which were written on Verus's exploits and, in it, explains how *not* to write history.

On his return to Samosata, Lucian persuaded his father to return with him to Athens. During the journey, Lucian met Alexander of Abonouteichos, a popular magician who claimed to have access to an oracle. Lucian's biting critique of Alexander, whom he considered a charlatan, can be found in the work entitled *Alexander; or the False Prophet*. This work provides a good example of Lucian's devastating wit and his abhorrence of fraud and deception of any kind. He remained in Athens for a while, but due to his proclivity for caustic satire, evidenced in his writings during this time such as *Timon, The Assembly of the Gods, Twice Accused,* and *The Auction of Lives,* he garnered few friends and became dissatisfied with Athenian life.

Through the help of a friend, Gaius Calvisius Statianus, prefect of Egypt from 170 to 175, Lucian obtained a post in Alexandria which could have led to a career in the civil service. However, feeling too old to start a new career and not enthralled with Alexandria, he returned to Athens. During this Alexandrian period, he wrote *Apology* and *On His Failure to Give Greetings*.

Back in Athens once again, Lucian devoted his time to speaking (usually at the Olympic Games) and writing. The works from this period of his life include *Lexiphanes, The Eunuch, The False Sophist,* and *The True History*. This last, written about 180, lampoons historical literature and satirizes the imaginations of historians and geographers. It is considered one of Lucian's greatest contributions.

Lucian died sometime after 180, leaving a wife and son. Although the details of his life are vague, his influence on modern writers is not. Rabelais took him as a model. The works of Fielding, Swift, Cyrano de Bergerac, and Voltaire illustrate Lucian's lasting influence. *Gulliver's Travels* and *Candide* attest to the impact of Lucian's work, especially *The True History*. Lucian was a master of the art of satire, and his writing is as witty and relevant for the modern reader as it was for those living during the second century.

The True History

Introduction

Athletes and physical trainers do not limit their attention to the questions of perfect condition and exercise; they say there is a time for relaxation also—which indeed they represent as the most important element in training. I hold it equally true for literary men that after severe study they should unbend the intellect, if it is to come perfectly efficient to its next task.

The rest they want will best be found in a course of literature which does not offer entertainment pure and simple, depending on mere wit or felicity, but is also capable of stirring an educated curiosity—in a way which I hope will be exemplified in the following pages. They are intended to have an attraction independent of any originality of subject, any happiness of general design, any verisimilitude in the piling up of fictions. This attraction is in the veiled reference underlying all the details of my narrative; they parody the cock-and-bull stories of ancient poets, historians, and philosophers; I have only refrained from adding a key because I could rely upon you to recognize as you read.

Ctesias, son of Ctesiochus of Cnidus, in his work on India and its characteristics, gives details for which he had neither the evidence of his eyes nor of hearsay. Iambulus's *Oceanica* is full of marvels; the whole thing is a manifest fiction, but at the same time pleasant reading. Many other writers have adopted the same plan, professing to relate their own travels, and describing monstrous beasts, savages, and strange ways of life. The fount and inspiration of their humour is the Homeric Odysseus, entertaining Alcinous's court with his prisoned winds, his men one-eyed or wild or cannibal, his beasts with many heads, and his metamorphosed comrades; the Phaeacians were simple folk, and he fooled them to the top of their bent.

When I come across a writer of this sort, I do not much mind his lying; the practice is much too well established for that, even with professed philosophers; I am only surprised at his expecting to escape detection. Now I am myself vain enough to cherish the hope of bequeathing something to posterity; I see no reason for resigning my right to that inventive freedom which others enjoy; and, as I have no truth to put on record, having lived a very humdrum life, I fall back on falsehood—but falsehood of a more consistent variety; for I now make the only true statement you are to expect—that I am a liar. This confession is, I consider, a full defence against all imputations. My subject is, then, what I have neither seen, experienced, nor been told, what neither exists nor could conceivably do so. I humbly solicit my readers' incredulity.

Book I

Starting on a certain date from the Pillars of Heracles, I sailed with a fair wind into the Atlantic. The motives of my voyage were a certain intellectual restlessness, a passion for novelty, a curiosity about the limits of the ocean and the peoples who might dwell beyond it. This being my design, I provisioned and watered my ship on a generous scale. My crew amounted to fifty, all men whose interests, as well as their years, corresponded with my own. I had further provided a good supply of arms, secured the best navigator to be had for money, and had the ship—a sloop—specially strengthened for a long and arduous voyage.

For a day and a night we were carried quietly along by the breeze, with land still in sight. But with the next day's dawn the wind rose to a gale, with a heavy sea and a dark sky; we found ourselves unable to take in sail. We surrendered ouselves to the elements, let her run, and were storm-driven for more than eleven weeks. On the eightieth day the sun came out quite suddenly, and we found ourselves close to a lofty wooded island, round which the waves were murmuring gently, the sea having almost fallen by this time. We brought her to land, disembarked, and after our long tossing lay a considerable time idle on shore; we at last made a start, however, and leaving thirty of our number to guard the ship I took the other twenty on a tour of inspection.

We had advanced half a mile inland through woods, when we came upon a brazen pillar, inscribed in Greek characters— which however were worn and dim—'Heracles and Dionysus reached this point.' Not far off were two footprints on rock; one might have been an acre in area, the other being smaller; and I conjecture that the latter was Dionysus's, and the other Heracles's; we did obeisance, and proceeded. Before we had gone far, we found ourselves on a river which ran wine; it was very like Chian; the stream full and copious, even navigable in parts. This evidence of Dionysus's sojourn was enough to convince us that the inscription on the pillar was authentic. Resolving to find the source, I followed the river up, and discovered, instead of a fountain, a number of huge vines covered with grapes; from the root of each there issued a trickle of perfectly clear wine, the joining of which made the river. It was well stocked with great fish, resembling wine both in colour and taste; catching and eating some, we at once found ourselves intoxicated; and indeed when opened the fish were full of wine-lees; presently it occurred to us to mix them with ordinary water fish, thus diluting the strength of our spirituous food.

We now crossed the river by a ford, and came to some vines of a most extraordinary kind. Out of the ground came a thick well-grown stem; but the upper part was a woman, complete from the loins upward. They were like our painters' representations of Daphne in the act of turning into a tree just as Apollo overtakes her. From the finger-tips sprang vine twigs, all loaded with grapes; the hair of their heads was tendrils, leaves, and grape-clusters. They greeted us and welcomed our approach, talking Lydian, Indian, and Greek, most of them the last. They went so far as to kiss us on the mouth; and whoever was kissed staggered like a drunken man. But they would not permit us to pluck their fruit, meeting the attempt with cries of pain. Some of them made further amorous advances; and two of my comrades who yielded to these solicitations found it impossible to extricate themselves again from their embraces; the man became one plant with the vine, striking root beside it; his fingers turned to vine twigs, the tendrils were all round him, and embryo grape-clusters were already visible on him.

We left them there and hurried back to the ship, where we told our tale, including our friends' experiment in viticulture. Then after taking some casks ashore and filling them with wine and water we bivouacked near the beach, and next morning set sail before a gentle breeze. But about midday, when we were out of sight of the island, a waterspout suddenly came upon us, which swept the ship round and up to a height of some three hundred and fifty miles above the earth. She did not fall back into the sea, but was suspended aloft, and at the same time carried along by a wind which struck and filled the sails.

For a whole week we pursued our airy course, and on the eighth day descried land; it was an island with air for sea, glistening, spherical, and bathed in light. We reached it, cast anchor, and landed; inspection soon showed that it was inhabited and cultivated. In the daytime nothing could be discerned outside of it; but night revealed many neighbouring islands, some larger and some smaller than ours; there was also another land below us containing cities, rivers, seas, forests, and mountains; and this we concluded to be our Earth.

We were intending to continue our voyage, when we were discovered and detained by the Horse-vultures, as they are called. These are men mounted on huge vultures, which they ride like horses; the great birds have ordinarily three heads. It will give you some idea of their size if I state that each of their quill-feathers is longer and thicker than the mast of a large merchantman. This corps is charged with the duty of patrolling the land, and bringing any strangers it may find to the king; this was what was now done with us. The king surveyed us, and, forming his conclusions from our dress, 'Strangers,' said he, 'you are Greeks, are you not?' we assented. 'And how did you traverse this vast space of air?' In answer we gave a full account of ourselves, to which he at once replied with his own history. It seemed he too was a mortal, named Endymion, who had been conveyed up from our Earth in his sleep, and after his arrival had become king of the country; this was, he told us, what we knew on our Earth as the moon. He bade us be of good cheer and entertain no apprehensions; all our needs should be supplied.

'And if I am victorious,' he added, 'in the campaign which I am now commencing against the inhabitants of the Sun, I promise you an extremely pleasant life at my court.' We asked about the enemy, and the quarrel. 'Phaethon,' he replied, 'king of the Sun (which is inhabited, like the Moon), has long been at war with us. The occasion was this: I wished at one time to collect the poorest of my subjects and send them as a colony to Lucifer, which is uninhabited. Phaethon took umbrage at this, met the emigrants half way with a troop of Horse-ants, and forbade them to proceed. On that occasion, being in inferior force, we were worsted and had to retreat; but I now intend to take the offensive and send my colony. I shall be glad if you will participate; I will provide your equipment

and mount you on vultures from the royal coops; the expedition starts to-morrow.' I expressed our readiness to do his pleasure.

That day we were entertained by the king; in the morning we took our place in the ranks as soon as we were up, our scouts having announced the approach of the enemy. Our army numbered 100,000 (exclusive of camp-followers, engineers, infantry, and allies), the Horse-vultures amounting to 80,000, and the remaining 20,000 being mounted on Salad-wings. These latter are also enormous birds, fledged with various herbs, and with quill-feathers resembling lettuce leaves. Next these were the Millet-throwers and the Garlic-men. Endymion had also a contingent from the North of 30,000 Flea-archers and 50,000 Wind-coursers. The former have their name from the great fleas, each of the bulk of a dozen elephants, which they ride. The Wind-coursers are infantry, moving through the air without wings; they effect this by so girding their shirts, which reach to the ankle, that they hold the wind like a sail and propel their wearers ship-fashion. These troops are usually employed as skirmishers. 70,000 Ostrich-slingers and 50,000 Horse-cranes were said to be on their way from the stars over Cappadocia. But as they failed to arrive I did not actually see them; and a description from hearsay I am not prepared to give, as the marvels related of them put some strain on belief.

Such was Endymion's force. They were all armed alike; their helmets were made of beans, which grow there of great size and hardness; the breastplates were of overlapping lupine-husks sewn together, these husks being as tough as horn; as to shields and swords, they were of the Greek type.

When the time came, the array was as follows: on the right were the Horse-vultures, and the King with the *élite* of his forces, including ourselves. The Salad-wings held the left, and in the centre were the various allies. The infantry were in round numbers 60,000,000; they were enabled to fall in thus: there are in the Moon great numbers of gigantic spiders, considerably larger than an average Aegean island; these were instructed to stretch webs across from the Moon to Lucifer; as soon as the work was done, the King drew up his infantry on this artificial plain, entrusting the command to Nightbat, son of Fairweather, with two lieutenants.

On the enemy's side, Phaethon occupied the left with his Horse-ants; they are great winged animals resembling our ants except in size; but the largest of them would measure a couple of acres. The fighting was done not only by their riders; they used their horns also; their numbers were stated as 50,000. On their right was about an equal force of Sky-gnats—archers mounted on great gnats; and next them the Sky-pirouetters, light-armed infantry only, but of some military value; they slung monstrous radishes at long range, a wound from which was almost immediately fatal, turning to gangrene at once; they were supposed to anoint their missiles with mallow juice. Next came the Stalk-fungi, 10,000 heavy-armed troops for close quarters; the explanation of their name is that their shields are mushrooms, and their spears asparagus stalks. Their neighbours were the Dog-acorns, Phaethon's contingent from Sirius. These were 5,000 in number, dog-faced men fighting on winged acorns. It was reported that Phaethon too was disappointed of the slingers whom he had summoned from the Milky Way, and of the Cloud-centaurs. These latter, however, arrived, most unfortunately for us, after the battle was decided; the slingers failed altogether, and are said to have felt the resentment of Phaethon, who wasted their territory with fire. Such was the force brought by the enemy.

As soon as the standards were raised and the asses on both sides (their trumpeters) had brayed, the engagement commenced. The Sunite left at once broke without awaiting the onset of the Horse-vultures, and we pursued, slaying them. On the other hand, their right had the better of our left, the Sky-gnats pressing on right up to our infantry. When these joined in, however, they turned and fled, chiefly owing to the moral effect of our success on the other flank. The rout became decisive, great numbers were taken and slain, and blood flowed in great quantities on to the clouds, staining them as red as we see them at sunset; much of it also dropped earthwards, and suggested to me that it was possibly some ancient event of the same kind which persuaded Homer that Zeus had rained blood at the death of Sarpedon.

Relinquishing the pursuit, we set up two trophies, one for the infantry engagement on the spiders' webs, and one on the clouds for the air-battle. It was while we were thus engaged that our scouts announced the approach of the Cloud-centaurs, whom Phaethon had expected in time for the battle. They were indeed close upon us, and a strange sight, being compounded of winged horses and men; the human part, from the middle upwards, was as tall as the Colossus of Rhodes, and the equine the size of a large merchantman. Their number I cannot bring myself to write down, for fear of exciting incredulity. They were commanded by Sagittarius. Finding their friends defeated, they sent a messenger after Phaethon to bring him back, and, themselves in perfect order, charged the disarrayed Moonites, who had left their ranks and were scattered in pursuit or pillage; they routed the whole of them, chased the King home, and killed the greater part of his birds; they tore up the trophies and overran the woven plain; I myself was taken, with two of my comrades. Phaethon now arrived, and trophies were erected on the enemy's part. We were taken off to the Sun the same day, our hands tied behind with a piece of the cobweb.

They decided not to lay siege to the city; but after their return they constructed a wall across the intervening space, cutting off the Sun's rays from the Moon. The wall was double, and built of clouds; the consequence was total eclipse of the Moon, which experienced a continuous night. This severity forced Endymion to negotiate. He entreated that the wall might be taken down, and his kingdom released from this life of darkness; he offered to pay tribute, conclude an alliance, abstain from hostilities in future, and give hostages for these engagements. The Sunites held two assemblies on the question, in the first of which they refused all concessions; on the second day, however, they relented, and peace was concluded on the following terms.

Articles of peace between the Sunites and their allies of the one part, and the Moonites and their allies of the other part.

1. The Sunites shall demolish the party-wall, shall make no further incursion into the Moon, and shall hold their captives to ransom at a fixed rate.

2. The Moonites shall restore to the other stars their autonomy, shall not bear arms against the Sunites, and shall conclude with them a mutual defensive alliance.

3. The King of the Moonites shall pay to the King of the Sunites, annually, a tribute of ten thousand jars of dew, and give ten thousand hostages of his subjects.

4. The high contracting parties shall found the colony of Lucifer in common, and shall permit persons of any other nationality to join the same.

5. These articles shall be engraved on a pillar of electrum, which shall be set up on the border in mid-air.

Sworn to on behalf of the Sun by Firebrace, Heaton, and Flashman; and on behalf of the Moon by Nightwell, Monday, and Shimmer.

Peace concluded, the removal of the wall and restoration of captives at once followed. As we reached the Moon, we were met and welcomed by our comrades and King Endymion, all weeping for joy. The King wished us to remain and take part in founding the colony, and, women not existing in the Moon, offered me his son in marriage. I refused, asking that we might be sent down to the sea again; and finding that he could not prevail, he entertained us for a week, and then sent us on our way.

I am now to put on record the novelties and singularities which attracted my notice during our stay in the Moon.

When a man becomes old, he does not die, but dissolves in smoke into the air. There is one universal diet; they light a fire, and in the embers roast frogs, great numbers of which are always flying in the air; they then sit round as at table, snuffing up the fumes which rise and serve them for food; their drink is air compressed in a cup till it gives off a moisture resembling dew. Beauty with them consists in a bald head and a hairless body; a good crop of hair is an abomination. On the comets, as I was told by some of their inhabitants who were there on a visit, this is reversed. They have beards, however, just above the knee; no toe-nails, and but one toe on each foot. They are all tailed, the tail being a large cabbage of an evergreen kind, which does not break if they fall upon it.

Their mucus is a pungent honey; and after hard work or exercise they sweat milk all over, which a drop or two of the honey curdles into cheese. The oil which they make from onions is very rich, and as fragrant as balsam. They have an abundance of water-producing vines, the stones of which resemble hailstones; and my own belief is that it is the shaking of these vines by hurricanes, and the consequent bursting of the grapes, that results in our hailstorms. They use the belly as a pouch in which to keep necessaries, being able to open and shut it. It contains no intestines or liver, only a soft hairy lining; their young, indeed, creep into it for protection from cold.

The clothing of the wealthy is soft glass, and of the poor, woven brass; the land is very rich in brass, which they work like wool after steeping it in water. It is with some hesitation that I describe their eyes, the thing being incredible enough to bring doubt upon my veracity. But the fact is that these organs are removable; any one can take out his eyes and do without till he wants them; then he has merely to put them in; I have known many cases of people losing their own and borrowing at need; and some—the rich, naturally—keep a large stock. Their ears are plane-leaves, except with the breed raised from acorns; theirs being of wood.

Another marvel I saw in the palace. There

is a large mirror suspended over a well of no great depth; any one going down the well can hear every word spoken on our Earth; and if he looks at the mirror, he sees every city and nation as plainly as though he were standing close above each. The time I was there, I surveyed my own people and the whole of my native country; whether they saw me also, I cannot say for certain. Any one who doubts the truth of this statement has only to go there himself, to be assured of my veracity.

When the time came, we took our leave of King and court, got on board, and weighed anchor. Endymion's parting gifts to me were two glass shirts, five of brass, and a suit of lupine armour, all of which, however, I afterwards left in the whale's belly; he also sent, as our escort for the first fifty miles, a thousand of his Horse-vultures.

We passed on our way many countries, and actually landed on Lucifer, now in process of settlement, to water. We then entered the Zodiac and passed the Sun on the left, coasting close by it. My crew were very desirous of landing, but the wind would not allow of this. We had a good view of the country, however, and found it covered with vegetation, rich, well-watered, and full of all good things. The Cloud-centaurs, now in Phaethon's pay, espied us and pounced upon the ship, but left us alone when they learned that we were parties to the treaty.

By this time our escort had gone home. We now took a downward course, and twenty-four hours' sailing brought us to Lampton. This lies between the atmospheres of the Pleiads and the Hyads, though in point of altitude it is considerably lower than the Zodiac. When we landed, we found no human beings, but numberless lamps bustling about or spending their time in the market-place and harbour; some were small, and might represent the lower classes, while a few, the great and powerful, were exceedingly bright and conspicuous. They all had their own homes or lodgings, and their individual names, like us; we heard them speak, and they did us no harm, offering us entertainment, on the contrary; but we were under

some apprehension, and none of us accepted either food or bed. There is a Government House in the middle of the city, where the Governor sits all night long calling the roll-call; any one not answering to his name is capitally punished as a deserter; that is to say, he is extinguished. We were present and witnessed the proceedings, and heard lamps defending their conduct and advancing reasons for their lateness. I there recognized our own house lamp, accosted him, and asked for news of my friends, in which he satisfied me. We stayed there that night, set sail next morning, and found ourselves sailing, now, nearly as low as the clouds. Here we were surprised to find Cloud-cuckoo-land; we were prevented from landing by the direction of the wind, but learned that the King's name was Crookbeak, son of Fitz-Ousel. I bethought me of Aristophanes, the learned and veracious poet whose statements had met with unmerited incredulity. Three days more, and we had a distinct view of the Ocean, though there was no land visible except the islands suspended in air; and these had now assumed a brilliant fiery hue. About noon on the fourth day the wind slackened and fell, and we were deposited upon the sea.

The joy and delight with which the touch of water affected us is indescribable; transported at our good fortune, we flung ourselves overboard and swam, the weather being calm and the sea smooth. Alas, how often is a change for the better no more than the beginning of disaster! We had but two days' delightful sail, and by the rising sun of the third we beheld a crowd of whales and marine monsters, and among them one far larger than the rest—some two hundred miles in length. It came on open-mouthed, agitating the sea far in front, bathed in foam, and exhibiting teeth whose length much surpassed the height of our great phallic images, all pointed like sharp stakes and white as elephants' tusks. We gave each other a last greeting, took a last embrace, and so awaited our doom. The monster was upon us; it sucked us in; it swallowed ship and crew entire. We escaped being ground by its teeth, the ship gliding in through the interstices.

Inside, all was darkness at first, in which we could distinguish nothing; but when it next opened its mouth, an enormous cavern was revealed, of great extent and height; a city of ten thousand inhabitants might have had room in it. Strewn about were small fish, the *disjecta membra* of many kinds of animal, ships' masts and anchors, human bones, and merchandise; in the centre was land with hillocks upon it, the alluvial deposit, I supposed, from what the whale swallowed. This was wooded with trees of all kinds, and vegetables were growing with all the appearance of cultivation. The coast might have measured thirty miles round. Sea-birds, such as gulls and halcyons, nested on the trees.

We spent some time weeping, but at last got our men up and had the ship made fast, while we rubbed wood to get a fire and prepared a meal out of the plentiful materials around us; there were fragments of various fish, and the water we had taken in at Lucifer was unexhausted. Upon getting up next day, we caught glimpses, as often as the whale opened his mouth, of land, of mountains, it might be of the sky alone, or often of islands; we realized that he was dashing at a great rate to every part of the sea. We grew accustomed to our condition in time, and I then took seven of my comrades and entered the wood in search of information. I had scarcely gone half a mile when I came upon a shrine, which its inscription showed to have been raised to Posidon; a little further were a number of graves with pillars upon them, and close by a spring of clear water; we also heard a dog bark, saw some distant smoke, and conjectured that there must be a habitation.

We accordingly pressed on, and found ourselves in presence of an old man and a younger one, who were working hard at a plot of ground and watering it by a channel from the spring. We stood still, divided between fear and delight. They were standing speechless, no doubt with much the same feelings. At length the old man spoke:— 'What are you, strangers; are you spirits of the sea, or unfortunate mortals like ourselves? As for us, we are men, bred on land; but now we have suffered a sea change, and swim about in this containing monster, scarce knowing how to describe our state; reason tells us we are dead, but instinct that we live.' This loosed my tongue in turn. 'We too, father,' I said, 'are men, just arrived; it is but a day or two since we were swallowed with our ship. And now we have come forth to explore the forest; for we saw that it was vast and dense. Methinks some heavenly guide has brought us to the sight of you, to the knowledge that we are not prisoned all alone in this monster. I pray you, let us know your tale, who you are and how you entered.' Then he said that, before he asked or answered questions, he must give us such entertainment as he could; so saying, he brought us to his house—a sufficient dwelling furnished with beds and what else he might need—, and set before us green-stuff and nuts and fish, with wine for drink. When we had eaten our fill, he asked for our story. I told him as it had passed, the storm, the island, the airy voyage, the war, and so to our descent into the whale.

It was very strange, he said, and then gave us his history in return. 'I am a Cyprian, gentlemen. I left my native land on a trading voyage with my son here and a number of servants. We had a fine ship, with a mixed cargo for Italy; you may have seen the wreckage in the whale's mouth. We had a fair voyage to Sicily, but on leaving it were caught in a gale, and carried in three days out to the Atlantic, where we fell in with the whale and were swallowed, ship and crew; of the latter we two alone survived. We buried our men, built a temple to Posidon, and now live this life, cultivating our garden, and feeding on fish and nuts. It is a great wood, as you see, and in it are vines in plenty, from which we get delicious wine; our spring you may have noticed; its water is of the purest and coldest. We use leaves for bedding, keep a good fire, snare the birds that fly in, and catch living fish by going out on the monster's gills; it is there also that we take our bath when we are disposed. There is moreover at no great distance a salt lake two or three miles round, producing all sorts of fish; in this we swim and sail, in a little boat of my building. It is now seven and twenty years since we were swallowed.

'Our lot might have been endurable enough, but we have bad and troublesome neighbours, unfriendly savages all.' 'What,' said I, 'are there other inhabitants?' 'A great many,' he replied, 'inhospitable and abhorrent to the sight. The western part of the wood (so to name the caudal region) is occupied by the Stockfish tribe; they have eels' eyes and lobster faces, are bold warriors, and eat their meat raw. Of the sides of the cavern, the right belongs to the Tritonomendetes, who from the waist upwards are human, and weazels below; their notions of justice are slightly less rudimentary than the others'. The left is in possession of the Crabhands and the Tunnyheads, two tribes in close alliance. The central part is inhabited by the Crays and the Flounderfoots, the latter warlike and extremely swift. As to this district near the mouth, the East, as it were, it is in great part desert, owing to frequent inundations. I hold it of the Flounderfoots, paying an annual tribute of five hundred oysters.

'Such is the land; and now it is for you to consider how we may make head against all these tribes, and what shall be our manner of life.' 'What may their numbers be, all told?' I asked. 'More than a thousand.' 'And how armed?' 'They have no arms but fishbones.' 'Why then,' I said, 'let us fight them by all means; we are armed, and they are not; and, if we win, we shall live secure.' We agreed on this course, and returned to the ship to make our preparations. The pretext for war was to be non-payment of the tribute, which was on the point of falling due. Messengers, in fact, shortly came to demand it, but the old man sent them about their business with an insolent answer. The Flounderfoots and Crays were enraged, and commenced operations with a tumultuous inroad upon Scintharus—this was our old man's name.

Expecting this, we were awaiting the attack

in full armour. We had put five and twenty men in ambush, with directions to fall on the enemy's rear as soon as they had passed; they executed their orders, and came on from behind cutting them down, while the rest of us—five and twenty also, including Scintharus and his son—met them face to face with a spirited and resolute attack. It was risky work, but in the end we routed and chased them to their dens. They left one hundred and seventy dead, while we lost only our navigating officer, stabbed in the back with a mullet rib, and one other.

We held the battlefield for the rest of that day and the night following, and erected a trophy consisting of a dolphin's backbone upright. Next day the news brought the other tribes out, with the Stockfish under a general called Slimer on the right, the Tunnyheads on the left, and the Crabhands in the centre; the Tritonomendetes stayed at home, preferring neutrality. We did not wait to be attacked, but charged them near Posidon's temple with loud shouts, which echoed as in a subterranean cave. Their want of armour gave us the victory; we pursued them to the wood, and were henceforth masters.

Soon after, they sent heralds to treat for recovery of their dead, and for peace. But we decided to make no terms with them, and marching out next day exterminated the whole, with the exception of the Tritonomendetes. These too, when they saw what was going on, made a rush for the gills, and cast themselves into the sea. We went over the country, now clear of enemies, and occupied it from that time in security. Our usual employments were exercise, hunting, vinedressing, and fruit-gathering; we were in the position of men in a vast prison from which escape is out of the question, but within which they have luxury and freedom of movement. This manner of life lasted for a year and eight months.

It was on the fifth of the next month, about the second gape (the whale, I should say, gaped regularly once an hour, and we reckoned time that way)—about the second gape, then, a sudden shouting and tumult became audible; it sounded like boatswains giving the time and oars beating. Much excited, we crept right out into our monster's mouth, stood inside the teeth, and beheld the most extraordinary spectacle I ever looked upon —giants of a hundred yards in height rowing great islands as we do triremes. I am aware that what I am to relate must sound improbable; but I cannot help it. Very long islands they were, but of no great height; the circumference of each would be about eleven miles; and its complement of giants was some hundred and twenty. Of these some sat along each side of the island, rowing with big cypresses, from which the branches and leaves were not stripped; in the stern, so to speak, was a considerable hillock, on which stood the helmsman with his hand on a brazen steering-oar of half a mile in length; and on the deck forward were forty in armour, the combatants; they resembled men except in their hair, which was flaming fire, so that they could dispense with helmets. The work of sails was done by the abundant forest on all the islands, which so caught and held the wind that it drove them where the steersman wished; there was a boatswain timing the stroke, and the islands jumped to it like great galleys.

We had seen only two or three at first; but there appeared afterwards as many as six hundred, which formed in two lines and commenced an action. Many crashed into each other stem to stem, many were rammed and sunk, others grappled, fought an obstinate duel, and could hardly get clear after it. Great courage was shown by the troops on deck, who boarded and dealt destruction, giving no quarter. Instead of grappling-irons, they used huge captive squids, which they swung out on to the hostile island; these grappled the wood and so held the island fast. Their missiles, effective enough, were oysters the size of waggons, and sponges which might cover an acre.

Aeolocentaur and Thalassopot were the names of the rival chiefs; and the question between them was one of plunder; Thalassopot was supposed to have driven off several herds of dolphins, the other's property; we could hear them vociferating the charge and calling out their Kings' names. Aeolocentaur's fleet finally won, sinking one hundred and fifty of the enemy's islands and capturing three with their crews; the remainder backed away, turned and fled. The victors pursued some way, but, as it was now evening, returned to the disabled ones, secured most of the enemy's, and recovered their own, of which as many as eighty had been sunk. As a trophy of victory they slung one of the enemy's islands to a stake which they planted in our whale's head. They lay moored round him that night, attaching cables to him or anchoring hard by; they had vast glass anchors, very strong. Next morning they sacrificed on the whale's back, buried their dead there, and sailed off rejoicing, with something corresponding to our paean. So ended the battle of the islands.

Book II

I now began to find life in the whale unendurable; I was tired to death of it, and concentrated my thoughts on plans of escape. Our first idea was to excavate a passage through the beast's right side, and go out through it. We actually began boring, but gave it up when we had penetrated half a mile without getting through. We then determined to set fire to the forest, our object being the death of the whale, which would remove all difficulties. We started burning from the tail end; but for a whole week he made no sign; on the eighth and ninth days it was apparent that he was unwell; his jaws opened only languidly, and each time closed again very soon. On the tenth and eleventh days mortification had set in, evidenced by a horrible stench; on the twelfth, it occurred to us, just in time, that we must take the next occasion of the mouth's being open to insert props between the upper and lower molars, and so prevent his closing it; else we should be imprisoned and perish in the dead body. We successfully used great beams for the purpose, and then got the ship ready with all the water and provisions we could manage. Scintharus was to navigate her. Next day the whale was dead.

We hauled the vessel up, brought her through one of the gaps, slung her to the teeth, and so let her gently down to the water. We then ascended the back, where we sacrificed to Posidon by the side of the trophy, and, as there was no wind, encamped there for three days. On the fourth day we were able to start. We found and came into contact with many corpses, the relics of the sea-fight, and our wonder was heightened when we measured them. For some days we enjoyed a moderate breeze, after which a violent north wind rose, bringing hard frost; the whole sea was frozen—not merely crusted over, but solidified to four hundred fathoms' depth; we got out and walked about. The continuance of the wind making life intolerable, we adopted the plan, suggested by Scintharus, of hewing an extensive cavern in the ice, in which we stayed a month, lighting fires and feeding on fish; we had only to dig these out. In the end, however, provisions ran short, and we came out; the ship was frozen in, but we got her free; we then hoisted sail, and were carried along as well as if we had been afloat, gliding smoothly and easily over the ice. After five days more the temperature rose, a thaw set in, and all was water again.

A stretch of five and thirty miles brought us to a small desert isle, where we got water —of which we were now in want—, and shot two wild bulls before we departed. These animals had their horns not on the top of the head, but, as Momus recommended, below the eyes. Not long after this, we entered a sea of milk, in which we observed an island, white in colour, and full of vines. The island was one great cheese, quite firm, as we afterwards ascertained by eating it, and three miles round. The vines were covered with fruit, but the drink we squeezed from it was milk instead of wine. In the centre of the island was a temple to Galatea the Nereid, as the inscription informed us. During our stay there, the ground itself served us for bread and meat, and the vine-milk for drink. We

learned that the queen of these regions was Tyro, daughter of Salmoneus, on whom Posidon had conferred this dignity at her decease.

After spending five days there we started again with a gentle breeze and a rippling sea. A few days later, when we had emerged from the milk into blue salt water, we saw numbers of men walking on the sea; they were like ourselves in shape and stature, with the one exception of the feet, which were of cork; whence, no doubt, their name of Corksoles. It struck us as curious that they did not sink in, but travelled quite comfortably clear of the water. Some of them came up and hailed us in Greek, saying that they were making their way to their native land of Cork. They ran alongside for some distance, and then turned off and went their own way, wishing us a pleasant voyage. A little further we saw several islands; close to us on the left was Cork, our friends' destination, consisting of a city founded on a vast round cork; at a greater distance, and a little to the right, were five others of considerable size and high out of the water, with great flames rising from them.

There was also a broad low one, as much as sixty miles in length, straight in our course. As we drew near it, a marvellous air was wafted to us, exquisitely fragrant, like the scent which Herodotus describes as coming from Arabia Felix. Its sweetness seemed compounded of rose, narcissus, hyacinth, lilies and violets, myrtle and bay and flowering vine. Ravished with the perfume, and hoping for reward of our long toils, we drew slowly near. Then were unfolded to us haven after haven, spacious and sheltered, and crystal rivers flowing placidly to the sea. There were meadows and groves and sweet birds, some singing on the shore, some on the branches; the whole bathed in limpid balmy air. Sweet zephyrs just stirred the woods with their breath, and brought whispering melody, delicious, incessant, from the swaying branches; it was like Pan-pipes heard in a desert place. And with it all there mingled a volume of human sound, a sound not of tumult, but rather of revels where some flute, and some praise the fluting, and some clap their hands commending flute or harp.

Drawn by the spell of it we came to land, moored the ship, and left her, in charge of Scintharus and two others. Taking our way through flowery meadows we came upon the guardians of the peace, who bound us with rose-garlands—their strongest fetters—and brought us to the governor. As we went they told us this was the island called of the Blest, and its governor the Cretan Rhadamanthus. When we reached the court, we found there were three cases to be taken before our turn would come.

The first was that of Ajax, son of Telamon, and the question was whether he was to be admitted to the company of Heroes; it was objected that he had been mad and taken his own life. After long pleadings Rhadamanthus gave his decision: he was to be put under the charge of Hippocrates the physician of Cos for the hellebore treatment, and, when he had recovered his wits, to be made free of the table.

The second was a matrimonial case, the parties Theseus and Menelaus, and the issue possession of Helen. Rhadamanthus gave it in favour of Menelaus, on the ground of the great toils and dangers the match had cost him—added to the fact that Theseus was provided with other wives in the Amazon queen and the daughters of Minos.

The third was a dispute for precedence between Alexander son of Philip and Hannibal the Carthaginian; it was won by the former, who had a seat assigned him next to Cyrus the elder.

It was now our turn. The judge asked by what right we set foot on his holy ground while yet alive. In answer we related our story. He then had us removed while he held a long consultation with his numerous assessors, among whom was the Athenian Aristides the Just. He finally reached a conclusion and gave judgement: on the charges of curiosity and travelling we were remanded till the date of our deaths; for the present we were to stay in the island, with admission to the Heroic society, for a fixed term, after which we must depart. The limit he appointed for our stay was seven months.

Our rose-chains now fell off of their own accord, we were released and taken into the city, and to the Table of the Blest. The whole of this city is built of gold, and the enclosing wall of emerald. It has seven gates, each made of a single cinnamon plank. The foundations of the houses, and all ground inside the wall, are ivory; temples are built of beryl, and each contains an altar of one amethyst block, on which they offer hecatombs. Round the city flows a river of the finest perfume, a hundred royal cubits in breadth, and fifty deep, so that there is good swimming. The baths, supplied with warm dew instead of ordinary water, are in great crystal domes heated with cinnamon wood.

Their raiment is fine cobweb, purple in colour. They have no bodies, but are intangible and unsubstantial—mere form without matter; but, though incorporeal, they stand and move, think and speak; in short, each is a naked soul, but carries about the semblance of body; one who did not touch them would never know that what he looked at was not substantial; they are shadows, but upright, and coloured. A man there does not grow old, but stays at whatever age he brought with him. There is no night, nor yet bright day; the morning twilight, just before sunrise, gives the best idea of the light that prevails. They have also but one season, perpetual spring, and the wind is always in the west.

The country abounds in every kind of flower, in shrubs and garden herbs. There are twelve vintages in the year, the grapes ripening every month; and they told us that pomegranates, apples, and other fruits were gathered thirteen times, the trees producing twice in their month Minous. Instead of grain, the corn develops loaves, shaped like mushrooms, at the top of the stalks. Round the city are 365 springs of water, the same of honey, and 500, less in volume however, of perfume. There are also seven rivers of milk and eight of wine.

The banqueting-place is arranged outside the city in the Elysian Plain. It is a fair lawn closed in with thick-grown trees of every kind, in the shadow of which the guests recline, on cushions of flowers. The waiting and handing is done by the winds, except only the filling of the wine-cup. That is a service not required; for all round stand great trees of pellucid crystal, whose fruit is drinking-cups of every shape and size. A guest arriving plucks a cup or two and sets them at his place, where they at once fill with wine. So for their drink; and instead of garlands, the nightingales and other singing birds pick flowers with their beaks from the meadows round, and fly over snowing the petals down and singing the while. Nor is perfume forgotten; thick clouds draw it up from the springs and river, and hanging overhead are gently squeezed by the winds till they spray it down in fine dew.

During the meal there is music and song. In the latter kind, Homer's verse is the favourite; he is himself a member of the festal company, reclining next above Odysseus. The choirs are of boys and girls, conducted and led by Eunomus the Locrian, Arion of Lesbos, Anacreon and Stesichorus; this last had made his peace with Helen, and I saw him there. When these have finished, a second choir succeeds, of swans and swallows and nightingales; and when their turn is done, all the trees begin to pipe, conducted by the winds.

I have still to add the most important element in their good cheer: there are two springs hard by, called the Fountain of Laughter, and the Fountain of Delight. They all take a draught of both these before the banquet begins, after which the time goes merrily and sweetly.

I should now like to name the famous persons I saw. To begin with, all the demi-gods, and the besiegers of Troy, with the exception of Ajax the Locrian; he, they said, was undergoing punishment in the place of the wicked. Of barbarians there were the two Cyruses, Anacharsis the Scythian, Zamolxis the Thracian, and the Latin Numa; and then Lycurgus the Spartan, Phocion and Tellus of Athens, and the Wise Men, but without Periander. And I saw Socrates son of Sophroniscus in converse with Nestor and Palamedes; clustered round him were Hyacinth the Spartan, Narcissus of Thespiae, Hylas, and many another comely boy. With Hyacinth I suspected that he was in love; at least he was for ever poking questions at him. I heard that Rhadamanthus was dissatisfied with Socrates, and had several times threatened him with expulsion, if he insisted on talking nonsense, and would not drop his irony and enjoy himself. Plato was the only one I missed, but I was told that he was living in his own Utopia, working the constitution and laws which he had drawn up.

For popularity, Aristippus and Epicurus bore the palm, in virtue of their kindliness, sociability, and good-fellowship. Aesop the Phrygian was there, and held the office of jester. Diogenes of Sinope was much changed; he had married Lais the courtesan, and often in his cups would oblige the company with a dance, or other mad pranks. The Stoics were not represented at all; they were supposed to be still climbing the steep hill of Virtue; and as to Chrysippus himself, we were told that he was not to set foot on the island till he had taken a fourth course of hellebore. The Academics contemplated coming, but were taking time for consideration; they could not yet regard it as a certainly that any such island existed. There was probably the added difficulty that they were not comfortable about the judgement of Rhadamanthus, having themselves disputed the possibility of judgement. It was stated that many of them had started to follow persons travelling to the island, but, their energy failing, had abandoned the journey half-way and gone back.

I have mentioned the most noteworthy of the company, and add that the most highly respected among them are, first Achilles, and second Theseus.

Before many days had passed, I accosted the poet Homer, when we were both disengaged, and asked him, among other things, where he came from; it was still a burning question with us, I explained. He said he was aware that some brought him from Chios, others from Smyrna, and others again from Colophon; the fact was, he was a Babylonian, generally known not as Homer, but as Tigranes; but when later in life he was given as a *homer* or hostage to the Greeks, that name clung to him. Another of my questions was about the so-called spurious lines; had he written them, or not? He said they were all genuine; so I now knew what to think of the critics Zenodotus and Aristarchus, and all their lucubrations. Having got a categorical answer on that point, I tried him next on his reason for starting the Iliad at the wrath of Achilles; he said he had no exquisite reason; it had just come into his head that way. Another thing I wanted to know was whether he had composed the Odyssey before the Iliad, as generally believed. He said this was not so. As to his reported blindness, I did not need to ask; he had his sight, so there was an end of that. It became a habit of mine, whenever I saw him at leisure, to go up and ask him things, and he answered quite readily—especially after his acquittal; a libel suit had been brought against him by Thersites, on the ground of the ridicule to which he is subjected in the poem; Homer had briefed Odysseus, and been acquitted.

It was during our sojourn that Pythagoras arrived; he had undergone seven transmigrations, lived the lives of that number of animals, and completed his psychic travels. It was the entire right half of him that was gold. He was at once given the franchise, but the question was still pending whether he was to be known as Pythagoras or Euphorbus. Empedocles also came, scorched all over and baked right through; but not all his entreaties could gain him admittance.

The progress of time brought round the Games of the Dead. The umpires were Achilles, holding that office for the fifth, and Theseus for the seventh time. A full report would take too long; but I will summarize the events. The wrestling went to Carus the Heraclid, who won the garland from Odys-

seus. The boxing resulted in a tie, the pair being the Egyptian Areus, whose grave is in Corinth, and Epeus. For mixed boxing and wrestling they have no prize. Who won the flat race, I have forgotten. In poetry, Homer really did much the best, but the award was for Hesiod. All prizes were plaited wreaths of peacock feathers.

Just after the Games were over, news came that the Damned had broken their fetters, overpowered their guard, and were on the point of invading the island, the ringleaders being Phalaris of Agrigentum, Busiris the Egyptian, Diomedes the Thracian, Sciron, and Pityocamptes. Rhadamanthus at once drew up the Heroes on the beach, giving the command to Theseus, Achilles, and Ajax Telamonius, now in his right senses. The battle was fought, and won by the Heroes, thanks especially to Achilles. Socrates, who was in the right wing, distinguished himself still more than in his lifetime at Delium, standing firm and showing no sign of trepidation as the enemy came on; he was afterwards given as a reward of valour a large and beautiful park in the outskirts, to which he invited his friends for conversation, naming it the Post-mortem Academy.

The defeated party was seized, re-fettered, and sent back for severer torments. Homer added to his poems a description of this battle, and at my departure handed me the MS. to bring back to the living world; but it was unfortunately lost with our other property. It began with the line:

Tell now, my Muse, how fought the mighty Dead.

According to their custom after successful war, they boiled beans, held the feast of victory, and kept high holiday. From this Pythagoras alone held aloof, fasting and sitting far off, in sign of his abhorrence of bean-eating.

We were in the middle of our seventh month, when an incident happened. Scintharus's son, Cinyras, a fine figure of a man, had fallen in love with Helen some time before, and it was obvious that she was very much taken with the young fellow; there used to be nods and becks and takings of wine between them at table, and they would go off by themselves for strolls in the wood. At last love and despair inspired Cinyras with the idea of an elopement. Helen consented, and they were to fly to one of the neighbouring islands, Cork or Cheese Island. They had taken three of the boldest of my crew into their confidence; Cinyras said not a word to his father, knowing that he would put a stop to it. The plan was carried out; under cover of night, and in my absence —I had fallen asleep at table—, they got Helen away unobserved and rowed off as hard as they could.

About midnight Menelaus woke up, and finding his wife's place empty raised an alarm, and got his brother to go with him to King Rhadamanthus. Just before dawn the look-outs announced that they could make out a boat, far out at sea. So Rhadamanthus sent fifty of the Heroes on board a boat hollowed out of an asphodel trunk, with orders to give chase. Pulling their best, they overtook the fugitives at noon, as they were entering the milky sea near the Isle of Cheese; so nearly was the escape effected. The boat was towed back with a chain of roses. Helen shed tears, and so felt her situation as to draw a veil over her face. As to Cinyras and his associates, Rhadamanthus interrogated them to find whether they had more accomplices, and, being assured to the contrary, had them whipped with mallow twigs, bound, and dismissed to the place of the wicked.

It was further determined that we should be expelled prematurely from the island; we were allowed only one day's grace. This drew from me loud laments and tears for the bliss that I was now to exchange for renewed wanderings. They consoled me for their sentence, however, by telling me that it would not be so many years before I should return to them, and assigning me my chair and my place at the table—a distinguished one—in anticipation. I then went to Rhadamanthus, and was urgent with him to reveal the future

to me, and give me directions for our voyage. He told me that I should come to my native land after many wanderings and perils, but as to the time of my return he would give me no certainty. He pointed, however, to the neighbouring islands, of which five were visible, besides one more distant, and informed me that the wicked inhabited these, the near ones, that is, 'from which you see the great flames rising; the sixth yonder is the City of Dreams; and beyond that again, but not visible at this distance, is Calypso's isle. When you have passed these, you will come to the great continent which is opposite your own; there you will have many adventures, traverse divers tribes, sojourn among inhospitable men, and at last reach your own continent.' That was all he would say.

But he pulled up a mallow root and handed it to me, bidding me invoke it at times of greatest danger. When I arrived in this world, he charged me to abstain from stirring fire with a knife, from lupines, and from the society of boys over eighteen; these things if I kept in mind, I might look for return to the island. That day I made ready for our voyage, and when the banquet hour came, I shared it. On the morrow I went to the poet Homer and besought him to write me a couplet for inscription; when he had done it, I carved it on a beryl pillar which I had set up close to the harbour; it ran thus:

This island, ere he took his homeward way,
The blissful Gods gave Lucian to survey.

I stayed out that day too, and next morning started, the Heroes attending to see me off. Odysseus took the opportunity to come unobserved by Penelope and give me a letter for Calypso in the isle Ogygia. Rhadamanthus sent on board with me the ferryman Nauplius, who, in case we were driven on to the islands, might secure us from seizure by guaranteeing that our destination was different. As soon as our progress brought us out of the scented air, it was succeeded by a horrible smell as of bitumen, brimstone, and pitch all burning together; mingled with this were the disgusting and intolerable fumes of roasting human flesh; the air was dark and thick, distilling a pitchy dew upon us; we could also hear the crack of whips and the yelling of many voices.

We only touched at one island, on which we also landed. It was completely surrounded by precipitous cliffs, arid, stony, rugged, treeless, unwatered. We contrived to clamber up the rocks, and advanced along a track beset with thorns and snags—a hideous scene. When we reached the prison and the place of punishment, what first drew our wonder was the character of the whole. The very ground stood thick with a crop of knife-blades and pointed stakes; and it was ringed round with rivers, one of slime, a second of blood, and the innermost of flame. This last was very broad and quite impassable; the flame flowed like water, swelled like the sea, and teemed with fish, some resembling fire-brands, and others, the small ones, live coals; these were called lamplets.

One narrow way led across all three; its gate was kept by Timon of Athens. Nauplius secured us admission, however, and then we saw the chastisement of many kings, and many common men; some were known to us; indeed there hung Cinyras, swinging in eddies of smoke. Our guides described the life and guilt of each culprit; the severest torments were reserved for those who in life had been liars and written false history; the class was numerous, and included Ctesias of Cnidus, and Herodotus. The fact was an encouragement to me, knowing that I had never told a lie.

I soon found the sight more than I could bear, and returning to the ship bade farewell to Nauplius and resumed the voyage. Very soon we seemed quite close to the Isle of Dreams, though there was a certain dimness and vagueness about its outline; but it had something dreamlike in its very nature; for as we approached it receded, and seemed to get further and further off. At last we reached it and sailed into Slumber, the port, close to the ivory gates where stands the temple of the Cock. It was evening when we landed, and upon proceeding to the city we saw many strange dreams. But I intend first to describe the city, as it has not been done before; Homer indeed mentions it, but gives no detailed description.

The whole place is embowered in wood, of which the trees are poppy and mandragora, all thronged with bats; this is the only winged thing that exists there. A river, called the Somnambule, flows close by, and there are two springs at the gates, one called Wakenot, and the other Nightlong. The rampart is lofty and of many colours, in the rainbow style. The gates are not two, as Homer says, but four, of which two look on to the plain Stupor; one of them is of iron, the other of pottery, and we were told that these are used by the grim, the murderous, and the cruel. The other pair face the sea and port, and are of horn—it was by this that we had entered—and of ivory. On the right as you enter the city stands the temple of Night, which deity divides with the Cock their chief allegiance; the temple of the latter is close to the port. On the left is the palace of Sleep. He is the governor, with two lieutenants, Nightmare, son of Whimsy, and Flittergold, son of Fantasy. A well in the middle of the market-place goes by the name of Heavyhead; beside which are the temples of Deceit and Truth. In the market also is the shrine in which oracles are given, the priest and prophet, by special appointment from Sleep, being Antiphon the dream-interpreter.

The dreams themselves differed widely in character and appearance. Some were well-grown, smooth-skinned, shapely, handsome fellows, others rough, short, and ugly, some apparently made of gold, others of common cheap stuff. Among them some were found with wings, and other strange variations; others again were like the mummers in a pageant, tricked out as kings or Gods or what not. Many of them we felt that we had seen in our world, and sure enough these came up and claimed us as old acquaintance; they took us under their charge, found us lodgings, entertained us with lavish kindness, and, not content with the magnificence of this present reception, promised us royalties and provinces. Some of them also took us to see our friends, doing the return trip all in the day.

For thirty days and nights we abode there —a very feast of sleep. Then on a sudden came a mighty clap of thunder: we woke; jumped up; provisioned; put off. In three days we were at the Isle of Ogygia, where we landed. Before delivering the letter, I opened and read it; here are the contents: *ODYSSEUS TO CALYPSO, GREETING. Know that in the faraway days when I built my raft and sailed away from you, I suffered shipwreck; I was hard put to it, but Leucothea brought me safe to the land of the Phaeacians; they gave me passage home, and there I found a great company suing for my wife's hand and living riotously upon our goods. All them I slew, and in after years was slain by Telegonus, the son that Circe bare me. And now I am in the Island of the Blest, ruing the day when I left the life I had with you, and the everlasting life you proffered. I watch for opportunity, and meditate escape and return.* Some words were added, commending us to her hospitality.

A little way from the sea I found the cave just as it is in Homer, and herself therein at her spinning. She took and read the letter, wept for a space, and then offered us entertainment; royally she feasted us, putting questions the while about Odysseus and Penelope; what were her looks? and was she as discreet as Odysseus had been used to vaunt her? To which we made such answers as we thought she would like.

Leaving her, we went on board, and spent the night at anchor just off shore; in the morning we started with a stiff breeze, which grew to a gale lasting two days; on the third day we fell in with the Pumpkin-pirates. These are savages of the neighbouring islands who prey upon passing ships. They use large boats made of pumpkins ninety feet long. The pumpkin is dried and hollowed out by removal of the pulp, and the boat is completed by the addition of cane masts and pumpkin-leaf sails. Two boatfuls of them engaged us, and we had many casualties from their pumpkin-seed missiles. The fight was

long and well matched; but about noon we saw a squadron of Nut-tars coming up in rear of the enemy. It turned out that the two parties were at war; for as soon as our assailants observed the others, they left us alone and turned to engage them.

Meanwhile we hoisted sail and made the best of our way off, leaving them to fight it out. It was clear that the Nut-tars must win, as they had both superior numbers—there were five sail of them—and stronger vessels. These were made of nutshells, halved and emptied, measuring ninety feet from stem to stern. As soon as they were hull down, we attended to our wounded; and from that time we made a practice of keeping on our armour, to be in instant readiness for an attack—no vain precaution either.

Before sunset, for instance, there assailed us from a bare island some twenty men mounted on large dolphins—pirates again. Their dolphins carried them quite well, curvetting and neighing. When they got near, they divided, and subjected us to a cross fire of dry cuttlefish and crab's eyes. But our arrows and javelins were too much for them, and they fled back to the island, few of them unwounded.

At midnight, in calm weather, we found ourselves colliding with an enormous halcyon's nest; it was full seven miles round. The halcyon was brooding, not much smaller herself than the nest. She got up, and very nearly capsized us with the fanning of her wings; however, she went off with a melancholy cry. When it was getting light, we got on to the nest, and found on examination that it was composed like a vast raft of large trees. There were five hundred eggs, larger in girth than a tun of Chian. We could make out the chicks inside and hear them croaking; we hewed open one egg with hatchets, and dug out an unfledged chick bulkier than twenty vultures.

Sailing on, we had left the nest some five and twenty miles behind, when a miracle happened. The wooden goose of our sternpost suddenly clapped its wings and started cackling; Scintharus, who was bald, recovered his hair; most striking of all, the ship's mast came to life, putting forth branches sideways, and fruit at the top; this fruit was figs, and a bunch of black grapes, not yet ripe. These sights naturally disturbed us, and we fell to praying the Gods to avert any disaster they might portend.

We had proceeded something less than fifty miles when we saw a great forest, thick with pines and cypresses. This we took for the mainland; but it was in fact deep sea, set with trees; they had no roots, but yet remained in their places, floating upright, as it were. When we came near and realized the state of the case, we could not tell what to do; it was impossible to sail between the trees, which were so close as to touch one another, and we did not like the thought of turning back. I climbed the tallest tree to get a good view, and found that the wood was five or six miles across, and was succeeded by open water. So we determined to hoist the ship on to the top of the foliage, which was very dense, and get her across to the other sea, if possible. It proved to be so. We attached a strong cable, got up on the tree-tops, and hauled her after us with some difficulty; then we laid her on the branches, hoisted sail, and floating thus were propelled by the wind. A line of Antimachus came into my head:

And as they voyaged thus the woodland through—

Well, we made our way over and reached the water, into which we let her down in the same way. We then sailed through clear transparent sea, till we found ourselves on the edge of a great gorge which divided water from water, like the land fissures which are often produced by earthquakes. We got the sails down and brought her to just in time to escape making the plunge. We could bend over and see an awful mysterious gulf perhaps a hundred miles deep, the water standing wall against wall. A glance round showed us not far off to the right a water bridge which spanned the chasm, and gave a moving surface crossing from one sea to the other. We got out the sweeps, pulled her to the bridge, and with great exertions effected that astonishing passage.

There followed a sail through smooth water, and then a small island, easy of approach, and inhabited; its occupants were the Ox-heads, savage men with horns, after the fashion of our poets' Minotaur. We landed and went in search of water and provisions, of which we were now in want. The water we found easily, but nothing else; we heard, however, not far off, a numerous lowing; supposing it to indicate a herd of cows, we went a little way towards it, and came upon these men. They gave chase as soon as they saw us, and seized three of my comrades, the rest of us getting off to sea. We then armed—for we would not leave our friends unavenged—and in full force fell on the Ox-heads as they were dividing our slaughtered men's flesh. Our combined shout put them to flight, and in the pursuit we killed about fifty, took two alive, and returned with our captives. We had found nothing to eat; the general opinion was for slaughtering the prisoners; but I refused to accede to this, and kept them in bonds till an embassy came from the Ox-heads to ransom them; so we understood the motions they made, and their tearful supplicatory lowings. The ransom consisted of a quantity of cheese, dried fish, onions, and four deer; these were three-footed, the two forefeet being joined into one. In exchange for all this we restored the prisoners, and after one day's further stay departed.

By this time we were beginning to observe fish, birds on the wing, and other signs of land not far off; and we shortly saw men, practising a mode of navigation new to us; for they were boat and crew in one. The method was this: they float on their backs, erect a sail, and then, holding the sheets with their hands, catch the wind. These were succeeded by others who sat on corks, to which were harnessed pairs of dolphins, driven with reins. They neither attacked nor avoided us, but drove along in all confidence and peace, admiring the shape of our craft and examining it all round.

That evening we touched at an island of no

great size. It was occupied by what we took for women, talking Greek. They came and greeted us with kisses, were attired like courtesans, all young and fair, and with long robes sweeping the ground. Cabbalusa was the name of the island, and Hydramardia the city's. These women paired off with us and led the way to their separate homes. I myself tarried a little, under the influence of some presentiment, and looking more closely observed quantities of human bones and skulls lying about. I did not care to raise an alarm, gather my men, and resort to arms; instead, I drew out my mallow, and prayed earnestly to it for escape from our perilous position. Shortly after, as my hostess was serving me, I saw that in place of human feet she had ass's hoofs; whereupon I drew my sword, seized, bound, and closely questioned her. Reluctantly enough she had to confess; they were sea-women called Ass-shanks, and their food was travellers. 'When we have made them drunk,' she said, 'and gone to rest with them, we overpower them in their sleep.' After this confession I left her there bound, went up on to the roof, and shouted for my comrades. When they appeared, I repeated it all to them, showed them the bones, and brought them in to see my prisoner; she at once vanished, turning to water; however, I thrust my sword into this experimentally, upon which the water became blood.

Then we marched hurriedly down to our ship and sailed away. With the first glimmering of dawn we made out a mainland, which we took for the continent that faces our own. We reverently saluted it, made prayer, and held counsel upon our best course. Some were for merely landing and turning back at once, others for leaving the ship, and going into the interior to make trial of the inhabitants. But while we were deliberating, a great storm arose, which dashed us, a complete wreck, on the shore. We managed to swim to land, each snatching up his arms and anything else he could.

Such are the adventures that befell me up to our arrival at that other continent: our sea-voyage; our cruise among the islands and in the air; then our experiences in and after the whale; with the Heroes; with the dreams; and finally with the Ox-heads and the Ass-shanks. Our fortunes on the continent will be the subject of the following books.

An Essay on Criticism

Alexander Pope

Editor's Introduction

Few literary figures have sustained as many ironies as Alexander Pope. Regarded both in his own time and since as the greatest English poet of the Augustan age, he devoted years to the translation of one poet greater than himself and wrote perhaps his finest work in candid imitation of another. All but a few of his poems were composed within a prosody of narrow limits, the so-called "heroic couplet" consisting of a pair of ten-syllable lines, rhymed at the end and repeated throughout. This he employed in poetic forms such as elegies, eulogies, epitaphs, and epigrams, in which it was all but impossible to transcend models fixed by long tradition and classical authority. And while some of his best work was brilliantly, even savagely satirical of certain of his contemporaries (who treated him in like fashion), until the name of "Mr. Pope" became a thing to reckon, he was in person a man abnormally short of stature and frail in health who was often reduced to surveying his domain, the literary London of his day, from a chair in which he had to be transported.

It was characteristic of him that he should have produced the *Essay on Criticism* (1711), a work that undertakes to set forth the rules of good writing as his age understood them, when he was only twenty-five—too young, one might suppose, to have provided much demonstration himself of the arts he criticizes. He was nothing, however, if not precocious. Born a Roman Catholic, which by the English laws of that time prevented him from any formal schooling, and subject from an early age to ailments of body and mind that limited his activity, he had educated himself with the intensity of one who had nothing else to do. Although his father's home was outside London, he managed to get to the city often, so that before he was twenty he had made the acquaintance, begun through correspondence, of Wycherley, Congreve, and other literary men of the day. By 1705 his earliest poems—certain "Pastorals," as he called them—were in circulation among these friends, along with other poems which in revised versions he published later in life. The *Essay on Criticism*, though incomparable in its command of the kind of verse it uses, was not an attempt at original thought but rather a sort of dissertation by which its author established his competence before the literary men of his day; indeed, the poem's most famous lines, as "A little learning is a dangerous thing," "To err is human, to forgive, divine," and "fools rush in where angels fear to tread," were all taken from other critics—Horace, Quintilian, Boileau—and in Pope's time would have been recognized as such.

Pope's greatest achievements were at this point still ahead of him. In 1714 he published *The Rape of the Lock,* a mock-epic that proved his wit. The following year appeared the first volume of his translation of the *Iliad,* a work that occupied him until 1720 and established his mastery of the tradition of heroic poetry his age so greatly admired. It also earned him a substantial amount of money, which he needed, for he was the first Englishman to depend entirely on his writings for his income, his religion making it impossible for him to receive the emoluments available before and since to other men.

In 1719 he moved to the country estate at Twickenham (then pronounced Twit'nam) near Richmond, some fifteen miles up the Thames from London, where he afterward remained except for occasional visits to the metropolis. These he sometimes managed, despite his physical handicaps, by a boat which he rowed himself. It was at Twickenham that, his estate being divided by a public road, he had constructed the famous underground passage that still exists, in which he set specimens of rare minerals, and which he called his "grotto." Notwithstanding the vanity of such a term (as Dr. Johnson thought it), Pope was seriously interested in landscape gardens and became a recognized authority on such works as well as a designer of them for his friends.

Following the publication of an edition of Shakespeare's plays which he edited (1725), Pope in 1728 commenced the satirical writings and the "Epistles" in imitation of Horace that manifest the perfection of his poetic art. They are remarkable as adaptations, in his own language for his own time, of the classic poet he admired most, whose quality he had captured in some famous lines:

> Horace still charms with graceful negligence,
> And without method talks us into sense,
> Will, like a friend, familiarly convey,
> The truest notions in the easiest way.

These works were Pope's chief occupation during the remainder of his life. He also completed his *Dunciad,* another mock-epic largely written by 1728 but finished only a few years before his death, in which he said all he could think to say against certain writers of his time whose unpardonable defect was the fact, as he thought, that they were dull. He was at work on the epic poem (not mock-epic) his critical principles almost obliged him to attempt, as he was on a revision of his poems for a new edition, when he died in 1744.

I

'Tis hard to say, if greater want of skill
  Appear in writing or in judging ill;
But, of the two, less dang'rous is th' offence,
To tire our patience, than mislead our sense.
Some few in that, but numbers err in this,   5
Ten censure wrong for one who writes amiss;
A fool might once himself alone expose,
Now one in verse makes many more in prose.
  'Tis with our judgments as our watches, none
Go just alike, yet each believes his own.   10
In Poets as true genius is but rare,
True taste as seldom is the Critic's share;
Both must alike from Heaven derive their light,
These born to judge, as well as those to write.
Let such teach others who themselves excel,   15
And censure freely who have written well.
Authors are partial to their wit, 'tis true,
But are not Critics to their judgment too?
  Yet if we look more closely, we shall find
Most have the seeds of judgment in their mind: 20
Nature affords at least a glimm'ring light;
The lines, tho' touched but faintly, are drawn right.
But as the slightest sketch, if justly traced, ⎫
Is by ill-colouring but the more disgraced, ⎬
So by false learning is good sense defaced: ⎭   25
Some are bewildered in the maze of schools,
And some made coxcombs Nature meant but fools.
In search of wit these lose their common sense,
And then turn Critics in their own defence:
Each burns alike, who can, or cannot write,   30
Or with a Rival's, or an Eunuch's spite.
All fools have still an itching to deride,
And fain would be upon the laughing side.
If Mævius scribble in Apollo's spite,
There are who judge still worse than he can write.   35
  Some have at first for Wits, then Poets past,
Turned Critics next, and proved plain fools at last.
Some neither can for Wits nor Critics pass,
As heavy mules are neither horse nor ass.
Those half-learn'd witlings, numerous in our isle,   40
As half-formed insects on the banks of Nile;
Unfinished things, one knows not what to call,

---

34. *Mævius:* a third-rate poet contemporary with Virgil.

Their generation's so equivocal:
To tell 'em, would a hundred tongues require,
Or one vain Wit's, that might a hundred tire.   45
    But you who seek to give and merit fame,
And justly bear a Critic's noble name,
Be sure yourself and your own reach to know,
How far your genius, taste, and learning go;
Launch not beyond your depth, but be discreet,   50
And mark that point where sense and dulness meet.
    Nature to all things fixed the limits fit,
And wisely curbed proud man's pretending wit.
As on the land while here the ocean gains,
In other parts it leaves wide sandy plains;   55
Thus in the soul while memory prevails,
The solid pow'r of understanding fails;
Where beams of warm imagination play,
The memory's soft figures melt away.
One science only will one genius fit;   60
So vast is art, so narrow human wit:
Not only bounded to peculiar arts,
But oft in those confined to single parts.
Like kings we lose the conquests gained before,
By vain ambition still to make them more;   65
Each might his sev'ral province well command,
Would all but stoop to what they understand.
    First follow Nature, and your judgment frame
By her just standard, which is still the same:
Unerring NATURE, still divinely bright,   70
One clear, unchanged, and universal light,
Life, force, and beauty, must to all impart,
At once the source, and end, and test of Art.
Art from that fund each just supply provides,
Works without show, and without pomp presides: 75
In some fair body thus th' informing soul
With spirits feeds, with vigour fills the whole,
Each motion guides, and ev'ry nerve sustains;
Itself unseen, but in th' effects, remains.
Some, to whom Heaven in wit has been profuse,   80
Want as much more, to turn it to its use;
For wit and judgment often are at strife,
Tho' meant each other's aid, like man and wife.
'Tis more to guide, than spur the Muse's steed;
Restrain his fury, than provoke his speed;   85
The wingèd courser, like a generous horse,
Shows most true mettle when you check his course.
    Those RULES of old discovered, not devised,

---

84. *Muse's steed:* Pegasus.

Are Nature still, but Nature methodized;
Nature, like liberty, is but restrained   90
By the same laws which first herself ordained.
 Hear how learn'd Greece her useful rules indites,
When to repress, and when indulge our flights:
High on Parnassus' top her sons she showed,
And pointed out those arduous paths they trod;   95
Held from afar, aloft, th' immortal prize,
And urged the rest by equal steps to rise.
Just precepts thus from great examples given,
She drew from them what they derived from Heaven.
The generous Critic fanned the Poet's fire,   100
And taught the world with reason to admire.
Then Criticism the Muses' handmaid proved,
To dress her charms, and make her more beloved:
But following Wits from that intention strayed,
Who could not win the mistress, wooed the maid;   105
Against the Poets their own arms they turned,
Sure to hate most the men from whom they learned.
So modern 'Pothecaries, taught the art
By Doctor's bills to play the Doctor's part,
Bold in the practice of mistaken rules,   110
Prescribe, apply, and call their masters fools.
Some on the leaves of ancient authors prey,
Nor time nor moths e'er spoiled so much as they.
Some drily plain, without invention's aid,
Write dull receipts how poems may be made.   115
These leave the sense, their learning to display,
And those explain the meaning quite away.
 You then whose judgment the right course would steer,
Know well each Ancient's proper character;
His fable, subject, scope in ev'ry page;   120
Religion, Country, genius of his Age:
Without all these at once before your eyes,
Cavil you may, but never criticize.
Be Homer's works your study and delight,
Read them by day, and meditate by night;   125
Thence form your judgment, thence your maxims bring,
And trace the Muses upward to their spring.
Still with itself compared, his text peruse;
And let your comment be the Mantuan Muse.
 When first young Maro in his boundless mind   130
A work t' outlast immortal Rome designed,
Perhaps he seemed above the critic's law,
And but from Nature's fountains scorned to draw:
But when t' examine every part he came,

---

129. *Mantuan Muse:* Virgil. 130 *Maro:* Virgil.

Nature and Homer were, he found, the same.   135
Convinced, amazed, he checks the bold design; ⎫
And rules as strict his laboured work confine, ⎬
As if the Stagirite o'erlooked each line.   ⎭
Learn hence for ancient rules a just esteem;
To copy nature is to copy them.   140
   Some beauties yet no Precepts can declare,
For there's a happiness as well as care.
Music resembles Poetry, in each   ⎫
Are nameless graces which no methods teach,   ⎬
And which a master-hand alone can reach.   ⎭   145
If, where the rules not far enough extend,
(Since rules were made but to promote their end)
Some lucky Licence answer to the full
Th' intent proposed, that Licence is a rule.
Thus, Pegasus, a nearer way to take,   150
May boldly deviate from the common track.
Great wits sometimes may gloriously offend,
And rise to faults true Critics dare not mend;
From vulgar bounds with brave disorder part,
And snatch a grace beyond the reach of art,   155
Which without passing thro' the judgment, gains
The heart, and all its end at once attains.
In prospects thus, some objects please our eyes, ⎫
Which out of nature's common order rise,   ⎬
The shapeless rock, or hanging precipice.   ⎭   160
But tho' the Ancients thus their rules invade,
(As Kings dispense with laws themselves have made)
Moderns, beware! or if you must offend
Against the precept, ne'er transgress its End;
Let it be seldom, and compelled by need;   165
And have, at least, their precedent to plead.
The Critic else proceeds without remorse,
Seizes your fame, and puts his laws in force.
   I know there are, to whose presumptuous thoughts
Those freer beauties, even in them, seem faults.   170
Some figures monstrous and mis-shaped appear,
Considered singly, or beheld too near,
Which, but proportioned to their light, or place,
Due distance reconciles to form and grace.
A prudent chief not always must display   175
His powers in equal ranks, and fair array,
But with th' occasion and the place comply,
Conceal his force, nay seem sometimes to fly.
Those oft are stratagems which errors seem,
Nor is it Homer nods, but we that dream.   180

_____

138. *the Stagirite:* Aristotle (so called from his birthplace, Stagyra).

Still green with bays each ancient Altar stands,
Above the reach of sacrilegious hands;
Secure from Flames, from Envy's fiercer rage,
Destructive War, and all-involving Age.
See, from each clime the learn'd their incense bring!   185
Hear, in all tongues consenting Pæans ring!
In praise so just let every voice be joined,
And fill the general chorus of mankind.
Hail, Bards triumphant! born in happier days;
Immortal heirs of universal praise!   190
Whose honours with increase of ages grow,
As streams roll down, enlarging as they flow;
Nations unborn your mighty names shall sound,
And worlds applaud that must not yet be found!
Oh may some spark of your celestial fire,   195
The last, the meanest of your sons inspire,
(That on weak wings, from far, pursues your flights;
Glows while he reads, but trembles as he writes)
To teach vain Wits a science little known,
T' admire superior sense, and doubt their own!   200

II

Of all the Causes which conspire to blind
Man's erring judgment, and misguide the mind,
What the weak head with strongest bias rules,
Is *Pride*, the never-failing vice of fools.
Whatever nature has in worth denied,   205
She gives in large recruits of needful pride;
For as in bodies, thus in souls, we find
What wants in blood and spirits, swelled with wind:
Pride, where wit fails, steps in to our defence,
And fills up all the mighty Void of sense.   210
If once right reason drives that cloud away,
Truth breaks upon us with resistless day.
Trust not yourself; but your defects to know,
Make use of every friend—and every foe.
  A *little learning* is a dangerous thing;   215
Drink deep, or taste not the Pierian spring.
There shallow draughts intoxicate the brain,
And drinking largely sobers us again.
Fired at first sight with what the Muse imparts,
In fearless youth we tempt the heights of Arts,   220
While from the bounded level of our mind
Short views we take, nor see the lengths behind;
But more advanced, behold with strange surprise
New distant scenes of endless science rise!
So pleased at first the towering Alps we try,   225

263

Mount o'er the vales, and seem to tread the sky,
Th' eternal snows appear already past,
And the first clouds and mountains seem the last;
But, those attained, we tremble to survey
The growing labours of the lengthened way, 230
Th' increasing prospect tires our wandering eyes,
Hills peep o'er hills, and Alps on Alps arise!
    A perfect Judge will read each work of wit
With the same spirit that its author writ:
Survey the WHOLE, nor seek slight faults to find 235
Where nature moves, and rapture warms the mind;
Nor lose, for that malignant dull delight,
The generous pleasure to be charmed with Wit.
But in such lays as neither ebb, nor flow,
Correctly cold, and regularly low, 240
That shunning faults, one quiet tenour keep,
We cannot blame indeed —— but we may sleep.
In wit, as nature, what affects our hearts
Is not th' exactness of peculiar parts;
'Tis not a lip, or eye, we beauty call, 245
But the joint force and full result of all.
Thus when we view some well-proportioned dome,
(The world's just wonder, and even thine, O Rome!)
No single parts unequally surprize,
All comes united to th' admiring eyes; 250
No monstrous height, or breadth, or length appear;
The Whole at once is bold, and regular.
    Whoever thinks a faultless piece to see,
Thinks what ne'er was, nor is, nor e'er shall be.
In every work regard the writer's End, 255
Since none can compass more than they intend;
And if the means be just, the conduct true,
Applause, in spite of trivial faults, is due;
As men of breeding, sometimes men of wit,
T' avoid great errors, must the less commit: 260
Neglect the rules each verbal Critic lays,
For not to know some trifles, is a praise.
Most Critics, fond of some subservient art,
Still make the Whole depend upon a Part:
They talk of principles, but notions prize, 265
And all to one loved Folly sacrifice.
    Once on a time, La Mancha's Knight, they say,
A certain bard encountering on the way,
Discoursed in terms as just, with looks as sage,
As e'er could Dennis of the Grecian stage; 270
Concluding all were desperate sots and fools,

---

267. *La Mancha's knight: Don Quixote.* 270. *Dennis:* a contemporary critic.

Who durst depart from Aristotle's rules.
Our Author, happy in a judge so nice,
Produced his Play, and begged the Knight's advice;
Made him observe the subject, and the plot,   275
The manners, passions, unities; what not?
All which, exact to rule, were brought about,
Were but a Combat in the lists left out.
"What! leave the Combat out?" exclaims the Knight;
Yes, or we must renounce the Stagirite.   280
"Not so by Heaven" (he answers in a rage),
"Knights, squires, and steeds, must enter on the stage."
So vast a throng the stage can ne'er contain.
"Then build a new, or act it in a plain."
   Thus Critics, of less judgment than caprice,   285
Curious not knowing, not exact but nice,
Form short Ideas; and offend in arts
(As most in manners) by a love to parts.
   Some to *Conceit* alone their taste confine,
And glittering thoughts struck out at every line;   290
Pleased with a work where nothing's just or fit;
One glaring Chaos and wild heap of wit.
Poets like painters, thus, unskilled to trace
The naked nature and the living grace,
With gold and jewels cover every part,   295
And hide with ornaments their want of art.
True Wit is Nature to advantage dressed,
What oft was thought, but ne'er so well expressed;
Something, whose truth convinced at sight we find,
That gives us back the image of our mind.   300
As shades more sweetly recommend the light,
So modest plainness sets off sprightly wit.
For works may have more wit than does 'em good,
As bodies perish thro' excess of blood.
   Others for *Language* all their care express,   305
And value books, as women men, for Dress:
Their praise is still,—the Style is excellent:
The Sense, they humbly take upon content.
Words are like leaves; and where they most abound,
Much fruit of sense beneath is rarely found: 310
False Eloquence, like the prismatic glass,
Its gaudy colours spreads on every place;
The face of Nature we no more survey,
All glares alike, without distinction gay:
But true expression, like th' unchanging Sun, ⎫   315
Clears and improves whate'er it shines upon, ⎬
It gilds all objects, but it alters none.   ⎭

---

289. *conceit:* an ingenious poetic figure or thought.

Expression is the dress of thought, and still
Appears more decent, as more suitable;
A vile conceit in pompous words expressed,   320
Is like a clown in regal purple dressed:
For different styles with different subjects sort,
As several garbs with country, town, and court.
Some by old words to fame have made pretence,
Ancients in phrase, mere moderns in their sense;   325
Such laboured nothings, in so strange a style,
Amaze th' unlearn'd, and make the learnèd smile.
Unlucky, as Fungoso in the play,
These sparks with awkward vanity display
What the fine gentleman wore yesterday;   330
And but so mimic ancient wits at best,
As apes our grandsires, in their doublets drest.
In words, as fashions, the same rule will hold;
Alike fantastic, if too new, or old:
Be not the first by whom the new are tried,   335
Nor yet the last to lay the old aside.
    But most by *Numbers* judge a Poet's song;
And smooth or rough, with them is right or wrong:
In the bright Muse, though thousand charms conspire,
Her voice is all these tuneful fools admire;   340
Who haunt Parnassus but to please their ear,
Not mend their minds; as some to Church repair,
Not for the doctrine, but the music there.
These equal syllables alone require,
Tho' oft the ear the open vowels tire;   345
While expletives their feeble aid do join;
And ten low words oft creep in one dull line:
While they ring round the same unvaried chimes,
With sure returns of still expected rhymes;
Where-e'er you find "the cooling western breeze,"   350
In the next line it "whispers through the trees:"
If crystal streams "with pleasing murmurs creep,"
The reader's threatened (not in vain) with "sleep:"
Then, at the last and only couplet fraught
With some unmeaning thing they call a thought,   355
A needless Alexandrine ends the song
That, like a wounded snake, drags its slow length along.
Leave such to tune their own dull rhymes, and know
What's roundly smooth or languishingly slow;
And praise the easy vigour of a line,   360
Where Denham's strength, and Waller's sweetness join.
True ease in writing comes from art, not chance,
As those move easiest who have learned to dance.

---

328. *play:* Ben Jonson's *Every Man Out of His Humour.* 337. *Numbers:* versification (especially the sound). 356. *Alexandrine:* a line of twelve syllables and six stresses (illustrated in 357).

'Tis not enough no harshness gives offence,
The sound must seem an Echo to the sense: 365
Soft is the strain when Zephyr gently blows,
And the smooth stream in smoother numbers flows;
But when loud surges lash the sounding shore,
The hoarse, rough verse should like the torrent roar:
When Ajax strives some rock's vast weight to throw,   370
The line too labours, and the words move slow;
Not so, when swift Camilla scours the plain,
Flies o'er the unbending corn, and skims along the main.
Hear how Timotheus' varied lays surprize,
And bid alternate passions fall and rise!   375
While, at each change, the son of Libyan Jove
Now burns with glory, and then melts with love,
Now his fierce eyes with sparkling fury glow,
Now sighs steal out, and tears begin to flow:
Persians and Greeks like turns of nature found,   380
And the world's victor stood subdued by Sound!
The power of Music all our hearts allow,
And what Timotheus was, is DRYDEN now.
     Avoid Extremes; and shun the fault of such,
Who still are pleased too little or too much.   385
At every trifle scorn to take offence—
That always shows great pride, or little sense;
Those heads, as stomachs, are not sure the best,
Which nauseate all, and nothing can digest.
Yet let not each gay turn thy rapture move;   390
For fools admire, but men of sense approve:
As things seem large which we thro' mists descry,
Dulness is ever apt to magnify.
     Some foreign writers, some our own despise;
The Ancients only, or the Moderns prize.   395
Thus Wit, like Faith, by each man is applied
To one small sect, and all are damned beside.
Meanly they seek the blessing to confine,
And force that sun but on a part to shine,
Which not alone the southern wit sublimes,   400
But ripens spirits in cold northern climes;
Which from the first has shone on ages past,
Enlights the present, and shall warm the last;
Tho' each may feel increases and decays,
And see now clearer and now darker days.   405
Regard not then if Wit be old or new,
But blame the false, and value still the true.
     Some ne'er advance a Judgment of their own,
But catch the spreading notion of the Town;

---

372. *Camilla:* described in Virgil's *Aeneid*, vii 808 ff. 374. *Timotheus:* musician to Alexander the Great. 376. *Jove:* Alexander the Great.

They reason and conclude by precedent,   410
And own stale nonsense which they ne'er invent.
Some judge of author's names, not works, and then
Nor praise nor blame the writings, but the men.
Of all this servile herd the worst is he
That in proud dulness joins with Quality: 415
A constant Critic at the great man's board,
To fetch and carry nonsense for my Lord.
What woful stuff this madrigal would be,
In some starved hackney sonneteer, or me?
But let a Lord once own the happy lines,   420
How the wit brightens! how the style refines!
Before his sacred name flies every fault,
And each exalted stanza teems with thought!
　　The Vulgar thus through Imitation err;
As oft the Learn'd by being singular;   425
So much they scorn the crowd, that if the throng
By chance go right, they purposely go wrong;
So Schismatics the plain believers quit,
And are but damned for having too much wit.
Some praise at morning what they blame at night;   430
But always think the last opinion right.
A Muse by these is like a mistress used,
This hour she's idolized, the next abused;
While their weak heads like towns unfortified,
'Twixt sense and nonsense daily change their side.   435
Ask them the cause; they're wiser still, they say;
And still to-morrow's wiser than to-day.
We think our fathers fools, so wise we grow,
Our wiser sons, no doubt, will think us so.
Once School-divines this zealous isle o'er-spread;   440
Who knew most Sentences, was deepest read;
Faith, Gospel, all, seemed made to be disputed,
And none had sense enough to be confuted:
Scotists and Thomists, now, in peace remain,
Amidst their kindred cobwebs in Duck-lane.   445
If Faith itself has different dresses worn,
What wonder modes in Wit should take their turn?
Oft, leaving what is natural and fit,
The current folly proves the ready wit;
And authors think their reputation safe,   450
Which lives as long as fools are pleased to laugh.
　　Some valuing those of their own side or mind,
Still make themselves the measure of mankind:
Fondly we think we honour merit then,
When we but praise ourselves in other men.   455

---

445. *Duck-lane:* London street where second-hand books were sold.

Parties in Wit attend on those of State,
And public faction doubles private hate.
Pride, Malice, Folly, against Dryden rose,
In various shapes of Parsons, Critics, Beaus;
But sense survived, when merry jests were past;   460
For rising merit will buoy up at last.
Might he return, and bless once more our eyes,
New Blackmores and new Milbourns must arise:
Nay should great Homer lift his awful head,
Zoilus again would start up from the dead.   465
Envy will merit, as its shade, pursue;
But like a shadow, proves the substance true;
For envied Wit, like Sol eclipsed, makes known
Th' opposing body's grossness, not its own,
When first that sun too powerful beams displays,   470
It draws up vapours which obscure its rays;
But even those clouds at last adorn its way,
Reflect new glories, and augment the day.
  Be thou the first true merit to befriend;
His praise is lost, who stays till all commend.   475
Short is the date, alas, of modern rhymes,
And 't is but just to let them live betimes.
No longer now that golden age appears,
When Patriarch-wits survived a thousand years:
Now length of Fame (our second life) is lost,   480
And bare threescore is all even that can boast;
Our sons their fathers' failing language see;
And such as Chaucer is, shall Dryden be.
So when the faithful pencil has designed
Some bright Idea of the master's mind,   485
Where a new world leaps out at his command,
And ready Nature waits upon his hand;
When the ripe colours soften and unite,
And sweetly melt into just shade and light;
When mellowing years their full perfection give,   490
And each bold figure just begins to live,
The treacherous colours the fair art betray,
And all the bright creation fades away!
  Unhappy Wit, like most mistaken things,
Atones not for that envy which it brings.   495
In youth alone its empty praise we boast,
But soon the short-lived vanity is lost:
Like some fair flower the early spring supplies,
That gaily blooms, but even in blooming dies.
What is this Wit, which must our cares employy?   500

---

463. Sir Richard *Blackmore* and Luke *Milbourn* were among those who attacked Dryden and his work. 465. *Zoilus:* ancient grammarian, whose strictures upon Homer have made his name synonymous with pedantry.

The owner's wife, that other men enjoy;
Then most our trouble still when most admired,
And still the more we give, the more required;
Whose fame with pains we guard, but lose with ease,
Sure some to vex, but never all to please;   505
'Tis what the vicious fear, the virtuous shun,
By fools 'tis hated, and by knaves undone!
   If Wit so much from Ignorance undergo,
Ah let not Learning too commence its foe!
Of old, those met rewards who could excel,   510
And such were praised who but endeavoured well:
Tho' triumphs were to generals only due,
Crowns were reserved to grace the soldiers too.
Now, they who reach Parnassus' lofty crown,
Employ their pains to spurn some others down;   515
And while self-love each jealous writer rules,
Contending wits become the sport of fools:
But still the worst with most regret commend,
For each ill Author is as bad a Friend.
To what base ends, and by what abject ways,   520
Are mortals urged thro' sacred lust of praise!
Ah ne'er so dire a thirst of glory boast,
Nor in the Critic let the Man be lost.
Good-nature and good-sense must ever join;
To err is human, to forgive, divine.   525
   But if in noble minds some dregs remain
Not yet purged off, of spleen and sour disdain;
Discharge that rage on more provoking crimes,
Nor fear a dearth in these flagitious times.
No pardon vile Obscenity should find,   530
Tho' wit and art conspire to move your mind;
But Dulness with Obscenity must prove
As shameful sure as Impotence in love.
In the fat age of pleasure, wealth, and ease,
Sprung the rank weed, and thrived with large increase: 535
When love was all an easy Monarch's care;
Seldom at council, never in a war:
Jilts ruled the state, and statesmen farces writ;
Nay Wits had pensions, and young Lords had wit:
The Fair sat panting at a Courtier's play,   540
And not a Mask went unimproved away:
The modest fan was lifted up no more,
And Virgins smiled at what they blushed before.
The following licence of a Foreign reign
Did all the dregs of bold Socinus drain;   545
Then unbelieving priests reformed the nation,

---

545. *Socinus:* founder of Unitarianism, denied the divinity of Christ.

And taught more pleasant methods of salvation;
Where Heaven's free subjects might their rights dispute,
Lest God himself should seem too absolute:
Pulpits their sacred satire learned to spare,   550
And Vice admired to find a flatterer there!
Encouraged thus, Wit's Titans braved the skies,
And the press groaned with licensed blasphemies.
These monsters, Critics! with your darts engage,
Here point your thunder, and exhaust your rage!   555
Yet shun their fault, who, scandalously nice,
Will needs mistake an author into vice;
All seems infected that th' infected spy,
As all looks yellow to the jaundiced eye.

III

Learn then what MORALS Critics ought to show,   560
For 'tis but half a Judge's task, to know.
'Tis not enough, taste, judgment, learning, join;
In all you speak, let truth and candour shine:
That not alone what to your sense is due
All may allow; but seek your friendship too.   565
  Be silent always when you doubt your sense;
And speak, tho' sure, with seeming diffidence:
Some positive, persisting fops we know,
Who, if once wrong, will needs be always so;
But you, with pleasure own your errors past,   570
And make each day a crítique on the last.
  'Tis not enough, your counsel still be true;
Blunt truths more mischief than nice falsehoods do;
Men must be taught as if you taught them not,
And things unknown proposed as things forgot.   575
Without Good Breeding, truth is disapproved;
That only makes superior sense beloved.
  Be niggards of advice on no pretence;
For the worst avarice is that of sense.
With mean complacence ne'er betray your trust,   580
Nor be so civil as to prove unjust.
Fear not the anger of the wise to raise;
Those best can bear reproof, who merit praise.
  'Twere well might critics still this freedom take,
But Appius reddens at each word you speak,   585
And stares, tremendous, with a threatening eye,
Like some fierce Tyrant in old tapestry.
Fear most to tax an Honourable fool,

---

585. *Appius:* John Dennis, a literary critic whose tragedy called *Appius and Virginia* had been
a failure.

Whose right it is, uncensured, to be dull;
Such, without wit, are Poets when they please,   590
As without learning they can take Degrees.
Leave dangerous truths to unsuccessful Satires,
And flattery to fulsome Dedicators,
Whom, when they praise, the world believes no more,
Than when they promise to give scribbling o'er.   595
'Tis best sometimes your censure to restrain,
And charitably let the dull be vain:
Your silence there is better than your spite,
For who can rail so long as they can write?
Still humming on, their drowsy course they keep,   600
And lashed so long, like tops, are lashed asleep.
False steps but help them to renew the race,
As, after stumbling, Jades will mend their pace.
What crowds of these, impenitently bold,
In sounds and jingling syllables grown old,   605
Still run on Poets, in a raging vein,
Even to the dregs and squeezings of the brain,
Strain out the last dull droppings of their sense,
And rhyme with all the rage of Impotence.
    Such shameless Bards we have; and yet 'tis true,   610
There are as mad abandoned Critics too.
The bookful blockhead, ignorantly read,
With loads of learnèd lumber in his head,
With his own tongue still edifies his ears,
And always listening to himself appears.   615
All books he reads, and all he reads assails,
From Dryden's Fables down to Durfey's Tales.
With him, most authors steal their works, or buy;
Garth did not write his own Dispensary.
Name a new Play, and he's the Poet's friend,   620
Nay, showed his faults—but when would Poets mend?
No place so sacred from such fops is barred,
Nor is Paul's church more safe than Paul's churchyard:
Nay, fly to altars; there they'll talk you dead:
For Fools rush in where Angels fear to tread.   625
Distrustful sense with modest caution speaks,   ⎫
It still looks home, and short excursions makes; ⎬
But rattling nonsense in full volleys breaks,   ⎭
And never shocked, and never turned aside,
Bursts out, resistless, with a thundering tide.   630
    But where's the man, who counsel can bestow,
Still pleased to teach, and yet not proud to know;
Unbiassed, or by favour, or by spite;
Not dully prepossessed, nor blindly right;

---

617. *Durfey:* Thomas Durfey, dramatist, song-writer, and literary hack. 619. *Dispensary:* the title of a poem by Pope's friend, Sir Samuel Garth.

Tho' learn'd, well-bred; and tho' well-bred, sincere,   635
Modestly bold, and humanly severe:
Who to a friend his faults can freely show,
And gladly praise the merit of a foe?
Blest with a taste exact, yet unconfined;
A knowledge both of books and human kind: 640
Generous converse; a soul exempt from pride;
And love to praise, with reason on his side?
   Such once were Critics; such the happy few,
Athens and Rome in better ages knew.
The mighty Stagirite first left the shore,   645
Spread all his sails, and durst the deeps explore:
He steered securely, and discovered far,
Led by the light of the Mæonian Star.
Poets, a race long unconfined, and free,
Still fond and proud of savage liberty,   650
Received his laws; and stood convinced 'twas fit,
Who conquered Nature, should preside o'er Wit.
   Horace still charms with graceful negligence,
And without method talks us into sense,
Will, like a friend, familiarly convey   655
The truest notions in the easiest way.
He, who supreme in judgment, as in wit,
Might boldly censure, as he boldly writ,
Yet judged with coolness, tho' he sung with fire;
His Precepts teach but what his works inspire.   660
Our Critics take a contrary extreme,
They judge with fury, but they write with fle'me:
Nor suffers Horace more in wrong Translations
By Wits, than Critics in as wrong Quotations.
   See Dionysius Homer's thoughts refine,   665
And call new beauties forth from every line!
   Fancy and art in gay Petronius please,
The scholar's learning, with the courtier's ease.
   In grave Quintilian's copious work, we find
The justest rules, and clearest method joined: 670
Thus useful arms in magazines we place,
All ranged in order, and disposed with grace,
But less to please the eye, than arm the hand,
Still fit for use, and ready at command.
   Thee, bold Longinus! all the Nine inspire,   675
And bless their Critic with a Poet's fire.
An ardent Judge, who zealous in his trust,
With warmth gives sentence, yet is always just;

---

648. *Mæonian star:* Homer. 666. *Dionysius:* Dionysius of Halicarnassus, Greek rhetorician and critic. 667. *Petronius:* Roman author whose *Satyricon* contains a small amount of criticism. 669. *Quintilian:* Roman author of a famous treatise of rhetoric, *De Institutione Oratoria.* 675. *Longinus:* attributed author of the treatise *On Elevated Style* (often called *On the Sublime*).

Whose own example strengthens all his laws;
And is himself that great Sublime he draws.   680
    Thus long succeeding Critics justly reigned,
Licence repressed, and useful laws ordained.
Learning and Rome alike in empire grew;
And Arts still followed where her Eagles flew;
From the same foes, at last, both felt their doom,   685
And the same age saw Learning fall, and Rome.
With Tyranny, then Superstition joined,
As that the body, this enslaved the mind;
Much was believed, but little understood,
And to be dull was construed to be good;   690
A second deluge Learning thus o'er-run,
And the Monks finished what the Goths begun.
    At length Erasmus, that great injured name,
(The glory of the Priesthood, and the shame!)
Stemmed the wild torrent of a barbarous age,   695
And drove those holy Vandals off the stage.
    But see! each Muse, in Leo's golden days,
Starts from her trance, and trims her withered bays,
Rome's ancient Genius, o'er its ruins spread,
Shakes off the dust, and rears his reverend head   700
Then Sculpture and her sister-arts revive;
Stones leaped to form, and rocks began to live;
With sweeter notes each rising Temple rung;
A Raphael painted, and a Vida sung.
Immortal Vida: on whose honoured brow   705
The Poet's bays and Critic's ivy grow:
Cremona now shall ever boast thy name,
As next in place to Mantua, next in fame!
    But soon by impious arms from Latium chased,
Their ancient bounds the banished Muses passed;   710
Thence Arts o'er all the northern world advance.
But Critic-learning flourished most in France:
The Rules, a nation born to serve obeys;
And Boileau still in right of Horace sways.
But we, brave Britons, foreign laws despised,   715
And kept unconquered, and uncivilized;
Fierce for the liberties of wit, and bold,
We still defied the Romans, as of old.
Yet some there were, among the sounder few
Of those who less presumed, and better knew,   720
Who durst assert the juster ancient cause,
And here restored Wit's fundamental laws.

---

698. *Leo:* Pope Leo X (1513–21) a great patron of the arts. 704. *Vida:* Renaissance Latin poet (1488–1566), author of a verse treatise on poetics. 707–8. *Cremona, Mantua:* Vida's and Virgil's birthplaces. 709. Rome was sacked by the French in 1527. 714. *Boileau:* Referring especially to his *L'Art poétique* (1673).

Such was the Muse, whose rules and practice tell,
"Nature's chief Master-piece is writing well."
Such was Roscommon, not more learn'd than good,   725
With manners generous as his noble blood;
To him the wit of Greece and Rome was known,
And every author's merit, but his own.
Such late was Walsh—the Muse's judge and friend,
Who justly knew to blame or to commend;   730
To failings mild, but zealous for desert;
The clearest head, and the sincerest heart.
This humble praise, lamented shade! receive,
This praise at least a grateful Muse may give:
The Muse, whose early voice you taught to sing,   735
Prescribed her heights, and pruned her tender wing,
(Her guide now lost) no more attempts to rise,
But in low numbers short excursions tries:
Content, if hence th' unlearn'd their wants may view,
The learn'd reflect on what before they knew: 740
Careless of censure, nor too fond of fame;
Still pleased to praise, yet not afraid to blame,
Averse alike to flatter, or offend;
Not free from faults, nor yet too vain to mend.

---

723. *the Muse:* John Sheffield (1648–1721). 725. *Roscommon:* Wentworth Dillon, Earl of Roscommon (1633?–85), author of a verse *Essay on Translated Verse.* 729. *Walsh:* William Walsh (1633–1708), critic and poet who had been Pope's early mentor.

The Autobiography of Edward Gibbon

Edward Gibbon

Editor's Introduction

Gibbon's *Autobiography*—or *Memoirs of My Life and Writings*, as its author would have called it had he lived to publish such a work—is, notwithstanding its preparation by another hand and the fact that it exists in no fewer than six unfinished drafts, among the classics of its kind, indeed one of the world's favorite books. Its fascination lies partly in its display of the ironic style, itself a celebrated thing, that Gibbon had perfected for his history of the Roman Empire, which is here adapted with happy effect to personal account. But it appeals also to the interest which every reader of the *Decline and Fall* must have in the person who, working entirely alone, could become the master of that tremendous subject, one of the most extraordinary achievements in the intellectual history of the Western world. "The public," Gibbon observed, "are always curious to know the men who have left behind them any image of their minds." To which he added, with characteristic candor, that he assumed the review of his own "moral and literary character" must be of particular concern.

The book as we have it was constructed by his friend and literary executor, Lord Sheffield, from sketches written by Gibbon between 1788 and 1793, the year before his death. Of these, the first was merely a family history, begun after the presentation to him of a book on heraldry written by a Gibbon he wrongly supposed had been his ancestor. Subsequent drafts dealt with his own upbringing, were extended to his middle life, went back and told the same story at greater length with the addition of what he called "observation and excursions." None of them goes beyond the completion of the *Decline and Fall,* when Gibbon was trying to decide what to do with the rest of his life, an interval he supposed would be longer than it turned out to be. In addition, he left what Sheffield called "notes and memoranda on loose unconnected papers and cards," of which that friend made use while stitching together, so far as possible, the accounts Gibbon had written into one continuous narrative supplemented, particularly at the end, by letters. Long after this appeared, and when examination of Gibbon's papers revealed the extent of the editorial job that Sheffield had done, the relevant documents including the six drafts were published also, but by then the work as Sheffield formed it had established itself as "Gibbon's Autobiography," and no recasting of the materials has ever succeeded in replacing it.

Not that the figure who emerges in the book is an altogether attractive one. Gibbon was a little man of large vanity, in later life very fat, who dressed like a fop and dominated rooms with talk to which he summoned the attention of the company by tapping on his snuffbox. He liked to look at the portrait of himself which had been painted by Reynolds, and which he hung at the house in Lausanne where he spent the latter part of his life; he spent more money than he could afford on lavish extravagances; he liked the company of men richer than himself, to whom he all but toadied. Among his contemporaries, Boswell, who belonged to the same London club, detested him, and Johnson, who was his opposite in everything except erudition, probably felt much the same way. Yet Gibbon was capable of enduring friendships, at least one of which may be said to have cost him something, for he insisted, not long before his death, hearing that Sheffield's wife had died, on making a difficult and circuitous journey from Switzerland across a France torn by revolution to be at his friend's side, when he was already suffering from the humiliating disease—a large hydrocele in the vicinity of what he called his "inexpressibles"—that ultimately killed him.

Whatever one may think of Gibbon, the story of his life is not without its poignant moments. Among these, one is his account of the afternoon in October 1764, while he was sitting on the steps overlooking the ruins of the capitol in Rome, when the subject to which he was to devote himself presented itself to him in all its magnitude; another is his description of the evening more than twenty years later when, having written the last line of the *Decline and Fall,* he got up from his table to take a walk around his Swiss garden, musing on the completion of the task that had occupied him for so long. That there is a kind of drama in these events is mysterious, for such episodes are not usually remarkable in scholars. But in Gibbon, the sense, first, of having been called to a great task, and second, of having seen it through despite every difficulty and discouragement, was very real, and we as readers come to share it. Not for nothing did he refer to himself in the third person as "the historian of the Roman Empire."

The text of the *Autobiography* (to give it its familiar name) reprinted here is substantially that which Sheffield published in 1796, and which has been reprinted many times since. Sheffield's notes are indicated by his initial. Omitted are, besides the letters to and from Gibbon which his friend added by way of providing some account of his last years, a number of letters and journal excerpts that Gibbon included in his drafts, often as footnotes. Many of these are in French, a language Gibbon knew as well as, and even, he sometimes thought, better than he knew his own.

The Autobiography of Edward Gibbon

In the fifty-second year of my age, after the completion of an arduous and successful work, I now propose to employ some moments of my leisure in reviewing the simple transactions of a private and literary life. Truth, naked, unblushing truth, the first virtue of more serious history, must be the sole recommendation of this personal narrative. The style shall be simple and familiar: but style is the image of character; and the habits of correct writing may produce, without labour or design, the appearance of art and study. My own amusement is my motive, and will be my reward: and if these sheets are communicated to some discreet and indulgent friends, they will be secreted from the public eye till the author shall be removed beyond the reach of criticism or ridicule.[1]

A lively desire of knowing and of recording our ancestors so generally prevails, that it must depend on the influence of some common principle in the minds of men. We seem to have lived in the persons of our forefathers; it is the labour and reward of vanity to extend the term of this ideal longevity. Our imagination is always active to enlarge the narrow circle in which nature has confined us. Fifty or an hundred years may be allotted to an individual; but we step forward beyond death with such hopes as religion and philosophy will suggest; and we fill up the silent vacancy that precedes our birth, by associating ourselves to the authors of our existence. Our calmer judgement will rather tend to moderate, than to suppress, the pride of an ancient and worthy race. The satirist may laugh, the philosopher may preach; but reason herself will respect the prejudices and habits, which have been consecrated by the experience of mankind. Few there are who can sincerely despise in others, an advantage of which they are secretly ambitious to partake. The knowledge of our own family from a remote period, will be always esteemed as an abstract pre-eminence, since it can never be promiscuously enjoyed; but the longest series of peasants and mechanics would not afford much gratification to the pride of their descendant. We wish to discover our ancestors, but we wish to discover them possessed of ample fortunes, adorned with honourable titles, and holding an eminent rank in the class of hereditary nobles, which has been maintained for the wisest and most beneficial purposes, in almost every climate of the globe, and in almost every modification of political society.

Wherever the distinction of birth is allowed to form a superior order in the state, education and example should always, and will often, produce among them a dignity of sentiment and propriety of conduct, which is guarded from dishonour by their own and the public esteem. If we read of some illustrious line so ancient that it has no beginning, so worthy that it ought to have no end, we sympathize in its various fortunes; nor can

---

[1] This passage is found in one only of the six sketches, and in that which seems to have been the first written, and which was laid aside among loose papers. Mr. Gibbon, in his communications with me on the subject of his Memoirs, a subject which he had not mentioned to any other person, expressed a determination of publishing them in his lifetime; and never appears to have departed from that resolution, excepting in one of his letters annexed, in which he intimates a doubt, though rather carelessly, whether in his time, or at any time, they would meet the eye of the public. In a conversation, however, not long before his death, I suggested to him, that, if he should make them a full image of his mind, he would not have nerves to publish them, and therefore that they should be posthumous. He answered, rather eagerly, that he was determined to publish them *in his lifetime*. S.

we blame the generous enthusiasm, or even the harmless vanity, of those who are allied to the honours of its name. For my own part, could I draw my pedigree from a general, a statesman, or a celebrated author, I should study their lives with the diligence of filial love. In the investigation of past events, our curiosity is stimulated by the immediate or indirect reference to ourselves; but in the estimate of honour we should learn to value the gifts of nature above those of fortune; to esteem in our ancestors the qualities that best promote the interests of society; and to pronounce the descendant of a king less truly noble than the offspring of a man of genius, whose writings will instruct or delight the latest posterity. The family of Confucius is, in my opinion, the most illustrious in the world. After a painful ascent of eight or ten centuries, our barons and princes of Europe are lost in the darkness of the middle ages; but, in the vast equality of the empire of China, the posterity of Confucius have maintained, above two thousand two hundred years, their peaceful honours and perpetual succession. The chief of the family is still revered, by the sovereign and the people, as the lively image of the wisest of mankind. The nobility of the Spencers has been illustrated and enriched by the trophies of Marlborough; but I exhort them to consider the *Fairy Queen*[2] as the most precious jewel of their coronet. Our immortal Fielding was of the younger branch of the Earls of Denbigh, who draw their origin from the Counts of Habsburg, the lineal descendants of Eltrico, in the seventh century, Duke of Alsace. Far different have been the fortunes of the English and German divisions of the family of Habsburg: the former, the knights and sheriffs of Leicestershire, have slowly risen to the dignity of a peerage; the latter, the Emperors of Germany, and Kings of Sapin, have threatened the liberty of the old, and invaded the treasures of the new world. The successors of Charles the Fifth may disdain their brethren of England; but the romance of *Tom Jones,* that exquisite picture of human manners, will outlive the palace of the Escurial, and the imperial eagle of the house of Austria.

That these sentiments are just, or at least natural, I am the more inclined to believe, as I am not myself interested in the cause; for I can derive from my ancestors neither glory nor shame. Yet a sincere and simple narrative of my own life may amuse some of my leisure hours; but it will subject me, and perhaps with justice, to the imputation of vanity. I may judge, however, from the experience both of past and of the present times, that the public are always curious to know the men who have left behind them any image of their minds: the most scanty accounts of such men are compiled with diligence, and perused with eagerness; and the student of every class may derive a lesson, or an example, from the lives most similar to his own. My name may hereafter be placed among the thousand articles of a *Biographia Britannica;* and I must be conscious that no one is so well qualified as myself to describe the series of my thoughts and actions. The authority of my masters, of the grave Thuanus, and the philosophic Hume, might be sufficient to justify my design; but it would not be difficult to produce a long list of ancients and moderns who, in various forms, have exhibited their own portraits. Such portraits are often the most interesting, and sometimes the only interesting parts of their writings; and if they be sincere, we seldom complain of the minuteness or prolixity of these personal memorials. The lives of the younger Pliny, of Petrarch, and of Erasmus, are expressed in the epistles which they themselves have given to the world. The essays of Montaigne and Sir William Temple bring us home to the houses and bosoms of the authors: we smile without contempt at the headstrong passions of Benvenuto Cellini, and the gay follies of Colley Cibber. The confessions of St. Austin and Rousseau disclose the secrets of the human heart: the commentaries of the learned

---

[2] Nor less praiseworthy are the ladies three,
The honour of that noble familie,
Of which I meanest boast myself to be.
Spenser, *Colin Clout,* &c., v. 538.

Huet have survived his evangelical demonstration; and the memoirs of Goldoni are more truly dramatic than his Italian comedies. The heretic and the churchman are strongly marked in the characters and fortunes of Whiston and Bishop Newton; and even the dullness of Michael de Marolles and Anthony Wood acquires some value from the faithful representation of men and manners. That I am equal or superior to some of these, the effects of modesty and affection cannot force me to dissemble.

My family is originally derived from the county of Kent. The southern district, which borders on Sussex and the sea, was formerly overspread with the great forest Anderida, and even now retains the denomination of the *Weald*, or Woodland. In this district, and in the hundred and parish of Rolvenden, the Gibbons were possessed of lands in the year one thousand three hundred and twenty-six; and the elder branch of the family, without much increase or diminution of property, still adheres to its native soil. Fourteen years after the first appearance of his name, John Gibbon is recorded as the Marmorarius or architect of King Edward the Third: the strong and stately castle of Queensborough, which guarded the entrance of the Medway, was a monument of his skill; and the grant of an hereditary toll on the passage from Sandwich to Stonar, in the Isle of Thanet, is the reward of no vulgar artist. In the visitations of the heralds, the Gibbons are frequently mentioned: they held the rank of Esquire in an age when that title was less promiscuously assumed: one of them, in the reign of Queen Elizabeth, was captain of the militia of Kent; and a free school, in the neighbouring town of Benenden, proclaims the charity and opulence of its founder. But time, or their own obscurity, has cast a veil of oblivion over the virtues and vices of my Kentish ancestors; their character or station confined them to the labours and pleasures of a rural life; nor is it in my power to follow the advice of the poet, in an inquiry after a name—

Go! search it there, where to be born, and die,
Of rich and poor makes all the history.[*]

so recent is the institution of our parish registers. In the beginning of the seventeenth century a younger branch of the Gibbons of Rolvenden migrated from the country to the city; and from this branch I do not blush to descend. The law requires some abilities; the church imposes some restraints; and before our army and navy, our civil establishments, and India empire, had opened so many paths of fortune, the mercantile profession was more frequently chosen by youths of a liberal race and education, who aspired to create their own independence. Our most respectable families have not disdained the counting-house, or even the shop; their names are enrolled in the Livery and Companies of London; and in England, as well as in the Italian commonweaths, heralds have been compelled to declare that gentility is not degraded by the exercise of trade.

The armorial ensigns which, in the times of chivalry, adorned the crest and shield of the soldier, are now become an empty decoration, which every man, who has money to build a carriage, may paint according to his fancy on the panels. My family arms are the same which were borne by the Gibbons of Kent in an age when the College of Heralds religiously guarded the distinctions of blood and name: a lion rampant gardant, between three escallop-shells Argent, on a field Azure.[3] I should not, however, have been tempted to blazon my coat of arms, were it not connected with a whimsical anecdote. About the reign of James the First, the three harmless escallop-shells were changed by Edmund Gibbon, Esq., into three *Ogresses,* or female cannibals, with a design of stigmatizing three ladies, his kinswomen, who had

---

[*] Alexander Pope, *Moral Essays,* iii, 287—Ed.

[3] The father of Lord Chancellor Hardwicke married an heiress of this family of Gibbon. The Chancellor's escutcheon in the Temple Hall quarters the arms of Gibbon, as does also that, in Lincoln's Inn Hall, of Charles York, Chancellor in 1770. S.

provoked him by an unjust lawsuit. But this singular mode of revenge, for which he obtained the sanction of Sir William Seagar, king-at-arms, soon expired with its author; and, on his own monument in the Temple Church, the monsters vanish, and the three escallop-shells resume their proper and hereditary place.

Our alliances by marriage it is not disgraceful to mention. The chief honour of my ancestry is James Fiens, Baron Say and Seale, and Lord High Treasurer of England, in the reign of Henry the Sixth; from whom by the Phelips, the Whetnalls, and the Cromers, I am lineally descended in the eleventh degree. His dismission and imprisonment in the Tower were insufficient to appease the popular clamour; and the Treasurer, with his son-in-law Cromer, was beheaded (1450), after a mock trial by the Kentish insurgents. The black list of his offences, as it is exhibited in Shakespeare, displays the ignorance and envy of a plebeian tyrant. Besides the vague reproaches of selling Maine and Normandy to the Dauphin, the Treasurer is specially accused of luxury, for riding on a foot-cloth, and of treason, for speaking French, the language of our enemies: 'Thou hast most traiterously corrupted the youth of the realm', says Jack Cade to the unfortunate lord, 'in erecting a grammar school; and whereas before, our forefathers had no other books than the score and the tally, thou hast caused printing to be used; and, contrary to the king, his crown, and dignity, thou hast built a paper-mill. It will be proved to thy face, that thou hast men about thee who usually talk of a noun and a verb, and such abominable words, as no Christian ear can endure to hear.'[*] Our dramatic poet is generally more attentive to character than to history; and I much fear that the art of printing was not introduced into England till several years after Lord Say's death: but of some of these meritorious crimes I should hope to find my ancestor guilty; and a man of letters may be proud of his descent from a patron and martyr of learning.

In the beginning of the last century, Robert Gibbon, Esq., of Rolvenden in Kent[4] (who died in 1618), had a son of the same name of Robert, who settled in London, and became a member of the Clothworkers' Company. His wife was a daughter of the Edgars, who flourished about four hundred years in the county of Suffolk, and produced an eminent and wealthy serjeant-at-law, Sir Gregory Edgar, in the reign of Henry the Seventh. Of the sons of Robert Gibbon (who died in 1643), Matthew did not aspire above the station of a linen-draper in Leadenhall Street; but John has given to the public some curious memorials of his existence, his character, and his family. He was born on the 3rd of November, in the year 1629; his education was liberal, at a grammar school, and afterwards in Jesus College at Cambridge; and he celebrates the retired content which he enjoyed at Allesborough in Worcestershire, in the house of Thomas Lord Coventry, where he was employed as a domestic tutor. But the spirit of my kinsman soon immerged into more active life; he visited foreign countries as a soldier and a traveller, acquired the knowledge of the French and Spanish languages; passed some time in the Isle of Jersey, crossed the Atlantic, and resided upwards of a twelvemonth (1659) in the rising colony of Virginia. In this remote province, his taste, or rather passion, for heraldry found a singular gratification at a war-dance of the native Indians. As they moved in measured steps, brandishing their tomahawks, his curious eye contemplated their little

---

[*] William Shakespeare, *Henry VI*, act 4, sc. 7: 35 —Ed.

[4] Robert Gibbon, my lineal ancestor, in the fifth degree, was captain of the Kentish militia, and as he died in the year 1618, it may be presumed that he had appeared in arms at the time of the Spanish invasion. His wife was Margaret Phillips, daughter of Edward Phillips de la Weld in Tenterden, and of Rose his wife, daughter of George Whitnell, of East Peckham, Esquire. Peckham, the seat of the Whitnells of Kent, is mentioned, not indeed much to its honour, in the *Memoires du Comte de Grammont*, a classical work, the delight of every man and woman of taste to whom the French language is familiar.

shields of bark, and their naked bodies, which were painted with the colours and symbols of his favourite science. 'At which (says he) I exceedingly wondered; and concluded that heraldry was ingrafted *naturally* into the sense of human race. If so, it deserves a greater esteem than nowadays is put upon it.' His return to England after the restoration was soon followed by his marriage—his settlement in a house in St. Catherine's Cloister, near the Tower, which devolved to my grandfather—and his introduction into the Heralds' College (in 1671) by the style and title of Blue-mantle Pursuivant-at-Arms. In this office he enjoyed near fifty years the rare felicity of uniting, in the same pursuit, his duty and inclination: his name is remembered in the College, and many of his letters are still preserved. Several of the most respectable characters of the age, Sir William Dugdale, Mr. Ashmole, Dr. John Betts, and Dr. Nehemiah Grew, were his friends; and in the society of such men, John Gibbon may be recorded without disgrace as the member of an astrological club. The study of hereditary honours is favourable to the Royal prerogative; and my kinsman, like most of his family, was a high Tory both in church and state. In the latter end of the reign of Charles the Second, his pen was exercised in the cause of the Duke of York: the Republican faction he most cordially detested; and as each animal is conscious of its proper arms, the herald's revenge was emblazoned on a most diabolical escutcheon. But the triumph of the Whig government checked the preferment of Blue-mantle; and he was even suspended from his office till his tongue could learn to pronounce the oath of abjuration. His life was prolonged to the age of ninety; and, in the expectation of the inevitable though uncertain hour, he wishes to preserve the blessings of health, competence, and virtue. In the year 1682 he published at London his *Introductio ad Latinam Blasoniam,* an original attempt, which Camden had desiderated, to define, in a Roman idiom, the terms and attributes of a Gothic institution. It is not two years since I acquired, in a foreign land,

some domestic intelligence of my own family; and this intelligence was conveyed to Switzerland from the heart of Germany. I had formed an acquaintance with Mr. Langer, a lively and ingenious scholar, while he resided at Lausanne as preceptor to the Hereditary Prince of Brunswick. On his return to his proper station of Librarian to the Ducal Library of Wolfenbuttel, he accidentally found among some literary rubbish a small old English volume of heraldry, inscribed with the name of John Gibbon. From the title only Mr. Langer judged that it might be an acceptable present to his friend; and he judged rightly. His manner is quaint and affected; his order is confused: but he displays some wit, more reading, and still more enthusiasm; and if an enthusiast be often absurd, he is never languid. An English text is perpetually interspersed with Latin sentences in prose and verse; but in his own poetry he claims an exemption from the laws of prosody. Amidst a profusion of genealogical knowledge, my kinsman could not be forgetful of his own name; and to him I am indebted for almost the whole information concerning the Gibbon family. From this small work (a duodecimo of one hundred and sixty-five pages) the author expected immortal fame: and at the conclusion of his labour he sings, in a strain of self-exultation:

Usque huc corrigitur Romana Blasonia per me;
Verborumque dehinc barbara forma cadat.
Hic liber, in meritum si forsitan incidet usum,
Testis rite meae sedulitatis erit.
Quicquid agat Zoilus, ventura fatebitur aetas
Artis quod fueram non Clypearis inops.[*]

Such are the hopes of authors! In the failure of those hopes John Gibbon has not been the

---

[*] The language of heraldic blazonry—heretofore fallen into a barbaric state—I have now set straight in Roman Latin. If this book should come into deserved use, it will rightly be a witness of my assiduous care. Whatever critic Zoilus may do, the age to come will acknowledge that it was not lacking in the art of Clypean distinction (such as to win me fame).—Ed.

first of his profession, and very possibly may not be the last of his name. His brother, Matthew Gibbon, the draper, had one daughter and two sons—my grandfather, Edward, who was born in the year 1666, and Thomas, afterwards Dean of Carlisle. According to the mercantile creed, that the best book is a profitable ledger, the writings of John the herald would be much less precious than those of his nephew Edward: but an author professes at least to write for the public benefit; and the slow balance of trade can be pleasing to those persons only to whom it is advantageous. The successful industry of my grandfather raised him above the level of his immediate ancestors; he appears to have launched into various and extensive dealings: even his opinions were subordinate to his interest; and I find him in Flanders clothing King William's troops, while he would have contracted with more pleasure, though not perhaps at a cheaper rate, for the service of King James. During his residence abroad, his concerns at home were managed by his mother Hester, an active and notable woman. Her second husband was a widower, of the name of Acton: they united the children of their first nuptials. After his marriage with the daughter of Richard Acton, goldsmith in Leadenhall Street, he gave his own sister to Sir Whitmore Acton, of Aldenham; and I am thus connected, by a triple alliance, with that ancient and loyal family of Shropshire baronets. It consisted about that time of seven brothers, all of gigantic stature; one of whom, a pigmy of six feet two inches, confessed himself the last and the least of the seven; adding, in the true spirit of party, that such men were not born since the Revolution. Under the Tory administration of the last four years of Queen Anne (1710–4), Mr. Edward Gibbon was appointed one of the Commissioners of the Customs; he sat at that Board with Prior: but the merchant was better qualified for his station than the poet; since Lord Bolingbroke has been heard to declare that he never conversed with a man who more clearly understood the commerce and finances of England. In the year 1716 he was elected one of the directors of the South Sea Company; and his books exhibited the proof that, before his acceptance of this fatal office, he had acquired an independent fortune of sixty thousand pounds.

But his fortune was overwhelmed in the shipwreck of the year twenty, and the labours of thirty years were blasted in a single day. Of the use or abuse of the South Sea scheme, of the guilt or innocence of my grandfather and his brother directors, I am neither a competent nor a disinterested judge. Yet the equity of modern times must condemn the violent and arbitrary proceedings, which would have disgraced the cause of justice, and would render injustice still more odious. No sooner had the nation awakened from its golden dream than a popular and even a parliamentary clamour demanded their victims: but it was acknowledged on all sides that the South Sea directors, however guilty, could not be touched by any known laws of the land. The speech of Lord Molesworth, the author of *The State of Denmark,* may show the temper, or rather the intemperance, of the House of Commons. 'Extraordinary crimes (exclaimed that ardent Whig) call aloud for extraordinary remedies. The Roman lawgivers had not foreseen the possible existence of a parricide: but as soon as the first monster appeared he was sewn in a sack, and cast headlong into the river; and I shall be content to inflict the same treatment on the authors of our present ruin.' His motion was not literally adopted; but a bill of pains and penalties was introduced, a retroactive statue, to punish the offences, which did not exist at the time they were committed. Such a pernicious violation of liberty and law can be excused only by the most imperious necessity; nor could it be defended on this occasion by the plea of impending danger or useful example. The legislature restrained the persons of the directors, imposed an exorbitant security for their appearance, and marked their characters with a previous note of ignominy: they were compelled to deliver, upon oath, the strict value of their estates; and were disabled from making any transfer or alienation of any part of their property. Against a bill of pains and penalties it is the common right of every subject to be heard by his counsel at the bar: they prayed to be heard; their prayer was refused; and their oppressors, who required no evidence, would listen to no defence. It had been at first proposed that one-eighth of their respective estates should be allowed for the future support of the directors; but it was speciously urged, that in the various shades of opulence and guilt such an unequal proportion would be too light for many, and for some might possibly be too heavy. The character and conduct of each man were separately weighed; but, instead of the calm solemnity of a judicial inquiry, the fortune and honour of three and thirty Englishmen were made the topic of hasty conversation, the sport of a lawless majority; and the basest member of the committee, by a malicious word or a silent vote, might indulge his general spleen or personal animosity. Injury was aggravated by insult, and insult was embittered by pleasantry. Allowances of twenty pounds, or one shilling, were facetiously moved. A vague report that a director had formerly been concerned in *another* project, by which some unknown persons had lost their money, was admitted as a proof of his actual guilt. One man was ruined because he had dropped a foolish speech, that his horses should feed upon gold; another because he was grown so proud, that, one day at the Treasury, he had refused a civil answer to persons much above him. All were condemned, absent and unheard, in arbitrary fines and forfeitures, which swept away the greatest part of their substance. Such bold oppression can scarcely be shielded by the omnipotence of parliament: and yet it may be seriously questioned, whether the judges of the South Sea directors were the true and legal representatives of their country. The first parliament of George the First had been chosen (1715) for three years; the term had elapsed, their trust was expired; and the four additional years (1718–22), during which they continued to sit, were derived

not from the people, but from themselves; from the strong measure of the septennial bill, which can only be paralleled by *il serar di consiglio* of the Venetian history. Yet candour will own that to the same parliament every Englishman is deeply indebted: the septennial act, so vicious in its origin, has been sanctioned by time, experience, and the national consent. Its first operation secured the House of Hanover on the throne, and its permanent influence maintains the peace and stability of government. As often as a repeal has been moved in the House of Commons, I have given in its defence a clear and conscientious vote.

My grandfather could not expect to be treated with more lenity than his companions. His Tory principles and connexions rendered him obnoxious to the ruling powers: his name is reported in a suspicious secret; and his well-known abilities could not plead the excuse of ignorance or error. In the first proceedings against the South Sea directors, Mr. Gibbon is one of the few who were taken into custody; and, in the final sentence, the measure of his fine proclaims him eminently guilty. The total estimate which he delivered on oath to the House of Commons amounted to one hundred and six thousand five hundred and forty-three pounds, five shillings, and sixpence, exclusive of antecedent settlements. Two different allowances of fifteen and of ten thousand pounds were moved for Mr. Gibbon; but, on the question being put, it was carried without a division for the smaller sum. On these ruins, with the skill and credit, of which parliament had not been able to despoil him, my grandfather at a mature age erected the edifice of a new fortune: the labours of sixteen years were amply rewarded; and I have reason to believe that the second structure was not much inferior to the first. He had realized a very considerable property in Sussex, Hampshire, Buckinghamshire, and the New River Company; and had acquired a spacious house, with gardens and land, at Putney, in Surrey, where he resided in decent hospitality. He died in December, 1736, at the age of seventy; and by his last will, at the expense of Edward, his only son (with whose marriage he was not perfectly reconciled), enriched his two daughters, Catherine and Hester. The former became the wife of Mr. Edward Elliston: their daughter and heiress Catherine was married in the year 1756 to Edward Eliot, Esq. (now Lord Eliot), of Port Eliot, in the county of Cornwall; and their three sons are my nearest male relations on the father's side. A life of devotion and celibacy was the choice of my aunt, Mrs. Hester Gibbon, who, at the age of eighty-five, still resides in a hermitage at Cliffe, in Northamptonshire; having long survived her spiritual guide and faithful companion Mr. William Law, who, at an advanced age, about the year 1761, died in her house. In our family he had left the reputation of a worthy and pious man, who believed all that he professed, and practised all that he enjoined. The character of a nonjuror, which he maintained to the last, is a sufficient evidence of his principles in church and state; and the sacrifice of interest to conscience will be always respectable. His theological writings, which our domestic connexion has tempted me to peruse, preserve an imperfect sort of life, and I can pronounce with more confidence and knowledge on the merits of the author. His last compositions are darkly tinctured by the incomprehensible visions of Jacob Behmen; and his discourse on the absolute unlawfulness of stage entertainments is sometimes quoted for a ridiculous intemperance of sentiment and language. 'The actors and spectators must all be damned: the playhouse is the porch of hell, the place of the devil's abode, where he holds his filthy court of evil spirits: a play is the devil's triumph, a sacrifice performed to his glory, as much as in the heathen temples of Bacchus or Venus', &c., &c. But these sallies of religious frenzy must not extinguish the praise which is due to Mr. William Law as a wit and a scholar. His argument on topics of less absurdity is specious and acute, his manner is lively, his style forcible and clear; and, had not his vigorous mind been clouded by enthusiasm, he might be ranked with the most agreeable and ingenious writers of the times. While the Bangorian controversy was a fashionable theme, he entered the lists on the subject of Christ's kingdom, and the authority of the priesthood: against the plain account of the sacrament of the Lord's Supper he resumed the combat with Bishop Hoadley, the object of Whig idolatry, and Tory abhorrence; and at every weapon of attack and defence the nonjuror, on the ground which is common to both, approves himself at least equal to the prelate. On the appearance of the Fable of the Bees, he drew his pen against the licentious doctrine that private vices are public benefits, and morality as well as religion must join in his applause. Mr. Law's master-work, the *Serious Call,* is still read as a popular and powerful book of devotion. His precepts are rigid, but they are founded on the gospel: his satire is sharp, but it is drawn from the knowledge of human life; and many of his portraits are not unworthy of the pen of La Bruyere. If he finds a spark of piety in his reader's mind, he will soon kindle it to a flame; and a philosopher must allow that he exposes, with equal severity and truth, the strange contradiction between the faith and practice of the Christian world. Under the names of Flavia and Miranda he has admirably described my two aunts —the heathen and the Christian sister.

My father, Edward Gibbon, was born in October, 1707: at the age of thirteen he could scarcely feel that he was disinherited by Act of Parliament; and, as he advanced towards manhood, new prospects of fortune opened to his view. A parent is most attentive to supply in his children the deficiencies of which he is conscious in himself: my grandfather's knowledge was derived from a strong understanding, and the experience of the ways of men; but my father enjoyed the benefits of a liberal education as a scholar and a gentleman. At Westminster School, and afterwards at Emmanuel College in Cambridge, he passed through a regular course of academical discipline; and the care of his learning and morals was entrusted to his private tutor, the same Mr. William Law. But the mind of a saint is above or below the present world; and while the pupil proceeded on his travels, the tutor remained at Putney, the much-honoured friend and spiritual director of the whole family. My father resided some time at Paris to acquire the fashionable exercises; and as his temper was warm and social, he indulged in those pleasures for which the strictness of his former education had given him a keener relish. He afterwards visited several provinces of France; but his excursions were neither long nor remote; and the slender knowlege, which he had gained of the French language, was gradually obliterated. His passage through Besançon is marked by a singular consequence in the chain of human events. In a dangerous illness Mr. Gibbon was attended, at his own request, by one of his kinsmen of the name of Acton, the younger brother of a younger brother, who had applied himself to the study of physic. During the slow recovery of his patient, the physician himself was attacked by the malady of love: he married his mistress, renounced his country and religion, settled at Besançon, and became the father of three sons; the eldest of whom, General Acton, is conspicuous in Europe as the principal Minister of the King of the Two Sicilies. By an uncle whom another stroke of fortune had transplanted to Leghorn, he was educated in the naval service of the Emperor; and his valour and conduct in the command of the Tuscan frigates protected the retreat of the Spaniards from Algiers. On my father's return to England he was chosen, in the general election of 1734, to serve in Parliament for the borough of Petersfield: a burgage tenure, of which my grandfather possessed a weighty share, till he alienated (I know not why) such important property. In the opposition to Sir Robert Walpole and the Pelhams, prejudice and society connected his son with the Tories,—shall I say Jacobites? or, as they were pleased to style themselves, the country gentlemen? with them he gave many a vote; with them he drank many a bottle. Without acquiring the fame of an orator or a statesman, he eagerly joined in the great opposition,

which, after a seven years' chase, hunted down Sir Robert Walpole: and in the pursuit of an unpopular minister, he gratified a private revenge against the oppressor of his family in the South Sea persecution.

I was born at Putney, in the county of Surrey, the 27th of April, Old Style, in the year one thousand seven hundred and thirty-seven; the first child of the marriage of Edward Gibbon, Esq., and of Judith Porten.[5] My lot might have been that of a slave, a savage, or a peasant; nor can I reflect without pleasure on the bounty of Nature, which cast my birth in a free and civilized country, in an age of science and philosophy, in a family of honourable rank, and decently endowed with the gifts of fortune. From my birth I have enjoyed the right of primogeniture; but I was succeeded by five brothers and one sister, all of whom were snatched away in their infancy. My five brothers, whose names may be found in the parish register of Putney, I shall not pretend to lament: but from my childhood to the present hour I have deeply and sincerely regretted my sister, whose life was somewhat prolonged, and whom I remember to have seen an amiable infant. The relation of a brother and a sister, especially if they do not marry, appears to me of a very singular nature. It is a familiar and tender friendship with a female, much about our own age; an affection perhaps softened by the secret influence of sex, but pure from any mixture of sensual desire, the sole species of Platonic love that can be indulged with truth, and without danger.

At the general election of 1741, Mr. Gibbon and Mr. Delmé stood an expensive and

---

[5] The union to which I owe my birth was a marriage of inclination and esteem. Mr. James Porten, a merchant of London, resided with his family at Putney, in a house adjoining to the bridge and churchyard, where I have passed many happy hours of my childhood. He left one son (the late Sir Stanier Porten) and three daughters: Catherine, who preserved her maiden name, and of whom I shall hereafter speak; another daughter married Mr. Darrel of Richmond, and left two sons, Edward and Robert: the youngest of the three sisters was Judith, my mother.

successful contest at Southampton, against Mr. Dummer and Mr. Henly, afterwards Lord Chancellor and Earl of Northington. The Whig candidate had a majority of the resident voters; but the corporation was firm in the Tory interest: a sudden creation of one hundred and seventy new freemen turned the scale; and a supply was readily obtained of respectable volunteers, who flocked from all parts of England to support the cause of their political friends. The new Parliament opened with the victory of an opposition, which was fortified by strong clamour and strange coalitions. From the event of the first divisions, Sir Robert Walpole perceived that he could no longer lead a majority in the House of Commons, and prudently resigned (after a dominion of one and twenty years) the guidance of the state (1742). But the fall of an unpopular minister was not succeeded, according to general expectation, by a millennium of happiness and virtue: some courtiers lost their places, some patriots lost their characters, Lord Orford's offences vanished with his power; and after a short vibration, the Pelham government was fixed on the old basis of the Whig aristocracy. In the year 1745, the throne and the constitution were attacked by a rebellion, which does not reflect much honour on the national spirit: since the English friends of the Pretender wanted courage to join his standard, and his enemies (the bulk of the people) allowed him to advance into the heart of the kingdom. Without daring, perhaps without desiring, to aid the rebels, my father invariably adhered to the Tory opposition. In the most critical season he accepted, for the service of the party, the office of alderman in the city of London: but the duties were so repugnant to his inclination and habits, that he resigned his gown at the end of a few months. The second Parliament in which he sat was prematurely dissolved (1747): and as he was unable or unwilling to maintain a second contest for Southampton, the life of the senator expired in that dissolution.

The death of a new-born child before that of its parents may seem an unnatural, but it is strictly a probable event: since of any given number the greater part are extinguished before their ninth year, before they possess the faculties of the mind or body. Without accusing the profuse waste or imperfect workmanship of Nature, I shall only observe, that this unfavourable chance was multiplied against my infant existence. So feeble was my constitution, so precarious my life, that, in the baptism of my brothers my father's prudence successively repeated my Christian name of Edward, that, in case of the departure of the eldest son, this patronymic appellation might be still perpetuated in the family.

———*Uno avulso non deficit alter.**

To preserve and to rear so frail a being, the most tender assiduity was scarcely sufficient; and my mother's attention was somewhat diverted by her frequent pregnancies, by an exclusive passion for her husband, and by the dissipation of the world, in which his taste and authority obliged her to mingle. But the maternal office was supplied by my aunt, Mrs. Catherine Porten; at whose name I feel a tear of gratitude trickling down my cheek. A life of celibacy transferred her vacant affection to her sister's first child: my weakness excited her pity; her attachment was fortified by labour and success: and if there be any, as I trust there are some, who rejoice that I live, to that dear and excellent woman they must hold themselves indebted. Many anxious and solitary days did she consume in the patient trial of every mode of relief and amusement. Many wakeful nights did she sit by my bedside in trembling expectation that each hour would be my last. Of the various and frequent disorders of my childhood my own recollection is dark; nor do I wish to expatiate on so disgusting a topic. Suffice it to say, that while every practitioner, from Sloane and Ward to the Chevalier Taylor, was successively summoned to torture or relieve

---

* Virgil *Aeneid.* vi. 143 [One being taken away, another is not lacking.]—Ed.

me, the care of my mind was too frequently neglected for that of my health: compassion always suggested an excuse for the indulgence of the master, or the idleness of the pupil; and the chain of my education was broken as often as I was recalled from the school of learning to the bed of sickness.

As soon as the use of speech had prepared my infant reason for the admission of knowledge, I was taught the arts of reading, writing, and arithmetic. So remote is the date, so vague is the memory of their origin in myself, that, were not the error corrected by analogy, I should be tempted to conceive them as innate. In my childhood I was praised for the readiness with which I could multiply and divide, by memory alone, two sums of several figures: such praise encouraged my growing talent; and had I persevered in this line of application, I might have acquired some fame in mathematical studies.

After this previous institution at home, or at a day-school at Putney, I was delivered at the age of seven into the hands of Mr. John Kirkby, who exercised about eighteen months the office of my domestic tutor. His own words, which I shall here transcribe, inspire in his favour a sentiment of pity and esteem. 'During my abode in my native county of Cumberland, in quality of an indigent curate, I used now and then in a summer, when the pleasantness of the season invited, to take a solitary walk to the seashore, which lies about two miles from the town where I lived. Here I would amuse myself, one while in viewing at large the agreeable prospect which surrounded me, and another while (confining my sight to nearer objects) in admiring the vast variety of beautiful shells thrown upon the beach, some of the choicest of which I always picked up, to divert my little ones upon my return. One time among the rest, taking such a journey in my head, I sat down upon the declivity of the beach with my face to the sea, which was now come up within a few yards of my feet, when immediately the sad thought of the wretched condition of my family, and the unsuccessfulness of all endeavours to amend it, came crowding

into my mind, which drove me into a deep melancholy, and ever and anon forced tears from my eyes.' Distress at last forced him to leave the country. His learning and virtue introduced him to my father; and at Putney he might have found at least a temporary shelter, had not an act of indiscretion again driven him into the world. One day, reading prayers in the parish church, he most unluckily forgot the name of King George: his patron, a loyal subject, dismissed him with some reluctance and a decent reward; and *how* the poor man ended his days I have never been able to learn. Mr. John Kirkby is the author of two small volumes—the *Life of Automathes* (London, 1745) and an *English and Latin Grammar* (London, 1746), which, as a testimony of gratitude, he dedicated (November 5, 1745) to my father. The books are before me: from them the pupil may judge the preceptor; and, upon the whole, his judgement will not be unfavourable. The grammar is executed with accuracy and skill, and I know not whether any better existed at the time in our language: but the *Life of Automathes* aspires to the honours of a philosophical fiction. It is the story of a youth, the son of a shipwrecked exile, who lives alone on a desert island from infancy to the age of manhood. A hind is his nurse; he inherits a cottage, with many useful and curious instruments; some ideas remain of the education of his two first years; some arts are borrowed from the beavers of a neighbouring lake; some truths are revealed in supernatural visions. With these helps, and his own industry, Automathes becomes a self-taught though speechless philosopher, who had investigated with success his own mind, the natural world, the abstract sciences, and the great principles of morality and religion. The author is not entitled to the merit of invention, since he has blended the English story of *Robinson Crusoe* with the Arabian romance of *Hai Ebn Yokhdan*, which he might have read in the Latin version of Pocock. In the *Automathes* I cannot praise either the depth of thought or elegance of style; but the book is not devoid of entertainment or instruction;

and among several interesting passages I would select the discovery of fire, which produces by accidental mischief the discovery of conscience. A man who had thought so much on the subjects of language and education was surely no ordinary preceptor: my childish years, and his hasty departure, prevented me from enjoying the full benefit of his lessons; but they enlarged my knowledge of arithmetic, and left me a clear impression of the English and Latin rudiments.

In my ninth year (January, 1746), in a lucid interval of comparative health, my father adopted the convenient and customary mode of English education; and I was sent to Kingston-upon-Thames, to a school of about seventy boys, which was kept by Dr. Wooddeson and his assistants. Every time I have since passed over Putney Common, I have always noticed the spot where my mother, as we drove along in the coach, admonished me that I was now going into the world, and must learn to think and act for myself. The expression may appear ludicrous; yet there is not, in the course of life, a more remarkable change than the removal of a child from the luxury and freedom of a wealthy house, to the frugal diet and strict subordination of a school; from the tenderness of parents and the obsequiousness of servants, to the rude familiarity of his equals, the insolent tyranny of his seniors, and the rod, perhaps, of a cruel and capricious pedagogue. Such hardships may steel the mind and body against the injuries of fortune; but my timid reserve was astonished by the crowd and tumult of the school; the want of strength and activity disqualified me for the sports of the playfield; nor have I forgotten how often in the year forty-six I was reviled and buffeted for the sins of my Tory ancestors. By the common methods of discipline, at the expense of many tears and some blood, I purchased the knowledge of the Latin syntax: and not long since I was possessed of the dirty volumes of Phaedrus and Cornelius Nepos, which I painfully construed and darkly understood. The choice of these authors is not injudicious. The *Lives* of Cornelius Nepos, the friend of Atticus and Cicero, are composed in the style of the purest age: his simplicity is elegant, his brevity copius: he exhibits a series of men and manners; and with such illustrations, as every pedant is not indeed qualified to give, this classic biographer may initiate a young student in the history of Greece and Rome. The use of fables or apologues has been approved in every age, from ancient India to modern Europe. They convey in familiar images the truths of morality and prudence; and the most childish understanding (I advert to the scruples of Rousseau) will not suppose either that beasts *do* speak, or that men *may* lie. A fable represents the genuine characters of animals; and a skilful master might extract from Pliny and Buffon some pleasing lessons of natural history, a science well adapted to the taste and capacity of children. The Latinity of Phaedrus is not exempt from an alloy of the silver age; but his manner is concise, terse, and sententious: the Thracian slave discreetly breathes the spirit of a freeman; and when the text is sound, the style is perspicuous. But his fables, after a long oblivion, were first published by Peter Pithou, from a corrupt manuscript. The labours of fifty editors confess the defects of the copy, as well as the value of the original; and the schoolboy may have been whipped for misapprehending a passage which Bentley could not restore, and which Burman could not explain.

My studies were too frequently interrupted by sickness; and after a real or nominal residence at Kingston school of near two years, I was finally recalled (December, 1747) by my mother's death, which was occasioned, in her thirty-eighth year, by the consequences of her last labour. I was too young to feel the importance of my loss; and the image of her person and conversation is faintly imprinted in my memory. The affectionate heart of my aunt, Catherine Porten, bewailed a sister and a friend; but my poor father was inconsolable, and the transport of grief seemed to threaten his life or his reason. I can never forget the scene of our first interview, some weeks after the fatal event;

the awful silence, the room hung with black, the midday tapers, his sighs and tears; his praises of my mother, a saint in heaven; his solemn adjuration that I would cherish her memory and imitate her virtues; and the fervour with which he kissed and blessed me as the sole surviving pledge of their loves. The storm of passion insensibly subsided into calmer melancholy. At a convivial meeting of his friends, Mr. Gibbon might affect or enjoy a gleam of cheerfulness; but his plan of happiness was for ever destroyed: and after the loss of his companion he was left alone in a world, of which the business and pleasures were to him irksome or insipid. After some unsuccessful trials he renounced the tumult of London and the hospitality of Putney, and buried himself in the rural or rather rustic solitude of Buriton; from which, during several years, he seldom emerged.

As far back as I can remember, the house near Putney Bridge and churchyard, of my maternal grandfather, appears in the light of my proper and native home. It was there that I was allowed to spend the greatest part of my time, in sickness or in health, during my school vacations and my parents' residence in London, and finally after my mother's death. Three months after that event, in the spring of 1748, the commercial ruin of her father, Mr. James Porten, was accomplished and declared. As his effects were not sold, nor the house evacuated, till the Christmas following, I enjoyed during the whole year the society of my aunt, without much consciousness of her impending fate. I feel a melancholy pleasure in repeating my obligations to that excellent woman, Mrs. Catherine Porten, the true mother of my mind as well as of my health. Her natural good sense was improved by the perusal of the best books in the English language; and if her reason was sometimes clouded by prejudice, her sentiments were never disguised by hypocrisy or affectation. Her indulgent tenderness, the frankness of her temper, and my innate rising curiosity, soon removed all distance between us; like friends of an equal age, we freely conversed on every topic, familiar or abstruse; and it was her delight and reward to observe the first shoots of my young ideas. Pain and languor were often soothed by the voice of instruction and amusement; and to her kind lessons I ascribe my early and invincible love of reading, which I would not exchange for the treasures of India. I should perhaps be astonished, were it possible to ascertain the date, at which a favourite tale was engraved, by frequent repetition, in my memory: the Cavern of the Winds; the Palace of Felicity; and the fatal moment, at the end of three months or centuries, when Prince Adolphus is overtaken by Time, who had worn out so many pair of wings in the pursuit. Before I left Kingston school I was well acquainted with Pope's *Homer* and the *Arabian Nights' Entertainments,* two books which will always please by the moving picture of human manners and specious miracles: nor was I then capable of discerning that Pope's translation is a portrait endowed with every merit, excepting that of likeness to the original. The verses of Pope accustomed my ear to the sound of poetic harmony: in the death of Hector, and the shipwreck of Ulysses, I tasted the new emotions of terror and pity; and seriously disputed with my aunt on the vices and virtues of the heroes of the Trojan war. From Pope's *Homer* to Dryden's *Virgil* was an easy transition; but I know not how, from some fault in the author, the translator, or the reader, the pious Aeneas did not so forcibly seize on my imagination; and I derived more pleasure from Ovid's *Metamorphoses,* especially in the fall of Phaeton, and the speeches of Ajax and Ulysses. My grandfather's flight unlocked the door of a tolerable library; and I turned over many English pages of poetry and romance, of history and travels. Where a title attracted my eye, without fear or awe I snatched the volume from the shelf; and Mrs. Porten, who indulged herself in moral and religious speculations, was more prone to encourage than to check a curiosity above the strength of a boy. This year (1748), the twelfth of my age, I shall note as the most propitious to the growth of my intellectual stature.

The relics of my grandfather's fortune afforded a bare annuity for his own maintenance; and his daughter, my worthy aunt, who had already passed her fortieth year, was left destitute. Her noble spirit scorned a life of obligation and dependance; and after revolving several schemes, she preferred the humble industry of keeping a boarding-house for Westminster School,[6] where she laboriously earned a competence for her old age. This singular opportunity of blending the advantages of private and public education decided my father. After the Christmas holidays, in January, 1749, I accompanied Mrs. Porten to her new house in College Street; and was immediately entered in the school, of which Dr. John Nicoll was at that time head master. At first I was alone: but my aunt's resolution was praised; her character was esteemed; her friends were numerous and active: in the course of some years she became the mother of forty or fifty boys, for the most part of family and fortune; and as her primitive habitation was too narrow, she built and occupied a spacious mansion in Dean's Yard. I shall always be ready to join in the common opinion, that our public schools, which have produced so many eminent characters, are the best adapted to the genius and constitution of the English people. A boy of spirit may acquire a previous and practical experience of the world; and his playfellows may be the future friends of his heart or his interest. In a free intercourse with his equals, the habits of truth, fortitude, and prudence will insensibly be matured. Birth and riches are measured by the standard of personal merit; and the mimic scene of a rebellion has displayed, in their true colours, the ministers and patriots of the rising generation. Our seminaries of learning do not exactly correspond with the precept of a Spartan king, 'that the child should be instructed in the arts which will be useful to the man'; since a finished scholar may emerge from the head of Westminster or Eton, in total ignorance of the business and conversation of English gentlemen in the latter end of the eighteenth century. But these schools may assume the merit of teaching all that they pretend to teach, the Latin and Greek languages: they deposit in the hands of a disciple the keys of two valuable chests; nor can he complain, if they are afterwards lost or neglected by his own fault. The necessity of leading in equal ranks so many unequal powers of capacity and application will prolong to eight or ten years the juvenile studies, which might be dispatched in half that time by the skilful master of a single pupil. Yet even the repetition of exercise and discipline contributes to fix in a vacant mind the verbal science of grammar and prosody: and the private or voluntary student, who possesses the sense and spirit of the classics, may offend, by a false quantity, the scrupulous ear of a well-flogged critic. For myself, I must be content with a very small share of the civil and literary fruits of a public school. In the space of two years (1749, 1750), interrupted by danger and debility, I painfully climbed into the third form; and my riper age was left to acquire the beauties of the Latin, and the rudiments of the Greek tongue. Instead of audaciously mingling in the sports, the quarrels, and the connexions of our little world, I was still cherished at home under the maternal wing of my aunt; and my removal from Westminster long preceded the approach of manhood.

The violence and variety of my complaints, which had excused my frequent absence from Westminster School, at length engaged Mrs. Porten, with the advice of physicians, to conduct me to Bath: at the end of the Michaelmas vacation (1750) she quitted me with reluctance, and I remained several months under the care of a trusty maid-servant. A strange nervous affection, which alternately contracted my legs, and produced, without any visible symptoms, the most excruciating pain, was ineffectually opposed by the various methods of bathing and pumping. From

---

[6] It is said in the family that she was principally induced to this undertaking by her affection for her nephew, whose weak constitution required her constant and unremitted attention. S.

Bath I was transported to Winchester, to the house of a physician; and after the failure of his medical skill, we had again recourse to the virtues of the Bath waters. During the intervals of these fits, I moved with my father to Buriton and Putney; and a short unsuccessful trial was attempted to renew my attendance at Westminster School. But my infirmities could not be reconciled with the hours and discipline of a public seminary; and instead of a domestic tutor, who might have watched the favourable moments, and gently advanced the progress of my learning, my father was too easily content with such occasional teachers as the different places of my residence could supply. I was never forced, and seldom was I persuaded, to admit these lessons: yet I read with a clergyman at Bath some odes of Horace, and several episodes of Virgil, which gave me an imperfect and transient enjoyment of the Latin poets. It might now be apprehended that I should continue for life an illiterate cripple: but, as I approached my sixteenth year, nature displayed in my favour her mysterious energies: my constitution was fortified and fixed; and my disorders, instead of growing with my growth and strengthening with my strength, most wonderfully vanished. I have never possessed or abused the insolence of health; but since that time few persons have been more exempt from real or imaginary ills; and, till I am admonished by the gout, the reader will no more be troubled with the history of my bodily complaints. My unexpected recovery again encouraged the hope of my education; and I was placed at Esher, in Surrey, in the house of the Reverend Mr. Philip Francis, in a pleasant spot, which promised to unite the various benefits of air, exercise, and study (January, 1752). The translator of Horace might have taught me to relish the Latin poets had not my friends discovered in a few weeks that he preferred the pleasures of London to the instruction of his pupils. My father's perplexity at this time, rather than his prudence, was urged to embrace a singular and desperate measure. Without preparation or delay he carried me to Oxford; and I was matriculated in the University as a gentleman-commoner of Magdalen College, before I had accomplished the fifteenth year of my age (April 3, 1752).

The curiosity which had been implanted in my infant mind was still alive and active; but my reason was not sufficiently informed to understand the value, or to lament the loss, of three precious years from my entrance at Westminster to my admission at Oxford. Instead of repining at my long and frequent confinement to the chamber or the couch, I secretly rejoiced in those infirmities, which delivered me from the exercises of the school and the society of my equals. As often as I was tolerably exempt from danger and pain, reading, free desultory reading, was the employment and comfort of my solitary hours. At Westminster my aunt sought only to amuse and indulge me; in my stations at Bath and Winchester, at Buriton and Putney, a false compassion respected my sufferings, and I was allowed, without control or advice, to gratify the wanderings of an unripe taste. My indiscriminate appetite subsided by degrees in the *historic* line: and since philosophy has exploded all innate ideas and natural propensities, I must ascribe this choice to the assiduous perusal of the *Universal History,* as the octavo volumes successively appeared. This unequal work, and a treatise of Hearne, the *Ductor historicus,* referred and introduced me to the Greek and Roman historians, to as many at least as were accessible to an English reader. All that I could find were greedily devoured, from Littlebury's lame Herodotus, and Spelman's valuable Xenophon, to the pompous folios of Gordon's Tacitus, and a ragged Procopius of the beginning of the last century. The cheap acquisition of so much knowledge confirmed my dislike to the study of languages; and I argued with Mrs. Porten, that, were I master of Greek and Latin, I must interpret to myself in English the thoughts of the original, and that such extemporary versions must be inferior to the elaborate translations of professed scholars; a silly sophism, which could not easily be confuted by a person ignorant of any other language than her own. From the ancient I leaped to the modern world: many crude lumps of Speed, Rapin, Mezeray, Davila, Machiavel, Father Paul, Bower, &c., I devoured like so many novels; and I swallowed with the same voracious appetite the descriptions of India and China, of Mexico and Peru.

My first introduction to the historic scenes, which have since engaged so many years of my life, must be ascribed to an accident. In the summer of 1751 I accompanied my father on a visit to Mr. Hoare's, in Wiltshire; but I was less delighted with the beauties of Stourhead than with discovering in the library a common book, the *Continuation of Echard's Roman History*, which is indeed executed with more skill and taste than the previous work. To me the reigns of the successors of Constantine were absolutely new; and I was immersed in the passage of the Goths over the Danube when the summons of the dinner-bell reluctantly dragged me from my intellectual feast. This transient glance served rather to irritate than to appease my curiosity; and as soon as I returned to Bath I procured the second and third volumes of Howel's *History of the World*, which exhibit the Byzantine period on a larger scale. Mahomet and his Saracens soon fixed my attention; and some instinct of criticism directed me to the genuine sources. Simon Ockley, an original in every sense, first opened my eyes; and I was led from one book to another, till I had ranged round the circle of Oriental history. Before I was sixteen, I had exhausted all that could be learned in English of the Arabs and Persians, the Tartars and Turks; and the same ardour urged me to guess at the French of D'Herbelot, and to construe the barbarous Latin of Pocock's *Abulfaragius*. Such vague and multifarious reading could not teach me to think, to write, or to act; and the only principle, that darted a ray of light into the indigested chaos, was an early and rational application to the order of time and place. The maps of Cellarius and Wells imprinted in my mind the picture of ancient geography: from Stranchius I imbibed the elements of chronology: the Tables

of Helvicus and Anderson, the Annals of Usher and Prideaux, distinguished the connexion of events, and engraved the multitude of names and dates in a clear and indelible series. But in the discussion of the first ages I overleaped the bounds of modesty and use. In my childish balance I presumed to weigh the systems of Scaliger and Petavius, of Marsham and Newton, which I could seldom study in the originals; and my sleep has been disturbed by the difficulty of reconciling the Septuagint with the Hebrew computation. I arrived at Oxford with a stock of erudition that might have puzzled a doctor, and a degree of ignorance of which a schoolboy would have been ashamed.

At the conclusion of this first period of my life, I am tempted to enter a protest against the trite and lavish praise of the happiness of our boyish years, which is echoed with so much affectation in the world. That happiness I have never known, that time I have never regretted; and were my poor aunt still alive, she would bear testimony to the early and constant uniformity of my sentiments. It will indeed be replied that *I* am not a competent judge; that pleasure is incompatible with pain; that joy is excluded from sickness; and that the felicity of a schoolboy consists in the perpetual motion of thoughtless and playful agility, in which I was never qualified to excel. My name, it is most true, could never be enrolled among the sprightly race, the idle progeny of Eton or Westminster,

Who foremost might delight to cleave,
With pliant arm, the glassy wave,
Or urge the flying ball.[*]

The poet may gaily describe the short hours of recreation; but he forgets the daily tedious labours of the school, which is approached each morning with anxious and reluctant steps.

A traveller who visits Oxford or Cambridge is surprised and edified by the appar-

---

[*] Thomas Gray, *Ode on a Distant Prospect of Eton College*—Ed.

ent order and tranquillity that prevail in the seats of the English muses. In the most celebrated Universities of Holland, Germany, and Italy, the students, who swarm from different countries, are loosely dispersed in private lodgings at the houses of the burghers: they dress according to their fancy and fortune; and in the intemperate quarrels of youth and wine, their *swords,* though less frequently than of old, are sometimes stained with each other's blood. The use of arms is banished from our English Universities; the uniform habit of the academics, the square cap and black gown, is adapted to the civil and even clerical professions; and from the doctor in divinity to the undergraduate, the degrees of learning and age are externally distinguished. Instead of being scattered in a town, the students of Oxford and Cambridge are united in colleges; their maintenance is provided at their own expense, or that of the founders; and the stated hours of the hall and chapel represent the discipline of a regular, and, as it were, a religious community. The eyes of the traveller are attracted by the size or beauty of the public edifices; and the principal colleges appear to be so many palaces, which a liberal nation has erected and endowed for the habitation of science. My own introduction to the University of Oxford forms a new era in my life; and at the distance of forty years I still remember my first emotions of surprise and satisfaction. In my fifteenth year I felt myself suddenly raised from a boy to a man: the persons, whom I respected as my superiors in age and academical rank, entertained me with every mark of attention and civility; and my vanity was flattered by the velvet cap and silk gown, which distinguish a gentleman-commoner from a plebeian student. A decent allowance, more money than a schoolboy had ever seen, was at my own disposal; and I might command, among the tradesmen of Oxford, an indefinite and dangerous latitude of credit. A key was delivered into my hands, which gave me the free use of a numerous and learned library: my apartment consisted of three elegant and well-furnished rooms in the new building, a stately pile, of Magdalen College; and the adjacent walks, had they been frequented by Plato's disciples, might have been compared to the Attic shade on the banks of the Ilissus. Such was the fair prospect of my entrance (April 3, 1752) into the University of Oxford.

A venerable prelate, whose taste and erudition must reflect honour on the society in which they were formed, has drawn a very interesting picture of his academical life:—'I was educated (says Bishop Lowth) in the University of Oxford. I enjoyed all the advantages, both public and private, which that famous seat of learning so largely affords. I spent many years in that illustrious society, in a well-regulated course of useful discipline and studies, and in the agreeable and improving commerce of gentlemen and of scholars; in a society where emulation without envy, ambition without jealousy, contention without animosity, incited industry, and awakened genius; where a liberal pursuit of knowledge and a genuine freedom of thought was raised, encouraged and pushed forward by example, by commendation, and by authority. I breathed the same atmosphere that the Hookers, the Chillingworths, and the Lockes had breathed before; whose benevolence and humanity were as extensive as their vast genius and comprehensive knowledge; who always treated their adversaries with civility and respect; who made candour, moderation, and liberal judgement as much the rule and law as the subject of their discourse. And do you reproach me with my education in this place, and with my relation to this most respectable body, which I shall always esteem my greatest advantage and my highest honour?' I transcribe with pleasure this eloquent passage, without examining what benefits or what rewards were derived by Hooker, or Chillingworth, or Locke, from their academical institution; without inquiring, whether in this angry controversy the spirit of Lowth himself is purified from the intolerant zeal which Warburton had ascribed to the genius of the place. It may indeed be observed that the atmosphere of

Oxford did not agree with Mr. Locke's constitution, and that the philosopher justly despised the academical bigots, who expelled his person and condemned his principles. The expression of gratitude is a virtue and a pleasure: a liberal mind will delight to cherish and celebrate the memory of its parents; and the teachers of science are the parents of the mind. I applaud the filial piety, which it is impossible for me to imitate; since I must not confess an imaginary debt, to assume the merit of a just or generous retribution. To the University of Oxford *I* acknowledge no obligation; and she will as cheerfully renounce me for a son, as I am willing to disclaim her for a mother. I spent fourteen months at Magdalen College; they proved the fourteen months the most idle and unprofitable of my whole life: the reader will pronounce between the school and the scholar: but I cannot affect to believe that nature had disqualified me for all literary pursuits. The specious and ready excuse of my tender age, imperfect preparation, and hasty departure, may doubtless be alleged; nor do I wish to defraud such excuses of their proper weight. Yet in my sixteenth year I was not devoid of capacity or application; even my childish reading had displayed an early though blind propensity for books; and the shallow flood might have been taught to flow in a deep channel and a clear stream. In the discipline of a well-constituted academy, under the guidance of skilful and vigilant professors, I should gradually have risen from translations to originals, from the Latin to the Greek classics, from dead languages to living science: my hours would have been occupied by useful and agreeable studies, the wanderings of fancy would have been restrained, and I should have escaped the temptations of idleness, which finally precipitated my departure from Oxford.

Perhaps in a separate annotation I may coolly examine the fabulous and real antiquities of our sister universities, a question which has kindled such fierce and foolish disputes among their fanatic sons. In the meanwhile it will be acknowledged that these venerable bodies are sufficiently old to partake of all the prejudices and infirmities of age. The schools of Oxford and Cambridge were founded in a dark age of false and barbarous science; and they are still tainted with the vices of their origin. Their primitive discipline was adapted to the education of priests and monks; and the government still remains in the hands of the clergy, an order of men whose manners are remote from the present world, and whose eyes are dazzled by the light of philosophy. The legal incorporation of these societies by the charters of popes and kings had given them a monopoly of the public instruction; and the spirit of monopolists is narrow, lazy, and oppressive: their work is more costly and less productive than that of independent artists; and the new improvements so eagerly grasped by the competition of freedom, are admitted with slow and sullen reluctance in those proud corporations, above the fear of a rival, and below the confession of an error. We may scarcely hope that any reformation will be a voluntary act; and so deeply are they rooted in law and prejudice, that even the omnipotence of Parliament would shrink from an inquiry into the state and abuses of the two Universities.

The use of academical degrees, as old as the thirteenth century, is visibly borrowed from the mechanic corporations; in which an apprentice, after serving his time, obtains a testimonial of his skill, and a licence to practise his trade and mystery. It is not my design to deprecate those honours, which could never gratify or disappoint my ambition; and I should applaud the institution, if the degrees of bachelor or licentiate were bestowed as the reward of manly and successful study: if the name and rank of doctor or master were strictly reserved for the professors of science, who have approved their title to the public esteem.

In all the Universities of Europe, excepting our own, the languages and sciences are distributed among a numerous list of effective professors: the students, according to their taste, their calling, and their diligence, apply themselves to the proper masters; and in the annual repetition of public and private lectures, these masters are assiduously employed. Our curiosity may inquire what number of professors has been instituted at Oxford (for I shall now confine myself to my own University)? by whom are they appointed, and what may be the probable chances of merit or incapacity? how many are stationed to the three faculties, and how many are left for the liberal arts? what is the form, and what the substance, of their lessons? But all these questions are silenced by one short and singular answer, 'That in the University of Oxford, the greater part of the public professors have for these many years given up altogether even the pretence of teaching'. Incredible as the fact may appear, I must rest my belief on the positive and impartial evidence of a master of moral and political wisdom, who had himself resided at Oxford. Dr. Adam Smith assigns as the cause of their indolence, that, instead of being paid by voluntary contributions, which would urge them to increase the number, and to deserve the gratitude of their pupils, the Oxford professors are secure in the enjoyment of a fixed stipend, without the necessity of labour, or the apprehension of control. It has indeed been observed, nor is the observation absurd, that excepting in experimental sciences, which demand a costly apparatus and a dexterous hand, the many valuable treatises that have been published on every subject of learning may now supersede the ancient mode of oral instruction. Were this principle true in its utmost latitude, I should only infer that the offices and salaries, which are become useless, ought without delay to be abolished. But there still remains a material difference between a book and a professor; the hour of the lecture enforces attendance; attention is fixed by the presence, the voice, and the occasional questions of the teacher; the most idle will carry something away; and the more diligent will compare the instructions which they have heard in the school, with the volumes which they peruse in their chamber. The advice of a skilful professor will adapt a course of reading to every mind and every situation; his authority will discover, admonish, and at last chastise the negligence of his disciples; and his vigilant inquiries will ascertain the steps of their literary progress. Whatever science he professes he may illustrate in a series of discourses, composed in the leisure of his closet, pronounced on public occasions, and finally delivered to the press. I observe with pleasure that in the University of Oxford Dr. Lowth, with equal eloquence and erudition, has executed this task in his incomparable *Praelectiones* on the Poetry of the Hebrews.

The College of St. Mary Magdalen was founded in the fifteenth century by Wainfleet, Bishop of Winchester; and now consists of a president, forty fellows, and a number of inferior students. It is esteemed one of the largest and most wealthy of our academical corporations, which may be compared to the Benedictine abbeys of Catholic countries; and I have loosely heard that the estates belonging to Magdalen College, which are leased by those indulgent landlords at small quit-rents and occasional fines, might be raised, in the hands of private avarice, to an annual revenue of nearly thirty thousand pounds. Our colleges are supposed to be schools of science, as well as of education; nor is it unreasonable to expect that a body of literary men, devoted to a life of celibacy, exempt from the care of their own subsistence, and amply provided with books, should devote their leisure to the prosecution of study, and that some effects of their studies should be manifested to the world. The shelves of their library groan under the weight of the Benedictine folios, of the editions of the fathers, and the collections of the middle ages, which have issued from the single abbey of St. Germain des Préz at Paris. A composition of genius must be the offspring of one mind; but such works of industry, as may be divided among many hands, and must be continued during many years, are the peculiar province of a laborious community. If I inquire into the manufactures of the monks of Magdalen, if I extend the inquiry to the other colleges of Oxford and Cambridge, a silent blush, or a scornful frown, will be the only reply. The fellows or monks of my time were decent easy men, who supinely enjoyed the gifts of the founder; their days were filled by a series of uniform employments; the chapel and the hall, the coffee-house and the common room, till they retired, weary and well satisfied, to a long slumber. From the oil of reading, or thinking, or writing, they had absolved their conscience; and the first shoots of learning and ingenuity withered on the ground, without yielding any fruits to the owners or the public. As a gentleman-commoner, I was admitted to the society of the fellows, and fondly expected that some questions of literature would be the amusing and instructive topics of their discourse. Their conversation stagnated in a round of college business, Tory politics, personal anecdotes, and private scandal: their dull and deep potations excused the brisk intemperance of youth: and their constitutional toasts were not expressive of the most lively loyalty for the house of Hanover. A general election was now approaching: the great Oxfordshire contest already blazed with all the malevolence of party zeal. Magdalen College was devoutly attached to the old interest! and the names of Wenman and Dashwood were more frequently pronounced, than those of Cicero and Chrysostom. The example of the senior fellows could not inspire the undergraduates with a liberal spirit or studious emulation; and I cannot describe, as I never knew, the discipline of college. Some duties may possibly have been imposed on the poor scholars, whose ambition aspired to the peaceful honours of a fellowship (*ascribi quietis ordinibus ... Deorum*); but no independent members were admitted below the rank of a gentleman-commoner, and our velvet cap was the cap of liberty. A tradition prevailed that some of our predecessors had spoken Latin declamations in the hall; but of this ancient custom no vestige remained: the obvious methods of public exercises and examinations were totally unknown; and I have never heard that either the president or the society interfered in the private economy of the tutors and their pupils.

The silence of the Oxford professors, which deprives the youth of public instruction, is imperfectly supplied by the tutors, as they are styled, of the several colleges. Instead of confining themselves to a single science, which had satisfied the ambition of Burman or Bernoulli, they teach, or promise to teach, either history or mathematics, or ancient literature, or moral philosophy; and as it is possible that they may be defective in all, it is highly probable that of some they will be ignorant. They are paid, indeed, by private contributions; but their appointment depends on the head of the house: their diligence is voluntary, and will consequently be languid, while the pupils themselves, or their parents, are not indulged in the liberty of choice or change. The first tutor into whose hands I was resigned appears to have been one of the best of the tribe: Dr. Waldegrave was a learned and pious man, of a mild disposition, strict morals, and abstemious life, who seldom mingled in the politics or the jollity of the college. But his knowledge of the world was confined to the University; his learning was of the last, rather than of the present age; his temper was indolent; his faculties, which were not of the first rate, had been relaxed by the climate, and he was satisfied, like his fellows, with the slight and superficial discharge of an important trust. As soon as my tutor had sounded the insufficiency of his disciple in school-learning, he proposed that we should read every morning from ten to eleven the comedies of Terence. The sum of my improvement in the University of Oxford is confined to three or four Latin plays; and even the study of an elegant classic, which might have been illustrated by a comparison of ancient and modern theatres, was reduced to a dry and literal interpretation of the author's text. During the first weeks I constantly attended these lessons in my tutor's room; but as they appeared equally devoid of profit and pleasure, I was once tempted to try the experiment of a formal apology. The apology was accepted with a smile. I repeated the offence with less ceremony; the excuse was admitted with the same indulgence: the slightest motive of laziness or indisposition, the most trifling avocation at home or abroad, was allowed as a worthy impediment; nor did my tutor appear conscious of my absence or neglect. Had the hour of lecture been constantly filled, a single hour was a small portion of my academic leisure. No plan of study was recommended for my use; no exercises were prescribed for his inspection; and, at the most precious season of youth, whole days and weeks were suffered to elapse without labour or amusement, without advice or account. I should have listened to the voice of reason and of my tutor; his mild behaviour had gained my confidence. I preferred his society to that of the younger students; and in our evening walks to the top of Headington Hill, we freely conversed on a variety of subjects. Since the days of Pocock and Hyde, oriental learning has always been the pride of Oxford, and I once expressed an inclination to study Arabic. His prudence discouraged this childish fancy; but he neglected the fair occasion of directing the ardour of a curious mind. During my absence in the summer vacation, Dr. Waldegrave accepted a college living at Washington in Sussex, and on my return I no longer found him at Oxford. From that time I have lost sight of my first tutor; but at the end of thirty years (1781) he was still alive; and the practice of exercise and temperance had entitled him to a healthy old age.

The long recess between the Trinity and Michaelmas terms empties the colleges of Oxford, as well as the courts of Westminster. I spent, at my father's house at Buriton in Hampshire, the two months of August and September. It is whimsical enough that as soon as I left Magdalen College, my taste for books began to revive; but it was the same blind and boyish taste for the pursuit of exotic history. Unprovided with original learning, unformed in the habits of thinking, unskilled in the arts of composition, I resolved—to write a book. The title of this first essay, *The Age of Sesostris*, was perhaps suggested by Voltaire's *Age of Lewis XIV*, which was new and popular; but my sole object was to investigate the probable date of the life and reign of the conqueror of Asia. I was then enamoured of Sir John Marsham's *Canon Chronicus;* an elaborate work, of whose merits and defects I was not yet qualified to judge. According to his specious, though narrow plan, I settled my hero about the time of Solomon, in the tenth century before the Christian era. It was therefore incumbent on me, unless I would adopt Sir Isaac Newton's shorter chronology, to remove a formidable objection; and my solution, for a youth of fifteen, is not devoid of ingenuity. In his version of the Sacred Books, Manetho the high priest had identified Sethosis, or Sesostris, with the elder brother of Danaus, who landed in Greece, according to the Parian Marble, fifteen hundred and ten years before Christ. But in my supposition the high priest is guilty of a voluntary error; flattery is the prolific parent of falsehood. Manetho's *History of Egypt* is dedicated to Ptolemy Philadelphus, who derived a fabulous or illegitimate pedigree from the Macedonian kings of the race of Hercules. Danaus is the ancestor of Hercules; and after the failure of the elder branch, his descendants, the Ptolemies, are the sole representatives of the royal family, and may claim by inheritance the kingdom which they hold by conquest. Such were my juvenile discoveries; at a riper age, I no longer presume to connect the Greek, the Jewish, and the Egyptian antiquities, which are lost in a distant cloud. Nor is this the only instance, in which the belief and knowledge of the child are superseded by the more rational ignorance of the man. During my stay at Buriton, my infant labour was diligently prosecuted, without much interruption from company or country diversions; and I already heard the music of public applause. The discovery of my own weakness was the first symptom of taste. On my return to Oxford, *The Age of Sesostris* was wisely relinquished; but the imperfect sheets remained twenty years at the bottom of a drawer, till, in a general clearance of papers (November, 1772), they were committed to the flames.

After the departure of Dr. Waldegrave, I was transferred, with his other pupils, to his academical heir, whose literary character did not command the respect of the college. Dr. Winchester well remembered that he had a salary to receive, and only forgot that he had a duty to perform. Instead of guiding the studies, and watching over the behaviour of his disciple, I was never summoned to attend even the ceremony of a lecture; and, excepting one voluntary visit to his rooms, during the eight months of his titular office, the tutor and pupil lived in the same college as strangers to each other. The want of experience, of advice, and of occupation, soon betrayed me into some improprieties of conduct, ill-chosen company, late hours, and inconsiderate expense. My growing debts might be secret; but my frequent absence was visible and scandalous: and a tour to Bath, a visit into Buckinghamshire, and four excursions to London in the same winter, were costly and dangerous frolics. They were, indeed, without a meaning, as without an excuse. The irksomeness of a cloistered life repeatedly tempted me to wander; but my chief pleasure was that of travelling; and I was too young and bashful to enjoy, like a manly Oxonian in town, the pleasures of London. In all these excursions I eloped from Oxford; I returned to college; in a few days I eloped again, as if I had been an independent stranger in a hired lodging, without once hearing the voice of admonition, without once feeling the hand of control. Yet my time was lost, my expenses were multiplied, my behaviour abroad was unknown; folly as well as vice should have awakened the attention of my superiors, and my tender years would have justified a more than ordinary degree of restraint and discipline.

It might at least be expected that an ecclesiastical school should inculcate the orthodox principles of religion. But our venerable mother had contrived to unite the opposite extremes of bigotry and indifference: an heretic, or unbeliever, was a monster in her eyes; but she was always, or often, or sometimes, remiss in the spiritual education of her own children. According to the statutes of the University, every student, before he is matriculated, must subscribe his assent to the thirty-nine articles of the Church of England, which are signed by more than read, and read by more than believe them. My insufficient age excused me, however, from the immediate performance of this legal ceremony; and the Vice-Chancellor directed me to return, as soon as I should have accomplished my fifteenth year; recommending me, in the meanwhile, to the instruction of my college. My college forgot to instruct: I forgot to return, and was myself forgotten by the first magistrate of the University. Without a single lecture, either public or private, either Christian or Protestant, without any academical subscription, without any episcopal confirmation, I was left by the dim light of my catechism to grope my way to the chapel and communion-table, where I was admitted, without a question, how far, or by what means, I might be qualified to receive the Sacrament. Such almost incredible neglect was productive of the worst mischiefs. From my childhood I had been fond of religious disputation: my poor aunt has been often puzzled by the mysteries which she strove to believe; nor had the elastic spring been totally broken by the weight of the atmosphere of Oxford. The blind activity of idleness urged me to advance without armour into the dangerous mazes of controversy; and at the age of sixteen, I bewildered myself in the errors of the Church of Rome.

The progress of my conversion may tend to illustrate, at least, the history of my own mind. It was not long since Dr. Middleton's *Free Inquiry* had sounded an alarm in the theological world; much ink and much gall had been spilt in the defence of the primitive miracles; and the two dullest of their champions were crowned with academic honours by the University of Oxford. The name of Middleton was unpopular; and his proscription very naturally led me to peruse his writings, and those of his antagonists. His bold criticism, which approaches the precipice of infidelity, produced on my mind a singular effect; and had I persevered in the communion of Rome, I should now apply to my own fortune the prediction of the Sibyl,

—Via prima salutis,
Quod minimè reris, Graiâ, pandetur ab urbe.[*]

The elegance of style and freedom of argument were repelled by the shield of prejudice. I still revered the character, or rather the names, of the saints and fathers whom Dr. Middleton exposes; nor could he destroy my implicit belief, that the gift of miraculous powers was continued in the Church during the first four or five centuries of Christianity. But I was unable to resist the weight of historical evidence, that within the same period most of the leading doctrines of Popery were already introduced in theory and practice: nor was my conclusion absurd, that miracles are the test of truth, and that the Church must be orthodox and pure, which was so often approved by the visible interposition of the Deity. The marvellous tales which are so boldly attested by the Basils and Chrysostoms, the Austins and Jeroms, compelled me to embrace the superior merits of celibacy, the institution of the monastic life, the use of the sign of the cross, of holy oil, and even of images, the invocation of saints, the worship of relics, the rudiments of purgatory in prayers for the dead, and the tremendous mystery of the sacrifice of the body and blood of Christ, which insensibly swelled into the prodigy of transubstantiation. In these dispositions, and already more than half a convert, I formed an unlucky intimacy with a young gentleman of our college. With a character less resolute, Mr. Molesworth had imbibed the same religious opinions; and some Popish books, I know not through what channel, were conveyed into his possession. I read, I applauded, I believed: the English translations of two famous works of Bossuet, Bishop of Meaux, the *Exposition of the Catholic Doctrine,*

and the *History of the Protestant Variations,* achieved my conversion, and I surely fell by a noble hand.[7] I have since examined the originals with a more discerning eye, and shall not hesitate to pronounce, that Bossuet is indeed a master of all the weapons of controversy. In the *Exposition,* a specious apology, the orator assumes, with consummate art, the tone of candour and simplicity; and the ten-horned monster is transformed, at his magic touch, into the milk-white hind, who must be loved as soon as she is seen. In the *History,* a bold and well-aimed attack, he displays, with a happy mixture of narrative and argument, the faults and follies, the changes and contradictions of our first reformers; whose variations (as he dexterously contends) are the mark of historical error, while the perpetual unity of the Catholic Church is the sign and test of infallible truth. To my present feelings it seems incredible that I should ever believe that I believed in transubstantiation. But my conqueror oppressed me with the sacramental words, 'Hoc est corpus meum' [This is my body], and dashed against each other the figurative half-meanings of the Protestant sects: every objection was resolved into omnipotence; and after repeating, at St. Mary's, the Athanasian creed, I humbly acquiesced in the mystery of the real pressence.

To take up half on trust, and half to try,
Name it not faith, but bungling bigotry.
Both knave and fool, the merchant we may call,
To pay great sums, and to compound the small,
For who would break with Heaven, and would not
*   break for all?*[†]

---

[*] Virgil *Aeneid.* 96–97 [The first way to safety will be opened to you, though you will scarce believe it, from a Grecian city.]—Ed.

[7] Mr. Gibbon never talked with me on the subject of his conversion to Popery but once: and then, he imputed his change to the works of Parsons the Jesuit, who lived in the reign of Elizabeth, and who, he said, had urged all the best arguments in favour of the Roman Catholic religion. S.

[†] John Dryden, *The Hind and the Panther,* I:141 — Ed.

No sooner had I settled my new religion than I resolved to profess myself a Catholic. Youth is sincere and impetuous; and a momentary glow of enthusiasm had raised me above all temporal considerations.[8]

By the keen Protestants, who would gladly retaliate the example of persecution, a clamour is raised of the increase of Popery: and they are always loud to declaim against the toleration of priests and jesuits, who pervert so many of his majesty's subjects from their religion and allegiance. On the present occasion, the fall of one or more of her sons directed this clamour against the University; and it was confidently affirmed that Popish missionaries were suffered, under various disguises, to introduce themselves into the colleges of Oxford. But justice obliges me to declare that, as far as relates to myself, the assertion is false; and that I never conversed with a priest, or even with a Papist, till my resolution from books was absolutely fixed. In my last excursion to London, I addressed myself to Mr. Lewis, a Roman Catholic bookseller in Russell Street, Covent Garden, who recommended me to a priest, of whose name and order I am at present ignorant.[9] In our first interview he soon discovered that persuasion was needless. After sounding the motives and merits of my conversion, he consented to admit me into the pale of the Church; and at his feet, on the 8th of June, 1753, I solemnly, though privately, abjured the errors of heresy. The seduction of an English youth of family and fortune was an act of as much danger as glory; but he bravely overlooked the danger, of which I was not then sufficiently informed. 'Where a person is reconciled to the See of Rome, or procures others to be reconciled, the offence (says Blackstone) amounts to high treason.' And if the humanity of the age would prevent the execution of this sanguinary statute, there were other laws of a less odious cast, which condemned the priest to perpetual imprisonment, and transferred the proselyte's estate to his nearest relation. An elaborate controversial epistle, approved by my director, and addressed to my father, announced and justified the step which I had taken. My father was neither a bigot nor a philosopher; but his affection deplored the loss of an only son; and his good sense was astonished at my strange departure from the religion of my country. In the first sally of passion he divulged a secret which prudence might have suppressed, and the gates of Magdalen College were for ever shut against my return. Many years afterwards, when the name of Gibbon was become as notorious as that of Middleton, it was industriously whispered at Oxford, that the historian had formerly 'turned Papist': my character stood exposed to the reproach of inconstancy; and this invidious topic would have been handled without mercy by my opponents, could they have separated my cause from that of the University. For my own part, I am proud of an honest sacrifice of interest to conscience. I can never blush, if my tender mind was entangled in the sophistry that seduced the acute and manly understandings of Chillingworth and Bayle, who afterwards emerged from superstition to scepticism.

While Charles the First governed England, and was himself governed by a Catholic queen, it cannot be denied that the missionaries of Rome laboured with impunity and success in the court, the country, and even the Universities. One of the sheep,

——*Whom the grim wolf with privy paw*
Daily devours apace, and nothing said,

is Mr. William Chillingworth, Master of Arts, and Fellow of Trinity College, Oxford; who, at the ripe age of twenty-eight years, was persuaded to elope from Oxford to the English

---

[8] He described the letter to his father, announcing his conversion, as written with all the pomp, the dignity, and self-satisfaction of a martyr. S.

[9] His name was Baker, a Jesuit, and one of the chaplains of the Sardinian Ambassador. Mr. Gibbon's conversion made some noise; and Mr. Lewis, the Roman Catholic bookseller of Russell Street, Covent Garden, was summoned before the Privy Council, and interrogated on the subject. This was communicated by Mr. Lewis's son. 1814. S.

seminary at Douay in Flanders. Some disputes with Fisher, a subtle Jesuit, might first awaken him from the prejudices of education; but he yielded to his own victorious argument, 'that there must be somewhere an infallible judge; and that the Church of Rome is the only Christian society which either does or can pretend to that character.' After a short trial of a few months, Mr. Chillingworth was again tormented by religious scruples: he returned home, resumed his studies, unravelled his mistakes, and delivered his mind from the yoke of authority and superstition. His new creed was built on the principle that the Bible is our sole judge, and private reason our sole interpreter: and he ably maintains this principle in *The Religion of a Protestant,* a book which, after startling the doctors of Oxford, is still esteemed the most solid defence of the Reformation. The learning, the virtue, the recent merits of the author, entitled him to a fair preferment: but the slave had now broken his fetters; and the more he weighed, the less was he disposed to subscribe to the thirty-nine articles of the Church of England. In a private letter he declares, with all the energy of language, that he could not subscribe to them without subscribing to his own damnation; and that if ever he should depart from his immovable resolution, he would allow his friends to think him a madman or an atheist. As the letter is without a date, we cannot ascertain the number of weeks or months that elapsed between this passionate abhorrence and the Salisbury Register, which is still extant. 'Ego Gulielmus Chillingworth, . . . omnibus hisce articulis, . . . et singulis in iisdem contentis, volens et ex animo subscribo, et consensum meum iisdem praebeo. 20 die Julii 1638' [I, William Chillingworth, freely and from my heart subscribe to all these articles and to everything contained in them, and give them my consent]. But, alas! the chancellor and prebendary of Sarum soon deviated from his own subscription: as he more deeply scrutinized the article of the Trinity, neither scripture nor the primitive fathers could long uphold his orthodox belief; and he could not

but confess, 'that the doctrine of Arius is either a truth, or at least no damnable heresy'. From this middle region of the air, the descent of his reason would naturally rest on the firmer ground of the Socinians: and if we may credit a doubtful story, and the popular opinion, his anxious inquiries at last subsided in philosophic indifference. So conspicuous, however, were the candour of his nature and the innocence of his heart, that this apparent levity did not affect the reputation of Chillingworth. His frequent changes proceeded from too nice an inquisition into truth. His doubts grew out of himself; he assisted them with all the strength of his reason: he was then too hard for himself; but finding as little quiet and repose in those victories, he quickly recovered, by a new appeal to his own judgement: so that in all his sallies and retreats, he was in fact his own convert.

Bayle was the son of a Calvinist minister in a remote province in France, at the foot of the Pyrenees. For the benefit of education, the Protestants were tempted to risk their children in the Catholic Universities; and in the twenty-second year of his age young Bayle was seduced by the arts and arguments of the Jesuits of Toulouse. He remained about seventeen months (March 19, 1699–August 19, 1670) in their hands, a voluntary captive; and a letter to his parents, which the new convert composed or subscribed (April 15, 1670), is darkly tinged with the spirit of Popery. But nature had designed him to think as he pleased, and to speak as he thought: his piety was offended by the excessive worship of creatures; and the study of physics convinced him of the impossibility of transubstantiation, which is abundantly refuted by the testimony of our senses. His return to the communion of a falling sect was a bold and disinterested step, that exposed him to the rigour of the laws; and a speedy flight to Geneva protected him from the resentment of his spiritual tyrants, unconscious as they were of the full value of the prize which they had lost. Had Bayle adhered to the Catholic Church, had he embraced the ecclesiastical profession, the genius and favour of such a proselyte might have aspired to wealth and honours in his native country: but the hypocrite would have found less happiness in the comforts of a benefice, or the dignity of a mitre, than he enjoyed at Rotterdam in a private state of exile, indigence, and freedom. Without a country, or a patron, or a prejudice, he claimed the liberty and subsisted by the labours of his pen: the inequality of his voluminous works is explained and excused by his alternately writing for himself, for the booksellers, and for posterity; and if a severe critic would reduce him to a single folio, that relic, like the books of the Sibyl, would become still more valuable. A calm and lofty spectator of the religious tempest, the philosopher of Rotterdam condemned with equal firmness the persecution of Lewis the Fourteenth, and the republican maxims of the Calvinists; their vain prophecies, and the intolerant bigotry which sometimes vexed his solitary retreat. In reviewing the controversies of the times, he turned against each other the arguments of the disputants; successively wielding the arms of the Catholics and Protestants, he proves that neither the way of authority nor the way of examination can afford the multitude any test of religious truth; and dexterously concludes that custom and education must be the sole grounds of popular belief. The ancient paradox of Plutarch, that atheism is less pernicious than superstition, acquires a tenfold vigour when it is adorned with the colours of his wit, and pointed with the acuteness of his logic. His critical dictionary is a vast repository of facts and opinions; and he balances the *false* religions in his sceptical scales, till the opposite quantities (if I may use the language of algebra) annihilate each other. The wonderful power which he so boldly exercised, of assembling doubts and objections, had tempted him jocosely to assume the title of the νεφεληγερετα Ζευς, the cloud-compelling Jove; and in a conversation with the ingenious Abbé (afterwards Cardinal) de Polignac, he freely disclosed his universal Pyrrhonism. 'I am most truly (said Bayle) a Protestant; for I protest indifferently against all systems and all sects.'

The academical resentment, which I may possibly have provoked, will prudently spare this plain narrative of my studies, or rather of my idleness; and of the unfortunate event which shortened the term of my residence at Oxford. But it may be suggested, that my father was unlucky in the choice of a society and the chance of a tutor. It will perhaps be asserted that in the lapse of forty years many improvements have taken place in the college and in the University. I am not unwilling to believe that some tutors might have been found more active than Dr. Waldegrave and less contemptible than Dr. Winchester. At a more recent period, many students have been attracted by the merit and reputation of Sir William Scott, then a tutor in University College, and now conspicuous in the profession of the civil law: my personal acquaintance with that gentleman has inspired me with a just esteem for his abilities and knowledge; and I am assured that his lectures on history would compose, were they give to the public, a most valuable treatise. Under the auspices of the late Deans, a more regular discipline has been introduced, as I am told, at Christ Church;[10] a course of classi-

---

[10] This was written on the information Mr. Gibbon had received, and the observation he had made, previous to his late residence at Lausanne. During his last visit to England, he had an opportunity of seeing at Sheffield Place some young men of the college above alluded to; he had great satisfaction in conversing with them, made many inquiries respecting their course of study, applauded the discipline of Christ Church, and the liberal attention shown by the Dean, to those whose only recommendation was their merit. Had Mr. Gibbon lived to revise this work, I am sure he would have mentioned the name of Dr. Jackson with the highest commendation: and also that of Dr. Bagot, Bishop of St. Asaph, whose attention to the duties of his office while he was Dean of Christ Church was unremitted; and to whom, perhaps, that college is more indebted for the good discipline introduced there, than to any other person whatever. There are other colleges at Oxford, with whose discipline my friend was unacquainted, to which, without doubt, he would willingly have allowed their due praise, particularly Brasenose and Oriel Colleges; the former under the care of Dr. Cleaver,

cal and philosophical studies is proposed, and even pursued, in that numerous seminary: learning has been made a duty, a pleasure, and even a fashion; and several young gentlemen do honour to the college in which they have been educated. According to the will of the donor, the profit of the second part of Lord Clarendon's *History* has been applied to the establishment of a riding-school, that the polite exercises might be taught, I known not with what success, in the University. The Vinerian professorship is of far more serious importance; the laws of his country are the first science of an Englishman of rank and fortune, who is called to be a magistrate, and may hope to be a legislator. This judicious institution was coldly entertained by the graver doctors, who complained (I have heard the complaint) that it would take the young people from their books: but Mr. Viner's benefaction is not unprofitable, since it has at least produced the excellent commentaries of Sir William Blackstone.

After carrying me to Putney, to the house of his friend Mr. Mallet[11], by whose philosophy I was rather scandalized than reclaimed, it was necessary for my father to form a new plan of education, and to devise some method which, if possible, might effect the cure of my spiritual malady. After much debate it was determined, from the advice and personal experience of Mr. Eliot (now Lord Eliot), to fix me, during some years, at Lausanne in Switzerland. Mr. Frey, a Swiss gentleman of Basil, undertook the conduct of the journey: we left London the 19th of June, crossed the sea from Dover to Calais, travelled post through several provinces of France, by the direct road of St. Quentin, Rheims, Langres, and Besançon, and arrived the 30th of June at Lausanne, where I was immediately settled under the roof and tuition of Mr. Pavilliard, a Calvinist minister.

The first marks of my father's displeasure rather astonished than afflicted me: when he treatened to banish, and disown, and disinherit, a rebellious son, I cherished a secret hope that he would not be able or willing to effect his menaces; and the pride of conscience encouraged me to sustain the hon-

---

Bishop of Chester, the latter under that of Dr. Eveleigh. It is still greatly to be wished that the general expense, or rather extravagance, of young men at our English Universities may be more effectually restrained. The expense, in which they are permitted to indulge, is inconsistent not only with a necessary degree of study, but with those habits of morality which should be promoted, by all means possible, at an early period of life. An academical education in England is at present an object of alarm and terror to every thinking parent of moderate fortune. It is the apprehension of the expense, of the dissipation, and other evil consequences which arise from the want of proper restraint at our own Universities, that forces a number of our English youths to those of Scotland, and utterly excludes many from any sort of academical instruction. If a charge be true, which I have heard insisted on, that the heads of our colleges in Oxford and Cambridge are vain of having under their care chiefly men of opulence, who may be supposed exempt from the necessity of economical control, they are indeed highly censurable; since the mischief of allowing early habits of expense and dissipation is great, in various respects, even to those possessed of large property; and the most serious evil from this indulgence must happen to youths of humbler fortune, who certainly form the majority of students both at Oxford and Cambridge. S.

Since these observations appeared, a Sermon, with very copious notes, has been published by the Reverend Dr. Parr, wherein he complains of the scantiness of praise bestowed on those who were educated at the Universities of England. I digressed merely to speak of the few heads of colleges of whom I had at that time heard, or with whom I was acquainted, and I did not allude to any others educated there. I have further to observe, that I have not met with any person who lived at the time of which Mr. Gibbon alludes, who was not of opinion that his representation, at least of his own college, was just: and such was the opinion of that accomplished, ingenious, and zealous friend of the University, the late Mr. Windham: but every man, acquainted with the former and present state of the University, will acknowledge the vast improvements which have of late been introduced into the plan and conduct of education in the University. S.

[11] The author of a *Life of Bacon*, which has been rated above its value; of some forgotten poems and plays; and of the pathetic ballad of William and Margaret. His tenets were deistical; perhaps a stronger term might have been used. S.

ourable and important part which I was now acting. My spirits were raised and kept alive by the rapid motion of my journey, the new and various scenes of the Continent, and the civility of Mr. Frey, a man of sense, who was not ignorant of books or the world. But after he had resigned me into Pavilliard's hands, and I was fixed in my new habitation, I had leisure to contemplate the strange and melancholy prospect before me. My first complaint arose from my ignorance of the language. In my childhood I had once studied the French grammar, and I could imperfectly understand the easy prose of a familiar subject. But when I was thus suddenly cast on a foreign land, I found myself deprived of the use of speech and of hearing; and, during some weeks, incapable not only of enjoying the pleasures of conversation, but even of asking or answering a question in the common intercourse of life. To a home-bred Englishman every object, every custom was offensive; but the native of any country might have been disgusted with the general aspect of his lodging and entertainment. I had now exchanged my elegant apartment in Magdalen College for a narrow, gloomy street, the most unfrequented of an unhandsome town, for an old inconvenient house, and for a small chamber ill-contrived and ill-furnished, which, on the approach of winter, instead of a companionable fire, must be warmed by the dull, invisible heat of a stove. From a man I was again degraded to the dependence of a schoolboy. Mr. Pavilliard managed my expenses, which had been reduced to a diminutive state: I received a small monthly allowance for my pocket-money; and helpless and awkward as I have ever been, I no longer enjoyed the indispensable comfort of a servant. My condition seemed as destitute of hope as it was devoid of pleasure: I was separated for an indefinite, which appeared an infinite term from my native country; and I have lost all connexion with my Catholic friends. I have since reflected with surprise, that as the Romish clergy of every part of Europe maintain a close correspondence with each other, they never attempted, by letters or messages, to rescue me from the hands of the heretics, or at least to confirm my zeal and constancy in the profession of the faith. Such was my first introduction to Lausanne; a place where I spent nearly five years with pleasure and profit, which I afterwards revisited without compulsion, and which I have finally selected as the most grateful retreat for the decline of my life.

But it is the peculiar felicity of youth that the most unpleasing objects and events seldom make a deep or lasting impression; it forgets the past, enjoys the present, and anticipates the future. At the flexible age of sixteen I soon learned to endure, and gradually to adopt, the new forms of arbitrary manners: the real hardships of my situation were alienated by time. Had I been sent abroad in a more splendid style, such as the fortune and bounty of my father might have supplied, I might have returned home with the same stock of language and science which our countrymen usually import from the Continent. An exile and a prisoner as I was, their example betrayed me into some irregularities of wine, of play, and of idle excursions: but I soon felt the impossibility of associating with them on equal terms; and after the departure of my first acquaintance, I held a cold and civil correspondence with their successors. This seclusion from English society was attended with the most solid benefits. In the *Pays de Vaud* [in Switzerland], the French language is used with less imperfection than in most of the distant provinces of France: in Pavilliard's family, necessity compelled me to listen and to speak; and if I was at first disheartened by the apparent slowness, in a few months I was astonished by the rapidity of my progress. My pronunciation was formed by the constant repetition of the same sounds; the variety of words and idioms, the rules of grammar, and distinctions of genders, were impressed in my memory: ease and freedom were obtained by practice; correctness and elegance by labour; and before I was recalled home, French, in which I spontaneously thought, was more familiar than English to my ear, my tongue, and my pen. The first effect of this opening knowledge was the revival of my love of reading, which had been chilled at Oxford; and I soon turned over, without much choice, almost all the French books in my tutor's library. Even these amusements were productive of real advantage: my taste and judgement were now somewhat riper. I was introduced to a new mode of style and literature: by the comparison of manners and opinions, my views were enlarged, my prejudices were corrected, and a copious voluntary abstract of the *Histoire de l'Eglise et de l'Empire,* by le Sueur, may be placed in a middle line between my childish and my manly studies. As soon as I was able to converse with the natives, I began to feel some satisfaction in their company: my awkward timidity was polished and emboldened; and I frequented, for the first time, assemblies of men and women. The acquaintance of the Pavilliards prepared me by degrees for more elegant society. I was received with kindness and indulgence in the best families of Lausanne; and it was in one of these that I formed an intimate and lasting connexion with Mr. Deyverdun, a young man of an amiable temper and excellent understanding. In the arts of fencing and dancing, small indeed was my proficiency; and some months were idly wasted in the riding-school. My unfitness to bodily exercise reconciled me to a sedentary life, and the horse, the favourite of my countrymen, never contributed to the pleasures of my youth.

My obligations to the lessons of Mr. Pavilliard, gratitude will not suffer me to forget: he was endowed with a clear head and a warm heart; his innate benevolence had assuaged the spirit of the Church; he was rational, because he was moderate: in the course of his studies he had acquired a just though superficial knowledge of most branches of literature; by long practice, he was skilled in the arts of teaching; and he laboured with assiduous patience to know the character, gain the affection, and open the mind of his English pupil. As soon as we began to understand each other, he gently led me, from a blind and undistinguishing love of reading, into the path of instruction. I consented with pleasure that a portion of the morning hours should be consecrated to a plan of modern history and geography, and to the critical perusal of the French and Latin classics; and at each step I felt myself invigorated by the habits of application and method. His prudence repressed and disembled some youthful sallies; and as soon as I was confirmed in the habits of industry and temperance, he gave the reins into my own hands. His favourable report of my behaviour and progress gradually obtained some latitude of action and expense; and he wished to alleviate the hardships of my lodging and entertainment. The principles of philosophy were associated with the examples of taste; and by a singular chance, the book, as well as the man, which contributed the most effectually to my education, has a stronger claim on my gratitude than on my admiration. Mr. De Crousaz, the adversary of Bayle and Pope, is not distinguished by lively fancy or profound reflection; and even in his own country, at the end of a few years, his name and writings are almost obliterated. But his philosophy had been formed in the school of Locke, his divinity in that of Limborch and Le Clerc; in a long and laborious life, several generations of pupils were taught to think, and even to write; his lessons rescued the academy of Lausanne from Calvinistic prejudice; and he had the rare merit of diffusing a more liberal spirit among the clergy and people of the Pays de Vaud. His system of logic, which in the last editions has swelled to six tedious and prolix volumes, may be praised as a clear and methodical abridgement of the art of reasoning, from our simple ideas to the most complex operations of the human understanding. This system I studied, and meditated, and abstracted, till I obtained the free command of an universal instrument, which I soon presumed to exercise on my Catholic opinions. Pavilliard was not unmindful that his first task, his most important duty, was to reclaim me from the errors of Popery. The intermixture of sects has rendered the Swiss clergy acute and learned on the topics of controversy; and I have some of his letters in which he celebrates the dexterity of his attack, and my gradual concessions, after a firm and well-managed defence.[12] I was willing, and I am now willing, to allow him a handsome share of the honour of my conversion: yet I must observe that it was principally effected by my private reflections; and I still remember my solitary transport at the discovery of a philosophical argument against the doctrine of transubstantiation: that the text of Scripture, which seem to inculcate the real presence, is attested only by a single sense—our sight; while the real presence itself is disproved by three of our senses—the sight, the touch, and the taste. The various articles of the Romish creed disappeared like a dream; and after a full conviction, on Christmas Day, 1754, I received the sacrament in the church of Lausanne. It was here that I suspended my religious inquiries, acquiescing with implicit belief in the tenets and mysteries which are adopted by the general consent of Catholics and Protestants.[13]

Such, from my arrival at Lausanne, during the first eighteen or twenty months (July 1753–March 1755), were my useful studies, the foundation of all my future improvements. But every man who rises above the common level has received two educations: the first from his teachers; the second, more personal and important, from himself. He will not, like the fanatics of the last age, define the moment of grace; but he cannot forget the era of his life in which his mind has expanded to its proper form and dimensions. My worthy tutor had the good sense and modesty to discern how far he could be useful: as soon as he felt that I advanced beyond his speed and measure, he wisely left me to my genius; and the hours of lesson were soon lost in voluntary labour of the whole morning, and sometimes of the whole day. The desire of prolonging my time gradually confirmed the salutary habit of early rising, to which I have always adhered, with some regard to seasons and situations; but it is happy for my eyes and my health, that my temperate ardour has never been seduced to trespass on the hours of the night. During the last three years of my residence at Lausanne, I may assume the merit of serious and solid application; but I am tempted to distinguish the last eight months of the year 1755 as the period of the most extraordinary diligence and rapid progress.[14] In my French

[12] M. Pavilliard has described to me the astonishment with which he gazed on Mr. Gibbon standing before him: a thin little figure, with a large head, disputing and urging, with the greatest ability, all the best arguments that had ever been used in favour of Popery. Mr. Gibbon many years ago became very fat and corpulent, but he had uncommonly small bones, and was very slightly made. S.

[13] FROM MR. GIBBON TO MRS. PORTEN.

DEAR MADAM,

I have at length good news to tell you. I am now good Protestant, and am extremely glad of it. I have in all my letters taken notice of the different movements of my mind, entirely Catholic when I came to Lausanne, wavering long time between the two systems, and at last fixed for the Protestant —when that conflict was over, I had still another difficulty—brought up with all the ideas of the Church of England, I could scarce resolve the communion with Presbyterians, as all the people of this country are. I at last got over it, for considering that whatever difference there may be between their churches and ours, in the government and discipline, they still regard us as brethren and profess the same faith as us—determined then in this design, I declared it to the ministers of the town, assembled at Mr. Pavilliard's, who having examined me, approved of it, and permitted me to receive the communion with them, which I did Christmas day from the hands of Mr. Pavilliard, who appeared extremely glad of it. I am so extremely myself—and do assure you feel a joy extremely pure, and the more so, as I know it to be not only innocent but laudable.

(This letter is curious: as it shows how short a time (not more than a year and a half) he had adopted the idiom of the French language and lost that of his own. S.)

[14] JOURNAL, December 1755.—In finishing this year, I must remark how favourable it was to my studies. In the space of eight months, from the beginning of April, I learnt the principles of drawing; made myself complete master of the French and Latin languages, with which I was very superficially acquainted before, and wrote and translated a great deal in both; read Cicero's *Epistles ad Familiares*, his *Brutus*, all his *Orations*, his *Dialogues de Amicitiá*, and *De Senectute*; Terence, twice; and Pliny's *Epistles*. In French, Giannone's *History of Na-*

and Latin translations I adopted an excellent method, which, from my own success, I would recommend to the imitation of students. I chose some classic writer, such as Cicero and Vertot, the most approved for purity and elegance of style. I translated, for instance, an epistle of Cicero into French; and after throwing it aside, till the words and phrases were obliterated from my memory, I re-translated my French into such Latin as I could find; and then compared each sentence of my imperfect version with the ease, the grace, the propriety of the Roman orator. A similar experiment was made on several pages of the Revolutions of Vertot; I turned them into Latin, returned them after a sufficient interval into my own French, and again scrutinized the resemblance or dissimilitude of the copy and the original. By degrees I was less ashamed, by degrees I was more satisfied with myself; and I preserved in the practice of these double translations, which filled several books, till I had acquired the knowledge of both idioms, and the command at least of a correct style. This useful exercise of writing was accompanied and succeeded by the more pleasing occupation of reading the best authors. The perusal of the Roman classics was at once my exercise and reward. Dr. Middleton's *History*, which I then appreciated above its true value, naturally directed me to the writings of Cicero. The most perfect editions, that of Olivet, which may adorn the shelves of the rich, that of Ernesti, which should lie on the table of the learned, were not within my reach. For the familiar epistles I used the text and English commentary of Bishop Ross; but my general edition was that of Verburgius, published at Amsterdam in two large volumes in folio, with an indifferent choice of various notes. I read, with application and pleasure, *all* the epistles, *all* the orations, and the most important treatises of rhetoric and philosophy; and as I read, I applauded the observation of Quintilian, that every student may judge his own proficiency, by the satisfaction which he receives from the Roman orator. I tasted the beauties of language, I breathed the spirit of

freedom, and I imbibed from his precepts and examples the public and private sense of a man. Cicero in Latin, and Xenophon in Greek, are indeed the two ancients whom I would first propose to a liberal scholar; not only for the merit of their style and sentiments, but for the admirable lessons, which may be applied almost to every situation of public and private life. Cicero's *Epistles* may in particular afford the models of every form of correspondence, from the careless effusions of tenderness and friendship, to the well-guarded declaration of discreet and dignified resentment. After finishing this great author, a library of eloquence and reason, I formed a more extensive plan of reviewing the Latin classics[15], under the four divisions of—(1) historians, (2) poets, (3) orators, and (4) philosophers, in a chronological series, from the days of Plautus and Sallust, to the decline of the language and empire of Rome: and this plan, in the last twenty-seven months of my residence at Lausanne (January, 1756–April, 1758), I *nearly* accomplished. Nor was this review, however rapid, either hasty or superficial. I indulged myself in a second and even a third perusal of Terence, Virgil, Horace, Tacitus, &c., and studied to imbibe the sense and spirit most congenial to my own. I never suffered a difficult or corrupt passage to escape, till I had viewed it in every light of which it was susceptible: though often disappointed, I always consulted the most learned or ingenious commentators, Torrentius and Dacier on Horace, Catrou and Servius on

ples, and l'Abbé Bannier's *Mythology,* and M. De Boehat's *Mémoires sur la Suisse,* and wrote a very ample relation of my tour. I likewise began to make very large collections of what I read. But what I esteem most of all, from the perusal and meditation of De Crousaz's *Logic,* I not only understood the principles of that science, but formed my mind to a habit of thinking and reasoning I had no idea of before.

[15] JOURNAL, January 1756.—I determined to read over the Latin authors in order; and read this year, Virgil, Sallust, Livy, Velleius Paterculus, Valerius Maximus, Tacitus, Suetonius, Quintus Curtius, Justin, Florus, Plautus, Terence, and Lucretius. I also read and meditated Locke upon the Understanding.

Virgil, Lipsius on Tacitus, Meziriac on Ovid, &c.; and in the ardour of my inquiries, I embraced a large circle of historical and critical erudition. My abstracts of each book were made in the French language: my observations often branched into particular essays; and I can still read, without contempt, a dissertation of eight folio pages on eight lines (287–294) of the fourth *Georgic* of Virgil. Mr. Deyverdun, my friend, whose name will be frequently repeated, had joined with equal zeal, though not with equal perseverance, in the same undertaking. To him every thought, every composition, was instantly communicated; with him I enjoyed the benefits of a free conversation on the topics of our common studies.

But it is scarcely possible for a mind endowed with any active curiosity to be long conversant with the Latin classics without aspiring to know the Greek originals, whom they celebrate as their masters, and of whom they so warmly recommend the study and imitation;

———*Vos exemplaria Graeca*
Nocturnâ versate manu, versate diurnâ.[*]

It was now that I regretted the early years which had been wasted in sickness or idleness, or mere idle reading; that I condemned the perverse method of our schoolmasters, who, by first teaching the mother language, might descend with so much ease and perspicuity to the origin and etymology of a derivative idiom. In the nineteenth year of my age I determined to supply this defect; and the lessons of Pavilliard again contributed to smooth the entrance of the way, the Greek alphabet, the grammar, and the pronunciation according to the French accent. At my earnest request we presumed to open the *Iliad;* and I had the pleasure of beholding, though darkly and through a glass, the true image of Homer, whom I had long since admired in an English dress. After my tutor had left me to myself, I worked my way through about half the *Iliad*, and afterwards interpreted alone a large portion of Xeno-

phon and Herodotus. But my ardour, destitute of aid and emulation, was gradually cooled, and, from the barren task of searching words in a lexicon, I withdrew to the free and familiar conversation of Virgil and Tacitus. Yet in my residence at Lausanne I had laid a solid foundation, which enabled me, in a more propitious season, to prosecute the study of Grecian literature.

From a blind idea of the usefulness of such abstract science, my father had been desirous, and even pressing, that I should devote some time to the mathematics; nor could I refuse to comply with so reasonable a wish. During two winters I attended the private lectures of Monsieur de Traytorrens, who explained the elements of algebra and geometry, as far as the conic sections of the Marquis de l'Hôpital, and appeared satisfied with my diligence and improvement.[16] But as my childish propensity for numbers and calculations was totally extinct, I was content to receive the passive impression of my professor's lectures, without any active exercise of my own powers. As soon as I understood the principles, I relinquished for ever the pursuit of the mathematics; nor can I lament that I desisted, before my mind was hardened by the habit of rigid demonstration, so destructive of the finer feelings of moral evidence,

---

[*] Horace *Ars Poetica.* 268–69 [To the Greek models, turn by night and day your hand.]—Ed.

[16] JOURNAL, January, 1757.—I began to study algebra under M. de Traytorrens, went through the elements of algebra and geometry, and the three first books of the Marquis de l'Hôpital's *Conic Sections.* I also read Tibullus, Catullus, Propertius, Horace (with Dacier's and Torrentius's notes), Virgil, Ovid's *Epistles,* with Meziriac's Commentary, the *Ars Amandi,* and the *Elegies;* likewise the Augustus and Tiberius of Suetonius, and a Latin translation of Dion Cassius, from the death of Julius Caesar to the death of Augustus. I also continued my correspondence begun last year with M. Allamand of Bex, and the Professor Breitinger of Zurich; and opened a new one with the Professor Gesner of Göttingen.

N.B.—Last year and this, I read St. John's Gospel, with part of Xenophon's *Cyropaedia;* the *Iliad,* and Herodotus: but, upon the whole, I rather neglected my Greek.

which must, however, determine the actions and opinions of our lives. I listened with more pleasure to the proposal of studying the law of nature and nations, which was taught in the academy of Lausanne by Mr. Vicat, a professor of some learning and reputation. But, instead of attending his public or private course, I preferred in my closet the lessons of his masters, and my own reason. Without being disgusted by Grotius or Puffendorf, I studied in their writings the duties of a man, the rights of a citizen, the theory of justice (it is, alas! a theory), and the laws of peace and war, which have had some influence on the practice of modern Europe. My fatigues were alleviated by the good sense of their commentator, Barbeyrac. Locke's *Treatise of Government* instructed me in the knowledge of Whig principles, which are rather founded in reason than experience; but my delight was in the frequent perusal of Montesquieu, whose energy of style, and boldness of hypothesis, were powerful to awaken and stimulate the genius of the age. The logic of De Crousaz had prepared me to engage with his master Locke, and his antagonist Bayle; of whom the former may be used as a bridle, and the latter as a spur, to the curiosity of a young philosopher. According to the nature of their respective works, the schools of argument and objection, I carefully went through the *Essay on Human Understanding*, and occasionally consulted the most interesting articles of the *Philosophic Dictionary*. In the infancy of my reason I turned over, as an idle amusement, the most serious and important treatise: in its maturity, the most trifling performance could exercise my taste or judgement; and more than once I have been led by a novel into a deep and instructive train of thinking. But I cannot forbear to mention three particular books, since they may have remotely contributed to form the historian of the Roman empire. (1) From the *Provincial Letters* of Pascal, which almost every year I have perused with new pleasure, I learned to manage the weapon of grave and temperate irony, even on subjects of ecclesiastical solemnity. (2) *The Life of Juli-*

an, by the Abbé de la Bléterie, first introduced me to the man and the times; and I should be glad to recover my first essay on the truth of the miracle which stopped the rebuilding of the Temple of Jerusalem. (3) In Giannone's *Civil History of Naples* I observed with a critical eye the progress and abuse of sacerdotal power, and the revolutions of Italy in the darker ages. This various reading, which I now conducted with discretion, was digested, according to the precept and model of Mr. Locke, into a large commonplace book; a practice, however, which I do not strenuously recommend. The action of the pen will doubtless imprint an idea on the mind as well as on the paper: but I much question whether the benefits of this laborious method are adequate to the waste of time; and I must agree with Dr. Johnson (*Idler*, No. 74), 'that what is twice read is commonly better remembered than what is transcribed'.

During two years, if I forget some boyish excursions of a day or a week, I was fixed at Lausanne; but at the end of the third summer, my father consented that I should make the tour of Switzerland with Pavilliard: and our short absence of one month (September 21–October 20, 1755) was a reward and relaxation of my assiduous studies.[17] The

---

[17] FROM EDWARD GIBBON TO MRS. PORTEN.

. . . Now for myself. As my father has given me leave to make a journey round Switzerland, we set out to-morrow. Buy a map of Switzerland, it will cost you but a shilling, and follow me. I go by Iverdun, Neufchâtel, Bienne or Biel, Soleurre or Solothurn, Bale or Basil, Bade, Zurich, Lucerne, and Bern. The voyage will be of about four weeks; so that *I hope to find a letter from you waiting for me.* As my father had given me leave to learn what I had a mind, I have learned to ride, and learn actually to dance and draw. Besides that, I often give ten or twelve hours a day to my studies. I find a great many agreeable people here; see them sometimes, and can say upon the whole, without vanity, that though I am the Englishman here who spends the least money, I am he who is the most generally liked. I told you that my father had promised to send me into France and Italy. I have thanked him for it; but if he would follow my plan, he won't do it yet awhile. I never liked young travellers; they go

fashion of climbing the mountains and reviewing the *Glaciers* had not yet been introduced by foreign travellers, who seek the sublime beauties of nature. But the political face of the country is not less diversified by the forms and spirit of so many various republics, from the jealous government of the *few* to the licentious freedom of the *many*. I contemplated with pleasure the new prospects of men and manners; though my conversation with the natives would have been more free and instructive had I possessed the German, as well as the French language. We passed through most of the principal towns in Switzerland; Neufchâtel, Bienne, Soleurre, Arau, Baden, Zurich, Basil, and Bern. In every place we visited the churches, arsenals, libraries, and all the most eminent persons; and after my return, I digested my notes in fourteen or fifteen sheets of a French journal, which I dispatched to my father, as a proof that my time and his money had not been misspent. Had I found this journal among his papers, I might be tempted to select some passages; but I will not transcribe the printed accounts, and it may be sufficient to notice a remarkable spot, which left a deep and lasting impression on my memory. From Zurich we proceeded to the Benedictine Abbey of Einsidlen, more commonly styled Our Lady of the Hermits. I was astonished by the profuse ostentation of riches in the poorest corner of Europe; amidst a savage scene of woods and mountains a palace appears to have been erected by magic; and it was erected by the potent magic of religion. A crowd of palmers and votaries was prostrate before the altar. The title and worship of the Mother of God provoked my indignation; and the lively naked image of superstition suggested to me, as in the same place it had done to Zuinglius, the most pressing argument for the reformation of the Church. About two years after this tour, I passed at Geneva a useful and agreeable month; but this excursion, and some short visits in the Pays de Vaud, did not materially interrupt my studious and sedentary life at Lausanne.

My thirst of improvement, and the languid state of science at Lausanne, soon prompted me to solicit a literary correspondence with several men of learning, whom I had not an opportunity of personally consulting. (1) In the perusal of Livy (xxx. 44) I had been stopped by a sentence in a speech of Hannibal, which cannot be reconciled by any torture with his character or argument. The commentators dissemble, or confess their perplexity. It occurred to me, that the change of a single letter, by substituting *otio* instead of *odio*, might restore a clear and consistent sense; but I wished to weigh my emendation in scales less partial than my own. I addressed myself to M. Crevier, the successor of Rollin, and a professor in the University of Paris, who had published a large and valuable edition of Livy. His answer was speedy and polite; he praised my ingenuity, and adopted my conjecture. (2) I maintained a Latin correspondence, at first anonymous, and afterwards in my own name, with Professor Breitinger of Zurich, the learned editor of a Septuagint Bible. In our frequent letters we discussed many questions of antiquity, many passages of the Latin classics. I pro-

---

too raw to make any great remarks, and they lose a time which is (in my opinion) the most precious part of a man's life. My scheme would be, to spend this winter at Lausanne: for though it is a very good place to acquire the air of good company and the French tongue, we have no good professors. To spend (I say) the winter at Lausanne; go into England to see my friends for a couple of months, and after that, finish my studies, either at Cambridge (for after what has passed one cannot think of Oxford), or at an University in Holland. If you liked the scheme, *could you not propose it to my father by Metcalf, or somebody* who has a *certain credit over him?* I forgot to ask you whether, in case my father writes to tell me of his marriage, would you advise me to compliment my mother-in-law? I think so. My health is so very regular, that I have nothing to say about it.

I have been the whole day writing this letter; the preparations for our voyage gave me a thousand interruptions. Besides that, I was obliged to write in English. This last reason will seem a paradox, but I assure you the French is much more familiar to me.

I am, &c.,
E. GIBBON.

Lausanne, Sept. 20, 1755.

posed my interpretations and amendments. His censures, for he did not spare my boldness of conjecture, were sharp and strong; and I was encouraged by the consciousness of my strength, when I could stand in free debate against a critic of such eminence and erudition. (3) I corresponded on similar topics with the celebrated Professor Matthew Gesner, of the University of Göttingen; and he accepted, as courteously as the two former, the invitation of an unknown youth. But his abilities might possibly be decayed; his elaborate letters were feeble and prolix; and when I asked his proper direction, the vain old man covered half a sheet of paper with the foolish enumeration of his titles and offices. (4) These professors of Paris, Zurich, and Göttingen were strangers, whom I presumed to address on the credit of their name; but Mr. Allamand, Minister at Bex, was my personal friend, with whom I maintained a more free and interesting correspondence. He was a master of language, of science, and, above all, of dispute; and his acute and flexible logic could support, with equal address, and perhaps with equal indifference, the adverse sides of every possible question. His spirit was active, but his pen had been indolent. Mr. Allamand had exposed himself to much scandal and reproach, by an anonymous letter (1745) to the Protestants of France, in which he labours to persuade them that *public* worship is the exclusive right and duty of the state, and that their numerous assemblies of dissenters and rebels were not authorized by the law or the gospel. His style is animated, his arguments specious; and if the Papist may seem to lurk under the mask of a Protestant, the philosopher is concealed under the disguise of a Papist. After some trials in France and Holland, which were defeated by his fortune or his character, a genius that might have enlightened or deluded the world, was buried in a country living, unknown to fame, and discontented with mankind. 'Est sacrificulus in pago, et rusticos decipit' [The sacrificing priest is in the country and ensnares the rustics]. As often as private or ecclesiastical business called him to Lausanne, I enjoyed the pleasure and benefit of his conversation, and we were mutually flattered by our attention to each other. Our correspondence, in his absence, chiefly turned on Locke's metaphysics, which he attacked, and I defended; the origin of ideas, the principles of evidence, and the doctrine of liberty;

And found no end, in wandering mazes lost. *

By fencing with so skilful a master, I acquired some dexterity in the use of my philosophic weapons; but I was still the slave of education and prejudice. He had some measures to keep; and I much suspect that he never showed me the true colours of his secret scepticism.

Before I was recalled from Switzerland, I had the satisfaction of seeing the most extraordinary man of the age; a poet, an historian, a philosopher, who has filled thirty quartos, of prose and verse, with his various productions, often excellent, and always entertaining. Need I add the name of Voltaire? After forfeiting, by his own misconduct, the friendship of the first of kings, he retired, at the age of sixty, with a plentiful fortune, to a free beautiful country, and resided two winters (1757 and 1758) in the town or neighbourhood of Lausanne. My desire of beholding Voltaire, whom I then rated above his real magnitude, was easily gratified. He received me with civility as an English youth; but I cannot boast of any peculiar notice or distinction, *Virgilium vidi tantum.*†

The ode which he composed on his first arrival on the banks of the Leman Lake, *O Maison d'Aristippe! O Jardin d'Epicure*, &c., had been imparted as a secret to the gentleman by whom I was introduced. He allowed me to read it twice; I knew it by heart; and as my discretion was not equal to my memory, the author was soon displeased by the circulation of a copy. In writing this trivial anecdote, I

---

* John Milton, *Paradise Lost*, ii, 561 — Ed.
† Ovid *Tristia*. 4. 10. 51 [I saw only Virgil.]—Ed.

wished to observe whether my memory was impaired, and I have the comfort of finding that every line of the poem is still engraved in fresh and indelible characters. The highest gratification which I derived from Voltaire's residence at Lausanne was the uncommon circumstance of hearing a great poet declaim his own productions on the stage. He had formed a company of gentlemen and ladies, some of whom were not destitute of talents. A decent theatre was framed at Monrepos, a country-house at the end of a suburb; dresses and scenes were provided at the expense of the actors; and the author directed the rehearsals with the zeal and attention of paternal love. In two successive winters his tragedies of *Zayre, Alzire, Zulime,* and his sentimental comedy of the *Enfant Prodigue,* were played at the theatre of Monrepos. Voltaire represented the characters best adapted to his years, Lusignan, Alvaréz, Benassar, Euphemon. His declamation was fashioned to the pomp and cadence of the old stage; and he expressed the enthusiasm of poetry, rather than the feelings of nature. My ardour, which soon became conspicuous, seldom failed of procuring me a ticket. The habits of pleasure fortified my taste for the French theatre, and that taste has perhaps abated my idolatry for the gigantic genius of Shakespeare, which is inculcated from our infancy as the first duty of an Englishman. The wit and philosophy of Voltaire, his table and theatre, refined, in a visible degree, the manners of Lausanne; and, however addicted to study, I enjoyed my share of the amusements of society. After the representation of Monrepos I sometimes supped with the actors. I was now familiar in some, and acquainted in many houses; and my evenings were generally devoted to cards and conversation, either in private parties or numerous assemblies.

I hesitate, from the apprehension of ridicule, when I approach the delicate subject of my early love. By this word I do not mean the polite attention, the gallantry, without hope or design, which has originated in the spirit of chivalry, and is interwoven with the texture of French manners. I understand by this passion the union of desire, friendship, and tenderness, which is inflamed by a single female, which prefers her to the rest of her sex, and which seeks her possession as the supreme or the sole happiness of our being. I need not blush at recollecting the object of my choice; and though my love was disappointed of success, I am rather proud that I was once capable of feeling such a pure and exalted sentiment. The personal attractions of Mademoiselle Susan Curchod were embellished by the virtues and talents of the mind. Her fortune was humble, but her family was respectable. Her mother, a native of France, had preferred her religion to her country. The profession of her father did not extinguish the moderation and philosophy of his temper, and he lived content with a small salary and laborious duty in the obscure lot of minister of Crassy, in the mountains that separate the Pays de Vaud from the county of Burgundy.[18] In the solitude of

---

[18] EXTRACTS FROM THE JOURNAL.

March 1757.	I wrote some critical observations upon Plautus.
March 8th.	I wrote a long dissertation on some lines of Virgil.
June.	I saw Mademoiselle Curchod— *Omnia vincit amor, et nos cedamus amori.*
August.	I went to Crassy, and staid two days.
Sept. 15th.	I went to Geneva.
Oct. 15th.	I came back to Lausanne, having passed through Crassy.
Nov. 1st.	I went to visit M. de Watteville Loin, and saw Mademoiselle Curchod in my way through Rolle.
Nov. 17th.	I went to Crassy, and staid there six days.
Jan. 1758.	In the three first months of this year I read Ovid's *Metamorphoses,* finished the conic sections with M. de Traytorrens, and went as far as the infinite series; I likewise read Sir Isaac Newton's *Chronology,* and wrote my critical observations upon it.
Jan. 23rd.	I saw *Alzire* acted by the society at Monrepos. Voltaire acted Alvarez; D'Hermanches, Zamore; de St. Cierge, Gusman; M. de Gentil, Monteze; and Madame Denys, Alzire.

a sequestered village he bestowed a liberal, and even learned, education on his only daughter. She surpassed his hopes by her proficiency in the sciences and languages; and in her short visits to some relations at Lausanne, the wit, the beauty, and erudition of Mademoiselle Curchod were the theme of universal applause. The report of such a prodigy awakened my curiosity; I saw and loved. I found her learned without pedantry, lively in conversation, pure in sentiment, and elegant in manners; and the first sudden emotion was fortified by the habits and knowledge of a more familiar acquaintance. She permitted me to make her two or three visits at her father's house. I passed some happy days there, in the mountains of Burgundy, and her parents honourably encouraged the connexion. In a calm retirement the gay vanity of youth no longer fluttered in her bosom; she listened to the voice of truth and passion, and I might presume to hope that I had made some impression on a virtuous heart. At Crassy and Lausanne I indulged my dream of felicity: but on my return to England, I soon discovered that my father would not hear of this strange alliance, and that without his consent I was myself destitute and helpless. After a painful struggle I yielded to my fate: I sighed as a lover, I obeyed as a son;[19] my wound was insensibly healed by time, absence, and the habits of a new life. My cure was accelerated by a faithful report of the tranquillity and cheerfulness of the lady herself, and my love subsided in friendship and esteem. The minister of Crassy soon afterwards died; his stipend died with him: his daughter retired to Geneva, where, by teaching young ladies, she earned a hard subsistence for herself and her mother; but in her lowest distress she maintained a spotless reputation, and a dignified behaviour. A rich banker of Paris, a citizen of Geneva, had the good fortune and good sense to discover and possess this inestimable treasure; and in the capital of taste and luxury she resisted the temptations of wealth, as she had sustained the hardships of indigence. The genius of her husband has exalted him to the most conspicuous station in Europe. In every change of prosperity and disgrace he has reclined on the bosom of a faithful friend; and Mademoiselle Curchod is now the wife of M. Necker, the minister, and perhaps the legislator, of the French monarchy.

Whatsoever have been the fruits of my education, they must be ascribed to the fortunate banishment which placed me at Lausanne. I have sometimes applied to my own fate the verses of Pindar, which remind an Olympic champion that his victory was the consequence of his exile; and that at home, like a domestic fowl, his days might have rolled away inactive or inglorious.

... ἦτοι καὶ τεά κεν,
'Ενδομάχας ἅτ' ἀλέκτωρ,
Συγγόνω παρ' ἑστίᾳ
'Ακλεὴς τιμὰ κατεφυλλορόησε ποδῶν·
Εἰ μὴ στάσις ἀντιάνειρα
Κνωσίας ἄμερσε πάτρας.[20]   Olymp. xii.

If my childish revolt against the religion of my country had not stripped me in time of my academic gown, the five important years, so liberally improved in the studies and conversation of Lausanne, would have been steeped in port and prejudice among the monks of Oxford. Had the fatigue of idleness compelled me to read, the path of learning would not have been enlightened by a ray of philosophic freedom. I should have grown to manhood ignorant of the life and language

---

[19] See *Oeuvres de Rousseau*, tom. xxxiii, pp. 88, 89, octave edition. As an author I shall not appeal from the judgement, or taste, or caprice of *Jean Jacques:* but that extraordinary man, whom I admire and pity, should have been less precipitate in condemning the moral character and conduct of a stranger.

[20] Thus, like the crested bird of Mars, at home
Engag'd in foul domestic jars,
And wasted with intestine wars,
Inglorious hadst thou spent thy vig'rous bloom;
Had not sedition's civil broils
Expell'd thee from thy native *Crete,*
And driv'n thee with more glorious toils
Th' *Olympic* crown in *Pisa's* plain to meet.
West's *Pind.* S.

of Europe, and my knowledge of the world would have been confined to an English cloister. But my religious error fixed me at Lausanne, in a state of banishment and disgrace. The rigid course of discipline and abstinence, to which I was condemned, invigorated the constitution of my mind and body; poverty and pride estranged me from my countrymen. One mischief, however, and in their eyes a serious and irreparable mischief, was derived from the success of my Swiss education: I had ceased to be an Englishman. At the flexible period of youth, from the age of sixteen to twenty-one, my opinions, habits, and sentiments were cast in a foreign mould; the faint and distant remembrance of England was almost obliterated; my native language was grown less familiar; and I should have cheerfully accepted the offer of a moderate independence on the terms of perpetual exile. By the good sense and temper of Pavilliard my yoke was insensibly lightened: he left me master of my time and actions; but he could neither change my situation, nor increase my allowance, and with the progress of my years and reason I impatiently sighed for the moment of my deliverance. At length, in the spring of the year 1758, my father signified his permission and his pleasure that I should immediately return home. We were then in the midst of a war: the resentment of the French at our taking their ships without a declaration had rendered that polite nation somewhat peevish and difficult. They denied a passage to English travellers, and the road through Germany was circuitous, toilsome, and, perhaps in the neighbourhood of the armies, exposed to some danger. In this perplexity, two Swiss officers of my acquaintance in the Dutch service, who were returning to their garrisons, offered to conduct me through France as one of their companions; nor did we sufficiently reflect that my borrowed name and regimentals might have been considered, in case of a discovery, in a very serious light. I took my leave of Lausanne on the 11th of April, 1758, with a mixture of joy and regret, in the firm resolution of revisiting, as a man, the persons and places which had been so dear to my youth. We travelled slowly, but pleasantly, in a hired coach, over the hills of Franche-compté and the fertile province of Lorraine, and passed, without accident or inquiry, through several fortified towns of the French frontier: from thence we entered the wild Ardennes of the Austrian duchy of Luxemburg; and after crossing the Meuse at Liège, we traversed the heaths of Brabant, and reached, on the fifteenth day, our Dutch garrison of Bois le Duc. In our passage through Nancy, my eye was gratified by the aspect of a regular and beautiful city, the work of Stanislaus, who, after the storms of Polish royalty, reposed in the love and gratitude of his new subjects of Lorraine. In our halt at Maestricht I visited Mr. de Beaufort, a learned critic, who was known to me by his specious arguments against the five first centuries of the *Roman History*. After dropping my regimental companions, I stepped aside to visit Rotterdam and the Hague. I wished to have observed a country, the monument of freedom and industry; but my days were numbered, and a longer delay would have been ungraceful. I hastened to embark at the Brill, landed the next day at Harwich, and proceeded to London, where my father awaited my arrival. The whole term of my first absence from England was four years ten months and fifteen days.

In the prayers of the Church our personal concerns are judiciously reduced to the threefold distinction of *mind, body,* and *estate.* The sentiments of the mind excite and exercise our social sympathy. The review of my moral and literary character is the most interesting to myself and to the public; and I may expatiate, without reproach, on my private studies; since they have produced the public writings, which can alone entitle me to the esteem and friendship of my readers. The experience of the world inculcates a discreet reserve on the subject of our person and estate, and we soon learn that a free disclosure of our riches or poverty would provoke the malice of envy, or encourage the insolence of contempt.

The only person in England whom I was impatient to see was my aunt Porten, the affectionate guardian of my tender years. I hastened to her house in College Street, Westminister; and the evening was spent in the effusions of joy and confidence. It was not without some awe and apprehension that I approached the presence of my father. My infancy, to speak the truth, had been neglected at home; the severity of his look and language at our last parting still dwelt on my memory; nor could I form any notion of his character, or my probable reception. They were both more agreeable than I could expect. The domestic discipline of our ancestors has been relaxed by the philosophy and softness of the age; and if my father remembered that he had trembled before a stern parent, it was only to adopt with his own son an opposite mode of behaviour. He received me as a man and a friend; all constraint was banished at our first interview, and we ever afterwards continued on the same terms of easy and equal politeness. He applauded the success of my education; every word and action was expressive of the most cordial affection; and our lives would have passed without a cloud, if his economy had been equal to his fortune, or if his fortune had been equal to his desire. During my absence he had married his second wife, Miss Dorothea Patton, who was introduced to me with the most unfavourable prejudice. I considered his second marriage as an act of displeasure, and I was disposed to hate the rival of my mother. But the injustice was in my own fancy, and the imaginary monster was an amiable and deserving woman. I could not be mistaken in the first view of her understanding, her knowledge, and the elegant spirit of her conversation: her polite welcome, and her assiduous care to study and gratify my wishes, announced at least that the surface would be smooth; and my suspicions of art and falsehood were gradually dispelled by the full discovery of her warm and exquisite sensibility. After some reserve on my side, our minds associated in confidence and friendship; and as Mrs. Gibbon had neither children nor the hopes of children, we more easily adopted the tender names and genuine characters of mother and of son. By the indulgence of these parents, I was left at liberty to consult my taste or reason in the choice of place, of company, and of amusements; and my excursions were bounded only by the limits of the island, and the measure of my income. Some faint efforts were made to procure me the employment of secretary to a foreign embassy; and I listened to a scheme which would again have transported me to the continent. Mrs. Gibbon, with seeming wisdom, exhorted me to take chambers in the Temple, and devote my leisure to the study of the law. I cannot repent of having neglected her advice. Few men, without the spur of necessity, have resolution to force their way through the thorns and thickets of that gloomy labyrinth. Nature had not endowed me with the bold and ready eloquence which makes itself heard amidst the tumult of the bar; and I should probably have been diverted from the labours of literature, without acquiring the fame or fortune of a successful pleader. I had no need to call to my aid the regular duties of a profession; every day, every hour, was agreeably filled; nor have I known, like so many of my countrymen, the tediousness of an idle life.

Of the two years (May, 1758–May, 1760), between my return to England and the embodying of the Hampshire militia, I passed about nine months in London, and the remainder in the country. The metropolis affords many amusements, which are open to all. It is itself an astonishing and perpetual spectacle to the curious eye; and each taste, each sense may be gratified by the variety of objects which will occur in the long circuit of a morning walk. I assiduously frequented the theatres at a very propitious era of the stage, when a constellation of excellent actors, both in tragedy and comedy, was eclipsed by the meridian brightness of Garrick in the maturity of his judgement and vigour of his performance. The pleasures of a town-life are within the reach of every man who is regardless of his health, his money, and his company. By the contagion of example I was sometimes seduced; but the better habits, which I had formed at Lausanne, induced me to seek a more elegant and rational society; and if my search was less easy and successful than I might have hoped, I shall at present impute the failure of the disadvantages of my situation and character. Had the rank and fortune of my parents given them an annual establishment in London, their own house would have introduced me to a numerous and polite circle of acquaintance. But my father's taste had always preferred the highest and the lowest company, for which he was equally qualified; and after a twelve years' retirement, he was no longer in the memory of the great with whom he had associated. I found myself a stranger in the midst of a vast and unknown city; and at my entrance into life I was reduced to some dull family parties, and some scattered connexions, which were not such as I should have chosen for myself. The most useful friends of my father were the Mallets: they received me with civility and kindness at first on his account, and afterwards on my own; and (if I may use Lord Chesterfield's words) I was soon *domesticated* in their house. Mr. Mallet, a name among the English poets, is praised by an unforgiving enemy, for the ease and elegance of his conversation, and his wife was not destitute of wit or learning. By his assistance I was introduced to Lady Hervey, the mother of the present Earl of Bristol. Her age and infirmities confined her at home; her dinners were select; in the evening her house was open to the best company of both sexes and all nations; nor was I displeased at her preference and affectation of the manners, the language, and the literature of France. But my progress in the English world was in general left to my own efforts, and those efforts were languid and slow. I had not been endowed by art or nature with those happy gifts of confidence and address, which unlock every door and every bosom; nor would it be reasonable to complain of the just consequences of my sickly childhood, foreign education, and reserved temper. While coaches were rattling through Bond Street, I have passed many a solitary evening in my lodging with my books. My studies were sometimes interrupted by a sigh, which I breathed towards Lausanne; and on the approach of spring, I withdrew without reluctance from the noisy and extensive scene of crowds without company, and dissipation without pleasure. In each of the twenty-five years of my acquaintance with London (1758–83), the prospect gradually brightened; and this unfavourable picture most properly belongs to the first period after my return from Switzerland.

My father's residence in Hampshire, where I have passed many light, and some heavy hours, was at Buriton near Petersfield, one mile from the Portsmouth road, and at the easy distance of fifty-eight miles from London. An old mansion, in a state of decay, had been converted into the fashion and convenience of a modern house; and if strangers had nothing to see, the inhabitants had little to desire. The spot was not happily chosen, at the end of the village and the bottom of the hill: but the aspect of the adjacent grounds was various and cheerful; the downs commanded a noble prospect, and the long hanging woods in sight of the house could not perhaps have been improved by art or expense. My father kept in his own hands the whole of the estate, and even rented some additional land; and whatsoever might be the balance of profit and loss, the farm supplied him with amusement and plenty. The produce maintained a number of men and horses, which were multiplied by the intermixture of domestic and rural servants; and in the intervals of labour the favourite team, a handsome set of bays or greys, was harnessed to the coach. The economy of the house was regulated by the taste and prudence of Mrs. Gibbon. She prided herself in the elegance of her occasional dinners; and from the uncleanly avarice of Madame Pavilliard, I was suddenly transported to the daily neatness and luxury of an English table. Our immediate neighbourhood was rare and rustic; but from the verge of our hills, as far as

Chichester and Goodwood, the western district of Sussex was interspersed with noble seats and hospitable families, with whom we cultivated a friendly, and might have enjoyed a very frequent, intercourse. As my stay at Buriton was always voluntary, I was received and dismissed with smiles; but the comforts of my retirement did not depend on the ordinary pleasures of the country. My father could never inspire me with his love and knowledge of farming. I never handled a gun, I seldom mounted a horse; and my philosophic walks were soon terminated by a shady bench, where I was long detained by the sedentary amusement of reading or meditation. At home I occupied a pleasant and spacious apartment; the library on the same floor was soon considered as my peculiar domain; and I might say with truth, that I was never less alone than when by myself. My sole complaint, which I piously suppressed, arose from the kind restraint imposed on the freedom of my time. By the habit of early rising I always secured a sacred portion of the day, and many scattered moments were stolen and employed by my studious industry. But the family hours of breakfast, of dinner, of tea, and of supper, were regular and long: after breakfast Mrs. Gibbon expected my company in her dressing-room; after tea my father claimed my conversation and the perusal of the newspapers; and in the midst of an interesting work I was often called down to receive the visit of some idle neighbours. Their dinners and visits required, in due season, a similar return; and I dreaded the period of the full moon, which was usually reserved for our more distant excursions. I could not refuse attending my father, in the summer of 1759, to the races at Stockbridge, Reading, and Odiam, where he had entered a horse for the hunters' plate; and I was not displeased with the sight of our Olympic games, the beauty of the spot, the fleetness of the horses, and the gay tumult of the numerous spectators. As soon as the militia business was agitated, many days were tediously consumed in meetings of deputy-lieutenants at Petersfield, Alton, and Winchester. In the close of the same year, 1759, Sir Simeon (then Mr.) Stewart attempted an unsuccessful contest for the county of Southampton, against Mr. Legge, Chancellor of the Exchequer: a well-known contest, in which Lord Bute's influence was first exerted and censured. Our canvass at Portsmouth and Gosport lasted several days; but the interruption of my studies was compensated in some degree by the spectacle of English manners, and the acquisition of some practical knowledge.

If in a more domestic or more dissipated scene my application was somewhat relaxed, the love of knowledge was inflamed and gratified by the command of books; and I compared the poverty of Lausanne with the plenty of London. My father's study at Buriton was stuffed with much trash of the last age, with much High Church divinity and politics, which have long since gone to their proper place; yet it contained some valuable editions of the classics and the fathers, the choice, as it should seem, of Mr. Law; and many English publications of the times had been occasionally added. From this slender beginning I have gradually formed a numerous and select library, the foundation of my works, and the best comfort of my life, both at home and abroad. On the receipt of the first quarter, a large share of my allowance was appropriated to my literary wants. I cannot forget the joy with which I exchanged a bank-note of twenty pounds for the twenty volumes of the *Memoirs of the Academy of Inscriptions*; nor would it have been easy, by any other expenditure of the same sum, to have procured so large and lasting a fund of rational amusement. . . . The review of my library must be reserved for the period of its maturity; but in this place I may allow myself to observe, that I am not conscious of having ever bought a book from a motive of ostentation, that every volume, before it was deposited on the shelf, was either read or sufficiently examined, and that I soon adopted the tolerating maxim of the elder Pliny, 'nullum esse librum tam malum ut non ex aliquâ parte prodesset.* I could not yet find leisure or courage to renew the pursuit of the Greek language, excepting by reading the lessons of the Old and New Testament every Sunday, when I attended the family to church. The series of my Latin authors was less strenuously completed; but the acquisition, by inheritance or purchase, of the best editions of Cicero, Quintilian, Livy, Tacitus, Ovid, &c., afforded a fair prospect, which I seldom neglected. I persevered in the useful method of abstracts and observations: and a single example may suffice, of a note which had almost swelled into a work. The solution of a passage of Livy (xxxviii, 38) involved me in the dry and dark treatises of Greaves, Arbuthnot, Hooper, Bernard, Eisenschmidt, Gronovius, La Barré, Freret, &c.; and in my French essay (chapter 20) I ridiculously send the reader to my own *manuscript* remarks on the weights, coins, and measures of the ancients, which were abruptly terminated by the militia drum.

As I am now entering on a more ample field of society and study, I can only hope to avoid a vain and prolix garrulity, by overlooking the vulgar crowd of my acquaintance, and confining myself to such intimate friends among books and men, as are best entitled to my notice by their own merit and reputation, or by the deep impression which they have left on my mind. Yet I will embrace this occasion of recommending to the young student a practice which about this time I myself adopted. After glancing my eye over the design and order of a new book, I suspended the perusal till I had finished the task of self-examination, till I had revolved, in a solitary walk, all that I knew or believed, or had thought on the subject of the whole work, or of some particular chapter: I was then qualified to discern how much the author added to my original stock; and if I was sometimes satisfied by the agreement, I was sometimes armed by the opposition of our ideas. The favourite companions of my leisure were our English writers since the Revolution: they breathe the spirit of reason and liberty; and they most seasonably contribut-

ed to restore the purity of my own language, which had been corrupted by the long use of a foreign idiom. By the judicious advice of Mr. Mallet, I was directed to the writings of Swift and Addison; wit and simplicity are their common attributes: but the style of Swift is supported by manly original vigour; that of Addison is adorned by the female graces of elegance and mildness. The old reproach, that no British altars had been raised to the muse of history, was recently disproved by the first performances of Robertson and Hume, the histories of Scotland and of the Stuarts. I will assume the presumption of saying that I was not unworthy to read them: nor will I disguise my different feelings in the repeated perusals. The perfect composition, the nervous language, the well-turned periods of Dr. Robertson, inflamed me to the ambitious hope that I might one day tread in his footsteps: the calm philosophy, the careless inimitable beauties of his friend and rival, often forced me to close the volume with a mixed sensation of delight and despair.

The design of my first work, the *Essay on the Study of Literature*, was suggested by a refinement of vanity, the desire of justifying and praising the object of a favourite pursuit. In France, to which my ideas were confined, the learning and language of Greece and Rome were neglected by a philosophic age. The guardian of those studies, the Academy of Inscriptions, was degraded to the lowest rank among the three royal societies of Paris: the new appellation of Erudits was contemptuously applied to the successors of Lipsius and Casaubon; and I was provoked to hear (see M. d'Alembert, *Discours préliminaire à l'Encyclopédie*) that the exercise of the memory, their sole merit, had been superseded by the nobler faculties of the imagination and the judgement. I was ambitious of proving by my own example, as well as by my precepts, that all the faculties of the mind may be exercised and displayed by the study of ancient

---

* Pliny the Younger *Letters.* 3.5 [No book is so bad that one cannot gain from part of it]—Ed.

literature; I began to select and adorn the various proofs and illustrations which had offered themselves in reading the classics and the first pages or chapters of my essay were composed before my departure from Lausanne. The hurry of the journey, and of the first weeks of my English life, suspended all thought of serious application: but my object was ever before my eyes; and no more than ten days, from the first to the eleventh of July, we suffered to elapse after my summer establishment at Buriton. My essay was finished in about six weeks; and as soon as a fair copy had been transcribed by one of the French prisoners at Petersfield, I looked round for a critic and judge of my first performance. A writer can seldom be content with the doubtful recompense of solitary approbation; but a youth ignorant of the world, and of himself, must desire to weigh his talents in some scales less partial than his own: my conduct was natural, my motive laudable, my choice of Dr. Maty judicious and fortunate. By descent and education, Dr. Maty, though born in Holland, might be considered as a Frenchman; but he was fixed in London by the practice of physic, and an office in the British Museum. His reputation was justly founded on the eighteen volumes of the *Journal Britannique*, which he had supported, almost alone, with perseverance and success. This humble though useful labour, which had once been dignified by the genius of Bayle and the learning of Le Clerc, was not disgraced by the taste, the knowledge, and the judgement of Maty: he exhibits a candid and pleasing view of the state of literature in England during a period of six years (January, 1750–December, 1755); and, far different from his angry son, he handles the rod of criticism with the tenderness and reluctance of a parent. The author of the *Journal Britannique* sometimes aspires to the character of a poet and philosopher: his style is pure and elegant; and in his virtues, or even in his defects, he may be ranked as one of the last disciples of the school of Fontenelle. His answer to my first letter was prompt and polite: after a careful examination he returned my manuscript, with some animadversion and much applause; and when I visited London in the ensuing winter, we discussed the design and execution in several free and familiar conversations. In a short excursion to Buriton I reviewed my essay, according to his friendly advice; and after suppressing a third, adding a third, and altering a third, I consummated my first labour by a short preface, which is dated February 3, 1759. Yet I still shrunk from the press with the terrors of virgin modesty: the manuscript was safely deposited in my desk; and as my attention was engaged by new objects, the delay might have been prolonged till I had fulfilled the precept of Horace, 'nonumque prematur in annum'.* Father Sirmond, a learned Jesuit, was still more rigid, since he advised a young friend to expect the mature age of fifty before he gave himself or his writings to the public (Olivet, *Histoire de l'Académie Françoise*, tom. ii, p. 143). The counsel was singular; but it is still more singular that it should have been approved by the example of the author. Sirmond was himself fifty-five years of age when he published (in 1614) his first work, an edition of *Sidonius Apollinaris*, with many valuable annotations. (See his life, before the great edition of his works in five volumes folio, Paris, 1696, e Typographia Regia.)

Two years elapsed in silence: but in the spring of 1761 I yielded to the authority of a parent, and complied, like a pious son, with the wish of my own heart.[21] My private re-

---

* Horace *Ars Poetica.* 388 [and let it be held until the ninth year]—Ed.

[21] JOURNAL, March 8, 1758.—I began my *Essai sur l'Étude de la Littérature*, and wrote the 23 first chapters (excepting the following ones, 11, 12, 13, 18, 19, 20, 21, 22) before I left Switzerland.

July 11. I again took in hand my Essay; and in about six weeks finished it, from C. 23–55 (excepting 27, 28, 29, 30, 31, 32, 33, and note to C. 38), besides a number of chapters from C. 55 to the end, which are now struck out.

Feb. 11, 1759. I wrote the chapters of my Essay, 27, 28, 29, 30, 31, the note to C. 38, and the first part of the preface.

April 23, 1761. Being at length, by my father's advice, determined to publish my Essay, I revised it with great care, made many alterations, struck

solves were influenced by the state of Europe. About this time the belligerent powers had made and accepted overtures of peace; our English plenipotentiaries were named to assist at the Congress of Augsburg, which never met: I wished to attend them as a gentleman or a secretary; and my father fondly believed that the proof of some literary talents might introduce me to public notice, and second the recommendations of my friends. After a last revisal I consulted with Mr. Mallet and Dr. Maty, who approved the design and promoted the execution. Mr. Mallet, after hearing me read my manuscript, received it from my hands, and delivered it into those of Becket, with whom he made an agreement in my name; an easy agreement: I required only a certain number of copies; and, without transferring my property, I devolved on the bookseller the charges and profits of the edition. Dr. Maty undertook, in my absence, to correct the sheets: he inserted, without my knowledge, an elegant and flattering epistle to the author; which is composed, however, with so much art, that, in case of a defeat, his favourable report might have been ascribed to the indulgence of a friend for the rash attempt of a *young English* gentleman. The work was printed and published, under the title of *Essai sur l'Étude de la Littérature,* à Londres, chez T. Becket et P. A. de Hondt, 1761, in a small volume in duodecimo: my dedication to my father, a proper and pious address, was composed the 28th of May: Dr. Maty's letter is dated the 16th of June; and I received the first copy (June 23) at Alresford, two days before I marched with the Hampshire militia. Some weeks afterwards, on the same ground, I presented my book to the late Duke of York, who breakfasted in Colonel Pitt's tent. By my father's direction, and Mallet's advice, my literary gifts were distributed to several eminent characters in England and France; two books were sent to the Count de Caylus, and the Duchesse d'Aiguillon, at Paris: I had reserved twenty copies for my friends at Lausanne, as the first fruits of my education, and a grateful token of my

remembrance: and on all these persons I levied an unavoidable tax of civility and compliment. It is not surprising that a work, of which the style and sentiments were so totally foreign, should have been more successful abroad than at home. I was delighted by the copious extracts, the warm commendations, and the flattering predictions of the journals of France and Holland: and the next year (1762) a new edition (I believe at Geneva) extended the fame, or at least the circulation, of the work. In England it was received with cold indifference, little read, and speedily forgotten: a small impression was slowly dispersed; the bookseller murmured, and the author (had his feelings been more exquisite) might have wept over the blunders and baldness of the English translation. The publication of my History fifteen years afterwards revived the memory of my first performance, and the Essay was eagerly sought in the shops. But I refused the permission which Becket solicited of reprinting it: the public curiosity was imperfectly satisfied by a pirated copy of the booksellers of Dublin; and when a copy of the original edition has been discovered in a sale, the primitive value of half-a-crown has risen to the fanciful price of a guinea or thirty shillings.

I have expatiated on the petty circumstances and period of my first publication, a memorable era in the life of a student, when he ventures to reveal the measure of his mind: his hopes and fears are multiplied by the idea of self-importance, and he believes

---

out a considerable part, and wrote the chapters from 57–78, which I was obliged myself to copy out fair.

June 10, 1761. Finding the printing of my book proceeded but slowly, I went up to town, where I found the whole was finished. I gave Becket orders for the presents: twenty for Lausanne; copies for the Duke of Richmond, Marquis of Carnavon, Lords Waldegrave, Litchfield, Bath, Granville, Bute, Shelbourn, Chesterfield, Hardwicke, Lady Hervey, Sir Joseph Yorke, Sir Matthew Featherstone, MM. Mallet, Maty, Scott, Wray, Lord Engremont, M. de Bussy, Mademoiselle la Duchesse d'Aiguillon, and M. le Comte de Caylus; great part of these were only my father's or Mallet's acquaintance.

for a while that the eyes of mankind are fixed on his person and performance. Whatever may be my present reputation, it no longer rests on the merit of this first essay; and at the end of twenty-eight years I may appreciate my juvenile work with the impartiality, and almost with the indifference of a stranger. In his answer to Lady Hervey, the Count de Caylus admires, or affects to admire, 'les livres sans nombre que Mr. Gibbon a lus et très bien lus' [the innumerable books Mr. Gibbon has read and read carefully at that]. But, alas! my stock of erudition at that time was scanty and superficial; and if I allow myself the liberty of naming the Greek masters, my genuine and personal acquaintance was confined to the Latin classics. The most serious defect of my Essay is a kind of obscurity and abruptness which always fatigues, and may often elude, the attention of the reader. Instead of a precise and proper definition of the title itself, the sense of the word *Littérature* is loosely and variously applied: a number of remarks and examples, historical, critical, philosphical, are heaped on each other without method or connexion; and if we except some introductory pages, all the remaining chapters might indifferently be reversed or transposed. The obscurity of many passages is often affected, 'brevis esse laboro, obscurus fio',[*] the desire of expressing perhaps a common idea with sententious and oracular brevity: alas! how fatal has been the imitation of Montesquieu! But this obscurity sometimes proceeds from a mixture of light and darkness in the author's mind; from a partial ray which strikes upon an angle, instead of spreading itself over the surface of an object. After this fair confession I shall presume to say that the Essay does credit to a young writer of two and twenty years of age, who had read with taste, who thinks with freedom, and who writes in a foreign language with spirit and elegance. The defence of the early History of Rome and the new Chronology of Sir Isaac Newton form a specious argument. The patriotic and political design of the Georgics is happily conceived; and any probable conjecture, which tends to raise the dignity of the poet and the poem, deserves to be adopted, without a rigid scrutiny. Some dawnings of a philosophic spirit enlighten the general remarks on the study of history and of man. I am not displeased with the inquiry into the origin and nature of the gods of polytheism, which might deserve the illustration of a riper judgement. Upon the whole, I may apply to the first labour of my pen the speech of a far superior artist, when he surveyed the first productions of his pencil. After viewing some portraits which he had painted in his youth, my friend Sir Joshua Reynolds acknowledged to me that he was rather humbled than flattered by the comparison with his present works; and that after so much time and study, he had conceived his improvement to be much greater than he found it to have been.

At Lausanne I composed the first chapters of my Essay in French, the familiar language of my conversation and studies, in which it was easier for me to write than in my mother tongue. After my return to England I continued the same practice, without any affectation, or design of repudiating (as Dr. Bentley would say) my vernacular idiom. But I should have escaped some anti-Gallican clamour, had I been content with the more natural character of an English author. I should have been more consistent had I rejected Mallet's advice, of prefixing an English dedication to a French book; a confusion of tongues that seemed to accuse the ignorance of my patron. The use of a foreign dialect might be excused by the hope of being employed as a negotiator, by the desire of being generally understood on the continent; but my true motive was doubtless the ambition of new and singular fame, an Englishman claiming a place among the writers of France. The Latin tongue had been consecrated by the service of the Church, it was refined by the imitation of the ancients; and in the fifteenth and sixteenth centuries the scholars

---

[*] Horace *Ars Poetica.* 25–26 [I labor to be brief and become obscure]—Ed.

of Europe enjoyed the advantage, which they have gradually resigned, of conversing and writing in a common and learned idiom. As that idiom was no longer in any country the vulgar speech, they all stood on a level with each other; yet a citizen of old Rome might have smiled at the best Latinity of the Germans and Britons; and we may learn from the *Ciceronianus* of Erasmus, how difficult it was found to steer a middle course between pedantry and barbarism. The Romans themselves had sometimes attempted a more perilous task, of writing in a living language, and appealing to the taste and judgement of the natives. The vanity of Tully was doubly interested in the Greek memoirs of his own consulship; and if he modestly supposes that some Latinisms might be detected in his style, he is confident of his own skill in the art of Isocrates and Aristotle; and he requests his friend Atticus to disperse the copies of his work at Athens, and in the other cities of Greece (*ad Atticum,* i. 19; ii, 1). But it must not be forgotten, that from infancy to manhood Cicero and his contemporaries had read and declaimed, and composed with equal diligence in both languages; and that he was not allowed to frequent a Latin school till he had imbibed the lessons of the Greek grammarians and rhetoricians. In modern times, the language of France has been diffused by the merit of her writers, the social manners of the natives, the influence of the monarchy, and the exile of the Protestants. Several foreigners have seized the opportunity of speaking to Europe in this common dialect, and Germany may plead the authority of Liebnitz and Frederic, of the first of her philosophers, and the greatest of her kings. The just pride and laudable prejudice of England has restrained this communication of idioms; and of all the nations on this side of the Alps, my countrymen are the least practised, and least perfect, in the exercise of the French tongue. By Sir William Temple and Lord Chesterfield it was only used on occasions of civility and business, and their printed letters will not be quoted as models of composition. Lord Bolingbroke may have published in

French a sketch of his *Reflections on Exile*: but his reputation now reposes on the address of Voltaire, 'Docte sermones utriusque linguae'; and by his English dedication to Queen Caroline, and his *Essay on Epic Poetry*, it should seem that Voltaire himself wished to deserve a return of the same compliment. The exception of Count Hamilton cannot fairly be urged; though an Irishman by birth, he was educated in France from his childhood. Yet I am surprised that a long residence in England, and the habits of domestic conversation, did not affect the ease and purity of his inimitable style; and I regret the omission of his English verses, which might have afforded an amusing object of comparison. I might therefore assume the *primus ego in patriam,* &c., but with what success I have explored this untrodden path must be left to the decision of my French readers. Dr. Maty, who might himself be questioned as a foreigner, has secured his retreat at my expense. 'Je ne crois pas que vous vous piquiez d'être moins facile à reconnoître pour un Anglois que Lucullus pour un Romain' [I do not believe you are any more offended to be taken with difficulty for an Englishman, than Lucullus would have been for a Roman]. My friends at Paris have been more indulgent, they received me as a countryman, or at least as a provincial; but they were friends and Parisians.[22] The defects which Maty insinuates, 'Ces traits saillans, ces figures hardies, ce sacrifice de la règle au sentiment, et de la cadence à la force' [These striking bursts of eloquence, these bold characters, the sacrifice of order to emotion and of rhythm to force], are the faults of the youth, rather than of the stranger: and after the long and laborious exercise of my own language, I am conscious that my French style has been ripened and improved.

---

[22] The copious extracts which were given in the *Journal Étranger* by Mr. Suard, a judicious critic, must satisfy both the author and the public. I may here observe that I have never seen in any literary review a tolerable account of my *History*. The manufacture of journals, at least on the continent, is miserably debased.

I have already hinted that the publication of my Essay was delayed till I had embraced the military profession. I shall now amuse myself with the recollection of an active scene, which bears no affinity to any other period of my studious and social life.

In the outset of a glorious war, the English people had been defended by the aid of German mercenaries. A national militia has been the cry of every patriot since the Revolution; and this measure, both in parliament and in the field, was supported by the country gentlemen or Tories, who insensibly transferred their loyalty to the house of Hanover: in the language of Mr. Burke, they have changed the idol, but they have preserved the idolatry. In the act of offering our names and receiving our commissions, as major and captain in the Hampshire regiment (June 12, 1759), we had not supposed that we should be dragged away, my father from his farm, myself from my books, and condemned, during two years and a half (May 10, 1760—December 23, 1762), to a wandering life of military servitude. But a weekly or monthly exercise of thirty thousand provincials would have left them useless and ridiculous; and after the pretence of an invasion had vanished, the popularity of Mr. Pitt gave a sanction to the illegal step of keeping them till the end of the war under arms, in constant pay and duty, and at a distance from their respective homes. When the King's order for our embodying came down, it was too late to retreat, and too soon to repent. The south battalion of the Hampshire militia was a small independent corps of four hundred and seventy-six, officers and men, commanded by Lieutenant-Colonel Sir Thomas Worsley, who, after a prolix and passionate contest, delivered us from the tyranny of the Lord Lieutenant, the Duke of Bolton. My proper station, as first captain, was at the head of my own, and afterwards of the grenadier company; but in the absence, or even in the presence, of the two field officers, I was entrusted by my friend and my father with the effective labour of dictating the orders, and exercising the battalion. With the

help of an original journal, I could write the history of my bloodless and inglorious campaigns; but as these events have lost much of their importance in my own eyes, they shall be dispatched in a few words. From Winchester, the first place of assembly (June 4, 1760), we were removed, at our own request, for the benefit of a foreign education. By the arbitrary, and often capricious orders of the War Office, the battalion successively marched to the pleasant and hospitable Blandford (June 17); to Hilsea barracks, a seat of disease and discord (September 1); to Cranbrook in the Weald of Kent (December 11); to the seacoast of Dover (December 27); to Winchester camp (June 25, 1761); to the populous and disorderly town of Devizes (October 23); to Salisbury (February 28, 1762); to our beloved Blandford a second time (March 9): and finally, to the fashionable resort of Southampton (June 2); where the colours were fixed till our final dissolution (December 23). On the beach at Dover we had exercised in sight of the Gallic shores. But the most splendid and useful scene of our life was a four months' encampment on Winchester Down, under the command of the Earl of Effingham. Our army consisted of the thirty-fourth regiment of foot and six militia corps. The consciousness of defects was stimulated by friendly emulation. We improved our time and opportunities in morning and evening field days; and in the general reviews the South Hampshire were rather a credit than a disgrace to the line. In our subsequent quarters of the Devizes and Blandford, we advanced with a quick step in our military studies; the ballot of the ensuing summer renewed our vigour and youth; and had the militia subsisted another year, we might have contested the prize with the most perfect of our brethen.

The loss of so many busy and idle hours was not compensated by any elegant pleasure; and my temper was insensibly soured by the society of our rustic officers. In every state there exists, however, a balance of good and evil. The habits of a sedentary life were usefully broken by the duties of an active profession: in the healthful exercise of the field I hunted with a battalion, instead of a pack; and at that time I was ready, at any hour of the day or night, to fly from quarters to London, from London to quarters, on the slightest call to private or regimental business. But my principal obligation to the militia was the making me an Englishman, and a soldier. After my foreign education, with my reserved temper, I should long have continued a stranger to my native country, had I not been shaken in this various scene of new faces and new friends: had not experience forced me to feel the characters of our leading men, the state of parties, the forms of office, and the operation of our civil and military system. In this peaceful service I imbibed the rudiments of the language, and science of tactics, which opened a new field of study and observation. I diligently read, and meditated, the *Mémoires Militaires* of Quintus Icilius, the only writer who has united the merits of a professor and a veteran. The discipline and evolutions of a modern battalion gave me a clearer notion of the phalanx and the legion; and the captain of the Hampshire grenadiers (the reader may smile) has not been useless to the historian of the Roman empire.

A youth of any spirit is fired even by the play of arms, and in the first sallies of my enthusiasm I had seriously attempted to embrace the regular profession of a soldier. But this military fever was cooled by the enjoyment of our mimic Bellona, who soon unveiled to my eyes her naked deformity. How often did I sigh for my proper station in society and letters! How often (a proud comparison) did I repeat the complaint of Cicero in the command of a provincial army! 'Clitellae bovi sunt impositae. Est incredibile quam me negotii taedeat. Non habet satis magnum campum ille tibi non ignotus cursus animi; et industriae meae praeclara opera cessat. Lucem, *libros,* urbem, domum, vos desidero. Sed feram, ut potero; sit modo annuum. Si prorogatur, actum est.'[23] From a service without danger I might indeed have retired without disgrace; but as often as I hinted a wish of resigning, my fetters were riveted by

the friendly entreaties of the colonel, the parental authority of the major, and my own regard for the honour and welfare of the battalion. When I felt that my personal escape was impracticable, I bowed my neck to the yoke: my servitude was protracted far beyond the annual patience of Cicero; and it was not till after the preliminaries of peace that I received my discharge from the act of government which disembodied the militia.[24]

[23] *Epist. ad Atticum,* lib. v, 15. [The saddles have been put on the wrong beast. You can't believe how sick I am of this business. My mind lacks a field big enough to run in as you know, and the notable effect of my industry is lost. I want light, *books,* the city, home, you. But I will bear it as I can provided it is but for a year. If that is the extent of it, so be it.]—Ed.

[24] JOURNAL, January 11, 1761.—In these seven or eight months of a most disagreeably active life, I have had no studies to set down; indeed, I hardly took a book in my hande the whole time. The first two months at Blandford, I might have done something; but the novelty of the thing, of which for some time I was so fond as to think of going into the army, our field-days, our dinners abroad, and the drinking and late hours we got into, prevented any serious reflections. From the day we marched from Blandford I had hardly a moment I could call my own, almost continually in motion; if I was fixed for a day, it was in the guard-room, a barrack, or an inn. Our disputes consumed the little time I had left. Every letter, every memorial relative to them fell to my share; and our evening conferences were used to hear all the morning hours strike. At last I got to Dover, and Sir Thomas left us for two months. The charm was over; I was sick of so hateful a service; I was settled in a comparatively quiet situation. Once more I began to taste the pleasure of thinking.

Recollecting some thoughts I had formerly had in relation to the System of Paganism, which I intended to make use of in my Essay, I resolved to read Tully *de Natura Deorum,* and finished it in about a month. I lost some time before I could recover my habit of application.

Oct. 23.—Our first design was to march through Marlborough; but finding on inquiry that it was a bad road, and a great way about, we resolved to push for the Devizes in one day, though nearly thirty miles. We accordingly arrived there about three o'clock in the afternoon.

Nov. 21.—I have very little to say for this and the following month. Nothing could be more uniform than the life I led there. The little civility of the neighbouring gentlemen gave us no opportunity of dining out; the time of year did not tempt us to

When I complain of the loss of time, justice to myself and to the militia must throw the greatest part of that reproach on the first

---

any excursions round the country; and at first my indolence, and afterwards a violent cold, prevented my going over to Bath. I believe in the two months I never dined or lay from quarters. I can therefore only set down what I did in the literary way. Designing to recover my Greek, which I had somewhat neglected, I set myself to read Homer, and finished the four first books of the *Iliad,* with Pope's translation and notes; at the same time, to understand the geography of the *Iliad,* and particularly the catalogue, I read the 8th, 9th, 10th, 12th, 13th, and 14th books of Strabo, in Casaubon's Latin translation: I likewise read Hume's *History of England to the Reign of Henry the Seventh,* just published, *ingenious but superficial;* and the *Journals des Scavans* for August, September, and October, 1761, with the *Bibliothèque des Sciences,* &c., from July to October: both these journals speak very handsomely of my book.

December 25, 1761.—When, upon finishing the year, I take a review of what I have done, I am not dissatisfied with what I did in it, upon making proper allowances. On the one hand, I could begin nothing before the middle of January. The Deal duty lost me part of February; although I was at home part of March, and all April, yet electioneering is no friend to the muses. May, indeed, though dissipated by our sea parties, was pretty quiet; but June was absolutely lost, upon the march, at Alton, and settling ourselves in camp. The four succeeding months in camp allowed me little leisure, and less quiet. November and December were indeed as much my own as any time can be whilst I remain in the militia; but still it is, at best, not a life for a man of letters. However, in this tumultuous year (besides smaller things which I have set down), I read four books of Homer in Greek, six of Strabo in Latin, Cicero *de Natura Deorum,* and the great philosophical and theological work of M. de Beausobre: I wrote in the same time a long dissertation on the succession of Naples; reviewed, fitted for the press, and augmented above a fourth, my *Essai sur l'Étude de la Littérature.*

In the six weeks I passed at Beriton, as I never stirred from it, every day was like the former. I had neither visits, hunting, nor walking. My only resources were myself, my books, and family conversations.—But to me these were great resources.

April 24, 1762.—I waited upon Colonel Harvey in the morning, to get him to apply for me to be brigade-major to Lord Effingham, as a post I should be very fond of, and for which I am not unfit. Harvey received me with great good nature and candour, told me he was both willing and able to serve me; that indeed he had already applied

seven or eight months, while I was obliged to learn as well as to teach. The dissipation of Blandford, and the disputes of Portsmouth,

to Lord Effingham for Leake, one of his own officers, and though there would be more than one brigade-major, he did not think he could properly recommend two; but that if I could get some other person to break the ice, he would second it, and believed he should succeed; should that fail, as Leake was in bad circumstances, he believed he could make a compromise with him (this was my desire) to let me do the duty without pay. I went from him to the Mallets, who promised to get Sir Charles Howard to speak to Lord Effingham.

August 22.—I went with Ballard to the French church, where I heard a most indifferent sermon preached by M. ******. A very bad style, a worse pronunciation and action, and a very great vacuity of ideas, composed this excellent performance. Upon the whole, which is preferable, the philosophic method of the English, or the rhetoric of the French preachers? The first (though less glorious) is certainly safer for the preacher. It is difficult for a man to make himself ridiculous, who proposes only to deliver plain sense on a subject he has thoroughly studied. But the instant he discovers the least pretensions towards the sublime or the pathetic, there is no medium; we must either admire or laugh; and there are so many various talents requisite to form the character of an orator, that it is more than probable we shall laugh. As to the advantage of the hearer, which ought to be the great consideration, the dilemma is much greater. Excepting in some particular cases, where we are blinded by popular prejudices, we are in general so well acquainted with our duty, that it is almost superfluous to convince us of it. It is the heart, and not the head, that holds out: and it is certainly possible, by a moving eloquence, to rouse the sleeping sentiments of that heart, and incite it to acts of virtue. Unluckily it is not so much acts, as habits of virtue, we should have in view; and the preacher who is inculcating, with the eloquence of a Bourdaloue, the necessity of a virtuous life, will dismiss his assembly full of emotions, which a variety of other objects, the coldness of our northern constitutions, and no immediate opportunity of exerting their good resolutions, will dissipate in a few moments.

August 24.—The same reason that carried so many people to the assembly to-night, was what kept me away; I mean the dancing.

28.—To-day Sir Thomas came to us to dinner. The Spa has done him a great deal of good, for he looks another man. Pleased to see him, we kept bumperizing till after roll-calling; Sir Thomas assuring us, every fresh bottle, how infinitely soberer he was grown.

consumed the hours which were not employed in the field; and amid the perpetual hurry of an inn, a barrack, or a guard-room,

---

29.—I felt the usual consequences of Sir Thomas's company, and lost a morning, because I had lost the day before. However, having finished Voltaire, I returned to Le Clerc (I mean for the amusement of my leisure hours); and laid aside for some time his *Bibliothèque Universelle* to look into the *Bibliothèque Choisie*, which is by far the better work.

September 23.—Colonel Wilkes, of the Buckinghamshire militia, dined with us, and renewed the acquaintance Sir Thomas and myself had begun with him at Reading. I scarcely ever met with a better companion; he has inexhaustible spirits, infinite wit and humour, and a great deal of knowledge; but a thorough profligate in principle as in practice, his life stained with every vice, and his conversation full of blasphemy and indecency. These morals he glories in—for shame is a weakness he has long since surmounted. He told us himself, that in this time of public dissension he was resolved to make his fortune. Upon this noble principle he has connected himself closely with Lord Temple and Mr. Pitt, commenced a public adversary to Lord Bute, whom he abuses weekly in the *North Briton* and other political papers in which he is concerned. This proved a very debauched day: we drank a good deal both after dinner and supper; and when at last Wilkes had retired, Sir Thomas and some others (of whom I was not one) broke into his room, and made him drink a bottle of claret in bed.

October 5.—The review, which lasted about three hours, concluded, as usual, with marching by Lord Effingham, by grand divisions. Upon the whole, considering the camp had done both the Winchester and the Gosport duties all the summer, they behaved very well, and made a fine appearance. As they marched by, I had my usual curiosity to count their files. The following is my

		No. of Files.	No. of Men.	Establishment.
Berkshire,	Grenadiers,	19	91	273	560
	Battalion,	72			
W. Essex,	Grenadiers,	15	95	285	480
	Battalion,	80			
S. Gloster,	Grenadiers,	20	104	312	600
	Battalion,	84			
N. Gloster,	Grenadiers,	13	65	195	360
	Battalion,	52			
Lancashire,	Grenadiers,	20	108	324	800
	Battalion,	88			
Wiltshire,	Grenadiers,	24	144	432	800
	Battalion,	120			
	Total		607	1821	3600

all literary ideas were banished from my mind. After this long fast, the longest which I have ever known, I once more tasted at field return: I think it a curiosity; I am sure it is more exact than is commonly made to a reviewing general.

N.B.—The Gosport detachment from the Lancashire consisted of two hundred and fifty men. The Buckinghamshire took the Winchester duty that day.

So that this camp in England, supposed complete, with only one detachment, had under arms, on the day of the grand review, little more than half their establishment. This amazing deficiency (though exemplified in every regiment I have seen) is an extraordinary military phenomenon: what must it be upon foreign service? I doubt whether a nominal army of an hundred thousand men often brings fifty [thousand] into the field.

Upon our return to Southampton in the evening, we found Sir Thomas Worsley.

October 21.—One of those impulses, which it is neither very easy nor very necessary to withstand, drew me from Longinus to a very different subject, the Greek Calendar. Last night, when in bed, I was thinking of a dissertation of M. de la Nauze upon the Roman Calendar, which I read last year. This led me to consider what was the Greek, and finding myself very ignorant of it, I determined to read a short, but very excellent abstract of Mr. Dodwell's book *de Cyclis,* by the famous Dr. Halley. It is only twenty-five pages; but as I meditated it thoroughly and verified all the calculations, it was a very good morning's work.

October 28.—I looked over a new Greek Lexicon which I had just received from London. It is that of Robert Constantine, Lugdun. 1637. It is a very large volume in folio, in two parts, comprising in the whole 1,785 pages. After the great *Thesaurus,* this is esteemed the best Greek Lexicon. It seems to be so. Of a variety of words for which I looked, I always found an exact definition; the various senses well distinguished, and properly supported, by the best authorities. However, I still prefer the radical method of Scapula to this alphabetical one.

December 11.—I have already given an idea of the Gosport duty; I shall only add a trait which characterizes admirably our unthinking sailors. At a time when they knew that they should infallibly be discharged in a few weeks, numbers, who had considerable wages due to them, were continually jumping over the walls, and risking the losing of it for a few hours' amusement at Portsmouth.

17.—We found old Captain Meard at Alresford, with the second division of the fourteenth. He and all his officers supped with us, and made the eve-

Dover the pleasures of reading and thinking; and the hungry appetite with which I opened a volume of Tully's philosophical works is still present to my memory. The last review of my Essay before its publication had prompted me to investigate the *nature of the gods;* my inquires led me to the *Histoire Critique du Manichéisme* of Beausobre, who discusses many deep questions of Pagan and Christian theology; and from this rich treasury of facts and opinions I deduced my own conse-

quences, beyond the holy circle of the author. After this recovery I never relapsed into indolence; and my example might prove that in the life most averse to study, some hours may be stolen, some minutes may be snatched. Amidst the tumult of Winchester camp I sometimes thought and read in my tent; in the more settled quarters of the Devizes, Blandford, and Southampton, I always secured a separate lodging, and the necessary books; and in the summer of 1762, while

---

ning rather a drunken one.

18.—About the same hour our two corps paraded to march off. They, an old corps of regulars, who had been two years quiet in Dover castle. We, part of a young body of militia, two-thirds of our men recruits, of four months' standing, two of which they had passed upon very disagreeable duty. Every advantage was on their side, and yet our superiority, both as to appearance and discipline, was so striking, that the most prejudiced regular could not have hesitated a moment. At the end of the town our two companies separated: my father's struck off for Petersfield, whilst I continued my route to Alton; into which place I marched my company about noon; two years six months and fifteen days after my first leaving it. I gave the men some beer at roll-calling which they received with great cheerfulness and decency. I dined and lay at Harrison's where I was received with that old-fashioned breeding, which is at once so honourable and so troublesome.

23.—Our two companies were disembodied; mine at Alton and my father's at Beriton. Smith marched them over from Petersfield: they fired three volleys, lodged the major's colours, delivered up their arms, received their money, partook of a dinner at the major's expense, and then separated with great cheerfulness and regularity. Thus ended the militia; I may say ended, since our annual assemblies in May are so very precarious, and can be of so little use. However, our sergeants and drums are still kept up, and quartered at the rendezvous of the company, and the adjutant remains at Southampton in full pay.

As this was an extraordinary scene of life, in which I was engaged above three years and a half from the date of my commission, and above two years and a half from the time of our embodying, I cannot take my leave of it without some few reflections. When I engaged in it, I was totally ignorant of its nature and consequences. I offered, because my father did, without ever imagining that we should be called out, till it was too late to retreat with honour. Indeed, I believe it happens throughout, that our most important actions have been

often determined by chance, caprice, or some very inadequate motive. After our embodying, many things contributed to make me support it with great impatience:—our continual disputes with the Duke of Bolton; our unsettled way of life, which hardly allowed me books or leisure for study; and, more than all, the disagreeable society in which I was forced to live.

After mentioning my sufferings, I must say something of what I found agreeable. Now it is over, I can make the separation much better than I could at the time. (1) The unsettled way of life itself had its advantages. The exercise and change of air and of objects amused me, at the same time that it fortified my health. (2) A new field of knowledge and amusement opened itself to me; that of military affairs, which, both in my studies and travels, will give me eyes for a new world of things, which before would have passed unheeded. Indeed, in that respect, I can hardly help wishing our battalion had continued another year. We had got a fine set of new men, all our difficulties were over; we were perfectly well clothed and appointed; and, from the progress our recruits had already made, we could promise ourselves that we should be one of the best militia corps by next summer: a circumstance that would have been the more agreeable to me, as I am now established the real acting major of the battalion. But what I value most is the knowledge it has given me of mankind in general, and of my own country in particular. The general system of our government, the methods of our several offices, the departments and powers of their respective officers, our provincial and municipal administration, the views of our several parties, the characters, connexions, and influence of our principal people, have been impressed on my mind, not by vain theory, but by the indelible lessons of action and experience. I have made a number of valuable acquaintance, and am myself much better known, than (with my reserved character) I should have been in ten years, passing regularly my summers at Beriton, and my winters in London. So that the sum of all is, that I am glad the militia has been, and glad that it is no more.

the new militia was raising, I enjoyed at Buriton two or three months of literary repose[25]. In forming a new plan of study, I hesitated between the mathematics and the Greek language; both of which I had neglected since my return from Lausanne. I consulted a learned and friendly mathematician, Mr. George Scott, a pupil of de Moivre; and his map of a country, which I have never explored, may perhaps be more serviceable to others. As soon as I had given the preference to Greek, the example of Scaliger and my own reason determined me on the choice of Homer, the father of poetry, and the Bible of the ancients: but Scaliger ran through the *Iliad* in one and twenty days; and I was not dissatisfied with my own diligence for performing the same labour in an equal number of weeks. After the first difficulties were surmounted, the language of nature and harmony soon became easy and familiar, and each day I sailed upon the ocean with a brisker gale and a more steady course.

Ἐν δ᾽ ἄνεμος πρῆσεν μέσον ἱστίον,
'ἀμφὶ δὲ κῦμα
Στείρῃ πορφύρεον μεγάλ᾽ ἴαχε, νηὸς
ἰούσης·
Ἡ δ᾽ ἔθεεν κατὰ κῦμα διαπρήσσουσα
κέλευθα.[26]

Iliad, A. 481.

In the study of a poet who has since become the most intimate of my friends, I successively applied many passages and fragments of Greek writers; and among these I shall notice a life of Homer, in the *Opuscula Mythologica* of Gale, several books of the geography of Strabo, and the entire treatise of Longinus, which, from the title and the style, is equally worthy of the epithet of *sublime*. My grammatical skill was improved, my vocabulary was enlarged; and in the militia I acquired a just and indelible knowledge of the first of languages. On every march, in every journey, Horace was always in my pocket, and often in my hand: but I should not mention his two critical epistles, the amusement of a morning, had they not been accompanied by the elaborate commentary of Dr. Hurd, now Bishop of Worcester. On the interesting subjects of composition and imitation of epic and dramatic poetry, I presumed to think for myself; and thirty close-written pages in folio could scarcely comprise my full and free discussion of the sense of the master and the pedantry of the servant.

After his oracle Dr. Johnson, my friend Sir Joshua Reynolds denies all original genius, any natural propensity of the mind to one art or science rather than another. Without engaging in a metaphysical or rather verbal dispute, I *know*, by experience, that from my early youth I aspired to the character of an historian. While I served in the militia, before and after the publication of my Essay, this idea ripened in my mind; nor can I paint in more lively colours the feelings of the moment, than by transcribing some passages,

---

[25] JOURNAL, May 8, 1762.—This was my birthday, on which I entered into the twenty-sixth year of my age. This gave me occasion to look a little into myself, and consider impartially my good and bad qualities. It appeared to me, upon this inquiry, that my character was virtuous, incapable of a base action, and formed for generous ones; but that it was proud, violent, and disagreeable in society. These qualities I must endeavour to cultivate, extirpate, or restrain, according to their different tendency. Wit I have none. My imagination is rather strong than pleasing. My memory both capacious and retentive. The shining qualities of my understanding are extensiveness and penetration; but I want both quickness and exactness. As to my situation in life, though I may sometimes repine at it, it perhaps is the best adapted to my character. I can command all the conveniencies of life, and I can command too that independence (that first earthy blessing), which is hardly to be met with in a higher or lower fortune. When I talk of my situation, I must exclude that temporary one, of being in the militia. Though I go through it with spirit and application, it is both unfit for, and unworthy of me.

[26] ——Fair wind, and blowing fresh,
Apollo sent them; quick they rear'd the mast,
Then spread th' unsullied canvas to the gale,
And the wind fill'd it. Roar'd the sable flood
Around the bark, that ever as she went
Dash'd wide the brine, and scudded swift away.
Cowper's *Homer*. S.

under their respective dates, from a journal which I kept at that time.

BURITON, APRIL 14, 1761
(In a short excursion from Dover).

'Having thought of several subjects for an historical composition, I chose the expedition of Charles VIII of France into Italy. I read two memoirs of Mr. de Forcemagne in the *Academy of Inscriptions* (tom. xvii, pp. 539–607), and abstracted them. I likewise finished this day a dissertation, in which I examine the right of Charles VIII to the crown of Naples, and the rival claims of the House of Anjou and Arragon: it consists of ten folio pages, besides large notes.'

BURITON, AUGUST 4, 1761
(In a week's excursion from Winchester camp).

'After having long revolved subjects for my intended historical essay, I renounced my first thought of the expedition of Charles VIII as too remote from us, and rather an introduction to great events, than great and important in itself. I successively chose and rejected the crusade of Richard I, the barons' wars against John and Henry III, the history of Edward the Black Prince, the lives and comparisons of Henry V and the Emperor Titus, the life of Sir Philip Sidney, and that of the Marquis of Montrose. At length I have fixed on Sir Walter Raleigh for my hero. His eventful story is varied by the characters of the soldier and sailor, the courtier and historian; and it may afford such a fund of materials as I desire, which have not yet been properly manufactured. At present I cannot attempt the execution of this work. Free leisure, and the opportunity of consulting many books, both printed and manuscript, are as necessary as they are impossible to be attained in my present way of life. However, to acquire a general insight into my subject and resources, I read the life of Sir Walter Raleigh by Dr. Birch, his copious article in the *General Dictionary* by the same hand, and the reigns of Queen Elizabeth and James I in Hume's *History of England.*'

BURITON, JANUARY, 1762
(In a month's absence from the Devizes).

'During this interval of repose, I again turned my thoughts to Sir Walter Raleigh, and looked more closely into my materials. I read the two volumes in quarto of the *Bacon Papers,* published by Dr. Birch; the *Fragmenta Regalia* of Sir Robert Naunton, Mallet's *Life of Lord Bacon,* and the political treatises of that great man in the first volume of his works, with many of his letters in the second; Sir William Monson's *Naval Tracts,* and the elaborate *Life of Sir Walter Raleigh,* which Mr. Oldys has prefixed to the best edition of his *History of the World.* My subject opens upon me, and in general improves upon a nearer prospect.'

BURITON, JULY 26, 1762
(During my summer residence).

'I am afraid of being reduced to drop my hero; but my time has not, however, been lost in the research of his story, and of a memorable era of our English annals. The *Life of Sir Walter Raleigh,* by Oldys, is a very poor performance; a servile panegyric, or flat apology, tediously minute, and composed in a dull and affected style. Yet the author was a man of diligence and learning, who had read everything relative to his subject, and whose ample collections are arranged with perspicuity and method. Excepting some anecdotes lately revealed in the Sidney and Bacon Papers I know not what I should be able to add. My ambition (exclusive of the uncertain merit of style and sentiment) must be confined to the hope of giving a good abridgement of Oldys. I have even the disappointment of finding some parts of this copious work very dry and barren; and these parts are unluckily some of the most characteristic: Raleigh's colony of Virginia, his quarrels with Essex, the true secret of his con-

331

spiracy, and, above all, the detail of his private life, the most essential and important to a biographer. My best resource would be in the circumjacent history of the times, and perhaps in some digressions artfully introduced, like the fortunes of the peripatetic philosophy in the portrait of Lord Bacon. But the reigns of Elizabeth and James I are the periods of English history which have been the most variously illustrated: and what new lights could I reflect on a subject which has exercised the accurate industry of Birch, the lively and curious acuteness of Walpole, the critical spirit of Hurd, the vigorous sense of Mallet and Robertson, and the impartial philosophy of Hume? Could I even surmount these obstacles, I should shrink with terror from the modern history of England, where every character is a problem, and every reader a friend or an enemy; where a writer is supposed to hoist a flag of party, and is devoted to damnation by the adverse faction. Such would be *my* reception at home: and abroad, the historian of Raleigh must encounter an indifference far more bitter than censure or reproach. The events of his life are interesting; but his character is ambiguous, his actions are obscure, his writings are English, and his fame is confined to the narrow limits of our language and our island. I must embrace a safer and more extensive theme.

'There is one which I should prefer to all others, *The History of the Liberty of the Swiss*, of that independence which a brave people rescued from the House of Austria, defended against a Dauphin of France, and finally sealed with the blood of Charles of Burgundy. From such a theme, so full of public spirit, of military glory, of examples of virtue, of lessons of government, the dullest stranger would catch fire: what might not *I* hope, whose talents, whatsoever they may be, would be inflamed with the seal of patriotism. But the materials of this history are inaccessible to me, fast locked in the obscurity of an old barbarous German dialect, of which I am totally ignorant, and which I cannot resolve to learn for this sole and peculiar purpose.

'I have another subject in view, which is the contrast of the former history: the one a poor, warlike, virtuous republic, which emerges into glory and freedom; the other a commonwealth, soft, opulent, and corrupt; which, by just degrees, is precipitated from the abuse to the loss of her liberty: both lessons are, perhaps, equally instructive. This second subject is, *The History of the Republic of Florence, under the House of Medicis*: a period of one hundred and fifty years, which rises or descends from the dregs of the Florentine democracy, to the title and dominion of Cosmo de Medicis in the Grand Duchy of Tuscany. I might deduce a chain of revolutions not unworthy of the pen of Vertot; singular men, and singular events; the Medicis four times expelled, and as often recalled; and the genius of freedom reluctantly yielding to the arms of Charles V and the policy of Cosmo. The character and fate of Savanarola, and the revival of arts and letters in Italy, will be essentially connected with the elevation of the family and the fall of the republic. The Medicis, 'stirps quasi fataliter nata ad instauranda vel fovenda studia' [a stock marked by fate for restoring and fostering learning] (*Lipsius ad Germanos et Gallos*, Epist. viii), were illustrated by the patronage of learning; and enthusiasm was the most formidable weapon of their adversaries. On this splendid subject I shall most probably fix; but *when*, or *where*, or *how* will it be executed? I behold in a dark and doubtful perspective;

Res altâ terrâ, et caligine mersas.[27]

The youthful habits of the language and manner of France had left in my mind an ardent desire of revisiting the continent on a

---

[27] [Virgil *Aeneid*. 6. 267: "Things immersed deep in earth and darkness."—Ed.] JOURNAL, July 27, 1762.—The reflections which I was making yesterday I continued and digested to-day. I don't absolutely look on that time as lost, but that it might have been better employed than in revolving schemes, the execution of which is so far distant. I must learn to check these wanderings of my imagination.

larger and more liberal plan. According to the law of custom, and perhaps of reason, foreign travel completes the education of an English gentleman: my father had consented to my wish, but I was detained above four years by my rash engagement in the militia.

Nov. 24.—I dined at the Cocoa Tree with Holt; who, under a great appearance of oddity, conceals more real honour, good sense, and even knowledge than half those who laugh at him. We went thence to the play (*The Spanish Friar*); and when it was over returned to the Cocoa Tree. That respectable body, of which I have the honour of being a member, affords every evening a sight truly English. Twenty or thirty, perhaps, of the first men in the kingdom, in point of fashion and fortune, supping at little tables covered with a napkin, in the middle of a coffee-room, upon a bit of cold meat, or a sandwich, and drinking a glass of punch. At present, we are full of king's counsellors and lords of the bedchamber; who, having jumped into the ministry, make a very singular medley of their old principles and language, with their modern ones.

26.—I went with Mallet to breakfast with Garrick; and thence to Drury Lane house, where I assisted at a very private rehearsal, in the Green Room, of a new tragedy of Mallet's, called *Elvira*. As I have since seen it acted, I shall defer my opinion of it till then; but I cannot help mentioning here the surprising versatility of Mrs. Pritchard's talents, who rehearsed, almost at the same time, the part of a furious queen in the Green Room, and that of a coquette on the stage, and passed several times from one to the other with the utmost ease and happiness.

Dec. 30.—Before I close the year I must balance my accounts—not of money, but of time. I may divide my studies into four branches: (1) Books that I have read for themselves, classic writers, or capital treatises upon any science; such books as ought to be perused with attention, and meditated with care. Of these I read *the twenty last books of the Iliad twice, the three first books of the Odyssey, the Life of Homer,* and *Longinus* περὶ Ὕψους. (2) Books which I have read, or consulted, to illustrate the former. Such as this year, *Blackwell's Inquiry into the Life and Writings of Homer, Burke's Sublime and Beautiful, Hurd's Horace, Guichardt's Mémoires Militaires,* a great variety of passages of the ancients occasionally useful: large extracts from *Mezeriac, Bayle,* and *Potter;* and many memoirs and abstracts from the *Academy of Belles Lettres:* among these I shall only mention here two long and curious suites of dissertations—*the one upon the Temple of Delphi, the Amphictyonic Council, and the Holy Wars, by MM. Hardion and de Valois; the other upon the Games of the Grecians, by MM.*

I eagerly grasped the first moments of freedom: three for four weeks in Hampshire and London were employed in the preparations of my journey, and the farewell visits of friendship and civility: my last act in town was to applaud Mallet's new tragedy of *Elvira*[28];

Burette, Gedoyne, and de la Barre. (3) Books of amusement and instruction, perused at my leisure hours, without any reference to a regular plan of study. Of these, perhaps, I read too many, since I went through the *Life of Erasmus,* by Le Clerc and Burigny, many extracts from *Le Clerc's Bibliothèques, The Ciceronianus,* and *Colloquies of Erasmus, Barclay's Argenis, Terasson's Sethos, Voltaire's Siècle de Louis XIV, Madame de Motteville's Memoirs,* and *Fontenelle's Works.* (4) Compositions of my own. I find hardly any except *this Journal,* and the *Extract of Hurd's Horace,* which (like a chapter of Montaigne) contains many things very different from its title. To these four heads I must this year add a fifth. (5) Those treatises of English history which I read in January, with a view to my now abortive scheme of the *Life of Sir Walter Raleigh.* I ought indeed to have known my own mind better before I undertook them. Upon the whole, after making proper allowances, I am not dissatisfied with the year.

The three weeks which I passed at Beriton, at the end of this and the beginning of the ensuing year, are almost a blank. I seldom went out; and as the scheme of my travelling was at last entirely settled, the hurry of impatience, the cares of preparations, and the tenderness of friends I was going to quit, allowed me hardly any moments for study.

[28] JOURNAL, January 11, 1763.—I called upon Dr. Maty in the morning. He told me that the Duke de Nivernois desired to be acquainted with me. It was indeed with that view that I had written to Maty from Beriton to present, in my name, a copy of my book to him. Thence I went to Becket, paid him his bill (fifty-four pounds), and gave him back his translation. It must be printed, though very indifferent. My comfort is, that my misfortune is not an uncommon one. We dined and supped at the Mallets.

12.—I went with Maty to visit the Duke in Albemarle Street. He is a little emaciated figure, but appears to possess a good understanding, taste, and knowledge. He offered me very politely letters for Paris. We dined at our lodgings. I went to Covent Garden to see Woodward in *Bobadil,* and supped with the Mallets at George Scott's.

19.—I waited upon Lady Hervey and the Duke de Nivernois, and received my credentials. Lady Hervey's are for M. le Comte de Caylus, and Madame Geoffrin. The Duke received me civilly, but (perhaps through Maty's fault) treated me

a post-chaise conveyed me to Dover, the packet to Boulogne, and such was my diligence, that I reached Paris on the 28th of January, 1763, only thirty-six days after the disbanding of the militia. Two or three years were loosely defined for the term of my absence; and I was left at liberty to spend that time in such places and in such a manner as was most agreeable to my taste and judgement.

In this first visit I passed three months and a half (January 28–May 9), and a much longer space might have been agreeably filled, without any intercourse with the natives. At home we are content to move in the daily round of pleasure and business; and a scene which is always present is supposed to be within our knowledge, or at least within our power. But in a foreign country, curiosity is our business and our pleasure; and the traveller, conscious of his ignorance, and covetous of his time, is diligent in the search and the view of every object that can deserve his attention. I devoted many hours of the morning to the circuit of Paris and the neighbourhood, to the visit of churches and palaces conspicuous by their architecture, to the royal manufactures, collections of books and pictures, and all the various treasures of art, or learning, and of luxury. An Englishman may hear without reluctance, that in these curious and costly articles Paris is superior to London; since the opulence of the French capital arises from the defects of its government and religion. In the absence of Louis XIV and his successors, the Louvre has been left unfinished: but the millions which have been lavished on the sands of Versailles, and the morass of Marli, could not be supplied by the legal allowance of a British king. The splendour of the French nobles is confined to their town residence; that of the English is more usefully distributed in their country seats; and we should be astonished at our own riches, if the labours of architecture, the spoils of Italy and Greece, which are now scattered from Inverary to Wilton, were accumulated in a few streets between Marylebone and Westminster. All superfluous orna-

ment is rejected by the cold frugality of the Protestants; but the Catholic superstition, which is always the enemy of reason, is often the parents of the arts. The wealthy communities of priests and monks expand their revenues in stately edifices; and the parish church of St. Sulpice, one of the noblest structures in Paris, was built and adorned by the private industry of a late curé. In this

---

more as a man of letters than as a man of fashion. His letters are entirely in that style; for the Count de Caylus and MM. de la Bléterie, de Ste Palaye, Caperonier, du Clos, de Forcemagne, and d'Alembert. I then undressed for the play. My father and I went to the Rose, in the passage of the playhouse, where we found Mallet, with about thirty friends. We dined together, and went thence into the pit, where we took our places in a body, ready to silence all opposition. However, we had no occasion to exert ourselves. Not withstanding the malice of party, Mallet's nation, connexions, and, indeed, imprudence, we heard nothing but applause. I think it was deserved. The plan was borrowed from M. de la Motte, but the details and language have great merit. A fine vein of dramatic poetry runs through the piece. The scenes between the father and son awaken almost every sensation of the human breast; and the counsel would have equally moved, but for the inconvenience unavoidable upon all theatres, that of entrusting fine speeches to indifferent actors. The perplexity of the catastrophe is much, and I believe justly, criticised. But another defect made a stronger impression upon me. When a poet ventures upon the dreadful situation of a father who condemns his son to death, there is no medium, the father must either be a monster or a hero. His obligations of justice, of the public good, must be as binding, as apparent, as perhaps those of the first Brutus. The cruel necessity consecrates his actions, and leaves no room for repentance. The thought is shocking; if not carried into action. In the execution of Brutus's sons I am sensible of that fatal necessity. Without such an example, the unsettled liberty of Rome would have perished the instant after its birth. But Alonzo might have pardoned his son for a rash attempt, the cause of which was a private injury, and whose consequences could never have disturbed an established government. He might have pardoned such a crime in any other subject; and as the laws could exact only an equal rigour for a son, a vain appetite for glory, and a mad affectation of heroism, could alone have influenced him to exert an unequal and superior severity.

outset, and still more in the sequel of my tour, my eye was amused; but the pleasing vision cannot be fixed by the pen; the particular images are darkly seen through the medium of five-and-twenty years, and the narrative of my life must not degenerate into a book of travels.

But the principal end of my journey was to enjoy the society of a polished and amiable people, in which favour I was strongly prejudiced, and to converse with some authors, whose conversation, as I fondly imagined, must be far more pleasing and instructive than their writings. The moment was happily chosen. At the close of a successful war the British name was respected on the continent:

——*Clarum et venerabile nomen
Gentibus.* [A name famous and venerable among the nations.]—Ed.

Our opinions, our fashions, even our games, were adopted in France; a ray of national glory illuminated each individual, and every Englishman was supposed to be born a patriot and a philosopher. For myself, I carried a special recommendation; my name and my Essay were already known; the compliment of having written in the French language entitled me to some returns of civility and gratitude. I was considered as a man of letters, who wrote for amusement. Before my departure I had obtained from the Duke de Nivernois, Lady Hervey, the Mallets, Mr. Walpole, &c., many letters of recommendation to their private or literary friends. Of these epistles the reception and success were determined by the character and situation of the persons by whom and to whom they were addressed: the seed was sometimes cast on a barren rock, and it sometimes multiplied an hundred fold in the production of new shoots, spreading branches, and exquisite fruit. But upon the whole, I had reason to praise the national urbanity, which from the court has diffused its gentle influence to the shop, the cottage, and the schools. Of the men of genius of the age, Montesquieu and Fontenelle were no more; Voltaire resided on his own estate near Geneva; Rousseau in the preceding year had been driven from his hermitage of Montmorency; and I blush at my having neglected to seek, in this journey, the acquaintance of Buffon. Among the men of letters whom I saw, d'Alembert and Diderot held the foremost rank in merit, or at least in fame. I shall content myself with enumerating the well-known names of the Count de Caylus, of the Abbé de la Blèterie, Barthélemy, Raynal, Arnaud, of Messieurs de la Condamine, du Clos, de Ste Palaye, de Bougainville, Caperonnier, de Guignes, Suard, &c., without attempting to discriminate the shades of their characters, or the degrees of our connexion. Alone, in a morning visit, I commonly found the artists and authors of Paris less vain, and more reasonable, than in the circles of their equals, with whom they mingle in the houses of the rich. Four days in a week I had a place, without invitation, at the hospitable tables of Mesdames Geoffrin and du Bocage, of the celebrated Helvetius, and of the Baron d'Olbach. In these symposia the pleasures of the table were improved by lively and liberal conversation; the company was select, though various and voluntary.

The society of Madame du Bocage was more soft and moderate than that of her rivals, and the evening conversations of M. de Forcemagne were supported by the good sense and learning of the principal members of the Academy of Inscriptions. The opera and the Italians I occasionally visited; but the French theatre, both in tragedy and comedy, was my daily and favourite amusement. Two famous actresses then divided the public applause. For my own part, I preferred the consummate art of the Clairon, to the intemperate sallies of the Dumesnil, which were extolled by her admirers as the genuine voice of nature and passion. Fourteen weeks insensibly stole away; but had I been rich and independent, I should have prolonged, and perhaps have fixed, my residence at Paris.

Between the expensive style of Paris and of Italy it was prudent to interpose some months of tranquil simplicity; and at the thoughts of Lausanne I again lived in the pleasures and studies of my early youth. Shaping my course through Dijon and Besançon, in the last of which places I was kindly entertained by my cousin Acton, I arrived in the month of May, 1763, on the banks of the Leman Lake. It had been my intention to pass the Alps in the autumn, but such are the simple attractions of the place, that the year had almost expired before my departure from Lausanne in the ensuing spring. An absence of five years had not made much alteration in manners, or even in persons. My old friends, of both sexes, hailed my voluntary return; the most genuine proof of my attachment. They had been flattered by the present of my book, the produce of their soil; and the good Pavilliard shed tears of joy as he embraced a pupil whose literary merit he might fairly impute to his own labours. To my old list I added some new acquaintance, and among the strangers I shall distinguish Prince Lewis of Wirtemberg, the brother of the reigning Duke, at whose country-house, near Lausanne, I frequently dined: a wandering meteor, and at length a falling star, his light and ambitious spirit had successively dropped from the firmament of Prussia, of France, and of Austria; and his faults, which he styled his misfortunes, had driven him into philosophic exile in the Pays de Vaud. He could now moralize on the vanity of the world, the equality of mankind, and the happiness of a private station. His address was affable and polite, and as he had shone in courts and armies, his memory could supply, and his eloquence could adorn, a copious fund of interesting anecdotes. His first enthusiasm was that of charity and agriculture; but the sage gradually lapsed in the saint, and Prince Lewis of Wirtemberg is now buried in a hermitage near Mayence, in the last stage of mystic devotion. By some ecclesiastical quarrel, Voltaire had been provoked to withdraw himself from Lausanne, and retire to his castle at Ferney, where I again visited the poet and the actor, without seeking his more intimate acquaintance, to which I might now have pleaded a better

title. But the theatre which he had founded, the actors whom he had formed, survived the loss of their master; and recent from Paris, I attended with pleasure at the representation of several tragedies and comedies. I shall not descend to specify particular names and characters; but I cannot forget a private institution, which will display the innocent freedom of Swiss manners. My favourite society had assumed, from the age of its members, the proud denomination of the spring (*la société du printemps*). It consisted of fifteen or twenty young unmarried ladies, of genteel, though not of the very first families; the eldest perhaps about twenty, all agreeable, several handsome, and two or three of exquisite beauty. At each other's houses they assembled almost every day, without the control, or even the presence, of a mother or an aunt; they were trusted to their own prudence, among a crowd of young men of very nation in Europe. They laughed, they sung, they danced, they played at cards, they acted comedies; but in the midst of this careless gaiety, they respected themselves, and were respected by the men; the invisible line between liberty and licentiousness was never transgressed by a gesture, a word, or a look, and their virgin chastity was never sullied by the breath of scandal or suspicion: a singular institution, expressive of the innocent simplicity of Swiss manners. After having tasted the luxury of England and Paris, I could not have returned with satisfaction to the coarse and homely table of Madame Pavilliard; nor was her husband offended that I now entered myself as a *pensionnaire,* or boarder, in the elegant house of Mr. de Mesery, which may be entitled to a short remembrance, as it has stood above twenty years, perhaps, without a parallel in Europe. The house in which we lodged was spacious and convenient, in the best street, and commanding, from behind, a noble prospect over the country and the lake. Our table was served with neatness and plenty; the boarders were select; we had the liberty of inviting any guests at a stated price; and in the summer the scene was occasionally transferred to a pleasant villa, about a league from Lausanne. The characters of master and mistress were happily suited to each other, and to their situation. At the age of seventy-five, Madame de Mesery, who has survived her husband, is still a graceful, I had almost said a handsome woman. She was alike qualified to preside in her kitchen and her drawing-room; and such was the equal propriety of her conduct, that of two or three hundred foreigners, none ever failed in respect, none could complain of her neglect, and none could ever boast of her favour. Mesery himself, of the noble family of De Crousaz, was a man of the world, a jovial companion, whose easy manners and natural sallies maintained the cheerfulness of his house. His wit could laugh at his own ignorance: he disguised, by an air of profusion, a strict attention to his interest; and in this situation, he appeared like a nobleman who spent his fortune and entertained his friends. In this agreeable society I resided nearly eleven months (May, 1763–April, 1764); and in this second visit to Lausanne, among a crowd of my English companions, I knew and esteemed Mr. Holroyd (now Lord Sheffield); and our mutual attachment was renewed and fortified in the subsequent stages of our Italian journey. Our lives are in the power of chance, and a slight variation on either side, in time or place, might have deprived me of a friend, whose activity in the ardour of youth was always prompted by a benevolent heart, and directed by a strong understanding.

If my studies at Paris had been confined to the study of the world, three or four months would not have been unprofitably spent. My visits, however superficial, to the Academy of Medals and the public libraries, opened a new field of inquiry; and the view of so many manuscripts of different ages and characters induced me to consult the two great Benedictine works, the *Diplomatica* of Mabillon, and the *Palaeographia* of Montfaucon. I studied the theory without attaining the practice of the art: nor should I complain of the intricacy of Greek abbreviations and Gothic alphabets, since every day, in a familiar language,

I am at a loss to decipher the hieroglyphics of a female note. In a tranquil scene, which revived the memory of my first studies, idleness would have been less pardonable: the public libraries of Lausanne and Geneva liberally supplied me with books; and if many hours were lost in dissipation, many more were employed in literary labour. In the country, Horace and Virgil, Juvenal and Ovid, were my assiduous companions: but in town, I formed and executed a plan of study for the use of my Transalpine expedition: the topography of old Rome, the ancient geography of Italy, and the science of medals. (1) I diligently read, almost always with a pen in my hand, the elaborate treatises of Nardini, Donatus, &c., which fill the fourth volume of the Roman Antiquities of Graevius. (2) I next undertook and finished the *Italia Antiqua* of Cluverius, a learned native of Prussia, who had measured, on foot, every spot, and has compiled and digested every passage of the ancient writers. These passages in Greek or Latin authors I perused in the text of Cluverius, in two folio volumes: but I separately read the descriptions of Italy by Strabo, Pliny, and Pomponius Mela, the Catalogues of the epic poets, the Itineraries of Wesseling's Antoninus, and the coasting Voyage of Rutilius Numatianus; and I studied two kindred subjects in the *Mesures Itinéraires* of d'Anville, and the copious work of Bergier, *Histoire des grands Chemins de l'Empire Romain*. From these materials I formed a table of roads and distances reduced to our English measure; filled a folio commonplace book with my collections and remarks on the geography of Italy; and inserted in my journal many long and learned notes on the insulae and populousness of Rome, the social war, the passage of the Alps by Hannibal, &c. (3) After glancing my eye over Addison's agreeable dialogues, I more seriously read the great work of Ezechiel Spanheim, *de Praestantia et Usu Numismatum*, [On the Use and Excellence of Ancient Coins], and applied with him the medals of the kings and emperors, the families and colonies, to the illustration of ancient history. And thus was

I armed for my Italian journey.

I shall advance with rapid brevity in the narrative of this tour, in which somewhat more than a year (April, 1764–May, 1765) was agreeably employed. Content with tracing my line of march, and slightly touching on my personal feelings, I shall waive the minute investigation of the scenes which have been viewed by thousands, and described by hundreds of our modern travellers. Rome is the great object of our pilgrimage: and first, the journey; second, the residence; and third, the return, will form the most proper and perspicuous division. (1) I climbed Mount Cenis, and descended into the plain of Piedmont, not on the back of an elephant, but on a light osier seat, in the hands of the dexterous and intrepid chairmen of the Alps. The architecture and government of Turin presented the same aspect of tame and tiresome uniformity; but the court was regulated with decent and splendid economy; and I was introduced to his Sardinian majesty, Charles Emanuel, who, after the incomparable Frederic, held the second rank (proximus longo tamen intervallo)* among the kings of Europe. The size and populousness of Milan could not surprise an inhabitant of London: but the fancy is amused by a visit to the Boromean Islands, an enchanted palace, a work of the fairies in the midst of a lake encompassed with mountains, and far removed from the haunts of men. I was less amused by the marble palaces of Genoa, than by the recent memorials of her deliverance (in December, 1746) from the Austrian tyranny; and I took a military survey of every scene of action within the enclosure of her double walls. My steps were detained at Parma and Modena, by the precious relics of the Farnese and Este collections: but, alas! the far greater part had been already transported, by inheritance or purchase, to Naples and Dresden. By the road of Bologna and the Apennine I at last reached Florence, where I reposed from June to September, during the heat of the summer months. In the Gallery, and especially in the Tribune, I first acknowledged, at the feet of the Venus of Medicis, that the chisel may dispute the pre-eminence with the pencil, a truth in the fine arts which cannot on this side of the Alps be felt or understood. At home I had taken some lessons of Italian; on the spot I read, with a learned native, the classics of the Tuscan idiom, but the shortness of my time, and the use of the French language, prevented my acquiring any facility of speaking; and I was a silent spectator in the conversations of our envoy, Sir Horace Mann, whose serious business was that of entertaining the English at his hospitable table. After leaving Florence I compared the solitude of Pisa with the industry of Lucca and Leghorn, and continued my journey through Sienna to Rome, where I arrived in the beginning of October. (2) My temper is not very susceptible of enthusiasm, and the enthusiasm which I do not feel I have ever scorned to affect. But, at the distance of twenty-five years, I can neither forget nor express the strong emotions which agitated my mind as I first approached and entered the *eternal city*. After a sleepless night, I trod, with a lofty step, the ruins of the Forum; each memorable spot where Romulus *stood,* or Tully spoke, or Caesar fell, was at once present to my eye; and several days of intoxication were lost or enjoyed before I could descend to a cool and minute investigation. My guide was Mr. Byers, a Scotch antiquary of experience and taste, but, in the daily labour of eighteen weeks, the powers of attention were sometimes fatigued, till I was myself qualified, in a last review, to select and study the capital works of ancient and modern art. Six weeks were borrowed for my tour of Naples, the most populous of cities, relative to its size, whose luxurious inhabitants seem to dwell on the confines of paradise and hellfire. I was presented to the boy-king [Ferdinand IV] by our new envoy, Sir William Hamilton; who, wisely diverting his correspondence from the Secretary of State to the Royal Society and British Museum, has eluci-

---

* Virgil *Aeneid*. 5. 320 [Second, but by a great distance]—Ed.

dated a country of such inestimable value to the naturalist and antiquarian. On my return, I fondly embraced, for the last time, the miracles of Rome; but I departed without kissing the foot of Rezzonico (Clement XIII), who neither possessed the wit of his predecessor Lambertini, nor the virtues of his successor Ganganelli. (3) In my pilgrimage from Rome to Loretto I again crossed the Apennine; from the coast of the Adriatic I traversed a fruitful and populous country, which could alone disprove the paradox of Montesquieu, that modern Italy is a desert. Without adopting the exclusive prejudice of the natives, I sincerely admire the paintings of the Bologna school. I hastened to escape from the sad solitude of Ferrara, which in the age of Caesar was still more desolate. The spectacle of Venice afforded some hours of astonishment; the University of Padua is a dying taper; but Verona still boasts her amphitheatre, and his native Vicenza is adorned by the classic architecture of Palladio: the road of Lombardy and Piedmont (did Montesquieu find them without inhabitants?) led me back to Milan, Turin, and the passage of Mount Cenis, where I again crossed the Alps in my way to Lyons.

The use of foreign travel has been often debated as a general question; but the conclusion must be finally applied to the character and circumstances of each individual. With the education of boys, *where* or *how* they may pass over some juvenile years with the least mischief to themselves or others, I have no concern. But after supposing the previous and indispensable requisites of age, judgement, a competent knowledge of men and books, and a freedom from domestic prejudices, I will briefly describe the qualifications which I deem most essential to a traveller. He should be endowed with an active, indefatigable vigour of mind and body, which can seize every mode of conveyance, and support, with a careless smile, every hardship of the road, the weather, or the inn. The benefits of foreign travel will correspond with the degrees of these qualifications; but, in this sketch, those to whom I am known will not accuse me of framing my own panegyric. It was at Rome, on the 15th of October, 1764, as I sat musing amidst the ruins of the Capitol, while the barefooted friars were singing vespers in the Temple of Jupiter[29], that the idea of writing the decline and fall of the city first started to my mind. But my original plan was circumscribed to the decay of the city rather than of the empire: and, though my reading and reflections began to point towards that object, some years elapsed, and several avocations intervened, before I was seriously engaged in the execution of that laborious work.

I had not totally renounced the southern provinces of France, but the letters which I found at Lyons were expressive of some impatience. Rome and Italy had satiated my curious appetite, and I was now ready to return to the peaceful retreat of my family and books. After a happy fortnight I reluctantly left Paris, embarked at Calais, again landed at Dover, after an interval of two years and five months, and hastily drove through the summer dust and solitude of London. On the 25th of June, 1765, I arrived at my father's house; and the five years and a half between my travels and my father's death (1770) are the portion of my life which I passed with the least enjoyment, and which I remember with the least satisfaction. Every spring I attended the monthly meeting and exercise of the militia at Southampton; and by the resignation of my father, and the death of Sir Thomas Worsley, I was successively promoted to the rank of major and lieutenant-colonel commandant; but I was each year more disgusted with the inn, the wine, the company, and the tiresome repetition of annual attendance and daily exercise. At home, the economy of the family and farm still maintained the same creditable appearance. My connexion with Mrs. Gibbon was mellowed into a warm and solid attachment; my growing years abolished the distance that might yet remain between a parent and a son, and my behaviour

---

[29] Now the church of the Zocolants, or Franciscan Friars. S.

satisfied my father, who was proud of the success, however imperfect in his own lifetime, of my literary talents. Our solitude was soon and often enlivened by the visit of the friend of my youth, Mr. Deyverdun, whose absence from Lausanne I had sincerely lamented. About three years after my first departure, he had emigrated from his native lake to the banks of the Oder in Germany. The *res angusta domi*, the waste of a decent patrimony, by an improvident father, obliged him, like many of his countrymen, to confide in his own industry; and he was entrusted with the education of a young prince, the grandson of the Margrave of Schavedt, of the Royal Family of Prussia. Our friendship was never cooled, our correspondence was sometimes interrupted; but I rather wished than hoped to obtain Mr. Deyverdun for the companion of my Italian tour. An unhappy, though honourable passion, drove him from his German court; and the attractions of hope and curiosity were fortified by the expectation of my speedy return to England. During four successive summers he passed several weeks or months at Buriton, and our free conversations, on every topic that could interest the heart or understanding, would have reconciled me to a desert or a prison. In the winter months of London my sphere of knowledge and action was somewhat enlarged, by the many new acquaintance which I had contracted in the militia and abroad; and I must regret, as more than an acquaintance, Mr. Godfrey Clarke of Derbyshire, an amiable and worthy young man, who was snatched away by an untimely death. A weekly convivial meeting was established by myself and other travellers, under the name of the Roman Club.[30]

The renewal, or perhaps the improvement, of my English life was embittered by the alteration of my own feelings. At the age of twenty-one I was, in my proper station of youth, delivered from the yoke of education, and delighted with the comparative state of liberty and affluence. My filial obedience was natural and easy; and in the gay prospect of futurity, my ambition did not extend beyond the enjoyment of my books, my leisure, and my patrimonial estate, undisturbed by the cares of a family and the duties of a profession. But in the militia I was armed with power; in my travels, I was exempt from control; and as I approached, as I gradually passed my thirtieth year, I began to feel the desire of being master in my own house. The most gentle authority will sometimes frown without reason, the most cheerful submission will sometimes murmur without cause; and such is the law of our imperfect nature, that we must either command or obey; that our personal liberty is supported by the obsequiousness of our own dependants. While so many of my acquaintance were married or in parliament, or advancing with a rapid step in the various roads of honour and fortune, I stood alone, immovable and insignificant; for after the monthly meeting of 1770, I had even withdrawn myself from the militia, by the resignation of an empty and barren commission. My temper is not susceptible of envy, and the view of successful merit has always excited my warmest applause. The miseries of a vacant life were never known to a man whose hours were insufficient for the inexhaustible pleasures of study. But I lamented that at the proper age I had not embraced the lucrative pursuits of the law or of trade, the chances of civil office or India adventure, or even the fat slumbers of the church; and my repentance became more lively as the loss of time was more irretrievable. Experience showed me the use of grafting my private consequence on the importance of a great professional body; the benefits of those firm connexions which are cemented by hope and interest, by gratitude and emulation, by the

---

[30] The members were Lord Mountstuart (now Marquis of Bute), Colonel Edmonstone, Wm. Weddal, Rev. Mr. Palgrave, Earl of Berkley, Godfrey Clarke (Member for Derbyshire), Holroyd (Lord Sheffield), Major Ridley, Thomas Charles Bigge, Sir William Guize, Sir John Aubrey, the late Earl of Abingdon, Hon. Peregrine Bertie, Rev. Mr. Cleaver, Hon. John Damer, Hon. George Damer (late Earl of Dorchester), Sir Thomas Gascoygne, Sir John Hort, E. Gibbon. S.

mutual exchange of services and favours. From the emoluments of a profession I might have derived an ample fortune, or a competent income, instead of being stinted to the same narrow allowance, to be increased only by an event which I sincerely deprecated. The progress and the knowledge of our domestic disorders aggravated my anxiety, and I began to apprehend that I might be left in my old age without the fruits either of industry or inheritance.

In the first summer after my return, whilst I enjoyed at Buriton the society of my friend · Deyverdun, our daily conversations expatiated over the field of ancient and modern literature; and we freely discussed my studies, my first Essay, and my future projects. The *Decline and Fall of Rome* I still contemplated at an awful distance: but the two historical designs which had balanced my choice were submitted to his taste; and in the parallel between the Revolutions of Florence and Switzerland, our common partiality for a country which was *his* by birth, and *mine* by adoption, inclined the scale in favour of the latter. According to the plan, which was soon conceived and digested, I embraced a period of two hundred years, from the association of the three peasants of the Alps to the plenitude and prosperity of the Helvetic body in the sixteenth century. I should have described the deliverance and victory of the Swiss, who have never shed the blood of their tyrants but in a field of battle; the laws and manners of the confederate states; the splendid trophies of the Austrian, Burgundian, and Italian wars; and the wisdom of a nation, which, after some sallies of martial adventure, has been content to guard the blessings of peace with the sword of freedom.

——*Manus haec inimica tyrannis*
Ense petit placidam sub libertate quietem.
[This hand an enemy to tyrants,
a sword that seeks a restful peace
   with liberty].

My judgement, as well as my enthusiasm, was satisfied with the glorious theme; and the as-sistance of Deyverdun seemed to remove an insuperable obstacle. The French or Latin memorials, of which I was not ignorant, are inconsiderable in number and weight; but in the perfect acquaintance of my friend with the German language, I found the key of a more valuable collection. The most necessary books were procured; he translated, for my own use, the folio volume of Schilling, a copious and contemporary relation of the war of Burgundy; we read and marked the most interesting parts of the great chronicle of Tschudi; and by his labour, or that of an inferior assistant, large extracts were made from the *History* of Lauffer and the *Dictionary* of Lew; yet such was the distance and delay, that two years elapsed in these preparatory steps; and it was late in the third summer (1767) before I entered, with these slender materials, on the more agreeable task of composition. A specimen of my History, the first book, was read the following winter in a literary society of foreigners in London; and as the author was unknown, I listened, without observation, to the free strictures, and unfavourable sentence, of my judges.[31] The

---

[31] Mr. Hume seems to have had a different opinion of this work.

FROM MR. HUME TO MR. GIBBON.
Sir,
   It is but a few days ago since M. Deyverdun put your manuscript into my hands, and I have perused it with great pleasure and satisfaction. I have only objection, derived from the language in which it is written. Why do you compose in French, and carry faggots into the wood, as Horace says with regard to Romans who wrote in Greek? I grant that you have a like motive to those Romans, and adopt a language much more generally diffused than your native tongue: but have you not remarked the fate of those two ancient languages in following ages? The Latin, though then less celebrated, and confined to more narrow limits, has in some measure outlived the Greek, and is now more generally understood by men of letters. Let the French, therefore, triumph in the present diffusion of their tongue. Our solid and increasing establishments in America, where we need less dread the inundation of Barbarians, promise a superior stability and duration to the English language.
   Your use of the French tongue has also led you into a style more poetical and figurative, and more

momentary sensation was painful; but their condemnation was ratified by my cooler thoughts. I delivered my imperfect sheets to the flames[32], and for ever renounced a design in which some expense, much labour, and more time, had been so vainly consumed. I cannot regret the loss of a slight and superficial essay, for such the work must have been in the hands of a stranger, uninformed by the scholars and statesmen, and remote from the libraries and archives of the Swiss republics. My ancient habits, and the presence of Deyverdun, encouraged me to write in French for the continent of Europe; but I was conscious myself that my style, above prose and below poetry, degenerated into a verbose and turgid declamation. Perhaps I may impute the failure to the injudicious choice of a foreign language. Perhaps I may suspect that the language itself is ill adapted to sustain the vigour and dignity of an important narrative. But if France, so rich in literary merit, had produced a great original historian, his genius would have formed and fixed the idiom to the proper tone, the peculiar mode of historical eloquence.

It was in search of some liberal and lucrative employment that my friend Deyverdun had visited England. His remittances from home were scanty and precarious. My purse was always open, but it was often empty; and I bitterly felt the want of riches and power, which might have enabled me to correct the errors of his fortune. His wishes and qualifications solicited the station of the travelling governor of some wealthy pupil; but every vacancy provoked so many eager candidates, that for a long time I struggled without success; nor was it till after much application that I could even place him as a clerk in the office of the Secretary of State. In a residence of several years he never acquired the just pronunciation and familiar use of the English tongue, but he read our most difficult authors with ease and taste: his critical knowledge of our language and poetry was such as few foreigners have possessed; and few of our countrymen could enjoy the theatre of Shakespeare and Garrick with more exqui-

site feeling and discernment. The consciousness of his own strength, and the assurance of my aid, emboldened him to imitate the example of Dr. Maty, whose *Journal Britannique* was esteemed and regretted; and to improve his model, by uniting with the transactions of literature a philosophic view of the arts and manners of the British nation. Our Journal for the year 1767, under the title of *Mémoires Littéraires de la Grande Bretagne,* was soon finished and sent to the press. For the first article, Lord Lyttelton's *History of Henry II,* I must own myself responsible; but the public has ratified my judgement of that voluminous work, in which sense and learning are not illuminated by a ray of genius. The next specimen was the choice of my friend, *The Bath Guide,* a light and whimsical performance, of local, and even verbal, pleasantry. I started at the attempt: he smiled at my fears: his courage was justified by success; and a master of both languages will applaud the curious felicity with which he has transfused into French prose the spirit, and even the humour, of the English verse. It is not my wish to deny how deeply I was interested in these Memoirs, of which I need not surely be ashamed; but at the distance of more than twenty years, it would be impossible for me to ascertain the respective shares of the two

---

highly coloured, than our language seems to admit of in historical productions: for such is the practice of French writers, particularly the more recent ones, who illuminate their pictures more than custom will permit us. On the whole, your History, in my opinion, is written with spirit and judgement; and I exhort you very earnestly to continue it. The objections that occurred to me on reading it were so frivolous, that I shall not trouble you with them, and should, I believe, have a difficulty to recollect them. I am, with great esteem,

Sir,

Your most obedient,

London, and most humble Servant,

24th of Oct. 1767 (Signed) DAVID HUME.

[32] He neglected to burn them. He left at Sheffield Place the introduction, or first book, in forty-three pages folio, written in a very small hand, besides a considerable number of notes. Mr. Hume's opinion, expressed in the letter in the last note, perhaps may justify the publication of it. S.

associates. A long and intimate communication of ideas had cast our sentiments and style in the same mould. In our social labours we composed and corrected by turns; and the praise which I might honestly bestow, would fall perhaps on some article or passage most properly my own. A second volume (for the year 1768) was published of these Memoirs. I will presume to say that their merit was superior to their reputation; but it is not less true that they were productive of more reputation than emolument. They introduced my friend to the protection, and myself to the acquaintance, of the Earl of Chesterfield, whose age and infirmities secluded him from the world; and of Mr. David Hume, who was under-secretary to the office in which Deyverdun was more humbly employed. The former accepted a dedication (April 12, 1769), and reserved the author for the future education of his successor: the latter enriched the Journal with a reply to Mr. Walpole's *Historical Doubts,* which he afterwards shaped into the form of a note. The materials of the third volume were almost completed, when I recommended Deyverdun as governor to Sir Richard Worsely, a youth, the son of my old lieutenant-colonel who was lately deceased. They set forwards on their travels, nor did they return to England till some time after my father's death.

My next publication was an accidental sally of love and resentment; of my reverence for modest genius, and my aversion for insolent pedantry. The sixth book of the *Aeneid* is the most pleasing and perfect composition of Latin poetry. The descent of Aeneas and the Sybil to the infernal regions, to the world of spirits, expands an awful and boundless prospect, from the nocturnal gloom of the Cumaean grot,

Ibant obscuri sola sub nocte per umbram,[*]

to the meridian brightness of the Elysian fields;

Largior hic campos aether et lumine vestit
Purpureo—[†]

from the dreams of simple nature, to the dreams, alas! of Egyptian theology, and the philosophy of the Greeks. But the final dismission of the hero through the ivory gate, whence

Falsa ad coelum mittunt insomnia manes,[‡]

seems to dissolve the whole enchantment and leaves the reader in a state of cold and anxious scepticism. This most lame and impotent conclusion has been variously imputed to the taste or irreligion of Virgil; but according to the more elaborate interpretation of Bishop Warburton, the descent to hell is not a false, but a mimic scene; which represents the initiation of Aeneas, in the character of a lawgiver, to the Eleusinian mysteries. This hypothesis, a singular chapter in the *Divine Legation of Moses,* had been admitted by many as true; it was praised by all as ingenious; nor had it been exposed, in a space of thirty years, to a fair and critical discussion. The learning and the abilities of the author had raised him to a just eminence; but he reigned the dictator and tyrant of the world of literature. The real merit of Warburton was degraded by the pride and presumption with which he pronounced his infallible decrees; in his polemic writings he lashed his antagonists without mercy or moderation; and his servile flatterers (see the base and malignant *Essay on the Delicacy of Friendship*[33]), exalting the master critic far above Aristotle and Longinus, assaulted every modest dissenter who refused to consult the oracle, and to adore the idol. In a land of liberty, such despotism must provoke a general opposition, and the zeal of opposition is seldom candid or impartial. A late professor of Oxford (Dr. Lowth), in a pointed and polished epistle (August 31, 1765), defended

---

[*] Virgil *Aeneid.* 6. 268 [They went obscurely through the gloom of the lonely night]—Ed.

[†] Virgil *Aeneid.* 6. 640 [Here a larger air clothes the fields with rosy light]—Ed.

[‡] Virgil *Aeneid.* 6. 896 [False the dreams the spirits send to heaven.]—Ed.

[33] By Hurd, afterwards Bishop of Worcester.

himself, and attacked the Bishop; and whatsoever might be the merits of an insignificant controversy, his victory was clearly established by the silent confusion of Warburton and his slaves. *I* too, without any private offence, was ambitious of breaking a lance against the giant's shield; and in the beginning of the year 1770, my *Critical Observations on the Sixth Book of the Aeneid* were sent, without my name, to the press. In this short essay, my first English publication, I aimed my strokes against the person and the hypothesis of Bishop Warburton. I proved, at least to my own satisfaction, *that* the ancient lawgivers did not invent the mysteries, and *that* Aeneas was never invested with the office of lawgiver: *that* there is not any argument, any circumstance, which can melt a fable into allegory, or remove the scene from the Lake Avernus to the Temple of Ceres: *that* such a wild supposition is equally injurious to the poet and the man: *that* if Virgil was not initiated he could not, if he were he would not, reveal the secrets of the initiation: *that* the anathema of Horace (*vetabo qui Cereris sacrum vulgarit,* &c.)* at once attests his own ignorance and the innocence of his friend. As the Bishop of Gloucester and his party maintained a discreet silence, my critical disquisition was soon lost among the pamphlets of the day; but the public coldness was overbalanced to my feelings by the weighty approbation of the last and best editor of Virgil, Professor Heyne of Göttingen, who acquiesces in my confutation, and styles the unknown author, *doctus . . . et elegantissimus Britannus.* But I cannot resist the temptation of transcribing the favourable judgement of Mr. Hayley, himself a poet and a scholar: 'An intricate hypothesis, twisted into a long and laboured chain of quotation and argument, the Dissertation on the Sixth Book of Virgil, remained some time unrefuted. . . . At length, a superior, but anonymous, critic arose, who, in one of the most judicious and spirited essays that our nation has produced, on a point of classical literature, completely overturned this ill-founded edifice, and exposed the arrogance and futility of its assuming architect'. He even condescends to

justify an acrimony of style, which had been gently blamed by the more unbiassed German; '*Paullo acrius quam velis . . . perstrinxit*'.[34] But I cannot forgive myself the contemptuous treatment of a man who, with all his faults, was entitled to my esteem[35]; and I can less forgive, in a personal attack, the cowardly concealment of my name and character.

In the fifteen years between my *Essay on the Study of Literature* and the first volume of the *Decline and Fall* (1761–1776), this criticism on Warburton, and some articles in the Journal, were my sole publications. It is more especially incumbent on me to mark the employment, or to confess the waste of time, from my travels to my father's death, an interval in which I was not diverted by any professional duties from the labours and pleasures of a studious life. (1) As soon as I was released from the fruitless task of the Swiss revolutions (1768), I began gradually to advance from the wish to the hope, from the hope to the design, from the design to the execution, of my historical work, of whose limits and extent I had yet a very inadequate notion. The Classics, as low as Tacitus, the younger Pliny, and Juvenal, were my old and familiar companions. I insensibly plunged into the ocean of Augustan history; and in the descending series I investigated, with my pen almost always in my hand, the original rec-

---

* Horace *Odes.* 3. 2. 26 [He who reveals the secret mysteries of Ceres, I will forbid entry to my house.] —Ed.

[34] The editor of the *Warburtonian Tracts*, Dr. Parr (p. 192), considers the allegorical interpretation 'as completely refuted in a most clear, elegant, and decisive work of criticism; which could not, indeed, derive authority from the greatest name: but to which the greatest name might with propriety have been affixed'.

[35] *The Divine Legation of Moses* is a monument, already crumbling in the dust, of the vigour and weakness of the human mind. If Warburton's new argument proved anything, it would be a demonstration against the legislator, who left his people without the knowledge of a future state. But some episodes of the work, on the Greek philosophy, the hieroglyphics of Egypt, &c., are entitled to the praise of learning, imagination, and discernment.

ords, both Greek and Latin, from Dion Cassius to Ammianus Marcellinus, from the reign of Trajan to the last age of the Western Caesars. The subsidiary rays of medals, and inscriptions of geography and chronology, were thrown on their proper objects; and I applied the collections of Tillemont, whose inimitable accuracy almost assumes the character of genius, to fix and arrange within my reach the loose and scattered atoms of historical information. Through the darkness of the middle ages I explored my way in the Annals and Antiquities of Italy of the learned Muratori; and diligently compared them with the parallel or transverse lines of Sigonius and Maffei, Baronius and Pagi, till I almost grasped the ruins of Rome in the fourteenth century, without suspecting that this final chapter must be attained by the labour of six quartos and twenty years. Among the books which I purchased, the Theodosian Code, with the commentary of James Godefroy, must be gratefully remembered; I used it (and much I used it) as a work of history, rather than of jurisprudence: but in every light it may be considered a full and capacious repository of the political state of the empire in the fourth and fifth centuries. As I believed, and as I still believe, that the propagation of the Gospel, and the triumph of the Church, are inseparably connected with the decline of the Roman monarchy, I weighed the causes and effects of the revolution, and contrasted the narratives and apologies of the Christians themselves, with the glances of candour or enmity which the Pagans have cast on the rising sects. The Jewish and heathen testimonies, as they are collected and illustrated by Dr. Lardner, directed, without superseding, my search of the originals; and in an ample dissertation on the miraculous darkness of the passion, I privately drew my conclusions from the silence of an unbelieving age. I have assembled the preparatory studies, directly or indirectly relative to my history; but, in strict equity, they must be spread beyond this period of my life, over the two summers (1771 and 1772) that elapsed between my father's death and my settlement in London. (2) In a free conversation with books and men, it would be endless to enumerate the names and characters of all who are introduced to our acquaintance; but in this general acquaintance we may select the degrees of friendship and esteem. According to the wise maxim, *Multum legere potius quam multa* [Read deeply and with discernment rather than widely and at random], I reviewed, again and again, the immortal works of the French and English, the Latin and Italian classics. My Greek studies (though less assiduous than I designed) maintained and extended my knowledge of that incomparable idiom. Homer and Xenophon were still my favourite authors; and I had almost prepared for the press an *Essay on the Cyropaedia*, which, in my own judgement, is not unhappily laboured. After a certain age, the new publications of merit are the sole food of the many; and the most austere student will often be tempted to break the line, for the sake of indulging his own curiosity, and of providing the topics of fashionable currency. A more respectable motive may be assigned for the third perusal of Blackstone's *Commentaries*, and a copious and critical abstract of that English work was my first serious production in my native language. (3) My literary leisure was much less complete and independent than it might appear to the eye of a stranger. In the hurry of London I was destitute of books; in the solitude of Hampshire I was not master of my time. My quiet was gradually disturbed by our domestic anxiety, and I should be ashamed of my unfeeling philosophy had I found much time to waste for study in the last fatal summer (1770) of my father's decay and dissolution.

The disembodying of the militia at the close of the war (1763) had restored the Major (a new Cincinnatus) to a life of agriculture. His labours were useful, his pleasures innocent, his wishes moderate; and my father *seemed* to enjoy the state of happiness which is celebrated by poets and philosophers, as the most agreeable to nature, and the least accessible to fortune.

Beatus ille, qui procul negotiis
(Ut prisca gens mortalium)
Paterna rura bubus exercet suis,
Solutus omni foenore.[36]   Hor. Epod. ii.

But the last indispensable condition, the freedom from debt, was wanting to my father's felicity; and the vanities of his youth were severely punished by the solicitude and sorrow of his declining age. The first mortgage, on my return from Lausanne (1758), had afforded him a partial and transient relief. The annual demand of interest and allowance was a heavy deduction from his income; the militia was a source of expense, the farm in his hands was not a profitable adventure, he was loaded with the costs and damages of an obsolete lawsuit; and each year multiplied the number, and exhausted the patience, of his creditors. Under these painful circumstances I consented to an additional mortgage, to the sale of Putney, and to every sacrifice that could alleviate his distress. But he was no longer capable of a rational effort, and his reluctant delays postponed not the evils themselves, but the remedies of those evils (remedia malorum potius quam mala differebat). The pangs of shame, tenderness, and self-reproach, incessantly preyed on his vitals; his constitution was broken; he lost his strength and his sight: the rapid progress of a dropsy admonished him of his end, and he sunk into the grave on the 10th of November, 1770, in the sixty-fourth year of his age. A family tradition insinuates that Mr. William Law had drawn his pupil in the light and inconstant character of Flatus, who is ever confident, and ever disappointed in the chase of happiness. But these constitutional failings were happily compensated by the virtues of the head and heart, by the warmest sentiments of honour and humanity. His graceful person, polite address, gentle manners, and unaffected cheerfulness, recommended him to the favour of every company; and in the change of times and opinions, his liberal spirit had long since delivered him from the zeal and prejudice of a Tory education. I submitted to the order of nature; and my grief was soothed by the conscious satisfaction that I had discharged all the duties of filial piety.

As soon as I had paid the last solemn duties to my father, and obtained, from time and reason, a tolerable composure of mind, I began to form a plan of an independent life, most adapted to my circumstances and inclination. Yet so intricate was the net, my efforts were so awkward and feeble, that nearly two years (November, 1770—October, 1772) were suffered to elapse before I could disentangle myself from the management of the farm, and transfer my residence from Buriton to a house in London. During this interval I continued to divide my year between town and the country; but my new situation was brightened by hope; my stay in London was prolonged into the summer; and the uniformity of the summer was occasionally broken by visits and excursions at a distance from home. The gratification of my desires (they were not immoderate) has been seldom disappointed by the want of money or credit; my pride was never insulted by the visit of an importunate tradesman; and my transient anxiety for the past or future has been dispelled by the studious or social occupation of the present hour. My conscience does not accuse me of any act of extravagance or injustice, and the remnant of my estate affords an ample and honourable provision for my declining age. I shall not expatiate on my economical affairs, which cannot be instructive or amusing to the reader. It is a rule of prudence, as well as of politeness, to reserve such confidence for the ear of a private friend, without exposing our situation to the envy or pity of strangers; for envy is productive of hatred, and pity borders too nearly on contempt. Yet I may believe, and even assert, that in circumstances more indigent or more wealthy, I should never have accomplished the task, or ac-

[36] Like the first mortals, blest is he,
From debts, and usury, and business free,
    With his own team who ploughs the soil,
Which grateful once confess'd his father's toil.
                                        Francis.

quired the fame, of an historian; that my spirit would have been broken by poverty and contempt, and that my industry might have been relaxed in the labour and luxury of a superfluous fortune.

I had now attained the first of earthly blessings, independence: I was the absolute master of my hours and actions: nor was I deceived in the hope that the establishment of my library in town would allow me to divide the day between study and society. Each year the circle of my acquaintance, the number of my dead and living companions, was enlarged. To a lover of books, the shops and sales of London present irresistible temptations; and the manufacture of my History required a various and growing stock of materials. The militia, my travels, the House of Commons, the fame of an author contributed to multiply my connexions: I was chosen a member of the fashionable clubs; and, before I left England in 1783, there were few persons of any eminence in the literary or political world to whom I was a stranger.[37] It would most assuredly be in my power to amuse the reader with a gallery of portraits and a collection of anecdotes. But I have always condemned the practice of transforming a private memorial into a vehicle of satire or praise. By my own choice I passed in town the greatest part of the year; but whenever I was desirous of breathing the air of the country, I possessed an hospitable retreat at Sheffield Place in Sussex, in the family of my valuable friend Mr. Holroyd, whose character, under the name Lord Sheffield, has since been more conspicuous to the public.

No sooner was I settled in my house and library, than I undertook the composition of the first volume of my *History*. At the outset all was dark and doubtful; even the title of the work, the true era of the *Decline and Fall of the Empire*, the limits of the introduction, the division of the chapters, and the order of the narrative; and I was often tempted to cast away the labour of seven years. The style of an author should be the image of his mind, but the choice and command of language is the fruit of exercise. Many experiments were made before I could hit the middle tone between a dull chronicle and a rhetorical declamation: three times did I compose the first chapter, and twice the second and third, before I was tolerably satisfied with their effect. In the remainder of the way I advanced with a more equal and easy pace; but the fifteenth and sixteenth chapters have been reduced by three successive revisals from a large volume to their present size; and they might still be compressed, without any loss of facts or sentiments. An opposite fault may be imputed to the concise and superficial narrative of the first reigns from Commodus to Alexander; a fault of which I have never heard, except from Mr. Hume in his last journey to London. Such an oracle might have been consulted and obeyed with rational devotion; but I was soon disgusted with the modest practice of reading the manuscript to my friends. Of such friends some will praise from politeness, and some will criticize from vanity. The author himself is the best judge of his own performance; no one has so deeply meditated on the subject; no one is so sincerely interested in the event.

By the friendship of Mr. (now Lord) Elliot, who had married my first cousin, I was returned at the general election for the borough of Leskeard. I took my seat at the beginning of the memorable contest between Great Britain and America, and supported, with many a sincere and silent vote, the rights, though not, perhaps, the interest, of the mother-country. After a fleeting illusive

---

[37] From the mixed, though polite company of Boodle's, White's and Brooks's, I must honourably distinguish a weekly society, which was instituted in the year 1764, and which still continues to flourish, under the title of the Literary Club. (Hawkins's *Life of Johnson*, p. 415; Boswell's *Tour to the Hebrides*, p. 97.) The names of Dr. Johnson, Mr. Burke, Mr. Topham Beauclerc, Mr. Garrick, Dr. Goldsmith, Sir Joshua Reynolds, Mr. Colman, Sir William Jones, Dr. Percy, Mr. Fox, Mr. Sheridan, Mr. Adam Smith, Mr. Steevens, Mr. Dunning, Sir Joseph Banks, Dr. Warton, and his brother Mr. Thomas Warton, Dr. Burney, &c., form a large and luminous constellation of British stars.

hope, prudence condemned me to acquiesce in the humble station of a mute. I was not armed by nature and education with the intrepid energy of mind and voice,

Vincentem strepitus, et natum rebus agendis. *

Timidity was fortified by pride, and even the success of my pen discouraged the trial of my voice.[38] But I assisted at the debates of a free assembly; I listened to the attack and defence of eloquence and reason; I had a near prospect of the characters, views, and passions of the first men of the age. The cause of government was ably vindicated by Lord North, a statesman of spotless integrity, a consummate master of debate, who could wield, with equal dexterity, the arms of reason and of ridicule. He was seated on the Treasury Bench between his Attorney and Solicitor-General, the two pillars of the law and state, *magis pares quam similes;* and the minister might indulge in a short slumber, whilst he was upholden on either hand by the majestic sense of Thurlow, and the skilful eloquence of Wedderburne. From the adverse side of the house an ardent and powerful opposition was supported by the lively declamation of Barré, the legal acuteness of Dunning, the profuse and philosophical fancy of Burke, and the argumentative vehemence of Fox, who, in the conduct of a party, approved himself equal to the conduct of an empire. By such men every operation of peace and war, every principle of justice or policy, every question of authority and freedom, was attacked and defended; and the subject of the momentous contest was the union or separation of Great Britain and America. The eight sessions that I sat in parliament were a school of civil prudence, the first and most essential virtue of an historian.

The volume of my *History,* which had been somewhat delayed by the novelty and tumult of a first session, was now ready for the press. After the perilous adventure had been declined by my friend Mr. Elmsly, I agreed, upon easy terms, with Mr. Thomas Cadell, a respectable bookseller, and Mr. William Stra-

han, an eminent printer; and they undertook the care and risk of the publication, which derived more credit from the name of the shop than from that of the author. The last revisal of the proofs was submitted to my vigilance; and many blemishes of style, which had been invisible in the manuscript, were discovered and corrected in the printed sheet. So moderate were our hopes, that the original impression had been stinted to five hundred, till the number was doubled by the prophetic taste of Mr. Strahan. During this awful interval I was neither elated by the ambition of fame, nor depressed by the apprehension of contempt. My diligence and accuracy were attested by my own conscience. History is the most popular species of writing, since it can adapt itself to the highest or the lowest capacity. I had chosen an illustrious subject. Rome is familiar to the schoolboy and the statesman; and my narrative was deduced from the last period of classical reading. I had likewise flattered myself, that an age of light and liberty would receive, without scandal, an inquiry into the human *causes* of the progress and establishment of Christianity.

I am at a loss how to describe the success of the work, without betraying the vanity of

---

* Horace *Ars Poetica.* 82 [A voice for prevailing and born for doing things.]—Ed.

[38] A French sketch of Mr. Gibbon's *Life,* written by himself, probably for the use of some foreign journalist or translator, contains no fact not mentioned in his English *Life.* He there describes himself with his usual candour. 'Depuis huit ans il a assisté aux délibérations les plus importantes, mais il ne s'est jamais trouvé *le courage,* ni *le talent,* de parler dans une assemblée publique [For eight years he was a part of the most important deliberations, but he never found the courage nor the talent to speak in a public assembly]. This sketch was written before the publication of his three last volumes, as in closing it he says of his *History:* 'Cette entreprise lui demande encore plusieurs années d'une application soutenue; mais quelqu'en soit le succès, il trouve dans cette application même un plaisir toujours varié et toujours renaissant' [This enterprise demands several more years of sustained effort; yet whatever be its success, he still finds in this effort an always varied and rejuvenating pleasure]. S.

the writer. The first impression was exhausted in a few days; a second and third edition were scarcely adequate to the demand; and the bookseller's property was twice invaded by the pirates of Dublin. My book was on every table, and almost on every toilette; the historian was crowned by the taste or fashion of the day; nor was the general voice disturbed by the barking of any *profane* critic. The favour of mankind is most freely bestowed on a new acquaintance of any original merit; and the mutual surprise of the public and their favourite is productive of those warm sensibilities, which at a second meeting can no longer be rekindled. If I listened to the music of praise, I was more seriously satisfied with the approbation of my judges. The candour of Dr. Robertson embraced his disciple. A letter from Mr. Hume overpaid the labour of ten years; but I have never presumed to accept a place in the triumvirate of British historians.

That curious and original letter will amuse the reader, and his gratitude should shield my free communication from the reproach of vanity.

'Edinburgh, March 18, 1776.
'Dear Sir,
'As I ran through your volume of history with great avidity and impatience, I cannot forbear discovering somewhat of the same impatience in returning you thanks for your agreeable present, and expressing the satisfaction which the performance has given me. Whether I consider the dignity of your style, the depth of your matter, or the extensiveness of your learning, I must regard the work as equally the object of esteem; and I own that if I had not previously had the happiness of your personal acquaintance, such a performance from an Englishman in our age would have given me some surprise. You may smile at this sentiment, but as it seems to me that your countrymen, for almost a whole generation, have given themselves up to barbarous and absurd faction, and have totally neglected all polite letters, I no longer expected any valuable production ever to come

from them. I know it will give you pleasure (as it did me) to find that all the men of letters in this place concur in their admiration of your work, and in their anxious desire of your continuing it.

'When I heard of your undertaking (which was some time ago), I own I was a little curious to see how you would extricate yourself from the subject of your two last chapters. I think you have observed a very prudent temperament; but it was impossible to treat the subject so as not to give grounds of suspicion against you, and you may expect that a clamour will arise. This, if anything, will retard your success with the public; for in every other respect your work is calculated to be popular. But among many other marks of decline, the prevalence of superstition in England prognosticates the fall of philosophy and decay of taste; and though nobody be more capable than you to revive them, you will probably find a struggle in your first advances.

'I see you entertain a great doubt with regard to the authenticity of the poems of Ossian. You are certainly right in so doing. It is indeed strange that any men of sense could have imagined it possible, that above twenty thousand verses, along with numberless historical facts, could have been preserved by oral tradition during fifty generations, by the rudest, perhaps, of all the European nations, the most necessitous, the most turbulent, and the most unsettled. Where a supposition is so contrary to common sense, any positive evidence of it ought never to be regarded. Men run with great avidity to give their evidence in favour of what flatters their passions and their national prejudices. You are therefore over and above indulgent to us in speaking of the matter with hesitation.

'I must inform you that we are all very anxious to hear that you have fully collected the materials for your second volume, and that you are even considerably advanced in the composition of it. I speak this more in the name of my friends than in my own, as I cannot expect to live so long as to see the publication of it. Your ensuing volume will be more delicate than the preceding, but I trust in your prudence for extricating you from the difficulties; and, in all events, you have courage to despise the clamour of bigots.

I am, with great regard,

Dear Sir,

Your most obedient, and most humble

Servant,

DAVID HUME.'

Some weeks afterwards I had the melancholy pleasure of seeing Mr. Hume in his passage through London: his body feeble, his mind firm. On the 25th of August of the same year (1776) he died, at Edinburgh, the death of a philosopher.

My second excursion to Paris was determined by the pressing invitation of M. and Madame Necker, who had visited England in the preceding summer. On my arrival I found M. Necker Director-General of the finances, in the first bloom of power and popularity. His private fortune enabled him to support a liberal establishment; and his wife, whose talents and virtues I had long admired, was admirably qualified to preside in the conversation of her table and drawing-room. As their friend, I was introduced to the best company of both sexes, to the foreign ministers of all nations, and to the first names and characters of France, who distinguished me by such marks of civility and kindness as gratitude will not suffer me to forget, and modesty will not allow me to enumerate. The fashionable suppers often broke into the morning hours; yet I occasionally consulted the Royal Library, and that of the Abbey of St. Germain, and in the free use of their books at home I had always reason to praise the liberality of those institutions. The society of men of letters I neither courted nor declined, but I was happy in the acquaintance of M. de Buffon, who united with a sublime genius the most amiable simplicity of mind and manners. At the table of my old friend, M. de Forcemagne, I was involved in a dispute with the Abbé de Mably; and his jealous irascible spirit revenged itself on a work which he was incapable of reading in the original.

Nearly two years had elapsed between the publication of my first and the commencement of my second volume; and the causes must be assigned of this long delay. (1) After a short holiday, I indulged my curiosity in some studies of a very different nature, a course of anatomy, which was demonstrated by Doctor Hunter, and some lessons of chemistry, which were delivered by Mr. Higgins. The principles of these sciences, and a taste for books of natural history, contributed to multiply my ideas and images; and the anatomist and chemist may sometimes track me in their own snow. (2) I dived, perhaps too deeply, into the mud of the Arian controversy; and many days of reading, thinking, and writing were consumed in the pursuit of a phantom. (3) It is difficult to arrange, with order and perspicuity, the various transactions of the age of Constantine; and so much was I displeased with the first essay, that I committed to the flames above fifty sheets. (4) The six months of Paris and pleasure must be deducted from the account. But when I resumed my task I felt my improvement; I was now master of my style and subject, and while the measure of my daily performance was enlarged, I discovered less reason to cancel or correct. It has always been my practice to cast a long paragraph in a single mould, to try it by my ear, to deposit it in my memory, but to suspend the action of the pen till I had given the last polish to my work. Shall I add, that I never found my mind more vigorous, nor my composition more happy, than in the winter hurry of society and parliament?

Had I believed that the majority of English readers were so fondly attached even to the name and shadow of Christianity; had I foreseen that the pious, the timid, and the prudent, would feel, or affect to feel, with such exquisite sensibility, I might, perhaps, have softened the two invidious chapters, which would create many enemies, and conciliate few friends. But the shaft was shot, the alarm was sounded, and I could only rejoice, that if the voice of our priests was clamorous and bitter, their hands were disarmed from the powers of persecution. I adhered to the wise resolution of trusting myself and my writings to the candour of the public, till Mr. Davies of Oxford presumed to attack, not the faith, but the fidelity, of the historian. *My Vindication,* expressive of less anger than contempt, amused for a moment the busy and idle metropolis; and the most rational part of the laity, and even of the clergy, appear to have been satisfied of my innocence and accuracy. I would not print this Vindication in quarto, lest it should be bound and preserved with the history itself. At the distance of twelve years, I calmly affirm my judgement of Davies, Chelsum &c. A victory over such antagonists was a sufficient humiliation. They, however, were rewarded in this world. Poor Chelsum was indeed neglected; and I dare not boast the making Dr. Watson a bishop; he is a prelate of a large mind and liberal spirit: but I enjoyed the pleasure of giving a royal pension to Mr. Davies, and of collating Dr. Apthorpe to an archiepiscopal living. Their success encouraged the zeal of Taylor the Arian[39], and Milner the Methodist[40], with many others, whom it would be difficult to remember, and tedious to rehearse. The list of my adversaries, however, was graced with the most respectable names of Dr. Priestley, Sir David Dalrymple, and Dr. White; and every polemic, of either University, discharged his sermon or pamphlet against the impenetrable silence of the Roman historian. In his *History of the Corruptions of Christianity,* Dr. Priestley threw down his two gauntlets to Bishop Hurd and Mr. Gibbon. I declined the challenge in a letter, exhorting my opponent to enlighten the world by his philosophical discoveries, and to remember that the merit of his predecessor Servetus is now reduced to a single passage, which indicates the smaller circulation of the blood through the lungs, from and to the heart. Instead of listening to this friendly advice, the dauntless philospher of Birmingham continued to fire away his double battery against those who believed too little, and those who believed too much. *From my* replies he has nothing to hope or fear: but his Socinian shield has repeatedly been pierced by the mighty spear of Horsley, and his trumpet of sedition may at length awaken the magistrates of a free country.

The profession and rank of Sir David Dalrymple (now a Lord of Session) has given a more decent colour to his style. But he scrutinized each separate passage of the two chapters with the dry minuteness of a special pleader; and as he was always solicitous to make, he may have succeeded sometimes in finding, a flaw. In his *Annals of Scotland,* he has shown himself a diligent collector and an accurate critic.

I have praised, and I still praise, the eloquent sermons which were preached in St. Mary's pulpit at Oxford by Dr. White. If he assaulted me with some degree of illiberal acrimony, in such a place, and before such an audience, he was obliged to speak the language of the country. I smiled at a passage in one of his private letters to Mr. Badcock: 'The part where we encounter Gibbon must be brilliant and striking'.

In a sermon preached before the University of Cambridge, Dr. Edwards complimented a work, 'which can only perish with the language itself'; and esteems the author a formidable enemy. He is, indeed, astonished that more learning and ingenuity has not been shown in the defence of Israel; that the prelates and dignitaries of the Church (alas, good man!) did not vie with each other whose stone should sink the deepest in the forehead of this Goliath.

'But the force of truth will oblige us to

---

[39] The stupendous title, *Thoughts on the Causes of the grand Apostasy,* at first agitated my nerves, till I discovered that it was the apostasy of the whole Church, since the Council of Nice, from Mr. Taylor's private religion. His book is a thorough mixture of *high* enthusiasm and *low* buffoonery, and the Millennium is a fundamental article of his creed.

[40] From his grammar school at Kingston-upon-Hull, Mr. Joseph Milner pronounces an anathema against all rational religion. *His* faith is a divine taste, a spiritual inspiration; *his* church is a mystic and invisible body; the *natural* Christians, such as Mr. Locke, who believe and interpret the Scriptures, are, in his judgement, no better than profane infidels.

confess, that in the attacks which have been levelled against our sceptical historian, we can discover but slender traces of profound and exquisite erudition, of solid criticism and accurate investigation; but we are too frequently disgusted by vague and inconclusive reasoning; by unseasonable banter and senseless witticisms; by embittered bigotry and enthusiastic jargon; by futile cavils and illiberal invectives. Proud and elated by the weakness of his antagonists, he condescends not to handle the sword of controversy'.

Let me frankly own that I was startled at the first discharge of ecclesiastical ordnance; but as soon as I found that this empty noise was mischievous only in the intention, my fear was converted into indignation; and every feeling of indignation or curiosity has long since subsided in pure and placid indifference.

The prosecution of my history was soon afterwards checked by another controversy of a very different kind. At the request of the Lord Chancellor, and of Lord Weymouth, then Secretary of State, I vindicated, against the French manifesto, the justice of the British arms. The whole correspondence of Lord Stormont, our late ambassador at Paris, was submitted to my inspection, and the *Mémoire Justificatif*, which I composed in French, was first approved by the Cabinet Ministers, and then delivered as a State paper to the courts of Europe. The style and manner are praised by Beaumarchais himself, who, in his private quarrel, attempted a reply; but he flatters me, by ascribing the memoir to Lord Stormont; and the grossness of his invective betrays the loss of temper and of wit; he acknowledged that *le style ne serait pas sans grace, ni la logique sans justesse* [the style would not be without grace, nor the logic without justice], &c., if the facts were true which he undertakes to disprove. For these facts my credit is not pledged; I spoke as a lawyer from my brief, but the veracity of Beaumarchais may be estimated from the assertion that France, by the treaty of Paris (1763), was limited to a certain number of ships of war. On the application of the Duke of Choiseul, he was

obliged to retract this daring falsehood.

Among the honourable connexions which I had formed, I may justly be proud of the friendship of Mr. Wedderburne, at that time Attorney-General, who now illustrates the title of Lord Loughborough, and the office of Chief Justice of the Common Pleas. By his strong recommendation, and the favourable disposition of Lord North, I was appointed one of the Lords Commissioners of Trade and Plantations; and my private income was enlarged by a clear addition of between seven and eight hundred pounds a year. The fancy of an hostile orator may paint, in the strong colours of ridicule, 'the perpetual virtual adjournment, and the unbroken sitting vacation of the Board of Trade'.[41] But it must be allowed that our duty was not intolerably severe, and that I enjoyed many days and weeks of repose, without being called away from my library to the office. My acceptance of a place provoked some of the leaders of the opposition, with whom I had lived in habits of intimacy[42]; and I was most unjustly ac-

---

[41] I can never forget the delight with which that diffusive and ingenious orator, Mr. Burke, was heard by all sides of the house, and even by those whose existence he proscribed. (See Mr. Burke's speech on the Bill of Reform, pp. 72–80.) The Lords of Trade blushed at their insignificancy, and Mr. Eden's appeal to the two thousand five hundred volumes of our Reports served only to excite a general laugh. I take this opportunity of certifying the correctness of Mr. Burke's printed speeches, which I have heard and read.

[42] It has always appeared to me, that nothing could be more unjustifiable than the manner in which some persons allowed themselves to speak of Mr. Gibbon's acceptance of an office at the Board of Trade. I can conceive that he may carelessly have used strong expressions in respect to some, or all parties; but he never meant that such expressions should be taken literally; and I know, beyond all possibility of question, that he was so far from being 'in a state of savage hostitility towards Lord North', as it is savagely expressed by Mr. Whitaker, that he always loved and esteemed him. I saw Mr. Gibbon constantly at this time, and was well acquainted with all his political opinions. And although he was not perfectly satisfied with *every* measure, yet he uniformly supported all the *principal* ones regarding the American war; and consid-

cused of deserting a party, in which I had never enlisted.[43]

The aspect of the next session of parliament was stormy and perilous; county meetings, petitions, and committees of correspondence, announced the public discontent; and instead of voting with a triumphant majority, the friends of government were often exposed to a struggle, and sometimes to a defeat. The House of Commons adopted Mr. Dunning's motion. 'That the influence of the Crown had increased, was increasing, and ought to be diminished': and Mr. Burke's bill of reform was framed with skill, introduced with eloquence and supported by numbers. Our late president, the American Secretary of State, very narrowly escaped the sentence of proscription; but the unfortunate Board of Trade was abolished in the committee by a small majority (207 to 199) of eight votes.

The storm, however, blew over for a time; a large defection of country gentlemen eluded the sanguine hopes of the patriots: the Lords of Trade were revived; administration recovered their strength and spirit; and the flames of London, which were kindled by a mischievous madman, admonished all thinking men of the danger of an appeal to the people. In the premature dissolution which followed this session of parliament I lost my seat. Mr. Elliot was now deeply engaged in the measures of opposition, and the electors of Leskeard[44] are commonly of the same opinion as Mr. Elliot.

In this interval of my senatorial life, I published the second and third volumes of the *Decline and Fall.* My ecclesiastical history still breathed the same spirit of freedom; but Protestant zeal is more indifferent to the characters and controversies of the fourth

---

ered himself, and, indeed, was a friend to Administration to the very period of his accepting office. He liked the brilliant society of a club, the most distinguished members of which were notorious for their opposition to Government, and might be led, in some degree, to join in their language; but Mr. Gibbon had little, I had almost said no political acrimony in his character. If the opposition of that or any other time could claim for their own every person who was not perfectly satisfied with all the measures of Government, their party would unquestionably have been more formidable. S.

[43] From Edward Gibbon, Esq., to Edward Elliot, Esq., of Port Elliot (afterwards Lord Elliot).

Dear Sir,   July 2, 1779.

Yesterday I received a very interesting communication from my friend the Attorney-General, whose kind and honourable behaviour towards me I must always remember with the highest gratitude. He informed me that, in consequence of an arrangement, a place at the Board of Trade was reserved for me, and that as soon as I signified my acceptance of it, he was satisfied no further difficulties would arise. My answer to him was sincere and explicit. I told him that I was far from approving all the past measures of the administration, even some of those in which I myself had silently concurred; that I saw, with the rest of the world, many capital defects in the characters of some of the present ministers, and was sorry that in so alarming a situation of public affairs, the country had not the assistance of several able and honest men who are now in opposition. But that I had not formed

with any of those persons in opposition any engagements or connexions which could in the least restrain or affect my parliamentary conduct; that I could not discover among them such superior advantages, either of measures or of abilities, as could make me consider it as a duty to attach myself to their cause; and that I clearly understood, from the publlc and private language of one of their leaders (Charles Fox), that in the actual state of the country, he himself was seriously of opinion that opposition could not tend to any good purpose, and might be productive of much mischief; that, for those reasons, I saw no objections which could prevent me from accepting an office under the present government, and that I was ready to take a step which I found to be consistent both with my interest and my honour.

It must now be decided whether I may continue to live in England or whether I must soon withdraw myself into a kind of philosophical exile in Switzerland. My father left his affairs in a state of embarrassment, and even of distress. My attempts to dispose of a part of my landed property have hitherto been disappointed, and are not likely at present to be more successful; and my plan of expense, though moderate in itself, deserves the name of extravagance, since it exceeds my real income. The addition of the salary which is now offered will make my situation perfectly easy; but I hope you will do me the justice to believe that my mind could not be so, unless I were satisfied of the rectitude of my own conduct. S.

[44] The borough which Mr. Gibbon had represented in parliament. S.

and fifth centuries. My obstinate silence had damped the ardour of the polemics. Dr. Watson, the most candid of my adversaries, assured me that he had no thoughts of renewing the attack, and my impartial balance of the virtues and vices of Julian was generally praised. This truce was interrupted only by some animadversions of the Catholics of Italy, and by some angry letters from Mr. Travis, who made me personally responsible for condemning, with the best critics, the spurious text of the three heavenly witnesses.

The piety or prudence of my Italian translator has provided an antidote against the poison of his original. The fifth and seventh volumes are armed with five letters from an anonymous divine to his friends, Foothead and Kirk, two English students at Rome; and this meritorious service is commended by Monsignor Stonor, a prelate of the same nation, who discovers much venom in the *fluid* and nervous style of Gibbon. The critical essay at the end of the third volume was furnished by the Abbate Nicola Spedalieri, whose zeal has gradually swelled to a more solid confutation in two quarto volumes.— Shall I be excused for not having read them?

The brutal insolence of Mr. Travis's challenge can only be excused by the absence of learning, judgement, and humanity; and to that excuse he has the fairest or foulest pretension. Compared with Archdeacon Travis, Chelsum and Davies assume the title of respectable enemies.

The bigoted advocate of popes and monks may be turned over even to the bigots of Oxford; and the wretched Travis still smarts under the lash of the merciless Porson. I consider Mr. Porson's answer to Archdeacon Travis as the most acute and accurate piece of criticism which as appeared since the days of Bentley. His strictures are founded in argument, enriched with learning, and enlivened with wit; and his adversary neither deserves nor finds any quarter at his hands. The evidence of the three heavenly witnesses would now be rejected in any court of justice: but prejudice is blind, authority is deaf, and

our vulgar bibles will ever be polluted by this spurious text, '*sedet aeternumque sedebit.*'* The more learned ecclesiastics will indeed have the secret satisfaction of reprobating in the closet what they read in the Church.

I perceived, and without surprise, the coldness and even prejudice of the town; nor could a whisper escape my ear that, in the judgement of many readers, my continuation was much inferior to the original attempts. An author who cannot ascend will always appear to sink: envy was now prepared for my reception, and the zeal of my religious was fortified by the motive of my political enemies. Bishop Newton, in writing his own life, was at full liberty to declare how much he himself and two eminent brethren were disgusted by Mr. Gibbon's prolixity, tediousness, and affectation. But the old man should not have indulged his zeal in a false and feeble charge against the historian[45], who had faithfully and even cautiously rendered Dr.

---

* Virgil *Aeneid*. 6. 617 [He sits and will sit forever.] —Ed.

[45] Extract from Mr. Gibbon's Commonplace Book.

Thomas Newton, Bishop of Bristol and Dean of St. Paul's, was born at Litchfield on the 21st of December, 1703, O.S. (January 1, 1704, N.S.), and died the 14th of February, 1782, in the seventy-ninth year of his age. A few days before his death he finished the memoirs of his own life, which have been prefixed to an edition of his posthumous works, first published in quarto, and since (1787) re-published in six volumes octavo.

Pp. 173, 174. 'Some books were published in 1781, which employed some of the Bishop's leisure hours, and during his illness. Mr. Gibbon's *History of the Decline and Fall of the Roman Empire* he read throughout, but it by no means answered his expectation; for he found it rather a prolix and tedious performance, his matter uninteresting, and his style affected; his testimonies not to be depended upon, and his frequent scoffs at religion offensive to every sober mind. He had before been convicted of making false quotations, which should have taught him more prudence and caution. But, without examining his authorities, there is one which must necessarily strike every man who has read Dr. Burnet's Treatise *de Statû Mortuorum*. In vol. iii, p. 99, Mr. G. has the following note:—"Burnett (*de S. M.*, pp. 56–84) collects the opinions of the Fathers, as far as they assert the sleep or repose of

Burnet's meaning by the alternative of 'sleep or repose'. That philosophic divine supposes, that, in the period between death and the resurrection, human souls exist without a body, endowed with internal consciousness, but destitute of all active or passive connexion with the external world. . . .

I was, however, encouraged by some domestic and foreign testimonies of applause; and the second and third volumes insensibly rose in sale and reputation to a level with the first. But the public is seldom wrong; and I am inclined to believe that, especially in the beginning, they are more prolix and less entertaining than the first: my efforts had not been relaxed by success, and I had rather deviated into the opposite fault of minute and superfluous diligence. On the Continent, my name and writings were slowly diffused: a French translation of the' first volume had disappointed the booksellers of Paris; and a passage in the third was

---

human souls till the day of judgement. He afterwards exposes (p. 91) the inconveniences which must arise if they possessed a more active and sensible existence. Who would not from hence infer that Dr. B. was an advocate for the sleep or insensible existence of the soul after death? whereas his doctrine is directly the contrary. He has employed some chapters in treating of the state of human souls in the interval between death and the resurrection; and after various proofs from reason, from scripture, and the Fathers, his conclusions are, that human souls exist after their separation from the body, that they are in a good or evil state according to their good or ill behaviour, but that neither their happiness nor their misery will be complete or perfect before the day of judgement. His argumentation is thus summed up at end of the fourth chapter — *Ex quibus constat primo, animas superesse extincto corpore; secundo, bonas bene, malas male se habituras; tertio, nec illis summam felicitatem, nec his summam miseriam, accessuram esse ante diem judicii.*" (The Bishop's reading the whole was a greater compliment to the work than was paid to it by two of the most eminent of his brethren for their learning and station. The one entered upon it, but was soon wearied, and laid it aside in disgust: the other returned it upon the bookseller's hands; and it is said that Mr. G. himself happened unluckily to be in the shop at the same time.)'

Does the Bishop comply with his own precept in the next page? (p. 175) 'Old age should lenify, should soften men's manners, and make them more mild and gentle: but often has the contrary effect, hardens their hearts, and makes them more sour and crabbed.'—He is speaking of Dr. Johnson.

Have I ever insinuated that preferment-hunting is the great occupation of an ecclesiastical life (Memoirs passim)? that a minister's influence and a bishop's patronage are sometimes pledged eleven deep (p. 151)? that a prebendary considers the audit week as the better part of the year (p. 127)? or that the most eminent of priests, the pope himself, would change religion, if anything better could be offered them (p. 56)? Such things are more than insinuated in the Bishop's *Life*, which afforded some scandal to the church, and some diversion to the profane laity.

None of the attacks from ecclesiastical antagonists were more malignant and illiberal than some strictures published in the *English Review*, October, 1788, &c., and afterwards reprinted in a separate volume, with the signature of John Whitaker, in 1791. I had mentioned them to Mr. Gibbon, when first published, but so far was he from supposing them worth his notice, that he did not see them till his late visit to England a few months before his death. If Mr. Whitaker had only pointed his bitterness against Mr. Gibbon's *opinions*, perhaps no inquiry would have been made into the possible source of his collected virulence and deliberate malignity.

I have in my possession very amicable letters from the Rev. Mr. Whitaker to Mr. Gibbon, written some time after he had read the offensive fifteenth and sixteenth chapters of the *Decline and Fall*. When Mr. Gibbon came to England, in 1787, he read Whitaker's *Mary Queen of Scots,* and I have heard him VERY *incautiously express his opinion of it. Some good-natured friend* mentioned it to Mr. Whitaker. It must be an extraordinary degree of resentment that could induce any person, of a liberal mind, to scrape together defamatory stories, true or false, and blend them with the defence of the most benign religion, whose precepts inculcate the very opposite practice. Religion receives her greatest injuries from those champions of the Church who, under the pretence of vindicating the Gospel, outrageously violate both the spirit and the letter of it.

Mr. Whitaker affects principally to review the fourth, fifth, and sixth volumes, but he has allotted the first month's review to an attack on the first three volumes, or rather on the first, which had been published twelve years and a half before it occurred to him that a review of it was necessary. S.

construed as a personal reflection on the reigning monarch.[46]

Before I could apply for a seat at the general election the list was already full; but Lord North's promise was sincere, his recommendation was effectual, and I was soon chosen on a vacancy for the borough of Lymington, in Hampshire. In the first session of the new parliament, administration stood their ground; their final overthrow was reserved for the second. The American war had once been the favourite of the country: the pride of England was irritated by the resistance of her colonies, and the executive power was driven by national clamour into the most vigorous and coercive measures. But the length of a fruitless contest, the loss of armies, the accumulation of debt and taxes, and the hostile confederacy of France, Spain, and Holland, indisposed the public to the American war, and the persons by whom it was conducted; the representatives of the people followed, at a slow distance, the changes of their opinion; and the ministers, who refused to bend, were broken by the tempest. As soon as Lord North had lost, or was about to lose, a majority in the House of Commons, he surrendered his office, and retired to a private station, with the tranquil assurance of a clear conscience and a cheerful temper: the old fabric was dissolved, and the posts of government were occupied by the victorious and veteran troops of opposition. The lords of trade were not immediately dismissed, but the board itself was abolished by Mr. Burke's bill, which decency had compelled the patriots to revive; and I was stripped of a convenient salary, after having enjoyed it about three years.

So flexible is the title of my *History*, that the final era might be fixed at my own choice; and I long hesitated whether I should be content with the three volumes, the fall of the Western empire, which fulfilled my first engagement with the public. In this interval of suspense, nearly a twelvemonth, I returned by a natural impulse to the Greek authors of antiquity; I read with new pleasure the *Iliad* and the *Odyssey*, the *Histories* of Herodotus,

Thucydides, and Xenophon, a large portion of the tragic and comic theatre of Athens, and many interesting dialogues of the Socratic school. Yet in the luxury of freedom I began to wish for the daily task, the active pursuit, which gave a value to every book, and an object to every inquiry: the preface of a new edition announced my design, and I dropped without reluctance from the age of Plato to that of Justinian. The original texts of Procopius and Agathias supplied the events and even the characters of this reign: but a laborious winter was devoted to the Codes, the Pandects, and the modern interpreters, before I presumed to form an abstract of the civil law. My skill was improved by practice, my diligence perhaps was quickened by the loss of office; and, excepting the last chapter, I had finished the fourth volume before I sought a retreat on the banks of the Leman Lake.

It is not the purpose of this narrative to expatiate on the public or secret history of the times: the schism which followed the death of the Marquis of Rockingham, the appointment of the Earl of Shelburne, the resignation of Mr. Fox, and his famous coalition with Lord North. But I may assert, with some degree of assurance, that in their political conflict those great antagonists had never felt any personal animosity to each other, that their reconciliation was easy and sincere, and that their friendship has never been clouded by the shadow of suspicion or jealousy. The most violent or venal of their respective followers embraced this fair occasion of revolt, but their alliance still commanded a majority in the House of Com-

---

[46] It may not be generally known that Louis the Sixteenth is a great reader, and a reader of English books. On perusing a passage of my *History* which seems to compare him to Arcadius or Honorius, he expressed his resentment to the Prince of B*****, from whom the intelligence was conveyed to me. I shall neither disclaim the allusion, nor examine the likeness; but the situation of the late King of France excludes all suspicion of flattery; and I am ready to declare that the concluding observations of my third volume were written before his accession to the throne.

mons; the peace was censured, Lord Shelburne resigned, and the two friends knelt on the same cushion to take the oath of Secretary of State. From a principle of gratitude I adhered to the coalition: my vote was counted in the day of battle, but I was overlooked in the division of the spoil. There were many claimants more deserving and importunate than myself: the Board of Trade could not be restored; and, while the list of places was curtailed, the number of candidates was doubled. An easy dismission to a secure seat at the Board of Customs or Excise was promised on the first vacancy: but the chance was distant and doubtful; nor could I solicit with much ardour an ignoble servitude, which would have robbed me of the most valuable of my studious hours[47]: at the same time the tumult of London, and the attendance on parliament, were grown more irksome; and, without some additional income, I could not long or prudently maintain the style of expense to which I was accustomed.

From my early acquaintance with Lausanne I had always cherished a secret wish that the school of my youth might become the retreat of my declining age. A moderate fortune would secure the blessings of ease, leisure, and independence: the country, the people, the manners, the language, were congenial to my taste; and I might indulge the hope of passing some years in the domestic society of a friend. After travelling with several English, Mr. Deyverdun was now settled at home, in a pleasant habitation, the gift of his deceased aunt: we had long been separated, we had long been silent; yet in my first letter I exposed, with the most perfect confidence, my situation, my sentiments, and my designs. His immediate answer was a warm and joyful acceptance: the picture of our future life provoked my impatience; and the terms of arrangement were short and simple, as he possessed the property, and I undertook the expense of our common house. Before I could break my English chain, it was incumbent on me to struggle with the feelings of my heart, the indolence of my temper, and the opinion of the world, which unanimously condemned this voluntary banishment. In the disposal of my effects, the library, a sacred deposit, was alone excepted. As my post-chaise moved over Westminster Bridge, I bade a long farewell to the 'fumum et opes strepitumque Romae'.[*] My journey by the direct road through France was not attended with any accident, and I arrived at Lausanne nearly twenty years after my second departure. Within less than three months the coalition struck on some hidden rocks: had I remained on board, I should have perished in the general shipwreck.

Since my establishment at Lausanne, more than seven years have elapsed; and if every day has not been equally soft and serene, not a day, not a moment, has occurred in which I have repented of my choice. During my absence, a long portion of human life, many changes had happened: my elder acquaintance had left the stage; virgins were ripened into matrons, and children were grown to the age of manhood. But the same manners were transmitted from one generation to another: my friend alone was an inestimable treasure; my name was not totally forgotten, and all were ambitious to welcome the arrival of a stranger and the return of a fellow-

---

[47] About the same time, it being in contemplation to send a secretary of embassy to Paris, Mr. Gibbon was a competitor for that office. (See Letter to and from Lord Thurlow.) The credit of being distinguished, and stopped by government when he was leaving England, the salary of £1,200 a year, the society of Paris, and the hope of a future provision for life, disposed him to renounce, though with much reluctance, an agreeable scheme on the point of execution; to engage, without experience, in a scene of business which he never liked; to give himself a master, or at least a principal, of an unknown, perhaps an unamiable character: to which might be added, the danger of the recall of the ambassador, or the change of ministry. Mr. Anthony Storer was preferred. Mr. Gibbon was somewhat indignant at the preference; but he never knew that it was the act of his friend Mr. Fox, contrary to the solicitations of Mr. Craufurd, and other of his friends. S.

[*] Horace *Odes*. 3. 29. 12 [The smoke and wealth and noise of Rome]—Ed.

citizen. The first winter was given to a general embrace, without any nice discrimination of persons and characters. After a more regular settlement, a more accurate survey, I discovered three solid and permanent benefits of my new situation. (1) My personal freedom had been somewhat impaired by the House of Commons and the Board of Trade; but I was now delivered from the chain of duty and dependence, from the hopes and fears of political adventure: my sober mind was no longer intoxicated by the fumes of party, and I rejoiced in my escape, as often as I read of the midnight debates which preceded the dissolution of parliament. (2) My English economy had been that of a solitary bachelor, who might afford some occasional dinners. In Switzerland I enjoyed at every meal, at every hour, the free and pleasant conversation of the friend of my youth; and my daily table was always provided for the reception of one or two extraordinary guests. Our importance in society is less a positive than a relative weight: in London I was lost in the crowd; I ranked with the first families of Lausanne, and my style of prudent expense enabled me to maintain a fair balance of reciprocal civilities. (3) Instead of a small house between a street and a stable-yard, I began to occupy a spacious and convenient mansion, connected on the north side with the city, and open on the south to a beautiful and boundless horizon. A garden of four acres had been laid out by the taste of Mr. Deyverdun: from the garden a rich scenery of meadows and vineyards descends to the Leman Lake, and the prospect far beyond the Lake is crowned by the stupendous mountains of Savoy. My books and my acquaintance had been first united in London; but this happy position of my library in town and country was finally reserved for Lausanne. Possessed of every comfort in this triple alliance, I could not be tempted to change my habitation with the changes of the seasons.

My friends had been kindly apprehensive that I should not be able to exist in a Swiss town at the foot of the Alps, after having so long conversed with the first men of the first cities of the world. Such lofty connexions may attract the curious, and gratify the vain; but I am too modest, or too proud, to rate my own value by that of my associates; and whatsoever may be the fame of learning of learning or genius, experience has shown me that the cheaper qualifications of politeness and good sense are of more useful currency in the commerce of life. By many, conversation is esteemed as theatre or a school: but after the morning has been occupied by the labours of the library, I wish to unbend rather than to exercise my mind; and in the interval between tea and supper I am far from disdaining the innocent amusement of a game at cards. Lausanne is peopled by a numerous gentry, whose companionable idleness is seldom disturbed by the pursuits of avarice or ambition: the women, though confined to a domestic education, are endowed for the most part with more taste and knowledge than their husbands and brothers: but the decent freedom of both sexes is equally remote from the extremes of simplicity and refinement. I shall add as a misfortune rather than a merit, that the situation and beauty of the Pays de Vaud, the long habits of the English, the medical reputation of Dr. Tissot, and the fashion of viewing the mountains and *Glaciers,* have opened us on all sides to the incursions of foreigners. The visits of Mr. and Madame Necker, of Prince Henry of Prussia, and of Mr. Fox, may form some pleasing exceptions; but, in general, Lausanne has appeared most agreeable in my eyes, when we have been abandoned to our own society. I had frequently seen Mr. Necker, in the summer of 1784, at a country house near Lausanne, where he composed his Treatise on the Administration of the Finances. I have since, in October, 1790, visited him in his present residence, the castle and barony of Copet, near Geneva. Of the merits and measures of that statesman various opinions may be entertained; but all impartial men must agree in their esteem of his integrity and patriotism.

In the month of August, 1784, Prince

Henry of Prussia, in his way to Paris, passed three days at Lausanne. His military conduct has been praised by professional men; his character has been vilified by the wit and malice of a demon[48]; but I was flattered by his affability, and entertained by his conversation.

In his tour to Switzerland (September, 1788) Mr. Fox gave me two days of free and private society. He seem to feel, and even to envy, the happiness of my situation; while I admired the powers of a superior man, as they are blended in his attractive character with the softness and simplicity of a child. Perhaps no human being was ever more perfectly exempt from the taint of malevolence, vanity, or falsehood.

My transmigration from London to Lausanne could not be effected without interrupting the course of my historical labours. The hurry of my departure, the joy of my arrival, the delay of my tools, suspended their progress; and a full twelvemonth was lost before I could resume the thread of regular and daily industry. A number of books most requisite and least common had been previously selected; the academical library at Lausanne, which I could use as my own, contained at least the fathers and councils; and I have derived some occasional succour from the public collections of Berne and Geneva. The fourth volume was soon terminated, by an abstract of the controversies of the Incarnation, which the learned Dr. Prideaux was apprehensive of exposing to profane eyes. It had been the original design of the learned Dean Prideaux to write the history of the ruin of the Eastern Church. In this work it would have been necessary, not only to unravel all those controversies which the Christians made about the hypostatical union, but also to unfold all the niceties and subtle notions which each sect entertained concerning it. The pious historian was apprehensive of exposing that incomprehensible mystery to the cavils and objections of unbelievers; and he durst not, 'seeing the nature of this book, venture it abroad in so wanton and lewd an age'.[49]

In the fifth and sixth volumes the revolutions of the empire and the world are the most rapid, various, and instructive; and the Greek or Roman historians are checked by the hostile narratives of the barbarians of the East and the West.[50]

It was not till after many designs, and many trials, that I preferred, as I still prefer, the method of grouping my picture by nations; and the seeming neglect of chronological order is surely compensated by the superior merits of interest and perspicuity. The style of the first volume is, in my opinion, somewhat crude and elaborate; in the second and third it is ripened into ease, correctness, and numbers; but in the three last I may have been seduced by the facility of my pen, and the constant habit of speaking one language and writing another may have infused some mixture of Gallic idioms. Happily for my eyes, I have always closed my studies with the day, and commonly with the morning; and a long, but temperate, labour has been accomplished, without fatiguing either the mind or the body; but when I computed the remainder of my time and my task, it was apparent that, according to the season of publication, the delay of a month would be productive of that of a year. I was now straining for the goal, and in the last winter many evenings were borrowed from the social pleasures of Lausanne. I could now wish that a pause, an interval, had been allowed for a serious revisal.

I have presumed to mark the moment of conception: I shall now commemorate the hour of my final deliverance. It was on the day, or rather night, of the 27th of June, 1787, between the hours of eleven and twelve, that I wrote the last lines of the last

---

[48] *Mémoire Secret de la Cour de Berlin*, by Mirabeau.
[49] See Preface to the *Life of Mahomet*, pp. 10, 11.
[50] I have followed the judicious precept of the Abbé de Mably (*Manière d'écrire l'Histoire*, p. 110), who advises the historian not to dwell too minutely on the decay of the eastern empire; but to consider the barbarian conquerors as a more worthy subject of his narrative. 'Fas est et ab hoste doceri' [One is permitted to learn from the enemy].

page, in a summer-house in my garden. After laying down my pen, I took several turns in a *berceau,* or covered walk of acacias, which commands a prospect of the country, the lake, and the mountains. The air was temperate, the sky was serene, the silver orb of the moon was reflected from the waters, and all nature was silent. I will not dissemble the first emotions of joy on recovery of my freedom, and, perhaps, the establishment of my fame. But my pride was soon humbled, and a sober melancholy was spread over my mind, by the idea that I had taken an everlasting leave of an old and agreeable companion, and that whatsoever might be the future date of my *History,* the life of the historian must be short and precarious. I will add two facts, which have seldom occurred in the composition of six, or at least of five quartos. (1) My first rough manuscript, without any intermediate copy, has been sent to the press. (2) Not a sheet has been seen by any human eyes, excepting those of the author and the printer: the faults and the merits are exclusively my own.[51]

I cannot help recollecting a much more extraordinary fact, which is affirmed of himself by Retif de la Bretorme, a voluminous and original writer of French novels. He laboured, and may still labour, in the humble office of corrector to a printing-house; but this office enabled him to transport an entire volume from his mind to the press; and his work was given to the public without ever having been written by the pen.

After a quiet residence of four years, during which I had never moved ten miles from Lausanne, it was not without some reluctance and terror that I undertook, in a journey of two hundred leagues, to cross the mountains and the sea. Yet this formidable adventure was achieved without danger or fatigue; and at the end of a fortnight I found myself in Lord Sheffield's house and library, safe, happy, and at home. The character of my friend (Mr. Holroyd) had recommended him to a seat in parliament for Coventry, the command of a regiment of light dragoons, and an Irish peerage. The sense and spirit of his

political writings have decided the public opinion on the great questions of our commercial interest with America and Ireland.[52]

The sale of his *Observations on the American States* was diffusive, their effect beneficial; the Navigation Act, the palladium of Britain, was defended, and perhaps saved, by his pen; and he proves, by the weight of fact and argument, that the mother-country may survive and flourish after the loss of Ameria. My friend has never cultivated the arts of composition but his materials are copious and correct, and he leaves on his paper the clear impression of an active and vigorous mind. His *Observations on the Trade, Manufactures, and present State of Ireland,* were intended to guide the industry, to correct the prejudices, and to assuage the passions of a country which seemed to forget that she could be free and prosperous only by a friendly connexion with Great Britain. The concluding observations are written with so much ease and spirit that they may be read by those who are the least interested in the subject.

He fell[53] (in 1784) with the unpopular coalition; but his merit has been acknowledged at the last general election, 1790, by the honourable invitation and free choice of the city of Bristol.[54] During the whole time of my

---

[51] Extract from Mr. Gibbon's Commonplace Book.

The fourth volume of the *History of the Decline and Fall of the Roman Empire*	begun March 1, 1782 —ended June, 1784.
The fifth volume ..	begun July, 1784—ended May 1, 1786.
The sixth volume ..	begun May 18, 1786—ended June 27, 1787.

These three volumes were sent to press August 15, 1787, and the whole impression was concluded April following.

[52] *Observations on the Commerce of the American States,* by John Lord Sheffield, the 6th edition, London, 1784, in 8 vo.

[53] It is not obvious from whence he fell; he never held nor desired any office of emolument whatever, unless his military commissions, and the command of a regiment of light dragoons, which he raised himself, and which was disbanded on the peace in 1783, should be deemed such. S.

[54] See a Letter from Mr. Gibbon to Lord Sheffield, Lausanne, August 7, 1790. S.

residence in England, I was entertained at Sheffield Place and in Downing Street, by his hospitable kindness; and the most pleasant period was that which I passed in the domestic society of the family. In the larger circle of the metropolis I observed the country and the inhabitants with the knowledge, and without the prejudices, of an Englishman; but I rejoiced in the apparent increase of wealth and prosperity, which might be fairly divided between the spirit of the nation and the wisdom of the minister. All party-resentment was now lost in oblivion; since I was no man's rival, no man was my enemy. I felt the dignity of independence, and as I asked no more, I was satisfied with the general civilities of the world. The house in London which I frequented with most pleasure and assiduity was that of Lord North. After the loss of power and of sight, he was still happy in himself and his friends, and my public tribute of gratitude and esteem could no longer be suspected of any interested motive. Before my departure from England, I was present at the august spectacle of Mr. Hastings's trial in Westminster Hall. It is not my province to absolve or condemn the Governor of India[55]; but Mr. Sheridan's eloquence commanded my applause; nor could I hear without emotion the personal compliment which he paid me in the presence of the British nation.[56]

From this display of genius, which blazed four successive days, I shall stoop to a very mechanical circumstance. As I was waiting in the manager's box, I had the curiosity to inquire of the shorthand writer, how many words a ready and a rapid orator might pronounce in an hour? From 7,000 to 7,500 was his answer. The medium of 7,200 will afford 120 words a minute, and two words in each second. But this computation will only apply to the English language.

As the publication of my three last volumes was the principal object, so it was the first care of my English journey. The previous arrangements with the bookseller and the printer were settled in my passage through London, and the proofs, which I returned more correct, were transmitted every post from the press to Sheffield Place. The length of the operation, and the leisure of the country, allowed some time to review my manuscript. Several rare and useful books, the *Assises de Jerusalem, Ramusius de Bello C. P^aro*, the *Greek Acts of the Synod of Florence*, the *Statuta Urbis Romae*, &c., were procured, and I introduced in their proper places the supplements which they afforded. The impression of the fourth volume had consumed three months. Our common interest required that we should move with a quicker pace; and Mr. Strahan fulfilled his engagement, which few printers could sustain, of delivering every week three thousand copies of nine sheets. The day of publication was, however, delayed, that it might coincide with the fifty-first anniversary of my own birthday; the double festival was celebrated by a cheerful literary dinner at Mr. Cadell's house; and I seemed to blush while they read an elegant compliment from Mr. Hayley,[57] whose poeti-

[55] He considered the *persecution* of that highly respectable person to have arisen from party views. S.

[56] He said the facts that made up the volume of narrative were unparalleled in atrociousness, and that nothing equal in criminality was to be traced, either in ancient or modern history, in the correct periods of Tacitus or the luminous page of Gibbon. *Morning Chronicle*, June 14, 1788. S.

[57] Occasional Stanzas, *by* Mr. Hayley, *read after the dinner at* Mr. Cadell's, May 8, 1788; *being the day of the publication of the three last volumes of* Mr. Gibbon's History, and his Birthday.

Genii of England, and of Rome!
In mutual triumph here assume
    The honours each may claim!
This social scene with smiles survey!
And consecrate the festive day
    To Friendship and to Fame!
Enough, by Desolation's tide,
With anguish, and indignant pride,
    Has Rome bewail'd her fate;
And mourn'd that Time, in Havoc's hour,
Defaced each monument of power
    To speak her truly great:
O'er maim'd Polybius, just and sage,
O'er Livy's mutilated page,
    How deep was her regret!
Touched by this Queen, in ruin grand,
See! Glory, by an English hand,
    Now pays a mighty debt:

cal talents had more than once been employed in the praise of his friend. Before Mr. Hayley inscribed with my name his epistles on history, I was not acquainted with that amiable man and elegant poet. He afterwards thanked me in verse for my second and third volumes[58]: and in the summer of 1781, the Roman Eagle[59] (a proud title) accepted the invitation of the English Sparrow, who chirped in the groves of Eartham, near Chichester. As most of the former purchasers were naturally desirous of completing their sets, the sale of the quarto edition was quick and easy; and an octavo size was printed to satisfy at a cheaper rate the public demand. The conclusion of my work was generally read, and variously judged. The style has been exposed to much academic criticism; a religious clamour was revived, and the reproach of indecency has been loudly echoed by the rigid censors of morals. I never could understand the clamour that has been raised against the indecency of my three last volumes. (1) An equal degree of freedom in the former part, especially in the first volume, had passed without reproach. (2) I am justified in painting the manners of the times; the vices of Theodora form an essential feature in the reign and character of Justinian; and the most naked tale in my history is told by the Rev. Mr. Joseph Warton, an

---

Lo! sacred to the Roman Name,
And raised, like Rome's immortal Fame,
  By Genius and by Toil,
The splendid Work is crown'd to-day,
On which Oblivion ne'er shall prey,
  Not Envy make her spoil!
England, exult! and view not now
With jealous glance each nation's brow,
  Where History's palm has spread!
In every path of liberal art,
Thy Sons to prime distinction start,
  And no superior dread.
Science for Thee a Newton raised;
For thy renown a Shakespeare blazed,
  Lord of the drama's sphere!
In different fields to equal praise
See History now thy Gibbon raise
  To shine without a peer!
Eager to honour living worth,
And bless to-day the double birth,

That proudest joy may claim,
Let artless Truth this homage pay,
And consecrate the festive day
  To Friendship and to Fame!

[58] Sonnet to Edward Gibbon, Esq.
On the Publication of his Second and Third Volumes,
1781.
With proud delight th' imperial founder gazed
  On the new beauty of his second Rome,
When on his eager eye rich temples blazed,
  And his fair city rose in youthful bloom:
A pride more noble may thy heart heart assume,
  O Gibbon! gazing on thy growing work,
In which, constructed for a happier doom,
  No hasty marks of vain ambition lurk:
Thou may'st deride both Time's destructive sway,
  And baser Envy's beauty-mangling dirk:
Thy gorgeous fabric, planned with wise delay,
  Shall baffle foes more savage than the Turk:
As ages multiply, its fame shall rise,
And earth must perish ere its splendour dies.

[59] A Card of Invitation to Mr. Gibbon at Brighthelmstone, 1781.
An English sparrow, pert and free,
Who chirps beneath his native tree,
Hearing the Roman eagles near,
And feeling more respect than fear,
Thus, with united love and awe,
Invites him to his shed of straw.
  Tho' he is but a twittering sparrow,
The field he hops is rather narrow,
When nobler plumes attract his view
He ever pays them homage due,
He looks with reverential wonder,
On him whose talons bear the thunder;
Nor could the Jackdaws e'er inveigle
His voice to vilify the eagle,
Tho' issuing from the holy towers,
In which they build their warmest bowers,
Their sovereign's haunt they slyly search,
In hopes to catch him on his perch
(For Pindar says, beside his God
The thunder-bearing bird will nod),
Then, peeping round his still retreat,
They pick from underneath his feet
Some molted feather he lets fall,
And swear he cannot fly at all.—
  Lord of the sky! whose pounce can tear
These croakers, that infest the air,
Trust him! the sparrow loves to sing
The praise of thy imperial wing!
He thinks thou'lt deem him, on his word,
An honest, though familiar bird;
And hopes thou soon wilt condescend
To look upon thy little friend;
That he may boast around his grove
A visit from the bird of Jove.

instructor of youth (*Essay on the Genius and Writings of Pope*, pp. 322–4). (3) My English text is chaste, and all licentious passages are left in the obscurity of a learned language. *Le Latin dans ses mots brave l'honnêteté,* says the correct Boileau, in a country and idiom more scrupulous than our own. Yet, upon the whole, the *History of the Decline and Fall* seems to have struck root, both at home and abroad, and may, perhaps, a hundred years hence still continue to be abused. I am less flattered by Mr. Porson's high encomium on the style and spirit of my history, than I am satisfied with his honourable testimony to my attention, diligence, and accuracy; those humble virtues, which religious zeal had most audaciously denied. . . .

The French, Italian, and German translations have been executed with various success; but, instead of patronizing, I should willingly suppress such imperfect copies, which injure the character, while they propagate the name of the author. The first volume had been feebly, though faithfully, translated into French by M. Le Clerc de Septchenes, a young gentleman of a studious character and liberal fortune. After his decease the work was continued by two manufacturers of Paris, MM. Desmuniers and Cantwell: but the former is now an active member of the National Assembly, and the undertaking languishes in the hands of his associate. The superior merit of the interpreter, or his language, inclines me to prefer the Italian version: but I wish that it were in my power to read the German, which is praised by the best judges. The Irish pirates are at once my friends and my enemies. But I cannot be displeased with the too numerous and correct impressions which have been published for the use of the Continent at Basil in Switzerland.[60] The conquests of our language and literature are not confined to Europe alone, and a writer who succeeds in London is speedily read on the banks of the Delaware and the Ganges.

In the preface of the fourth volume, while I gloried in the name of an Englishman, I announced my approaching return to the neighbourhood of the Lake of Lausanne. This last trial confirmed my assurance that I had wisely chosen for my own happiness; nor did I once, in a year's visit, entertain a wish of settling in my native country. Britain is the free and fortunate island; but where is the spot in which I could unite the comforts and beauties of my establishment at Lausanne? The tumult of London astonished my eyes and ears; the amusements of public places were no longer adequate to the trouble; the clubs and assemblies were filled with new faces and young men; and our best society, our long and late dinners, would soon have been prejudicial to my health. Without any share in the political wheel, I must be idle and insignificant: yet the most splendid temptations would not have enticed me to engage a second time in the servitude of Parliament or office. At Tunbridge, some weeks after the publication of my *History,* I reluctantly quitted Lord and Lady Sheffield, and, with a young Swiss friend[61], whom I had introduced to the English world, I pursued the road of Dover and Lausanne. My habitation was embellished in my absence, and the last division of books, which followed my steps, increased my chosen library to the number of between six and seven thousand volumes. My seraglio was ample, my choice was free, my appetite was keen. After a full repast on Homer and Aristophanes, I involved myself in the philosophic maze of the writings of Plato, of which the dramatic is, perhaps, more interesting than the argumentative part: but I stepped aside into every path of inquiry which reading or reflection accidentally opened.

Alas! the joy of my return, and my studious ardour, were soon damped by the melancholy state of my friend Mr. Deyverdun. His health and spirits had long suffered a gradual decline, a succession of apoplectic fits announced his dissolution, and before he ex-

---

[60] Of their fourteen octavo volumes, the two last include the whole body of the notes. The public importunity had forced *me* to remove them from the end of the volume to the bottom of the page; but I have often repented of my compliance.

[61] M. Wilhelm de Severy. S.

pired, those who loved him could not wish for the continuance of his life. The voice of reason might congratulate his deliverance, but the feelings of nature and friendship could be subdued only by time: his amiable character was still alive in my remembrance; each room, each walk, was imprinted with out common footsteps; and I should blush at my own philosophy, if a long interval of study had not preceded and followed the death of my friend. By his last will he left to me the option of purchasing his house and garden, or of possessing them during my life, on the payment either of a stipulated price, or of an easy retribution to his kinsman and heir. I should probably have been tempted by the demon of property, if some legal difficulties had not been started against my title; a contest would have been vexatious, doubtful, and invidious; and the heir most gratefully subscribed an agreement, which rendered my life-possession more perfect, and his future condition more advantageous. Yet I had often revolved the judicious lines in which Pope answers the objections of his long-sighted friend:

Pity to build without or child or wife;
Why, you'll enjoy it only all your life:
Well, if the use be mine, does it concern one,
Whether the name belong to Pope or Vernon? *

The certainty of my tenure has allowed me to lay out a considerable sum in improvements and alterations: they have been executed with skill and taste; and few men of letters, perhaps, in Europe, are so desirably lodged as myself. But I feel, and with the decline of years I shall more painfully feel, that I am alone in paradise. Among the circle of my acquaintance at Lausanne, I have gradually acquired the solid and tender friendship of a respectable family[62]; the four persons of whom it is composed are all endowed with the virtues best adapted to their age and situation; and I am encouraged to love the parents as a brother, and the children as a father. Every day we seek and find the opportunities of meeting: yet even this valuable connexion cannot supply the loss of domestic society.

Within the last two or three years our tranquillity has been clouded by the disorders of France; many families at Lausanne were alarmed and affected by the terrors of an impending bankruptcy; but the revolution, or rather the dissolution of the kingdom, has been heard and felt in the adjacent lands.

I beg leave to subscribe my assent to Mr. Burke's creed on the revolution of France. I admire his eloquence, I approve his politics, I adore his chivalry, and I can almost excuse his reverence for church establishments. I have sometimes though of writing a dialogue of the dead, in which Lucian, Erasmus, and Voltaire should mutually acknowledge the danger of exposing an old superstition to the contempt of the blind and fanatic multitude.

A swarm of emigrants of both sexes, who escaped from the public ruin, has been attracted by the vicinity, the manners, and the language of Lausanne; and our narrow habitations in town and country are now occupied by the first names and titles of the departed monarchy. These noble fugitives are entitled to our pity; they may claim our esteem, but they cannot, in their present state of mind and fortune, much contribute to our amusement. Instead of looking down as calm and idle spectators on the theatre of Europe, our domestic harmony is somewhat embittered by the infusion of party spirit: our ladies and gentlemen assume the character of self-taught politicians; and the sober dictates of wisdom and experience are silenced by the clamour of the triumphant *democrates*. The fanatic missionaries of sedition have scattered the seeds of discontent in our cities and villages, which have flourished above two hundred and fifty years without fearing the approach of war or feeling the weight of government. Many individuals, and some communities, appear to be infected with the Gallic frenzy, the wild theories of equal and boundless freedom; but I trust that the body

---

* Alexander Pope, *Imitations of Horace*, ii, 2:163.
[62] The family of de Severy. S.

of the people will be faithful to their sovereign and to themselves; and I am satisfied that the failure or success of a revolt would equally terminate in the ruin of the country. While the aristocracy of Berne protects the happiness, it is superfluous to inquire whether it be founded in the rights of man: the economy of the State is liberally supplied without the aid of taxes; and the magistrates *must* reign with prudence and equity, since they are unarmed in the midst of an armed nation.

The revenue of Berne, excepting some small duties, is derived from church lands, tithes, feudal rights, and interest of money. The republic has nearly £500,000 sterling in English funds, and the amount of their treasure is unknown to the citizens themselves. For myself (may the omen be averted!) I can only declare that the first stroke of a rebel drum would be the signal of my immediate departure.

When I contemplate the common lot of mortality, I must acknowledge that I have drawn a high prize in the lottery of life. The far greater part of the globe is overspread with barbarism or slavery: in the civilized world, the most numerous class is condemned to ignorance and poverty; and the double fortune of my birth is a free and enlightened country, in an honourable and wealthy family, is the lucky chance of an unit against millions. The general probability is about three to one that a new-born infant will not live to complete his fiftieth year.[63] I have now passed that age, and may fairly estimate the present value of my existence in the threefold division of mind, body, and estate.

(1) The first and indispensable requisite of happiness is a clear conscience, unsullied by the reproach or remembrance of an unworthy action.

——*Hic murus aheneus esto,*
Nil conscire sibi, nulla pallescere culpa.[*]

I am endowed with a cheerful temper, a moderate sensibility, and a natural disposition to repose rather than to activity: some mischievous appetites and habits have perhaps been corrected by philosophy or time. The love of study, a passion which derives fresh vigour from enjoyment, supplies each day, each hour, with a perpetual source of independent and rational pleasure; and I am not sensible of any decay of the mental faculties. The original soil has been highly improved by cultivation; but it may be questioned whether some flowers of fancy, some grateful errors, have not been eradicated with the weeds of prejudice. (2) Since I have escaped from the long perils of my childhood, the serious advice of a physician has seldom been requisite. 'The madness of superfluous health' I have never known, but my tender constitution has been fortified by time, and the inestimable gift of the sound and peaceful slumbers of infancy may be imputed both to the mind and body. (3) I have already described the merits of my society and situation; but these enjoyments would be tasteless or bitter if their possession were not assured by an annual and adequate supply. According to the scale of Switzerland, I am a rich man; and I am indeed rich, since my income is superior to my expense, and my expense is equal to my wishes. My friend Lord Sheffield has kindly relieved me from the cares to which my taste and temper are most adverse: shall I add, that since the failure of my first wishes, I have never entertained any serious thoughts of a matrimonial connexion?

I am disgusted with the affectation of men of letters, who complain that they have renounced a substance for a shadow, and that their fame (which sometimes is no insupportable weight) affords a poor compensation for envy, censure, and persecution.[64] My own ex-

---

[63] See Buffon, *Supplement à l'Histoire Naturelle*, tom. vii, pp. 158–64: Of a given number of new-born infants, one half, by the fault of nature or man, is extinguished before the age of puberty and reason—a melancholy calculation!

[*] Horace *Epistles.* 1. 1. 60–61. [Let this be our wall of bronze: a clear conscience and no fault to make us pale]—Ed.

[64] Mr. d'Alembert relates, that as he was walking in the gardens of Sans Souci with the King of

perience, at least, has taught me a very different lesson; twenty happy years have been animated by the labour of my *History,* and its success has given me a name, a rank, a character, in the world, to which I should not otherwise have been entitled. The freedom of my writings has indeed provoked an implacable tribe; but, as I was safe from the stings, I was soon accustomed to the buzzing of the hornets: my nerves are not tremblingly alive, and my literary temper is so happily framed, that I am less sensible of pain than of pleasure. The rational pride of an author may be offended, rather than flattered, by vague indiscriminate praise; but he cannot, he should not, be indifferent to the fair testimonies of private and public esteem. Even his moral sympathy may be gratified by the idea, that now, in the present hour, he is imparting some degree of amusement or knowledge to his friends in a distant land: that one day his mind will be familiar to the grandchildren of those who are yet unborn.[65] I cannot boast of the friendship or favour of princes; the patronage of English literature has long since been devolved on our booksellers, and the measure of their liberality is the least ambiguous test of our common success. Perhaps the golden mediocrity of my fortune has contributed to fortify my application.

The present is a fleeting moment, the past is no more; and our prospect of futurity is dark and doubtful. This day may *possibly* be my last: but the laws of probability, so true in general, so fallacious in particular, still allow about fifteen years.[66] I shall soon enter into the period which, as the most agreeable of his long life, was selected by the judgement and experience of the sage Fontenelle. His choice is approved by the eloquent historian of nature, who fixes our moral happiness to the mature season in which our passions are supposed to be calmed, our duties fulfilled, our ambition satisfied, our fame and fortune established on a solid basis.[67] In private conversation, that great and amiable man added the weight of his own experience; and this autumnal felicity might be exemplified in the lives of Voltaire, Hume, and many other men of letters. I am far more inclined to embrace than to dispute this comfortable doctrine. I will not suppose any premature decay of the mind or body; but I must reluctantly observe the two causes, the abbreviation of time, and the failure of hope, will always tinge with a browner shade the evening of life.[68]

Prussia, Frederic said to him, 'Do you see that old woman, a poor weeder, asleep on that sunny bank? she is probably a more happy being than either of us.' The king and the philosopher may speak for themselves; for my part I do not envy the old woman.

[65] In the first of ancient or modern romances (*Tom Jones*), this proud sentiment, this feast of fancy, is enjoyed by the genius of Fielding.— 'Come, bright love of fame, &c., fill my ravished fancy with the hopes of charming ages yet to come. Foretell me that some tender maid, whose grandmother is yet unborn, hereafter, when, under the fictitious name of Sophia, she reads the real worth which once existed in my Charlotte, shall from her sympathetic breast send forth a heaving sigh. Do thou teach me not only to foresee but to enjoy, nay even to feed on future praise. Comfort me by the solemn assurance, that, when the little parlour in which I sit at this moment shall be reduced to a worse furnished box, I shall be read with honour by those who never knew nor saw me, and whom I shall neither know nor see.' Book xiii, Chap. 1.

[66] Mr. Buffon, from our disregard of the possibility of death within the four and twenty hours, concludes that a chance, which falls below or rises above ten thousand to one, will never affect the hopes or fears of a reasonable man. The fact is true, but our courage is the effect of thoughtlessness, rather than of reflection. If a public lottery were drawn for the choice of an immediate victim, and if our name were incribed on one of the ten thousand tickets, should we be perfectly easy?

[67] See Buffon.

[68] The proportion of a part to the whole is the only standard by which we can measure the length of our existence. At the age of twenty, one year is a tenth, perhaps, of the time which has elapsed within our consciousness and memory: at the age of fifty it is no more than the fortieth, and this relative value continues to decrease till the last sands are shaken by the hand of death. This reasoning may seem metaphysical; but on a trial it will be found satisfactory and just. The warm desires, the long expectations of youth, are founded on the

ignorance of themselves and of the world: they are gradually damped by time and experience, by disappointment and possession; and after the middle season the crowd must be content to remain at the foot of the mountain; while the few who have climbed the summit aspire to descend or expect to fall. In old age, the consolation of hope is reserved for the tenderness of parents, who commence a new life in their children; the faith of enthusiasts, who sing Hallelujahs above the clouds; and the vanity of authors, who presume the immortality of their name and writings.

Candide

Voltaire

Editor's Introduction

The greatest French writer of his age—in some respects, perhaps, of any age—Voltaire was at once its most enlightened and its most subversive spirit. His enlightenment lay in his perception of the injustices of that age, its superstitions, its barbarities, even the enervated exactitude of its arts, to which he called attention with a pen so brilliant that the excitement of his words endures long after most of the objects of them have been forgotten. His subversions were less clearly beneficial. The civilization he attacked was in the end brought down by those who like himself sought to purge it of its defects, the tyranny he hated was given terrible occasion by the revolution he helped to bring about, the life of the mind was gravely damaged by his scorn of speculation, and the literary arts he called in question were overwhelmed by a Romanticism he lived to regret. Such results could be justified before the bar of heaven, or at least of history, only if the man who produced them was supremely serious, we may think. Whether Voltaire was that serious—whether, that is, he always knew how to mean what he said—is something that, whatever heaven's judgment may be, history is still considering.

Like Candide, the hero of his most famous tale, Voltaire was an exile and a wanderer for much of his life. The earliest of his exiles, brought about through a quarrel with a nobleman who had felt the sting of his satiric pen, provided an important lesson for him. Forced to spend three years (1726–29) in England, he discovered what he regarded as a country far more vigorous and enlightened (if in some ways also barbarous, to a Frenchman) than his own, characteristics he attributed to its tolerance of freedom of thought. The book he subsequently wrote about this, *Philosophical Letters on the British Nation* (1734), asserted the superiority of Locke and Newton over his countrymen, Descartes and Pascal—and the greater virtue, generally, of empirical as compared with *a priori* reasoning—on the conviction that human happiness is achieved not through introspection and penitence but through progess in the arts and sciences. The *Letters* thus embody not only "the philosophy of the 18th century," as the current *Encyclopædia Britannica* puts it, "but . . . also the essential direction of the modern mind."

Subsequent sojourns abroad, for the most part in Germany or Switzerland, occasioned by scandals in Voltaire's personal life or offenses he caused with his writings to both church and state in his own country, were longer, but hardly less productive. One of them, spent at Berlin under the protection of his protegé, Frederick the Great, saw the publication of his *History of the Century of Louis XIV* (1751), followed (in 1756) by his *Essay on Customs* — really a kind of world history from the fall of the Roman Empire — which, taken together, justify his reputation as the father of modern historical thought. He also offended opinion of the learned at Geneva, where he later repaired, by publishing a mock-heroic poem about St. Joan, as well as an account of the ministers of that city, intended for Diderot's Encyclopædia, which praised some of them for doubts as to the divinity of Christ. This pattern of extraordinary achievement accompanied by consistent but imprudent activities more appropriate to a mere troublemaker was repeated often throughout his career.

The works for which he is now chiefly remembered — and which, notwithstanding his innumerable plays, historical writings, and other works, are all that continue to be read — are the tales Voltaire began to write only after he was fifty. Of these, the best known are *Micromegas* (1752), treating of the presumption of man save as he acquires scientific knowledge, *Zadig* (1747), which says all Voltaire could think to say for the idea of a beneficent Providence, and *Candide, or Optimism* (1759). This was written following the devastating personal loss to him in the death of his mistress and collaborator, Mme du Châtelet, and also the shocking destruction of the Lisbon earthquake (1755), an event that had an unsettling effect upon his age somewhat like that of the atomic bomb upon our own.

Voltaire's last years were spent at Ferney, in Switzerland, near the French border, on an estate where he acted as lord of the manor, which he made a model of agricultural reform, and where he served as host to the learned of Europe who came to visit what was by then the most famous figure in the world. His writings of this period were directed against the bigotries and injustices of the day, especially those of the church, to the end of greater prosperity for both men and nations, and to the abolition of torture and judicial cruelty. His motto for these works was *"ecrasez l'enfame,"* which means "crush infamy," but which in effect was rendered some time later by Thomas Jefferson when he said that he had "sworn eternal hostility against every form of tyranny over the mind of man."

Ironically, it was not what he wrote but what he did that proved Voltaire's undoing. Always an activist, despising what he scorned as idle speculation, he took it upon himself, particularly during the years at Ferney, to give aid and comfort to victims of injustice and persecution whose cause he had defended with his pen. It was for this, more than for anything he had said, that he was given the frenzied hero's welcome he received in 1778, after his longest exile, upon his return to Paris, where he succumbed three months later, at the age of eighty-four, to exhaustion brought on by the endless festivities created in his honor.

Candide

I

How Candide Was Brought Up in a Fine Castle, and How He Was Expelled from Thence

There lived in Westphalia, in the castle of my Lord the Baron of Thunder-ten-tronckh, a young man, on whom nature had bestowed the most agreeable manners. His face was the index to his mind. He had an upright heart, with an easy frankness; which, I believe, was the reason he got the name of *Candide*. He was suspected, by the old servants of the family, to be the son of my Lord the Baron's sister, by a very honest gentleman of the neighborhood, whom the young lady declined to marry, because he could only produce seventy-one armorial quarterings; the rest of his genealogical tree having been destroyed through the injuries of time.

The Baron was one of the most powerful lords in Westphalia; his castle had both a gate and windows; and his great hall was even adorned with tapestry. The dogs of his outer yard composed his hunting pack upon occasion, his grooms were his huntsmen, and the vicar of the parish was his chief almoner. He was called My Lord by everybody, and everyone laughed when he told his stories.

My Lady the Baroness, who weighed about three hundred and fifty pounds, attracted, by that means, very great attention, and did the honors of the house with a dignity that rendered her still more respectable. Her daughter Cunegonde, aged about seventeen years, was of a ruddy complexion, fresh, plump, and well calculated to excite the passions. The Baron's son appeared to be in every respect worthy of his father. The preceptor, Pangloss, was the oracle of the house, and little Candide listened to his lectures with all the simplicity that was suitable to his age and character.

Pangloss taught metaphysico-theologo-cosmolonigology. He proved most admirably, that there could not be an effect without a cause; that, in this best of possible worlds, my Lord the Baron's castle was the most magnificent of castles, and my Lady the best of Baronesses that possibly could be.

"It is demonstrable," said he, "that things cannot be otherwise than they are: for all things having been made for some end, they must necessarily be for the best end. Observe well, that the nose has been made for carrying spectacles; therefore we have spectacles. The legs are visibly designed for stockings, and therefore we have stockings. Stones have been formed to be hewn, and make castles; therefore my Lord has a very fine castle; the greatest baron of the province ought to be the best accommodated. Swine were made to be eaten; therefore we eat pork all the year round: consequently, those who have merely asserted that all is good have said a very foolish thing; they should have said all is the best possible."

Candide listened attentively, and believed implicitly; for he thought Miss Cunegonde extremely handsome, though he never had the courage to tell her so. He concluded, that next to the good fortune of being Baron of Thunder-ten-tronckh, the second degree of happiness was that of being Miss Cunegonde, the third to see her every day, and the fourth to listen to the teachings of Master Pangloss, the greatest philosopher of the province, and consequently of the whole world.

One day Cunegonde having taken a walk in the environs of the castle, in a little wood, which they called a park, espied Doctor Pangloss giving a lesson in experimental philosophy to her mother's chambermaid; a little brown wench, very handsome, and very docile. As Miss Cunegonde had a strong inclination for the sciences, she observed, without making any noise, the reiterated experiments that were going on before her eyes; she saw very clearly the sufficient reason of the Doctor, the effects and the causes; and she returned greatly flurried, quite pensive, and full of desire to be learned; imagining that she might be a sufficient reason for young Candide, who also, might be the same to her.

On her return to the castle, she met Candide, and blushed; Candide also blushed; she wished him good morrow with a faltering voice, and Candide answered her, hardly knowing what he said. The next day, after dinner, as they arose from table, Cunegonde and Candide happened to get behind the screen. Cunegonde dropped her handkerchief, and Candide picked it up; she, not thinking any harm, took hold of his hand; and the young man, not thinking any harm either, kissed the hand of the young lady, with an eagerness, a sensibility, and grace, very particular; their lips met, their eyes sparkled, their knees trembled, their hands strayed.—The Baron of Thunder-ten-tronckh happening to pass close by the screen, and observing this cause and effect, thrust Candide out of the castle, with lusty kicks. Cunegonde fell into a swoon and as soon as she came to herself, was heartily cuffed on the ears by my Lady the Baroness. Thus all was thrown into confusion in the finest and most agreeable castle possible.

II
What Became of Candide among the Bulgarians

Candide being expelled the terrestrial paradise, rambled a long while without knowing where, weeping, and lifting up his eyes to heaven, and sometimes turning them towards the finest of castles, which contained the handsomest of baronesses. He laid himself down, without his supper, in the open field, between two furrows, while the snow fell in great flakes. Candide, almost frozen to death, crawled next morning to the neighboring village, which was called Walberghoff-trarbk-dikdorff. Having no money, and almost dying with hunger and fatigue, he stopped in a directed posture before the gate of an inn. Two men, dressed in blue, observing him in such a situation, "Brother," says one of them to the other, "there is a young fellow well built, and of a proper height." They accosted Candide, and invited him very civilly to dinner.

"Gentlemen," replied Candide, with an agreeable modesty, "you do me much honor, but I have no money to pay my shot."

"O sir," said one of the blues, "persons of your appearance and merit never pay anything; are you not five feet five inches high?"

"Yes, gentlemen, that is my height," returned he, making a bow.

"Come, sir, sit down at table; we will not only treat you, but we will never let such a man as you want money; men are made to assist one another."

"You are in the right," said Candide; "that is what Pangloss always told me, and I see plainly that everything is for the best."

They entreated him to take a few crowns, which he accepted, and would have given them his note; but they refused it, and sat down to table.

"Do not you tenderly love—?"

"O yes," replied he, "I tenderly love Miss Cunegonde."

"No," said one of the gentlemen; "we ask you if you do tenderly love the King of the Bulgarians?"

"Not at all," said he, "for I never saw him."

"How! he is the most charming of kings, and you must drink his health."

"O, with all my heart, gentlemen," and drinks.

"That is enough," said they to him; "you are now the bulwark, the support, the defender, the hero of the Bulgarians; your for-

"The Baron of Thunder-ten-tronckh happening to pass close by the screen, and observing this cause and effect, thrust Candide out of the castle, with lusty kicks."

tune is made, and you are certain of glory." Instantly they put him in irons, and carried him to the regiment. They made him turn to the right, to the left, draw the rammer, return the rammer, present, fire, step double; and they gave him thirty blows with a cudgel. The next day, he performed his exercises not quite so badly, and received but twenty blows; the third day the blows were restricted to ten, and he was looked upon by his fellow-soldiers as a kind of prodigy.

Candide, quite stupefied, could not well conceive how he had become a hero. One fine Spring day he took it into his head to walk out, going straight forward, imagining that the human, as well as the animal species, were entitled to make whatever use they pleased of their limbs. He had not travelled two leagues, when four other heroes, six feet high, came up to him, bound him, and put him into a dungeon. He is asked by a Court-martial, whether he chooses to be whipped six and thirty times through the whole regiment, or receive at once twelve bullets through the forehead? He in vain argued that the will is free, and that he chose neither the one nor the other; he was obliged to make a choice; he therefore resolved, in virtue of God's gift called *free-will*, to run the gauntlet six and thirty times. He underwent this discipline twice. The regiment being composed of two thousand men, he received four thousand lashes, which laid open all his muscles and nerves from the nape of the neck to the back. As they were proceeding to a third course, Candide, being quite spent, begged as a favor that they would be so kind as to shoot him; he obtained his request; they hoodwinked him, and made him kneel; the King of the Bulgarians, passing by, inquired into the crime of the delinquent; and as this prince was a person of great penetration, he discovered from what he heard of Candide, that he was a young metaphysician, entirely ignorant of the things of this world; and he granted him his pardon, with a clemency which will be extolled in all histories, and throughout all ages. An experienced surgeon cured Candide in three weeks, with emollients prescribed by no less master than Dioscorides. His skin had already begun to grow again, and he was able to walk, when the King of the Bulgarians gave battle to the King of the Abares.

III
How Candide Made His Escape from the Bulgarians, and What Afterwards Befell Him

Nothing could be so fine, so neat, so brilliant, so well ordered, as the two armies. The trumpets, fifes, hautboys, drums, and cannon,

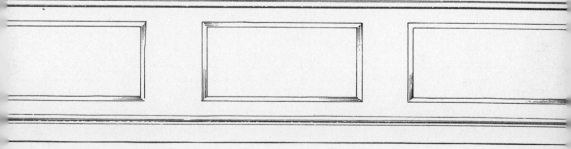

formed an harmony superior to what hell itself could invent. The cannon swept off at first about six thousand men on each side; afterwards, the musketry carried away from the best of worlds, about nine or ten thousand rascals that infected its surface. The bayonet was likewise the sufficient reason of the death of some thousands of men. The whole number might amount to about thirty thousand souls. Candide, who trembled like a philosopher, hid himself as well as he could, during this heroic butchery.

At last, while each of the two kings were causing *Te Deum*—glory to God—to be sung in their respective camps, he resolved to go somewhere else, to reason upon the effects and causes. He walked over heaps of the dead and dying; he came at first to a neighboring village belonging to the Abares, but found it in ashes; for it had been burnt by the Bulgarians, according to the law of nations. Here were to be seen old men full of wounds, casting their eyes on their murdered wives, who were holding their infants to their bloody breasts. You might see in another place virgins outraged after they had satisfied the natural desires of some of those heroes, whilst breathing out their last sighs. Others, half-burnt, praying earnestly for instant death. The whole field was covered with brains, and with legs and arms lopped off.

Candide betook himself with all speed to another village. It belonged to the Bulgarians, and had met with the same treatment from the Arabian heroes. Candide, walking still forward over quivering limbs, or through rubbish of houses, got at last out of the theatre of war, having some small quantity of provisions in his knapsack, and never forgetting Miss Cunegonde. His provisions failed him when he arrived in Holland; but having heard that every one was rich in that country, and that they were Christians, he did not doubt but he should be as well treated there as he had been in my Lord the Baron's castle, before he had been expelled thence on account of Miss Cunegonde's sparkling eyes.

He asked alms from several grave looking persons, who all replied, that if he continued that trade, they would confine him in a house of correction, where he should learn to earn his bread.

He replied afterwards to a man, who for a whole hour had been discoursing on the subject of charity, before a large assembly. This orator, looking at him askance, said to him: "What are you doing here? Are you for the good cause?"

"There is no effect without a cause," replied Candide, modestly; "all is necessarily linked, and ordered for the best. A necessity banished me from Miss Cunegonde; a necessity forced me to run the gauntlet; another necessity makes me beg my bread, till I can get into some business by which to earn it. All this could not be otherwise."

"My friend," said the orator to him, "do you believe that the Anti-Christ is alive?"

"I never heard whether he is or not," replied Candide; "but whether he is, or is not, I want bread!"

"You do not deserve to eat," said the other; "get you gone, you rogue; get you gone, you wretch; never in thy life come near me again!"

The orator's wife, having popped her head out of the chamber window, and seeing a man who doubted whether Anti-Christ was alive, poured on his head a full vessel of dirty water. Oh heavens! to what excess does religious zeal transport the fair sex!

A man who had not been baptized, a good Anabaptist, named *James*, saw the barbarous and ignominious manner with which they treated one of his brethren, a being with two feet, without feathers, and endowed with a rational soul. He took him home with him, cleaned him, gave him bread and beer, made him a present of two florins, and offered to teach him the method of working in his manufactories of Persian stuffs, which are fabricated in Holland. Candide, prostrating himself almost to the ground, cried out, "Master Pangloss argued well when he said that everything is for the best in this world; for I am infinitely more affected with your very great generosity, than by the hard-heartedness of that gentleman with the cloak, and the lady his wife."

Next day, as he was taking a walk, he met a beggar, all covered over with sores, his eyes half dead, the tip of his nose eaten off, his mouth turned to one side of his face, his teeth black, speaking through his throat, tormented with a violent cough, with gums so rotten, that his teeth came near falling out every time he spit.

IV
How Candide Met His Old Master of Philosophy, Dr. Pangloss, and What Happened to Them

Candide moved still more with compassion than with horror, gave this frightful mendicant the two florins which he had received of his honest Anabaptist James. The spectre fixed his eyes attentively upon him, dropt some tears, and was going to fall upon his neck. Candide, affrighted, drew back.

"Alas!" said the one wretch to the other, "don't you know your dear Pangloss?"

"What do I hear! Is it you, my dear master! you in this dreadful condition! What misfortune has befallen you? Why are you no longer in the most magnificent of castles? What has become of Miss Cunegonde, the nonpareil of the fair sex, the master-piece of nature?"

"I have no more strength," said Pangloss.

Candide immediately carried him to the Anabaptist's stable, where he gave him a little bread to eat. When Pangloss was refreshed a little, "Well," said Candide, "what has become of Cunegonde?"

"She is dead," replied the other.

Candide fainted away at this word; but his friend recovered his senses, with a little bad vinegar which he found by chance in the stable.

Candide, opening his eyes, cried out, "Cunegonde is dead! Ah, best of worlds, where art thou now? But of what distemper did she die? Was not the cause her seeing me

driven out of the castle by my Lord, her father, with such hard kicks on the breech?"

"No," said Pangloss, "she was gutted by some Bulgarian soldiers, after having been barbarously ravished. They knocked my Lord the Baron on the head for attempting to protect her; my Lady the Baroness was cut in pieces; my poor pupil was treated like his sister; and as for the castle, there is not one stone left upon another, nor a barn, nor a sheep, nor a duck, nor a tree. But we have been sufficiently revenged; for the Abarians have done the very same thing to a neighboring barony, which belonged to a Bulgarian Lord."

At this discourse, Candide fainted away a second time, but coming to himself, and having said all that he ought to say, he enquired into the cause and the effect, and into the sufficient reason that had reduced Pangloss to so deplorable a condition. "Alas," said the other, "it was love; love, the comforter of the human race, the preserver of the universe, the soul of all sensible beings, tender love." "Alas!" said Candide, "I know this love, the sovereign of hearts, the soul of our soul; yet it never cost me more than a kiss, and twenty kicks. But how could this charming cause produce in you so abominable an effect?"

Pangloss made answer as follows: "Oh my dear Candide, you knew Paquetta, the pretty attendant on our noble Baroness; I tasted in her arms the delights of Paradise, which produced those torments of hell with which you see me devoured. She was infected, and perhaps she is dead. Paquetta received this present from a very learned cavalier, who had it from an old countess, who received it from a captain of horse, who was indebted for it to a marchioness, who got it from a Spaniard. For my part, I shall give it to nobody, for I am dying."

"Oh Pangloss!" cried Candide, "what a strange genealogy! Was not the devil at the head of it?" "Not at all," replied the great man; "it was a thing indispensable; a necessary ingredient in the best of worlds; for if the Spaniard had not catched, in an island of America, this distemper, we should have had

"What do I hear! Is it you, my dear master! you in this dreadful condition!
What misfortune has befallen you?"

neither chocolate nor cochineal. It may also be observed, that to this day, upon our continent, this malady is as peculiar to us, as is religious controversy. The Turks, the Indians, the Persians, the Chinese, the Siamese, and the Japanese know nothing of it yet. But there is sufficient reason why they, in their turn, should become acquainted with it, a few centuries hence. In the mean time, it has made marvellous progress among us, and especially in those great armies composed of honest hirelings, well disciplined, who decide the fate of states; for we may rest assured, that when thirty thousand men in a pitched battle fight against troops equal to them in number, there are about twenty thousand of them on each side who have the pox."

"That is admirable," said Candide; "but you must be cured." "Ah! how can I?" said Pangloss; "I have not a penny, my friend; and throughout the whole extent of this globe, we cannot get any one to bleed us, or give us a glister, without paying for it, or getting some other person to pay for us."

This last speech determined Candide. He went and threw himself at the feet of his charitable Anabaptist James, and gave him so touching a description of the state his friend was reduced to, that the good man did not hesitate to entertain Dr. Pangloss, and he had him cured at his own expense. During the cure, Pangloss lost only an eye and an ear. As he wrote well, and understood arithmetic perfectly, the Anabaptist made him his bookkeeper. At the end of two months, being obliged to go to Lisbon on account of his business, he took the two philosophers along with him, in his ship. Pangloss explained to him how every thing was such as it could not be better; but James was not of this opinion. "Mankind," said he, "must have somewhat corrupted their nature, for they were not born wolves, and yet they have become wolves; God has given them neither cannon of twenty-four pounds, nor bayonets; and yet they have made cannon and bayonets to destroy one another: I might throw into the account bankrupts; and the law which seizes on the effects of bankrupts only to bilk the creditors." "All this was indispensable," replied the one-eyed doctor, "and private misfortunes constitute the general good; so that the more private misfortunes there are, the whole is better." While he was thus reasoning, the air grew dark, the winds blew from the four quarters of the world, and the ship was attacked by a dreadful storm, within sight of the harbor of Lisbon.

V
Tempest, Shipwreck, Earthquake and What Became of Dr. Pangloss, Candide and James the Anabaptist

One half of the passengers being weakened, and ready to breathe their last, with the inconceivable anguish which the rolling of the ship conveyed through the nerves and all the humors of the body, which were quite disordered, were not capable of being alarmed at the danger they were in. The other half uttered cries and made prayers; the sails were rent, the masts broken, and the ship became leaky. Every one worked that was able, nobody cared for any thing, and no order was kept. The Anabaptist contributed his assistance to work the ship. As he was upon deck, a furious sailor rudely struck him, and laid him sprawling on the planks; but with the blow he gave him, he himself was so violently jolted, that he tumbled overboard with his head foremost, and remained suspended by a piece of a broken mast. Honest James ran to his assistance, and helped him on deck again; but in the attempt, he fell into the sea, in the sight of the sailor, who suffered him to perish, without deigning to look upon him. Candide drew near and saw his benefactor, one moment emerging, and the next swallowed up for ever. He was just going to throw himself into the sea after him, when the philosopher Pangloss hindered him, by demonstrating to him, that the road to Lisbon had been made on purpose for this Anabaptist to be drowned in. While he was proving this, *a priori,* the vessel foundered, and all perished except Pangloss, Candide, and the brutal sailor, who drowned the virtuous Anabaptist. The villain luckily swam ashore, whither Pangloss and Candide were carried on a plank.

When they had recovered themselves a little, they walked towards Lisbon. They had some money left, with which they hoped to save themselves from hunger, after having escaped from the storm.

Scarce had they set foot in the city, bewailing the death of their benefactor, when they perceived the earth to tremble under their feet, and saw the sea swell in the harbor, and dash to pieces the ships that were at anchor. The whirling flames and ashes covered the streets and public places, the houses tottered, and their roofs fell to the foundations, and the foundations were scattered; thirty thousand inhabitants of all ages and sexes were crushed to death in the ruins. The sailor, whistling and swearing, said: "There is some booty to be got here." "What can be the sufficient reason for this phenomenon?" said Pangloss. "This is certainly the last day of the world," cried Candide. The sailor ran quickly into the midst of the ruins, encountered death to find money, found it, laid hold of it, got drunk, and having slept himself sober, purchased the favors of the first willing girl he met with, among the ruins of the demolished houses, and in the midst of the dying and the dead. While he was thus engaged, Pangloss pulled him by the sleeve. "My friend," said he, "this is not right; you trespass against universal reason, you choose your time badly." "Brains and blood!" answered the other; "I am a sailor, and was born at Batavia; you have mistaken your man, this time, with your universal reason."

Some pieces of stone having wounded Candide, he lay sprawling in the street, and covered with rubbish. "Alas!" said he to Pangloss, "get me a little wine and oil; I am dying." "This trembling of the earth is no new thing," answered Pangloss. "The City of Lima, in America, experienced the same concussions last year; the same cause has the same effects; there is certainly a train of sulphur under the earth, from Lima to Lisbon." "Nothing is more probable," said Candide; "but, for God's sake, a little oil and wine." "How probable?" replied the philosopher; "I maintain that the thing is demonstrable." Candide lost all sense, and Pangloss brought him a little water from a neighboring fountain.

The day following, having found some provisions, in rummaging through the rubbish, they recruited their strength a little. Afterwards, they employed themselves like others, in administering relief to the inhabitants that had escaped from death. Some citizens that had been relieved by them gave them as good a dinner as could be expected amidst such a disaster. It is true that the repast was mournful, and the guests watered their bread with their tears. But Pangloss consoled them by the assurance that things could not be otherwise, "For," said he, "all this must necessarily be for the best. As this volcano is at Lisbon, it could not be elsewhere; as it is impossible that things should not be what they are, as all is good."

A little man clad in black, who belonged to the inquisition, and sat at his side, took him up very politely, and said: "It seems, sir, you do not believe in original sin; for if all is for the best, then there has been neither fall nor punishment."

"I most humbly ask your excellency's pardon," answered Pangloss, still more politely; "for the fall of man and the curse necessarily entered into the best of worlds possible." "Then, sir, you do not believe there is liberty," said the inquisitor. "Your excellency will excuse me," said Pangloss; "liberty can consist with absolute necessity; for it was necessary we should be free; because, in short, the determinate will—"

Pangloss was in the middle of his proposition, when the inquisitor made a signal with his head to the tall armed footman in a cloak, who waited upon him, to bring him a glass of port wine.

VI

How a Fine Inquisition Was Celebrated to Prevent Earthquakes, and How Candide Was Whipped

After the earthquake, which had destroyed three-fourths of Lisbon, the sages of the country could not find any means more effectual to prevent a total destruction, than to give the people a splendid inquisition. It had been decided by the university of Coimbra, that the spectacle of some persons burnt to death by a slow fire, with great ceremony, was an infallible antidote for earthquakes.

In consequence of this resolution, they had seized a Biscayan, convicted of having married his godmother, and two Portuguese, who, in eating a pullet, had stripped off the lard. After dinner, they came and secured Dr. Pangloss, and his disciple Candide; the one for having spoken too freely, and the other for having heard with an air of approbation. They were both conducted to separate apartments, extremely damp, and never incommoded with the sun. Eight days after, they were both clothed with a gown and had their heads—adorned with paper crowns. Candide's crown and gown were painted with inverted flames, and with devils that had neither tails nor claws; but Pangloss' devils had claws and tails, and the flames were pointed upwards. Being thus dressed, they marched in procession, and heard a very pathetic speech followed by fine music on a squeaking organ. Candide was whipped on the back in cadence, while they were singing; the Biscayan, and the two men who would not eat lard, were burnt; and Pangloss, though it was contrary to custom, was hanged. The same day, the earth shook anew, with a most dreadful noise.

Candide, affrighted, interdicted, astonished, all bloody, all panting, said to himself: "If this is the best of possible worlds, what then are the rest? Supposing I had not been whipped now, I have been so, among the Bulgarians; but, oh, my dear Pangloss, thou greatest of philosophers, that it should be my fate to see thee hanged without knowing for what! Oh! my dear Anabaptist! thou best of men, that it should be thy fate to be drowned in the harbor! Oh! Miss Cunegonde! the jewel of ladies, that it should be thy fate to have been outraged and slain!"

He returned, with difficulty, supporting himself, after being lectured, whipped, absolved, and blessed, when an old woman accosted him, and said: "Child, take courage, and follow me."

VII

How an Old Woman Took Care of Candide, and How He Found the Object He Loved

Candide did not take courage, but he followed the old woman to a ruinated house. She gave him a pot of pomatum to anoint himself, left him something to eat and drink, and showed him a very neat little bed, near which was a complete suit of clothes. "Eat, drink, and sleep," said she to him, "and may God take care of you. I will be back to-morrow." Candide, astonished at all he had seen, at all he had suffered, and still more at the charity of the old woman, offered to kiss her hand. "You must not kiss my hand," said the old woman, "I will be back to-morrow. Rub yourself with the pomatum, eat and take rest."

Candide, notwithstanding so many misfortunes, ate, and went to sleep. Next morning, the old woman brought him his breakfast, looked at his back, and rubbed it herself with another ointment; she afterwards brought him his dinner; and she returned at night, and brought him his supper. The day following she performed the same ceremonies. "Who are you?" would Candide always say to her. "Who has inspired you with so much goodness? What thanks can I render you?" The good woman made no answer; she returned in the evening, but brought him no supper. "Come along with me," said she,

"Eight days after, they were both clothed with a gown and had their heads—adorned with paper crowns. Candide's crown and gown were painted with inverted flames, and with devils that had neither tails nor claws; but Pangloss' devils had claws and tails, and the flames were pointed upwards."

"and say not a word." She took him by the arm, and walked with him into the country about a quarter of a mile; they arrived at a house that stood by itself; surrounded with gardens and canals. The old woman knocked at a little door, which being opened, she conducted Candide by a private stair-case into a gilded closet, and leaving him on a brocade couch, shut the door and went her way. Candide thought he was in a revery, and looked upon all his life as an unlucky dream, but at the present moment, a very agreeable vision.

The old woman returned very soon supporting with difficulty a woman trembling, of a majestic port, glittering with jewels, and covered with a veil. "Take off that veil," said the old woman to Candide. The young man approached and took off the veil with a trembling hand. What joy! what surprise! he thought he saw Miss Cunegonde; he saw her indeed! It was she herself. His strength failed him, he could not utter a word, but fell down at her feet. Cunegonde fell upon the carpet. The old woman applied aromatic waters; they recovered their senses, and spoke to one another. At first, their words were broken, their questions and answers crossed each other, amidst sighs, tears and cries. The old woman recommended them to make less noise, and then left them to themselves. "How! is it you?" said Candide; "are you still alive? do I find you again in Portugal? You were not ravished then, as the philosopher Pangloss assured me?" "Yes, all this was so," said the lovely Cunegonde; "but death does not always follow from these two accidents." "But your father and mother! were they not killed?" "It is but too true," answered Cunegonde, weeping. "And your brother?" "My brother was killed too." "And why are you in Portugal? And how did you know that I was here? and by what strange adventure did you contrive to bring me to this house?" "I will tell you all that, presently," replied the lady; "but first you must inform me of all that has happened to you, since the harmless kiss you gave me, and the rude kicking which you received for it."

Candide obeyed her with the most profound respect; and though he was forbidden to speak, though his voice was weak and faltering, and though his back still pained him, yet he related to her, in the most artless manner, every thing that had befallen him since the moment of their separation. Cunegonde lifted up her eyes to heaven; she shed tears at the death of the good Anabaptist, and of Pangloss; after which she thus related her adventures to Candide, who lost not a word, but looked on her, as if he would devour her with his eyes.

VIII
The History of Cunegonde

"I was in my bed and fast asleep, when it pleased heaven to send the Bulgarians to our fine castle of Thunder-ten-tronckh; they murdered my father and my brother, and cut my mother to pieces. A huge Bulgarian, six feet high, perceiving the horrible sight had deprived me of my senses, set himself to ravish me. This abuse made me come to myself; I recovered my senses, I cried, I struggled, I bit, I scratched, I wanted to tear out the huge Bulgarian's eyes, not considering that what had happened in my father's castle was a common thing in war. The brute gave me a cut with his hanger, the mark of which I still bear about me." "Ah! I anxiously wish to see it," said the simple Candide. "You shall," answered Cunegonde; "but let me finish my story." "Do so," replied Candide.

She then resumed the thread of her story, as follows: "A Bulgarian captain came in, and saw me bleeding; but the soldier was not at all disconcerted. The Captain flew into a passion at the little respect the brute showed him, and killed him upon my body. He then caused me to be dressed, and carried me as a prisoner of war to his own quarters. I washed the scanty linen he had, and cooked his victuals. He found me very pretty, I must say it; and I cannot deny but he was well shaped, and that he had a white, soft skin; but for the rest, he had little sense or philosophy; one could plainly see that he was not bred under Dr. Pangloss. At the end of three months, having lost all his money, and being grown out of conceit with me, he sold me to a Jew, named *Don Issachar,* who traded to Holland and Portugal, and had a most violent passion for women. This Jew laid close seige to my person, but could not triumph over me; I have resisted him better than I did the Bulgarian soldier. A woman of honor may be ravished once, but her virtue gathers strength from such rudeness. The Jew, in order to render me more tractable, brought me to this country-house that you see. I always imagined hitherto that no place on earth was so fine as the castle of Thunder-ten-tronckh; but I am now undeceived.

"The grand inquisitor, observing me one day, ogled me very strongly, and sent me a note, saying he wanted to speak with me upon private business. Being conducted to his palace, I informed him of my birth; upon which he represented to me how much it was below my family to belong to an Israelite. A proposal was then made by him to Don Issachar, to yield me up to my Lord. But Don Issachar, who is the court-banker, and a man of credit, would not come into his measures. The inquisitor threatened him. At last, my Jew, being affrighted, concluded a bargain, by which the house and myself should belong to them both in common; the Jew to have possession Monday, Friday, and Saturday, and the inquisitor, the other days of the week. This agreement has now continued six months. It has not, however, been without quarrels; for it has been often disputed whether Saturday night or Sunday belonged to the old, or to the new law. For my part, I have hitherto disagreed with them both: and I believe that this is the reason I am still beloved by them.

"At length, to avert the scourge of earthquakes and to intimidate Don Issachar, it pleased his Lordship the Inquisitor to celebrate. He did me the honor to invite me to it. I got a very fine seat, and the ladies were served with refreshments between the ceremonies. I was seized with horror at seeing them burn the two Jews, and the honest Biscayan who married his godmother; but how great was my surprise, my consternation, my anguish, when I saw in a sanbenito and mitre, a person that somewhat resembled Pangloss! I rubbed my eyes, I looked upon him very attentively and I saw him hanged. I fell into a swoon, and scarce had I recovered my senses, when I saw you stripped stark naked; this was the height of horror, consternation, grief, and despair. I will frankly own to you that your skin is still whiter, and of a better complexion than that of my Bulgarian captain. This sight increased all the sensation that oppressed and distracted my soul. I cried out, I was going to say stop, barbarians; but my voice failed me, and all my cries would have been to no purpose. When you had been severely whipped: How is it possible, said I, that the amiable Candide, and the sage Pangloss, should both be at Lisbon—the one to receive a hundred lashes and the other to be hanged by order of my Lord the Inquisitor, by whom I am so greatly beloved? Pangloss certainly deceived me most cruelly, when he said that everything was for the best in this world.

"Agitated, astonished, sometimes beside myself, and sometimes ready to die with weakness; my head filled with the massacre of my father, my mother, and my brother, the insolence of the vile Bulgarian soldier, the stab he gave me with his hanger, my abject servitude, and my acting as cook to the Bulgarian captain; the rascal Don Issachar, my abominable inquisitor, the execution of Dr. Pangloss, the grand music on the organ while you were whipped, and especially the kiss I gave you behind the screen, the last day I saw you. I praised the Lord for having restored you to me after so many trials. I charged my old woman to take care of you, and to bring you hither as soon as she could. She has executed her commission very well; I have tasted the inexpressible pleasure of seeing you, hearing you, and speaking to you. You must have a ravenous appetite, by this time; I am hungry myself, too; let us therefore, sit down to supper."

On this, they both sat down to table; and after supper, they seated themselves on the fine couch before mentioned. They were there, when Signor Don Issachar, one of the masters of the house, came in. It was his Sabbath day, and he came to enjoy his right, and to express his tender love.

IX
What Happened to Cunegonde, Candide, the Grand Inquisitor and the Jew

This Issachar was the most choleric Hebrew that had been seen in Israel since the captivity in Babylon. "What," said he, "you dog of a Galilean, is it not enough to share with Monsieur the Inquisitor? but must this varlet also share with me?" When he had thus spoke, he drew out a long poniard, which he always carried about him, and not suspecting that his antagonist had any weapons, he fell upon Candide; but our honest Westphalian had received a fine sword from the old woman, along with his full suit. He drew his rapier, and in spite of his amiable temper, he laid the Israelite dead upon the spot, at the feet of Cunegonde.

"My God," cried she; "what will become of us? a man murdered in my apartment! If the peace-officer comes in, we are ruined." "If Pangloss had not been hanged," said Candide, "he would have given us excellent advice in this emergency; for he was a great philosopher. In this extremity, let us consult the old woman"—she was a very prudent woman, and began to give her advice, when another little door opened. It was now about one o'clock in the morning, and consequently the beginning of Sunday. This day was allotted to my Lord the Inquisitor. Entering, he saw the kicked Candide with a sword in his hand, a dead body stretched on the floor, Cunegonde in a dreadful fright, and the old woman giving advice.

See now what passed in Candide's mind at this instant, and how he reasoned: "If this holy man calls in assistance, he will infallibly have me roasted alive; he may treat Cunegonde in the same manner; he has caused me to be whipped without mercy; he is my rival; I am already in for manslaughter; there is no time to hesitate." This reasoning was clear and rapid; and without giving time to the inquisitor to recover from his surprise, he ran through the body, and laid him by the side of the Jew. "Behold, a second kill!" said Cunegonde; "there is no pardon for us; we are damned, our last hour is come. How could you, who are so very gentle, kill a Jew and a lord in two minutes' time?" "My fair Lady," answered Candide, "when a man is in love, jealous, and has been whipped by the inquisition, he does not know what he does."

The old woman then put in her word, and said, "There are three Andalusian horses in the stable, with their saddles and bridles; which the gallant Candide may get ready; Madam has some money and jewels; let us get on horseback without delay, and let us go to Cadiz; the weather is delightful, and very pleasant it is to travel in the cool of night."

Candide immediately saddled the three horses. Cunegonde, the old woman, and he travelled thirty miles on a stretch. While they were making the best of their way, the citizenry came to the house; they buried my Lord in a magnificent church and threw Issachar into a common sewer.

Candide, Cunegonde, and the old woman had now got to the little town of Avacena, in the middle of the mountains of Sierra Morena; having put up at an inn, they talked on affairs as follows.

X
In What Distress Candide, Cunegonde, and the Old Woman Arrived at Cadiz and of Their Embarkation

"Who could have robbed me of my pistoles and my diamonds?" said Cunegonde, with tears in her eyes; "what shall we live on? What shall we do? Where shall I find inquisitors and Jews to give me more money and jewels?" "Alas," said the old woman, "I strongly suspect a cavalier who slept yesterday in the same inn with us at Badajos. God preserve me from judging rashly, but he came twice into our chamber, and went away a long time before us." "Ah!" said Candide, "the good Pangloss has often demonstrated to me, that the goods of this world are common to all men, and that every one has an equal right to them. According to these principles, the cavalier ought to have left us enough to carry us to our journey's end. Have you nothing at all left then, my pretty Cunegonde?" "Not a farthing," said she. "What course shall we take?" said Candide. "Let us sell one of the horses," said the woman; "I can ride behind Miss, and we shall thus manage to reach Cadiz."

In the same inn was a Benedictine prior, who bought the horse very cheap. Candide, Cunegonde, and the old woman passed through Lucena, Chillas and Lebrixa and arrived at length at Cadiz, where they were fitting out a fleet, and assembling troops for bringing to reason the reverend fathers, the Jesuits of Parragua, who were accused of having excited one of their hordes, near the city of St. Sacrament, to revolt from their allegiance to the Kings of Spain and Portugal. Candide having served among the Bulgarians, performed the military exercise of that nation before the commander of this little army, with so much grace, celerity, address, dexterity and agility, that he gave him command of a company of infantry. Being now made a captain, he embarked with Miss Cunegonde, the old woman, two valets, and the two Andalusian horses, which had belonged to his Lordship, the grand Inquisitor of Portugal.

During the whole voyage, they argued a great deal on the philosophy of poor Pangloss. "We are going to another world," said Candide; "it is there, without doubt, that every thing is for the best. For it must be con-fessed that one has reason to be a little uneasy at what passes in this world, with respect to both physics and morals." "I love you with all my heart," said Cunegonde, "but my mind is still terrified at what I have seen and experienced." "All will be well," replied Candide; "the seas of the new world are preferable to those of Europe; they are more calm and the winds are more constant. Certainly, the new world is the best of all possible worlds."

"God grant it," said Cunegonde; "but I have been so terribly unfortunate here, that my heart is almost shut up against hope." "You complain, indeed," said the old woman; "alas! you have not met with such misfortunes as I have."

Cunegonde was almost ready to fall a laughing, and thought the old woman very comical, for pretending to be more unfortunate than herself.

"Alas, my good dame," said Cunegonde; "unless you have been ravished by two Bulgarians, and received two cuts with a hangar, and had two castles demolished, and had two fathers and two mothers murdered, and have seen two lovers whipped, I cannot see how you can have the advantage of me. Add to this, that I was born a baroness, with seventy-two armorial quarterings, and that I have, nevertheless, been a cook-maid." "My Lady," answered the old woman, "you know nothing of my ancestry, and were I to show you my back, you would not talk as you do, but would suspend your judgment." This discourse having raised an insatiable curiosity in the minds of Cunegonde and Candide, the old woman related her story as follows.

XI
The History of the Old Woman

My eyes have not always been bleared, and bordered with scarlet; my nose has not always touched my chin; nor have I been always a servant. I am the daughter of a king, and the Princess of Palestrina. I was brought up, till I was fourteen, in a palace, to which all the castles of your German barons would not have served for stables, and one of my robes cost more than all the magnificence in Westphalia. I increased in beauty, in charms, and in fine accomplishments, amidst pleasures, homages, and high expectations. I began to captivate every heart. My neck was formed—oh, what a neck! white, firm and shaped like that of the Venus de Medici. And what eyes; what eyelids! what fine black eyebrows! what flames sparkled from my eyeballs; the poets of my country told me they eclipsed the twinkling of the stars! The maids who dressed and undressed me fell into an ecstasy when they viewed me, and all the men would gladly have been in their places.

I was bethrothed to a prince, the sovereign of Massa Carara. What a prince! as handsome as myself, all sweetness and charms, of a witty mind, and burning with love. I loved him, as one always loves for the first time, with idolatry, with transport. Preparations were made for our nuptials. The pomp and magnificence were inconceivable; nothing but continual feasts, carousals, and operas; and all Italy made sonnets upon me, of which there was scarce one tolerable. I was just on the point of reaching the summit of happiness, when an old marchioness, who had been mistress to my prince, invited him to drink chocolate at her house. He died there in less than two hours' time in terrible convulsions. But this is only a mere trifle. My mother, in despair, and yet less afflicted than I was, resolved to retreat for some time from so mournful a place. She had a very fine country-seat near Gaeta. We embarked on board a galley of the country, gilt equal to the altar of St. Peter at Rome. We were scarcely at sea, when a corsair of Sallee fell upon and boarded us. Our soldiers defended themselves like true soldiers; they all fell upon their knees, after throwing away their arms, and asked pardon, *in articulo mortis,* of the corsair.

We were instantly stripped naked as monkeys; my mother, our maids of honor, and myself too, meeting with no better usage. It is a very surprising thing with what expedition these pirate gentry undress people. But what surprised me most was that they should touch us where we women do not ordinarily allow. This ceremony appeared very strange to me; but so we judge of everything that is not done in our own country. I soon learned that the search was to find out whether we had not concealed some of our jewels there. It is a custom established time out of mind among civilized nations that scour the sea. I know that those gentlemen, the pious knights of Malta, never omit to practice it, when they capture Turks of either sex. It is one of the laws of nations, from which they never deviate.

I need not tell you how great a hardship it is for a young princess and her mother to be carried slaves to Morocco. You may easily form a notion of what we underwent on board the vessel of the corsair. My mother was still very handsome, our maids of honor, nay, our plain chambermaids, had more charms than are to be found throughout all Africa. As for myself, I was all attraction, I was all beauty, and all charms; nay, more, I was a virgin. However, I was not one for long; for this flower, which had been reserved for the accomplished Prince of Massa Carara, was taken from me by the captain of the corsair. He was an ugly negro, but fancied he did me a great deal of honor. Indeed Her Highness, the Princess of Palestrina, and myself must have been very strong to resist all the violence we met with till our arrival at Morocco. But let me pass over that; these things are so very common that they are hardly worth the mentioning.

Morocco overflowed with blood when we arrived there. Fifty sons of the Emperor Muley Ismael had each their adherents; this produced, in effect, fifty civil wars, of blacks against blacks, of blacks against tawnies, of tawnies against tawnies, and of mulattoes against mulattoes. In a word, there was one continued carnage all over the empire.

No sooner were we landed than the blacks

of a party adverse to that of my corsair made an attempt to rob him of his booty. Next to the jewels and the gold, we were the most valuable things he had. I was here witness to such a battle as you never saw in your European climates. The people of the north have not so much fire in their blood, nor have they that raging passion for women that is so common in Africa. One would think that you Europeans had nothing but milk in your veins; but it is vitriol and fire that runs in those of the inhabitants of Mount Atlas and the neighboring countries. They fought with the fury of lions, tigers, and serpents of the country, to determine who should have us. A Moor seized my mother by the right arm, while my captain's lieutenant held her by the left; a Moorish soldier took hold of her by one leg, and our pirates held her by the other. All our women found themselves almost in a moment seized thus by four soldiers. My captain kept me concealed at his back. He had a scimitar in his hand, and killed every one that opposed his fury. In short, I saw all our Italian women and my mother torn to pieces, hacked and mangled by the brutes that fought for them. My fellow-prisoners, those who had taken them, soldiers, sailors, black, whites, mulattoes, and lastly my captain himself, were all killed; and I remained expiring upon a heap of dead bodies. These barbarous scenes extended, as every one knows, over more than three hundred leagues, without the perpetrators ever omitting the five prayers a day ordained by Mahomet.

I disengaged myself with great difficulty from the weight of so many dead, bloody carcasses heaped upon me, and made shift to crawl to a large orange-tree on the bank of a neighboring rivulet, where I sank down oppressed with fear, fatigue, horror, despair, and hunger. Soon after, my senses being overpowered, I fell into a sleep, which resembled a fainting fit rather than sleep. I was in this state of weakness and insensibility, between death and life, when I felt myself pressed by something that moved near my body. I opened my eyes, and saw a white man of a very good mien, who sighed, and muttered between his teeth in my own speech.

XII
The Sequel of the Old Woman's Adventures

Astonished, and transported with joy, to hear my own country language, I roused myself and determined to relate the great misfortunes that had befallen me. I then gave him a short account of the horrid scenes I had undergone, and relapsed again into a swoon. He carried me to a neighboring house, caused me to be put to bed, gave me something to eat, waited upon me, comforted and flattered me, and said that he had never seen any one so handsome as I was. "I was born at Naples," said he, "where they castrate two or three thousand children every year; some die of the operation, others acquire a finer voice than that of any woman, and others become governors of states. This operation was performed on me with great success, and I became a singer in the chapel of her Highness, the Princess of Palestrina." "Of my mother!" cried I. "Of your mother?" cried he again, shedding tears. "What! are you that young princess, whom I had the care of bringing up till she was six years old, and who bid fair, even then, to be as handsome as you are now?" "It is myself; my mother lies about four hundred paces from hence, cut into four quarters, under a heap of dead bodies."

I related to him all that had befallen me; he likewise told me his adventures, and informed me that he was sent to the King of Morocco, by a Christian prince, to conclude a treaty with that monarch, by which he was to furnish him with ammunition, artillery, and ships, to enable him entirely to destroy the commerce of other Christians. "My commission is fulfilled," said the honest eunuch to me; "I am going to embark at Ceuta, and will carry you to Italy."

I thanked him with tears of gratitude; but

"We were instantly stripped naked as monkeys;
my mother, our maids of honor, and myself too,
meeting with no better usage. It is a very
surprising thing with what expedition
these pirate gentry undress people."

instead of conducting me to Italy, he carried me to Algiers, and sold me to the Dey of that province. Scarce was I sold, when the plague, which had made the tour of Africa, Asia, and Europe, broke out at Algiers with great fury. You have seen earthquakes; but pray, Miss, have you ever had the plague! "Never," answered the Baroness.

"Had you had it," replied the old woman, "you would confess that it is far more terrible than an earthquake." It is very common in Africa; I was seized with it. Figure to yourself the situation of a king's daughter, about fifteen years of age, who, in the space of three months, had undergone poverty and slavery, had been ravished almost every day, had seen her mother cut into four quarters, had experienced both famine and war, and was dying of the plague at Algiers. I did not die for all that. But my eunuch, and the Dey, and almost all the seraglio at Algiers perished.

When the first ravages of this dreadful pestilence were over, they sold the slaves belonging to the Dey. A merchant purchased me, and carried me to Tunis. There he sold me to another merchant, who sold me again at Tripoli; from Tripoli, I was sold again at Alexandria; from Alexandria, I was sold again at Smyrna; and from Smyrna at Constantinople. At last, I became the property of an Aga of the Janissaries, who was soon after ordered to go to the defence of Asoph, then besieged by the Russians.

The Aga, who was a man of great gallantry, took all his seraglio along with him, and lodged us in a small fort on the Palus Maeotis, under the guard of two black eunuchs and twenty soldiers. We killed a great number of the Russians, who returned the compliment with interest. Asoph was put to fire and sword, and no regard was paid to age or sex. There remained only our little fort, which the enemy resolved to reduce by famine. The twenty Janissaries had sworn that they would never surrender. The extremities of famine to which they were reduced, obliged them to eat our two eunuchs, for fear of violating their oath; and a few days after, they resolved to devour the women.

We had an Iman, a very religious and humane man. He preached an excellent sermon to them, in which he dissuaded them from killing us all at once. "Cut only one of the backs of these ladies," said he, "and you will fare excellently well; if you must come to it again, you will have the same entertainment a few days hence. Heaven will bless you for so charitable an action, and you will find relief."

As he had an eloquent tongue, he easily persuaded them. This horrible operation was performed upon us, and the Iman applied the same balsam to us that is applied to children. We were all ready to die.

The Janissaries had scarce finished the feast with which we had supplied them, when the Russians came in their flat bottomed boats, and not a single Janissary escaped. The Russians showed no concern about the condition we were in. As there are French surgeons in every country, one of them who was a person of very great skill took us under his care and cured us; and I shall remember as long as I live that when my wounds were pretty well healed, he made me amorous proposals. To be short, he told us all to cheer up, and assured us that the like misfortune had happened in several sieges; and that it was the law of war.

As soon as my companions were able to walk, they were obliged to go to Moscow. I fell to the lot of a Boyard, who made me his gardener, and gave me twenty lashes with his whip every day. But my lord having been broke on the wheel, within two years after, along with thirty more Boyards, on account of some quarrel at court, I availed myself of this event, and made my escape. After traversing over all Russia, I was a long time servant to an innkeeper at Riga, afterwards at Rostock, Wismar, Leipsic, Cassel, Utrecht, Leyden, the Hague, and Rotterdam. I grew old in misery and disgrace, having only one half of my back, but still remembering that I was a king's daughter. A hundred times have I had thoughts of killing myself; but still I was fond of life. This ridiculous weakness is perhaps one of our most melancholy foibles. For can anything be more stupid than to be desirous of continually carrying a burden, which one has a good mind to throw down on the ground? to dread existence, and yet preserve it? in a word, to caress the serpent that devours us, till he has gnawed our very heart out?

In the countries through which it has been my fate to travel, and in the inns where I have been a servant, I have seen a prodigious number of people who looked upon their own existence as a curse; but I never knew of more than eight who voluntarily put an end to their misery, *viz.*, three negroes, four Englishmen, and a German professor named *Robeck*. My last service was with Don Issachar the Jew, who placed me near your person, my fair lady. I am resolved to share your fate; and I have been more affected with your misfortunes than with my own. I should never have spoken of my sufferings, if you had not vexed me a little, and if it had not been customary, on board a ship, to tell stories, by way of amusement. In short, Miss, I have a good deal of experience, and I have known the world. Divert yourself, and prevail upon each passenger to tell you his story; and if there is one found who has not frequently cursed his life, and has not as often said to himself, that he was the unhappiest of mortals, I will give you leave to throw me into the sea, head foremost.

XIII

How Candide Was Obliged to Part from the Fair Cunegonde and the Old Woman

The beautiful Cunegonde having heard the old woman's story, paid her all the civilities that were due to a person of her rank and merit. She approved of her proposal, and engaged all the passengers, one after another, to relate their adventures, and then both Candide and she confessed that the old woman was in the right. "It is a great pity," said Candide, "that the sage Pangloss was hanged, contrary to custom, for he would tell us most surprising things concerning the physical and moral evils which cover both land and sea; and I should be bold enough, with due respect, to propose some objections."

While each passenger was relating his story, the ship advanced in her voyage. They landed at Buenos-Ayres. Cunegonde, Capt. Candide, and the old woman, waited on the governor, Don Fernandes d'Ibaraa, y Figueora, y Mascarenes, y Lampourdos, y Souza. This nobleman was possessed of pride suitable to a person dignified with so many titles. He spoke to other people with so noble a disdain, turned up his nose, carried his head so high, raised his voice so intolerably, assumed so imperious an air, and affected so lofty a gait, that all those who saluted him were tempted to beat him. He was an excessive lover of the fair sex. Cunegonde appeared to him the prettiest woman he had ever seen. The first thing he did, was to ask whether she was not the Captain's wife? The manner in which he put the question alarmed Candide. He durst not say that she was his wife, because, in reality she was not. He durst not tell him that she was his sister, because she was not that either, and though this officious lie might have been of service to him, yet his soul was too refined to betray the truth. "Miss Cunegonde," said he, "intends me the honor of marrying me, and we beseech your Excellency to grace our nuptials with your presence."

Don Fernandes d'Ibaraa, y Figueora, y Mascarenes, y Lampourdos, y Souza, turning up his mustaches, forced a grim smile, and ordered Capt. Candide to go and review his company. Candide obeyed, and the Governor remained alone with Miss Cunegonde. He declared his passion, protested that he would marry her the next day in the face of the church, or otherwise, as it should be agreeable to a person of her charms. Cunegonde desired a quarter of an hour to consider the proposal, to consult with the old woman, and to make up her mind.

Said the old woman, to Cunegonde, "Miss,

you can reckon up seventy-two descents in your family, and not one farthing in your pocket. It is now in your power to be the wife of the greatest lord in South America, who has very pretty whiskers; and what occasion have you to pique yourself upon inviolable fidelity? You have been ravished by the Bulgarians; a Jew and an inquisitor have been in your good graces. Misfortunes have no law on their side. I confess, that were I in your place, I should have no scruples to marry the governor, and make the fortune of Capt. Candide."

While the old woman was thus speaking, with all the prudence which age and experience dictated, they descried a small vessel entering the port, which had on board an alcald and alguazils. The occasion of their voyage was this.

The old woman had shrewdly guessed, that it was a cavalier with a big sleeve that stole the money and jewels from Cunegonde in the city of Badajos, when she and Candide were making their escape. The man having offered to sell some of the diamonds to a jeweller, the latter recognized them as the inquisitor's. The cavalier, before he was hanged, confessed he had stolen them. He described the persons he had stolen them from, and told the route they had taken. The flight of Cunegonde and Candide being by this means discovered, they were traced to Cadiz, where a vessel was immediately sent in pursuit of them; and now the vessel was in the port of Buenos-Ayres. A report was spread, that an Alcald was going to land, and that he was in pursuit of the murderers of my lord the grand inquisitor. The old woman saw in a moment what was to be done. "You cannot run away," said she to Cunegonde, "and you have nothing to fear; it was not you that killed my lord; and besides, the governor, who is in love with you, will not suffer you to be ill treated. Therefore stay here." She then ran to Candide: "Fly," said she, "or in an hour you will be burnt alive." He had not a moment to lose; but how could he part from Cunegonde, and where could he fly to for shelter?

XIV
How Candide and Cacambo Were Received by the Clerics of Paraguay

Candide had brought such a valet with him from Cadiz, as one often meets with on the coasts of Spain, and in the colonies. He was a quarter-blooded Spaniard, born of a mongrel in Tucuman, and had been a singing-boy, a sexton, a sailor, a factor, a soldier, and a lacquey. His name was *Cacambo,* and he had a strong love for his master, because his master was a very good sort of man. Having saddled the two Andalusian horses with all expedition: "Let us go, Master, let us follow the old woman's advice, let us set off, and run without looking behind us." Candide dropped some tears: "Oh, my dear Cunegonde," said he, "must I leave you just at the time when the governor was going to have us married! Cunegonde, what will become of you in this strange country?" "She will do as well as she can," said Cacambo; "women are never at a loss; God will provide for her; let us run." "Whither art thou carrying me?" said Candide; "where are we going? what shall I do without Cunegonde?" "By St. James of Compostella," said Cacambo, "you were going to fight against the clerics; now let us go and fight *for* them. I know the road perfectly well; I will conduct you to their kingdom; they will be charmed to have a captain that knows the Bulgarian exercise; you will make a prodigious fortune; though one cannot find his account in one world, he may in another. It is a great pleasure to see new sights and perform new exploits."

"Have you been in Paraguay?" said Candide.

"Yes, in truth, I have," said Cacambo. "I was usher to the college and am acquainted with the government of the good clerics as well as I am with the streets of Cadiz. It is an admirable sort of government. The kingdom is upwards of three hundred leagues in diameter, and divided into thirty provinces. The rulers there are masters of everything, and the people have nothing. It is the masterpiece of reason and justice. For my part I see nothing so divine as the clerics who wage war here against the Kings of Spain and Portugal, and in Europe are their advisers, who in this country, kill Spaniards, and at Madrid, send them counsel. This transports me; let us therefore push forward; you are going to be the happiest of mortals. What pleasure will it be to those rulers when they know that a captain who understands the Bulgarian exercise comes to offer them his service!"

As soon as they reached the first barrier, Cacambo told the advanced guard, that a captain desired to speak with my lord the commandant. They went to inform the chief guard of it. A Paraguayan officer ran on foot to the commandant, to impart the news to him. Candide and Cacambo were at first disarmed, and their two Andalusian horses were seized. The two strangers were introduced between two files of musketeers; the commandant was at the further end, with a cap on his head, his gown tucked up, a sword by his side, and a staff in his hand. He made a signal, and straightway four and twenty soldiers surrounded the newcomers. A serjeant told them they must wait; that the commandant could not speak to them; that the lord ruler does not permit any Spaniard to open his mouth but in his presence, or to stay above three hours in the province. "And where is the lord ruler?" said Cacambo. "He is upon the parade," answered the serjeant: "and you cannot kiss his spurs in less than three hours." "But," said Cacambo, "my master, the Captain, who is ready to die for hunger as well as myself, is not a Spaniard, but a German; cannot we have something for breakfast, while we wait for his lordship?"

The serjeant went to give an account of this discourse to the commandant. "God be praised," said the commandant; "since he is a German, I may speak with him; bring him into my arbor." Candide was immediately conducted into a green pavilion, decorated with a very handsome balustrade of green and gilt marble, with intertextures of vines, containing parrots, humming-birds, fly-birds, Guinea-hens, and all other sorts of rare birds. An excellent breakfast was pro-

vided in vessels of gold, and while the Paraguayans were eating Indian corn mush out of wooden dishes, in the open fields, exposed to the sultry heat of the sun, the commandant retired to his arbor.

He was a very handsome young man, with a full face, tolerably fair, fresh colored, his eyebrows were arched, his eyes full of fire, his ears red, his lips like vermillion; his hair was somewhat fierce, but of a fierceness which differed both from that of a Spaniard and Cleric. They now returned to Candide and Cacambo the arms, which had been taken from them, together with the two Andalusian horses, which Cacambo took the liberty to feed near the arbor, keeping his eye upon them, for fear of a surprise.

Candide immediately kissed the hem of the commandant's garment; after which, they both sat down to table. "You are a German, then?" said the cleric to him, in that language. "Yes," said Candide. In pronouncing these words, they looked at each other with extreme surprise, which they were not able to account for. "And what part of Germany do you belong to?" said the Cleric. "To the lower part of Westphalia," said Candide; "I was born in the Castle of Thunder-ten-tronckh." "Heavens! is it possible!" cried the commandant. "What a miracle is this!" cried Candide. "Is it You?" said the commandant, " 'Tis impossible!" said Candide. On this they both fell backwards; but getting up again, they embraced each other, and shed tears of joy. "What! is it you, you! the brother of the fair Cunegonde! you that was slain by the Bulgarians! you, the Baron's son! are you a ruler at Paraguay? I must confess, that this is a strange world indeed! Ah! Pangloss! Pangloss! how pleased you would now be, if you had not been hanged."

The commandant ordered the negro slaves, and the Paraguayans, that poured out the liquor in cups of rock crystal, to retire. He thanked God, a thousand times; folded Candide in his arms: their faces being all the while bathed in tears. "You will be more astonished, more affected, more out of your wits," said Candide, "when I tell you that Miss

Cunegonde, your sister, who you thought was dead is as well as I am." "Where?" "In your neighborhood; at the house of the governor of Buenos-Ayres; and I came here to fight against you." Every word they spoke in this long conversation heaped surprise upon surprise. Their souls dwelt upon their tongues, listened in their ears, and sparkled in their eyes. As they were Germans, they made a long meal (according to custom), waiting for the lord ruler, when the commandant thus addressed their dear Candide.

XV

How Candide Killed the Brother of His Dear Cunegonde

"I shall ever have present to my memory," said the baron, "that horrible day, wherein I saw my father and mother killed, and my sister ravished. When the Bulgarians were gone, my sweet sister was nowhere to be found; and I, together with my father and mother, two maids, and three little lads that were murdered, were flung into a cart, in order to be buried in a chapel, which belonged to the clerics, about two leagues distant from our family-castle. A cleric sprinkled us with holy water, which being very salty, and some drops falling into my eyes, he could perceive my eye-balls move; on which he put his hand on my side, and felt my heart beat; I was taken care of, and, in about three weeks time, no one would have thought that any thing had ailed me. You know very well my dear Candide, I was very handsome, but I grew more so; on which account, the superior of the house conceived a very great affection for me, and some time after sent me to training. The superior was then looking out for a recruit of young men from Germany. For the rulers of Paraguay take as few Spanish as they can; but choose foreigners, because they think they can tyrannize over them as they please. I was therefore made choice of, as a proper person to go to work in this vineyard. I set sail in company with a Polander and a Tirolesian. On my arrival, I was honored with a lieutenancy. At present I am a colonel. We shall give the King of Spain's army a warm reception; I can assure you that they will be beaten. Providence has sent you hither to assist us. But is it true, that my dear sister Cunegonde is in our neighborhood, at the governor of Buenos-Ayres's house?" Candide swore that it was as true as the gospel. On this their tears gushed out afresh.

The Baron could not refrain from embracing Candide, whom he called his brother, and his protector. "Ah, perhaps," said he, "we two may enter the city in triumph, and recover my sister Cunegonde." "There is nothing I could wish for more," said Candide, "for I expected to be married to her, and I have some hopes I shall yet." "The insolence of the fellow!" replied the Baron. "Can you dare to think of marrying my sister, who can show seventy-two quarterings in her coat of arms? How dare you have the effrontery to speak to me thus!" Candide being quite thunderstruck at this, replied, "my revered father, all the quarterings in the world do not signify a farthing. I have delivered your sister from the hands of a Jew, and an inquisitor; she lies under a great many obligations to me, and is willing to marry me. Master Pangloss always told me that all men are equal. I am determined to marry her." "We will see whether you will, you villain!" said the cleric Baron of Thunder-ten-tronckh, at the same time giving him a blow on the face with the flat part of his sword. Candide drew his weapon immediately, and plunged it up to the hilt in the Baron's body; but drawing it out again, and looking upon it as it reeked, he cried out, "O God! I have killed my old master, my friend, my brother-in-law. I am one of the best-natured men in the world, yet I have killed three men."

Cacambo, who stood sentry at the door of the arbor, and who heard the noise, ran in. "We have nothing now to do but to sell our lives as dearly as we can," said his master to him; "and if they should force their way into the arbor, let us at least die with our arms in our hands."

Cacambo, who had been in circumstances of a similar nature, did not stand long to rack his brains for an expedient, but took the dress which the Baron wore, put it upon Candide, gave him the dead man's cap, and made him mount his horse. All this was done in the twinkling of an eye. "Let us gallop away, master," says he; "everybody will take you for some cleric that is going express, and we shall get to the frontiers before they can overtake us."

They fled like lightning, before these words were quite out of his mouth, crying out in Spanish, "Make way, make way for the Colonel."

XVI
What Passed Between Our Two Travellers and Two Girls, Two Monkeys, and the Savages Called Oreillons

Candide and his valet had got beyond the pass, before any person in the camp got the least intimation of the death of the German. The provident Cacambo had taken care to fill his wallet with bread, chocolate, ham, and some bottles of wine. They pushed with their Andalusian horses into a strange country, where they could not discover any path or road. At last, a pleasant meadow, which was divided by a river, presented itself to their eyes. Our two travellers turned their horses out to graze, and Cacambo proposed to his master to eat a bit, at the same time setting him the example. "Do you think," said Candide, "that I can feast upon ham, when I have killed the Baron's son, and find myself under a necessity never to see Cunegonde again as long as I live? What signifies it to prolong my days in misery, since I must spend them far away from her, a prey to remorse and despair? and what will the Journal of Trevoux say of me?"

Having thus spoke, he refused to eat a morsel. The sun was now set, when our two wanderers, to their very great surprise, heard faint cries, which seemed to come from women. It was not easy to determine these cries; they rose immediately, with all the anxiety and apprehension to which people are subject in a strange place, and immediately discovered that the noise was made by two girls, who ran, unclothed, on the banks of the meadow, pursued by two large monkeys. Candide was moved with pity, and as he had learned to shoot, among the Bulgarians, and was so good a marksman that he could hit a nut in a bush without touching the leaves, he took up his Spanish fuzee, which was double-charged, and killed the two monkeys. "God be praised, my dear Cacambo," said he; "I have delivered the two poor girls from this great danger. If I have been guilty of a sin in killing the inquisitor, I have now made ample amends for it by saving the lives of two innocent girls. They may chance to prove a couple of ladies of rank; and who knows but this adventure may do us great service, in this country?"

He was going on at this rate, thinking that he had done a great feat, but how great was his surprise, when he saw the two girls, instead of rejoicing, embrace the monkeys with marks of the most tender affection! they bathed their bodies with tears, and filled the air with shrieks that testified the deepest distress. "I never expected to have seen such a sight as this," said he to Cacambo; who replied, "You have done a fine piece of work, indeed, Sir, you have killed the ladies' sweethearts." "Their sweethearts! is it possible? Surely you are in jest, Cacambo; who the deuce could believe you to be in earnest?" "My dear Sir," replied Cacambo, "you are always for making mountains of mole-hills; why should you think it incredible that in some countries monkeys enjoy the favors of the ladies?" "Ay," replied Candide, "now I recollect, Mr. Pangloss has told me, that there may be many an instance of this kind, and that these mixtures gave birth to the Egipans, Fauns, and Satyrs; that a great many of the ancients had seen them with their own eyes; but I always looked upon it as a mere

"... immediately discovered that the noise was made by two girls, who ran, unclothed, on the banks of the meadow, pursued by two large monkeys."

romance." "You ought, at present, to see your mistake," said Cacambo, "and own that the doctor was in the right for once. And you may see what those people do, who have not received a particular education. All I am afraid of is, that these ladies will play us some spiteful trick." These wise reflections induced Candide to quit the meadow, and take to a wood; where he and Cacambo supped together; and, after heartily cursing the Portuguese inquisitor, the governor of Buenos-Ayres, and the Baron, they fell asleep.

On waking, they found that they could not stir, for the Oreillons, the inhabitants of the country, whom the two lasses had informed of their adventure, had bound them in the nighttime with cords made of the bark of a tree. They were surrounded by a body of fifty Oreillons, stark naked, armed with arrows, clubs, and hatchets made of flint. Some of them were making a great cauldron boil, others preparing spits, and all of them crying out, "He's a cleric, he's a cleric; we will make him pay sauce for it; we will pick his bones for him; let us eat the cleric, let us eat the cleric."

"You may remember I told you my dear master," cried Cacambo, in a lamentable tone, "that those two lasses would play us some spiteful trick."

Candide perceiving the cauldron and the spits, cried out, "O lord! we are certainly going to be roasted or boiled. Ah! if Mr. Pangloss had seen nature without disguise, would he have said whatever is, is right? It may be so; but I must confess it is a sad thing to have lost Miss Cunegonde, and to be roasted or boiled for food by the Oreillons."

Cacambo was never at a loss for an invention; "Never despair," said he to the disconsolate Candide. "I understand the jargon of these people a little, and am going to speak to them." "Don't fail," said Candide, "to represent to them the inhumanity of cooking men, and what an unchristian practice it is."

"Gentlemen," says Cacambo, "you fancy that you are going to feast on a cleric to-day; a very good dish, I make no doubt, nor is there any thing more just than to serve

one's enemies so. In effect, the law of nature teaches us to kill our fellow creatures, and it is a principle which is put in practice all over the globe. If we do not make use of the right of eating him, it is because we have plenty of victuals without it; but as you have not that advantage, it must certainly be better for you to eat your enemies than to fling away the fruit of your victories a feast to crows and ravens. But, Gentlemen, I suppose you would not relish to eat your friends. You fancy you are going to spit or boil a cleric, but, believe me, I assure you, it is your defender, it is the enemy of your enemies, that you are preparing to treat thus. As to myself, I was born among you. The gentleman you see here is my master, and so far from being a cleric, he has just now killed a cleric, and he is only dressed in his spoils, which is the cause of your mistake. In order to confirm my assertion, let one of you take his gown off, carry it to the first pass of the government of the fathers, and inform himself whether my master has not killed a cleric officer. It is an affair that won't take up much time, and you may always have it in your power to eat us, if you catch me in a lie. But if I have told you the truth, and nothing but the truth, you are too well acquainted with the principles of natural right, morality and law, not to show us some favor."

The Oreillons were so fully convinced of the reasonableness of this proposal, that they deputed two of their chief to go and inform themselves of the truth of what he had told them. The two deputies acquitted themselves of their charge like men of sense, and returned soon with a favorable account. The Oreillons then unbound the prisoners, showed them a thousand civilities, offered them women, gave them refreshments, and conducted them back again to the confines of their state, crying all the while, like madmen, "He is no cleric, he is no cleric."

Candide could not help admiring the subject of his deliverance. "What a people!" said he; "what men! what manners! If I had not had the good luck to run Miss Cunegonde's brother through the body, I should inevitably have been eaten up. But, after all, the dictates of pure nature are always best, since this people, instead of eating me, showed me a thousand civilities as soon as they knew that I was not a cleric."

XVII
The Arrival of Candide and His Man at the Country of Eldorado

When they had reached the frontiers of the Oreillons, "You see now," said Cacambo to Candide, "that this part of the world is not one pin better than the other. Take a fool's advice for once, and let us return to Europe as fast as ever we can." "How is that possible?" said Candide; "and pray what part of it would you have us go to? If I go to my own country, the Bulgarians and Arabians kill all they meet with there; if I return to Portugal, I am sure I shall be burnt alive; if we stay in this country, we run the hazard of being roasted every moment. And again, how can I think of leaving that part of the globe where Miss Cunegonde lives?"

"Why, then, let us take our course towards Cayenne," said Cacambo; "we shall meet with some Frenchmen there, for you know they are to be met with all over the globe; perhaps they will give us some relief, and God may have pity upon us."

It was no easy matter for them to go to Cayenne, as they did not know whereabouts it lay; besides, mountains, rivers, precipices, banditti, and savages, were difficulties they were sure to encounter in their journey. Their horses died with fatigue, and their provisions were soon consumed. After having lived a whole month on the wild fruits, they found themselves on the banks of a small river, which was bordered by cocoa trees, which both preserved their lives and kept up their hopes.

Cacambo, who was on all occasions as good a counsellor as the old woman, said to Candide, "We can hold out no longer; we have

walked enough already, and here's an empty canoe upon the shore, let's fill it with cocoa, then get on board, and let it drift with the stream. A river always runs to some inhabited place. If we don't meet with what we like, we are sure to meet with something new." "Why, what you say is very right, e'en let us go," said Candide, "and recommend ourselves to the care of Providence."

They rowed some leagues between the two banks, which were enamelled with flowers in some places, in others barren, in some parts level, and in others very steep. The river grew broader as they proceeded, and at last, lost itself in a vault of frightful rocks, which reached as high as the clouds. Our two travellers still had the courage to trust themselves to the stream. The river now growing narrower drove them along with such rapidity and noise as filled them with the utmost horror. In about four and twenty hours they got sight of daylight again, but their canoe was dashed in pieces against the breakers. They were obliged to crawl from one rock to another for a whole league; after which they came in sight of a spacious plain, bounded with inaccessible mountains. The country was highly cultivated, both for pleasure and profit; the useful and the ornamental were most agreeably blended. The roads were covered, or, more properly speaking, were adorned, with carriages, whose figures and materials were very brilliant, they were full of men and women, of an extraordinary beauty, and were drawn with great swiftness, by large red sheep, which, for fleetness, surpassed the finest horses of Andalusia, Tetuan, or Mequinez.

"This certainly," said Candide, "is a better country than Westphalia." He and Cacambo got on shore near the first village they came to. The very children of the village were dressed in gold brocades, all tattered, playing at quoits, at the entrance of the town. Our two travellers from the other world amused themselves with looking at them. The quoits were made of large round pieces, yellow, red, and green, and cast a surprising light. Our travellers' hands itched prodigiously to be fingering some of them; for they were almost certain that they were either gold, emeralds, or rubies; the least of which, would have been no small ornament to the throne of the Great Mogul. "To be sure," said Cacambo, "these must be the children of the king of the country, diverting themselves at quoits." The master of the village, coming at that instant to call them to school; "That's the preceptor to the royal family," cried Candide.

The little brats immediately quitted their play, leaving their quoits and other playthings behind them. Candide picked them up, ran to the schoolmaster, and presented them to him with a great deal of humility, acquainting him, by signs, that their Royal Highnesses had forgot their gold and jewels. The master of the village smiled, and flung them upon the ground; and having stared at Candide with some degree of surprise, walked off.

Our travellers did not fail immediately to pick up the gold, rubies, and emeralds. "Where have we got to now?" cried Candide. "The princes of the blood must certainly be well educated here, since they are taught to despise both gold and jewels." Cacambo was as much surprised as Candide. At length they drew near to the first house in the village, which was built like one of our European palaces. There was a vast crowd of people at the door, and still a greater within. They heard very good music, and their nostrils were saluted by a most refreshing smell from the kitchen.

Cacambo went up to the door, and heard them speaking the Peruvian language, which was his mother-tongue; for every one of my readers knows that Cacambo was born at Tucuman, a village where they make use of no other language. "I'll be your interpreter, master," cried Cacambo, in the greatest rapture, "this is a tavern, in with you, in with you."

Immediately, two waiters and two maids that belonged to the house, dressed in cloths of gold tissue, and having their hair tied back with ribbands, invited them to sit down to table with the landlord. They served up four soups, each garnished with two parroquets, a boiled vulture that weighed about two hundred pounds, two apes roasted, of an excellent taste, three hundred humming birds in one plate, and six hundred flybirds in another; together with exquisite ragouts, and the most delicious tarts, all in plates of a species of rock-crystal. After which, the lads and lasses served them with a great variety of liquors made from the sugar cane.

The guests were mostly tradesmen and carriers, all extremely polite, who asked some questions of Cacambo, with the greatest discretion and circumspection, and received satisfactory answers.

When the repast was ended, Cacambo and Candide thought to discharge their reckoning, by putting down two of the large pieces of gold which they had picked up. But the landlord and landlady burst into a loud fit of laughing, and could not restrain it for some time. Recovering themselves at last; "Gentlemen," says the landlord, "we can see pretty well that you are strangers, we are not much used to such guests here. Pardon us for laughing, when you offered us the stones of our highways in discharge of your reckoning. It is plain, you have got none of the money of this kingdom; but there is no occasion for it, in order to dine here. All the inns, which are established for the conveniency of trade, are maintained by the government. You have had but a sorry entertainment here, because this is but a poor village; but anywhere else, you will be sure to be received in a manner suitable to your merit."

Cacambo explained the host's speech to Candide, who heard it with as much astonishment and wonder as his friend Cacambo interpreted it. "What country can this be," said they to each other, "which is unknown to the rest of world, and of so different a nature from ours? it is probably that country where everything really is for the best; for it is absolutely necessary that there should be one of that sort. And in spite of all Doctor Pangloss' arguments, I could not help thinking that things were very bad in Westphalia."

XVIII
What They Saw in the Country of Eldorado

Cacambo could not conceal his curiosity from his landlord. "For my part," said the latter to him, "I am very ignorant, and I am well aware of it; but we have an old man here, who has retired from court, and is reckoned both the wisest and most communicative person in the kingdom." So saying, without any more ado, he conducted Cacambo to the old man's house. Candide acted now only the second personage, and followed his servant. They entered into a very plain house, for the door was nothing but silver, and the ceilings nothing but gold, but finished with so much taste, that the handsomest ceilings of Europe did not surpass them. The ante-chamber was indeed only covered with rubies and emeralds, but the order in which every thing was arranged made amends for this great simplicity.

The old gentleman received the two strangers on a sofa stuffed with the feathers of humming birds, and ordered them to be served with liquors in vessels of diamond; after which he satisfied their curiosity in the following manner.

"I am now in my hundred and seventy-second year, and I have heard my deceased father, who was groom to his Majesty, mention the surprising revolutions of Peru, of which he was an eye-witness. The kingdom we are in at present is the ancient country of the Incas, who left it very indiscreetly, in order to conquer one part of the world; instead of doing which, they themselves were all destroyed by the Spaniards.

"The princes of their family who remained in their native country were more wise; they made a law, by the unanimous consent of their whole nation, that none of our inhabitants should ever go out of our little kingdom; and it is owing to this that we have preserved both our innocence and our happiness. The Spaniards have had some confused idea of this country, and have called it *Eldorado;* and an Englishman, named Sir *Walter Raleigh,* has been on our coasts, above a hundred years ago; but as we are surrounded by inaccessible rocks and precipices, we have hitherto been sheltered from the rapacity of the European nations, who are inspired with an insensate rage for the stones and dirt of our land; to possess these, I verily believe they would not hesitate a moment to murder us all."

The conference between Candide and the old man was pretty long, and turned upon the form of government, the manners, the women, the public amusements, and the arts of Eldorado. At last, Candide, who had always a taste for Metaphysics, bid Cacambo ask if there was any religion in that country?

The old gentleman, reddening a little, "How is it possible," said he, "that you should question it? Do you take us for ungrateful wretches?" Cacambo then humbly asked him, what the religion of Eldorado was? This made the old gentleman redden again. "Can there be more religions than one?" said he; "we profess, I believe, the religion of the whole world; we worship the deity from evening to morning." "Do you worship one God?" said Cacambo, who still acted as interpreter in explaining Candide's doubts. "You may be sure we do," said the old man, "since it is evident there can be neither two, nor three, nor four. I must say, that the people of your world propose very odd questions." Candide was not yet wearied in interrogating the good old man; he wanted to know how they prayed to God in Eldorado. "We never pray at all," said the respectable sage; "we have nothing to ask of him; he has given us all we need, and we incessantly return him thanks."

Candide had a curiosity to see their priests, and bid Cacambo ask, where they were. This made the old gentleman smile. "My friends," said he, "we are all of us priests; the king, and the heads of each family, sing their songs of thanksgiving every morning, accompanied by five or six thousand musicians." "What!" said Cacambo, "have you no clerics to preach, to dispute, to tyrannize, to set people together by the ears, and to get

403

those burnt who are not of the same opinions as themselves?" "We must be very great fools indeed if we had," said the old gentleman; "we are all of us of the same opinion, here, and we don't understand what you mean by clerics."

Candide was in an ecstasy during all this discourse, and said to himself, "This place is vastly different from Westphalia, and my lord the Baron's castle. If our friend Pangloss had seen Eldorado, he would never have maintained, that nothing upon earth could surpass the castle of Thunder-ten-tronckh. It is plain that everybody should travel."

After this long conversation was finished, the good old man ordered a coach and six sheep to be got ready, and twelve of his domestics to conduct the travellers to the court. "Excuse me," says he to them, "if my age deprives me of the honor of attending you. The king will receive you in a manner that you will not be displeased with, and you will, I doubt not, make allowance for the customs of the country, if you should meet with anything that you disapprove of."

Candide and Cacambo got into the coach, and the six sheep were so fleet, that in less than four hours they reached the King's palace, which was situated at one end of the metropolis. The gate was two hundred and twenty feet high, and one hundred broad; it is impossible to describe the materials it was composed of. But one may easily guess, that it must have prodigiously surpassed those stones, and the sand which we call gold and jewels.

Candide and Cacambo, on their alighting from the coach, were received by twenty maids of honor, of an exquisite beauty, who conducted them to the baths, and presented them with robes made of the down of humming-birds; after which, the great officers and their ladies introduced them into his Majesty's apartment, between two rows of musicians, consisting of a thousand in each, according to the custom of the country.

When they approached the foot of the throne, Cacambo asked one of the great officers in what manner they were to behave when they went to pay their respects to his Majesty; whether they were to fall down on their knees, or their bellies; whether they were to put their hands upon their heads or upon their backs; whether they were to lick up the dust of the room; and, in a word, what the ceremony was? "The custom is," said the great officer, "to embrace the King, and kiss him on both cheeks." Candide and Cacambo accordingly clasped his Majesty round the neck, who received them in the most polite manner imaginable, and very genteelly invited them to sup with him.

In the interim, they showed them the city, the public edifices, that seemed almost to touch the clouds; the market places, embellished with a thousand columns; fountains of pure water, besides others of rose-water, and the liquors that are extracted from the sugar canes, which played continually in the squares, which were paved with a kind of precious stones, that diffused a fragrance like that of cloves or cinnamon. Candide asking them to show them their courts of justice, and their parliament house, they told him they had none, and that they were strangers to law-suits. He then inquired if they had any prisons, and was told they had not. What surprised him most, and gave him the greatest pleasure, was the palace of sciences, in which he saw a gallery two thousand paces in length, full of mathematical instruments and scientific apparatus.

After having spent the afternoon in going over about a thousandth part of the city, they were re-conducted to the palace. Candide seated himself at table with his Majesty, his valet Cacambo, and a great many ladies. Never was there a better entertainment; and never was more wit shown at table than what his Majesty displayed. Cacambo interpreted the King's repartees to Candide, and though they were translated, they appeared excellent repartees still; a thing which surprised Candide about as much as anything else.

They spent a whole month in this hospitable manner; Candide continually remarking to Cacambo, "I must say it again and again, my friend, that the castle where I was born

"Candide and Cacambo, on their alighting from the coach, were received by twenty maids of honor, of an exquisite beauty, who conducted them to the baths, and presented them with robes made of the down of humming-birds; . . ."

was nothing in comparison to the country where we are now; but yet Miss Cunegonde is not here, and without doubt you have left a sweetheart behind you in Europe. If we stay where we are, we shall be looked upon only as other folks; whereas, if we return to our own world, only with twelve sheep loaded with pebbles of Eldorado, we shall be richer than all the kings put together; we shall have no need to be afraid of the inquisitors, and we may easily recover Miss Cunegonde."

This proposal was extremely agreeable to Cacambo; so fond are we of running about, of making a figure among our countrymen, of telling our exploits, and what we have seen in our travels, that these two really happy men resolved to be no longer so, and accordingly asked his Majesty's leave to depart.

"You are very foolish," said his Majesty to them. "I am not ignorant that my country is a small affair, but when one is well off it's best to keep so. I certainly have no right to detain strangers; it is a degree of tyranny inconsistent with our customs and laws; all men are free; you may depart when you please; but you cannot get away without the greatest difficulty. It is impossible to go against the current up the rapid river which runs under the rocks; your passage hither was a kind of miracle. The mountains which surround my kingdom are a thousand feet high, and as steep as a wall; they are at least ten leagues over, and their descent is a succession of precipices. However, since you seem determined to leave us, I will immediately give orders to the constructors of my machines, to make one to transport you comfortably. When they have conveyed you to the other side of the mountains, no one must attend you; because my subjects have made a vow never to pass beyond them, and they are too wise to break it. There is nothing else you can ask of me which shall not be granted." "We ask your Majesty," said Cacambo, very eagerly, "only a few sheep loaded with provisions, together with some of the common stones and dirt of your country."

The King laughed heartily; "I cannot," said he, "conceive what pleasure you Europeans find in our yellow clay; but you are welcome to take as much of it as you please, and much good may it do you."

He gave immediate orders to his engineers to construct a machine to hoist up and transport these two extraordinary persons out of his kingdom. Three thousand able mechanics set to work, and in a fortnight's time the machine was completed, which cost no more than twenty millions sterling of their currency.

Candide and Cacambo were both placed on the machine, together with two large red sheep bridled and saddled for them to ride on, when they were over the mountains, twenty sheep of burden, loaded with provisions, thirty with the greatest curiosities of the country, by way of present, and fifty with gold, precious stones, and diamonds. The King, after tenderly embracing the two vagabonds, took his leave of them.

It was a very fine spectacle to see them depart, and the ingenious manner in which they and the sheep were hoisted over the mountains. The contrivers of the machine took their leave of them, after having got them safe over, and now Candide had no other desire and no other aim, than to go to present his sheep to Miss Cunegonde. "We have now got enough," said he, "to pay for the ransom of Miss Cunegonde, no matter what price the governor of Buenos-Ayres puts upon her. Let us march towards Cayenne, there take shipping, and then we will determine what kingdom to make a purchase of."

XIX
What Happened to Them at Surinam, and How Candide Became Acquainted with Martin

The first day's journey of our two travellers was very agreeable, they being elated with the idea of finding themselves masters of more treasure than Asia, Europe or Africa could scrape together. Candide was so transported, that he carved the name of Cunegonde upon almost every tree that he came to. The second day, two of their sheep sank in a morass, and were lost, with all that they carried; two others died of fatigue a few days after; seven or eight died at once of want, in a desert; and some few days after, some others fell down a precipice. In short, after a march of one hundred days, their whole flock amounted to no more than two sheep.

"My friend," said Candide to Cacambo, "you see how perishable the riches of this world are; there is nothing durable, nothing to be depended on but virtue, and the happiness of once more seeing Miss Cunegonde." "I grant it," said Cacambo; "but we have still two sheep left, besides more treasure than ever the King of Spain was master of; and I see a town a good way off, that I take to be Surinam, belonging to the Dutch. We are at the end of our troubles, and at the beginning of our happiness."

As they drew nigh to the city, they saw a negro stretched on the ground, more than half naked, having only a pair of drawers of blue cloth; the poor fellow had lost his left leg and his right hand. "Good God!" said Candide to him, in Dutch, "what do you here, in this terrible condition?" "I am waiting for my master, Mynheer Vanderdendur, the great merchant," replied the negro. "And was it Mynheer Vanderdendur that used you in this manner?" said Candide. "Yes sir," said the negro, "it is the custom of the country. They give us a pair of linen drawers for our whole clothing twice a year. If we should chance to have one of our fingers caught in the mill, as we are working in the sugar-houses, they cut off our hand; if we offer to run away, they cut off one of our legs; and I have had the misfortune to be found guilty of both these offences. Such are the conditions on which you eat sugar in Europe! Yet when my mother sold me for ten crowns at Patagonia on the coast of Guinea, she said to me, My dear boy, bless our fetiches, adore them always, they will make you live happily. You have the honor to be a slave to our lords, the whites, and will by that means be in a way of making the fortunes both of your father and your mother. Alas! I do not know whether I have made their fortunes, but I am sure they have not made mine. The dogs, monkeys, and parrots are a thousand times less wretched than we. The Dutch missionaries who converted me, told me every Sunday, that we all are sons of Adam, both blacks and whites. I am not a genealogist, myself; but if these preachers speak the truth, we are all cousins-german; and you must own that it is a shocking thing to use one's relations in this barbarous manner."

"Ah! Pangloss," cried Candide, "you never dreamed of such an abominable piece of cruelty and villainy! there is an end of the matter; I see I must at last renounce your optimism." "What do you mean by optimism?" said Cacambo. "Why," said Candide, "it is the folly of maintaining that everything is right, when it is wrong." He then looked upon the negro with tears in his eyes, and entered Surinam weeping.

Their first business was to inquire whether there was any vessel in the harbor wherein they could hire a passage for Buenos-Ayres. The person they applied to was no other than a Spanish commander, who offered to make an honorable bargain with them. He appointed to meet them at an inn, whither Candide and the faithful Cacambo went to wait for him with their two sheep.

Candide whose heart was always on his lips, told the Spaniard his adventures, and confessed that he was determined to run away with Miss Cunegonde. "I shall take care how I carry you to Buenos-Ayres, if that is the case," said the captain; "for I should be hanged, and so would you. The fair Cunegonde is my Lord's favorite mistress."

This was a thunder-clap to Candide; he wept a long time, but at last, drawing Cacambo aside, "I will tell you, my dear friend," said he, "what I would have you do. We have each of us about five or six millions of diamonds in our pocket; and as you are smarter at a bargain than I am, go you and fetch Miss

Cunegonde from Buenos-Ayres. If the governor should make any objection, give him a million diamonds; if that does not succeed, give him two millions. As you did not murder the inquisitor, they will have no complaint against you; in the mean time, I will fit out another vessel, and go and wait for you at Venice; that is a safe place, and I need not be afraid there of Bulgarians, Abares, Jews, or Inquisitors." Cacambo applauded this sage resolution. He was, indeed, under great concern at leaving so good a master, who used him like a familiar friend; but the pleasure of being serviceable to him soon got the better of the sorrow he felt in parting with him.

They took leave of each other with tears; Candide recommending to him at the same time not to forget their good old woman. The same day Cacambo set sail. This Cacambo was a very honest fellow.

Candide stayed some time at Surinam, waiting for another vessel to carry him and the two remaining sheep to Italy. He hired servants, and purchased everything necessary for so long a voyage; at last, Mynheer Vanderdendur, the master of a large vessel, came and offered his service. "What will you charge?" said he to the Dutchman, "for carrying me, my servants, goods, and the two sheep you see here, directly to Venice?" The master of the vessel asked ten thousand piastres; Candide made no objection.

"Oh, oh," said the crafty Vanderdendur to himself, after he had left him, "if this stranger can give ten thousand piastres, without any words about it, he must be immensely rich." Returning a few minutes after, he let him know that he could not go for less than twenty thousand. "Well, you shall have twenty thousand then," said Candide.

"Odso," said the captain with a low voice, "this man makes no more of twenty thousand piastres than he did of ten!" He then returned a second time, and said that he could not carry him to Venice for less than thirty thousand piastres. "You shall have thirty thousand then," replied Candide.

"Oh, oh," said the Dutch trader again to himself, "this man makes nothing of thirty thousand piastres; no doubt but the two sheep are loaded with immense treasures; let us stand out no longer; let us, however, finger the thirty thousand piastres first, and then we shall see."

Candide sold two small diamonds, the least of which was worth more than what the captain had asked. He advanced him the money. The two sheep were put aboard the vessel. Candide followed in a small wherry, intending to join the vessel in the road. But the captain improved his opportunity, unfurled sails, and unmoored. The wind being favorable, Candide, distracted and out of his wits, soon lost sight of him. "Ah!" cried he, "this is a trick worthy of the old world." He returned on shore, overwhelmed with sorrow; for he had lost more than would have made the fortunes of twenty princes.

He ran immediately to the Dutch judge, and as he hardly knew what he was about, knocked very loud at the door; he went in, told his case, and raised his voice a little higher than became him. The judge began by making him pay ten thousand piastres for the noise he had made; after which he heard him very patiently, and promised to examine into the affair, as soon as ever the trader should return; at the same time, making him pay ten thousand piastres more for the expense of hearing his case.

This proceeding made Candide stark mad. He had indeed experienced misfortunes a thousand times more affecting, but the coolness of the judge, and the knavish trick of the master of the vessel who had robbed him, fired his spirits, and plunged him into a profound melancholy. The villainy of mankind presented itself to his mind in all its deformity, and he dwelt upon nothing but the most dismal ideas. At last, a French vessel being ready to sail for Bordeaux, as he had no sheep loaded with diamonds to carry with him, he paid the common price as a cabin passenger, and ordered the crier to give notice all over the city, that he would pay the passage and board of any honest man that would go the voyage with him, and give him two thousand piastres besides, on condition that he would make it appear, that he was the most disgusted with his condition, and the most wretched person in that province.

A vast multitude of candidates presented themselves, enough to have manned a fleet. Candide selected twenty from among them, who seemed to have the best pretensions, and to be the most sociable. But as every one of them thought the preference due to himself, he invited them all to his inn, and gave them a supper, on condition that each one of them should take an oath, that he would relate his adventures faithfully, promising to choose that person who seemed to be the greatest object of pity, and had the greatest reason to be dissatisfied with his lot, and to give a small present to the rest, as a recompense for their trouble.

The assembly continued till four o'clock the next morning. As Candide was employed in hearing their adventures, he could not help recollecting what the old woman had told him during their voyage to Buenos-Ayres, and the bet she had made, that there was not a single person in the ship that had not experienced some terrible misfortune. He thought of Pangloss at every adventure that was related. "That Pangloss," said he, "would be hard put to it to defend his system now. I wish he was but here. Indeed, if everything is ordered for the best, it must be at Eldorado, but nowhere else on earth." At last, he decided in favor of a poor scholar, who had written ten years for the booksellers at Amsterdam. For he thought there could not be a more disagreeable employment in the world.

This scholar, though in other respects a good sort of a man, had been robbed by his wife, beat by his son, abandoned by his daughter, who got a Portuguese to run away with her; had been stripped of a small employment, which was all he had to subsist on, and was persecuted by the clerics at Surinam, because they took him for a Socinian.

It must indeed be confessed, that most of the other candidates were as unhappy as he; but he met with a preference, because Candide thought that a scholar was best calculated to amuse him during the voyage. All his competitors thought that Candide did them a great piece of injustice; but he appeased them by giving each of them a hundred piastres.

XX
What Happened to Candide and Martin at Sea

The old scholar, who was named *Martin,* embarked for Bordeaux along with Candide. They had both of them seen and suffered a great deal; and if the vessel had been going to sail from Surinam to Japan, by the way of the Cape of Good Hope, they would have found enough wherewith to entertain themselves on the subject of physical and moral evil, during the whole voyage.

Candide, however, had one great advantage over Martin, which was, that he still hoped to see Miss Cunegonde again; but as for Martin, he had nothing to hope for; to which we may add, that Candide had both gold and diamonds; and though he had lost a hundred large red sheep, loaded with the greatest treasure that the earth could produce, though the knavery of the Dutch captain was always uppermost in his thoughts, yet when he reflected upon what he had still left in his pockets, and when he talked about Cunegonde, especially toward the latter end of a hearty meal, he inclined to Pangloss' hypothesis.

"But you, Mr. Martin," said he to the scholar, "what is your opinion? what is your notion of physical and moral evil?" "Sir," replied Martin, "the clerics have accused me of being a Socinian; but the truth is I am a Manichean."

"You are in jest, sure," said Candide; "there are no longer any Manicheans in the world!" "I am one, though," said Martin; "I cannot well account for it, but yet I am not able to think otherwise." "The devil must be in you, then," said Candide. "He concerns himself so much in the affairs of this world," said Martin, "that he may possibly be in me as well as anywhere else; but I must confess that when I cast my eyes over this globe, or rather over this globule, I cannot help thinking that God has abandoned it to some malignant being: I always except Eldorado. I never met with a city that did not wish the destruction of its neighbor city, nor one family that did not desire to exterminate another family. All over the world, the poor curse the rich, to whom they are obliged to cringe; and the rich treat the poor like so many sheep, whose wool and flesh is sold to the highest bidder. A million assassins, formed into regiments, scour Europe from one extremity to another, committing murder and rapine systematically and according to discipline, for their bread, because they cannot find a more honest or honorable profession; and in those cities which seem to enjoy the blessings of peace, and where the arts are cultivated, mankind are devoured with greater envy, care and disquietude, than a city meets with when it is besieged. Private torments are still more insupportable than public calamities. In a word, I have seen and experienced so much that I have become a Manichean."

"There's some good in the world, for all that," replied Candide. "That may be," said Martin, "but I do not know where to find it."

In the midst of this dispute, they heard the report of cannon. The noise increasing every moment, each person took out his spy-glass, and soon clearly discovered two vessels about three miles distant, engaged in battle. The wind brought the combatants so near the French vessel that they had the pleasure of seeing the fight very clearly. At length one of the vessels gave the other a broadside between wind and water, which sunk it to the bottom. Candide and Martin plainly perceived about a hundred men on the deck of the ship which was sinking, lifting up their hands towards heaven, and making the most dismal lamentations; and in an instant they were all swallowed up by the sea.

"Well," said Martin, "see how mankind treat one another." "It is true," said Candide, "there's something diabolical in this affair." As he was saying this, he perceived something red and glittering swimming near his ship. They immediately sent the longboat to see what it could be, when it proved to be one of those red sheep. Candide felt more of joy at the recovery of this sheep, than he had of trouble at the loss of a hundred such, loaded with the large diamonds of Eldorado.

The French captain soon found that the captain of the conquering vessel was a Spaniard, and that the commander of the vessel which was sunk was a Dutch pirate, and the very same who had robbed Candide. The immense riches which the villain had amassed were buried in the sea along with him and there was only a single sheep saved.

"You see," said Candide to Martin, "that wickedness sometimes meets with condign punishment; that rascal, the Dutch commander, has met with the fate he merited." "Yes," said Martin; "but why should the passengers on board of his ship also perish together with him? God indeed has punished the villain, but he has permitted the devil to drown the rest."

In the mean time, the Frenchman and the Spaniard continued their course, and Candide pursued his debates with Martin. They disputed fifteen days without intermission; and, at the end of the fifteen days, both were as far from being convinced as when they began. But they chatted, intercommunicated their ideas, and amused each other reciprocally. Candide caressing his sheep, "Since I have found you," said he, "I have some hopes of recovering Cunegonde."

XXI
Candide and Martin Draw Near to the Coast of France and Continue to Discuss

At length they descried the coast of France. "Have you ever been in France, Mr. Martin?" said Candide. "Yes," said Martin, "I have travelled over several of its provinces. In some, half the inhabitants are mere fools; in others, they are too cunning; in others, either very polite and good natured, or very brutish; in others, they affect to be wits; and in all of them the chief occupation is love, the next lying, and the third to talk nonsense." "But, Mr. Martin, have you ever been in Paris?" "Yes, I have; the people are just the same there; it is a mere chaos; a crowd in which every one is in search after pleasure, but no one finds it, as far as I have been able to discover. I spent a few days there on my arrival, and I was robbed of all I had, by some sharpers, at the fair of St. Germain. Nay, I myself was taken up for a robber, and was eight days in prison; after which I turned corrector of the press, to get a small matter to carry me on foot to Holland. I know the whole tribe of scribblers, with malcontents and fanatics. They say the people are very polite in that city; I wish I could believe them."

"For my part, I have no curiosity to see France," said Candide; "you may easily fancy that when a person has once spent a month at Eldorado, he is very indifferent whether he sees anything else on earth, except Miss Cunegonde. I am going to wait for her at Venice; we will go through France, in our way towards Italy. Won't you bear me company?" "With all my heart," said Martin; "they say that Venice is not for any but the noble Venetians; but, for all that, they receive strangers very well, provided they have a good deal of money. I have none; you have; therefore, I'll follow you all the world over." "Now I think of it," said Candide, "do you imagine that the earth was originally nothing but water, as is asserted in the great book belonging to the Captain?" "I don't believe a word of it," said Martin, "no more than I do of all the reveries that have been published for some time." "But for what end was the world created, then?" said Candide. "To make people mad," replied Martin. "Were not you greatly surprised," continued Candide, "at the story I told you of the passion which the two girls in the country of the Oreillons had for those two apes?" "Not at all," said Martin; "I see nothing strange in that passion; for I have seen so many strange things already, that I can look upon nothing as extraordinary." "Do you believe," said Candide, "that mankind have always been cutting one another's throats; that they were always liars, knaves, treacherous and ungrateful; always thieves, sharpers, highwaymen, lazy, envious and gluttons; always drunkards, misers, ambitious and bloodthirsty; always backbiters, debauchees, fanatics, hypocrites and fools?" "Do you not believe," said Martin, "that hawks have always preyed upon pigeons, when they could light upon them?" "Certainly," said Candide. "Well, then," said Martin, "if the hawks have always had the same nature, what reason can you give why mankind should have changed theirs?" "Oh!" said Candide, "there is a great deal of difference, because free-will * * *."

In the midst of this dispute, they arrived at Bordeaux.

XXII
What Happened in France to Candide and Martin

Candide stayed no longer at Bordeaux than till he could dispose of some of the pebbles of Eldorado, and furnish himself with a post-chaise large enough to hold two persons; for he could not part with his philosopher Martin. He was indeed very sorry to part with his sheep, which he left at the Academy of Sciences at Bordeaux, which proposed for the subject of this year's prize, the reason why this sheep's wool was red; and the prize was adjudged to a learned man in the North, who demonstrated, by A *plus* B !mz6minus C divided by Z, that the sheep must be red, and die of the rot.

In the meantime, all the travellers whom Candide met in the inns on the road, telling him they were going to Paris, this general eagerness to see the capital inspired him, at length, with the same desire, as it was not

much out of the way in his journey towards
Venice.

He entered Paris by the suburb of St. Marçeau, and fancied himself to be in the dirtiest
village in Westphalia.

Candide had scarce got to his inn, when he
was seized by a slight indisposition, caused by
his fatigues. As he had a very large diamond
on his finger, and the people had taken notice of a pretty heavy box among his baggage,
in a moment's time he had no less than two
physicians to attend him, who did not wait to
be sent for; a few intimate friends, that never
left him, sat up with him together with a
couple of female friends that took care to
have his broths warmed. "I remember," said
Martin, "that when I was sick at Paris, in my
first journey, I was very poor, and could meet
neither with friends, nurses, nor physicians;
but I recovered."

Meanwhile, by medicines and bleedings,
Candide's disorder grew more serious, and
the clerk of the town came, with great modesty to ask a bill for the other world, payable to
the bearer. Candide refused to accord it: the
nurses assured him that it was a new fashion.
Candide replied, that he was resolved not to
follow the fashion. Martin was going to throw
the clerk out of the window. The clerk swore
that Candide should not be buried. Martin
swore he would bury the clerk, if he continued to be troublesome. The quarrel grew
high, and Martin took the clerk by the shoulders, and pushed him out of doors. This occasioned a great deal of scandal, and an action was commenced against him.

Candide recovered, and while he was con-
valescent, had the best company to sup with
him. They gamed high and Candide was very
much surprised that he never could throw
an ace; but Martin was not surprised at all.

Among those who did him the honors of
the city was a little cleric of Perigord, one of
those people that are always busy, always
alert, always ready to do one service, forward, fawning, and accommodating themselves to every one's humor; who watch for
strangers on their journey, tell them the
scandalous history of the town, and offer

them help at all prices. This man took Candide and Martin to the playhouse, where a
new tragedy was to be acted. Candide found
himself seated near the critics, but this did
not prevent him from weeping at some
scenes that were well acted. One of these critics, who stood at his elbow, said to him, in the
midst of one of the acts, "You were in the
wrong to shed tears; that's a shocking actress,
the actor who plays with her is worse than
she is, and the piece is still worse than the
actors. The author does not understand a
single word of Arabic, and yet the scene lies
in Arabia; but besides, he is a man who does
not believe that our ideas are innate. I'll
bring you twenty pamphlets against him to-
morrow."

"Pray sir," said Candide, to the cleric, "how
many theatrical pieces have you in France?"
"Five or six thousand," replied the other.
"Indeed! that is a great many," said Candide;
"but how many good ones are there among
them?" "Some fifteen or sixteen," was the
reply. "Oh, that is a great many," said Martin.

Candide was greatly taken with an actress
who played Queen Elizabeth in a dull kind of
tragedy, that was occasionally put on the
stage. "That actress," said he to Martin,
"pleases me greatly. She has some sort of
resemblance to Miss Cunegonde. I should be
very glad to pay my respects to her." The
cleric of Perigord offered his services to introduce him to her at her own house. Candide, who was brought up in Germany,
desired to be informed as to the ceremony
used on these occasions, and how a queen of
England was treated in France. "There is a
distinction to be observed in these matters,"
said the cleric. "In the country towns, we take
them to a tavern; here, in Paris, they are
treated with great respect during their lifetime, provided they are handsome; and
when they die, we throw their bodies on a
dunghill." "How!" said Candide, "throw a
queen's body on a dunghill?" "The gentleman is quite correct," said Martin; "he tells
you nothing but the truth. I happened to be
in Paris when Miss Mevina made her exit, as
they say, from this world to the other. She

"He entered Paris by the suburb of St. Marçeau, and fancied himself to be in the dirtiest village in Westphalia."

was refused what they here call the rights of sepulture: that is, to say, she was denied the privilege of rotting in a church-yard with all the beggars in the parish. They buried her at the corner of Burgundy Street, which most certainly would have shocked her extremely, for she was very high spirited." "This was a very unfeeling act," said Candide. "What would you do?" said Martin. "It is the way of these people. Figure to yourself all the contradictions, and all the absurdities possible, and you will find them in the church, in the government, in the tribunals, and in the theatres, of this droll nation." "Is it true that the Parisians are always laughing?" said Candide. "Yes," said the cleric, "but it is with hearts full of anger. They complain amidst bursts of laughter; they even commit the most detestable actions, laughing all the while."

"Who," said Candide, "was that ill-mannered hog, who spoke so disparagingly of the scene in the play that made me weep, and of the actors who gave me so much pleasure?" "It is a miserable creature," replied the cleric, "who gets his living by running down all the new plays and all the new books. He hates those who meet with success, as eunuchs hate all who enjoy themselves. He is one of those literary serpents who nourish themselves on venom. He is a pamphleteer." "What do you call a pamphleteer?" said Candide. "It is," said the cleric, "a maker of pamphlets; a Freron."

Thus Candide, Martin and the Perigordin conversed together, on the stairway, whilst seeing the spectators go out of the theatre. "Although I am very anxious to see Miss Cunegonde, I would like to sup with Mademoiselle Clairon, she appears so amiable," said Candide.

The cleric was not the man to approach Mademoiselle Clairon, who received only the best company. "She is engaged this evening," said he; "but permit me the honor to introduce you to a lady of quality, who will make you as well acquainted with Paris as though you had lived there four years."

Candide who was naturally curious, allowed himself to be taken to the house of the lady, situated in the faubourg Saint Honore; the company was playing at faro; twelve melancholy looking punters held each in their hands a small pack of cards, with the corners turned down, as if to register their losses. Profound silence reigned. The faces of all the punters were very pale, he who held the bank was the very picture of anxiety, and the lady of the house, seated near this pitiless man, observed with the eyes of a lynx every word, every *sept-et-le-va* with which each player of the company bent the corners of his cards; she made them straighten them out again; and was very strict in that respect, yet very polite, for fear of losing their custom. The lady assumed the title of Marchioness of Parolignac. Her daughter, about fifteen years of age, was one of the punters, and notified her mother by a wink of her eye of the little tricks the poor people they were victimizing resorted to in trying to repair their losses.

Candide and Martin enter. No one rises, no one salutes them, nobody even looks at them; all are intensely occupied with their cards. "Madame the Baroness of Thunderten-tronckh was more polite," thought Candide.

Meanwhile, the cleric whispered in the ear of the marchioness, who, partly rising, honored Candide with a gracious smile, and Martin with a majestic nod. She ordered a seat and a hand of cards to be given to Candide, who lost fifty thousand francs in two deals. After which, they supped very merrily, and all the company were astonished that Candide was not in the least cast down by his losses. The waiters came to the conclusion among themselves that he must be some English lord.

The supper was, like most suppers at Paris, begun in silence; afterwards, there was a noise of words that no one could distinguish. Then came insipid jokes, false news, and bad arguments; a little politics, and a great deal of scandal. They even conversed about new books. "Have you seen the romance of Mr. Gauchet, professor of philosophy?" said the cleric of Perigord. "Yes," replied one of the company, "but I couldn't finish reading it. We have a crowd of impertinent writers, but all of them together don't come up to the impertinence of Gauchet, professor of philosophy. I am so disgusted with this immensity of detestable books with which we are inundated, that I have taken to playing faro."

"And the Miscellanies of Troublet, what do you think of them?" said the cleric. "Ah!" said Madame de Parolignac; "the tiresome creature! How curiously he tells you what all the world knows. How weightily he discusses what is not worth being ever so lightly remarked. How he appropriates the genius of others without having the least genius himself. How he spoils what he steals; how he disgusts me; but he will disgust me no more; it is enough to have read a few pages."

There was at table a man of learning and taste, who inclined to what the marchioness had said. The conversation turning on tragedies, the lady asked how it happened that there were tragedies which were sometimes played, that nobody cared to read. The man of taste explained how a play could be somewhat interesting, yet have scarcely any merit. He proved, in a few words, that "it is not enough to introduce one or two of those scenes which are found in all the romances, and which always seduce the spectators. It is necessary to be new without being fickle, often sublime, and always natural; to understand the human heart, and make it speak; to be a good poet, without letting any character in the play appear like one; to be perfectly acquainted with language, to speak it with purity and continuous harmony, and never sacrifice sense to rhyme. Whoever," added he, "does not observe all these rules, may write one or two tragedies that will be applauded at the theatre, but he will never rank among good writers. There are very few good tragedies. Some are idyls in dialogue, well written and well rhymed; others are political reasonings which put us to sleep, or amplifications which repel us; others are dreams of demoniacs in barbarous style, desultory talk, long apostrophes to the gods because the author does not understand how to talk to men, false maxims and bombast."

Candide listened to all this with attention, and conceived a high opinion of the discourser; and as the marchioness had taken care to place him at her side, he took the liberty of asking, in a whisper, who this man was, who spoke so well. "It is a scholar," said the lady, "who never puntes, and whom the cleric sometimes brings along with him to supper. He is perfectly acquainted with tragedies and books, he has written a hissed tragedy, and a book which he dedicated to me; but the only copy that has ever seen the outside of the publisher's store is the one he presented to me." "The great man!" said Candide, "he is another Pangloss."

Then turning to him, he said: "Sir, you believe, no doubt, that all is for the best in the physical and moral world, and that nothing can be otherwise?" "Me," replied the scholar, "I don't think anything of the kind. I find that all goes contrary with us, that no one knows what is his rank, or what is his employment, or what he does, or what he ought to do; and except entertainments which are very gay, and over which there appears to be considerable union, all the rest of the time passes in impertinent quarrels, Jansenists against Molinists, members of parliament against dignitaries of the church, men of letters against men of letters, courtezans against courtezans, financiers against the people, wives against husbands, relations against relations; it is a continual warfare."

"I have seen the worst," replied Candide, "but a very great philosopher, who had the misfortune to be hanged, has taught me that all this is wonderfully well; a mere shadow on a very fine picture." "Your philosopher who has been hanged made a great fool of himself," said Martin; "your shadows are horrible blemishes." "It is men who make the blemishes," said Candide, "and they can't help it." "Then it is not their fault," said Martin. Most of the punters, who understood nothing of this language employed their time in drinking. Martin kept on reasoning with the scholar, and Candide related a part of his adventures to the lady of the house.

After supper, the marchioness conducted Candide into her private room, and seated him on a sofa. "Ah, well, you love Miss Cunegonde, of Thunder-ten-tronckh, to distraction." "Yes, Madam," said Candide. To this the marchioness replied with a tender smile, "You answer me just like a young Westphalian; a Frenchman would have said:—'It is true that I did love Mademoiselle Cunegonde, but having seen you, Madam, I fear I shall never love her any more.'" "Well, Madam," said Candide, "I will answer thus if you wish." "Your passion for her," said the marchioness, "commenced in picking up her handkerchief; will you please to pick up my garter?" "With all my heart," said Candide, and he picked it up. "Now I want you to tie it on," said the lady; and Candide tied it on. "Look you," said the lady, "you are a stranger; I sometimes make my Parisian lovers languish a fortnight, but I surrender to you the first night, *parce qu'il faut faire les honneurs de son pays* to a young man from Westphalia." The lady perceiving two enormous diamonds worn by her young stranger, praised them so much that they immediately passed from the fingers of Candide to those of the marchioness.

Candide, in returning with the cleric of Perigord, expressed remorse for having been guilty of infidelity towards Miss Cunegonde; the cleric consoled him; he had only a small part of the fifty thousand francs which Candide lost at play, and of the value of the two brilliants, half given, half extorted. His design was to profit as much as he could from the advantages Candide's acquaintanceship might procure him. He talked continually of Cunegonde, and Candide assured him that he would ask pardon of this beauty when he should meet her at Venice.

The cleric redoubled his politeness and attentions, and took a very tender interest in all Candide said, in all he did, and in all he wished to do.

"You have then, sir," said he, "a *rendez vous* at Venice?" "Yes, Mr. Cleric," said Candide, "I must certainly go there, to find Miss Cunegonde." Then, led away by the pleasure of speaking of one he so loved, he related, as was his custom, a part of his adventures with this illustrious Westphalian.

"I fancy," said the cleric, "that Miss Cunegonde is a lady of very great accomplishments, that she writes charming letters?" "I never received any letters from her," said Candide, "for, being driven out of the castle on account of my passion for her, I could not write to her; soon after, I heard she was dead; afterwards, I found her, and lost her; and I have now sent an express to her about two thousand five hundred leagues from hence, and wait for an answer."

The cleric heard him with great attention, and appeared to be a little thoughtful. He soon took leave of the two strangers, after a most affectionate embrace. The next day, as soon as Candide awoke, he received a letter couched in the following terms.

"My dearest love, I have been ill these eight days in this town, and have learned that you are here. I would fly to your arms, if I were able to stir. I knew of your passage to Bordeaux, where I have left the faithful Cacambo and the old woman, who are to follow me very soon. The governor of Buenos-Ayres has taken all from me, but your heart is still left me. Come; your presence will restore me to life, unless it kills me with pleasure."

This charming and unexpected letter transported Candide with inexpressible joy, whilst the sickness of his dear Cunegonde overwhelmed him with sorrow. Distracted between these two passions, he took his gold and diamonds, and got somebody to conduct him and Martin to the house where Miss Cunegonde was lodged.

On his entrance, he trembled in every limb, his heart beat quick, and his voice was choked-up with sighs; he asked them to bring a light, and was going to open the curtains of the bed. "Take care, sir," said the nurse, "she can't bear light, it would kill her"; and immediately she drew the curtains close again. "My dear Cunegonde," said Candide, weeping, "how do you find yourself? though you can't see me, you may speak to me, at least." "She cannot speak," said the maid. The sick lady then put a plump little hand out of the bed, which Candide for some time bathed with his tears, and afterwards filled with diamonds, leaving a bag full of gold upon the easy chair.

In the midst of his transports, a lifeguardman came in, followed by the Perigordin cleric and a file of soldiers. "There," said he, "are the two suspected foreigners." He caused them to be immediately seized, and ordered his men to drag them to prison. "It is not thus they treat travellers at Eldorado," said Candide. "I am more a Manichean than ever," said Martin. "But pray, sir, where are you going to carry us?" said Candide. "To a hole in the lowest dungeon," said the lifeguardman.

Martin having recovered his usual coolness, saw at once that the lass who pretended to be Cunegonde was a cheat; that the Perigordin cleric was an impostor, who had taken advantage of Candide's simplicity; and that the lifeguardman was another sharper, whom they might easily get clear of.

Rather than expose himself before a court of justice, Candide, by his counsellor's advice, and besides, being very impatient to see the real Cunegonde, offered the lifeguardman three small diamonds, worth about 3,000 pistoles each. "Ah, sir" said the man with the ivory baton, "though you had committed all the crimes that can be imagined, this would make me think you the most honest gentleman in the world! Three diamonds! worth 3,000 pistoles apiece! Sir, instead of putting you in a dungeon, I would lose my life for you; all strangers are arrested here, but let me alone for that; I have a brother at Dieppe in Normandy; I'll conduct you thither, and if you have any diamonds to give him, he will take as good care of you as I would myself."

"And why do they put all strangers under arrest?" said Candide. The cleric of Perigord then put in his word: "Because," said he, "a knave of Atrebatia listened to some foolish stories, which made him commit a parricide, not like that in May, 1610, but like that in December, 1594; and just like those that a great many other knaves have been guilty of, in other months and other years, after listening to foolish stories.

The lifeguardman then gave him a more particular account of their crimes. "Oh! the monsters," cried Candide; "are there then such terrible crimes among people who dance and sing? Can I not immediately get out of this country, where monkeys provoke tigers? I have seen bears in my own country, but I never met with men except at Eldorado. In the name of God, Mr. Officer, conduct me to Venice, where I am to wait for Miss Cunegonde." "I can conduct you no where except to Lower Normandy," said the mock officer. Immediately he ordered his irons to be struck off, said he was under a mistake, discharged his men, conducted Candide and Martin to Dieppe, and left them in the hands of his brother.

There was then a small Holland trader in the harbor. The Norman, by means of three more diamonds, became the most serviceable man in the world, put Candide and his attendants safe on board the vessel, which was ready to sail for Portsmouth, in England.

This was not the way to Venice; but Candide thought he had escaped from hell, and resolved to resume his voyage towards Venice the first opportunity that offered.

XXIII
Candide and Martin Go to the English Coast, and What They Saw There

"Ah! Pangloss! Ah! Martin! Martin! ah! my dear Cunegonde! what a world is this!" said Candide on board the Dutch ship. "A very foolish and abominable one indeed," replied Martin. "You are acquainted with England, then," said Candide; "are they as great fools there as in France?" "They have a different kind of folly," said Martin. "You know that these two nations are at war about a few acres of snow in Canada, and that they have spent a great deal more upon this war than all Canada is worth. To tell you precisely whether there are more people who ought to be confined in a madhouse in one country than in the other, is more than my weak capacity is able to perform. I only know in general that the people we are going to see are very melancholic."

As they were talking in this manner, they arrived at Portsmouth. The shore was covered with a multitude of people, who were looking very attentively at a pretty stout man who was kneeling, with his eyes bandaged, on the deck of a ship of war; four soldiers, that were placed opposite to him, shot three balls apiece through his head, with the greatest coolness imaginable, and the whole assembly went away very well satisfied. "What is the meaning of this?" said Candide; "and what demon is it that exercises his dominion all over the globe?"

He inquired who the stout gentleman was that was killed with so much ceremony. "He is an admiral," replied some of them. "And why was this admiral killed?" "Because," said they, "he did not kill men enough himself. He attacked the French admiral, and was found guilty of not being near enough to him." "But then," said Candide, "was not the French admiral as far off from the English admiral, as he was from him?" "That is what cannot be doubted," replied they. "But in this country it is of very great service to kill an admiral now and then, in order to make the rest fight better."

Candide was so astonished and shocked at what he had seen and heard, that he would not set foot on shore, but agreed with the master of the Dutch vessel (though he was sure to be robbed by him, as he had been by his countryman at Surinam) to carry him directly to Venice.

The master was ready in two days. They coasted all along France. Passing within sight of Lisbon, Candide gave a very deep groan. They passed the Straits, entered the Medi-terranean, and at last arrived at Venice.

"The Lord be praised," said Candide, embracing Martin, "it is here that I shall see the fair Cunegonde again! I have as good an opinion of Cacambo, as of myself. Everything is right, everything goes well; everything is the best that it can possibly be."

XXIV
Concerning Paquetta and Girofflee

As soon as they arrived at Venice, he caused search for Cacambo in all the inns, in all of the coffeehouses, and among all the girls of the town, but could not find him. He sent every day to all the ships and barks that arrived; but no news of Cacambo. "Well," said he to Martin, "I have had time enough to go from Surinam to Bordeaux, from Bordeaux to Paris, from Paris to Dieppe, from Dieppe to Portsmouth; after that I have coasted along Portugal and Spain, and traversed the Mediterranean, and have now been some months at Venice, and yet, for all that, the lovely Cunegonde is not come. Instead of her, I have only met with a cheating hussy, and a treacherous man of Perigord. Cunegonde is certainly dead, and I have nothing to do but to die also. Ah! it would have been far better for me to have stayed in that paradise, Dorado, than to have returned again to this cursed Europe. You are certainly right, my dear Martin, all is illusion and misery here."

He fell into a deep melancholy, and never frequented the opera, or the other diversions of the carnival; nay, he was proof against all the charms of the fair sex. Martin said to him, "You are very simple indeed, to fancy that a mongrel valet, with five or six millions in his pocket, would go to the end of the world in quest of your mistress, and bring her to Venice. If he meets with her, he'll keep her for himself; if he cannot find her, he'll get somebody else. Let me advise you to forget both your valet Cacambo and your mistress Cunegonde." Martin was a most wretched comforter. The melancholy of Candide increased; and Martin never ceased preaching that there was but very little virtue, and as little happiness, to be found on earth, excepting, perhaps, at Eldorado, where it was almost impossible for any one to go.

Whilst they were disputing on this important subject, and waiting for Cunegonde, Candide perceived a young guard in the Place St. Mark, with his arm around a young girl. He looked fresh, plump, and full of vigor; his eyes were sparkling, his air bold, his mien lofty, and his gait firm. This girl was tolerably handsome, and was singing a song; she ogled her companion with a great deal of passion, and now and then would give his fat cheeks a pinch.

"At least, you will grant me," said Candide to Martin, "that these two folks are happy. I have never found any but unhappy wretches till now, all over this habitable globe, excepting at Eldorado; but as for the girl and the guard, I will lay any wager that they are as happy as happy can be." "I will lay a wager that they are not," said Martin. "Let us invite them to dinner," said Candide, "then we shall see whether I am mistaken or not."

He immediately accosted them, made them a bow, and invited them to his inn to eat macaroni, partridges of Lombardy, and caviare, and to drink montepulciano, Cyprus and Samos wine. The girl blushed; the guard accepted the invitation, and the girl followed him, looking at Candide with surprise and confusion, whilst the tears trickled down her cheeks. Scarce had she entered into Candide's room, when she said to him, "What! does not Mr. Candide know his old friend Paquetta again?" At these words, Candide, who had not yet looked at her with any degree of attention, because Cunegonde engrossed all his thoughts, said to her, "Ah! my poor girl, is it you? you, who reduced Dr. Pangloss to the dreadful plight in which I saw him?"

"Ah, Sir! 'tis I myself," said Paquetta; "I find you know the whole story; and I have been informed of all the terrible disasters which have happened to the family of my Lady the Baroness, and the fair Cunegonde.

My fate, I assure you, has not been less melancholy. I was very innocent when you knew me. A cavalier easily seduced me. The effects of it were terrible. I was obliged to leave the castle some time after the Baron kicked and thrust you out of the door. If a celebrated quack had not taken pity on me, I should have perished. I was the quack's mistress for some time by way of recompense. His wife, who was as jealous as the devil, beat me every day, most unmercifully; she was a very fiend of hell. The doctor was one of the ugliest fellows I ever saw in my life, and I one of the most wretched creatures that ever existed, to be beat every day for the sake of a man whom I hated. You know how dangerous it is for a jealous woman to be married to a doctor. Being quite exasperated with his wife's behavior, he gave her one day so efficacious a remedy to cure her of a slight cold she had, that she died two hours after in the most horrid convulsions. My mistress's relations entered a criminal action against my master; he took to his heels and I was carried to jail. My innocence would never have saved me, if I had not been so handsome. The Judge acquitted me, on condition of his succeeding the doctor. I was soon afterwards supplanted by a rival, driven out of doors without any recompense, and obliged to continue this abominable occupation, which appears so pleasant to you men, while it is to us women the very abyss of misery. I am come to practice my profession at Venice. Ah, Sir, if you could imagine what it is to be obliged to caress indifferently, an old merchant, a counsellor, a gondolier; to be exposed to all sorts of insults and outrages; to be often reduced to borrow a petticoat, to have it rudely pulled up by a disagreeable rascal; to be robbed by one gallant of what one has got from another; to be fleeced by the officers of justice, and to have nothing in prospect but a frightful old age, a hospital, and a dunghill for a sepulchre, you would confess that I am one of the most unfortunate creatures in the world."

Paquetta opened her mind in this manner to the good Candide, in his closet, in the

" 'At least, you will grant me', said Candide to Martin, 'that these two folks are happy. I have never found any but unhappy wretches till now, . . .' "

presence of Martin; who said to Candide, "You see I have won half the wager already."

Girofflee waited in the dining-room, and drank a glass or two while he was waiting for dinner. "But," said Candide, to Paquetta, "you had an air so gay, so content, when I first met you, you sung, and caressed the guard with so much warmth, that you seemed to be as happy then as you pretend to be miserable now." "Ah, Sir," replied Paquetta, "this is one of the miseries of the trade. Yesterday, I was robbed and beaten by an officer, and to-day I am obliged to appear in good humor to please a guard." Candide wanted no more, to be satisfied, and he owned that Martin was in the right. They sat down to table with Paquetta and the soldier; the repast was very entertaining, and towards the end they began to speak to each other with some degree of confidence. "My man," said Candide to the guard, "you seem to enjoy a state that all the world might look on with envy. The flower of health blossoms on your countenance, and your physiognomy speaks nothing but happiness; you have a very pretty girl to divert you, and you seem to be well satisfied with your station as a guard."

"Faith, Sir," said Girofflee, "I wish that all the guards were at the bottom of the sea. I have been tempted an hundred times to set fire to the camp, and go and turn Turk. My parents forced me, at the age of fifteen, to put on this cursed uniform, to increase the fortune of an elder brother of mine, whom God confound. Jealousy, discord, and fury reside there. It is true, indeed, I have brought me in a little money; one part of which the commander robbed me of, and the rest serves me to spend with the girls; but every evening, when I enter the camp, I am ready to dash out my brains against the walls; and all the rest are in the same case."

Martin turned towards Candide, with his usual coolness, "Well," said he to him, "have not I won the whole wager now?" Candide gave two thousand piastres to Paquetta, and one thousand to Girofflee. "I'll answer for it," said he, "this will make them happy." "I don't

believe a word of it," said Martin; "you may perhaps make them a great deal more miserable by your piastres." "Be that as it may," said Candide; "but one thing comforts me, I see that one often finds those persons whom one never expected to find any more; and as I have found my red sheep and Paquetta again, it may be I may find Cunegonde again too." "I wish," said Martin, "that she may one day make you happy; but it is what I very much question." "You are very incredulous," said Candide. "That is what I always was," said Martin.

"But only look on these gondoliers," said Candide; "are they not perpetually singing?" "You don't see them at home with their wives, and their monkeys of children," said Martin. "The Doge has his inquietudes, and the gondoliers have theirs. Indeed, generally speaking, the condition of a gondolier is preferable to that of a doge; but I believe that the difference is so small, that it is not worth the trouble of examining into."

"People speak," said Candide, "of Seignior Pococurante, who lives in that fine palace upon the Brenta, and who entertains strangers in the most polite manner. They pretend that this man never felt any uneasiness." "I should be glad to see so extraordinary a phenomenon," said Martin. On which Candide instantly sent to Seignior Pococurante, to get permission to pay him a visit the next day.

XXV
The Visit to Seignior Pococurante, the Noble Venetian

Candide and Martin went in a gondola on the Brenta, and arrived at the palace of the noble Pococurante. His gardens were very spacious and ornamented with fine statues of marble, and the palace itself was a piece of excellent architecture. The master of the house, a very rich man, of about threescore, received our two inquisitives very politely, but with very little heartiness; which, though it confused Candide, did not give the least uneasiness to Martin.

At first, two young girls, handsome, and

very neatly dressed, served them with chocolate, which was frothed extremely well. Candide could not help dropping them a compliment on their beauty, their politeness, and their address. "The creatures are well enough," said the senator Pococurante: "I sometimes make them sleep with me; for I am quite disgusted with the ladies of the town; their coquetry, their jealousies, quarrels, humors, monkey-tricks, pride, follies, and the sonnets one is obliged to make, or hire others to make for them; but, after all, these two girls begin to grow tiresome to me."

After breakfast, Candide, taking a walk in a long gallery, was charmed with the beauty of the pictures. He asked by what master were the two first. "They are by Raphael," said the senator; "I bought them at a very high price, merely out of vanity, some years ago. They are said to be the finest paintings in Italy: but they do not please me at all; the colors are dead, the figures not finished, and do not appear with *relief* enough; the drapery is very bad. In short, let people say what they will, I do not find there a true imitation of nature. I do not like a piece, unless it makes me think I see nature itself; but there are no such pieces to be met with. I have, indeed, a great many pictures, but I do not value them at all."

While they were waiting for dinner, Pococurante entertained them with a concert; Candide was quite charmed with the music. "This *noise*," said Pococurante, "might divert one for half an hour, or so; but if it were to last any longer, it would grow tiresome to everybody, though no soul durst own it. Music is, now-a-days, nothing else but the art of executing difficulties; and what has nothing but difficulty to recommend it, does not please in the long run.

"I might, perhaps, take more pleasure in the opera, if they had not found out the secret of making such a monster of it as shocks me. Let those go that will to see wretched tragedies set to music, where the scenes are composed for no other end than to lug in by the head and ears two or three ridiculous

songs, in order to show off the throat of an actress to advantage. Let who will, or can, swoon away with pleasure, at hearing a eunuch trill out the part of Caesar and Cato, while strutting upon the stage with a ridiculous and affected air. For my part, I have long ago bid adieu to those paltry entertainments, which constitute the glory of Italy, and are purchased so extravagantly dear." Candide disputed the point a little, but with great discretion. Martin was entirely of the same sentiments with the senator. They sat down to table, and after an excellent dinner, went into the library. Candide, casting his eyes upon a Homer very handsomely bound, praised his High Mightiness for the goodness of his taste. "There," said he, "is a book that was the delight of the good Pangloss, the greatest philosopher in Germany." "It doesn't delight me," said Pococurante, with utter indifference; "I was made to believe formerly that I took a pleasure in reading Homer. But his continued repetition of battles that resemble each other; his gods, who are always very busy without bringing anything to a decision; his Helen, who is the subject of the war, and has scarce anything to do in the whole piece; I say all these defects give me the greatest disgust. I have asked some learned men, if they perused him with as little pleasure as I did? Those who were candid confessed to me that they could not bear to touch the book, but that they were obliged to give it a place in their libraries, as a monument of antiquity, as they do old rusty medals, which are of no use in commerce."

"Your Excellence does not entertain the same opinion of Virgil?" said Candide. "I confess," replied Pococurante, "that the second, the fourth, and the sixth book of his Æneid are excellent; but as for his pious Æneas, his brave Cloanthus, his friend Achates, the little Ascanius, the infirm King Latinus, the burgess Amata, and the insipid Lavinia, I do not think any thing can be more frigid or more disagreeable. I prefer Tasso, and Ariosto's soporiferous tales far before him."

"Shall I presume to ask you, sir," said Candide, "whether you do not enjoy a great deal of pleasure in perusing Horace?" "He has some maxims," said Pococurante, "which may be of a little service to a man who knows the world, and being delivered in expressive numbers, are imprinted more easily on the memory. But I set little value on his voyage to Brundusium, his description of his bad dinner, and the Billingsgate squabble between one Pupillus, whose speech he said was full of filthy stuff, and another whose words were as sharp as vinegar. I never could read without great disgust his indelicate lines against old women and witches; and I cannot see any merit in his telling his friend Maecenas, that if he should be ranked by him amongst the lyric poets, he would strike the stars with his sublime brow. Some fools admire everything in an author of reputation; for my part, I read only for myself; I approve nothing but what suits my own taste." Candide, having been taught to judge of nothing for himself, was very much surprised at what he heard; but Martin looked upon the sentiment of Pococurante as very rational.

"Oh, there's Cicero," said Candide; "this great man, I fancy, you are never tired of reading." "I never read him at all," replied the Venetian. "What is it to me, whether he pleads for Rabirius or Cluentius? I have trials enough of my own. I might, indeed, have been a greater friend to his philosophical works, but when I found he doubted of everything, I concluded I knew as much as he did, and that I had no need of a tutor to learn ignorance."

"Well! here are four and twenty volumes of the Academy of Sciences," cried Martin; "it is possible there may be something valuable in them." "There might be," said Pococurante, "if a single one of the authors of this hodge-podge had been even the inventor of the art of making pins; but there is nothing in all those volumes but chimerical systems, and scarce a single article of real use."

"What a prodigious number of theatrical pieces you have got here," said Candide, "in Italian, Spanish, and French!" "Yes," said the Senator, "there are about three thousand, and not three dozen good ones among them all. As for that collection of sermons, which all together are not worth one page of Seneca, and all those huge volumes of divinity, you may be sure they are never opened either by me or anybody else."

Martin perceiving some of the shelves filled with English books; "I fancy," said he, "a republican, as you are, must certainly be pleased with compositions that are writ with so great a degree of freedom." "Yes," said Pococurante, "it is commendable to write what one thinks; it is the privilege of man. But all over our Italy they write nothing but what they don't think. Those who now inhabit the country of the Caesars and Antonines, dare not have a single idea, without taking out a license from a Jacobin. I should be very well satisfied with the freedom that breathes in the English writers, if passion and the spirit of party did not corrupt all that was valuable in it."

Candide discovering a Milton, asked him if he did not look upon that author as a great genius? "What!" said Pococurante, "that blockhead, that has made a long commentary in ten books of rough verse, on the first chapter of Genesis? that gross imitator of the Greeks, who has disfigured the creation, and who, when Moses has represented the Eternal producing the world by a word, makes the Messiah take a large pair of compasses from the armory of God, to mark out his work? How can I have any esteem for one who has spoiled the hell and devils of Tasso; who turns Lucifer sometimes into a toad, and sometimes into a pigmy; makes him deliver the same speech a hundred times over; represents him disputing on divinity; and who, by a serious imitation of Ariosto's comic invention of firearms, represents the devils letting off their cannon in heaven? Neither myself, nor any one else in Italy, can be pleased at these outrages against common sense; but the marriage of Sin and Death, and the adders of which Sin was brought to bed, are enough to make every person of the least delicacy or taste vomit. This obscure, fantastical, and disgusting poem was despised at its first publication; and I only treat the author now in the same manner as he was treated in his own country by his contemporaries. By the by, I speak what I think; and I give myself no uneasiness whether other people think as I do, or not."

Candide was vexed at this discourse; for he respected Homer, and was fond of Milton. "Ah!" said he, whispering to Martin, "I am very much afraid that this strange man has a sovereign contempt for our German poets." "There would be no great harm in that," said Martin. "Oh, what an extraordinary man!" said Candide, muttering to himself. "What a great genius is this Pococurante! nothing can please him."

After having thus reviewed all the books, they went down into the garden. Candide expatiated upon its beauties. "I never knew anything laid out in such bad taste," said the master; "we have nothing but trifles here; but a day or two hence, I shall have one laid out upon a more noble plan."

When our two inquisitives had taken their leave of his Excellency, "Now, surely," said Candide to Martin, "you will confess that he is one of the happiest men upon earth, for he is above everything that he has." "Do not you see," said Martin, "that he is disgusted with everything that he has? Plato has said a long time ago, that the best stomachs are not those which cast up all sorts of victuals." "But," said Candide, "is not there pleasure in criticising everything? in perceiving defects where other people fancy they see beauties?" "That is to say," replied Martin, "that there is pleasure in having no pleasure." "Ah, well," said Candide, "no person will be so happy as myself, when I see Miss Cunegonde again." "It is always best to hope," said Martin.

In the mean time, days and weeks passed away, but no Cacambo was to be found. And Candide was so immersed in grief, that he did not recollect that Paquetta and Giroflee never so much as once came to return him thanks.

XXVI
Of Candide and Martin Supping with Six Strangers, and Who They Were

One night as Candide, followed by Martin, was going to seat himself at table with some strangers who lodged in the same hotel, a man with a face black as soot came behind him, and taking him by the arm, said, "Get ready to start with us immediately; don't fail!" He turned his head and saw Cacambo. Nothing but the sight of Cunegonde could have surprised or pleased him more. He was ready to run mad for joy. Embracing his dear friend, "Cunegonde is here," said he, "without doubt; where is she? Carry me to her, that I may die with joy in her company!" "Cunegonde is not here," said Cacambo, "she is at Constantinople." "Oh, Heavens! at Constantinople? But, if she was in China, I would fly thither; let us begone." "We will go after supper," replied Cacambo; "I can tell you no more; I am a slave; my master expects me, and I must go and wait at table; say not a word; go to supper and hold yourself in readiness."

Candide, distracted between joy and grief, charmed at having seen his trusty agent, astonished at beholding him a slave, full of the idea of finding his mistress again, his heart palpitating, and his understanding confused, set himself down at the table with Martin (who looked on all these adventures without the least emotion), and with six strangers that were come to spend the carnival at Venice.

Cacambo, who poured out wine for one of the six strangers, drew near to his master, towards the end of the repast, and whispered him in the ear, "Sire, your Majesty may set out when you think proper, the ship is ready." On saying these words, he went out. The guests looked at each other in surprise, without speaking a word; when another servant approaching his master, said to him, "Sire, your Majesty's chaise is at Padua, and the yacht is ready." The master gave a nod, and the domestic retired. All the guests stared at one another again, and their mutual surprise was increased. A third servant approaching the third stranger, said to him, "Sire, believe me, your Majesty must not stay here any longer; I am going to get everything ready"; and immediately he disappeared.

Candide and Martin had by this time concluded that this was a masquerade of the carnival. A fourth domestic said to the fourth master: "Your Majesty may depart whenever you please"; and went out as the others had done. The fifth servant said the same to the fifth master; but the sixth servant spoke in a different manner to the sixth stranger, who sat near Candide: "'Faith, sire," said he, "no one will trust your Majesty any longer, nor myself neither; and we may both be sent to jail this very night; I shall, however, take care of myself. Adieu."

All the domestics having disappeared, the six strangers, with Candide and Martin, remained in a profound silence. At last Candide broke the silence; "Gentlemen," said he, "this is something very droll; but why should you be all Kings? For my part, I own to you, that I am not, neither is Martin."

Cacambo's master answered very gravely in Italian, "I assure you that I am not in jest; I am Achmet III. I was Grand Sultan for several years; I dethroned my brother; my nephew dethroned me; my viziers were beheaded; I pass my life in the old seraglio. But my nephew, the Grand Sultan Mahmoud, permits me to take a voyage sometimes for the benefit of my health, and I have come to pass the carnival at Venice."

A young man who sat near Achmet spoke next; "My name is *Ivan;* I was Emperor of all the Russians; I was dethroned in my cradle; my father and mother were imprisoned; I was brought up in prison. I have sometimes permission to travel, accompanied by two persons as guards; I am also come to pass the carnival at Venice."

The third said, "I am Charles Edward, King of England; my father ceded his rights to the throne to me. I have sought to defend them; eight hundred of my adherents had

their hearts torn out alive, and their heads struck off. I myself have been in prison; I am going to Rome, to pay a visit to my father, who has been dethroned, as well as myself and my grandfather, and am come to Venice to celebrate the carnival."

The fourth then said, "I was King of Poland; the fortune of war has deprived me of my hereditary dominion; my father experienced the same reverse; I resign myself to providence, like the Sultan Achmet, the Emperor Ivan, and Charles Edward, whom God long preserve; and I am come to pass the carnival at Venice."

The fifth said, "I was King of Poland; I lost my kingdom twice; but providence has given me another government, in which I have done more good than all the kings of the Sarmatians put together have been able to do on the banks of the Vistula. I resign myself to providence, and am come to pass the carnival at Venice."

It was now the sixth monarch's turn to speak. "Gentlemen," said he, "I am not so great a prince as any of you; but for all that, I have been a King, as well as the best of you. I am Theodore; I was elected King of Corsica; I was once called *Your Majesty,* but at present am scarce allowed the title of *Sir.* I have caused money to be coined, but am not master at present of a farthing. I have had two secretaries of state, but now have scarce a single servant. I have been myself on a throne, and have for some time lain upon straw in a common jail in London. I am afraid I shall meet with the same treatment here, although I came hither, like your Majesties, to pass the carnival at Venice.

The five other kings heard this speech with a noble compassion. Each of them gave King Theodore twenty sequins to buy him some clothes and shirts, and Candide made him a present of a diamond worth two thousand sequins. "Who," said the five kings, "can this person be, who is able to give, and really has given an hundred times as much as either of us?" "Sir, are you also a King?" "No gentlemen," said Candide, "nor have I any desire to be one."

At the instant they rose from the table there arrived at the same inn four Serene Highnesses, who had also lost their dominions by the fortune of war, and were come to pass the carnival at Venice. But Candide took no notice of these new comers, his thoughts being wholly taken up with going to Constantinople in search of his dear Cunegonde.

XXVII
Candide's Voyage to Constantinople

The faithful Cacambo had already prevailed on the Turkish captain who was going to carry Sultan Achmet back again to Constantinople, to receive Candide and Martin on board. They both of them embarked, after they had prostrated themselves before his miserable Highness. As Candide was on his way, he said to Martin, "There were six dethroned kings that we supped with; and what is still more, among these six kings there was one that I gave alms to. Perhaps there may be a great many other princes more unfortunate still. For my own part, I have lost only one hundred sheep, and am flying to the arms of Cunegonde. My dear Martin, I must still say, Pangloss was in the right; all things are for the best." "I wish they were," said Martin. "But," said Candide, "the adventure we met with at Venice is something romantic. Such a thing was never before either seen or heard of, that six dethroned kings should sup together at a common inn." "This is not more extraordinary," replied Martin, "than most of the things that have happened to us. It is a common thing for kings to be dethroned; and with respect to the honor that we had of supping with them, it is a trifle that does not merit our attention."

Scarce had Candide got on board, when he fell on the neck of his old servant and friend Cacambo. "Well," said he, "what news of Cunegonde? is she still a miracle of beauty? does she love me still? how does she do? No doubt but you have bought a palace for her at Constantinople?"

"My dear master," replied Cacambo, "Cunegonde washes dishes on the banks of the Propontis, for a prince who has very few to wash; she is a slave in the house of an ancient sovereign named *Ragotsky*, to whom the Grand Turk allows three crowns a day to support him in his asylum; but, what is worse than all, she has lost her beauty, and is become shockingly ugly." "Well, handsome or ugly," replied Candide, "I am a man of honor, and it is my duty to love her still. But how came she to be reduced to so abject a condition, with the five or six millions that you carried her?" "Well," said Cacambo, "was I not to give two millions to Signor Don Fernandes d'Ibaraa, y Figueora, y Mascarenes, y Lampourdos, y Souza, the governor of Buenos-Ayres, for permission to take Miss Cunegonde back again? and did not a pirate rob us of all the rest? Did not this pirate carry us to Cape Matapan, to Milo, to Nicaria, to Samos, to Dardanelles, to Marmora, to Scutari? Cunegonde and the old woman are servants to the prince I told you of, and I am a slave of the dethroned sultan." "What a chain of shocking calamities!" said Candide. "But, after all, I have some diamonds, I shall easily purchase Cunegonde's liberty. It is a pity that she is grown so ugly."

Then, turning himself to Martin, "Who do you think," says he, "is most to be pitied; the Sultan Achmet, the Emperor Ivan, King Charles Edward, or myself?" "I cannot tell," said Martin, "I must look into your hearts to be able to tell." "Ah!" said Candide, "if Pangloss were here, he would know and tell us." "I know not," replied Martin, "in what sort of scales your Pangloss would weigh the misfortunes of mankind, and how he would appraise their sorrows. All that I can venture to say is, that there are millions of men upon earth a hundred times more to be pitied than King Charles Edward, the Emperor Ivan, or Sultan Achmet."

"That may be so," said Candide.

In a few days they reached the Black Sea. Candide began with ransoming Cacambo at an extravagant price; and, without loss of time, he got into a galley with his companions to go to the banks of the Propontis, in search

" 'My dear master', replied Cacambo, 'Cunegonde washes dishes on the banks of the Propontis, for a prince who has very few to wash; she is a slave in the house of an ancient sovereign named Ragotsky, . . . ' "

of Cunegonde, however ugly she might have become.

Among the crew, there were two slaves that rowed very badly, to whose bare shoulders the Levant trader would now and then apply severe strokes with a bull's pizzle. Candide, by a natural sympathy, looked at them more attentively than at the rest of the galley-slaves, and went up to them with a heart full of pity. The features of two of their faces, though very much disfigured, seemed to bear some resemblance to those of Pangloss, and the unfortunate Baron, the brother of Miss Cunegonde. This fancy made him feel very sad. He looked at them again more attentively. "Really," said he to Cacambo, "if I had not seen the good Pangloss hanged, and had not had the misfortune to kill the Baron myself, I should think it was they who are rowing in this galley."

At the names of the Baron and Pangloss, the two galley-slaves gave a loud shriek, became as if petrified in their seats, and let their oars drop. The master of the Levanter ran up to them, and redoubled the lashes of the bull's pizzle upon them. "Hold! Hold! Seignior," cried Candide, "I will give you what money you please." "What! it is Candide!" said one of the galley-slaves. "Oh! it is Candide!" said the other. "Do I dream?" said Candide; "am I awake? am I in this galley? is that Master Baron whom I killed? is that Master Pangloss whom I saw hanged?"

"It is ourselves! It is our very selves!" they exlaimed. What! "is that the great philosopher?" said Martin. "Harkee, Master Levant Captain," said Candide, "what will you take for the ransom of Monsieur Thunder-ten-tronckh, one of the first Barons of the empire, together with Master Pangloss, the most profound metaphysician of Germany?" "You Christian dog," said the Levant captain, "since these two dogs of Christian slaves are a baron and a metaphysician, which, without doubt, are high dignities in their own country, you shall give me fifty thousand sequins." "You shall have the money, sir; carry me back again, like lightning, to Constantinople, and you shall be paid directly. But stop, carry me to Miss Cunegonde first." The Levant captain, on the first offer of Candide, had turned the head of the vessel towards the city, and made the other slaves row faster than a bird cleaves the air.

Candide embraced the Baron and Pangloss a hundred times. "How happened it that I did not kill you, my dear Baron? and, my dear Pangloss, how came you to life again, after being hanged? and how came both of you to be galley-slaves in Turkey?" "Is it true that my dear sister is in this country?" said the Baron. "Yes," replied Cacambo. "Then I see my dear Candide once more," said Pangloss.

Candide presented Martin and Cacambo to them; the whole party mutually embraced, and all spoke at the same time. The galley flew like lightning, and they were already in the port. A Jew was sent for, to whom Candide sold a diamond for fifty thousand sequins, which was worth a hundred thousand, the Israelite swearing by Abraham that he could not give any more. He immediately paid the ransom of the Baron and Pangloss. The latter threw himself at the feet of his deliverer, and bathed them with his tears; as for the other, he thanked him with a nod, and promised to repay him the money the first opportunity. "But is it possible that my sister is in Turkey?" said he. "Nothing is more possible," replied Cacambo; "for she scours dishes in the house of a prince of Transylvania!" Two more Jews were instantly sent for, to whom Candide sold some more diamonds; and he and his party all set out again, in another galley, to go and deliver Cunegonde.

XXVIII
What Happened to Candide, Cunegonde, Pangloss, Martin, Etc.

"I ask your pardon once more," said Candide to the Baron. "I ask pardon for having thrust my sword through your body." "Don't let us say any more about it," said the Baron; "I was a little too hasty, I must confess. But since you desire to know by what fatality I came to be a galley-slave, I will inform you. After I was cured of my wound, by a brother who was apothecary, I was attacked and carried off by a party of Spaniards, who confined me in prison at Buenos-Ayres, at the very time my sister was setting out from thence. I demanded leave to return to Europe. I was nominated to go as almoner to Constantinople, with the French ambassador. I had not been eight days engaged in this employment, when one day I met with a young, well-made Icoglan. It was then very hot; the young man went to bathe himself, and I took the opportunity to bathe myself too. I did not know that it was a capital crime for a Christian to be found naked with a young Mussulman. A cadi ordered me to receive a hundred strokes of the bastinado on the soles of my feet, and condemned me to the galleys. I do not think there ever was a greater act of injustice. But I should be glad to know how it comes about, that my sister is dish-washer in the kitchen of a Transylvania prince, who is a refugee among the Turks."

"But you, my dear Pangloss," said Candide, "how came I ever to set eyes on you again!" "It is true, indeed," said Pangloss, "that you saw me hanged; I ought naturally to have been burnt; but you may remember, that it rained prodigiously when they were going to roast me; the storm was so violent that they despaired of lighting the fire. I was therefore hanged because they could do no better. A surgeon bought my body, carried it home with him, and began to dissect me. He first made a crucial incision. No one could have been more slovenly hanged than I was. The executioner of the inquisition burnt people marvellously well, but he was not used to the art of hanging them. The cord being wet did not slip properly, and the noose was badly tied: in short, I still drew my breath. The crucial incision made me give such a dreadful shriek, that my surgeon fell down backwards, and fancying he was dissecting the devil, he ran away, ready to die with the fright, and fell down a second time on the stair-case, as he was making off. His wife ran out of an adjacent closet, on hearing the noise, saw me extended on the table with my crucial incision, and being more frightened than her husband, fled also, and tumbled over him. When they were come to themselves a little, I heard the surgeon's wife say to him, "My dear, how came you to be so foolish as to venture to dissect a heretic? Don't you know that the devil always takes possession of the bodies of such people? I will go immediately and fetch a priest to exorcise him." I shuddered at this proposal, and mustered up what little strength I had left to cry out, Oh! have pity upon me! At length the Portuguese barber took courage, sewed up my skin, and his wife nursed me so well, that I was upon my feet again in about fifteen days. The barber got me a place, to be footman to a knight of Malta, who was going to Venice; but my master not being able to pay me my wages, I engaged in the service of a Venetian merchant, and went along with him to Constantinople.

"One day I took a fancy to go into a mosque. There was nobody there but an old iman, and a very handsome young devotee saying her prayers. Her breast was uncovered; she had in her bosom a beautiful nosegay of tulips, anemones, ranunculuses, hyacinths, and auriculas; she let her nosegay fall; I took it up, and presented it to her with the most profound reverence. However, I was so long in handing it to her, that the iman fell into a passion, and seeing I was a Christian, called out for help. They carried me before the cadi, who ordered me a hundred bastinadoes, and to be sent to the galleys. I was chained to the same galley and the same bench with the Baron. There were on board this galley four young men from Marseilles, five Neapolitan priests and two monks of Corfu, who told us that the like adventures happened every day. The Baron pretended that he had suffered more injustice than I; and I insisted that it was far more innocent to put a nosegay into a young woman's bosom, than to be found stark naked with an Icoglan. We were perpetually disputing, and we received twenty lashes every day with a bull's pizzle, when the concatenation of events in this universe brought you to our galley, and you ransomed us."

"Well, my dear Pangloss," said Candide, "when you were hanged, dissected, severely beaten, and tugging at the oar in the galley, did you always think that things in this world were all for the best?" "I am still as I always have been, of my first opinion," answered Pangloss; "for as I am a philosopher, it would be inconsistent with my character to contradict myself; especially as Liebnitz could not be in the wrong; and his pre-established harmony is certainly the finest system in the world, as well as his gross and subtle manner."

XXIX
How Candide Found Cunegonde and the Old Woman Again

While Candide, the Baron, Pangloss, Martin, and Cacambo, were relating their adventures to each other, and disputing about the contingent and non-contingent events of this world, and while they were arguing upon effects and causes, on moral and physical evil, on liberty and necessity, and on the consolations a person may experience in the galleys in Turkey, they arrive on the banks of the Propontis, at the house of the Prince of Transylvania. The first objects which presented themselves were Cunegonde and the old woman, hanging out some table-linen on the line to dry.

The Baron grew pale at this sight. Even Candide, the affectionate lover, on seeing his fair Cunegonde awfully tanned, with her eyelids reversed, her neck withered, her cheeks wrinkled, her arms red and rough, was seized with horror, jumped near three yards backwards, but afterwards advanced to her, but with more politeness than passion. She embraced Candide and her brother, who, each of them, embraced the old woman, and Candide ransomed them both.

There was a little farm in the neighborhood, which the old woman advised Candide to hire, till they could meet with better ac-

commodations for their whole company. As Cunegonde did not know that she had grown ugly, nobody having told her of it, she put Candide in mind of his promise to marry her, in so peremptory a manner, that he durst not refuse her. But when this thing was intimated to the Baron: "I will never suffer," said he, "such meanness on her part, nor such insolence on yours. With this infamy I will never be reproached. The children of my sister shall never be enrolled in the chapters of Germany. No; my sister shall never marry any but a Baron of the empire." Cunegonde threw herself at her brother's feet, and bathed them with her tears, but he remained inflexible. "You ungrateful puppy, you," said Candide to him. "I have delivered you from the galleys; I have paid your ransom; I have also paid that of your sister, who was a scullion here, and is very homely; I have the goodness, however, to make her my wife, and you are fool enough to oppose it; I have a good mind to kill you again, you make me so angry." "You may indeed kill me again," said the Baron; "but you shall never marry my sister, while I have breath."

XXX
Conclusion

Candide had no great desire, at the bottom of his heart, to marry Cunegonde. But the extreme impertinence of the Baron determined him to conclude the match, and Cunegonde pressed it so earnestly, that he could not retract. He advised with Pangloss, Martin, and the trusty Cacambo. Pangloss drew up on excellent memoir, in which he proved, that the Baron had no right over his sister, and that she might, according to all the laws of the empire, espouse Candide with her left hand. Martin was for throwing the Baron into the sea: Cacambo was of opinion that it would be best to send him back again to the Levant captain, and make him work at the galleys. This advice was thought good; the old woman approved it, and nothing was said to his sister about it. The scheme was put in execution for a little money, and so they had the pleasure of punishing the pride of a German Baron.

It is natural to imagine that Candide, after so many disasters, married to his sweetheart, living with the philosopher Pangloss, the philosopher Martin, the discreet Cacambo, and the old woman, and especially as he had brought so many diamonds from the country of the ancient Incas, must live the most agreeable life of any man in the whole world. But he had been so cheated by the Jews, that he had nothing left but the small farm; and his wife, growing still more ugly, turned peevish and insupportable. The old woman was very infirm, and worse humored than Cunegonde herself. Cacambo, who worked in the garden, and went to Constantinople to sell its productions, was worn out with labor, and cursed his fate. Pangloss was ready to despair, because he did not shine at the head of some university in Germany. As for Martin, as he was firmly persuaded that all was equally bad throughout, he bore things with patience. Candide, Martin, and Pangloss, disputed sometimes about metaphysics and ethics. They often saw passing under the windows of the farm-house boats full of effendis, bashaws, and cadis, who were going into banishment to Lemnos, Mitylene, and Erzerum. They observed that other cadis, bashaws, and effendis, succeeded in the posts of those who were exiled, only to be banished themselves in turn. They saw heads nicely impaled, to be presented to the Sublime Porte. These spectacles increased the number of their disputations; and when they were not disputing, their *ennui* was so tiresome that the old woman would often say to them, "I want to know which is the worst;—to be ravished an hundred times by negro pirates, to run the gauntlet among the Bulgarians, to be whipped and hanged, to be dissected, to row in the galleys; in a word, to have suffered all the miseries we have undergone, or to stay here, without doing anything?" "That is a great question," said Candide.

This discourse gave rise to new reflections, and Martin concluded, upon the whole, that mankind were born to live either in the distractions of inquietude, or in the lethargy of disgust. Candide did not agree with that opinion, but remained in a state of suspense. Pangloss confessed, that he had always suffered dreadfully; but having once maintained that all things went wonderfully well, he still kept firm to his hypothesis, though it was quite opposed to his real feelings.

What contributed to confirm Martin in his shocking principles, to make Candide stagger more than ever, and to embarrass Pangloss, was, that one day they saw Paquetta and Giroflee, who were in the greatest distress, at their farm. They had quickly squandered away their three thousand piastres, had parted, were reconciled, quarrelled again, had been confined in prison, had made their escape, and Giroflee had at length turned Turk. Paquetta continued her trade wherever she went, but made nothing by it. "I could easily foresee," said Martin to Candide, "that your presents would soon be squandered away, and would render them more miserable. You and Cacambo have spent millions of piastres, and are not a bit happier than Giroflee and Paquetta." "Ha! ha!" said Pangloss to Paquetta, "has Providence then brought you amongst us again, my poor child? Know, then, that you have cost me the tip of my nose, one eye, and one of my ears, as you see. What a world this is!" This new adventure set them a philosophizing more than ever.

There lived in the neighborhood a very famous dervise, who passed for the greatest philosopher in Turkey. They went to consult him. Pangloss was chosen speaker, and said to him, "Master, we are come to desire you would tell us, why so strange an animal as man was created."

"What's that to you?" said the dervise; "is it any business of thine?" "But, my reverend father," said Candide, "there is a horrible amount of evil in the world." "What signifies," said the dervise, "whether there be good or evil? When his Sublime Highness send a vessel to Egypt, does it trouble him, whether the mice on board are at their ease or not?" "What would you have one do then?" said Pangloss. "Hold your tongue," said the dervise. "I promised myself the pleasure," said Pangloss, "of reasoning with you upon effects and causes, the best of possible worlds, the origin of evil, the nature of the soul, and the pre-established harmony."— The dervise, at these words, shut the door in their faces.

During this conference, news was brought that two viziers and a mufti were strangled at Constantinople, and a great many of their friends impaled. This catastrophe made a great noise for several hours. Pangloss, Candide, and Martin, on their way back to the little farm, met a good-looking old man, taking the air at his door, under an arbor of orange trees. Pangloss, who had as much curiosity as philosophy, asked him the name of the mufti who was lately strangled. "I know nothing at all about it," said the good man; "and what's more, I never knew the name of a single mufti, or a single vizier, in my life. I am an entire stranger to the story you mention; and presume that, generally speaking, they who trouble their heads with state affairs, sometimes die shocking deaths, not without deserving it. But I never trouble my head about what is doing at Constantinople; I content myself with sending my fruits thither, the produce of my garden, which I cultivate with my own hands!" Having said these words, he introduced the strangers into his house. His two daughters and two sons served them with several kinds of sherbet, which they made themselves, besides caymac, enriched with the peels of candied citrons, oranges, lemons, bananas, pistachio nuts, and Mocoa coffee, unadulterated with the bad coffee of Batavia and the isles. After which, the two daughters of this good Mussulman perfumed the beards of Candide, Pangloss, and Martin.

"You must certainly," said Candide to the Turk, "have a very large and very opulent estate!" "I have only twenty acres," said the Turk; "which I, with my children, cultivate. Labor keeps us free from three of the greatest evils: tiresomeness, vice, and want."

As Candide returned to his farm, he made deep reflections on the discourse of the Turk. Said he to Pangloss and Martin, "The condition of this good old man seems to me preferable to that of the six kings with whom we had the honor to sup." "The grandeurs of royalty," said Pangloss, "are very precarious, in the opinion of all philosophers. For, in short, Eglon, king of the Moabites, was assassinated by Ehud; Absalom was hung by the hair of his head, and pierced through with three darts; King Nadab, the son of Jeroboam, was killed by Baasha; King Elah by Zimri; Ahaziah by Jehu; Athaliah by Jehoiadah; the kings Joachim, Jechonias, and Zedekias, were carried into captivity. You know the fates of Croesus, Astyages, Darius, Dionysius of Syracuse, Pyrrhus, Perseus, Hannibal, Jugurtha, Ariovistus, Caesar, Pompey, Nero, Otho, Vitellius, Domitian, Richard II., Edward II., Henry VI., Richard III., Mary Stuart, Charles I. of England, the three Henrys of France, and the Emperor Henry IV. You know—" "I know very well," said Candide, "that we ought to look after our garden." "You are in the right," said Pangloss, "for when man was placed in the garden of Eden, he was placed there, *ut operatur cum*, to cultivate it; which proves that mankind are not created to be idle." "Let us work," said Martin, "without disputing; it is the only way to render life supportable."

All their little society entered into this laudable design, according to their different abilities. Their little piece of ground produced a plentiful crop. Cunegonde was indeed very homely, but she became an excellent pastry cook. Paquetta worked at embroidery, and the old woman took care of the linen. There was no idle person in the company, not excepting even Giroflee; he made a very good carpenter, and became a very honest man.

As to Pangloss, he evidently had a lurking consciousness that his theory required unceasing exertions, and all his ingenuity, to sustain it. Yet he stuck to it to the last; his thinking and talking faculties could hardly be diverted from it for a moment. He seized every occasion to say to Candide, "All the events in this best of possible worlds are admirably connected. If a single link in the great chain were omitted, the harmony of the entire universe would be destroyed. If you had not been expelled from that beautiful castle, with those cruel kicks, for your love to Miss Cunegonde; if you had not been imprisoned by the inquisition; if you had not travelled over a great portion of America on foot; if you had not plunged your sword through the baron; if you had not lost all the sheep you brought from that fine country, Eldorado, together with the riches with which they were laden, you would not be here to-day, eating preserved citrons, and pistachio nuts."

"That's very well said, and may all be true," said Candide; "but let's cultivate our garden."

The Great Instauration

Francis Bacon

Editor's Introduction

Appearing elsewhere in this volume of *The Great Ideas Today* is an article by Stephen Toulmin that invites us to think about a new kind of science appropriate to the aims and structures of the post-modern age. Over three hundred and fifty years ago, Francis Bacon, one of the most famous scientific thinkers in history, presented his own plan for a total reevaluation and renovation of the sciences. He has often been cited as the founder of the modern scientific method, a procedure based upon experimentation and induction. The aim of his endeavors was to discover principles of knowledge which would direct action in ultimately overcoming the misery arising from the human condition. For Bacon, the end of science was knowledge, and knowledge was power; by understanding the principles of nature, we could finally possess the power to command them.

The work for which Bacon is most remembered and in which he revealed his plan for the restoration of science is *The Great Instauration,* the main part of which, *The Novum Organum,* was published in 1620. However, in 1605, Bacon published *The Advancement of Learning,* where he criticized those tendencies which impede a true understanding of nature, namely the reliance upon accepted authorities, the bias of specialists, and the "reduction of knowledge into arts." His answer to this perceived lack of a true method by which man can come to know anything can be found in *The Great Instauration.* It is here that Bacon propounded his plan to replace the practice of citing authorities (such as Aristotle) with a procedure that would eliminate prejudice and inexactitude.

Although Bacon is best known for his contribution to the philosophy of science, his life was not that of an aloof contemplative, disengaged from the political and social arenas. To the contrary, much of his energy and writing were devoted to securing positions of political prominence in the courts of Elizabeth I and James I.

He was born in London on January 22, 1561, the son of Sir Nicholas Bacon, Lord Keeper of the Seal, and Anne Cooke, an erudite woman with political connections of her own. In 1573 Bacon entered Trinity College at Cambridge, where he acquired a distaste for Aristotelian philosophy and scholastic life, and left after two years due to ill health. He went to Paris in 1576 with the British ambassador as preparation for a political career. In the same year, he was admitted to Gray's Inn for a legal education. His father died in 1579, leaving him with a meager inheritance and financial problems which were to plague him for years. (He was arrested for debt in 1598.) In 1582 Bacon became a barrister and progressed to the position of king's counsel extraordinary to the solicitor general; two years later he sat in Parliament as a leading member of the House of Commons. Although Bacon had prominent political connections and wrote a series of letters to the Queen applying for support and preferment, he never attained importance in Elizabeth's court because of his objection to her request of Parliament for subsidies to meet her war expenses in Spain.

It was during Elizabeth's reign that Bacon's controversial involvement with Robert Devereux, the Earl of Essex and the Queen's favorite, came about. The two met in 1591 and Bacon fostered the friendship with much advice and wisdom, Essex reciprocating with recommendations to the Queen for Bacon's advancement, although to no avail. Bacon advised Essex to direct his attention to Ireland where there was much rebellion against the Crown, but Essex failed miserably there and returned against orders. Essex was tried with Bacon as the prosecutor, but even afterward Essex felt no ill will toward his former adviser. However, after Essex attempted rebellion in February 1601, Bacon considered Essex a traitor and wrote the official report against him, entitled *A Declaration of the Practices and Treasons attempted and committed by Robert, late Earle of Essex.* In 1604 he wrote *Apologie in certaine imputations concerning the late Earle of Essex* as a defense of his seeming betrayal of Essex, but never seemed to have had any regrets about having been his official accuser.

Bacon's career in the court of James I advanced rapidly; he moved from solicitor-general in 1607 to Lord Chancellor in 1618, and was made Baron Verulam in 1618 and Viscount St. Albans in 1621. Bacon supported James in his struggles with Parliament, defending the royal prerogative, and wrote remarkable papers of advice to him on affairs of state, in particular, on the relations between the Crown and Parliament, all of which was rewarded by James. During this period, Bacon also wrote some three dozen plays and completed twelve drafts of the *Novum Organum.*

In 1621 two charges of bribery were brought against Bacon. He acknowledged receipt but claimed to have been unaffected by it. His defense was not fairly considered, and he was obliged to accept a punishment which entailed a fine of £40,000, imprisonment in the Tower of London, and exclusion from state office and Parliament. Bacon never regained his political status after that but devoted the rest of his life to writing on everything from law to educational reforms. In 1623 he published *De Augmentis Scientiarum,* a Latin translation of the *Advancement of Learning,* and *Historia Vitæ* ("History of Life and Death"). During this time, he also wrote *History of Henry VII.* The final edition of his *Essayes* appeared in 1625.

Prooemium

FRANCIS OF VERULAM *reasoned thus with himself, and judged it to be for the interest of the present and future generations that they should be made acquainted with his thoughts*

Being convinced that the human intellect makes its own difficulties, not using the true helps which are at man's disposal soberly and judiciously; whence follows manifold ignorance of things, and by reason of that ignorance mischiefs innumerable; he thought all trial should be made, whether that commerce between the mind of man and the nature of things, which is more precious than anything on earth, or at least than anything that is of the earth, might by any means be restored to its perfect and original condition, or if that may not be, yet reduced to a better condition than that in which it now is. Now that the errors which have hitherto prevailed, and which will prevail for ever, should (if the mind be left to go its own way), either by the natural force of the understanding or by help of the aids and instruments of Logic, one by one correct themselves, was a thing not to be hoped for: because the primary notions of things which the mind readily and passively imbibes, stores up, and accumulates (and it is from them that all the rest flow) are false, confused, and overhastily abstracted from the facts; nor are the secondary and subsequent notions less arbitrary and inconstant; whence it follows that the entire fabric of human reason which we employ in the inquisition of nature, is badly put together and built up, and like some magnificent structure without any foundation. For while men are occupied in admiring and applauding the false powers of the mind, they pass by and throw away those true powers, which, if it be supplied with the proper aids and can itself be content to wait upon nature instead of vainly affecting to overrule her, are within its reach. There was but one course left, therefore,—to try the whole thing anew upon a better plan, and to commence a total reconstruction of sciences, arts, and all human knowledge, raised upon the proper foundations. And this, though in the project and undertaking it may seem a thing infinite and beyond the powers of man, yet when it comes to be dealt with it will be found sound and sober, more so than what has been done hitherto. For of this there is some issue; whereas in what is now done in the matter of science there is only a whirling round about, and perpetual agitation, ending where it began. And although he was well aware how solitary an enterprise it is, and how hard a thing to win faith and credit for, nevertheless he was resolved not to abandon either it or himself; nor to be deterred from trying and entering upon that one path which is alone open to the human mind. For better it is to make a beginning of that which may lead to something, than to engage in a perpetual struggle and pursuit in courses which have no exit. And certainly the two ways of contemplation are much like those two ways of action, so much celebrated, in this—that the one, arduous and difficult in the beginning, leads out at last into the open country; while the other, seeming at first sight easy and free from obstruction, leads to pathless and precipitous places.

Moreover, because he knew not how long it might be before these things would occur to any one else, judging especially from this, that he has found no man hitherto who has applied his mind to the like, he resolved to publish at once so much as he has been able to complete. The cause of which haste was not ambition for himself, but solicitude for the work; that in case of his death there might remain some outline and project of that which he had conceived, and some evidence likewise of his honest mind and inclination towards the benefit of the human race. Certain it is that all other ambition whatsoever seemed poor in his eyes compared with the work which he had in hand; seeing that the matter at issue is either nothing, or a thing so great that it may well be content with its own merit, without seeking other recompense.

Preface

That the state of knowledge is not prosperous nor greatly advancing; and that a way must be opened for the human understanding entirely different from any hitherto known, and other helps provided, in order that the mind may exercise over the nature of things the authority which properly belongs to it.

It seems to me that men do not rightly understand either their store or their strength, but overrate the one and underrate the other. Hence it follows, that either from an extravagant estimate of the value of the arts which they possess, they seek no further; or else from too mean an estimate of their own powers, they spend their strength in small matters and never put it fairly to the trial in those which go to the main. These are as the pillars of fate set in the path of knowledge; for men have neither desire nor hope to encourage them to penetrate further. And since opinion of store is one of the chief causes of want, and satisfaction with the present induces neglect of provision for the future, it becomes a thing not only useful, but absolutely necessary, that the excess of honour and admiration with which our existing stock of inventions is regarded be in the very entrance and threshold of the work, and that frankly and without circumlocution, stripped off, and men be duly warned not to exaggerate or make too much of them. For let a man look carefully into all that variety of books with which the arts and sciences abound, he will find everywhere endless repetitions of the same thing, varying in the method of treatment, but not new in substance, insomuch that the whole stock, numerous as it appears at first view, proves on examination to be but scanty. And for its value and utility it must be plainly avowed that that wisdom which we have derived principally from the Greeks is but like the boyhood of knowledge, and has the characteristic property of boys: it can talk, but it cannot generate; for it is fruitful of controversies but barren of works. So that the state of learning as it now is appears to be represented to the life in the old fable of Scylla, who had the head and face of a virgin, but her womb was hung round with barking monsters, from which she could not be delivered. For in like manner the sciences to which we are accustomed have certain general positions which are specious and flattering; but as soon as they come to particulars, which are as the parts of generation, when they should produce fruit and works, then arise contentions and barking disputations, which are the end of the matter and all the issue they can yield. Observe also, that if sciences of this kind had any life in them, that could never have come to pass which has been the case now for many ages—that they stand almost at a stay, without receiving any augmentations worthy of the human race; insomuch that many times not only what was asserted once is asserted still, but what was a question once is a question still, and instead of being resolved by discussion is only fixed and fed; and all the tradition and succession of schools is still a succession of masters and scholars, not of inventors and those who bring to further perfection the things invented. In the mechanical arts we do not find it so; they, on the contrary, as having in them some breath of life, are continually growing and becoming more perfect. As originally invented they are commonly rude, clumsy, and shapeless; afterwards they acquire new powers and more commodious arrangements and constructions; in so far that men shall sooner leave the study and pursuit of them and turn to something else, than they arrive at the ultimate perfection of which they are capable. Philosophy and the intellectual sciences, on the contrary, stand like statues, worshipped and celebrated, but not moved or advanced. Nay, they sometimes flourish most in the hands of the first author, and afterwards degenerate. For when men have once made over their judgments to others' keeping, and (like those senators whom they called *Pedarii*) have agreed to support some one person's opinion, from that time they make no enlargement of the sciences themselves, but fall to the servile office of embellishing certain individual authors and increasing their retinue. And let it not be said that the sciences have been growing gradually till they have at last reached their full stature, and so (their course being completed) have settled in the works of a few writers; and that there being now no room for the invention of better, all that remains is to embellish and cultivate those things which have been invented already. Would it were so! But the truth is that this appropriating of the sciences has its origin in nothing better than the confidence of a few persons and the sloth and indolence of the rest. For after the sciences had been in several parts perhaps cultivated and handled diligently, there has risen up some man of bold disposition, and famous for methods and short ways which people like, who has in appearance reduced them to an art, while he has in fact only spoiled all that the others had done. And yet this is what posterity like, because it makes the work short and easy, and saves further

inquiry, of which they are weary and impatient. And if any one take this general acquiescence and consent for an argument of weight, as being the judgment of Time, let me tell him that the reasoning on which he relies is most fallacious and weak. For, first, we are far from knowing all that in the matter of sciences and arts has in various ages and places been brought to light and published; much less, all that has been by private persons secretly attempted and stirred; so neither the births nor the miscarriages of Time are entered in our records. Nor, secondly, is the consent itself and the time it has continued a consideration of much worth. For however various are the forms of civil polities, there is but one form of polity in the sciences; and that always has been and always will be popular. Now the doctrines which find most favour with the populace are those which are either contentious and pugnacious, or specious and empty; such, I say, as either entangle assent or tickle it. And therefore no doubt the greatest wits in each successive age have been forced out of their own course; men of capacity and intellect above the vulgar having been fain, for reputation's sake, to bow to the judgment of the time and the multitude; and thus if any contemplations of a higher order took light anywhere, they were presently blown out by the winds of vulgar opinions. So that Time is like a river, which has brought down to us things light and puffed up, while those which are weighty and solid have sunk. Nay, those very authors who have usurped a kind of dictatorship in the sciences and taken upon them to lay down the law with such confidence, yet when from time to time they come to themselves again, they fall to complaints of the subtlety of nature, the hiding-places of truth, the obscurity of things, the entanglement of causes, the weakness of the human mind; wherein nevertheless they show themselves never the more modest, seeing that they will rather lay the blame upon the common condition of men and nature than upon themselves. And then whatever any art fails to attain, they ever set it down upon the authority of that art itself as impossible of attainment; and how can art be found guilty when it is judge in its own cause? So it is but a device for exempting ignorance from ignominy. Now for those things which are delivered and received, this is their condition: barren of works, full of questions; in point of enlargement slow and languid; carrying a show of perfection in the whole, but in the parts ill filled up; in selection popular, and unsatisfactory even to those who propound them; and therefore fenced round and set forth with sundry artifices. And if there be any who have determined to make trial for themselves, and put their own strength to the work of advancing the boundaries of the sciences, yet have they not ventured to cast themselves completely loose from received opinions or to seek their knowledge at the fountain; but they think they have done some great thing if they do but add and introduce into the existing sum of science something of their own; prudently considering with themselves that by making the addition they can assert their liberty, while they retain the credit of modesty by assenting to the rest. But these mediocrities and middle ways so much praised, in deferring to opinions and customs, turn to the great detriment of the sciences. For it is hardly possible at once to admire an author and to go beyond him; knowledge being as water, which will not rise above the level from which it fell. Men of this kind, therefore, amend some things, but advance little; and improve the condition of knowledge, but do not extend its range. Some, indeed, there have been who have gone more boldly to work, and taking it all for an open matter and giving their genius full play, have made a passage for themselves and their own opinions by pulling down and demolishing former ones; and yet all their stir has but little advanced the matter; since their aim has been not to extend philosophy and the arts in substance and value, but only to change doctrines and transfer the kingdom of opinions to themselves; whereby little has indeed been gained, for though the error be the opposite of the other, the causes

of erring are the same in both. And if there have been any who, not binding themselves either to other men's opinions or to their own, but loving liberty, have desired to engage others along with themselves in search, these, though honest in intention, have been weak in endeavour. For they have been content to follow probable reasons, and are carried round in a whirl of arguments, and in the promiscuous liberty of search have relaxed the severity of inquiry. There is none who has dwelt upon experience and the facts of nature as long as is necessary. Some there are indeed who have committed themselves to the waves of experience, and almost turned mechanics; yet these again have in their very experiments pursued a kind of wandering inquiry, without any regular system of operations. And besides they have mostly proposed to themselves certain petty tasks, taking it for a great matter to work out some single discovery;—a course of proceeding at once poor in aim and unskilful in design. For no man can rightly and successfully investigate the nature of anything in the thing itself; let him vary his experiments as laboriously as he will, he never comes to a resting-place, but still finds something to seek beyond. And there is another thing to be remembered; namely, that all industry in experimenting has begun with proposing to itself certain definite works to be accomplished, and has pursued them with premature and unseasonable eagerness; it has sought, I say, experiments of Fruit, not experiments of Light; not imitating the divine procedure, which in its first day's work created light only and assigned to it one entire day; on which day it produced no material work, but proceeded to that on the days following. As for those who have given the first place to Logic, supposing that the surest helps to the sciences were to be found in that, they have indeed most truly and excellently perceived that the human intellect left to its own course is not to be trusted; but then the remedy is altogether too weak for the disease; nor is it without evil in itself. For the Logic which is received, though it be very properly applied to civil business and to those arts which rest in discourse and opinion, is not nearly subtle enough to deal with nature; and in offering at what it cannot master, has done more to establish and perpetuate error than to open the way to truth.

Upon the whole therefore, it seems that men have not been happy hitherto either in the trust which they have placed in others or in their own industry with regard to the sciences; especially as neither the demonstrations nor the experiments as yet known are much to be relied upon. But the universe to the eye of the human understanding is framed like a labyrinth; presenting as it does on every side so many ambiguities of way, such deceitful resemblances of objects and signs, natures so irregular in their lines, and so knotted and entangled. And then the way is still to be made by the uncertain light of the sense, sometimes shining out, sometimes clouded over, through the woods of experience and particulars; while those who offer themselves for guides are (as was said) themselves also puzzled, and increase the number of errors and wanderers. In circumstances so difficult neither the natural force of man's judgment nor even any accidental felicity offers any chance of success. No excellence of wit, no repetition of chance experiments, can overcome such difficulties as these. Our steps must be guided by a clue, and the whole way from the very first perception of the senses must be laid out upon a sure plan. Not that I would be understood to mean that nothing whatever has been done in so many ages by so great labours. We have no reason to be ashamed of the discoveries which have been made, and no doubt the ancients proved themselves in everything that turns on wit and abstract meditation, wonderful men. But as in former ages when men sailed only by observation of the stars, they could indeed coast along the shores of the old continent or cross a few small and mediterranean seas; but before the ocean could be traversed and the new world discovered, the use of the mariner's needle, as a more faithful and certain guide, had to be found out; in like manner the discoveries which have been hitherto made in the arts and sciences are such as might be made by practice, meditation, observation, argumentation,—for they lay near to the senses, and immediately beneath common notions; but before we can reach the remoter and more hidden parts of nature, it is necessary that a more perfect use and application of the human mind and intellect be introduced.

For my own part at least, in obedience to the everlasting love of truth, I have committed myself to the uncertainties and difficulties and solitudes of the ways, and relying on the divine assistance have upheld my mind both against the shocks and embattled ranks of opinion, and against my own private and inward hesitations and scruples, and against the fogs and clouds of nature, and the phantoms flitting about on every side; in the hope of providing at last for the present and future generations guidance more faithful and secure. Wherein if I have made any progress, the way has been opened to me by no other means than the true and legitimate humiliation of the human spirit. For all those who before me have applied themselves to the invention of arts have but cast a glance or two upon facts and examples and experience, and straightway proceeded, as if invention were nothing more than an exercise of thought, to invoke their own spirits to give them oracles. I, on the contrary, dwelling purely and constantly among the facts of nature, withdraw my intellect from them no further than may suffice to let the images and rays of natural objects meet in a point, as they do in the sense of vision; whence it follows that the strength and excellency of the wit has but little to do in the matter. And the same humility which I use in inventing I employ likewise in teaching. For I do not endeavour either by triumphs of confutation, or pleadings of antiquity, or assumption of authority, or even by the veil of obscurity, to invest these inventions of mine with any majesty; which might easily be done by one who sought to give lustre to his own name rather than light to other men's minds. I have not sought (I say) nor do I seek either to force or ensnare men's judgments, but I lead them to things themselves and the concordances of things, that they may see for themselves what they have, what they can dispute, what they can add and contribute to the common stock. And for myself, if in anything I have been either too credulous or too little awake and attentive, or if I have fallen off by the way and left the inquiry incomplete, nevertheless I so present these things naked and open, that my errors can be marked and set aside before the mass of knowledge be further infected by them; and it will be easy also for others to continue and carry on my labours. And by these means I suppose that I have established for ever a true and lawful marriage between the empirical and the rational faculty, the unkind and ill-starred divorce and separation of which has thrown into confusion all the affairs of the human family.

Wherefore, seeing that these things do not depend upon myself, at the outset of the work I most humbly and fervently pray to God the Father, God the Son, and God the Holy Ghost, that remembering the sorrows of mankind and the pilgrimage of this our life wherein we wear out days few and evil, they will vouchsafe through my hands to endow the human family with new mercies. This likewise I humbly pray, that things human may not interfere with things divine, and that from the opening of the ways of sense and the increase of natural light there may arise in our minds no incredulity or darkness with regard to the divine mysteries; but rather that the understanding being thereby purified and purged of fancies and vanity, and yet not the less subject and entirely submissive to the divine oracles, may give to faith that which is faith's. Lastly, that knowledge being now discharged of that venom which the serpent infused into it, and which makes the mind of man to swell, we may not be wise above measure and sobriety, but cultivate truth in charity.

And now having said my prayers I turn to men; to whom I have certain salutary admonitions to offer and certain fair requests to make. My first admonition (which was also my prayer) is that men confine the sense within the limits of duty in respect of things divine: for the sense is like the sun, which reveals the face of earth, but seals and shuts up the face of heaven. My next, that in flying from this evil they fall not into the opposite error, which they will surely do if they think that the inquisition of nature is in any part interdicted or forbidden. For it was not that pure and uncorrupted natural knowledge whereby Adam gave names to the creatures according to their propriety, which gave occasion to the fall. It was the ambitious and proud desire of moral knowledge to judge of good and evil, to the end that man may revolt from God and give laws to himself, which was the form and manner of the temptation. Whereas of the sciences which regard nature, the divine philosopher declares that "it is the glory of God to conceal a thing, but it is the glory of the King to find a thing out." Even as though the divine nature took pleasure in the innocent and kindly sport of children playing at hide and seek, and vouchsafed of his kindness and goodness to admit the human spirit for his playfellow at that game. Lastly, I would address one general admonition to all; that they consider what are the true ends of knowledge, and that they seek it not either for pleasure of the mind, or for contention, or for superiority to others, or for profit, or fame, or power, or any of these inferior things; but for the benefit and use of life; and that they perfect and govern it in charity. For it was from lust of power that the angels fell, from lust of knowledge that man fell; but of charity there can be no excess, neither did angel or man ever come in danger by it.

The requests I have to make are these. Of myself I say nothing; but in behalf of the business which is in hand I entreat men to believe that it is not an opinion to be held, but a work to be done; and to be well assured that I am labouring to lay the foundation, not of any sect or doctrine, but of human utility and power. Next, I ask them to deal fairly by their own interests, and laying aside all emulations and prejudices in favour of this or that opinion, to join in consultation for the common good; and being now freed and guarded by the securities and helps which I offer from the errors and impediments of the way, to come forward themselves and take part in that which remains to be done. Moreover, to be of good hope, nor to imagine that this Instauration of mine is a thing infinite and beyond the power of man, when it is in fact the true end and termination of infinite error; and seeing also that it is by no means forgetful of the conditions of mortality and humanity, (for it does not suppose that the work can be altogether completed within one generation, but provides for its being taken up by another); and finally that it seeks for the sciences not arrogantly in the little cells of human wit, but with reverence in the greater world. But it is the empty things that are vast: things solid are most contracted and lie in little room. And now I have only one favour more to ask (else injustice to me may perhaps imperil the business itself)—that men will consider well how far, upon that which I must needs assert (if I am to be consistent with myself), they are entitled to judge and decide upon these doctrines of mine; inasmuch as all that premature human reasoning which anticipates inquiry, and is abstracted from the facts rashly and sooner than is fit, is by me rejected (so far as the inquisition of nature is concerned), as a thing uncertain, confused, and ill built up; and I cannot be fairly asked to abide by the decision of a tribunal which is itself on its trial.

The Plan of the Work

The work is in six Parts:—

1. *The Divisions of the Sciences.*
2. *The New Organon; or Directions concerning the Interpretation of Nature.*
3. *The Phenomena of the Universe; or a Natural and Experimental History for the foundation of Philosophy.*
4. *The Ladder of the Intellect.*
5. *The Forerunners; or Anticipations of the New Philosophy.*
6. *The New Philosophy; or Active Science.*

The Arguments of the several Parts

It being part of my design to set everything forth, as far as may be, plainly and perspicuously (for nakedness of the mind is still, as nakedness of the body once was, the companion of innocence and simplicity), let me first explain the order and plan of the work. I distribute it into six parts.

The first part exhibits a summary or general description of the knowledge which the human race at present possesses. For I thought it good to make some pause upon that which is received; that thereby the old may be more easily made perfect and the new more easily approached. And I hold the improvement of that which we have to be as much an object as the acquisition of more. Besides which it will make me the better listened to; for "He that is ignorant (says the proverb) receives not the words of knowledge, unless thou first tell him that which is in his own heart." We will therefore make a coasting voyage along the shores of the arts and sciences received; not without importing into them some useful things by the way.

In laying out the divisions of the sciences

however, I take into account not only things already invented and known, but likewise things omitted which ought to be there. For there are found in the intellectual as in the terrestrial globe waste regions as well as cultivated ones. It is no wonder therefore if I am sometimes obliged to depart from the ordinary divisions. For in adding to the total you necessarily alter the parts and sections; and the received divisions of the sciences are fitted only to the received sum of them as it stands now.

With regard to those things which I shall mark as omitted, I intend not merely to set down a simple title or a concise argument of that which is wanted. For as often as I have occasion to report anything as deficient, the nature of which is at all obscure, so that men may not perhaps easily understand what I mean or what the work is which I have in my head, I shall always (provided it be a matter of any worth) take care to subjoin either directions for the execution of such work, or else a portion of the work itself executed by myself as a sample of the whole: thus giving assistance in every case either by work or by counsel. For if it were for the sake of my own reputation only and other men's interests were not concerned in it, I would not have any man think that in such cases merely some light and vague notion has crossed my mind, and that the things which I desire and offer at are no better than wishes; when they are in fact things which men may certainly command if they will, and of which I have formed in my own mind a clear and detailed conception. For I do not propose merely to survey these regions in my mind, like an augur taking auspices, but to enter them like a general who means to take possession.—So much for the first part of the work.

Having thus coasted past the ancient arts, the next point is to equip the intellect for passing beyond. To the second part therefore belongs the doctrine concerning the better and more perfect use of human reason in the inquisition of things, and the true helps of the understanding: that thereby (as far as the condition of mortality and humanity allows) the intellect may be raised and exalted, and made capable of overcoming the difficulties and obscurities of nature. The art which I introduce with this view (which I call *Interpretation of Nature*) is a kind of logic; though the difference between it and the ordinary logic is great; indeed immense. For the ordinary logic professes to contrive and prepare helps and guards for the understanding, as mine does; and in this one point they agree. But mine differs from it in three points especially; viz. in the end aimed at; in the order of demonstration; and in the starting point of the inquiry.

For the end which this science of mine proposes is the invention not of arguments but of arts; not of things in accordance with principles, but of principles themselves; not of probable reasons, but of designations and directions for works. And as the intention is different, so accordingly is the effect; the effect of the one being to overcome an opponent in argument, of the other to command nature in action.

In accordance with this end is also the nature and order of the demonstrations. For in the ordinary logic almost all the work is spent about the syllogism. Of induction the logicians seem hardly to have taken any serious thought, but they pass it by with a slight notice, and hasten on to the formulae of disputation. I on the contrary reject demonstration by syllogism, as acting too confusedly, and letting nature slip out of its hands. For although no one can doubt that things which agree in a middle term agree with one another (which is a proposition of mathematical certainty), yet it leaves an opening for deception; which is this. The syllogism consists of propositions; propositions of words; and words are the tokens and signs of notions. Now if the very notions of the mind (which are as the soul of words and the basis of the whole structure) be improperly and overhastily abstracted from facts, vague, not sufficiently definite, faulty in short in many ways, the whole edifice tumbles. I therefore reject the syllogism; and that not only as regards principles (for to principles the logicians themselves do not apply it) but also as regards middle propositions; which, though obtainable no doubt by the syllogism, are, when so obtained, barren of works, remote from practice, and altogether unavailable for the active department of the sciences. Although therefore I leave to the syllogism and these famous and boasted modes of demonstration their jurisdiction over popular arts and such as are matter of opinion (in which department I leave all as it is), yet in dealing with the nature of things I use induction throughout, and that in the minor propositions as well as the major. For I consider induction to be that form of demonstration which upholds the sense, and closes with nature, and comes to the very brink of operation, if it does not actually deal with it.

Hence it follows that the order of demonstration is likewise inverted. For hitherto the proceeding has been to fly at once from the sense and particulars up to the most general propositions, as certain fixed poles for the argument to turn upon, and from these to derive the rest by middle terms: a short way, no doubt, but precipitate; and one which will never lead to nature, though it offers an easy and ready way to disputation. Now my plan is to proceed regularly and gradually from one axiom to another, so that the most general are not reached till the last: but then when you do come to them you find them to be not empty notions, but well defined, and such as nature would really recognise as her first principles, and such as lie at the heart and marrow of things.

But the greatest change I introduce is in the form itself of induction and the judgment made thereby. For the induction of which the logicians speak, which proceeds by simple enumeration, is a puerile thing; concludes at hazard; is always liable to be upset by a contradictory instance; takes into account only what is known and ordinary; and leads to no result.

Now what the sciences stand in need of is a form of induction which shall analyse experience and take it to pieces, and by a due process of exclusion and rejection lead to an inevitable conclusion. And if that ordinary mode of judgment practised by the logicians was so laborious, and found exercise for such great wits, how much more labour must we be prepared to bestow upon this other, which is extracted not merely out of the depths of the mind, but out of the very bowels of nature.

Nor is this all. For I also sink the foundations of the sciences deeper and firmer; and I begin the inquiry nearer the source than men have done heretofore; submitting to examination those things which the common logic takes on trust. For first, the logicians borrow the principles of each science from the science itself; secondly, they hold in reverence the first notions of the mind; and lastly, they receive as conclusive the immediate informations of the sense, when well disposed. Now upon the first point, I hold that true logic ought to enter the several provinces of science armed with a higher authority than belongs to the principles of those sciences themselves, and ought to call those putative principles to account until they are fully established. Then with regard to the first notions of the intellect; there is not one of the impressions taken by the intellect when left to go its own way, but I hold it for suspected, and no way established, until it has submitted to a new trial and a fresh judgment has been thereupon pronounced. And lastly, the information of the sense itself I sift and examine in many ways. For certain it is that the senses deceive; but then at the same time they supply the means of discovering their own errors; only the errors are here, the means of discovery are to seek.

The sense fails in two ways. Sometimes it gives no information, sometimes it gives false information. For first, there are very many things which escape the sense, even when best disposed and no way obstructed; by reason either of the subtlety of the whole body, or the minuteness of the parts, or distance of place, or slowness or else swiftness of motion, or familiarity of the object, or other causes. And again when the sense does apprehend a thing its apprehension is not much to be relied upon. For the testimony and information of the sense has reference always to man, not to the universe; and it is a great error to assert that the sense is the measure of things.

To meet these difficulties, I have sought on all sides diligently and faithfully to provide helps for the sense—substitutes to supply its failures, rectifications to correct its errors; and this I endeavour to accomplish not so much by instruments as by experiments. For the subtlety of experiments is far greater than that of the sense itself, even when assisted by exquisite instruments; such experiments, I mean, as are skilfully and artificially devised for the express purpose of determining the point in question. To the immediate and proper perception of the sense therefore I do not give much weight; but I contrive that the office of the sense shall be only to judge of the experiment, and that the experiment itself shall judge of the thing. And thus I conceive that I perform the office of a true priest of the sense (from which all knowledge in nature must be sought, unless men mean to go mad) and a not unskilful interpreter of its oracles; and that while others only profess to uphold and cultivate the sense, I do so in fact. Such then are the provisions I make for finding the genuine light of nature and kindling and bringing it to bear. And they would be sufficient of themselves, if the human intellect were even, and like a fair sheet of paper with no writing on it. But since the minds of men are strangely possessed and beset, so that there is no true and even surface left to reflect the genuine rays of things, it is necessary to seek a remedy for this also.

Now the idols, or phantoms, by which the mind is occupied are either adventitious or innate. The adventitious come into the mind from without; namely, either from the doctrines and sects of philosophers, or from perverse rules of demonstration. But the innate are inherent in the very nature of the intellect, which is far more prone to error than the sense is. For let men please themselves as they will in admiring and almost adoring the human mind, this is certain: that as an un-

even mirror distorts the rays of objects according to its own figure and section, so the mind, when it receives impressions of objects through the sense, cannot be trusted to report them truly, but in forming its notions mixes up its own nature with the nature of things.

And as the first two kinds of idols are hard to eradicate, so idols of this last kind cannot be eradicated at all. All that can be done is to point them out, so that this insidious action of the mind may be marked and reproved (else as fast as old errors are destroyed new ones will spring up out of the ill complexion of the mind itself, and so we shall have but a change of errors, and not a clearance); and to lay it down once for all as a fixed and established maxim, that the intellect is not qualified to judge except by means of induction, and induction in its legitimate form. This doctrine then of the expurgation of the intellect to qualify it for dealing with truth, is comprised in three refutations: the refutation of the Philosophies; the refutation of the Demonstrations; and the refutation of the Natural Human Reason. The explanation of which things, and of the true relation between the nature of things and the nature of the mind, is as the strewing and decoration of the bridal chamber of the Mind and the Universe, the Divine Goodness assisting; out of which marriage let us hope (and be this the prayer of the bridal song) there may spring helps to man, and a line and race of inventions that may in some degree subdue and overcome the necessities and miseries of humanity. This is the second part of the work.

But I design not only to indicate and mark out the ways, but also to enter them. And therefore the third part of the work embraces the Phenomena of the Universe; that is to say, experience of every kind, and such a natural history as may serve for a foundation to build philosophy upon. For a good method of demonstration or form of interpreting nature may keep the mind from going astray or stumbling, but it is not any excellence of method that can supply it with the material of knowledge. Those however who aspire not to guess and divine, but to discover and know; who propose not to devise mimic and fabulous worlds of their own, but to examine and dissect the nature of this very world itself; must go to facts themselves for everything. Nor can the place of this labour and search and worldwide perambulation be supplied by any genius or meditation or argumentation; no, not if all men's wits could meet in one. This therefore we must have, or the business must be for ever abandoned. But up to this day such has been the condition of men in this manner, that it is no wonder if nature will not give herself into their hands.

For first, the information of the sense itself, sometimes failing, sometimes false; observation, careless, irregular, and led by chance; tradition, vain and fed on rumour; practice, slavishly bent upon its work; experiment, blind, stupid, vague, and prematurely broken off; lastly, natural history trivial and poor;—all these have contributed to supply the understanding with very bad materials for philosophy and the sciences.

Then an attempt is made to mend the matter by a preposterous subtlety and winnowing of argument. But this comes too late, the case being already past remedy; and is far from setting the business right or sifting away the errors. The only hope therefore of any greater increase or progress lies in a reconstruction of the sciences.

Of this reconstruction the foundation must be laid in natural history, and that of a new kind and gathered on a new principle. For it is in vain that you polish the mirror if there are no images to be reflected; and it is as necessary that the intellect should be supplied with fit matter to work upon, as with safeguards to guide its working. But my history differs from that in use (as my logic does) in many things,—in end and office, in mass and composition, in subtlety, in selection also and setting forth, with a view to the operations which are to follow.

For first, the object of the natural history which I propose is not so much to delight with variety of matter or to help with present use of experiments, as to give light to the discovery of causes and supply a suckling philosophy with its first food. For though it be true that I am principally in pursuit of works and the active department of the sciences, yet I wait for harvest-time, and do not attempt to mow the moss or to reap the green corn. For I well know that axioms once rightly discovered will carry whole troops of works along with them, and produce them, not here and there one, but in clusters. And that unseasonable and puerile hurry to snatch by way of earnest at the first works which come within reach, I utterly condemn and reject, as an Atalanta's apple that hinders the race. Such then is the office of this natural history of mine.

Next, with regard to the mass and composition of it: I mean it to be a history not only of nature free and at large (when she is left to her own course and does her work her own way),—such as that of the heavenly bodies, meteors, earth and sea, minerals, plants, animals,—but much more of nature under constraint and vexed; that is to say, when by art and the hand of man she is forced out of her natural state, and squeezed and moulded. Therefore I set down at length all experiments of the mechanical arts, of the operative part of the liberal arts, of the many crafts which have not yet grown into arts properly so called, so far as I have been able to examine them and as they conduce to the end in view. Nay (to say the plain truth) I do in fact (low and vulgar as men may think it) count more upon this part both for helps and safeguards than upon the other; seeing that the nature of things betrays itself more readily under the vexations of art than in its natural freedom.

Nor do I confine the history to Bodies; but I have thought it my duty besides to make a separate history of such Virtues as may be considered cardinal in nature. I mean those original passions or desires of matter which constitute the primary elements of nature; such as Dense and Rare, Hot and Cold, Solid and Fluid, Heavy and Light, and several others.

Then again, to speak of subtlety: I seek out and get together a kind of experiments much subtler and simpler than those which occur accidentally. For I drag into light many things which no one who was not proceeding by a regular and certain way to the discovery of causes would have thought of inquiring after; being indeed in themselves of no great use; which shows that they were not sought for on their own account; but having just the same relation to things and works which the letters of the alphabet have to speech and words—which, though in themselves useless, are the elements of which all discourse is made up.

Further, in the selection of the relation and experiments I conceive I have been a more cautious purveyor than those who have hitherto dealt with natural history. For I admit nothing but on the faith of eyes, or at least of careful and severe examination; so that nothing is exaggerated for wonder's sake, but what I state is sound and without mixture of fables or vanity. All received or current falsehoods also (which by strange negligence have been allowed for many ages to prevail and become established) I proscribe and brand by name; that the sciences may be no more troubled with them. For it has been well observed that the fables and superstitions and follies which nurses instil into children do serious injury to their minds; and the same consideration makes me anxious, having the management of the childhood as it were of philosophy in its course of natural history, not to let it accustom itself in the beginning to any vanity. Moreover, whenever I come to a new experiment of any subtlety (though it be in my own opinion certain and approved), I nevertheless subjoin a clear account of the manner in which I made it; that men knowing exactly how each point was made out, may see whether there be any error connected with it, and may arouse themselves to devise proofs more trustworthy and exquisite, if such can be found; and finally I interpose

everywhere admonitions and scruples and cautions, with a religous care to eject, repress, and as it were exorcise every kind of phantasm.

Lastly, knowing how much the sight of man's mind is distracted by experience and history, and how hard it is at the first (especially for minds either tender or preoccupied) to become familiar with nature, I not unfrequently subjoin observations of my own, being as the first offers, inclinations, and as it were glances of history towards philosophy; both by way of an assurance to men that they will not be kept for ever tossing on the waves of experience, and also that when the time comes for the intellect to begin its work, it may find everything the more ready. By such a natural history then as I have described, I conceive that a safe and convenient approach may be made to nature, and matter supplied of good quality and well prepared for the understanding to work upon.

And now that we have surrounded the intellect with faithful helps and guards, and got together with most careful selection a regular army of divine works, it may seem that we have no more to do but to proceed to philosophy itself. And yet in a matter so difficult and doubtful there are still some things which it seems necessary to premise, partly for convenience of explanation, partly for present use.

Of these the first is to set forth examples of inquiry and invention according to my method, exhibited by anticipation in some particular subjects; choosing such subjects as are at once the most noble in themselves among those under inquiry, and most different one from another; that there may be an example in every kind. I do not speak of those examples which are joined to the several precepts and rules by way of illustration (for of these I have given plenty in the second part of the work); but I mean actual types and models, by which the entire process of the mind and the whole fabric and order of invention from the beginning to the end, in certain subjects, and those various and remarkable, should be set as it were before the eyes. For I remember that in the mathematics it is easy to follow the demonstration when you have a machine beside you; whereas without that help all appears involved and more subtle than it really is. To examples of this kind,—being in fact nothing more than an application of the second part in detail and at large,—the fourth part of the work is devoted.

The fifth part is for temporary use only, pending the completion of the rest; like interest payable from time to time until the principal be forthcoming. For I do not make so blindly for the end of my journey, as to neglect anything useful that may turn up by the way. And therefore I include in this fifth part such things as I have myself discovered, proved, or added,—not however according to the true rules and methods of interpretation, but by the ordinary use of the understanding in inquiring and discovering. For besides that I hope my speculations may in virtue of my continual conversancy with nature have a value beyond the pretensions of my wit, they will serve in the meantime for wayside inns, in which the mind may rest and refresh itself on its journey to more certain conclusions. Nevertheless I wish it to be understood in the meantime that they are conclusions by which (as not being discovered and proved by the true form of interpretation) I do not at all mean to bind myself. Nor need any one be alarmed at such suspension of judgment, in one who maintains not simply that nothing can be known, but only that nothing can be known except in a certain course and way; and yet establishes provisionally certain degrees of assurance, for use and relief until the mind shall arrive at a knowledge of causes in which it can rest. For even those schools of philosophy which held the absolute impossibility of knowing anything were not inferior to those which took upon them to pronounce. But then they did not provide helps for the sense and understanding, as I have done, but simply took away all their authority: which is quite a different thing—almost the reverse.

The sixth part of my work (to which the rest is subservient and ministrant) discloses and sets forth that philosophy which by the legitimate, chaste, and severe course of inquiry which I have explained and provided is at length developed and established. The completion however of this last part is a thing both above my strength and beyond my hopes. I have made a beginning of the work —a beginning, as I hope, not unimportant:— the fortune of the human race will give the issue;—such an issue, it may be, as in the present condition of things and men's minds cannot easily be conceived or imagined. For the matter in hand is no mere felicity of speculation, but the real business and fortunes of the human race, and all power of operation. For man is but the servant and interpreter of nature: what he does and what he knows is only what he has observed of nature's order in fact or in thought; beyond this he knows nothing and can do nothing. For the chain of causes cannot by any force be loosed or broken, nor can nature be commanded except by being obeyed. And so those twin objects, human Knowledge and human Power, do really meet in one; and it is from ignorance of causes that operation fails.

And all depends on keeping the eye steadily fixed upon the facts of nature and so receiving their images simply as they are. For God forbid that we should give out a dream of our own imagination for a pattern of the world; rather may he graciously grant to us to write an apocalypse or true vision of the footsteps of the Creator imprinted on his creatures.

Therefore do thou, O Father, who gavest the visible light as the first fruits of creation, and didst breathe into the face of man the intellectual light as the crown and consummation thereof, guard and protect this work, which coming from thy goodness returneth to thy glory. Thou when thou turnedst to look upon the works which thy hands had made, sawest that all was very good, and didst rest from thy labours. But man, when he turned to look upon the work which his hands had made, saw that all was vanity and vexation of spirit, and could find no rest therein. Wherefore if we labour in thy works with the sweat of our brows thou wilt make us partakers of thy vision and thy sabbath.

Humbly we pray that this mind may be steadfast in us, and that through these our hands, and the hands of others to whom thou shalt give the same spirit, thou wilt vouchsafe to endow the human family with new mercies.

On the Aims and Instruments of Scientific Thought

William Kingdon Clifford

Editor's Introduction

William Kingdon Clifford, who was one of the most gifted mathematicians of his time, had also a fine speculative intelligence that he applied to subjects as various as ethics and scientific theory, on both of which he left writings of lasting interest. Of these, the best known is a work he did not live to finish in which he sought to explain the first principles of mathematics to those who are not mathematical; this was completed after his early death by his friend Karl Pearson, a distinguished mathematician in his own right, and published as *The Common Sense of the Exact Sciences*. The essay reprinted here, "On the Aims and Instruments of Scientific Thought," which undertakes to define the intellectual basis of the scientific enterprise, is one of Clifford's lectures included in a collection of his shorter pieces, also posthumous, called *The Ethics of Belief and Other Essays*.

Clifford was born at Exeter, England, on May 4, 1845, the son of a well-known citizen of the town and a justice of the peace. Virtually nothing is known of his early life save the fact that his mother, from whom he apparently inherited the tendency to tuberculosis that caused his death at thirty-three, died herself when he was nine. From a local school he went to King's College, London, where his mathematical abilities were quickly recognized, and then to Trinity College, Cambridge, where in 1867, unwilling to invest the months of special preparation that might have enabled him to win first prize in the examinations, he nevertheless walked in cold and placed second. On the strength of this, in 1868, he was made a fellow of Trinity College. Three years later he was appointed professor of applied mathematics at University College, London, and in 1874 he was elected a fellow of the Royal Society, having refused earlier election because he said he did not "wish to be respectable yet."

Given to hard work and scornful of its effect upon his system, Clifford produced a number of important technical papers and prepared many ambitious and thoughtful lectures during this period, only to discover, following a physical collapse in 1876, that he had ruined his health. Extended intervals in southern climates restored him only partly, and in 1878 he suffered a relapse from which he never rallied, though he survived, cheerful as to himself and unfailingly considerate of others, until the following year, when on March 3, after a last unavailing journey to Madeira, his strength gave out and he died.

Something of the range of his interests can be gathered from the fact that in addition to his command of mathematics and science Clifford was well read in the classics, modern history, and English literature, and was devoted besides to gymnastic exercises and strenuous athletics; as a student he once suspended himself by his toes from a cross-bar laid across a church steeple. In a day when student dress and behavior were rigidly conventional he was also given to eccentricities of clothing and conduct, none of which seemed, however, to cause offense, any more than did his fervent advocacy of unpopular causes in collegiate debate; on the contrary, he was much admired for his independence of mind, as he was for the fact that along with his other involvements he somehow managed to learn six languages, among them Arabic, Greek, and Sanskrit, and mastered hieroglyphics, shorthand, and Morse code on the side. These varied accomplishments were not all undertaken with the same seriousness, perhaps. But that together they amounted to something more than the diversions of a dilettante is attested not only by Clifford's writings but by the fact that in the course of his short life he came to know Clerk Maxwell, Frederick Pollock, Leslie Stephen, Alfred Marshall, and Henry Sidgwick, who were among the greatest men of their time in science, jurisprudence, letters, economics, and philosophy, and who regarded him in each case as one of their closest friends.

Clifford was celebrated as a lecturer for his ability to expound difficult subjects with clarity and grace. Among the matters he did much to help his generation understand were what in anticipation of Einstein he called "the theory of space-curvature," which he suggested "hints at a possibility of describing matter and motion in terms of extension only." He had also studied the non-Euclidian geometries of Lobachevsky and Riemann and was one of the first to point out that, as they showed that the geometry of Euclid is not universally true, so we cannot assume that the laws of nature are everywhere mathematically exact—a very modern notion. In these expositions Clifford apparently spoke with the same effectiveness he brought to the lecture that appears here and which is to be found at greater length in *The Common Sense of the Exact Sciences*. Of this book Bertrand Russell once said, in what might well be Clifford's epitaph, that it exhibits "an art of clarity such as belongs only to a very few great men—not the pseudo-clarity of the popularizer, which is achieved by ignoring or glozing over the difficult points, but that clarity that comes of profound and orderly understanding, by virtue of which principles become luminous and deductions easy." For comment on Clifford's ethical writings, *see* William James, *Principles of Psychology* (*GBWW*, Volume 53, pp. 85–87), and also "The Sentiment of Rationality" in *GGB*, Volume 10, pp. 75–79.

On the Aims and Instruments of Scientific Thought[1]

It may have occurred (and very naturally too) to such as have had the curiosity to read the title of this lecture, that it must necessarily be a very dry and difficult subject; interesting to very few, intelligible to still fewer, and, above all, utterly incapable of adequate treatment within the limits of a discourse like this. It is quite true that a complete setting-forth of my subject would require a comprehensive treatise on logic, with incidental discussion of the main questions of metaphysics; that it would deal with ideas demanding close study for their apprehension, and investigations requiring a peculiar taste to relish them. It is not my intention now to present you with such a treatise.

The British Association, like the world in general, contains three classes of persons. In the first place, it contains scientific thinkers; that is to say, persons whose thoughts have very frequently the characters which I shall presently describe. Secondly, it contains persons who are engaged in work upon what are called scientific subjects, but who in general do not, and are not expected to, think about these subjects in a scientific manner. Lastly, it contains persons who suppose that their work and their thoughts are unscientific, but who would like to know something about the business of the other two classes aforesaid. Now, to anyone who belonging to one of these classes considers either of the other two, it will be apparent that there is a certain gulf between him and them; that he does not quite understand them, nor they him; and that an opportunity for sympathy and comradeship is lost through this want of understanding. It is this gulf that I desire to bridge over, to the best of my power. That the scientific thinker may consider his business in relation to the great life of mankind; that the noble army of practical workers may recognise their fellowship with the outer world, and the spirit which must guide both; that this so-called outer world may see in the work of science only the putting in evidence of all that is excellent in its own work—may feel that the kingdom of science is within it: these are the objects of the present discourse. And they compel me to choose such portions of my vast subject as shall be intelligible to all, while they ought at least to command an interest universal, personal, and profound.

In the first place, then, what is meant by scientific thought? You may have heard some of it expressed in the various Sections this morning. You have probably also heard expressed in the same places a great deal of unscientific thought; notwithstanding that it was about mechanical energy, or about hydrocarbons, or about eocene deposits, or about malacopterygii. For scientific thought does not mean thought about scientific subjects with long names. There are no scientific subjects. The subject of science is the human universe; that is to say, everything that is, or has been, or may be related to man. Let us then, taking several topics in succession, endeavour to make out in what cases thought about them is scientific, and in what cases not.

Ancient astronomers observed that the relative motions of the sun and moon re-

[1] A Lecture delivered before the members of the British Association, at Brighton, on August 19, 1872.

curred all over again in the same order about every nineteen years. They were thus enabled to predict the time at which eclipses would take place. A calculator at one of our observatories can do a great deal more than this. Like them, he makes use of past experience to predict the future; but he knows of a great number of other cycles besides that one of the nineteen years, and takes account of all of them; and he can tell about the solar eclipse of six years hence exactly when it will be visible, and how much of the sun's surface will be covered at each place, and, to a second, at what time of day it will begin and finish there. This prediction involves technical skill of the highest order; but it does not involve scientific thought, as any astronomer will tell you.

By such calculations the places of the planet Uranus at different times of the year had been predicted and set down. The predictions were not fulfilled. Then arose Adams, and from these errors in the prediction he calculated the place of an entirely new planet, that had never yet been suspected; and you all know how the new planet was actually found in that place. Now this prediction does involve scientific thought, as anyone who has studied it will tell you.

Here then are two cases of thought about the same subject, both predicting events by the application of previous experience, yet we say one is *technical* and the other *scientific.*

Now let us take an example from the building of bridges and roofs. When an opening is to be spanned over by a material construction, which must bear a certain weight without bending enough to injure itself, there are two forms in which this construction can be made, the arch and the chain. Every part of an arch is compressed or pushed by the other parts; every part of a chain is in a state of tension, or is pulled by the other parts. In many cases these forms are united. A girder consists of two main pieces or booms, of which the upper one acts as an arch and is compressed, while the lower one acts as a chain and is pulled; and this is true even when both the pieces are quite

straight. They are enabled to act in this way by being tied together, or braced, as it is called, by cross pieces, which you must often have seen. Now suppose that any good practical engineer makes a bridge or roof upon some approved pattern which has been made before. He designs the size and shape of it to suit the opening which has to be spanned; selects his material according to the locality; assigns the strength which must be given to the several parts of the structure according to the load which it will have to bear. There is a great deal of thought in the making of this design whose success is predicted by the application of previous experience; it requires technical skill of a very high order; but it is not scientific thought. On the other hand, Mr. Fleeming Jenkin[2] designs a roof consisting of two arches braced together, instead of an arch and a chain braced together; and although this form is quite different from any known structure, yet before it is built he assigns with accuracy the amount of material that must be put into every part of the structure in order to make it bear the required load, and this prediction may be trusted with perfect security. What is the natural comment on this? Why, that Mr. Fleeming Jenkin is a scientific engineer.

Now it seems to me that the difference between scientific and merely technical thought, not only in these but in all other instances which I have considered, is just this: Both of them make use of experience to direct human action; but while technical thought or skill enables a man to deal with the same circumstances that he has met with before, scientific thought enables him to deal with different circumstances that he has never met with before. But how can experience of one thing enable us to deal with another quite different thing? To answer this question we shall have to consider more closely the nature of scientific thought.

Let us take another example. You know that if you make a dot on a piece of paper,

---

[2] *On Braced Arches and Suspension Bridges.* Edinburgh: Neill, 1870.

and then hold a piece of Iceland spar over it, you will see not one dot but two. A mineralogist, by measuring the angles of a crystal, can tell you whether or no it possesses this property without looking through it. He requires no scientific thought to do that. But Sir William Rowan Hamilton, the late Astronomer-Royal of Ireland, knowing these facts and also the explanation of them which Fresnel had given, thought about the subject, and he predicted that by looking through certain crystals in a particular direction we should see not two dots but a continuous circle. Mr. Lloyd made the experiment, and saw the circle, a result which had never been even suspected. This has always been considered one of the most signal instances of scientific thought in the domain of physics. It is most distinctly an application of experience gained under certain circumstances to entirely different circumstances.

Now suppose that the night before coming down to Brighton you had dreamed of a railway accident caused by the engine getting frightened at a flock of sheep and jumping suddenly back over all the carriages; the result of which was that your head was unfortunately cut off, so that you had to put it in your hat-box and take it back home to be mended. There are, I fear, many persons even at this day, who would tell you that after such a dream it was unwise to travel by railway to Brighton. This is a proposal that you should take experience gained while you are asleep, when you have no common sense,—experience about a phantom railway, and apply it to guide you when you are awake and have common sense, in your dealings with a real railway. And yet this proposal is not dictated by scientific thought.

Now let us take the great example of Biology. I pass over the process of classification, which itself requires a great deal of scientific thought; in particular when a naturalist who has studied and monographed a fauna or a flora rather than a family is able at once to pick out the distinguishing characters required for the subdivision of an order quite new to him. Suppose that we possess all this minute and comprehensive knowledge of plants and animals and intermediate organisms, their affinities and differences, their structures and functions—a vast body of experience, collected by incalculable labour and devotion. Then comes Mr. Herbert Spencer: he takes that experience of life which is not human, which is apparently stationary, going on in exactly the same way from year to year, and he applies that to tell us how to deal with the changing characters of human nature and human society. How is it that experience of this sort, vast as it is, can guide us in a matter so different from itself? How does scientific thought, applied to the development of a kangaroo foetus or the movement of the sap in exogens, make prediction possible for the first time in that most important of all sciences, the relations of man with man?

In the dark or unscientific ages men had another way of applying experience to altered circumstances. They believed, for example, that the plant called Jew's-ear, which does bear a certain resemblance to the human ear, was a useful cure for diseases of that organ: This doctrine of "signatures," as it was called, exercised an enormous influence on the medicine of the time. I need hardly tell you that it is hopelessly unscientific: yet it agrees with those other examples that we have been considering in this particular; that it applies experience about the shape of a plant—which is one circumstance connected with it—to dealings with its medicinal properties, which are other and different circumstances. Again, suppose that you had been frightened by a thunderstorm on land, or your heart had failed you in a storm at sea; if anyone then told you that in consequence of this you should always cultivate an unpleasant sensation in the pit of your stomach, till you took delight in it, that you should regulate your sane and sober life by the sensations of a moment of unreasoning terror: this advice would not be an example of scientific thought, yet it would be an application of past experience to new and different circumstances.

But you will already have observed what is the additional clause that we must add to our definition in order to describe scientific thought and that only. The step between experience about animals and dealings with changing humanity is the law of evolution. The step from errors in the calculated places of Uranus to the existence of Neptune is the law of gravitation. The step from the observed behaviour of crystals to conical refraction is made up of laws of light and geometry. The step from old bridges to new ones is the laws of elasticity and the strength of materials.

The step, then, from past experience to new circumstances must be made in accordance with an observed uniformity in the order of events. This uniformity has held good in the past in certain places; if it should also hold good in the future and in other places, then, being combined with our experience of the past, it enables us to predict the future, and to know what is going on elsewhere; so that we are able to regulate our conduct in accordance with this knowledge.

The aim of scientific thought, then, is to apply past experience to new circumstances; the instrument is an observed uniformity in the course of events. By the use of this instrument it gives us information transcending our experience, it enables us to infer things that we have not seen from things that we have seen; and the evidence for the truth of that information depends on our supposing that the uniformity holds good beyond our experience. I now want to consider this uniformity a little more closely; to show how the character of scientific thought and the force of its inferences depend upon the character of the uniformity of Nature. I cannot of course tell you all that is known of this character without writing an encyclopaedia; but I shall confine myself to two points of it about which it seems to me that just now there is something to be said. I want to find out what we mean when we say that the uniformity of Nature is *exact;* and what we mean when we say that it is *reasonable.*

When a student is first introduced to those sciences which have come under the dominion of mathematics, a new and wonderful aspect of Nature bursts upon his view. He has been accustomed to regard things as essentially more or less vague. All the facts that he has hitherto known have been expressed qualitatively, with a little allowance for error on either side. Things which are let go fall to the ground. A very observant man may know also that they fall faster as they go along. But our student is shown that, after falling for one second in a vacuum, a body is going at the rate of thirty-two feet per second, that after falling for two seconds it is going twice as fast, after going two and a half seconds two and a half times as fast. If he makes the experiment, and finds a single inch per second too much or too little in the rate, one of two things must have happened: either the law of falling bodies has been wrongly stated, or the experiment is not accurate—there is some mistake. He finds reason to think that the latter is always the case; the more carefully he goes to work, the more of the error turns out to belong to the experiment. Again, he may know that water consists of two gases, oxygen and hydrogen, combined; but he now learns that two pints of steam at a temperature of 150° centigrade will always make two pints of hydrogen and one pint of oxygen at the same temperature, all of them being pressed as much as the atmosphere is pressed. If he makes the experiment and gets rather more or less than a pint of oxygen, is the law disproved? No; the steam was impure, or there was some mistake. Myriads of analyses attest the law of combining volumes; the more carefully they are made, the more nearly they coincide with it. The aspects of the faces of a crystal are connected together by a geometrical law, by which, four of them being given, the rest can be found. The place of a planet at a given time is calculated by the law of gravitation; if it is half a second wrong, the fault is in the instrument, the observer, the clock, or the law; now, the more observations are made, the more of this fault is brought home to the instrument, the observer, and the clock. It is no wonder, then, that our student, contemplating these and many like instances, should be led to say: "I have been shortsighted; but I have now put on the spectacles of science which Nature had prepared for my eyes; I see that things have definite outlines, that the world is ruled by exact and rigid mathematical laws; χαι, σύ, θεός, γεω-μετρεῖς." It is our business to consider whether he is right in so concluding. Is the uniformity of Nature absolutely exact, or only more exact than our experiments?

At this point we have to make a very important distinction. There are two ways in which a law may be inaccurate. The first way is exemplified by that law of Galileo which I mentioned just now: that a body falling *in vacuo* acquires equal increase in velocity in equal times. No matter how many feet per second it is going, after an interval of a second it will be going thirty-two *more* feet per second. We now know that this rate of increase is not exactly the same at different heights, that it depends upon the distance of the body from the centre of the earth; so that the law is only approximate; instead of the increase of velocity being exactly *equal* in equal times, it itself increases very slowly as the body falls. We know also that this variation of the law from the truth is *too small to be perceived* by direct observation on the change of velocity. But suppose we have invented means for observing this, and have verified that the increase of velocity is inversely as the squared distance from the earth's centre. Still the law is not accurate; for the earth does not attract accurately towards her centre, and the direction of attraction is continually varying with the motion of the sea; the body will not even fall in a straight line. The sun and the planets, too, especially the moon, will produce deviations; yet the sum of all these errors will escape our new process of observation by being a great deal smaller than the necessary errors of that observation. But when these again have been allowed for, there is still the influence of the stars. In this case, however, we only give up one exact law for another. It may still be held that if the effect of every particle of matter in the uni-verse on the falling body were calculated according to the law of gravitation, the body would move exactly as this calculation required. And if it were objected that the body must be slightly magnetic or diamagnetic, while there are magnets not an infinite way off; that a very minute repulsion, even at sensible distances, accompanies the attraction; it might be replied that these phenomena are themselves subject to exact laws, and that when *all* the laws have been taken into account, the actual motion will exactly correspond with the calculated motion.

I suppose there is hardly a physical student (unless he has specially considered the matter) who would not at once assent to the statement I have just made; that if we knew all about it, Nature would be found universally subject to exact numerical laws. But let us just consider for another moment what this means.

The word "exact" has a practical and a theoretical meaning. When a grocer weighs you out a certain quantity of sugar very carefully and says it is exactly a pound, he means that the difference between the mass of the sugar and that of the pound weight he employs is too small to be detected by his scales. If a chemist had made a special investigation, wishing to be as accurate as he could, and told you this was exactly a pound of sugar, he would mean that the mass of the sugar differed from that of a certain standard piece of platinum by a quantity too small to be detected by *his* means of weighing, which are a thousandfold more accurate than the grocer's. But what would a mathematician mean, if he made the same statement? He would mean this. Suppose the mass of the standard pound to be represented by a length, say a foot, measured on a certain line; so that half a pound would be represented by six inches, and so on. And let the difference between the mass of the sugar and that of the standard pound be drawn upon the same line to the same scale. Then, if that difference were magnified an infinite number of times, it would still be invisible. This is the theoretical meaning of exactness; the practical meaning is only very close approximation; *how* close, depends upon the circumstances. The knowledge then of an exact law in the theoretical sense would be equivalent to an infinite observation. I do not say that such knowledge is impossible to man; but I do say that it would be absolutely different in kind from any knowledge that we possess at present.

I shall be told, no doubt, that we do possess a great deal of knowledge of this kind, in the form of geometry and mechanics; and that it is just the example of these sciences that has led men to look for exactness in other quarters. If this had been said to me in the last century, I should not have known what to reply. But it happens that about the beginning of the present century the foundations of geometry were criticised independently by two mathematicians, Lobatschewsky[3] and the immortal Gauss;[4] whose results have been extended and generalised more recently by Riemann[5] and Helmholtz.[6] And the conclusion to which these investigations lead is that, although the assumptions which were very properly made by the ancient geometers are practically exact—that is to say, more exact than experiment can be—for such finite things as we have to deal with, and such portions of space as we can reach; yet the truth of them for very much larger things, or very much smaller things, or parts of space which are at present beyond our reach, is a matter to be decided by experiment, when its powers are considerably increased. I want to make as clear as possible the real state of this question at present, because it is often supposed to be a question of words or metaphysics, whereas it is a very distinct and simple question of fact. I am supposed to know then that the three angles of a rectilinear triangle are exactly equal to two right angles. Now suppose that three points are taken in space, distant from one another as far as the Sun is from α Centauri, and that the shortest distances between these points are drawn so as to form a triangle. And suppose the angles of this triangle to be very accurately measured and added together; this can at present be done so accurately that the error shall

certainly be less than one minute, less therefore than the five-thousandth part of a right angle. Then I do not know that this sum would differ at all from two right angles; but also I do not know that the difference would be less than ten degrees, or the ninth part of a right angle.[7] And I have reasons for not knowing.

This example is exceedingly important as showing the connection between exactness and universality. It is found that the deviation if it exists must be nearly proportional to the area of the triangle. So that the error in the case of a triangle whose sides are a mile long would be obtained by dividing that in the case I have just been considering by four hundred quadrillions; the result must be a quantity inconceivably small which no experiment could detect. But, between this inconceivably small error and no error at all, there is fixed an enormous gulf; the gulf between practical and theoretical exactness, and, what is even more important, the gulf between what is practically universal and what is theoretically universal. I say that a law is practically universal which is more exact than experiment for all cases that might be got at by such experiments as we can make. We assume this kind of universality, and we find that it pays us to assume it. But a law would be theoretically universal if it were true of all cases whatever; and this is what we do not know of any law at all.

I said there were two ways in which a law might be inexact. There is a law of gases

---

[3] *Geometrische Untersuchungen zur Theorie der Parallellinien.* Berlin, 1840. Translated by Hoüel. Gauthier-Villars, 1866.

[4] Letter to Schumacher, Nov. 28, 1846 (refers to 1792).

[5] *Über die Hypothesen welche der Geometrie zugrunde liegen.* Göttingen, Abhandl., 1866–67. Translated by Hoüel in *Annali di Matematica*, Milan, vol. iii.

[6] *The Axioms of Geometry*, Academy, vol. i. p. 128 (a popular exposition). [And see now his article in *Mind*, No. III.]

[7] Assuming that parallax observations prove the deviation less than half a second for a triangle whose vertex is at the star and base a diameter of the earth's orbit.

which asserts that when you compress a perfect gas the pressure of the gas increases exactly in the proportion in which the volume diminishes. Exactly; that is to say, the law is more accurate than the experiment, and experiments are corrected by means of the law. But it so happens that this law has been explained; we know precisely what it is that happens when a gas is compressed. We know that a gas consists of a vast number of separate molecules, rushing about in all directions with all manner of velocities, but so that the mean velocity of the molecules of air in this room, for example, is about twenty miles a minute. The pressure of the gas on any surface with which it is in contact is nothing more than the impact of these small particles upon it. On any surface large enough to be seen there are millions of these impacts in a second. If the space in which the gas is confined be diminished, the average rate at which the impacts take place will be increased in the same proportion; and because of the enormous number of them, the actual rate is always exceedingly close to the average. But the law is one of statistics; its accuracy depends on the enormous numbers involved; and so, from the nature of the case, its exactness cannot be theoretical or absolute.

Nearly all the laws of gases have received these statistical explanations; electric and magnetic attraction and repulsion have been treated in a similar manner; and an hypothesis of this sort has been suggested even for the law of gravity. On the other hand the manner in which the molecules of a gas interfere with each other proves that they repel one another inversely as the fifth power of the distance; so that we here find at the basis of a statistical explanation a law which has the form of theoretical exactness. Which of these forms is to win? It seems to me again that we do not know, and that the recognition of our ignorance is the surest way to get rid of it.

The world in general has made just the remark that I have attributed to a fresh student of the applied sciences. As the discoveries of Galileo, Kepler, Newton, Dalton, Cavendish, Gauss, displayed ever new phenomena following mathematical laws, the theoretical exactness of the physical universe was taken for granted. Now, when people are hopelessly ignorant of a thing, they quarrel about the source of their knowledge. Accordingly, many maintained that we know these exact laws by intuition. These said always one true thing, that we did not know them from experience. Others said that they were really given in the facts, and adopted ingenious ways of hiding the gulf between the two. Others again deduced from transcendental considerations sometimes the laws themselves, and sometimes what through imperfect information they supposed to be the laws. But more serious consequences arose when these conceptions derived from Physics were carried over into the field of Biology. Sharp lines of division were made between kingdoms and classes and orders; an animal was described as a miracle to the vegetable world; specific differences which are practically permanent within the range of history were regarded as permanent through all time; a sharp line was drawn between organic and inorganic matter. Further investigation, however, has shown that accuracy had been prematurely attributed to the science, and has filled up all the gulfs and gaps that hasty observers had invented. The animal and vegetable kingdoms have a debatable ground between them, occupied by beings that have the characters of both and yet belong distinctly to neither. Classes and orders shade into one another all along their common boundary. Specific differences turn out to be the work of time. The line dividing organic matter from inorganic, if drawn today, must be moved to-morrow to another place; and the chemist will tell you that the distinction has now no place in his science except in a technical sense for the convenience of studying carbon compounds by themselves. In Geology the same tendency gave birth to the doctrine of distinct periods, marked out by the character of the strata deposited in them all over the sea; a doctrine than which, perhaps, no ancient cosmogony has been further from the truth, or done more harm to the progress of science. Refuted many years ago by Mr. Herbert Spencer,[8] it has now fairly yielded to an attack from all sides at once, and may be left in peace.

When then we say that the uniformity which we observe in the course of events is exact and universal, we mean no more than this: that we are able to state general rules which are far more exact than direct experiment, and which apply to all cases that we are at present likely to come across. It is important to notice, however, the effect of such exactness as we observe upon the nature of inference. When a telegram arrived stating that Dr. Livingstone had been found by Mr. Stanley, what was the process by which you inferred the finding of Dr. Livingstone from the appearance of the telegram? You assumed over and over again the existence of uniformity in nature. That the newspapers had behaved as they generally do in regard to telegraphic messages; that the clerks had followed the known laws of the action of clerks; that electricity had behaved in the cable exactly as it behaves in the laboratory; that the actions of Mr. Stanley were related to his motives by the same uniformities that affect the actions of other men; that Dr. Livingstone's handwriting conformed to the curious rule by which an ordinary man's handwriting may be recognised as having persistent characteristics even at different periods of his life. But you had a right to be much more sure about some of these inferences than about others. The law of electricity was known with practical exactness, and the conclusions derived from it were the surest things of all. The law about the handwriting, belonging to a portion of physiology which is unconnected with consciousness, was known with less, but still with considerable accuracy. But the laws of human action in which consciousness is concerned are still so far from being completely analysed and reduced to an exact form that the inferences which you made by their help were felt to have only a provisional force. It is possible

that by and by, when psychology has made enormous advances and become an exact science, we may be able to give to testimony the sort of weight which we give to the inferences of physical science. It will then be possible to conceive a case which will show how completely the whole process of inference depends on our assumption of uniformity. Suppose that testimony, having reached the ideal force I have imagined, were to assert that a certain river runs uphill. You could infer nothing at all. The arm of inference would be paralysed, and the sword of truth broken in its grasp; and reason could only sit down and wait until recovery restored her limb, and further experience gave her new weapons.

I want in the next place to consider what we mean when we say that the uniformity which we have observed in the course of events is *reasonable* as well as exact.

No doubt the first form of this idea was suggested by the marvellous adaptation of certain natural structures to special functions. The first impression of those who studied comparative anatomy was that every part of the animal frame was fitted with extraordinary completeness for the work that it had to do. I say extraordinary, because at the time the most familiar examples of this adaptation were manufactures produced by human ingenuity; and the completeness and minuteness of natural adaptations were seen to be far in advance of these. The mechanism of limbs and joints was seen to be adapted, far better than any existing ironwork, to those motions and combinations of motion which were most useful to the particular organisms. The beautiful and complicated apparatus of sensation caught up indications from the surrounding medium, sorted them, analysed them, and transmitted the results to the brain in a manner with which, at the time I am speaking of, no artificial contrivance could compete. Hence the belief grew amongst physiologists that every structure

---

[8] "Illogical Geology," in *Essays*, vol. i. Originally published in 1859.

which they found must have its function and subserve some useful purpose; a belief which was not without its foundation in fact, and which certainly (as Dr. Whewell remarks) has done admirable service in promoting the growth of physiology. Like all beliefs found successful in one subject, it was carried over into another, of which a notable example is given in the speculations of Count Rumford about the physical properties of water. Pure water attains its greatest density at a temperature of about $39\frac{1}{2}°$ Fahrenheit; it expands and becomes lighter whether it is cooled or heated, so as to alter that temperature. Hence it was concluded that water in this state must be at the bottom of the sea, and that by such means the sea was kept from freezing all through; as it was supposed must happen if the greatest density had been that of ice. Here then was a substance whose properties were eminently adapted to secure an end essential to the maintenance of life upon the earth. In short, men came to the conclusion that the order of nature was reasonable in the sense that everything was adapted to some good end.

Further consideration, however, has led men out of that conclusion in two different ways. First, it was seen that the facts of the case had been wrongly stated. Cases were found of wonderfully complicated structures that served no purpose at all; like the teeth of that whale of which you heard in Section D the other day, or of the Dugong, which has a horny palate covering them all up and used instead of them; like the eyes of the unborn mole, that are never used, though perfect as those of a mouse until the skull opening closes up, cutting them off from the brain, when they dry up and become incapable of use; like the outsides of your own ears, which are absolutely of no use to you. And when human contrivances were more advanced it became clear that the natural adaptations were subject to criticism. The eye, regarded as an optical instrument of human manufacture, was thus described by Helmholtz—the physiologist who learned physics for the sake of his physiology, and mathematics for the

sake of his physics, and is now in the first rank of all three. He said, "If an optician sent me that as an instrument, I should send it back to him with grave reproaches for the carelessness of his work, and demand the return of my money."

The extensions of the doctrine into Physics were found to be still more at fault. That remarkable property of pure water, which was to have kept the sea from freezing, does not belong to salt water, of which the sea itself is composed. It was found, in fact, that the idea of a reasonable adaptation of means to ends, useful as it had been in its proper sphere, could yet not be called universal, or applied to the order of nature as a whole.

Secondly, this idea has given way because it has been superseded by a higher and more general idea of what is reasonable, which has the advantage of being applicable to a large portion of physical phenomena besides. Both the adaptation and the non-adaptation which occur in organic structures have been *explained*. The scientific thought of Dr. Darwin, of Mr. Herbert Spencer, and of Mr. Wallace, has described that hitherto unknown process of adaptation as consisting of perfectly well-known and familiar processes. There are two kinds of these: the direct processes, in which the physical changes required to produce a structure are worked out by the very actions for which that structure becomes adapted—as the backbone or notochord has been modified from generation to generation by the bendings which it has undergone; and the indirect processes included under the head of Natural Selection—the reproduction of children slightly different from their parents, and the survival of those which are best fitted to hold their own in the struggle for existence. Naturalists might give you some idea of the rate at which we are getting explanations of the evolution of all parts of animals and plants—the growth of the skeleton, of the nervous system and its mind, of leaf and flower. But what then do we mean by *explanation*?

We were considering just now an explanation of a law of gases—the law according to which pressure increases in the same proportion in which volume diminishes. The explanation consisted in supposing that a gas is made up of a vast number of minute particles always flying about and striking against one another, and then showing that the rate of impact of such a crowd of particles on the sides of the vessel containing them would vary exactly as the pressure is found to vary. Suppose the vessel to have parallel sides, and that there is only one particle rushing backwards and forwards between them; then it is clear that if we bring the sides together to half the distance, the particle will hit each of them twice as often, or the pressure will be doubled. Now it turns out that this would be just as true for millions of particles as for one, and when they are flying in all directions instead of only in one direction and its opposite. Observe now; it is a perfectly well-known and familiar thing that a body should strike against an opposing surface and bound off again; and it is a mere everyday occurrence that what has only half so far to go should be back in half the time; but that pressure should be strictly proportional to density is a comparatively strange, unfamiliar phenomenon. The explanation describes the unknown and unfamiliar as being made up of the known and the familiar; and this, it seems to me, is the true meaning of explanation.[9]

Here is another instance. If small pieces of camphor are dropped into water, they will begin to spin round and swim about in a most marvellous way. Mr. Tomlinson gave, I believe, the explanation of this. We must observe, to begin with, that every liquid has a skin which holds it; you can see that to be true in the case of a drop, which looks as if it were held in a bag. But the tension of this skin is greater in some liquids than in others; and it is greater in camphor and water than in pure water. When the camphor is dropped into water it begins to dissolve and get surrounded with camphor and water instead of water. If the fragment of camphor were exactly symmetrical, nothing more would happen; the tension would be greater in its immediate neighbourhood, but no mo-

tion would follow. The camphor, however, is irregular in shape; it dissolves more on one side than the other: and consequently gets pulled about, because the tension of the skin is greater where the camphor is most dissolved. Now it is probable that this is not nearly so satisfactory an explanation to you as it was to me when I was first told of it; and for this reason. By that time I was already perfectly familiar with the notion of a skin upon the surface of liquids, and I had been taught by means of it to work out problems in capillarity. The explanation was therefore a description of the unknown phenomenon which I did not know how to deal with as made up of known phenomena which I did know how to deal with. But to many of you possibly the liquid skin may seem quite as strange and unaccountable as the motion of camphor on water.

And this brings me to consider the source of the pleasure we derive from an explanation. By known and familiar I mean that which we know how to deal with, either by action in the ordinary sense, or by active thought. When, therefore, that which we do not know how to deal with is described as made up of things that we do know how to deal with, we have that sense of increased power which is the basis of all higher pleasures. Of course we may afterwards, by association, come to take pleasure in explanation for its own sake. Are we then to say that the observed order of events is reasonable, in the sense that all of it admits of explanation? That a process may be capable of explanation, it must break up into simpler constituents which are already familiar to us. Now, first, the process may itself be simple, and not break up; secondly, it may break up into elements which are as unfamiliar and impracticable as the original process.

---

[9] This view differs from those of Mr. J. S. Mill and Mr. Herbert Spencer in requiring every explanation to contain an addition to our knowledge about the thing explained. Both these writers regard subsumption under a general law as a species of explanation. See also Ferrier's *Remains*, vol. ii, p. 436.

It is an explanation of the moon's motion to say that she is a falling body, only she is going so fast and is so far off that she falls quite round to the other side of the earth, instead of hitting it; and so goes on for ever. But it is no explanation to say that a body falls because of gravitation. That means that the motion of the body may be resolved into a motion of every one of its particles towards every one of the particles of the earth, with an acceleration inversely as the square of the distance between them. But this attraction of two particles must always, I think, be less familiar than the original falling body, however early the children of the future begin to read their Newton. Can the attraction itself be explained? Le Sage said that there is an everlasting hail of innumerable small ether-particles from all sides, and that the two material particles shield each other from this and so get pushed together. This is an explanation; it may or may not be a true one. The attraction may be an ultimate simple fact; or it may be made up of simpler facts utterly unlike anything that we know at present; and in either of these cases there is no explanation. We have no right to conclude, then, that the order of events is always capable of being explained.

There is yet another way in which it is said that Nature is reasonable; namely, inasmuch as every effect has a cause. What do we mean by this?

In asking this question, we have entered upon an appalling task. The word represented by "cause" has sixty-four meanings in Plato and forty-eight in Aristotle. These were men who liked to know as near as might be what they meant; but how many meanings it has had in the writings of the myriads of people who have not tried to know what they meant by it will, I hope, never be counted. It would not only be the height of presumption in me to attempt to fix the meaning of a word which has been used by so grave authority in so many and various senses; but it would seem a thankless task to do that once more which has been done so often at sundry times and in divers manners before. And yet with-out this we cannot determine what we mean by saying that the order of nature is reasonable. I shall evade the difficulty by telling you Mr. Grote's opinion.[10] You come to a scarecrow and ask, What is the cause of this? You find that a man made it to frighten the birds. You go away and say to yourself: "Everything resembles this scarecrow. Everything has a purpose." And from that day the word "cause" means for you what Aristotle meant by "final cause." Or you go into a hairdresser's shop, and wonder what turns the wheel to which the rotatory brush is attached. On investigating other parts of the premises, you find a man working away at a handle. Then you go away and say: "Everything is like that wheel. If I investigated enough, I should always find a man at a handle." And the man at the handle, or whatever corresponds to him, is from henceforth known to you as "cause."

And so generally. When you have made out any sequence of events to your entire satisfaction, so that you know all about it, the laws involved being so familiar that you seem to see how the beginning must have been followed by the end, then you apply that as a simile to all other events whatever, and your idea of cause is determined by it. Only when a case arises, as it always must, to which the simile will not apply, you do not confess to yourself that it was only a simile and need not apply to everything, but you say: "The cause of that event is a mystery which must remain for ever unknown to me." On equally just grounds the nervous system of my umbrella is a mystery which must remain for ever unknown to me. My umbrella has no nervous system; and the event to which your simile did not apply has no cause in your sense of the word. When we say then that every effect has a cause, we mean that every event is connected with something in a way that might make somebody call that the cause of it. But I, at least, have never yet seen any single meaning of the word that could be

---

[10] Plato, vol. ii (*Phaedo*) [*GBWW*, Vol. 7, pp. 220–51.]

fairly applied to the *whole* order of nature.

From this remark I cannot even except an attempt recently made by Mr. Bain to give the word a universal meaning, though I desire to speak of that attempt with the greatest respect. Mr. Bain[11] wishes to make the word "cause" hang on in some way to what we call the law of energy; but though I speak with great diffidence I do think a careful consideration will show that the introduction of this word "cause" can only bring confusion into a matter which is distinct and clear enough to those who have taken the trouble to understand what energy means. It would be impossible to explain that this evening; but I may mention that "energy" is a technical term out of mathematical physics, which requires of most men a good deal of careful study to understand it accurately.

Let us pass on to consider, with all the reverence which it demands, another opinion held by great numbers of the philosophers who have lived in the Brightening Ages of Europe; the opinion that at the basis of the natural order there is something which we can know to be *unreasonable,* to evade the processes of human thought. The opinion is set forth first by Kant, so far as I know, in the form of his famous doctrine of the antinomies or contradictions, a later form[12] of which I will endeavour to explain to you. It is said, then, that space must either be infinite or have a boundary. Now you cannot conceive infinite space; and you cannot conceive that there should be any end to it. Here, then, are two things, one of which must be true, while each of them is inconceivable; so that our thoughts about space are hedged in as it were, by a contradiction. Again, it is said that matter must either be infinitely divisible, or must consist of small particles incapable of further division. Now you cannot conceive a piece of matter divided into an infinite number of parts, while, on the other hand, you cannot conceive a piece of matter, however small, which absolutely cannot be divided into two pieces; for, however great the forces are which join the parts of it

together, you can imagine stronger forces able to tear it in pieces. Here, again, there are two statements, one of which must be true, while each of them is separately inconceivable; so that our thoughts about matter also are hedged in by a contradiction. There are several other cases of the same thing, but I have selected these two as instructive examples. And the conclusion to which philosophers were led by the contemplation of them was that on every side, when we approach the limits of existence a contradiction must stare us in the face. The doctrine has been developed and extended by the great successors of Kant; and this unreasonable, or unknowable, which is also called the absolute and the unconditioned, has been set forth in various ways as that which we know to be the true basis of all things. As I said before, I approach this doctrine with all the reverence which should be felt for that which has guided the thoughts of so many of the wisest of mankind. Nevertheless, I shall endeavour to show that in these cases of supposed contradiction there is always something which we do not know now, but of which we cannot be sure that we shall be ignorant next year. The doctrine is an attempt to found a positive statement upon this ignorance, which can hardly be regarded as justifiable. Spinoza said, "A free man thinks of nothing so little as of death"; it seems to me we may parallel this maxim in the case of thought, and say, "A wise man only remembers his ignorance in order to destroy it." A boundary is that which divides two adjacent portions of space. The question, then, "Has space (in general) a boundary?" involves a contradiction in terms, and is, therefore, unmeaning. But the question, "Does space contain a finite number of cubic miles, or an infinite number?" is

---

[11] *Inductive Logic,* chap. iv.

[12] That of Mr. Herbert Spencer, *First Principles.* I believe Kant himself would have admitted that the antinomies do not exist for the empiricist. [Much less does he say that either of a pair of antinomies must be true. The real Kantian position is that both assertions are illegitimate.]

a perfectly intelligible and reasonable question which remains to be answered by experiment.[13] The surface of the sea would still contain a finite number of square miles, if there were no land to bound it. Whether or no the space in which we live is of this nature remains to be seen. If its extent is finite, we may quite possibly be able to assign that extent next year; if, on the other hand, it has no end, it is true that the knowledge of that fact would be quite different from any knowledge we at present possess, but we have no right to say that such knowledge is impossible. Either the question will be settled once for all, or the extent of space will be shown to be greater than a quantity which will increase from year to year with the improvement of our sources of knowledge. Either alternative is perfectly conceivable, and there is no contradiction. Observe especially that the supposed contradiction arises from the assumption of theoretical exactness in the laws of geometry. The other case that I mentioned has a very similar origin. The idea of a piece of matter the parts of which are held together by forces, and are capable of being torn asunder by greater forces, is entirely derived from the large pieces of matter which we have to deal with. We do not know whether this idea applies in any sense even to the *molecules* of gases; still less can we apply it to the *atoms* of which they are composed. The word "force" is used of two phenomena: the pressure, which when two bodies are in contact connects the motion of each with the position of the other; and attraction or repulsion,—that is to say, a change of velocity in one body depending on the position of some other body which is not in contact with it. We do not know that there is anything corresponding to either of these phenomena in the case of a molecule. A meaning can, however, be given to the question of the divisibility of matter in this way. We may ask if there is any piece of matter so small that its properties as matter depend upon its remaining all in one piece. This question is reasonable; but we cannot answer it at present, though we

are not at all sure that we shall be equally ignorant next year. If there is no such piece of matter, no such limit to the division which shall leave it matter, the knowledge of that fact would be different from any of our present knowledge; but we have no right to say that it is impossible. If, on the other hand, there *is* a limit, it is quite possible that we may have measured it by the time the Association meets at Bradford. Again, when we are told that the infinite extent of space, for example, is something that we cannot conceive at present, we may reply that this is only natural, since our experience has never yet supplied us with the means of conceiving such things. But then we cannot be sure that the facts will not make us learn to conceive them; in which case they will cease to be inconceivable. In fact, the putting of limits to human conception must always involve the assumption that our previous experience is universally valid in a theoretical sense; an assumption which we have already seen reason to reject. Now you will see that our consideration of this opinion has led us to the true sense of the assertion that the Order of Nature is reasonable. If you will allow me to define a reasonable question as one which is asked in terms of ideas justified by previous experience, without itself contradicting that experience, then we may say, as the result of our investigation, that to every reasonable question there is an intelligible answer which either we or posterity may know.

We have, then, come some how to the following conclusions. By scientific thought we mean the application of past experience to new circumstances by means of an observed order of events. By saying that this order of events is exact we mean that it is exact enough to correct experiments by, but we do not mean that it is theoretically or absolutely exact, because we do not know. The process of inference we found to be in itself an as-

---

[13] The very important distinction between *unboundedness* and *infinite extent* is made by Riemann, *loc. cit.*

sumption of uniformity, and we found that, as the known exactness of the uniformity became greater, the stringency of the inference increased. By saying that the order of events is reasonable we do not mean that everything has a purpose, or that everything can be explained, or that everything has a cause; for neither of these is true. But we mean that to every reasonable question there is an intelligible answer, which either we or posterity may know *by the exercise of scientific thought.*

For I specially wish you not to go away with the idea that the exercise of scientific thought is properly confined to the subjects from which my illustrations have been chiefly drawn to-night. When the Roman jurists applied their experience of Roman citizens to dealings between citizens and aliens, showing by the difference of their actions that they regarded the circumstances as essentially different, they laid the foundations of that great structure which has guided the social progress of Europe. That procedure was an instance of strictly scientific thought. When a poet finds that he has to move a strange new world which his predecessors have not moved; when, nevertheless, he catches fire from their flashes, arms from their armoury, sustentation from their footprints, the procedure by which he applies old experience to new circumstances is nothing greater or less than scientific thought. When the moralist, studying the conditions of society and the ideas of right and wrong which have come down to us from a time when war was the normal condition of man and success in war the only chance of survival, evolves from them the conditions and ideas which must accompany a time of peace, when the comradeship of equals is the condition of national success; the process by which he does this is scientific thought and nothing else. Remember, then, that it is the guide of action; that the truth which it arrives at is not that which we can ideally contemplate without error, but that which we may act upon without fear; and you cannot fail to see that scientific thought is not an accompaniment or condition of human progress, but human progress itself. And for this reason the question what its characters are, of which I have so inadequately endeavoured to give you some glimpse, is the question of all questions for the human race.

PICTURE CREDITS

Key to abbreviations used to indicate location of pictures on page: r.—right; l.—left; t.—top; b.—bottom; c.—center; *—courtesy. Abbreviations are combined to indicate unusual placement.

—**FRONTISPIECE** Windsor, Royal Collection— *Copyright Reserved* —**8** (t.) * Oslo Kommunes Kunstsamlinger, Munch-Museet, Oslo —**8** (b.) David Magarshack —**9** * Munch-Museet, Oslo; photograph, O. Vaering —**13** Culver Pictures —**17** Tass/Sovfoto —**20** Mordecai Gorelik Collection —**21** * Collection of American Literature, Yale University Library —**24** The Bettmann Archive —**29** © Gisèle Freund —**34** (t.) The Bettmann Archive —**34** (b.) Raymond Mander & Joe Mitchenson Theatre Collection, London —**35** Culver Pictures —**36** * Trustees of the British Museum; photograph, J. R. Freeman & Co. Ltd. —**38** * Library of Congress, Washington, D.C. —**40** Sovfoto —**42** Raymond Mander & Joe Mitchenson Theatre Collection, London —**44** Billy Rose Theatre Collection, New York Public Library at Lincoln Center, Astor, Lenox and Tilden Foundations —**46** * Theatre Collection, New York Public Library at Lincoln Center, Astor, Lenox and Tilden Foundation —**47** Peter A. Juley & Son —**48** Raymond Mander & Joe Mitchenson Theatre Collection, London —**49** Raymond Mander & Joe Mitchenson Theatre Collection, London —**52-53** * Society for Cultural Relations with the U.S.S.R. —**56** Victoria and Albert Museum —**58** (t.), (b.) Schweizerische Theatersammlung, Bern —**60** Ullstein Bilderdienst, Berlin —**62** Denise Colomb — J. P. Ziolo —**68** John Wells —**160** Jeannine Deubel —**188** (l.), (r.) Jeannine Deubel —**204** Jeannine Deubel —**219** Jeannine Deubel —**256** * National Portrait Gallery, London —**276** * National Portrait Gallery, London —**368** Cliché des Musées Nationaux, Paris —**371, 374-375, 378, 382-383, 390-391, 398-399, 405, 413, 420-421, 428, 434-435** Drawings by Ron Villani —**436** * National Portrait Gallery, London —**454** * National Portrait Gallery, London

*T*o extend the tradition of excellence of your Britannica Great Books educational program, you may also avail yourself of other aids for your home reference center.

*D*escribed on the next page is a companion product—the Britannica 3 bookcase—that is designed to help you and your family. It will add attractiveness and value to your home library, as it keeps it well organized.

*S*hould you wish to order it, or to obtain further information, please write to us at

Britannica Home Library Service
Att: Year Book Department
P.O. Box 4928
Chicago, Illinois 60680

Britannica 3
custom-designed
BOOKCASE

- requires less than 1 x 3-ft. floor space

- laminated pecan finish resists burns, stains, scratches

- Early American styling enriches any setting

- case size: $35^{3}/_{4}''$ wide, $9^{3}/_{4}''$ deep, $27^{5}/_{8}''$ high